DEVIL'S Bargains

DEVELOPMENT OF WESTERN RESOURCES

The Development of Western Resources is an interdisciplinary series focusing on the use and misuse of resources in the American West. Written for a broad readership of humanists, social scientists, and resource specialists, the books in this series emphasize both historical and contemporary perspectives as they explore the interplay between resource exploitation and economic, social, and political experiences.

John G. Clark, *University of Kansas, Founding Editor*

Hal K. Rothman, *University of Nevada, Las Vegas, Series Editor*

DEVIL'S Bargains

Tourism in the Twentieth-Century American West

Hal K. Rothman

UNIVERSITY PRESS OF KANSAS

Published by the University Press of Kansas (Lawrence, Kansas 66049), which was organized by the Kansas Board of Regents and is operated and funded by Emporia State University, Fort Hays State University, Kansas State University, Pittsburg State University, the University of Kansas, and Wichita State University

Library of Congress
Cataloging-in-Publication Data

Rothman, Hal, 1958–
Devil's bargains : tourism in the twentieth century American West / Hal K. Rothman.
p. cm. — (Development of western resources)
Includes bibliographical references and index.
ISBN 0-7006-0910-5 (cloth)
1. Tourist trade — West (U.S.) I. Title. II. Series.
G155.U6R66 1998
338.4'791780433 — dc21 98-18520
CIP

British Library Cataloguing in Publication Data is available.

Printed in the United States of America

10 9 8 7 6 5 4 3 2 1

The paper used in this publication meets the minimum requirements of the American National Standard for Permanence of Paper for Printed Library Materials Z39.48-1984.

As always,

for Lauralee, Talia, and Brent

and for Earl Pomeroy

CONTENTS

ACKNOWLEDGMENTS

This book could not have been written without the help, support, and interest of an enormous cast of people in an incredible number of places. Peggy Shaffer took time from her own important work to read the manuscript, not once but twice. The cultural history dimension of this project results from her urging me to rethink and refine my ideas. Char Miller, Elliott West, Bill Philpott, and Jessica Teisch read large chunks of the manuscript and offered valuable ideas. Richard White offered a helpful critique of the finished manuscript. Bill Cronon read the introduction and encouraged me. David Nye added his valuable insights about technology, nature, and culture. Bill deBuys read the Santa Fe and Grand Canyon sections and offered his characteristically insightful comments. Steve Pyne offered his thoughts on the Grand Canyon. Mike Anderson let me read his work on the Grand Canyon. Tom Latousek read the Aspen sections and circulated them among his family members, many of whom have been in Aspen for three decades or more. They offered comments and provided additional sources and insights that only neonatives would know. Tom introduced me to Whip Jones, and the three of us had a marvelous dinner and discussion. Angus Thuermer Jr. and I had long discussions about the nature of tourism and its impact; he also let me stay at his house in Jackson. Gene Moehring was always willing to listen to me talk about his city. Mike Davis and Bob Gottlieb both proved to be excellent sounding boards. Dwight Pitcaithley offered cogent commentary on an intellectual history version of the Grand Canyon section. John Rember kindly offered his insights on the Sun Valley material. Michael Duchemin and Paivi Hoikkala provided insights into Los Angeles and escorted me through its maze. John Findlay gave me a venue at his conference, "Power and Place in the North American West," and an ongoing critique of my thinking. Willard Rollings read the Native American sections and offered his typically pointed and well-reasoned comments. Colin Loader and Elizabeth White both offered me the benefit of their wisdom on cultural history. A generation of my graduate students endured my long digressions into the nature of tourism. Rich Mingus, Cathleen Dooley, Brian Frehner, and Tom Latousek have gone on to better things, but I still appreciate their interest and willingness to listen during the rollicking discussions we enjoyed at our ongoing Friday afternoon symposium. Rich Wandschneider and the gang at Fishtrap provided a pleasant venue for the discussion of ideas. Patty Limerick, Pat Long, and Bill Reibsame at the University of Colorado, Boulder, arranged a marvelous symposium on tourism and were kind enough to include me. There I met Myles Rademan, the Prophet of Boom, and Raye Ringholz, both of whom have provided me with insight into the processes I describe here. Bob Righter and Sherry Smith were always willing to discuss tourism and its impact. Bob commented on the first paper I presented on the subject nearly a decade ago, noting then that my way was not the only way to look at tourism. My response then (but less so now) was that our points of view were different because he was gentry, a landowner, and I was a mere serf. Bob and Sherry have been my friends for more than a decade; the raft trip we took from their house facing Grand Teton made for a memorable afternoon. Marla and Steve Polott offered the benefit of their long experience with Las Vegas. Nancy Scott at the University Press of Kansas has been an exemplary editor. All authors should be so fortunate to have editors with her precision and enthusiasm.

Throughout the West, archivists opened their doors to me in an effort to make my work easier. Barbara Walton at the Denver Public Library; Ramon Powers at the Kansas State Historical Society; Jody McCabe at the Aspen Historical Society; Angus Thuermer of the *Jackson Hole News;* my good friend Bill Tydeman, a veteran of numerous of my other projects, and Tomas Jaehn at the Idaho Historical Society; Mike Devine at the American Heritage Center in Laramie; and the people at the Bud Werner Memorial Library in Steamboat Springs and at the Grand Canyon National Park Research Library made my life easier. Our friends Marcia, Howard, Amy, and Corey Fine made their home outside Boulder a haven for me as I traveled. Ann, Bill, Katie, and Dave deBuys made my trips to Santa Fe an occasion always to look forward to. The Original Santa Fe Margarita Sampling Club (OSFMSC) needs to begin monthly convocations. There are certainly other people to thank; any omissions are the fault of the slow leak in my short-term memory. Everyone who helped with this project has my unending gratitude.

The University of Nevada, Las Vegas (UNLV), and its History Department have been the most congenial and supportive place I can imagine to teach, research, and write history. My three chairs here, Larry Klein, Sue Fawn Chung, and Elspeth Whitney, and my excellent colleagues have tolerated my frequent absences and have helped arrange for all kinds of funding to support this project. On more than one occasion, I have depleted the department's travel resources; my colleagues have been quite generous in allowing me to do so. The University Grants and Fellowships Committee supported my research with substantial stipends for two consecutive summers; the Nevada Humanities Committee also awarded me a fellowship to complete this work. The university also granted me a faculty development leave in support of this project. UNLV itself has been kind enough to award my efforts on two separate occasions; this kind of encouragement has no equal in the confidence it inspires.

In the end it comes down to family; there is little else of real meaning in the world. My wife, Lauralee, endures much so that I can pursue projects such as this. Our children, Talia and Brent, enjoy the travel but don't quite understand why daddy is always asking other people questions. Without them I couldn't do it; there simply wouldn't be any reason. As is everything I do, this book is for them, with all my love and affection, in the hopes that it will make up in some small way for the time they let me take from them.

The people of Aspen in Wagner Park, next to the decade of their arrival in town. The importance of longevity in claiming a town cannot be overestimated. (Photo courtesy of the Aspen Historical Society.)

1970
1960

MAUI REDUX

Each winter, the humpback whales arrive in Lahaina Harbor off the island of Maui in search of warmer waters in which to breed as airplanes disgorge countless visitors to the islands. The whales have always come, appearing in Hawaiian legend and the earliest Anglo American accounts, gracing the art and cultural imagery of the islands. The tourists have come in numbers only since the end of World War II. The whales have great symbolic power, investing legend and fiction with meaning for as long as humans have seen them. In recent years, they have become the focus of protective legislation; fines are levied for coming too close when these stunning creatures cavort in the sea and engage in their mating ritual. They have become an attraction for visitors to the island, who buy tickets on all manner of seacraft, from large sloops to the fourteen-foot Zodiac pontoon raft my wife and I boarded, in an effort to photograph or even catch a glimpse of these now rare mammals. As the boat sped out into the harbor, I watched my fellow tourists as much as I watched the water. Cameras in hand, we all sought to capture an image of these beings, as if our interest alone will be sufficient to preserve a species decimated by more than 150 years of commercial hunting.

Once, Lahaina Harbor sheltered other forms of commerce. Two commodities dominated the mid-nineteenth century, the trade in souls converted by the God-fearing Protestant missionaries who first descended upon Hawaii during the 1820s and rest and revelry, the byproducts of the commerce in the meat, fat, oil, and skin from the whales sheltering there in winter. These two outside cultural and economic forms pressed against each other, squeezing Hawaiians between them. The missionaries sought to convert the islanders en masse; the whalers experienced more success enjoying the spoils of their slaughter throughout the northern Pacific Ocean. Neither legislation nor sermon saved these ocean creatures. Only the replacement of whale oil with petroleum products prevented the extinction of the magnificent species that wintered in the Hawaiian Islands.

As modern tourists, we revel in viewing the whales, in the act of communing with what we see as pure nature. We become ecotourists, people who share in an experience that is pleasurable. If we choose, we can easily define this viewing as a social good. The often outrageous sums such voyaging costs we rationalize as a part of the process of saving the planet for future generations. By investing in an experience we can only see, not take home with us, we give the whales and other endangered species a place in the human future. We go to see, not to harpoon these creatures, a situation we interpret as evidence of the spread of the liberal value system of the industrial world. Our ancestors used their power to kill whales; we choose to protect and appreciate them. There is a certainty born of arrogance and too much money entwined with wonder in many of us who disembark like I did, bandy-legged and sunburned, from water craft after an afternoon's whale-watching.[1]

Most of the tourists miss the scene behind them as they gaze at the water in search of these mysterious whales and the meaning they see embodied in them. Caught up by their interest, playing the lead role in a script written to affirm their choices, they become mesmerized by their own presence in the scene their culture and their imagination constructs. They play the roles in the script as if they are real. Lulled, they fail to see and understand the industrial and postindustrial worlds that grant this pleasure and give meaning to this ritual, regarding their self-defined enlightened behavior as a natural result of human endeavor, not as a commercial process of creating and consuming commodities in its own right.

I turned to look at the shore from the water and saw in full bloom the complicated structures and processes of modern tourism. The shoreline reveals an economic and cultural geography of tourism, a process of designing and defining intangible commodities that can be psychologically possessed through spending. It illustrates the importance of tourism as an industry and its preeminence in the Hawaiian economy. If in the Southwest, as the writer Ross Calvin once suggested, sky determines, on Maui, elevation determines.[2] Along the shoreline sprawl the communities of Kaanapali and Lahaina, dominated by the many shops, luxury hotels, restaurants, and other amenities essential to support modern tourists as they experience the islands. Here is a world visitors comprehend. It refracts them to themselves; they see it on their own terms.

Above this plane but intimately tied to it are the sugarcane fields and workers cutting the silver green stalks. Sugar became a major colonial industry in the islands, its leaders ousting the last Hawaiian queen, Liliuokalani, and much later financing resort development. Proximate to the tourist amenities, the cane fields so essential in the history of Hawaii show the tentacles of tourism creeping over them. Through the adjacent fields chugged the Sugar Cane Train, complete with its singing conductor Glen Foster, who cheerily crooned an odd combination of nostalgic mainland melodies, "Oh,

Susannah" and "Sweet Betsy from Pike," and Hawaiian worksongs as we rode along. The train took us on a one-hour tour amid sweating laborers hard at work in the fields. The songs, the ambience, the frivolity of the ride tell a story of this space that is about the visitor and not the fields. The ambience pulls tourists' attention from the physical labor of reality to the scenic sights and stories of mythic Maui. Most of the tourists look at the harbor, the hotels, the golf courses, and the sea, and when they see the labor around them, it is exotic or romantic rather than essential, sweaty, or backbreaking. Looking too closely at the workers themselves seemed dislocating, anachronistic, out of place in this carefully scripted scene.

Above the cane fields, above this liminal zone worked and visited but made into part of a romantic mise-en-scène, cattle roam the hillsides farther from town but still distinctly visible from the sea. Herdsmen round up animals for branding and castrating, away from the salt air and humidity of the lower elevations. Once part of the empires of great barons, the cattle are now an anachronism, an important economic activity to specific families but far less important in the shape of the island economy. Yet the romance remains, a feeling of human endeavor in a lush environment and a simpler time, constructed meaning for observers who seek a mythological Hawaii and a livelihood for those few fortunate enough to retain employment in the industry.

At the highest elevations, the volcanoes beckon to visitors, and the steady stream of automobiles on the narrow roads to the top of volcanic craters again attests to the visitor-based economy amid the clouds that shroud Maui's mountain peaks. Restaurants dot the sides of the roads along the climb, and the complexion of the people we passed changed from the bronze, brown, and golden hues of cane workers and cowboys to the sun-burned red of visitors like us. In the thin air of these pinnacles, visitors feel intimidated. The power of the volcano saps our confidence, challenges our illusion of control. Only the road tells us we remain powerful and important, in tune with nature and part of a culture that successfully subjugated these places. This is the tourist's illusion, a way of seeing that comes from guidebooks and brief jaunts to far away places instead of venturing beyond convenience.[3]

The geography of tourism illustrates the economic history of the island. A linear progression of activities unfolds in Maui's history, a series of colonial processes whose skeletons remain along the shoreline, impressing a complex network of relationships on existing local norms. Whaling came first, and Lahaina testifies to it. Sugar and cattle followed, raw materials exported to the mainland in classic colonial fashion. Then came tourism, capping and underpinning other economic forms. Its geography is logical, predictable, and organized, from beaches to golf courses to volcano national parks. It is a template placed upon, or perhaps over, local life and local ways, the prism through which the world sees Maui.

South of Lahaina, along the dry leeward coast of Maui rises the resort destination of Wailea, a more than 1,500-acre ancient lava bed covered by a forest of spiny kiawe and graced with stunning white sand beaches. Exquisite resorts enclose acres of public beaches in an area of the island that experienced little historic habitation. As late as the early 1970s, miles of untrammeled beaches stretched south from Ma'alea Bay past Wailea south to Makena. One jeep road led there, and a family might find themselves alone on an entire beach. Alexander and Baldwin (A&B), one of the great sugar giants, owned the area, and by 1970 they began a development program. A&B partnered with Northwestern Mutual Life Insurance Company, and a high-end project emerged along the once-open shore.[4]

Wailea is the driest part of the island, a desert with an average annual rainfall of approximately ten inches. The emergence of resorts there coincided with the development of a more sophisticated tourism strategy in the Hawaiian islands, as international corporations and worldwide capital took over the industry. On Maui, Kahului on the north coast once housed guests, but the heavy surf of the open north shore proved daunting for inexperienced mainland visitors. Lahaina, which had remained an "ordinary town," in the words of one longtime resident, well into the 1970s, added a development to the north, Kaanapali, where visitors could enjoy the softer waters. American Factors (AMFAC), which traced its roots to German traders who first arrived in 1849 and had become one of the largest sugar conglomerates in the islands, owned the area, rife with white sand beaches and clear and usually calm water. AMFAC developed the region as a one-owner resort, where control began and stayed with the company.[5]

Kaanapali too had problems that stymied the rapidly growing industry. Every afternoon, the clouds that surrounded the volcano dropped rain on the small coastal plain, sending visitors scurrying for cover and limiting the appeal of its resorts. Nor were there enough rooms to meet the demands spurred by the remarkable growth in visitation to the islands. Between 1960 and 1989, the 9,522 hotel rooms in Hawaii grew to more than 68,000; the number of visitors grew from 300,000 to 6.6 million. Competition and the need to offer perfect experience pushed developers toward new locales, which soon blossomed as self-contained megaresorts, each striving for more elite status.[6] Major hotel conglomerates responded by seeking a new location on Maui, avoiding the drawbacks of the existing locations.

The lack of rainfall that inhibited historic settlement and economic enterprise at Wailea became an advantage in the race to attract tourists. The desertlike flora and the annual ten-inch rainfall ensured that bathers on the southern Maui coast rarely had to worry about midafternoon showers ruining their fun. Growing interest in golf filled out the picture. The best sites at Kaanapali already sported the golf courses so attractive to Japanese investors, who supplied $6.8 billion of the $8.4 billion in foreign investment in Hawaii between 1970 and 1989.[7] Wailea was born, with its impressive and sometimes extravagant hotels, countless restaurants, and numerous golf courses. Even a nearby service community is filled with condominiums, apartments, and quaint shops; called Kihei, its name has historic provenance but little relationship to the condominiums that stand on its ground. The lack of rainfall that limited historic settlement proved an asset for the postextractive economy. Wailea has become the dominant resort area on Maui.

Wailea reveals important changes in the economic geography and demography of the island. The hotels along the coast include the Inter-Continental, a staple of worldwide resort destinations, the Four Seasons, and others. During the late 1980s, a "mind-boggling frenzy" of real-estate buying and selling occurred in Hawaii. Japanese investment, in no small part resulting from a favorable yen-to-dollar exchange rate, the exorbitant land prices of Japan, and the growth of Japanese tourism, grew to unprecedented levels. Although Hawaii's average price for a single-family home was at or near the top of all American cities, one study showed that the Japanese typically paid a premium of more than 21 percent over market value stemming from a favorable yen-dollar exchange rate, encouraging owners to sell as outrageous profit overcame jingoism and subsequently forced up the cost of resort amenities. On Maui, the island with the longest tradition of serving outsiders, tension resulted as Americans found themselves resenting the "colonization" of the Japanese.[8]

This colonization also reveals a kind of *West Side Story* segmentation of visitors and their experiences. As the globalization of capital and shifting wealth in the 1990s transformed economic demography, Japan Air Lines and later Korean Air Lines purchased Hawaiian hotels for their Far Eastern clients.[9] The social demography that tourism often spawns followed. As they passed through lobbies designed for their comfort, sunburned mainlanders spoke to their own kind about the matters of substance important to vacationing Americans in the 1990s. Far Eastern companies created a Hawaiian experience at odds with the American traditions of the place, structured and organized so completely that these visitors needed only vouchers issued through the companies, not American greenbacks, during their stay. Japanese tour companies imported their own service personnel instead of using American-born but Japanese-speaking Issei and Nisei, creating a closed experience, entirely at odds with American conceptions of vacation travel. Pacific Rim visitors were sheltered not only from the aspect they feared about American life, its unpredictability, but they were also sheltered from any but predigested experience.

Against this backdrop, American-owned companies assessed options; some sold, some competed. The Hyatt Regency chain built a Grand Hyatt at Wailea, one of approximately twelve such hotels in the world. Built in the style of the opulent nineteenth-century hotels, the Grand Hyatt featured a Fernand Botero sculpture garden, a hand-crafted tile floor, exquisite flower beds, an artistic mosaic swimming pool, and a chapel built in the New England style, a thinly disguised historical allusion to the northeastern missionaries who settled nineteenth-century Hawaii. In a style more spectacular than believable, this church is adorned with teak, mahogany, and other hardwoods. Instead of a place to save souls, it was available for rent and became a chapel where wealthy tourists married.

Vacationers on Wailea easily and often intentionally overlooked the superstructure of tourism. Resort destinations reveal clear patterns of labor. People whom visitors assume are local—often residents of Kahului or nearby Kihei, itself transformed—carry bags, wait tables, and mow the grass. Anglo Americans manage the hotels, and as the percentage of Japanese travelers to the island increased, bilingual Japanese were imported to cater to them. A glass ceiling existed. Making money as a bellman or bartender was not difficult, but the sometimes lucrative jobs had little status attached. Hawaiian tourism workers who completed a college degree found themselves looking at a cut in pay to take a skilled job.

The workers provide an illusion of their own. Many of the supposed Hawaiian natives who work the hotels originate in California or are Filipinos and Southeast Asians who can pass for locals to unschooled mainland eyes. "Give a guy a tan, an aloha shirt, three months on the job, and he's a transplanted local," remarks University of Hawaii Urban and Regional Planning professor Karl Kim, himself a neonative with more than a decade in the islands.[10] To the mainlanders, the workers are all the same, part of the mythical polyglot of Hawaii. Their confidence in knowing what they see obscures the complicated and convoluted interethnic relationships inherent in tourism.

Hawaiian natives and neonatives fill the service positions, offering smiles and friendly advice for tips. They put on a figurative mask to deal with tourists, knowing that the visitors expect certain behavior from them. Some seek to educate their charges: "Maui Mike," a gregarious attendant at the Inter-Continental Hotel, purchased by the Japanese for $90 million, promises to show visitors how the locals live. He is willing to offer a glimpse into what he touts as the "real Maui," reporting to me that few visitors take him up on the offer.

Always wearing a mask has consequences. Hawaiians became less and less enchanted by the prospect of tourist-industry labor, and labor shortages loomed. In sugar and other plantation work in the islands, companies resorted to foreign workers. Hawaii recruited tourist workers from around the Pacific Basin as it once imported Portuguese, Japanese, and other sugar-industry workers.[11] The result kept wages low, arguably improved service, and created further dislocation among native Hawaiian workers.

There are ways for visitors to penetrate closer to the heart of Maui, and my wife and I inadvertently stumbled on one. Attending a conference at an upscale hotel well beyond our budget, we slipped out to a local grocery store, the Ooka, to purchase days' worth of fruit, cereal, and other sundries for less than half the price of breakfast for two at the hotel. When we returned with the groceries in our rental car, the valet noticed the two bags: "The Ooka?" he asked, smiling in disbelief. "Hey, look," he shouted to his co-workers. "They found the Ooka." We rose in their estimation.

As a result of the differentiation in incomes and the desirability of Wailea's amenities, a local underground market flourishes. An illegal trade in the wristbands that allow visitors use of the exquisite hotel pools and grounds at Wailea, which the hotels sell to nonguests at the cost of seventy dollars per day, is ongoing. Locals exchange them among themselves and sell them to tourists for as little as twenty-five dollars at a small park in the middle of Kihei. The place has the romance of a mideastern bazaar; cultures, economies, and values meet and are transformed. The daily color of the wristband, purported to be secret, is always available for a price. During summer 1995, when I last visited, the pool at the Grand Wailea was filled with wristbanded swimmers, among them certainly some locals—the first rule of tourism is that locals always get in free—and tourists masquerading as paying visitors while hotel officials sought to stem the illicit trade. Visitors who could not afford the luxury resort but wanted to share in the experience of Wailea became the beneficiaries. Wristbanding was only one of the innumerable strategies that people used to invert the class and structural divisions of tourism. Hardly an attempt to equalize the gross disparity between the incomes of service workers and the wealthy, it illustrated the complex relationship between status and amenity that tourism ultimately spawns.

Wailea was never inexpensive, and it remained vulnerable to fluctuations in economic conditions around the world. In the mid-1990s room rates topped $230 per day at all the hotels. Some cost in excess of $400 per night, and most Americans who visited came as part of a convention package. The profit margins at such resorts were slim, and demand waxed and waned. Overbuilding also hurt, especially the high-end resorts with the most limited markets. The spectacular Grand Hyatt routinely posted large losses and became too expensive for the company to operate. In the mid-1990s it was sold at a loss to a Japanese conglomerate and became the Grand Wailea; the tourists who married in the faux New England chapel were almost exclusively Japanese. By 1995, with a weak dollar against the Japanese yen, the hotel's clientele overwhelmingly originated in the Far East. Maui seemed colonized once again, this time by the well-off of Japan. Citizens of other emergent economic powers on the Pacific Rim cast their eyes east, seeking the rewards that modern popular culture deemed the trappings of their success. This outcome, both predictable and unnerving, repeated an ongoing process in the history of Hawaii and of tourism.

The island most conditioned to a colonial service regime, Maui serves as a paradigm in its experience with tourism that ultimately puts an end to claims of exceptionalism about the American West. Maui's tourism typifies the industry in the West. Neither first nor last, extraordinary nor outstanding, Maui is archetypal; its patterns are those of the American West writ large over the global landscape. Because of its historic economic patterns and its mythic meaning, the West offers a clearer lens through which to see the emergence of the patterns of postindustrial economies in their paradigmatic form. On Maui, tourism actually and metaphorically sandwiches other economies and roles with the vagaries of economic fluctuation in a manner that defines the American West and indeed the pre-, non- and postindustrial worlds.

Hardly unique to Hawaii, tourism in the twentieth century has become one of the most important industries in the American West. From Santa Fe to Alaska, from San Antonio to Mt. Rainier, western communities and states depend on the revenue from visitors to sustain local services, develop infrastructure, support schools, and keep taxes low. In many western states, tourism has been the second or third most important source of income throughout the post–World War II period. In Nevada as in Hawaii, tourism is the foundation upon which the prosperity of the state economy rests. Marketing a place and its heritage, natural attributes, or constructed reality has become standard western fare, as typical as the steak and potatoes or biscuits and gravy served across the region or the poi and pig served at luaus to generations of visitors to the islands of Hawaii. As yet, no one has systematically addressed its social, cultural, environmental, and economic costs. The dance with tourism, in the West spanning more than the twentieth century, reveals the challenges of the postindustrial world. Across the sweep of the century, tourism's combination of promise and threat, of dislocation and relocation, becomes clear. The history of tourism in the West serves as a blueprint for the future of this most colonized and most mythical region of the nation.

NOTES

1. Mark Kurlansky, *Cod: A Biography of the Fish that Changed the World* (New York: Walker and Company, 1997), 231–32, makes much the same point from the perspective of displaced fishermen.
2. Ross Calvin, *Sky Determines: An Interpretation of the Southwest* (New York: Macmillan Company, 1934), 1–33.
3. Timothy Mitchell, *Colonizing Egypt* (New York: Cambridge University Press, 1988); Russell Banks, *Affliction* (New York: Harper and Row, 1989), addresses this theme directly.
4. Cummins E. Speakman Jr., *Mowee: An Informal History of the Hawaiian Island* (San Rafael, CA: Pueo Press, 1978), 189.
5. Speakman, *Mowee,* 186–87; Douglas Pearce, *Tourist Development,* 2d ed. (New York: John Wiley and Sons, 1989), 67–70, defines the concept of a one-owner resort.
6. Karl Kim, "Tourism on Our Terms: Tourism Planning in Hawaii," report, Western Governors' Association, 1991, 9–10.
7. Karl Kim, "The Political Economy of Foreign Investment in Hawai'i," *Social Process in Hawaii* 35 (1994): 42.
8. Ibid., 45–46; N. Ordway, "A Study of Foreign Investment in Real Property and Its Impact on the State" (Honolulu: University of Hawaii Center for Real Estate, 1990).
9. Speakman, *Mowee,* 188–89; conversation with Karl Kim, May 2, 1997.
10. Karl Kim to Hal Rothman, e-mail, June 27, 1997, copy in possession of author.
11. Kim, "Tourism on Our Terms," 12.

Introduction

Tourism is a devil's bargain, not only in the twentieth-century American West but throughout the nation and the world. Despite its reputation as a panacea for the economic ills of places that have lost their way in the postindustrial world or for those that never found it, tourism typically fails to meet the expectations of communities and regions that embrace it as an economic strategy. Regions, communities, and locales welcome tourism as an economic boon, only to find that it irrevocably changes them in unanticipated and uncontrollable ways. From this one enormous devil's bargain flows an entire collection of closely related conditions that complement the process of change in overt and subtle ways. Tourism transforms culture into something new and foreign; it may or may not rescue economies.

As a viable option for moribund or declining places, tourism promises much but delivers only a little, often in forms different from what its advocates anticipate. Its local beneficiaries come from a small segment of the population, "the growth coalition," the landowners, developers, planners, builders, real estate sales and management interests, bankers, brokers, and others.[1] The capital that sustains these interests comes from elsewhere, changing local relationships and the values that underpin them and their vision of place. Other residents flounder, finding their land their greatest asset and their labor lightly valued. With tourism comes unanticipated and irreversible consequences, social, cultural, economic, demographic, environmental, and political consequences that communities, their leaders, and their residents typically face unprepared. This coupling of promise and problem defies the usual mitigation processes of American society, the planning, zoning, and community sanction that historically combine to limit the impact of change.

The embrace of tourism triggers a contest for the soul of a place. Although an amorphous concept, it holds one piece of the core of the devil's bargain of tourism as a form of living. All places, even open prairies or rugged deserts, have identities; people see and define them, they have intrinsic characteristics, and they welcome or repel according to people's definitions of them as much as by their innate characteristics. Human-shaped places, cities and national parks, marinas and farms, closely guard their identities. Their people are located within them in ways that create not only national, regional, and local affiliation but also a powerful sense of self and place in the world. That identity depends on the context of the place and is linked to its social shape as well as to its economy, environment, and culture. Challenges to it threaten the status quo, especially when they pull on the bonds of community by pitting different elements, especially those that shared previous alliances against one another. As these bonds fray, subrosa tension, buried in the fictions of social arrangements, surfaces as the impact of change throws the soul of the place, any place, up for grabs.

In the twentieth-century American West, tourism initiates this contest as it generates myriad patterns that challenge the existing structure of communities and regions and reshape them. The initial development of tourism often seems innocuous, "beneath the radar" of outside interests, lucrative but not transformative. As places acquire the cachet of desirability, they draw people and money; the redistribution of wealth, power, and status follows, complicating local arrangements. When tourism creates sufficient wealth, it becomes too important to be left to the locals. Power moves away from local decision makers, even those who psychically and socially invest in the new system that tourism creates, and toward outside capital and its local representatives. This redistribution changes internal relations as it eventually consolidates into a dominant template or overlay for the places it develops. The new shape disenfranchises most locals even as it makes some natives and most neonatives—those who are attracted to the places that have become tourist towns because of the traits of these transformed places—economically better off and creates a place that becomes a mirror image of itself as its identity is marketed. A series of characteristic and oft-repeated consequences results, leaving all but a few people in tourist communities questioning whether they were better off in the economic doldrums that preceded tourism.

Tourism is the most colonial of colonial economies, not because of the sheer physical difficulty or the pain or humiliation intrinsic in its labor but because of its psychic and social impact on people and their places. Tourism and the social structure it provides transform locals into people who look like themselves but who act and believe differently as they learn to market their place and its, and their, identity. They change as much as did African workers in the copper mines of the Congo or the diamond mines of South Africa, men from rural homelands who became industrial cannon fodder. Unlike laborers in these colonial enterprises, who lived in obscurity as they labored, tourist workers face an enormous contradiction: who and what they are is crucial to visitors in the abstract; who they are as service workers is entirely meaningless. Tourist workers quickly learn that one of the most essential traits of their service is to mirror onto the guest what that visitor wants from them and from their place in a way that affirms the visitor's self-image.

Here begins a dilemma. Locals must be what visitors want them to be in order to feed and clothe themselves and their families, but they also must guard themselves, their souls, and their places from people who less appreciate its special traits. They negotiate these boundaries, creating a series of boxes between themselves and visitors, rooms where locals encourage visitors to feel that they have become of the place but where the locals also subtly guide visitors away from the essence of being local. The Sugar Cane Train in Maui nods in this direction as the conductor tells us his story; tourists do not much care about the stories of the cane cutters outside the train window.[2] In this process, the visited change, becoming different from who they were as they exchange the privilege of their identity. This offer to share an image of their sense of belonging for coin becomes a far more comprehensive and often more perplexing bargain than merely exchanging labor and the assets in their land for their sustenance.

This process of scripting space, both physically and psychically, defines tourist towns and resorts. All places have scripted space. The scripting of space is essential to the organizing of the physical and social world for the purpose of perpetuation. Like commercial space, tourist space is specially scripted to keep visitors at the center of the picture while simultaneously cloaking, manipulating, and even deceiving them into believing that their experience is the locals' life, reality, and view of the world. "Wasn't it wonderful [in Hawaii] before Captain Cook showed up," a friend said to me over dinner at an exquisite shoreside restaurant in Ma'alea Bay, Maui, thoroughly swallowing the fiction of the scripted space of tourism.[3]

Despite often seductively quaint and romantic settings, seeming harmlessness, and a reputation as a "clean" industry, tourism belongs to the modern and postindustrial, postmodern worlds; its social structures and cultural ways are those of an extractive industry. Though its environmental by-products are not the tailings piles of uranium mining, in the West they include the spread of real estate development, the gobbling up of open space in narrow mountain valleys, the traffic and sprawl of expansive suburban communities, and the transformation of the physical environment into roads and reservoirs that provide activity and convenience for visitors. Tourism offers visitors romanticized visions of the historic past, the natural world, popular culture, and especially of themselves. The sale of these messages, even in their most innocent form, is what iconoclastic author Edward Abbey called "industrial tourism," the packaging and marketing of experience as commodity within the boundaries of the accepted level of convenience to the public.[4]

The most postmodern of such devices, the ones that meld the technologies, attitudes, and styles of the Age of Information, the era of the global transmission of knowledge that followed 1980, go even further. They purposely create another level of experience that masquerades or prepares for so-called authentic experience, blurring any line that may remain and often making the replica more seductive than the original. Using experience to script space in another way, to design artificial controls that seem natural and ordinary as they highlight the activity by subtly persuading visitors that the activity is their own, this postmodern form shatters historical distinctions between the real and the unreal by producing faux replicas of experience independent of the activity from which they derive.

Las Vegas has best defined this practice in its redefinition of space, time, and meaning into constructs that serve the visitor, but the form has become ubiquitous. The climbing gym, which offers indoor mountain climbing and training for the initiated and uninitiated alike, fuses these concepts. A seventy-five-foot-high climbable rock face, Surge Rock, sponsored by Coca-Cola as a promotion for its newest soft drink, Surge, is at SKG Gameworks in Showcase, a prototype upscale entertainment and commercial development that opened in 1997 on the Las Vegas Strip. As the project debuted, Showcase developer and entrepreneur Barry Fieldman climbed the rockface. Family and friends arriving at his six-year-old's birthday party watched him ascend as they rode the elevator down to the first floor, where other climbers assembled.[5]

Given the varieties of experience available in the postmodern world, all tourism—Surge Rock, the Eiffel Tower, an African safari, backpacking in the Bob Marshall Wilderness in Montana, or following in the footsteps of protoarchaeologist Heinrich Schliemann—is scripted industrial tourism. The wealth of industrial society, its transportation technologies, its consumer goods, the emphasis on convenience, and the values of a postmodern, postconsumption culture create the surplus that allows people to select any experience they choose. The goal is not experience but fulfillment—making the chooser feel important, strong, powerful, a member of the right crowd, or whatever else they crave. The people determined to leave mainstream society in search of an individual sense of travel are scripted into believing that backpacking in the Bob Marshall makes them unique or at least part of a rare breed, intellectually and morally above other tourists. This conceit is common among elites—academics and environmentalists among them—who believe they are more knowledgeable than others.

This embrace of the inherently fraudulent ecotourism, a codeword for an activity that parallels the colonial tourism of Theodore Roosevelt in Africa, in the hopes of creating a better world reveals a stunning naivete. Finding the little out-of-the-way inn in rural Ireland no more invents a unique experience than does taking a bus tour of Las Vegas or the Universal Studios tour in Los Angeles. Instead it offers a wrapper that promises a self-affirming authentic experience in the viewer's terms. This delusion of distance from society and superiority of spirit and skill clearly exists for the climbers of Mount Everest. Rob Hall, the vaunted New Zealander guide of the Himalayas, recognized his death was imminent during a tragic May 1996 ascent and spoke to his eight-months-pregnant wife on a satellite phone, minimizing the idea that any form of tourism can be other than that of the global market. The expedition took place so that people who could afford it could feel personally satisfied; a total of eight people died as a result.[6] "Bagging trophy," as some people caustically refer to the status side of postmodern tourism, can be dangerous as well as exhilarating.

For Americans, the geographic and cultural landscapes of a mythic American West hold these psychic trophies. The West is the location of the American creation myth, the national *sipapu*, the figurative hole in the earth from which Pueblo Indian people emerged in their story of the beginning of the world. The image of the West, especially in the conquest that occurred between 1848 and 1890, serves that same mythic purpose for Americans. The Revolutionary War has distant meaning, but in the late twentieth century, the West holds mythic sway. In the post–Civil War West, the United States emerged anew and reinvented itself, shedding slavery, sectionalism, and states' rights and becoming the American nation that persisted until its post-Watergate fragmentation. The new nation embodied in the West transcended the inherent flaws of the first Republic, impaled on its own inconsistencies by the shelling of Fort Sumter. The West healed the hole in the heart of the nation born anew after its epic and cataclysmic tragedy. The revised national creation myth gave the West primacy in American life and thinking that grew from innocence and the potential for reinvention, a prestige further marking the region's importance in a postindustrial world increasingly dependent on tourism. When Americans paid homage to their national and nationalistic roots, they did not look to Independence Hall; they went West, like their forefathers, to find self and to create society, to build anew from the detritus of the old.[7] This need for redefinition explains the historic and modern fixation on the West in the United States and even in Europe.

Western tourism stands at the heart of the American drama precisely because it occurs on the same stage as the national drama of self-affirmation. To Americans the West is their refuge, the home of the "last best place," according to William Kittredge and Annick Smith, home to the mythic landscapes where Americans become whole again in the aftermath of personal or national cataclysm. This virtue and incredible burden makes tourism in the West more tantalizing, more fraught with tension and anxiety, and more full of text, subtext, and depth than anywhere else in the nation. The same activity in the West means more than elsewhere; the myth of exceptionalism has a life of its own as the Rockies rise in front of westward-bound travelers, even as late as Jack Kerouac's adventures in the 1950s.[8] That peculiar standing makes western tourism a crucible in which the powers that drive American capitalism mix with growing and increasingly disparate and random forces, economic, social, cultural, and political, shaking the foundations of the modern world.

Different parts of the American West react to tourism in disparate ways. One West, urban and rural, is tourist-dependent. In Nevada and Hawaii, which depend on tourism to the exclusion of other economic strategies, it has become an extension of state government. In both, tourism has paid the bills as it framed a postindustrial economy and postmodern culture. Both states also show traits of being plantation economies, run by outside capital and local overseers at the expense of the local public.[9] The identity of such places became what they marketed. Tourism there was studied, measured, and surveyed in an attempt to balance its impact with its profits without alienating visitors.

In another West, rural, rooted, and increasingly challenged by changing economic conditions, tourism has long been a by-product, a somewhat improbable shadow economy. To many people, especially those possessed of the myths of individualism that permeate American culture, it seemed ephemeral and unimportant, less substantive than making things, growing food, or raising animals. In places such as 1920s Jackson Hole, Wyoming, or southern Utah at the proclamation of the Grand Staircase–Escalante National Monument in 1996, the outright dismissal of tourism's significance and its amorphousness allowed it to develop with little input, to function autonomously, apart from other more thoroughly measured parts of the regional economy.

A third West, urban, more affluent, and more cosmopolitan, regarded tourism as an integral part of the regional mix, an essential sector of the economy similar to the industrial sector or other service endeavors. Los Angeles and San Francisco reflexively cater to tourism as just another economic undertaking. Almost without the recognition of the larger regional society, both visitor and visited, tourism acquired distinct forms in such places.

Despite their differences in geography and activity, the forms of tourism create similar patterns of life. In origins, economic structure, hierarchical organization, dependence on corridors of transportation, and transformative impact on existing communities, a diverse range of places from the Grand Canyon to Las Vegas and Disneyland offer numerous parallels. Tourism is barely distinguishable from other forms of colonial economies. Typically founded by resident protoentrepreneurs, the industry expands beyond local control, becomes institutionalized by large-scale forces of capital, and then grows to mirror not the values of the place but those of the traveling public. The malleability of the industry makes these places more pliable, creating pockets of prosperity within localities that are typically limited to incoming neonatives. Existing elites find themselves facing a trade-off: accept profitable but diminished status or fight against outside forces. For ordinary people who typically limped along in many of these locales, tourism offered the promise of panacea but delivered far less. Many residents gave up long-standing patterns of life, expecting tourism to provide better material sustenance without diminishing their sense of self or place. Often it did not, leaving people who had once accepted their position in an unsettled mood and economically only barely better off. As a salvation for social, cultural, and economic problems, tourism has typically fallen short, its success in some cases even more devastating than failure. Tourism's economic results range from good to disastrous. From a social perspective, no one it touches remains unchanged.

The selection of tourism involves a sequence of imperfect choices. It is not inherently bad for people, communities, or regions, but as William Dean Howells once observed, choice could be a curse. For many places in the American West of the 1990s, tourism offers the best available economic strategy to maintain community fabric. Yet those who seek it forget that the places that embraced tourism earlier in western history chose it because they had few other economic options. Tourism's greatest danger is its image as a panacea. Community leaders make imperfect choices based on insufficient information without recognizing the potential consequences. Only the benefits, the successes, the flow of revenue to state, county, and local coffers, occupy their thoughts, not the increase in expenditures and the changing social picture. The economist's fallacious dream of rational choice based on perfect information collapses as unanticipated consequences overwhelm expectations in tourist communities.[10]

Tourism is where modern capitalism ends and its postmodern equivalent, a compelling rendering of the post-1980s cultural and economic landscape, begins. The view of the shore from Lahaina Bay offers a legible geography that operates within a series of conventions apparently intelligible to inhabitants of an industrial sociocultural and economic landscape but that are really quite different. On Maui, experience is the commodity for sale. Viewing the whales epitomizes this process yet is simultaneously irrelevant. Maui connotes relaxation and renewal; its scripting is designed to promote comfort, convenience, and security even as it emphasizes the experience of being above the comforts it offers. It is postmodern script, placing the visitor at the center of the picture and encouraging concern with the self far beyond any interaction with the world. On Maui, the physical world is merely the backdrop to the self.

Postmodern capitalism is new terrain, largely unrecognizable except to the people who experience it. It is not the capitalism of Andrew Carnegie, J. P. Morgan, Henry Ford, Armand Hammer, or J. Paul Getty but more that of Walt Disney, Bill Gates, and gaming impresario Steve Wynn. It is not national or nationalistic but transnational and global. Its emphasis is not on the tangible of making things, of ever-larger assembly lines and production processes, but on the marketing of images, of information, of spectacle. It creates information and information-processing systems and the accoutrements that turn regional and national economic endeavor into a global commodity. Of equal significance, postmodern, postindustrial capitalism produces images that convey emotions, chiefly hope and contentment, and conduits for information. It is a form at once substantial and inconsequential, crucial yet trivial, meaningful yet ephemeral. Its sociocultural impact is vast; in its ability to move information, and consequently to move more traditional forms of economic endeavor such as assembly-line work, postmodern global capitalism is truly revolutionary. Postindustrial capitalism has changed the very meaning of economic endeavor, providing new ways to produce wealth in a transformation as profound as the industrial revolution.

Industrial capitalism began in a productive ethos, a work ethic rightly or wrongly labeled Protestant and an ideal of producing goods with an ebullient joy that helped make their consumption an afterthought. Pragmatism permeated the production phase of American capitalism, that great expansion of productivity associated with the years between 1865 and 1914. It focused on the transformation of raw material into useable commodities such as steel or finished products such as sewing machines and telephones. The shelves of goods available in the "palaces of consumption," department stores, were the signature of the age. Utility defined this phase of capitalism, manifested in the time and motion studies of Frederick Winslow Taylor, in the subsequent invention of the assembly line, and in transportation systems such as railroads and electric street cars dependent on industrial technologies.[11]

Intimately connected to production was consumption, the dominant feature of the stage of industrialization that gathered momentum following World War I. The spectacular consumption of the late nineteenth century, labeled "conspicuous" by social critic Thorstein Veblen, triggered an emphasis on the status rather than on the utility of goods. This trend continued with the advent of mass technologies such as the radio, the moving picture, and later television and reached its pinnacle in the refinement of details that marked the planned obsolescence built into the graciously lined and finned vehicles of the immediate post–World War II era. Consumption became first a means to an end in American society and later an end in itself. Consumption was about using and enjoying the largesse of American economic development, a concept foreign when industrialization began in the United States but that grew significantly in fits and starts until it gathered full force during the 1920s. That enjoyment went hand in hand with the rise of advertising, the widespread availability of credit, and the increased social importance of the self. It reached a pinnacle during the American Cultural Revolution of the 1960s, articulated with a razor-sharp edge by Tom Wolfe in "The Me Decade."[12] The needs of the individual ruled without social checks. The ethic of tangible consumption dominated as the nation transformed from a society that avowed deferred gratification to one that collectively and individually sought instant fulfillment.

Industrial-age Americans made things; then they bought them. In the postindustrial world, Americans became consumers not only of tangible goods but also of the spirit and meaning of things. What Americans of a certain class could touch and hold no longer exclusively granted the security and importance to which its possessors were accustomed. When anyone could lease a BMW, the elite needed more: the control of feelings, emotion, identity, and modes of understanding that signified status, a way to differentiate themselves from the increasingly luxurious mass cultural norm. In a world short on time, where only the very rich and the very poor possessed it and only the former had the means to use it, a new way to define the self as special emerged. In turn, a new form of commodification came to dominate the American and the international landscape. Corporations packaged and people purchased what they felt granted them identity, but that identity ceased to follow traditional iconography and became a product of the international culture marketplace.[13] Modernism had been about finding the individual's place in the world of machines; the mergers and downsizing of postindustrialism rendered the individual irrelevant as postmodernism made the self the only meaningful reference point. Ultimately, this affirmed a series of trappings, tangible and shapeless, that proclaimed an identity of the self, a far cry from the national identity of the production ethos. Adorning the self became a goal, but not only with jewelry and clothing. An intangible dimension gained great significance.

Tourism, through which people acquire intangibles—experience, cachet, proximity to celebrity—became the successor to industrial capitalism, the endpoint in a process that transcended consumption and made living a function of accoutrements. It created a culture, languid and bittersweet, and as writer Mark Edmundson puts it, "very, very self-contained. . . . There's little fire, little passion to be found" that had as its object participation in consumption.[14] Yet even the young recognized that this culture was equally post-tangible, not about consuming things but about possessing experience. Material goods no longer fulfilled and created status in the United States and Europe. Only a very few products were so elite that they could not be widely owned, and even those few could be suitably copied. Goods were insufficient; status became a function of time spent, of context, of address, of place, of a table in a restaurant. Although the water was the same and the towels no softer and only marginally fluffier at the Grand Wailea's pool than at any other, that pool contained a schooled aestheticism that Americans, and world citizens, mistake for better. The pilfered wristbands provided entrée, the look of prosperity and status, wrapped around the intangible of presence in the right places. In the postindustrial, postmodern world, people collect the difference embodied in travel experience as others once collected Fabergé eggs. The act of travel, especially on terms dictated by the self, has come to mark the self-proclaimed well rounded and has allowed individuals to define themselves as unique. Travel as a defining experience has become a new form of religion, a new way to value the self. Bumper stickers will soon sport sayings like "she who has been the most places and stayed in luxury in all of them wins" instead of the more passé "he who dies with the most toys wins."

Tourism is the archetype of the service economy, the market of the future. Its form resembles that of the industrial world and derives wealth from it, but tourism is postindustrial in the way it competes economically and in the transnational global patterns of capital distribution it reveals. The seemingly nondescript Sunnyside Inn lodge and restaurant on the shores of Lake Tahoe appears certain to be a one-owner lodge, an old time resort. Here in a home built by a Captain Kendrick of the Schlage Lock Company early in the century, visitors receive an elegant and relaxing experience, real hospitality, just as the captains of industry once received. A close look at the walls reveals a line of photos of peer restaurants, other members of the T S Restaurant chain—in Kaanapali, Lahaina, Malibu, and Huntington Beach.[15] The Sunnyside Inn had not belonged to family operators since 1986, when San Francisco restauranteurs bought the inn and restored it to its former elegance. Sunnyside Inn was one of more than a dozen restaurants scripted to offer unique experience and simultaneously to obviate the traces of that scripting. This faux chain, precisely unlike chain restaurants such as Denny's in the diversity of ambience but adhering to the formula, demonstrates that activities packaged as distinct have structural parallels. These too are networks, shaped by the scripting of space and formed by capital, influence, power, and attraction, but they deny their association with each other in a way that industrial networks never did.

Nor is participation in this economy the same as in its industrial counterpart. Selling ambience, experience, and identity has little in common with selling durable goods except for the selling itself. Little that can be touched and handled changes hands in the tourist transaction; the souvenirs are big business, but they are emblems and not the point itself. The exchange is more complicated and ambiguous than a typical material sales transaction. A feeling is transmitted and perhaps shared; a way of living is expressed. A mode of behavior, be it the ethos of skiing, the appreciation of the Mona Lisa, or the way to hold your cards at the Blackjack table, is offered and recognized if not always understood. These markers of belonging, of being part of the fashionable, the exciting, the new, are critical in a world where most earlier indicators of status have become easily attainable. In this new form of exchange, an entity meaningful but intangible, typically the identity, way of life, or feel of a place and its people seems to be offered up for a price. But not always.

A view of tourism from the perspective of the visited highlights a different set of relationships. For locals and incoming neonative workers, people who accepted the constructed ethos of a place and generally are willing to be underemployed there, the embrace of tourism leads to significant changes. A world in which people apparently do the same thing but in a different way, with a different feel, becomes first characteristic and then overwhelming. Sun Valley, Idaho, native John Rember describes this situation: "There are worse lives than those lived in museums," he mused about his own fate, "worse shortcomings than a lack of authenticity."[16] As problematic as is the concept of authenticity, Rember's definition holds much weight. "Authentic" to him is a world that serves its residents ahead of outsiders, where people grow crops, hunt animals for the table instead of sport, and are tuned to the rhythms of the land. It is a world agricultural and industrial, the forms called first and second nature by William Cronon.[17] The tourist world inverts that principle, opening a new realm of existence, a third nature, much to the distress of Edward Abbey, who made a living writing about experience without acknowledging his own role in creating change, and of locals, who remember a time before tourism descended upon them and altered their lives.

The world Rember remembers contains Cronon's first and second nature. First nature, the prehuman landscape, and I would add its organization by humans for subsistence purposes, contained essentially hunting and gathering, herding, and small-scale agrarian regimes. It is not devoid of humans, which would render it meaningless and abstract. Instead first nature describes hundreds of centuries of relationship between a species and their world, which they typically could affect only in small ways. The prototype for second nature became Cronon's Chicago, a place apart from first nature but intrinsically tied to it, its utility transformed by protoindustrial and later by heavy industrial processes, forms of organization, and physical and intellectual structures and symbols.[18] If first nature was organized to feed and clothe the self and the family, second nature's forms were designed to market to the world.

Third nature, like postindustrial economies and postmodern thinking, focuses on what can be felt in a personal and an emotional sense. It is a natural world organized to acquire intangibles, experience, and cachet, to grant identity, to regard nature as a fount of psychic energy and emotion. Faux or real, scenery evokes powerful emotions. The fin de siècle tourist understood the Grand Canyon as an affirmation of the nation. The postmodern tourist measures it by its impact on the self. Surge Rock is real to people who see El Capitan only as a climbing rock; Surge Rock provokes similar respect because it shares the same purpose with El Capitan. Third nature is intangible, ethereal; only in the mind and perhaps in the heart can its significance exist.

Yet even the people who remember a world before the tourism of third nature and sometimes resent the present cannot live without tourism, for it provides them a promise of permanence in place, a kind of importance, and income. In places where Rember's ways of making a living never existed or have become tenuous, where the power of social structure has weakened and frayed, where many people or even most have little to anticipate except the drudgery of poverty and irrelevance, the promise of tourism, and often the physical changes and attendant growth it creates, provides hope and the glimmer of a future. Tourism begins as a panacea but becomes addictive. Its promise of vitality appears to offer a better way, a way to hope in a reality that stays much the same. It is as seductive as is a tourist's view from a Zodiac in Lahaina Harbor.

These multiple tensions play in ambiguous and multifaceted ways in the development of a tourist economy. The selection or acceptance of tourism as a strategy forces a new characterization of the virtues of place. When AMFAC developed Kaanapali as a resort, it evaluated the area differently than it did for sugar production. The new viewpoint also illuminates a working description of the local power structure, which tourism soon changes. These two features define place, often to the consternation of people who perceive their position differently. Here Rember's fictional characters live, here the "real" of the local world separates from the perceived real that visitors are encouraged to embrace. Here the tension between the various polarities of these different worldviews is manifested.

Tourism transforms place and people, but few can do without its benefits. It brings new neighbors, who often do not share existing values, but those newcomers are a source of prosperity. In the West tourism encourages the marketing of an entity different from the beef grazed on local grass, the timber in nearby forests, or the riches buried deep in the ground. Though these too can bring about exercises in colonialism that impress a structure upon a town, they require only local backs, not hearts or minds. In tourism, the very identity of place becomes its economic sustenance, and in that transformation is a complicated and paradoxical situation for the people of that place.

Three basic, overlapping, and intertwined types of tourism have evolved and become integrated during the twentieth century in the American West. They existed in various forms from the beginning of the era of mass transportation. They rose to dominance, in no small part based on the cultural values of the moment, the distribution of wealth, and the availability of transportation to the destinations that defined the ethos of the moment. Each revealed specific attributes of the dominant thinking of their time, superseding the other forms of tourism that coexisted. In this respect, the different forms of tourism became cumulative rather than sequential. Each successive stage of dominance embodied previous traits, including those attributes in the new shape that reflected changing American values.

The first type to develop was heritage or cultural tourism, the marketing of the historic, scenic, and mythic past. Long before the turn of the twentieth century, Americans defined a cultural heritage for themselves apart from the European legacy they revered and emulated and to which they felt inferior. Cultural values and a need for a national iconography made a reverential approach both to the past and the spectacular scenic attributes of the West a cultural necessity. The art of Thomas Moran, Albert Bierstadt, and others reflected that mythic formulation and conceptually—and through the railroad, physically—generations embraced it. As long as travel remained an upper-middle- and upper-class phenomenon, heritage and cultural tourism exemplified its dominant ethos.

This class-based tourism reflected and resulted from the industrialization of the late nineteenth century. It embodied the simultaneous confidence and insecurity of the industrial age, the tremendous pride in the accomplishments of industrial society, and the myriad benefits it brought as well as the uneasiness caused by the changes it wrought. In the initial phase of national tourism, the industry manifested a class-based affirmation of the power and virtues of the modern while providing a context for a critique of industrial society. In ascribing nationwide meaning to place, tourism served an important conceptual role in American society. Western tourism, so closely allied with the idea of Manifest Destiny, the quest for the sublime, and the desire to know that marked fin de siècle America, became an integral part of reassuring the powerful of their place in a rapidly changing world.

During the 1920s and after broader distribution of increased wealth, better transportation systems, and easier access to remote places initiated the rapid development of nationally marketed recreational tourism. This phenomenon involved physical experience in the outdoors instead of the museumlike appreciation for cultural and natural features that characterized heritage tourism. Recreational tourism melded the amenities required by elite nineteenth-century tourists with activities that appealed to a broader public, less status conscious but more affluent and having greater amounts of leisure time after World War II. Hunting was the first great recreational tourism in the American West; the practice even enjoyed cultural and heritage meaning during the 1890s. The development of the ski industry and the emergence of prewar resorts such as Sun Valley, Idaho, and in the postwar years, Aspen, Colorado, granted new significance to the sport in American society.

As the infrastructure that supported travel developed, as roads stretched toward the horizon in the American West and tourist camps and motor courts appeared, travel became democratized. No longer were the wealthy the only people who could arrive at desirable destinations. The social spread in automobile ownership ensured that a wider range of people visited a broader spectrum of places and passed through a far more diverse world on the way, expanding the impact of tourism but diluting the intensity of its message. The new traveler, more middle class and by the 1920s less tuned to the tastes of the American elite, enjoyed different activities. The hegemonic influence of cultural and heritage tourism gave way to the sheer experience of recreation.

The growth in population and employment opportunities in the post–World War II era, technological innovations such as air travel and air-conditioning, and the rise of a society that placed a premium on leisure and had the discretionary capital to fund that obsession helped inaugurate the third phase, entertainment tourism. Between 1945 and 1973 the United States experienced economic growth of such great proportion that it altered American expectations. The combination of wealth and technology allowed Americans unparalleled freedom and changed the way they experienced the world. Television contributed greatly to this conceptual reformulation as did the panoply of popular culture devices, from cable television to the VCR, boombox, Walkman, and personal computer. In this changing cultural self-pronouncement, the West retained great significance. It became a playground, the American dreamscape, historic, mythic, and actual, spawning a complex industry with the ability to transform places as it created an economy for destitute and flourishing communities alike. The development of Las Vegas, Disneyland, and their range of imitators characterized this phase. In the post–1945 United States, travel to accomplish personal objectives acquired the status of national birthright, and changing modes of transportation and accommodation made its forms accessible to a broader range of people than ever before.

In the postwar era, the three basic forms of tourism melded into images of their earlier incarnations. Heritage and recreational tourism in the West, historically linked by geography, developed closer ties as the tastes of the American public changed. Entertainment tourism eventually included both recreational and heritage tourism within its broad dimensions, packaging experience in resorts and national parks and mimicking what these forms offered in the packaged unreality of Disneyland, theme parks, and even Las Vegas. The result was an industry that was sufficiently malleable to weave straw into gold. But there was a steep price to pay for the trick: the cultural, environmental, and psychic transformation of place. Tourism made new places that looked like their predecessors and occupied the same geography, but ultimately the past and future shared only the physical attributes of the place.

The approach of tourism also frayed the bonds of community. Ties within communities exist on two levels: actual bonds of connection and agreed-upon fictions. In the latter, people paper over the differences between them in an effort to maintain the semblance of community. They stipulate that their disagreements are matters of conscience and belief that divide people of good character and intent. The embrace of tourism shatters such fictions, pitting different elements against each other—those who stand to benefit from the changes against those whose economic status will decline. Such tension is not unusual in any kind of community. Particularly in small tourist or resort towns, the destruction of the fiction that everyone has the best interests of the community at heart leads to a rending of the social fabric. The members of the growth coalition, who stand to benefit, embrace the new, sometimes with terrifying alacrity. Those whom this economic change leaves in stasis or decline seethe, resent, and sometimes resist.

Members of the latter group band together and develop a range of strategies to halt, slow, deflect, or reverse the changes that tourism brings. A continuum of response among those threatened has evolved, from resistance to negotiation to acceptance to denial, as places defined themselves in terms of their past. In highly educated and sophisticated communities, filled with neonatives from the elite groups in American society, such resistance could be powerful and all-encompassing. The loosely defined rubric "quality of life" served as the concept behind such efforts. In communities more inclined to accept power from above, with fewer people who felt control over the fate of their place, such actions often consisted of grumbling disguised as social critique. In all cases, the right to challenge change was conveyed through self-identification rituals that had social, cultural, and sometimes economic traits. These rituals — ranging from photographs of the people of Aspen lined up on the local rugby field next to markers connoting the year they arrived to commercials reminding Las Vegans of "how it used to be before the volcano, before the pyramid" — proved local and neonative identity and strengthened ties within the wide group ambivalent about the changes tourism caused.[19]

As a solution to social and economic problems, tourism has vast limitations. The last resort of moribund communities and states, tourism is employed by local leaders as a remedy for the problems of places with declining industries. Tourism required no special skill of its employees, save a willingness to be gracious and attentive. Operators of tourist enterprises rarely requested tax abatements and local dollars to support the industry, and the retail trade generated by tourism filled the coffers of most western states with sales tax revenue. Tourism often functioned as a response to economic desperation, serving as a replacement economy for declining industries. Viewed through the rosiest of lenses, it promised that a community could retain its fabric and character as it brought prosperity.

Unlike traditional industries, which often brought a labor force that became socialized to local norms, tourism came replete with transient newcomers. Labor followed tourism, as did managers and other supervisory personnel. So did neonatives, who found themselves embracing a fixed moment in local time. The tourists themselves became a strong influence, objects of contempt and gratitude but harbingers of a range of experience beyond that of most locals. The need for tourists to experience an event they defined as real but that they could quickly understand compelled change. Locals who expected to be who they were became who their visitors wanted them to be; increasingly, these purveyors of local service ceased to be local at all. Neonatives replaced locals, creating the oddly postmodern spectacle of newcomers imitating locals for visitors to give the outsiders what they were paying for: reality as the tourist understood it.

A paradox resulted: local communities that embraced tourism expected to be visited by many people but generally thought their lives would remain the same. They did not anticipate, nor were they prepared for, the ways in which tourism would change them, the rising cost of property in their town, the traffic, the self-perception that the work they did was unimportant, the diminishing sense of pride in work and ultimately in community, and the tears in the social fabric that followed. Many locals found selling themselves more complicated than selling their minerals or their beef. But given their dwindling options, tourism was sometimes the only choice.

Western tourism typifies the impact of the industry. With the exception of the belt from Seattle to San Diego, the West remains an economic colony, supported by federal and outside dollars, subject to both extraregional and intraregional influences, seeking to assert independence and to control its destiny. It finds itself with the economic structure and sociocultural issues of a colony hardened beyond transfiguration. The structure of these communities and their evolution, the way they use transient and semipermanent labor, and the way they constantly are reinvented highlight the problems of tourist-based economies. Identity becomes malleable as national chains, many of them resort-based, replace local businesses. These stores become ubiquitous, obscuring local business and culture to a traveling public that is seeing just what it saw at home in a different setting and in the process, affirming home, travel destination, and self. This homogenization and increasing uniformity reflect rather than foreshadow transformation. Although the arrival of such businesses illustrates the increased economic importance of tourist communities, it also spells the end of existing cultures. Often this arrival amounts to killing the goose that laid the golden egg. The inherent problem of communities that succeed in attracting so many people is that their very presence destroys the cultural and environmental amenities that made the place special.

This is the core of the complicated devil's bargain. Success creates the seeds of its own destruction as more and more people seek the experience of an authentic place transformed to seem more authentic. In search of lifestyle instead of life, these seekers of identity and amenity transform what they touch beyond recognition. Things that look the same are not the same; actions that are the same acquire different meaning. In the process, tourists validate the transformations they cause; local will must bend to them as it deflects them, fostering a grumbling social critique often indistinguishable from nostalgia for the world they have demolished. The tensions of industrial capitalism take on new shape. Third nature, nature as spectacle, develops an ethos that claims similarity to first nature rather than to the industrial second nature that provides its wealth. Tourism complicates; it defines and redefines life after industrialization. It is different yet the same. Western tourism sells us what we are, what we as a nation of individuals need to validate ourselves, to make us what we want to be. In that process, we as tourists change all that we encounter. Making us what we want to be means shaping other places and people along with ourselves. This is the fault line of tourism, its Grand Canyon.

2

Tourism and the Framing of a Culture

Tourism as a modern pursuit resulted from the affluence that accompanied the mercantile and industrial revolutions and from the broadening intellectual curiosity that followed the Enlightenment. Travel has always been possible for human beings; tourism possessed distinctly different traits and purposes. Both wealth and intellectual attitude were necessary prerequisites for early tourism. People had to want experience, had to crave the different, both close and far away. They had to define the activities they chose, including the means of conveyance, in specific ways to become tourists. A product of revolutions in thinking and economic endeavor, the tourist was at once a new being with uncommon ideas and attitudes and a traditional one, descended from travelers and holding the intellectual idea of travel as a broadening experience. The merging of the two created a new and amorphous category so that people craved not only experience but self-affirmation, not only distance from home but their customary amenities. The tourist became an actor on the stage of the industrial and postindustrial world, the observer and the observed.

Although the world's wealthy have always enjoyed the privilege of travel, the concept of tourism expresses more than mere movement to new and different places for pleasure or cultural gain. Tourism is unlike other forms of human movement across space. Tourists travel differently; they may travel in the same plane, train, boat, or automobile, but they pack differently, live differently, and see and act differently. They take fewer possessions with them, worry less about what they will find, recognize that any part of their experience is transitory, and value the process more than the end.[1] Tourism may precede or even spur the permanent movement of people from one place to another, but it is not the travel of migration. Tourism is an entirely different activity that operates under a set of conventions much newer in human experience than those of immigration. The industrial world shapes its rule and defines its boundaries. Even those who push beyond these limits are tied to them. The conventions of tourism and the social and economic structures it encourages are products of mercantile and industrial wealth and the leisure they create. Without the technological transformation that accompanied industrialization, without the transportation networks, the broader distribution of goods, and the spread of cultural conventions through newly invented media, the combination of enlightenment, affirmation, recreation, and leisure that is twentieth-century tourism would not exist.

In the modern era, tourism has become a process, an activity through which masses of people experience places other than their homes in a system of institutions designed to convey them on their journey in whatever degree of comfort or privation they choose. Not incidentally, the process shapes—or scripts—how tourists think about the places they encounter. By definition, tourists do not depend on social and familial connections. Instead they enter the travel market as purchasers of goods, services, and ultimately the intangibles that hold the essence of place. They choose, an activity that connotes freedom in significant ways; conversely, tourism is also a social activity in that people make selections based on the preferences of their socioeconomic and status peers.[2] Tourists come and go, within the confines of available choices about activities, accommodations, transportation, cuisine, and especially socialization. This experience, including wide ranges of behavior and conversely narrow sets of options as well as the self- and externally imposed constraints of culture, defines tourism as a modern and postmodern endeavor.

Not all travelers in history have been tourists. Crusaders were no more tourists than Moslem pilgrims who make the *haj* to Mecca and Medina. Although both groups make decisions along the way, the nature of those choices is dictated not by the individual but by the overarching purpose. From global traveler Marco Polo, the thirteenth- and fourteen-century explorer and trader, to Tecumseh, who traveled the Old Northwest and the Great Plains in search of allies for his pan-Indian confederacy, from Spanish explorer Francisco Vásquez de Coronado to explorers Lewis and Clark and scientist Alexander von Humboldt, most people traveled for reasons other than pleasure or recreation. "Sojourners" provides a more apt description of such people. Their travel had little to do with leisure. They went to trade, as did Polo; to build political alliances, in the manner of Tecumseh; to conquer, in the case of Vásquez de Coronado; to map and assess the economic value of the land they found, as did Lewis and Clark; or to seek to know and quantify the universe, in the case of Humboldt. That they returned with stories to tell that encouraged others to follow added to the spice of travel but hardly made these progenitors into tourists in the modern sense.

The travelers of the preindustrial world passed alone through unfamiliar places, assisted by a loosely connected web of commercial connections that extended over a large area or simply guided by people previously unknown to them. They could not avail themselves of the scripts of modern tourism, of the effortless and sometimes purposely effort-laden means of conveyance, accommodation, and experience. They did not know where the comfortable hotels were, how they could find the best road, or whom they could trust. Nor did they believe that their wealth could solve any predicament. Like the British imperial explorer Henry Pottinger, who reconnoitered approach roads to India disguised as a holy man and a horse trader, these sojourners encountered the world without social, cultural, or institutional support, without a cell phone to call their travel agent or a railroad car in which to retire.[3] Although some traveled for leisure or recreational pursuits, these individuals more appropriately might be labeled prototourists. When fifteenth-century merchants visited Venice to see its splendor, they approached the rationale that underpinned tourism. The activities they engaged in were similar to those of the hordes of tourists who followed, but the nature of their experience was different because the filters between them and the unfamiliar world they encountered were fewer and initially less developed.

Travel for the express purpose of leisure became possible and necessary for more people than a privileged elite as a result of the wealth, the technology, and, in the United States especially, the dislocation that first the market revolution and later industrialization produced.[4] Like many other benefits derived from technological innovation, tourism followed an old dictum: people became tourists because they could. The circumstances of their lives provided the wealth, the time, the conceptual need—for whatever reasons—and the opportunity to visit places that soon catered to their tastes. Their sense of self and their society placed a value on the experience of travel, often to specific locations that possessed social and cultural cachet or significance.[5] This scenario foreshadowed the self-fulfilling prophecy of the economic development of the tourist industry. With the creation of a class of Americans who shared the attributes of wealth and time, organized systems to accomplish their goals for a profitable fee were not far off. As tourism became a possibility for more than a very few, it took shape as an industry.

Tourism as a modern activity emerged in the United States early in the nineteenth century. Privileged Americans believed that they required a trip to the Continent to polish themselves. Later the same rite of passage became mandatory for their young; the tales of eighteenth- and nineteenth-century Americans in Europe, from Benjamin Franklin and Thomas Jefferson to Jane Addams, were legion. Domestic travel also became a social goal. For the wealthy, especially in the South, travel to selected resorts provided escape from the hot, humid summers as they decamped for cooler, higher elevations. Northerners pursued first the built environment, the institutions of the American Republic, and later what they deemed "nature," constructing significance in the world around them as the guidebooks they read shaped their sense of meaning. This practice became codified in the "fashionable tour," the trip up the Hudson River to Albany, west on the Erie Canal and finally to Niagara Falls. By the 1830s an industry emerged at Niagara Falls. Within a decade, travel had been transformed from a pursuit that, at least for the urban upper classes, depended not on the social and preexisting economic connections that had always driven it but on a web of status-oriented, commercially motivated endeavor. There had to be things to see and places to stay, activities and inns and restaurants. Sometimes these necessities for travel existed before and even in place of the structures of community. A pattern soon developed; people saw what they set out to see, interpreting it within the context of their background and the values of their culture.[6] At its very inception as an industry, tourism became self-fulfilling. It worked to confirm the understanding that people already had about the world around them.

Early tourism showed some of the traits of the later industry but was distant from it in many ways. After traveling to see human accomplishment, a theme echoed in later tourism, tourists became representations of the popular culture of their time. They imitated their predecessors as they viewed the achievements of their society. Only after infatuation with the built environment did American tourists learn to view nature, and only then as a result of a changing cultural scenario. With the concept of nature as an understood construct, the progeny of industrial wealth could mimic their romantic heroes, and like Lord Byron, could extol the beauty of nature and its meaning. Americans shifted their focus from the built and toward nature as they recast an identity in indigenous art forms. The writings of James Fenimore Cooper and Washington Irving contributed to creating an American intellectual ethos, answering the question that hung over the intellectual life of the early Republic: "Who in the world reads in an American book?" This view of the New World long confounded Europeans; the famed exchanges between the Comte Georges Louis LeClerc de Buffon and Thomas Jefferson provided a context for the lack of understanding on the Continent. After Cooper and Irving, an indigenous style of presenting the American world existed, albeit largely in a literary mode.[7]

Yet the nature presented in such works was both real and a construction of value systems. From Cooper, whose native, aristocratic, and liminal characters in novels such as *The Pioneers* might be termed protoecologists, to Charles Brockden Brown, in whose novel *Wieland* the characters build a cupola on the divide between farmed land and its untamed counterpart they call wilderness, a distinct view of the meaning of the natural world developed. Tourists learned to view the nature they saw in the terms of such cultural conventions. They understood what they were supposed to see from guidebooks and other forms of information, and they saw what they understood they would see. Between 1827 and 1939, the White Mountains in northern New Hampshire attracted most of the literary and artistic luminaries of the time, becoming the measure by which Americans understood nature. The emergence of the Hudson River School of painters, which included White Mountain tourists such as painter Thomas Cole, who searched for scenery to paint that would make him famous, helped make the outdoors even more fashionable, more powerful. Ever after the sublime, the picturesque, and the pastoral shaped the cosmology of American travelers.[8]

This protoindustrial travel became dominant in New England. Mirroring regional cultural differences, a more leisure-based tourism followed in the South. Hot springs and mountain elevations were at its center; the economically productive lowlands were misery for Anglo Americans in the summers. Besides heat and humidity, the threat of disease, often the undefined bilious fever, drove people to cooler, higher elevations where resorts had been created to offer respite from the summers. Initially these resorts were difficult to reach, but as more and more of the affluent desired to visit throughout the antebellum period, road access improved. They were the exclusive province of the wealthy, those with the combination of time and money that allowed them to get away and stay away during the languid summers.[9]

The Civil War changed the vectors of American tourism as it did nearly everything else about the nation. The older distinction of North and South became archaic. Not only had the war shattered that dichotomy, but it also reframed American debate in a tripartite formulation. Now there were three;

the West belonged in the mix, a place both mythic and real, an intellectual and physical locale where Americans could reinvent themselves if they chose. In the West, a Yankee or a rebel past was only as important as its bearer chose to make it, a tie to a world shattered by strife. As Indian people were removed from their lands by settlement and the military, former southerners, their sympathizers, so-called "galvanized Yankees," Free-Soilers, and even freedmen and women spread westward, seeking the redemption of reinvention and the prosperity they thought the western ground held.

In this process, the West became the national *sipapu,* the figurative hole in the earth from which the modern American nation sprang. The West was certainly a real place, defined by its impressive and varied physical nature, its subregional aridity, its various topographies, and its illusion of being free of the staid institutions and traditions of the Northeast and the South. It was also a mythic place, the crucible for the idea of a modern unified nation held together by its parts. It became a seedbed for democracy, in the sentiment of historian Frederick Jackson Turner, a place in which Americans hoped to find their true essence after sectional strife and the industrial age robbed them of it. Post–Civil War westerners were equally new and old, intellectually and actually divided between Yankee roots in crusty individualist entrepreneurship and southern antecedents in the concept of states' rights. This quirky mix melded iconoclasm and independence, local custom and culture, and dogmatic ferociousness in the westerner, the new American who answered Hector St. Jean de Crevecoeur's perplexing question about the nature of the nation.

The antebellum view of the Republic was anachronistic in the post–Civil War climate. Union became the national purpose, realized by the golden spike linking the continent by rail and repeated in many other places and ways. The founding of the news magazine the *Nation* was typical; conceptually, one unified nation held together by a powerful central government was a post–Civil War concept. Earlier, the question of the sovereignty of individual states and their relationship to the national government loomed large. Even the name of the most important postwar railroad, the Union Pacific, with its red, white, and blue coat of arms, indicated the change in national consciousness.

The mythic nature of the West served as a magnet for this postwar culture as it redefined its parameters. The West was unformed and malleable in the eyes of nineteenth-century America, a place with mythic meaning and promise of prosperity but without physical and conceptual shape. It seemed a canvas on which to paint the newest nation, to cover the errors of the past, drawing attention away from the calamity of sectionalism and moving on with the concept of Manifest Destiny and the odd combination of individualism and group endeavor it embodied. Like many other mythic locales, the West became intellectually amorphous, a place to become whatever one wanted to be, a place less real than a representation of qualities missing in mainstream society. Tourism in the West permitted, indeed promoted the filling of this void.

The post–Civil War emergence of western tourism was distinctly different from the roots of Anglo-European travel in the region. Throughout the nineteenth century, travelers visited, creating an impressive record of its attributes. But this travel remained idiosyncratic both in method and purpose, defined by the individuals who undertook it and their objectives. Intrepid travelers—Henry Marie Brackenridge, a writer and statesman who traveled up the Mississippi and Missouri Rivers with fur trader Manuel Lisa in June 1811; George Catlin, who set out to chronicle native people before they disappeared and not incidentally profit from his ventures; Prince Maximilian of Wied, who in 1833 undertook a scientific expedition for which the Swiss illustrator Karl Bodmer served as artist; the raconteur Capt. William Drummond Stewart, who in 1837 employed Alfred Jacob Miller in a parallel capacity to Bodmer—initiated a pattern of intellectual transmission of a mythic West made real by its geography and cultural history. Ethnographers as well as sojourners, these early travelers created powerful images of the region and its peoples that the nation began to digest.[10]

These initial visitors, prototourists really, were part of a European colonial tradition repeated around the globe. They had come to the West to follow in the conventions of their elite world, to understand and interpret the resources and peoples of this enticing region through the lens of their assumptions and presumptions. Prince Maximilian proved notable in this respect. Prior to coming West, he spent three years tramping through the heat and humidity of the Brazilian Amazon. Exotic places were his forte, his passion, in a manner typical of some segments of European nobility. In the taxonomic tradition, they collected and recorded knowledge for posterity and not incidentally for their own glorification. The entire history of the British Royal Geographic Society thoroughly attested to the self-aggrandizement that was part of the process of elite travel as did the midcentury battles among American botanists. Others such as Stewart were at odds with the privileged world from which they came but thoroughly imbued with its tradition. Selecting

Miller, Stewart guaranteed that his adventures and his prowess would be recorded, that a testimony to the triumph of the outcast would someday decorate the walls of Murthley Castle in Scotland.[11]

The goals of these travelers matched their time, an era in which knowing and understanding were closely intertwined with seeing and touching. Herman Melville's success with *Typee* in 1846 accented the spirit of the age. The story both titillated and enlightened, taught and mocked, shocked and affirmed. Melville showed his peers a world they could only imagine, replete with sailors, islanders who practiced a range of personal and social behaviors that astounded the Christian Northeast, and vistas, places, and scenarios beyond their wildest expectations. To his readers, Melville penetrated the veil of otherness that defined the non-Christian world. *Typee* was real and unreal simultaneously; it felt and sounded true, but its descriptions were so at odds with the expectations of its audience that it defied belief. The smashing success of the novel underscored not only the importance of understanding the interiorscape of the human condition but also the expanding horizons of midcentury. Part travelogue, part novel, and part work of neosocial realism, *Typee* reflected the growing obsession with the world beyond the reach of the urban and the urbane, the rural and the gentrified.[12]

Like Herman Melville in the Marquesa Islands, sojourners such as Maximilian and Catlin were part of a vanguard that had little choice about whether to experience the West on its own terms. They embraced the difficulties of their adventure as an aspect of its meaning, but such a trip was not for everyone in mid- or late-nineteenth-century America. There were no railroads or hotels in which to stay, no way to travel except in the means of conveyance the inhabitants of the region, native or otherwise used. Like Melville, Prince Maximilian was accustomed to the hardships of travel. His sojourn in tropical Brazil was more difficult than the American West could ever be. Stewart was a skilled horseman and military officer who took pride in his ability to adapt to conditions on the plains and in the mountains. Only places such as Sublette's Fort, later Fort Laramie, built in 1834 and later taken over by the American Fur Company, offered respite from the rigors of travel, and then only at gougers' prices. Francis Parkman, who traveled the West in 1846, was appalled that $.05 worth of tobacco in Boston cost $1.50 at Fort Laramie.[13] But travelers such as Parkman had no recourse. They were among the first to be gouged by their own kind in remote locations; ever after, the kinship of common intellectual, national, and physical origins meant little when profit on the periphery was at stake.

The pivotal fictional figure in the transition from sojourner to tourist traveler was Phileas Fogg, the methodical protagonist of Jules Verne's *Around the World in Eighty Days.* In response to a combination of wager and dare offered while he sat playing cards at his club in London, Fogg set out to prove that someone could circumnavigate the globe in eighty days. Verne nailed the obsession of his moment; the novel, set late in 1872, straddled an instant of transition in the uses and meaning of travel. Fogg both preceded tourism and followed it. His journey was a sort of leisure, but strangely a business arrangement—a wager of £20,000. It depended on the technologies of the late nineteenth century, the railroad, the steamship, and yachts as well as on camels and other more exotic conveyances. Although the potential existed, Fogg hardly looked through the tourist's lens; in Suez, Fogg "sat quietly down to breakfast, never once thinking of inspecting the town, being one of those Englishmen who are wont to see foreign countries through the eyes of their domestics."[14] Like *Typee,* Verne's widely popular book whetted the appetite for travel. Neither tourist, explorer, nor truly businessman, Fogg provided both a glimpse of the future and a summation of the past.

As Fogg's fictional endeavor took place, Americans cleared their West of all but the remnants of its past. They eliminated animal species, created reservations for persistent native peoples, and impressed a railroad-inspired grid across the nation, clearing the way for new kinds of travel in the region. Instead of seeing the West as did mountain men and explorers, wealthy Americans now had a range of options to experience the region. They embraced these choices, believing they saw through the eyes of the mountain man. Railroads created new categories of travelers. Much more than a parade of Maximilians and Catlins followed the tracks.[15] Travelers in the West became more like Fogg, less interested in their surroundings and more interested in their experience in making the journey. Railroads made travel available to those who could afford the fare but who never before would have attempted a sojourn, considering a wagon or stagecoach trip across the West excruciating.

Railroads began as mere conveyances, beneath the level of amenity the wealthy expected. Initially railroad cars were mere wooden boxes, dangerous ones at that. In one of the seemingly infinite instances of horror associated with the early years of American railroading, Benjamin Pierce, the eight-year-old son of president-elect Franklin K. Pierce, was killed in an 1853 train accident in which his parents escaped uninjured. The physical danger of train travel remained quite real, and comfort lagged as well. Into the 1870s, conditions of train travel were outstanding if passengers were merely uncomfortable. The food served along train lines was abominable. To avoid eating horribly prepared and often rancid food, many travelers brought their own provisions. Before 1876 the axiom for riders on the Atchison, Topeka, and Santa Fe (AT&SF) was "bring your own or go hungry." The accommodations matched the food. One British observer noted that there was no difference between first class and second class on American trains. They were all second class.[16]

After the Civil War, the quality of train travel rapidly improved, and the prospect of travel in the American West became palatable as railroads allowed affluent Americans a combination of comfort and mobility. Train gauges were standardized, a process that began during the Civil War and culminated in 1886 with the integration of the five-foot track gauge in the South into the national grid. By 1870, faster, more luxurious passenger cars became standard. In that year, the New York Central line offered sleeping cars on its service to the hinterlands of the Midwest. The 900-mile trip to Chicago took two days and one night. Wagner Palace and Pullman cars were common additions, especially on transcontinental or other longer journeys. Sleeping-car porters traveled along to make the trip easier for this class of travelers, although some visitors were dubious of their value. Even the food improved, especially after a transplanted Englishman named Fred Harvey shook hands with an AT&SF official and initiated a series of lunch kitchens that turned first into restaurants and later into hotels that were among the premier institutions of their kind in that era. The transcontinental links meant that train travelers could ride with comforts for which they were willing to pay. For the wealthiest, those who could afford the roughly $300 coast-to-coast and return fare in an era when a schoolteacher might earn $200 in a year, the rails provided an existence that differed from their customary routine only in the confinement of the width of the railcar and the incessant rhythmic sound of the train wheels.[17]

The 1880s were the heyday of the Pullman cars, a moment of luxury between the dangerous cattle cars that preceded them and the middle-class passenger cars that followed as train travel became more widely affordable. The Pullmans offered a more limited form of travel, running only through populated areas or to special places. The AT&SF and Atlantic and Pacific Railroad had not yet reached the coast, leaving the Union Pacific as the only cross-country track. Those who rode the trains, except for the few who sought exotic adventure such as the journalist Sylvester Baxter, simply rode to well-known destinations: the hot springs along the AT&SF tracks, the famous California hotels such as the Hotel Del Monte in Monterey, the Hotel Del Coronado in San Diego, and later the Hotel Raymond in Pasadena, and other similar places.[18] Such travel showed a limited geography tied to cultural symbolism, still fundamentally evocative of Europe. Only when people no longer routinely compared the landscape of the American West to Europe could an indigenous iconography that celebrated the American nation take shape.

The railroad differed from any preceding form of travel. Not only did it comfortably convey larger numbers of people greater distances than ever before, but for the first time, people passed through a landscape yet did not necessarily engage it. Passengers commented on the phenomenon of going to sleep in the gray northern winter and waking up among the sagebrush of the western desert. This was disconcerting to some, as they felt separated from the world they traversed. They became observers, not participants, willing or otherwise, in all that rolled by outside their train window. In a stagecoach or a wagon travelers experienced their surroundings. Inside the train, the cold did not always make them cold and the rain did not drench their clothes although often the heat in a passenger car was as bad or worse than outside.[19] Train travelers were insulated. They could see the world as they passed it by at the unheard-of pace of twenty to thirty miles per hour, but they were not part of it. This was a new experience, appropriate to the distinctions of the industrial age; it separated travelers not only from each other but also from the world they viewed, delivering them only to their chosen destinations.

The railroad made tourists out of travelers, especially in the western United States. The act of tourism required distance from home, the ability to see a new place within the context of outside experience rather than entirely inside its intellectual, cultural, and social parameters. To be a tourist meant to be divorced from the realities of any visited place, to re-create its essence in the context of the cultural baggage a traveler brought along in a manner previously impossible. George Catlin could never have been a tourist. Even though he could not help applying the prism of his culture as he attempted to portray Indian people as he saw them, his involvement with people and places was too intimate to allow the necessary refracting of his reality onto theirs. Even the very first passengers to ride West on the UP or the AT&SF lines experienced a corridor transformed by the railroad from which they could depart and to which they could always return. This ability to terminate experience and return to the world so close to that from which they came was crucial to the distinction between tourists and sojourners. The malleability associated with this movement was also intrinsic to the creation of a socioculturally significant tourism.

At approximately the same time, iconographic changes in national cosmology and growing nationalistic sentiments placed a premium on the celebration of the special features of the American nation, a precursor of the transformation of tourism into an activity that resonated throughout society. The spectacular scenery of the American West, its deep canyons, rugged mountain peaks, and its post–Civil War development, seemingly devoid of the fractures of sectionalism, became symbolic of the nation's grandeur. Pity poor Thomas Jefferson! Only a century before, he had been forced to ship the carcass of a seven-foot-tall moose to Paris to defend the New World against pronouncements of its degeneracy and inferiority from his old friend Buffon; the evidence was insufficient for the French naturalist, who refused to retract his condemnation. By 1900 Americans were content that their geography equaled Europe's cultural past. Some daringly referred to Switzerland as the Colorado of Europe, inverting a historic American sense of inadequacy in the face of Europe's attractions.[20] The West offered more than a counter; it granted physical superiority, a magnificence for which the previous century of European exploration around the globe created an understanding.

The comprehension of this West occurred at precisely the moment Americans began the excruciating but exciting prospect of defining an American landscape worthy of intellectual independence from European antecedents. In politics and social organization, the new nation had been an innovator. In identity derived from culture, art, and literature, Americans floundered. As romantic consciousness exploded on the intellectual landscape, driven by the overwhelming physical forms of the American West, first reported by Meriwether Lewis and William Clark and later codified in lore through the reports of John C. Frémont—typically authored by his wife, Jesse Benton Frémont—Americans defined a New World cultural identity that matched its social organization. Words and images created a new meaning for the West. It focused not on the utility of the region for economic purposes, Thomas Jefferson's original charge to Lewis and Clark, but instead on the seemingly aberrant nature of the physical West. The reports of hot water shooting into the air, of multicolored formations that dripped steaming water, of wide rivers, and of mountains so high they did not seem to bend toward a peak before clouds enveloped them made the West seem preternatural, magnificent yet mysterious, knowable yet incomprehensible.[21]

Following the lead of the painters of the Hudson River School, thinkers, explorers, surveyors—Alexander von Humboldt and the U.S. Army Corps of Topographical Engineers—artists, writers, scientists, photographers, and others defined a romantic West that they could above all know and understand. This West remained mysterious, apart and different, but it could be measured and understood in the terms of nineteenth-century discourse.

Purveyors of the leading forms of the era's popular culture featured western locales in their work; even exciting new technologies such as daguerreotypes and stereopticons used western panoramas to illustrate their innovation and accentuate their significance. Thomas Moran joined the many artists who painted exquisite western vistas on a greater and grander scale than Hudson River School painters ever imagined, rivaling the spectacular work of romanticists such as Frederick Church and far surpassing even the most famous artistic depictions of romantic Europe. Compared to the art of J. W. R. Turner and other Europeans, Moran's work showed more exquisite scenery on a grander, more spectacular and sublime scale. Eadweard Muybridge's pictures of Yosemite and William Henry Jackson's glass plates taken in the West became photographs and stereopticon slides that developed wide currency. Explorers and scientists such as John Wesley Powell, the one-armed Civil War brevet major who rafted the Grand Canyon in 1869 and became a leader in American science, and Ferdinand Vandiveer Hayden, who performed important surveys throughout the West, announced their exploits with pride and passion; interest in the special features of the region grew. Nathaniel Pitt "National Park" Langford promoted the wonders of the Yellowstone region, advocating its inclusion in a publicly owned park or reservation. Old Faithful geyser and Tower Falls in Yellowstone National Park, created in 1872, the massive and spectacular El Capitan in Yosemite, which achieved national park status in the 1890s, and other places developed grand cultural meaning. John Muir, known as John of the Mountains as a result of his intimate connection to Yosemite, touched a chord with his evocative writing about the sentience of the natural world. Americans saw themselves as "nature's nation," with an updated appreciation for their own technological prowess.[22]

As the American West became the psychic location of the national creation myth, Americans understood their experience and identity as a people as being formed anew and refashioned. First the geography of the West and later, after the end of the Indian Wars and the creation of the reservation system, its ethnography became the subject of a romantic yet simultaneously utilitarian national lore. The artists and writers of the era fashioned the mythic American West that Frederick Jackson Turner later epitomized with the articulation of his frontier thesis. Conceptually the images and the words matched, fitting together to affirm the direction of industrial America, the values and nationalism inherent in its conquest of the continent, the empiricism enunciated in its description of science, and the supposed mystery that enveloped romantic depictions of its territory. Americans came to fathom what they perceived as their unique relationship to the natural world, a firm bond between this visually exceptional region and the people who believed they had mastered it. They learned to revere the physical features that served as the backdrop for their national myths as much as if they had been castles in Europe or the battlefields of the eastern seaboard.

Place, that most essential component of American identity, became definitive in American culture, part and parcel of the remains of the antebellum states' rights philosophy transported West and equally of the Free-Soil mythology that inspired westward settlement on the plains and in the mountains. In late nineteenth-century America, individual identity remained closely tied to property ownership. Building a home in a place conferred more than traditional concepts of individuality; it meant total and complete domination of the farmstead, or in more visible cases, the 100,000-acre-or-more ranch. No government could encroach on this mythic strata, no one but the owner could allow or prohibit there. Paradoxically yet symbiotically, the post–Civil War West held room for recalcitrant former Confederates and ebullient homesteaders, for those who saw open spaces as an invitation to defy law and those who equated ownership of land with independence. At precisely this moment ownership of the means of production, not land, held the key to the economic future. To many Americans and most westerners, place meant individuality, a way of distinguishing the self that contained a strong antigovernment, antiauthoritarian streak.[23]

A significant difference remained between the meaning of American and European places: late nineteenth-century Americans saw their mythic past as real and alive in actual and mythic ways, a condition that stemmed from its proximity in time and space to their lives and from the emergence of the concept of union. In the West, Indian people roamed the landscape into the 1890s, when the massacre at Wounded Knee drew a figurative line between past and future. The Indian presence, albeit on reservations, reflected the newness of the nation in actual and symbolic terms. The preservation of huge areas, such as Yellowstone and Glacier National Park, created an authenticated landscape, where people of an industrial culture could see the physical environment in which their predecessors, the actual conquerors, had proved their mettle. The only difference was that these sacred landscapes were cleansed of Indians, the human history erased as the romanticism of American natural history became national iconography.[24]

Romanticism focused tourism in the West and gave it a purpose. Before the development of a full-blown romantic consciousness in the United States, tourists interpreted through a diffuse range of lenses. Romanticism and knowledge of the West fused into a central conceptualization of tourism.

This image provided a range of explanations that superseded the personal, a series of reasons that combined nationalism and expiation, affirmation of self and society, and physical, material, and technological triumph as the foundation for systematized, class-based travel. The West earned specific symbolic meaning at the moment that sufficient wealth and technology made visits from sizable numbers of the affluent possible. Railroad travel in the West manifested the power of American wealth, creating a pattern in which the act of tourism affirmed American society.

In the process of fashioning a new intellectual construction of their land, of creating this tourism of reverence, the forces of capitalism and culture fused to create a form of endeavor that echoed the dialogue elsewhere evident in American society. Places that were shaped by the self-pronounced Manifest Destiny of the American nation embodied national instincts. They promised the expiation and rejuvenation necessary in the aftermath of the Civil War, and on many levels, from intellectual messages to forms of organization, they affirmed the values, progress, and order of fin de siècle American society. Tourism mirrored the cultural values of the traveling classes at the turn of the century. It showed the American aristocracy what they wanted to see, and more important, helped invent tangible views of what its members sought to believe. The tourism of the era replicated the structure and values of the world of industrial America in a different form. It drew attention to the spectacular features of the landscape through the means of the new technologies, allowing tourists who sought experience to reach these features without sacrificing their amenities. Turn-of-the-century tourism showed vistas in comfort as it transmitted the values of industrial society.

This framing served as an overlay upon the Other, upon the different and disparate physical forms of the West, and upon the people who preceded English-speakers in the region. The template was hierarchical, as was the top-down culture of the Victorian world that wealthy Americans embraced with the ascent of industrialism, but it had an added virtue. It created a context in which English-speakers, possessed of the confidence that physical conquest imbued, could seek to order Indian, Hispano, and other lives and could integrate those experiences into the top-to-bottom philosophical organization of fin de siècle American society. The blueprint that tourism both needed and created allowed Anglo Americans to "understand" the western past and the cultures they encountered from their railroad car window, typically on their own exclusive terms. The overlay made the distinct cultural mores and values of different groups in the West comprehensible, even if in the most narrow and often pejorative terms. Tourism and its organizational structure helped create the lens that allowed Americans to come to grips with the world of the western past and present.

The message embodied in this fin de siècle western tourism melded three distinctly different and sometimes contradictory concepts: the idea of sublimity at the core of romanticism, the power of conquest embodied in Manifest Destiny, and the conception of empiricism that lay at the heart of post-Darwinian science. With only a little prompting transmitted through art and literature, visitors understood the vistas to which they were conveyed as uplifting intellectual experiences, beyond the sheer emotional value of the visual impact of mountains, canyons, and spectacular lakes. Turn-of-the-century writers and artists routinely linked the spectacle of landscapes to the achievements of the American nation. They sought to measure, quantify, and define place as they revered the beauty of the West. The locales that excited their consciousness, and especially the ability to deliver people to them in style, proved the knowledge, power, and grace of industrial civilization. For a people who believed themselves victorious in their conquest of the continent, the ultimate triumph was to experience the mysteries of the sublime in comfort.[25]

Before 1900 tourists could easily reach many of these scenic wonderlands and cultural refuges. The West had been linked to the nation. An infrastructure that supported tourism extended up and down the California coast and along the rail lines that crisscrossed the interior of the West. These steel rails created corridors of access to the machined miracles of the modern world. They conveyed goods and people across the countryside, altering the economy and often the culture of the places they touched. From Rincon, New Mexico, and Hillsboro, Kansas, both unremarkable in the sweep of American history except for their shared distinction of physically changing locations to take advantage of the installation of nearby railroad tracks, to the countless communities that were born or received new amenities and experienced cultural or economic transformations, the railroad clearly served as the dominant catalyst of change after 1850.[26]

The ribbons of rail across the landscape created a culture of protourbanity wherever they went. Railstops became towns, and nearby, new communities were founded and grew up to take advantage of the new access to the outside world. Economic regimes became viable with the availability of transportation. A hierarchy of communities followed, the ones on the rail lines typically being most significant. The railroad functioned like a stone dropped into a pool of water; it created ripples. The rails pulled everything in their reach—people, capital, natural resources—toward them, creating spheres of influence.[27] This clustering was essential. It helped create the institutions that could support organized tourism for economic profit.

The railroad also spread to places that, because of their significance, demanded the expansion of rail corridors, even to remote locations. The great mining finds of the post–Civil War era typified this process. Communities such as Butte, Montana, Kennecott, Alaska, and countless others pulled the railroad to them. The discovery of their mineral riches made their importance so great and the potential profit for the creation of a transportation network so vast that either an existing railroad built a spur to reach the location or the company that ran the mines built a line to the trunk line, sometimes as much as 100 miles away.[28] Success in extractive industry depended upon access; the raw materials of remote places had to be integrated into the market. For tourism, the converse was true. People had to be able to reach the spectacular but often remote places that contained cultural meaning.

Economic endeavor drove each form of expansion, and as some tourist attractions developed the pull inspired by national mythology and good promotion, rails to tourist destinations magically appeared. The routes that promoted local and regional visitation, such as the Madison River and the Yellowstone River, both of which led south from Montana into Yellowstone National Park, and the National Park Free Wagon Road and the Horseback Trail, which approached from the west, were soon superseded by railroads. First the rails came within 100 miles or so of places such as Yellowstone; the narrow gauge Utah Northern line reached Beaver Canyon, Idaho, now called Monida, late in the 1870s. In 1883 the Northern Pacific Railroad arrived in Livingston, Montana, a mere fifty-six miles from Yellowstone, and a six-month project constructed a branch line to the park. When completed, the first rail line specifically to a tourist destination in the western United States began operation.[29]

The branch line from Livingston to Yellowstone illustrated the growing economic value of tourism. Until the railroad, tourism in the Yellowstone area had been primarily a local and regional affair. People from Montana, Wyoming, and Idaho visited, and they camped, hunted, and otherwise lived off the land during a large part of their journey. Such travelers mirrored the practices and behavior of earlier sojourners, from John Colter, who may have first seen the geyser basins early in the nineteenth century, to National Park Langford and his crew. These regional tourists also faced similar hardships even within the boundaries of a national park. Late in the 1870s, sightings of Bannock Indians in the western part of the park were common. In 1877, when Chief Joseph and his people traversed Yellowstone in their vain attempt to escape the pursuing military, the Nez Perce captured visitors within the park. Called the Radersburg tourists, after their village thirty-five miles south of Helena, Montana, these captives traveled on their own conveyances, farm wagons, buggies, or horses, only to find themselves surrounded by the Nez Perce.[30] They were not buying rail tickets and staying at hotels; they hunted their food within park boundaries as they did outside. This was prototypical local tourism, its terms dictated by local conditions and its experience different from riding the rails, not only because of the choice of destination but in every aspect of the journey. The transportation, the accommodations, and the message of travel were distinctly local. The Radersburg tourists and their peers shared in none of the common affirmative traits of railroad travel.

With the opening of the park branch line in 1883, the picture of Yellowstone tourism changed. Rail lines were expensive, and railroad magnates did not build them expecting to lose money or to have their visitors threatened. Northern Pacific Railroad builder Henry Villard sought to bring wealthy passengers along his branch to Yellowstone. The approximately 2,000 people who lived in Livingston, where the branch departed for the park, shared the same expectations. They welcomed the economic might of the Northern Pacific, seeing its delivery of visitors as a salve for their ongoing economic woes. The Northern Pacific had already transformed the Yellowstone Valley as its rails traversed the region. Its impact on the park itself surely would be no less.[31]

Like the underground minerals, tourism seemed an economic resource worthy of consideration when regional economies proved unstable. The Madison Valley near the park typified much rural western land. Its environment provided a kind of subsistence that was increasingly transformed into a part of the national market by the rails. Its Anglo American settlers, persuaded of the economic efficacy and cultural independence of their status as landowning ranchers and farmers, embraced an animal husbandry regime at the precise moment in American history when the ownership of small tracts of land routinely offered greater symbolic than economic potential for advancement. In the valleys that surrounded Yellowstone, most settlers remained economically marginal despite their attempts to better their lives. They could not count on rising prices for livestock to ensure a brighter future. Given the fluctuation of the market for animals, tourism offered another source of income.[32] A symmetry existed in this relationship, an unarticulated understanding that if local people played into the expectations of visitors, they could anticipate being rewarded by a seasonal industry with the potential to carry them through the long Montana winters.

The people who visited Yellowstone after the arrival of the railroad were almost exclusively of one class: the monied who could afford the expense of travel and who possessed the time to enjoy the long and luxurious train trips. Most tourists who rode the rails during the late nineteenth century were beneficiaries of the transformation from a mercantile economy to industrial capitalism. Those who owned the means of production and their families and friends set out for the remote parts of the nation in their fancy railroad cars. The first railroad cars to travel the branch line to Yellowstone in 1884 were the Northern Pacific luxury car, the *Montana,* and a Louisville and Nashville Railroad luxury car. Later that first afternoon, the train pulled the *Railway Age,* said to be the finest railroad car of its era.[33] Only the most wealthy could afford an extravagance that so perfectly defined the symbolism of travel during the Gilded Age.

Yellowstone was not alone among destinations that drew the railroad. The Hotel Del Monte, a creation of the Southern Pacific Railroad completed in 1880 at the southern end of Monterey Bay in California, was another example of the luxurious fusion of railroads and resorts. Initially the hotel drew a local crowd. The wealthy of the San Francisco area descended upon it in all their splendor, challenging the observation of Caroline Dall, an early visitor, who remarked that the hotel was "intended for a public that does not yet exist."[34] That public did exist; it merely lived closer than the traveling Dall recognized. The hotel quickly became a stop for Walter Raymond's tour syndicate, which added to its local prestige and to its cachet with national travelers, its local constituency expanding to include a national one.[35]

Tourism met other psychic needs in fin de siècle America. Especially after the pronouncement of the closing of the frontier in the aftermath of the 1890 Census, Americans yearned for a salve for their sociocultural wounds, the malaise that defined their condition. Industrialization offered much, as the World's Columbian Exposition, opening in Chicago in 1893, showed, but it destroyed much as well. Americans felt ambivalence, collectively strengthened and individually weakened by the power of machines, by the nature of cities; their art and literature reflected this anxiety. In the spectacular vistas of the West, in a growing obsession with native peoples and their arts, Americans used a geographic place as mythical space to work out tensions. Traversing that space in a railcar granted power, but the act of travel also defiled the place. Tourism embodied a contradiction as it renewed and rejuvenated an industrial nation. The tourists needed to reach special places, but in so doing they changed them. Tourism had to provide the comforts without seeming to trample the primal nature of a region, special because

Americans wanted its physical nature to defy the efforts of civilization. This dualism meant that the West immediately divided into sacred and profane space, the latter of railroad corridors and towns, and the former of mountain peaks, wide-open landscapes, and Indian villages. Through the profane to the sacred came tourists, seeking in a vision of a naturally noble past the essence of their society. Tourism embodied a love-hate relationship with the power of the modern world, as did other ramifications of industrialization.

Early western tourism mirrored the history of American travel. As Mark Twain's *Innocents Abroad* so clearly demonstrated, Americans were always adventurous and self-involved.[36] Tourism acquired the trappings of status, and as individuals within the nation became wealthy, they expected a level of pampering that was foreign to all other travelers in the nineteenth century save royalty. Especially in the West, they wanted "eastern life in a western environment," as one visitor to Colorado Springs observed.[37] Luxury railroad cars testified to the conflicting impulses of adventure and amenity that tugged at the wealthy traveler.

As the physical organization of travel developed, its message remained embryonic. Before the 1890s tour syndicates delivered travelers along the routes illustrated in guidebooks. Railroads and resorts offered an increasing measure of comfort, but intellectually, tourism remained diffuse. Almost a full generation after Langford promoted Yellowstone, after the surveys of the Grand Canyon, after the mythifying of the region in lore and legend, tourism followed the railroads instead of the cultural vectors that regional mythology, national iconography, and powerful bombast dictated. In the West, people traveled to a range of curious and exciting places, inspiring and beautiful such as Yellowstone or Yosemite, more difficult to reach before the railroad arrived at nearby El Portal in 1907; the hot springs and the accompanying Montezuma Hotel in Las Vegas, New Mexico, or the famed Antlers Hotel in Colorado Springs, Colorado. They traveled because they could, rather than for any larger social or cultural purpose. No systematic intellectual organization of these places yet existed. The West and westering as a concept possessed enormous cachet in American society, but its constituent parts, its mountains, rivers, crevasses, and even national parks did not. Nor were resorts set up to impart cultural values—except for the practice of mimicking the patterns of behavior, such as dressing for breakfast, that typified the tonier resorts of the East Coast.[38] The combination of social conditions that granted western tourism a meaningful place in American culture, the availability of luxury travel, and a sizable wealthy population had not yet coalesced.

Despite the myriad reasons for which they traveled, these early travelers were transformative. The rails that brought them, the hotels where they stayed, and their needs required the organization of capital, the application of standards, and a range of changes in the nature of local places. Fierce competition, itself transformative, to offer amenities to visitors ensued as the stakes rose. In the American West, these needs changed travel into tourism. They imposed the institutions and accoutrements of industrial society on the concept of seeing the continent, reflecting the tendency of dominant culture to highlight its achievements in symbolic events and foreshadowing the complicated messages of fin de siècle American society.

By 1900 the disjointed tourism of the late nineteenth-century West had been transformed into an organized activity, not only along the coast but also along the railroad tracks that cut through the region. Western travel ceased to be an individualistic activity of a limited elite and instead became part of the process of official affirmation of American society. Tourism had become intrinsically linked to the formulation of the industrial age, to the combination of Manifest Destiny, empirical knowledge, and romantic thinking that typified the fin de siècle. These expressions, with their transformative powers, peaked in different ways at the Grand Canyon and in Santa Fe.

3

The Tourism of Hegemony I

Railroads, Elites, and the Grand Canyon

No place spoke to fin de siècle America like the Grand Canyon. The Great Chasm of the Colorado, the Grand Cañon, and its other superlatives seemingly embodied the identity Americans sought as they fashioned their place among the nations of the world. Its dizzying vistas, its rich and moving colors, its mystery, and Americans' ability to master it confirmed to them that their continent had substance and depth. Here was the entire package, a place the people of the time regarded as God's handiwork that reflected what Americans wanted themselves and their nation to be. It offered assurance and wonder, power and humility intertwined; it became the icon of the moment that explained Americans' complicated relationship with the land they possessed.

Before 1860 the Grand Canyon was simply an obstacle to travel, an enormous hole in the ground. The intellectual approach that made its fantastic landscapes, vast loneliness, and remarkable topography meaningful simply did not have currency in the Western world. European accounts of the canyon demonstrated that lack of understanding. Spanish explorer García López de Cárdenas, who in 1540 guided a contingent of the Vásquez de Coronado expedition to its rim, looked over the edge and perceived not the beauty, mystery, and power of the canyon but only the obvious: its condition as a barrier to forward movement. López de Cárdenas withdrew disappointed, and he, his men, and ultimately Spanish culture remained indifferent to the intellectual possibilities of the canyon. This response in the face of wonder was hardly callous; it presaged a hard-nosed Spanish intellectual and cultural resistance to the Enlightenment, the scientific revolution, and the empiricism that accompanied it. López de Cárdenas's indifference typified a view that can best be described as dogmatically premodern. Only the combination of the empirical and the sublime, laced with the articulation of science and progress, that defined nineteenth-century thought precipitated an alteration of this outlook. When it came, it stemmed from the American Republic, chock full of expansionist enthusiasm. When John Wesley Powell rafted the canyon in 1869, he and his men feared and revered it. By 1880 the context coalesced in which Anglo Americans learned to appreciate and later to understand a distilled version of the Grand Canyon.[1]

Geologist Clarence E. Dutton chiefly created this modern understanding of the canyon. A Yale University graduate, Civil War veteran and career army officer, an accomplished raconteur, and a cofounder with Powell of the pivotal Cosmos Club in Washington, DC, Dutton typified the tradition of military exploration in the intellectual and physical sense. He was both a thinker and a doer. Dutton worked closely with Powell, providing much of the scientific power underpinning Powell's *Report on the Arid Lands.* Dutton's own writing won renown. *The Tertiary History of the Grand Canyon,* a U.S. Geological Survey report, retained lasting significance.[2]

The Tertiary History defined the Grand Canyon for literate America. Dutton placed the canyon firmly within the cosmology of romantic America, complementing the spectacular scenes described by Alexander von Humboldt and painted by Frederick Church and Thomas Coles. Dutton described the canyon in the tripartite terms of the late nineteenth century. He brought its land forms within the realm of scientific explanation while appreciating its sublime power and beauty. The very act of defining the Grand Canyon reflected the third facet of late nineteenth-century American culture, the hefty baggage of Manifest Destiny. By defining the unknowable in empirical terms, the conquering culture codified this special place.[3] Dutton explained the empiricism, mystery, and power of the Grand Canyon, an overlay that any literate American of the 1880s could use to place the canyon in the romanticized worldview springing from the rigid hierarchies of industrialization.

It took time for this image to disseminate widely. In the 1880s few Anglo Americans had seen the Grand Canyon. The primary conveyance of the era, the railroad, did not cross northern Arizona, restricting the opportunities for all but the most intrepid. Even after Dutton, the Grand Canyon remained as remote as the Andes, as far away and as well understood in a scientific sense as the South Seas. When rails first traversed the region in 1882, they passed through Williams, Arizona, more than sixty miles to the south of the rim of the canyon. For extractive economic purposes at least, the Grand Canyon did not merit a major investment of capital.[4]

Before a rail line reached the canyon, individual enterprises served the few visitors who ventured there. Around 1883, John "Captain" Hance became the first Anglo American resident on the rim. A colorful storyteller with a checkered personal history, Hance initiated a pattern that typified tourist endeavors near the canyon. He filed a mining claim on a piece of land about four miles east of Grandview Point and located an asbestos mine there, but his real business was to entertain visitors with his roguish collection of stories and tales. J. Wilbur Thurber's stage from Flagstaff brought people for a twenty-dollar fee, as did William W. Bass, who settled in Williams in 1883 and became obsessed with the canyon. Bass started a guide business that conveyed people from Ashfork and Williams. So did Sanford H. Rowe, whose livery business in Williams frequently brought him to the canyon. While being guided there by a venerated Havasupai Indian, Big Jim, Rowe spotted damp ground that indicated a seep. There he staked a mining claim, having already used his homestead claim near Williams, and struggled to prove up. Others followed, often pretending to mine and almost always seeking ways to bring more visitors to the canyon. Locals all, these guides took only the brave and sometimes the foolhardy over the rutted tracks to the rim of the canyon.[5]

These enterprises created geographically diverse locations along the rim, and no central location for tourists emerged. The path of the stage established patterns of travel, and as new homesteads and mining claims developed, where people sold rooms, views, food, and occasionally tours, the stage reached these locations, too. Considerable spontaneity characterized early development. A number of small-scale entrepreneurs who engaged in other economic activities also offered services to visitors. They did little to promote the canyon or to improve the scant amenities available there, relying instead on a growing sense in America that the canyon had great moral and cultural significance. These protoresorts were as idiosyncratic as the people who owned them. No one location, individual, or company dominated tourism at the Grand Canyon although the competition among proprietors sometimes was fierce. The scale of tourism remained small, and the few purveyors of rooms and trips grappled only for visitors, not to dominate the trade and exclude competitors.[6]

By the early 1890s economic interests in Flagstaff invested in the resources of the canyon, but they emphasized mining, not tourism. Ralph Henry Cameron, a "down-east Yankee" from Maine who arrived in Flagstaff in 1883 and built a political machine in Coconino County, served as catalyst. Cameron linked up with another transplant, Peter D. Berry, who moved to northern Arizona in 1888 to handle his murdered brother's affairs. Berry kept a saloon, and his earlier mining experience attracted the entrepreneurial Cameron and his brother, Niles Cameron. The three worked as partners on mining claims in the canyon as early as 1890.[7]

The power in this triumvirate centered on Ralph Henry Cameron, who had resources, political savvy, and vast aspirations. Cameron became sheriff of Coconino County and used his office to economic advantage. Niles Cameron deferred to his more astute brother. Berry ran the mining operation. In 1890–1891 the group widened an old Havasupai track and created the Bright Angel Trail, clearing it as far as Indian Gardens below the rim. The Last Chance Mine, a vein of high-grade copper below Horseshoe Mesa so excellent that it won prizes at the World's Columbian Exposition in Chicago in 1893, inspired the creation of the Grandview Trail twelve miles east of the Bright Angel and linked Berry's mill site with the mine below.[8]

By the mid-1890s the canyon possessed great cultural significance. Dutton's descriptions gained great currency. Thomas Moran, who first painted the canyon in 1873 at John Wesley Powell's request, returned in the 1880s to color illustrations for *The Tertiary History* drawn by artist and ethnographer William Henry Holmes, and J. K. Hillers's photographs helped illustrate its meaning. Dutton, Moran, and Powell provided American elites with their interpretation of the Grand Canyon, information that had to be passed to the public. The great popularizer of the canyon was editor, author, and traveler Charles F. Lummis, who during the 1880s made the Southwest the focus of a concerted effort to present an exotic but uniquely American past excluding Europe and its castles. His writing attracted wide attention, for it melded the themes of the era with an appreciation for the exotic. Lummis did not attempt to describe the canyon after his first visit. "There it is; go see it for yourself," he wrote in *A Tramp Across the Country*, investing the canyon with a meaning beyond words and simultaneously issuing a challenge to modern America.[9] The visitors who descended on Berry's mining camp were imbued with the spirit of Powell's explorations, Dutton's intellectual mapping, Moran's and Hillers's art, and the combination of nationalism and exhilaration tinged with self-doubt that so affected the privileged of the age. Tourists must have greatly perplexed these miners, scraping out a living in the gorgeous setting but finding no aesthetic or sociocultural meaning.[10]

Increased demand soon changed tourism. Professionals replaced the smallest and most idiosyncratic operators. Profit, at least on a small scale, became a distinct prospect as more visitors came, and regional entrepreneurs saw the canyon as a source of revenue. John Hance sold first, inaugurating a pattern that came to define tourism throughout the American West. In 1895 Thurber, who owned the stage from Flagstaff, bought sixty-seven-year-old Hance's property. An outside interest from within the region supplanted a local one, and the venerated Hance began his initial semiretirement. It lasted until 1897, when he became the first postmaster at the canyon. The post office was aptly named Tourist, Arizona.[11]

As the century closed, an awkward situation existed at the Grand Canyon. Intellectually delineated and enjoying a role in American culture, the canyon held a firm place in the gallery of the extraordinary that Americans relied on to persuade themselves that they controlled an expansive continent. This idea was part of the cosmology of affirmation, along with the set of signs and symbols that convinced Americans that all was right in their world—when abundant evidence to the contrary existed. The Grand Canyon represented the scope and scale of American civilization and reminded Americans of the spectacular beauty of their continent and the importance of the nation. Despite this cultural significance, the canyon lacked the amenities associated with meaningful places in the late nineteenth century. No Hotel Del Coronado sat on its rim. Its accommodations were crude and rough in an era before the traveling classes found the lack of comfort culturally persuasive. Its various enterprises were poorly run. Even reaching the canyon was an ordeal. The trip from Flagstaff to Hance's ranch and back could take three excruciating days of bouncing on rutted roads. Although many would have paid to see it, in 1900 few would endure the rigors of the trip. The mythic qualities of the place were enhanced, but the growth of tourism was hamstrung by the absence of a consistent, comfortable, and efficient form of transportation.[12]

A railroad to the canyon was the most feasible solution. In 1890 mining dominated economic endeavor, and tourism remained a largely unorganized sideline. As late as 1898, local leaders opposed a national park at the Grand Canyon; they believed it would eliminate prospecting and depopulate the area.[13] As tourism became an important southwestern economic staple during the 1890s, AT&SF president E. P. Ripley recognized both the vast economic potential of tourist rail traffic and the meaning of the Grand Canyon. The AT&SF purchased the old A&P track through Williams and awaited the demise of a small mining railroad. When it went bankrupt, the AT&SF bought it and finished a spur to bring tourists, not to transport copper out of the canyon.[14] On September 17, 1901, a scheduled train made its initial trip from Williams to the Grand Canyon. A ticket for the comfortable three-hour

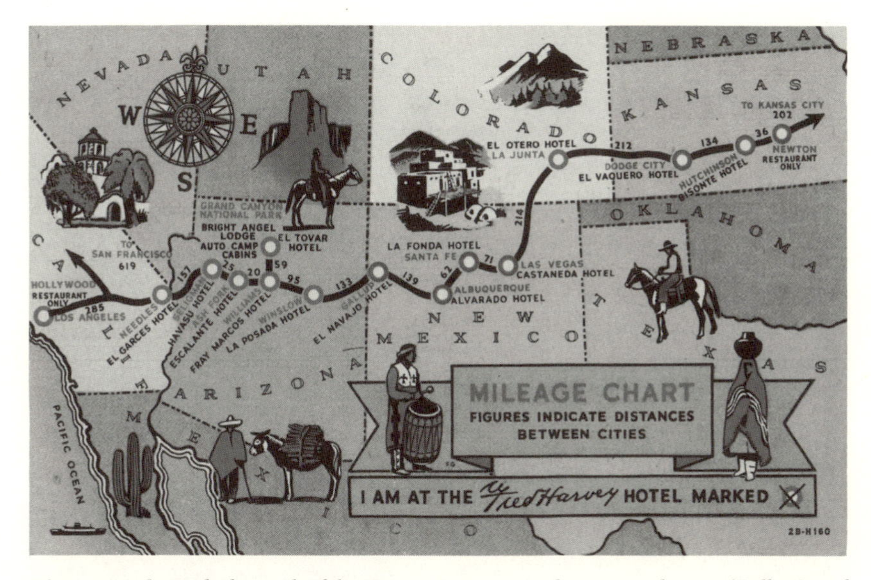

This postcard reveals the reach of the Harvey Company in the 1910s and 1920s. (Collection of the author.)

trip cost $3.95, substantially less than the $20.00 price of the day-long stage ride on rutted roads that departed three times each week from Flagstaff.[15]

The train that reached the rim created the catalytic moment in the modern history of the Grand Canyon, the moment when the canyon and the cultural, intellectual, social, and economic currents of fin de siècle America met in transformative embrace. The purchase of the local railroad by a national corporation with the power, capital, and impetus to invent a consumable Grand Canyon changed the trajectory of local and regional history. Instead of remaining an out-of-the-way symbol, the canyon quickly became an American cultural institution, a place that elite Americans could reach and felt they must see. Before the AT&SF, the Grand Canyon stayed literally and figuratively distant. Neither the ways to it nor its services met the expectations of any but the most adventurous of the elite. With the AT&SF in charge, upper-class and upper-middle-class Americans could visit it on their own terms, in comfort.

After the demise of the local railroad, the AT&SF and its offshoot, the Fred Harvey Company, took control. A British immigrant, Fred Harvey found a niche in rail service. He made his living by offering western travelers good food in a decent environment, and by the end of the 1870s, he operated eating establishments along the AT&SF tracks. By 1889 Harvey was the

The lobby of the El Navajo Hotel, Gallup, New Mexico, shows the plush, regional feel of the Harvey Hotels. (Postcard collection of the author.)

prime purveyor of food and lodging along the AT&SF; he enjoyed the first choice of hotel and restaurant sites along any AT&SF–owned or –leased line. Fred Harvey became an institution, the only universally recognized name among Western travelers. When the AT&SF built the Grand Canyon terminal, Harvey Houses, as his establishments were called, were fixtures along AT&SF tracks. Harvey's fifteen hotels, forty-seven lunchrooms and dining rooms, and thirty railroad dining cars on the new deluxe trains led the industry.[16]

The Grand Canyon was a prime location for the Harvey Company, but it differed from Gallup or Amarillo or any of the other places that enjoyed Harvey Houses. One constituency, tourists, existed at the canyon, creating a zero-sum situation in the nascent service industry. Harvey's food and accommodations were superior, and the company quickly offered services in all price ranges. No one wanted to patronize his competitors, and the Harvey Company managed to meet almost everyone's needs. Existing providers felt squeezed; they could not rely on locals or even on the growing number of employees at the canyon to offset Harvey's advantages. Visitors remained the sole source of significant revenue at the Grand Canyon, and the Harvey Company seemed to serve them all. Its appearance became a declaration of war on existing concerns. Tourist operators had to join forces with or against this powerful entity or be swept aside. Local elites typically faced two choices:

they could exchange their preeminence for a lessened but still respected and profitable role in the new arrangement, or they could battle against the powerful forces of change. This devil's bargain altered the status quo.[17]

The coming of the railroad signified the changing economic value of the canyon and confirmed its growing importance in national culture. Even the prescient Ralph Henry Cameron initially did not recognize that the rails that moved copper out might also bring in large numbers of visitors. As the 1890s ended, he understood that tourism had become a viable economic strategy. When the AT&SF announced its hotel on the rim, Cameron accelerated his efforts to acquire more land and defend what he already possessed. Cameron first entered mining claims in the late 1890s. After 1900 he filed dozens of new claims indiscriminately, giving himself preemptive rights to more than 7,000 acres of the canyon. In 1907 alone Cameron entered thirty-nine claims. Many were located on or near the rim or included trails to the bottom; two, the Cape Horn and Golden Eagle claims, lay just west of the railroad terminus on the south rim. Other claims covered the spring at Indian Gardens and three other places essential to reaching the bottom of the canyon. With confirmed claims, Cameron would control the primary path to the bottom and four of the most strategic places along the route to the Colorado River.[18] The AT&SF might have power and influence, but Cameron knew that landownership and his political status could translate into a windfall as industrial tourism approached the rim.

Cameron's actions took on greater significance as national interest in the Grand Canyon grew; tension about control existed almost from the moment Anglo Americans recognized the canyon as a special place. Efforts to codify its legal status reflected the sense of significance. In 1882 Sen. Benjamin Harrison of Indiana first proposed the canyon for national park status. Twice more during the 1880s, national park proposals went forward. In 1893, as he left the White House, President Harrison used lame-duck executive power to designate the Grand Canyon as a forest reserve. The designation permitted mining claims but did little to alleviate growing competition. Although the executive proclamation of forest reserves anticipated later national-local tension, in 1893 it remained a paper proclamation. Conversant in law and politics, Cameron devised a strategy to secure the many mining claims within the Grand Canyon and instructed Berry in ways to engage federal representatives sent to survey and assess their holdings.[19]

Mollifying government representatives while subtly reminding them of local power succeeded in the prerailroad era. Persuading federal field agents that the operation was a valid mining claim won only a portion of the battle for Cameron and his friends. Swaying visiting General Land Office (GLO) agents and others presented few difficulties; to such officials, Cameron appeared the most powerful person in northern Arizona and federal officials rarely challenged local elites. Cameron worked at a cooperative relationship with the men and they reciprocated. His power held as long as they perceived him as the dominant legitimate source of power in the Grand Canyon area.[20]

The advent of the AT&SF and the Harvey Company altered Cameron's position. The railroad offered much to the isolated hoteliers of the canyon, and even Cameron's closest associates, including Berry, traded with the AT&SF. The railroad, the Harvey Company, and Berry initially enjoyed commercial arrangements for marketing views of the canyon, but the relationship soon grew strained. The railroad diminished Berry's status and threatened his existing relationships. His clients also worked with the railroad and gained even greater profit. In a typical instance, one photographer informed Berry that if "Harvey buys my [photographic] views . . . he has a right to job them if he wants." Berry also found himself buying potable water, a scarce and dear commodity at the canyon, from the AT&SF.[21] The independence and dominance he once enjoyed as a result of his affiliation with Cameron quickly disappeared.

The shift in the local balance of power created considerable tension. The AT&SF expected to control the canyon and established a classic late nineteenth-century hierarchy of services, amenities, and accommodations. From the Harvey Company's perspective, Cameron and his friends stood in the way of progress. From Cameron's point of view, the canyon was his, and he had the perfected titles to mining claims and ongoing relationships with federal field officers to prove it. The presence of the AT&SF irrevocably altered the status quo; Cameron's access to real power in American society paled in comparison to the influence that the Fred Harvey Company and the AT&SF routinely exercised.

The location of a terminal ultimately determined the central tourist district at the canyon. In 1898 Congress granted land on the rim for a terminal, and the AT&SF acquired this parcel as part of their purchase of the defunct railroad. Despite a challenge from Cameron, who filed a mining claim on the same tract in hopes of controlling the incoming rail trade, the AT&SF built the station about 500 yards east of the Bright Angel Lodge and less than that from a spectacular view of the canyon. This situation compelled hotel owners near the terminal to choose. They could cooperate with the railroad and accept a limited role in an expanded industry, or they could engage a large, powerful, and influential conglomerate in economic battle.

Cooperation offered clear benefits. By 1904, Martin Buggeln, a longtime independent in the canyon vicinity, ran the Bright Angel Lodge, managing it with the AT&SF. He received free use of the station grounds and widespread advertising in exchange for a small percentage of his receipts. In contrast, the railroad's influence ensured that Cameron and Berry's facilities were not mentioned in regional newspapers except in purchased advertising.[22] Smaller entrepreneurs rushed to accommodate the incoming powers; they either cooperated or found their enterprises under what was effectively economic siege.

The cornerstone of the AT&SF development program was El Tovar, a rustic and ornate $250,000 hotel built on the very edge of the canyon. When it opened in 1905, the four-story, 325-foot wide, 218-foot deep hotel contained 100 well-appointed rooms, replete with hot and cold running water, electric lights, and steam heat. Its only deficiency was the single bath on each of the four floors, for which guests required reservations. In its expansive dining room, visitors could dine on fresh salmon from the Pacific Coast, California fruit, Michigan celery, Camembert cheese, and other delectables of industrial America.[23]

El Tovar became the harbinger of the new at the Grand Canyon. Its accommodations were more luxurious and sophisticated than those of any existing operators. Before the railroad arrived, proprietors struggled to provide clean sheets and tasty meals. The amenities at El Tovar ensured that anyone who could afford its rates would choose it. El Tovar also foretold a hierarchy of service, in which gradations of less expensive accommodations providing better amenities than previously offered at the canyon were imminent. Not as lavish as El Tovar, such accommodations competed directly with each of the lodges scattered along the south rim.

Although Berry felt compelled to ask the AT&SF why he encountered such "unfriendly treatment" from the railroad, the astute Cameron watched the construction of El Tovar with a sinking feeling. The coming of the railroad threatened existing proprietors. It certainly changed the way they operated. Slipshod standards and practices, typified by Berry's remarkable failure to respond to the request of the Sierra Club to accommodate twenty-five of its members and guide them to the canyon floor in 1902, would not help them survive. In the new environment, small operators had to be efficient and professional to have even a glimmer of a chance. By 1905, when the Bright Angel Lodge reopened as the Bright Angel Camp under the auspices of the Fred Harvey Company, Cameron understood how these newcomers would reshape local economics. Buggeln's relationship with the AT&SF prompted the railroad to shift its tracks a few hundred feet to the east so that guests would disembark closer to his establishment than to Cameron's tent camp. The railroad forbade Cameron's operatives from soliciting business at the train station, and a miniwar followed. Legal skirmishes continued for more than a decade, and for a time, men from both sides carried guns as they hailed and usually harangued incoming trains crammed with visitors.[24]

Accommodations and status became intertwined. The prosperous stayed at El Tovar, which had all the trappings of rustic aristocracy. The Bright Angel Camp, at seventy-five cents per day, European plan, aimed at cost-conscious visitors. This pattern of interrelated but essentially noncompeting resorts owned by one large entity typified tourism accommodations. By 1900 markets included clearly defined niches, based on the amounts people were willing to pay. Cameron remained outside the existing structure, his hotel and camps invisible to all but locals. Even when he sought to elicit sympathy with advertisements that claimed he stood alone against an overwhelming monopoly, he faced the classic problem of small businesses fighting larger corporations. Despite a money-back guarantee, despite rooms and tents that Cameron assured potential customers were "neater and cozier" than any others, despite even his plea to visitors to patronize an individual rather than a "greedy, grasping corporation," Cameron's share of the tourist trade failed to increase. Although people may have sympathized with him, the railroad-subsidized rate at Buggeln's establishment remained twenty-five cents per night less expensive.[25] To most visitors, the price difference outweighed any principle that might be at stake.

Cameron stood his ground and battled head-on with incoming power for more than two decades. He regularly engaged the Harvey Company, the AT&SF, the Forest Service, and after the Grand Canyon became a national park in 1919, the National Park Service. In his view, they conspired to deprive him of what he considered his primacy at the canyon. Cameron's rising political stature gave him the illusion of successful resistance and ultimate vindication. After 1908, in Washington, DC, as Arizona's territorial delegate, Cameron believed he could "commence to show the 'powers that be' . . . the conditions [at the Grand Canyon] in their true light." Federal officials disagreed with that assessment. In 1909 Secretary of the Interior James R. Garfield invalidated many of Cameron's mining claims. By 1914 Cameron felt besieged by the Forest Service, believing the agency and the AT&SF joined against "us people who have to live in that region." Despite Berry's waning enthusiasm and William Randolph Hearst's pending offer to purchase Grandview for a summer cottage, the intrepid Cameron told Berry he intended to stay no matter what the consequences and expressed his philosophy, "*Never say die,*" time and again. Cameron retained some of his holdings into the 1920s, but individualist enterprises such as his own became increasingly marginalized. National power and corporate influence prevailed over personal and local interests.[26]

The tension between Cameron and the AT&SF mirrored similar situations throughout the West that pitted the older American ethos of antebellum commercial culture, Yankee individualism, and states' rights against the postbellum view of a nation with transcontinental scope, needs, reach, and objectives. Cameron and the railroad re-created the conflicts that preceded the Civil War. Recast at the Grand Canyon, these tensions looked much like intransigent locals battling incoming national entities. Cameron's perspective reflected local control, with his roots in Maine, individualism, and a large measure of the idea of economic states' rights. He epitomized the older American ethos in all its contradictory manifestations; he was both Yankee entrepreneur and an advocate of states' rights local control. Cameron ran hard against the dominant currents of his time: the idea of national values and national interest. In the post–Civil War formulation that became Progressivism, his individual desires and even "ownership" of parts of the canyon became less important than scripting the canyon in national mythology. The AT&SF and the Harvey Company represented modern industrial capitalism, lacking geographic boundaries and establishing homogenizing networks that evinced a national rather than a regional sensibility. In concert with the nascent Progressivism sweeping the land during the early twentieth century, the linkages established by national corporations and the national ethos they represented remained the dominant feature of American economic and cultural life and a major concern in intellectual circles.

Whether merely avaricious or philosophically an individualist, Cameron faced the primary issue of the era: in the age of Theodore Roosevelt, social good defined by the privileged and powerful classes became more important than individual desire for wealth. Although Roosevelt could define "good" and "bad" monopolies, he was not prepared to allow the Ralph H. Camerons of the world to make similar distinctions. The combined weight of the railroad and the government proved the most potent force at the Grand Canyon. After Roosevelt's 1903 visit—when he proclaimed that no "building of any kind, not a summer cottage, a hotel [should be permitted] to mar the wonderful grandeur, the sublimity, the great loneliness, and beauty of the Canyon,"—the nascent federal preservation system focused on the canyon.

Progressivism and its emphasis on social responsibility most directly threatened the dominance of local elites. From major cities to remote places such as the Grand Canyon, the proponents of Progressivism sought to recast power relationships in what they deemed more equitable forms. To local elites, especially on the peripheries, central authority smacked of tyranny and vicious intrusion, and they grappled to maintain their hard-won status and power. Such conflicts took many forms, often translating into political battles in the guise of a principled stance. At the Grand Canyon, the issues stood defined in stark relief in the struggle between the corporations, supported by a weak federal bureaucracy, and Cameron, battling for local power, to see who would control a powerful symbol of the American nation.

The Grand Canyon's legal standing and its place in national culture were incongruous. Even as it became an icon, its legal status reflected only the value of its natural resources. By the 1890s the public clamored to see it, but weak mechanisms for its protection paralleled the ineffectual transportation systems that delivered visitors. Lack of access protected the Grand Canyon, but that same remote character allowed Cameron to file claims and turn them into legal title. The canyon's status first as a forest reserve and subsequently as a mining reserve failed to prohibit other uses of reserved land.[27] Before 1905 Cameron held legally filed mining claims. As long as the canyon had vast economic potential as a tourist destination and a canny politician could easily claim it for extractive purposes, problems ensued.

The railroad also benefited from the minimal legal structure. Even though Theodore Roosevelt demanded a rim devoid of development, El Tovar soon stood at almost the exact spot where he had spoken. The Grand Canyon became the first forest reserve to have a hotel and a railroad terminus. In 1908 it passed to the next level of protection after Forest Service chief and leading conservationist Gifford Pinchot told Theodore Roosevelt of David Rust, another Grand Canyon miner, and his plan to construct a tramway to the bottom. Still, the canyon remained wide open. Roosevelt thwarted the project by proclaiming more than 800,000 acres as a national monument under the terms of the Antiquities Act of 1906, but that status hardly secured protection from intrusions and economic development. Each step, however tentative, did limit Cameron's options, but the changes came slowly.[28]

The railroad, not the government, made the initial inroads in curtailing Cameron's power. Capital played an important role; by 1909 the Harvey Company's accommodations completely overshadowed Cameron's. The Santa Fe Land Improvement Company (SFLIC), an AT&SF offshoot, developed the Santa Maria Trail, which provided an alternative to Cameron's Bright Angel Trail. The SFLIC was the only source of funding for road construction on the south rim. The $6,000 it spent to build a road to Hopi Point in 1907 and 1908 had been the single greatest capital expenditure for road construction. The road to Grandview became impassable during the winter and the wet portion of spring, isolating not only Berry but everyone else east of the terminus. Visitors never reached Grandview easily, but in El Tovar's nicely appointed carriages, Hopi Point was always accessible on the improved road. Access determined the fate of Grandview. In 1909 only a few thousand visitors enjoyed its breathtaking panorama, but the numbers at El Tovar and the Bright Angel Lodge swelled.[29]

The AT&SF and the Harvey Company so quickly established dominance that even some foresters criticized the situation. In 1909, sixteen years after the creation of the forest reserve at the canyon, the Forest Service still lacked a meaningful presence there. Two uniformed rangers were stationed on the south rim, one located three miles west of the railroad depot and the other three miles east of Grandview. In the twenty miles between them private concerns firmly controlled access, lodging, service, and everything else. Most visitors never saw the rangers, whose primary responsibilities only peripherally addressed the stream of tourists. Existing roads remained private, comprising the trails cut by Rowe, Bass, Berry, Hance, and others and the two-and-a-half-mile stretch from the depot to Hopi Point that the SFLIC graded. Even the water had to be freighted in, 100,000 gallons a day on the rails. "Practically all the existing improvements are the results of private enterprise and capital," forest examiner W. R. Mattoon noted in 1909. Development was "too great in its proportions and . . . too world wide in its significance . . . to be handed over to or attempted by private enterprises." Pinchot's agency, imbued with an ethos of Progressivism, did attempt to shape the location.[30]

Despite its legal position of power, the Forest Service accomplished its directives by negotiation rather than by assertion. This decision revealed both strategy and a recognition of fait accompli. As elsewhere in the nation, foresters at the grassroots levels interpreted agency directives in the context of local custom and culture. At the Grand Canyon, they recognized the infinitely greater resources of the railroad and the Harvey company, and after Pinchot's departure from the Forest Service in 1910, their cachet. Even as foresters implemented a rudimentary program of fire control, communications, and road and trail construction, they relied on Berry, Brant, and the others to implement their planning. Foresters did not regard this situation as unusual; at the time it typified the agency's practices.[31]

Negotiated leadership reflected the convoluted status of the Grand Canyon. Approximately twelve years stood between Cameron's initial efforts to mine and the construction of El Tovar; six more passed before the Forest Service developed its first plan. When foresters asserted their claim to administrative control, their procedures were little more than an overlay on the existing battle between national and local commercial interests. Despite Mattoon's rhetoric, the Forest Service allied with the Harvey Company and the railroad against Cameron and Berry. Cameron's obsessive suspiciousness of government agencies contributed to the choice, but not significantly. The Forest Service was responsible for the Grand Canyon, but the railroad and the Harvey Company enjoyed on-the-ground control. For a decentralized agency with a history of carefully reading relationships, the outcome was not surprising.

The Harvey Company forced small, local entrepreneurs either to find a niche or change occupations. Lacking Cameron's political power and supreme confidence, they were in no position to resist. Those who could made arrangements; Buggeln was the best example. Others, such as Sanford Rowe, took advantage of the presence of the Harvey Company in small ways. Since the 1880s Rowe transported visitors. After the coming of the railroad, he and a partner, Edward Hamilton, began an autocamp at Rowe Wells. The first automobile, driven by Oliver Lippincott and carrying Los Angeles reporter Winfield C. Hogaboom, arrived at the canyon in 1902, and despite abysmal conditions, more visitors drove their own conveyances. By 1910 a substantial auto trade existed, but the Harvey Company regarded it as unimportant. From Rowe's perspective, there were enough visitors to go around. Needing only a few, he drew them from auto campers, a constituency the railroad did not serve, and the occasional spillover from the hotels. A grizzled old-timer, Rowe also fashioned his camp as an experience distant from modern amenities. There was some truth to that, but the distance was not always intentional. His lack of capital and the difficulty in securing goods accounted for many of the limits his visitors faced. Rowe's predicament was typical. The railroad changed the terrain where he and his peers operated. There were consequences; by 1917 the Forest Service described these businesspeople as "critical and dissatisfied." This mirrored the visitors' views of the service they received from small operators the same way; the Harvey Company fared much better.[32]

The most significant battle between the Harvey Company and local operators involved the Kolb brothers, Emory and Ellsworth. In 1902 the Kolbs arrived at the Grand Canyon. Ellsworth Kolb became a bellhop at the Bright Angel Lodge; Emory Kolb unsuccessfully sought work as a miner. In 1904 they purchased a photographic studio in Williams for $425 and relocated it on the rim. Acquiring land at the head of Bright Angel Trail from Cameron, the brothers built a log structure and started a business photographing expeditions to the canyon bottom. In 1911 the two descended the Colorado River in a raft, an expedition they filmed. Upon their return, Emory Kolb began a lecture tour including slides and a motion picture to packed audiences across the country. By 1915 they had erected a showroom at the top of the Bright Angel Trail, and Emory Kolb continued his lectures; their studio continued to grow. But the Kolbs faced the institutionalization of the Grand Canyon as unhappily as Cameron. The Forest Service plan of 1909 recommended limiting construction on the rim, which precipitated a battle between the Kolbs and the AT&SF/Harvey Company. Later the Forest Service became the subject of the brothers' rancor.[33]

The Kolbs became pivotal figures at the Grand Canyon. More than anyone else, they recognized both sides of the cultural and intellectual gulf that accompanied the tourist transformation. The brothers embraced an antebellum individualist ethos and also grasped the notion of the national audience that eluded Cameron. They understood that the romance of their trip had great resonance, a timbre that was enhanced as such adventures became rare. The Kolbs capitalized on sentiments they aroused, first for profit and later for public support against what they perceived as attacks on their independence.

A struggle for the affection of the public ensued. The Kolbs understood an important lesson long before it became conventional wisdom in the United States: if government or a large economic entity encroaches on a specific niche, reach for the national public. Emory Kolb's lecture tours and the subsequent book in 1914 by Ellsworth Kolb, *Through the Grand Canyon from Wyoming to Mexico,* gave the brothers a status that even Ralph H. Cameron could not match. Despite the Forest Service's strongly held sense that the Kolb's structure was architecturally inappropriate and its anxiety that the brothers distorted the situation in their accounts, the agency had little power over them. Nominally subject to its regulation, the brothers purchased their property from Cameron and could ignore Forest Service and railroad strictures. The fray escalated in 1914, when the Harvey Company built a competing photography studio, the Lookout, designed by schoolteacher-turned-architect/designer Mary Elizabeth Jane Colter, on the rim less than 100 yards away. The Kolbs ever after believed that the government instigated a conspiracy against them. Each time the Forest Service cajoled the Kolbs, the brothers added disparaging remarks about the foresters, the Harvey Company, and even the U.S. Geological Survey, which had no presence at the canyon, to their lectures. Hamstrung by the Kolbs' audience and its own decentralized and cooperative management tradition, the Forest Service simply endured. Only much later did the Kolb brothers become the avuncularly charming, autograph-signing pair who enthralled the post–World War II traveling public.[34]

Other entrepreneurs felt threatened as the Harvey Company and its offshoots developed a comprehensive operation. The livery operators faced the greatest challenge. Once they enjoyed a monopoly on transportation, but the railroad altered their standing. When automobiles came to the canyon in significant numbers, and independent operators and the Camerons offered competing services, long-standing but extraneous livery operators found themselves in search of clientele. W. W. Bass was hurt the most, claiming that the Forest Service failed to safeguard his concession. He believed new operators received advantages unavailable to him. For a time, the Forest Service appeased Bass; rangers allowed him to book his passengers at the agency office and provided him additional support. Nothing helped. In 1917, Bass sued. By the mid-1920s, the disappointed man left the canyon area and settled in Wickenburg, Arizona, which became a center of dude ranching.[35]

As the Forest Service solidified control of the Grand Canyon, it also sought to restore some of the perceived authenticity of the location. With Dutton and Lummis, the canyon had become a representation of the unique nature of the North American continent and the people who deemed themselves its possessors. Mythic place names abounded, but they related more to the meaning of the Grand Canyon in fin de siècle America than to its reality. In creating such names, Clarence Dutton had seen the canyon as exemplifying romanticism and had used that language. Thor Temple, Zoroaster Temple, the Tower of Ra, Confucius Temple, and Shiva Temple formed an intellectual crust for Dutton's *Tertiary History.* Forest Supervisor Don P. Johnston and Forest Examiner Aldo Leopold objected on pragmatic and intellectual grounds. The names were examples of "bad taste," their report averred, causing problems for hotel personnel, who were compelled regularly to explain the bizarre names, and marring the natural splendor of the canyon. Johnston and Leopold believed Indian names would serve better.[36]

This redefinition signaled change, regulation, and the location of the canyon in a twentieth-century cosmos. Dutton's canyon expressed the classical illusions of romanticism, the full-blown identification of the curiosities of world heritage with the cultural past. With Johnston and Leopold's renaming, the canyon assumed the more sedate nomenclature of the Progressive Era, emphasizing a temporal instead of a mythic past and the empirical accuracy of the age. Dutton's canyon evoked the nineteenth-century obsessions with the Orient and the sublime; the Forest Service's canyon embraced the very essence of American society, reflecting its own pragmatic ethic.

Much of the tension in relations between local operators and the Forest Service stemmed from the foresters' need to impress a Progressive Era order on the chaotic situation at the south rim. This reprised the tension between the older antebellum ethic and the postbellum world view. Development at the Grand Canyon was, in forest examiner Frank Waugh's terms, "in many ways abnormal." The local institutions that usually supported growth, banks, developers, shopkeepers, and others were absent, partly because of its remote location and partly because of the transience of people and leadership and the iconoclastic character of local powerholders. When Progressives came head to head with raw individualists, friction resulted. As the Grand Canyon became too intellectually, culturally, and financially important to be left to locals, the zero-sum traits in the situation clarified.[37]

The rivalries on the south rim severely hampered the community-building efforts of the Forest Service. Competition and attendant conflict long preceded the agency. The battle between Cameron and the railroad had existed since 1900, and the internecine conflicts between different people on the rim dated at least to the opening of El Tovar and the railroad terminal in 1905. Well-intended Forest Service's attempts to create community, another of the goals of Progressive Era theorists that required negotiation and modification, remained largely futile at the Grand Canyon.

The on-going human presence and the tension associated with it concerned the Forest Service, which had little experience with such situations. Despite the valiant efforts of Johnston, Leopold, and Waugh, the Forest Service actively sought to convert the Grand Canyon to national park status. The agency's willingness to let permits for summer homes along the canyon exacerbated its problems, and Secretary of Agriculture David F. Houston, Chief Forester Henry Graves, and a range of other high-level officials believed that the skills of the Forest Service did not fit a tourist venue. The AT&SF favored the National Park Service, founded in 1916, to administer the park. The rapid increase in the population of feral burros running loose in the canyon, a result of animals lost or escaped from mining operations or pack trips to the bottom, also indicated that the Park Service might be better suited to manage the canyon. Foresters had much experience with grazing but little with managing an explosion of nonnative species and gladly ceded such issues to the new service. A budding rivalry between the two services hampered cooperation, but the Grand Canyon appeared so thoroughly within the purview of the Park Service that the transfer occurred with little of the acrimony that typified interagency relations during that era.[38]

The arrival of the Park Service instituted another level of organization at the canyon. Only three years old in 1919, the Park Service aimed to become a premier tourist-service agency. NPS officials developed expectations about running the parks and were eager to add the Grand Canyon to their list. An intense construction program followed the February 1919 transfer, with visitor accommodations, staff comforts, and the implementation of visitor-control strategies paramount. The Park Service standardized tourism at the Grand Canyon well beyond the limits of Forest Service efforts.[39]

Conceived and created in the spirit of the Progressive Era and promotion-oriented Jazz-age flashiness, the Park Service approached the public on new terms. Unlike foresters, who came from a decentralized tradition and needed the cooperation of locals to effect their duties, the Park Service managed comparatively small areas according to the needs of outsiders, not locals. Director Stephen T. Mather was a promotional wizard who made his fortune marketing borax; he remained a well-connected individual. He knew power, where to find it, and how to make it work for him. The *Brooklyn Daily Eagle,* hoping to fund the construction of a gateway entrance, gave one of the first private donations to the canyon. Mather instead persuaded the newspaper to build an information booth. With access to outside funding, a promotional campaign in full swing, and the clout of the railroad and the Harvey Company behind him, Mather ignored the complaints of locals.[40]

The Park Service supported the programs of the Harvey Company with a great deal more enthusiasm than had the Forest Service. With Mather at the helm, it valued the national well above the local, and not only at the Grand Canyon. Seeking professional operators and standardized service, the NPS pressured the remaining local entrepreneurs. Mather himself vehemently advocated regulated monopolies. Securing such control meant wrangling with landowners within the park's boundaries who preceded the park's establishment. These legitimate private claims were anathema as the Park Service established its presence.[41] Mather's agency found itself confronting a range of interests, from Cameron to the Kolbs to Rowe, who claimed parts of the canyon, and they clearly associated the Park Service with the railroad and the Harvey Company.

Faced with this even more powerful onslaught of outside power, the locals had few resources. Capitulation was out of the question; like Cameron, individuals such as Rowe believed in the first-in-time, first-in-right doctrine of the nineteenth-century West, the quirky combination of stubborn Yankee self-confidence and southern states' rights philosophy. The Grand Canyon belonged to them, Progressive Era rhetoric about shared resources notwithstanding, and they intended to keep it. Cameron kept the locals riled up, and they engaged in a number of strategies designed to impede the plans of the Harvey Company, the railroad, and eventually the Park Service.

Most prominent among these tactics were a series of complaints directed at the Harvey Company, and during the first two years of NPS administration, they were sent to the Park Service. Some of these concerns were shared by the new administration: poor quality roads and absent paving, a lack of protection to prevent cars from careening over the edge, breakdowns of tour vehicles, and other similar complaints. Objections concerning service were often directed at the Harvey Company. Problems with ride concessionaires, inadequate supplies, excessive fees, and a range of other vexations plagued visitors. One such letter, concerned with high prices, asserted that the Grand Canyon was a "robber's roost owned and countenanced by the government."[42]

The Park Service regarded itself as a regulatory force and invested time and effort in ensuring adequate services. Officials cracked down on easily fixed problems; in one instance, at the Park Service's urging, R. Hunter Clarkson of the Harvey Company simply replaced a decrepit seven-year-old Pierce Arrow with new White Motor Company touring cars. Individual concessions such as the Babbitt-Polson store, a general store that supplied the growing number of auto campers, received repeated warnings to keep their shelves stocked and their doors open.[43] The Park Service's reputation for quality service preceded it, and at the Grand Canyon, arguably its most important individual location, there could be no compromises. Consistent pressure on the lax was part of the obligation of administering a regulated monopoly.

Another type of complaint was equally common but far more vexing. Almost from the moment the Park Service arrived, locals who complained that the Harvey Company conspired to force them out of business inundated agency officials. Such people expected the Park Service to become their ally, and their first missives beseeched the agency to intervene against the stranglehold of the railroad. After the announcement of a twenty-year contract between the Park Service and the Harvey Company early in 1920, the tone of the letters changed, excoriating the Park Service for its part in a perceived conspiracy against small businessowners. Josephine Henson, who was involved in a dispute over Rowe Wells, best expressed this perspective: "It seems this wonderful handiwork of *God* has been conceded to Fred Harvey and unless one patronizes said company one is not entitled to the privileges of a [U.S.] citizen."[44]

Although Henson spoke from her personal position, the Harvey Company clearly shaped the direction of the Grand Canyon's development. By 1919 the company enjoyed a fifteen-year lead in the development of facilities. Largely because of the design work of Mary Elizabeth Jane Colter, it placed a signature imprint on the south rim. The Park Service accepted this architectural style and mirrored it in its own construction whenever possible. The agency's acquiescence acknowledged the fait accompli of the Harvey Company's control. The arrangement offered an odd form of incongruity; as the Park Service accepted the idea of "parkitecture," the concept that NPS facilities should reflect indigenous architectural styles, it granted a regional style predominance over a local one.

The Harvey Company's architecture had its roots in the pueblos of New Mexico. NPS associate director Arno B. Cammerer called it the "adobe architecture indigenous to that section," but it was a telescoping of the artistic construction of a range of styles from around the Southwest. The indigenous people of the region, the Havasupai who lived in Cataract Canyon, a side canyon of the Grand Canyon to the west of the south rim, lived in *jacal* homes called "hawas," mud and stick structures, not the adobe or masonry of the pueblos. As local representation, the adobe style Colter grafted onto the Grand Canyon was a jumble. Anglo American architects borrowed it from places as diverse as Santa Fe and the Hopi mesas. As regional consolidation, it managed to hold the interest of a public largely uninterested in discriminating among the varieties of mythic Indian people.[45]

To the disadvantage of the peoples of the canyon region, the railroad and the Harvey Company engaged in a clear mythification process that mirrored their combined efforts elsewhere in the Southwest. This mythic southwestern overlay privileged Hopi and pueblo culture above Navajo, and Navajo above Havasupai, Yavapai, and Hualapai. Crafts sold at the Grand Canyon followed the architectural styles the Harvey Company and the railroad framed for the traveling public. They too were regional, not local, tied to the emerging cross-tribal manifestation of a polyglot Indian culture that followed the tracks of the AT&SF. From one mythic location to another, from Santo Domingo to Zuñi and Hopi, a dominant local culture appeared in the arts. Each place marketed its own distinctive crafts. Only at the Grand Canyon among nonurban locations were the craft work and jewelry of local peoples slighted in favor of those with mythic regional cachet. In the eyes of visitors, Hopi replaced Havasupai as the dominant Indian people of the canyon.

The Hopi articulated a long-standing claim to the Grand Canyon, but its strength had been diminished over time. Hopi religion teaches that they ascended from their *sipapu* within the Grand Canyon. Despite their claims, little archaeological or historical evidence supported any kind of consistent Hopi occupation anywhere in the region. The approximately 150 miles to the Hopi mesas suggested that their presence there occurred most often because of calamities that affected sustenance. In the 1770s, one Spanish explorer reported that a few Hopi had gone to live with the Havasupai as a result of a severe drought, but other reports of Hopi residence in the canyon are scarce. Yet the Hopi traveled to the canyon to collect salt as late as the 1880s, according to tradition and mythology, following the path that the ancients had taken when they came up from the *sipapu*. During the week-long trip, each traveler inscribed his clan's sign on a rock near the descent to the salt caves, leaving accumulated evidence of their culturally and spiritually significant journey. The row of clan signs attested to the visits but hardly made a claim for Hopi dominance or control of the canyon.[46]

The power of the Hopi presence at the Grand Canyon emanated from the widespread exposure to their art that began in the 1870s with the work of the prolific ethnographer Frank Cushing. The railroad also played upon the remote nature of the Hopi and their seeming lack of resistance to Anglo American encroachment. The Hopi mesas were far from the tracks, yet in the pattern of Santa Fe, that made the Hopi seem more "Indian" in a mythic sense than did Indian people adjacent to rail lines. The Hopi were quickly deemed as mythically "pure," uncontaminated by their limited contact with the white world. Their art acquired particular cachet. In 1893 the World's Columbian Exposition featured a replica of a Hopi altar made by H. R. Voth, a Mennonite missionary to the Hopi. The Santa Fe railroad exhibit featured Nampeyo, who became the most famous of Hopi potters and the initiator of the Sikyatki Revival style. In 1898 Walter Hough of the Bureau of American Ethnology published a pamphlet, "The Moqui Snake Dance," for the railroad, which in 1903 commissioned artist Louis Akin to paint Hopi people for an advertising campaign. Nor did the Hopi people, renowned for their desire to keep outsiders from their ceremonies, strenuously object to visitors coming to see the Snake Dance. During the early 1900s a transportation service that carried visitors from the rail stop to the Hopi mesas for the dances made this distant place more accessible.[47] Before the opening of El Tovar and the Hopi House, Indian ceremony and art had become commodified. Whether such marketing trampled on religious beliefs or not, the Hopi enjoyed a place in the pageant of the American mythic.

At the Grand Canyon, the commodification of Hopi crafts became institutionalized. The construction of the faux pueblo Hopi House in 1905, the first project designed by Colter, was the precursor of a pattern of treatment of native peoples. A combination of reverence for the mythical with disregard for the actual permeated Indian-white relations at the canyon. Colter's work elevated Indian architecture, creating for the world of the traveler an image of Indianness that could be easily assimilated in fin de siècle culture. At Hopi House, Colter replicated a part of the Hopi community at Old Oraibi, creating a place for Hopi people to live and make crafts for sale as visitors watched. Despite the famed Oraibi split, which ended with the departure of a traditionalist group from First Mesa in 1906, families from the three mesas participated in crafts work at the Grand Canyon. Visitors saw a range of Hopi arts and crafts. Families from the village of Hotevilla displayed their silversmithing skills on the rim. Nampeyo sat in front of El Tovar and showed her Sikyatki Revival pottery to thousands of visitors.[48]

Nampeyo played a paradoxical role in the revival of Hopi crafts. Although zoologist-archaeologist Jesse Walter Fewkes claimed that Nampeyo had discovered the motifs that made up the Sikyatki Revival in the discarded pot shards of his excavation at Sikyatki, the talented potter probably first reproduced ancient designs at the behest of ethnologist Alexander Stephen and trader Thomas V. Keam more than a decade before the Fewkes excavation. Keam played an instrumental role in the creation of Hopi painted pottery, even making tile molds for Hopi artisans to use, and he and Stephen helped create the revived form by paying Hopi to reproduce ancient forms and designs while simultaneously developing a market for their creations. William Henry Jackson photographed Nampeyo making pots in 1875 or 1876, when she was about fifteen years old, preceding Fewkes's first appearance by more than a decade.[49] The Hopi crafts that so entranced visitors at the Grand Canyon were part of the overlay created to facilitate interpretation, but the revival occurred to serve the needs of the market rather than the Hopi.

For Hopi people, life at the Grand Canyon had all the trade-offs of integration into mainstream culture. By the mid-1920s, they congregated in the second-floor Hopi House apartment of Jane Nichols, a Hopi woman from Sipaulovi born into the Secakukus family, the only Hopi traders on Second Mesa. The apartment was a social center for Hopi at the canyon. Jane Nichols fed single people who arrived at the canyon, some on work crews and others in the tourist industry. Her hospitality offered a community that mirrored the practices of the Hopi mesas but that differed in many ways. Instead of characteristic Hopi foods such as Piki, cornmeal gruel baked on rock and rolled while hot into a thin wafer twelve inches long and one inch in diameter, the food at the Grand Canyon was termed by one observer "Hopi-American style, with very tasty mutton stews containing squash or onions and with homemade bread of white flour made in round loaves with a thick crust." An Anglo, Hopi Smith, ran Hopi House for the Harvey Company, serving as a cultural interpreter between the Hopi and visitors and creating a version of culture as workplace for Hopis at the Grand Canyon. In this environment, acculturation occurred rapidly if not always thoroughly. Despite access to their own tribal healers, some Hopis approached Old Doc Jones, the AT&SF railroad physician, for nostrums for their ills. In one instance, a Hopi man who had his ear shorn off in an automobile mishap brought the detached appendage to Jones in a handkerchief, thinking the doctor could reattach it.[50] This cultural amalgamation typified the experience of Hopi at the canyon; they sought to maintain the order of their villages but found the attractions of their new lives both enticing and distracting. Most were drawn back to their mythic role at 5:00 P.M. each day, when they were expected to perform dances in front of Hopi House for the edification of tourists.

More complex were Hopi roles located between typical labor and ceremonial activity such as craftmaking. Hopi who worked at labor or service jobs were invisible as Indians; only in regalia or in the Hopi House did they connect with the tourists' perception of what an Indian should be. Hopi Sam from Second Mesa was an unusually visible example of an Indian who worked in such a capacity. As he scurried to collect the bags of incoming train passengers in the 1920s, he was known to visitors as the "smiling bellhop," not as the smiling Indian bellhop. Engaged in an ordinary endeavor, Hopi Sam and the numerous other workers simply could not be "Indian" in twentieth-century society. A Hopi carrying a bag from the train station or working on a road crew had no place in the Anglo American overlay of the Grand Canyon. Such instances created genuine incongruity and seeming aphasia. Paul Nichols, Jane Nichols's husband, ran the newsstand at the old Bright Angel Lodge. Located in the original log cabin where John Hance had spun his tall tales before the crude stone fireplace for the amusement of visitors, the newsstand juxtaposed variations of the mythic; the tale-telling old frontiersman and the quiet Hopi businessman persuaded separate generations of visitors that they found genuine experience when they visited Grand Canyon Village.[51]

Hopi House brought a different Indian culture to the Grand Canyon, the rule-bound culture of the Hopi mesas. Despite the reverence Colter intended in her design, Hopi House also served as cultural exploitation. The building and its appearance of authenticity helped superimpose the Hopi culture on the Havasupai but in a manner that the typical visitor would not grasp. In 1905 the Hopi were well established as commercial artisans. The Havasupai were less known to the outside world, perhaps accounting for the emphasis on Hopi crafts at the shop. Clearly and unsurprisingly, the Harvey Company's motive was profit, not visitor education, and Colter's fine architectural sensitivity blurred the important distinctions between the two cultures as it commodified the Hopi presence.[52]

The imagery associated with the Hopi was unavailable to the Havasupai people, who lived about thirty miles to the west of the south rim. Despite their long history in the region, including a period of time before Anglo arrival when they farmed on what became the Bright Angel Trail, the Havasupai attracted little of the interest and cachet that simultaneously plagued and benefited the Hopi. Even Big Jim, the noted Havasupai who once guided Sanford Rowe, never acquired more than local mythic importance. As late as 1918, when ethnologist Leslie Spier visited, the Havasupai led an isolated life. A few stories of contacts with the outside appeared in the ethnographic literature, but generally, Havasupai stories concerned conflict with other Indian groups, not with the white world. The Havasupai did not so much resist Anglo culture as avoid it. For at least a while, their agricultural regime in Cataract Canyon sustained them, and the attractions of the outside world held little appeal. They "remained unobtrusive but always present," as Elizabeth Compton Hegemann observed.[53]

The arrival of the AT&SF and the Harvey Company at the south rim changed Havasupai life. Especially in the early years, an on-going need for labor drove the canyon's economy. Roads, trails, and other facilities had to be built, and no labor force existed close at hand. A number of Havasupai and some Navajo were attracted to these jobs, and when Spier arrived, a clear tradition of Havasupai work on the rim existed. Most such labor was unspectacular and decidedly not mythic; the one Havasupai endeavor Anglo Americans noticed and attached significance to occurred in 1928, during the construction of the Kaibab Bridge. During summer, all work at the canyon bottom was accomplished primarily at night. Havasupai men hoisted the cables that supported the bridge on their shoulders and traversed the seven miles of steep trails to the bottom like a centipede.[54]

Havasupai labor offered none of the mythic characteristics of Hopi crafts, Indian dancing, or other kinds of ceremonial activities. The Havasupai performed ordinary jobs, the men laboring at construction and building, the women undertaking domestic and kitchen work. The long isolation of the

Havasupai meant that they were not part of the Indian myth created along the AT&SF. Most tourists barely differentiated among Indian people, and few had ever pronounced the name Havasupai. Compared to the Hopi, the Havasupai lacked a clear profile in the minds of visitors.

Nor did the labor have the impact on the Havasupai community or its people that the craft work had on the Hopi. Into the 1920s, Havasupai people simply put in their time on the rim, using the cash earned to supplement the crops grown in their canyon. The Havasupai did not typically regard work on the rim as a special activity. It was barely important in their cosmology. They lived economically on the rim, building only their cedar bark and juniper shelters. When fields needed tending, they headed to the canyons; when peaches ripened, they went to their orchards. Observers on the rim and in the canyon commented on the dedication of the Havasupai to their agriculture. Before 1925 only a few Havasupai acquired the habits of the white world during their time on the rim.[55]

The proximity of the Havasupai village and the seasonal nature of most of their work contributed to dismal living conditions on the rim. Unlike the Hopi, the Havasupai seemed local. Park Service officials did not plan housing for them. Nor did the Havasupai see their residences at the canyon as anything more than a camp. Although before 1920 they resided along the rim, by the early 1920s they were consolidated at a location about two miles southwest of Grand Canyon Village. They built shacks of material found at the Grand Canyon dump—scrap lumber, packing material, rusted tin, and paper cartons—and fashioned an existence that drew negative attention from the Anglo world on the rare occasions anyone noticed.[56]

The Havasupai housing situation was not the only such problem for the Park Service, but it remained an issue longer than did any other similar situation. A camp of "unsightly box-cars and shacks," mostly made of wood and corrugated metal and lined with cardboard, existed along the railroad right-of-way for employees of the railroad and the Harvey Company. It was removed in 1931, long after the Park Service built snug little houses for its own personnel. The one-mile distance between the Grand Canyon Village and the Supai camp meant that only a few concerned people saw the squalid conditions there. The presumption that Havasupai people "chose" to live this way also remained strong. Long after the Park Service invested heavily in turning Grand Canyon Village into a showcase, just down the road abysmal living conditions, replete with rampant attacks of controllable disease, flourished.[57]

By the 1930s the situation at the Supai camp reflected the changes in Havasupai life brought on by the growth of tourism. Initially Havasupai men worked and lived alone on the rim for short periods. As more work became available, they stayed longer and longer, and by the 1920s, their families came along. The living conditions did not improve, and the camp grew "by accretion and without system, planning or supervision," according to Grand Canyon National Park superintendent Minor R. Tillotson. In 1936, "It stood as a monument to a communal Indian life," Tillotson insisted, "which is absorbing little of the real advantages of civilization, yet is rapidly acquiring many of the less desirable aspects." Tillotson understated the case. U.S. Public Health Service senior sanitary engineer Henry S. Hommon recognized the problem as early as 1922 and attributed the lack of improvement to the poverty of the Havasupai. Hommon's observation captured only part of the problem. Clearly, Havasupai people regarded their sojourn on the rim as temporary and may not have considered it wise to invest their resources in more comprehensive shelter.[58]

In the early 1930s, the highway that passed in front of the Supai camp was improved, more tourists traveled it, and the Park Service faced repercussions. Conditions at the camp became common knowledge, to the consternation of the Park Service. Visitors commented on it, and officials responded with their typical aplomb. The Park Service initiated a plan, the Bureau of Indian Affairs joined the project, and efforts to resolve not only housing problems but also water supply, lack of medical personnel, and the search for a camp supervisor began. Housing was the first and easiest problem to solve. In July 1936 construction began on seven cabins for the Havasupai; only six were completed. By early 1937 government-issue houses awaited the Havasupai who worked at the South Rim.[59]

But they could not move in. The Park Service, the Havasupai, and the Bureau of Indian Affairs found themselves in a stalemate. The Park Service wanted the Indian Service to provide supervision for the new houses and insisted that before anyone move in the existing hawas be torn down so that incoming Indian people could not occupy them and compound the problem the new houses had been built to correct. The Indian Service claimed that the matter was beyond its jurisdiction. The Havasupai were not going to tear down their makeshift structures without the guarantee that the new ones would be open to them. For almost three years, the Havasupai remained in the hawas they had built; only in May 1939 did they move into the six cabins.[60]

The camp story revealed the priorities of the Park Service. Codification of its procedures was the paramount goal, and even fifteen years after the transfer of the park to the agency, much work remained before the park both functioned and appeared as the Park Service expected. The Havasupai situation was the last to be addressed. Agency, railroad, and Harvey Company workers received better living quarters before the Indians did, a function of culture and location. The former had complained; the Havasupai did not. The Park Service's priority had been Grand Canyon Village, and the Supai camp was not in the village proper. Until it attracted visitors' attention, the camp, long described as unobtrusive, was left alone. The Hopi were central to the public scheme of the Grand Canyon, but the Havasupai remained on its intellectual and cultural periphery.

Their situation typified the treatment of people regarded as peripheral in a symbolic setting. Unlike the Hopi, the Havasupai were incidental to the mythologizing of the canyon; their eyesore of a camp remained invisible from the cultural overlay of the canyon, hidden from the script that fashioned it. Over time, the market economy—the jobs on the south rim—drew in the Havasupai. They spent less time in the canyon tending their crops and became closer to the white world. Little acknowledgment of the change, especially in the form of services, followed. Embrace of the market had consequences. Native practices fell by the wayside, as individuals found employment or customers for their wares and discovered that for a price, the market economy would provide their material needs.

Such a situation mirrored the age-old response of Native Americans and other preindustrial people to the coming of more expensive but far more utilitarian mass-produced market goods. As industrialization and its accoutrements spread across the country, such people faced a choice: participate in the market economy, reap the benefits of material culture, and risk second-class economic and cultural status or eschew such goods, enjoy fewer material benefits, and maintain traditional identity, culture, values, and practices. A few could successfully negotiate this transformation, but for most, it inaugurated irrevocable changes. For the Havasupai who lived in the canyon, the experience was pronounced. For Native Americans at the Grand Canyon, there were few ways to win.[61]

Anglo neonatives at the Grand Canyon experienced similar patterns. Although they understood the options better, they were still people from the periphery, remote to the central vectors of wealth and power of the early twentieth century. As the old-timers were displaced, an entirely new group, tied closely to the Harvey Company and the railroad, took precedence at the canyon. This group regarded the location as an economic opportunity, and in some cases, as an escape from the drudgery of rural and agricultural life.

The canyon held promise of economic opportunity and social mobility, of the miracles of the modern world. The number of people, especially young women, who embraced this chance was vast.

Working at the Grand Canyon offered the appearance of a better life for young women. By 1907 the Harvey Company employed more than 2,000 women along the AT&SF lines. Most perceived the Grand Canyon as one of the best places to work. Described by one of their peers as "from farms, from cities, everywhere," the girls found themselves in an enjoyable work environment with access to a particularly appealing pool of potential marriage partners, the wealthy young men who visited the canyon. The routine company prohibition against fraternization was dropped at the Harvey Houses of the Grand Canyon, and many of the waitresses found that male Harvey House workers, cowboys, sightseeing-car drivers, and others made good partners. The combination of similarity in class and daily proximity led to a significant number of marriages between workers instead of with the wealthier, more transitory visitors. In employment, upward advancement remained atypical. The company required specialized skill for its best management and even service positions. The Harvey Houses "served as a sort of normal school for the training of managers and domestics of every sort," in the estimation of one observer of the process. The company hired and trained their own cooks, "Frenchmen and Germans who enter their employ when young."[62] Tourism offered opportunity within limited realms, but it could not fulfill all the dreams of its workers.

Even the most powerful people in the region faced the complicated negotiation of status, influence, and wealth that tourism brought. Cameron could not maintain his presence in the canyon after the arrival of the AT&SF, the Harvey Company, and the Park Service. He was compelled to sell his tracts to the government or face condemnation under the power of eminent domain. A powerful individual in northern Arizona, Cameron was no match for the combined force of the government, the railroads, and the burgeoning travel industry. Although he became a noted obstacle for the federal agencies that managed land in the West, even his election as U.S. Senator from Arizona in 1920 could not alter his circumstances. Sanford Rowe eventually abandoned the canyon and moved to the edge of the western Navajo reservation, where he sunk a well, cut timber, and remained a pioneer. Although Elizabeth Compton Hegemann believed Rowe cared little for the modern world, like the mythic Daniel Boone, much of his disregard stemmed from his loss of position and status.[63] From top to bottom, local Anglo American society was rearranged by tourism at the Grand Canyon.

National park status created a new neonative community at the canyon. Park Service personnel and their families resided there, as did the employees of the railroad and the Harvey Company. It was an idyllic experience, especially during the off-season, when fewer tourists encroached on their special playground. "We lay supreme in Our little world flanked by the great depths of the Canyon and the miles of pine-covered plateau stretching south to the San Francisco Peaks" beyond Flagstaff, Elizabeth Compton Hegemann remembered. "A single track of steel bound us to the main artery of travel at Williams, over which each morning came Our precious water supply in tank cars on the regular freight train. . . . It was Our lifeline." Dependent on the railroad, people at the canyon knew they were fortunate to have its beauty to themselves for even some of the year.[64]

Membership in this little community had to be earned. Hegemann acquired her status when she married park ranger Michael Harrison, "stepping across an invisible but definite line of demarcation" that distinguished visitors from worker-residents. The boundaries were clear. No Grand Canyon resident would mistake a ranger in uniform sans the trademark Park Service Stetson hat for a paperboy, as one tourist did on seeing the small, slight, and youthful Harrison. Nor would visitors be invited to the revelry of local parties, such as the one held in the El Tovar coffeeshop one New Year's Eve that finished moments before the ritual 7:00 A.M. opening. The residents of Grand Canyon felt special and believed that they had not only a unique attachment to the place but also an exceptional appreciation of it. "It was a fascinating and almost unreal background in which to make one's home, if all the beckoning potentialities were to be explored," Hegemann wrote. "We not only welcomed the new, but savored the old ways of the pioneer life which was passing into history right under Our noses. . . . The surrounding country became a part of us or at least we became an integral part of it."[65]

The people at the Grand Canyon shared a strong sense of community. Much like soldiers on the front, a closeness developed among them, predicated on their common experiences and circumstances. They were part of a script, not wholly of the place but truly of it. Between the world of visitors and the people of all backgrounds who came before them, they played crucial roles in seeing that the canyon served the intellectual needs of the ever-expanding number of visitors. They were also interlopers, as most of them recognized, and between the world that preceded them and the visitors to whom they catered, they had only each other. This shared feeling gave their lives the qualities of some combination of summer camp, college dormitory, and collective living experience.[66]

By the mid-1920s the transformation of the Grand Canyon was complete. Its sublime characteristics had been packaged and promoted for an upper- and upper-middle-class audience, who could find the amenities they wanted and enjoy an experience they regarded as genuine. The Harvey Company offered a level of service that appealed to the so-called "better class of people." The first airplane landed and took off from the bottom of the canyon in 1922, a harbinger of the future. At nearly the same time, the Oklahoma State Supreme Court upheld the Harvey Company rule that required men to wear suit coats in company dining cars and dining rooms. The Park Service instituted rules and procedures that managed not only the canyon but also the people who came to see it. An onslaught of automobiles had just begun. The Harvey-run Hopi House at Grand Canyon Village sold baskets, blankets, and other crafts to visitors; it did not trade with Indian peoples. To get Pendleton robes, Stetson hats, Levis, or other goods, Native Americans had to go to the nearby Babbitt Brothers trading post.[67] "Park Indians," Havasupais from the immediate area, Navajos and Hopis from the vicinity, and others, had been pulled into the tourist economy. They were only a step away from being twentieth-century stereotypical agency Indians. The once-vaunted Cameron was reduced to holding Senate hearings denouncing the federal bureaucracy.

The combination of entrepreneurial activity embodied in the Fred Harvey Company and the AT&SF, and the rise of the Grand Canyon as national symbol, created a special kind of meaning. To the people of the time, the Grand Canyon was much more than the immense hole in the ground that explorer García López de Cárdenas perceived. The canyon represented the grandeur of the American continent and the hardy people who believed they had conquered it. This perspective, the railroad spur from Williams, and the opulent El Tovar allowed the cultural symbolism of the era to meld with the appropriate level of amenity, creating a symbol with vast resonance in American society. The first western national tourist destination had been invented, mirroring the nation's structures and blending the values of the Progressive Era with the benefits of industrialization.

4

The Tourism of Hegemony II

The Railroad, Neonativity, and Santa Fe

At the base of the Sangre de Cristo Mountains in northern New Mexico, Santa Fe experienced a transformation that paralleled that of the Grand Canyon. Between 1880 and 1925, its role as governmental center disappeared, and its status grew as a place that fashioned itself as unique in an age obsessed with mass production. The territorial capital of New Mexico, an anomaly among American holdings on the continent in its demography, tricultural heritage, and even its patterns of language, Santa Fe held an inverted promise for industrial America. Instead of the affirmation associated with the Grand Canyon, Santa Fe proposed a challenge, one seemingly sincere and severe but intentionally muted. In the invented Santa Fe, upper-class Americans dissatisfied with their culture could discover a world that seemed different from the one they left but that measured its distance in style rather than substance. Santa Fe promised a different formula than did industrial America, but ultimately it only recapitulated the same structure behind a seductive and well-organized mask.

As it had at the Grand Canyon, the railroad played a catalytic role in making Santa Fe accessible, but real change stemmed from the vision of an Anglo American neonative entrepreneur who fashioned a new city of cultural significance from the detritus of a declining nineteenth-century economy. Instead of a physical transformation, this feat required the repackaging of Santa Fe's most obvious attributes—the foreignness, its largely intact historic fabric, and the presence of Indian people—into a script that American travelers could simultaneously interpret as different and as tacitly unthreatening. Santa Fe embraced tourism because the community and its region had few options. It had little else to offer the industrial world, few ways to avoid the slow decline of communities that modernity overlooked.

Although by the 1920s Santa Fe owned powerful cachet based on the perception of its cultural difference from the American mainstream, in the late nineteenth century the town barely escaped oblivion. The AT&SF bypassed it in the 1880s, and its only rail service was the Chili Line, a narrow-gauge offshoot of the Denver, Western, and Rio Grande (D&RG) that ran from Antonito, Colorado, down the Rio Grande Valley to the Buckman Crossing south of the Otowi Bridge and then climbed the mesas to Santa Fe. The Chili Line provided an economic link, but it served a predominantly local and regional audience. A few tourists traveled up the Rio Grande Valley to Española and beyond, but most of the traffic consisted of produce brought down from villages along the route. The chiles, sheepskins, mutton, and wool from the Rio Grande Valley were insufficient to ward off economic doldrums, and by 1900 Santa Fe seemed consigned to the scrapheap of western history, slightly beyond but thoroughly outside the pale of the cross-continental steel rails that drove economic expansion. Its commercial role replaced by the budding rail junction of Albuquerque almost seventy miles to the south, the town faced difficult times. By 1910 more than 20 percent of its population in 1880 had moved on, leaving Santa Fe with a population roughly 80 percent of its size in 1817. In the technological selection process that determined the future of the West, Santa Fe had been left behind.[1]

Like the rest of New Mexico, Santa Fe was poorly prepared for the advent of Anglo American railroad-connected market economics. In the 1880s New Mexico, especially in the north, lacked even a rudimentary middle class. Subsistence agriculture and animal husbandry dominated the Rio Arriba region. *Extranjero* (foreign) families, German-Jewish emigrés prominent among them, constituted the merchant class, which played the dominant role in capital formation, intermarried with local people, and traded extensively but possessed the goals of an individualist mercantile culture instead of the community orientation of their Hispano neighbors. The colonial nature of trade in the peripheries of the Southwest gradually transferred agriculturalists' tangible assets to merchants, revealing one dimension of the well-documented larger picture of the alienation of Hispano land and property. Softened by American law, in which they typically were not conversant, Hispanos found their assets disappearing. By 1900 a process that centralized wealth in the hands of a few, converting the many from ownership to tenancy, was well under way. As it occurred, most of Spanish-speaking northern New Mexico became poorer and more dependent. Without access to the wages of industrialization or the skills to fit in the new marketplace, the chance to consume the goods that industrialization produced was illusory.[2]

By 1900 Santa Fe had long since ceased to be the Hispanic trading town of myth. Transformation followed the American conquest in 1846; especially in the 1870s and 1880s, northern New Mexico's ties to the world of industrialization grew stronger, bringing outside capital and power. The railroad, which reached Albuquerque in the early 1880s, changed the geographic trajectory of trade and the value of land, which in turn meant that long-standing patterns of ownership and social and economic behavior came under severe stress. An ongoing influx of Anglo Americans followed 1846, and the coming of the railroad accelerated their impact. In Santa Fe, the initial wave included the protomiddle class of industrialization, shopkeepers and clerks, and those more typical of the vanguard of industrialization, railroad workers, track-layers, schedulers, and others. Closely behind followed the fly-by-night entrepreneurs who made their living off the expansion of the railroad infrastructure. Extralocal timbermen became a particular menace to Hispano landowners. Lawyers also became a prominent feature of Santa Fe, drawn both by the territorial capital and the numerous rapacious lawsuits directed at confiscating Hispano property. These newcomers became the clearest features of Americanization and created a form of cyclic economic expansion. New Mexico was opened to a different legal, cultural, and economic system, and its offerings were subjected to a quick plucking by the denizens of the incoming culture. Such resources were few in the high desert of the Rio Arriba, and this rush lasted briefly, completed by 1900. It left economic and cultural shambles in its wake, and even the territorial capital scrambled for economic sustenance. Bypassed by the railroad, superseded by Albuquerque, and seemingly destined for irrelevance, Santa Fe was in the doldrums.

Culture rescued Santa Fe, providing it an economy at a time when few other options existed. Before 1910 Hispanos, Indians, and Anglos alike had used and overused the best grazing lands in the area. Agriculture in the region remained tentative at best, and a large-scale mining economy did not exist. New Mexico's status as a territory diminished Santa Fe's political importance as the capital, and the rise of Albuquerque further impinged on its status. Santa Fe's days as an important commercial trading center ended when the railroad passed it by, and the local newspaper was reduced to repeatedly trumpeting the attributes of the community in the hope someone significant would notice. "Nature has marked Santa Fe as the sanitarium of the world," one frequently reprinted turn-of-the-century article announced as it attempted to capture a share of the tuberculosis trade for northern New Mexico.[3] With a dim economic future, the town reflected the difficulties common among communities with only tentative access to the railroad corridors to link them to the twentieth century.

One cultural entrepreneur, Edgar L. Hewett, rescued Santa Fe and transformed it into a place with a special resonance in American culture. After being fired from the presidency of New Mexico Normal School—now New Mexico Highlands University—in Las Vegas, New Mexico, in 1903, Hewett began his career as a promoter of culture. Born on a farm in Illinois, he became a teacher at Missouri's Tarkio College, rising to the position of college president. On the way, he became an avid amateur archaeologist, and after arriving in Santa Fe, he turned his attention to the nearby Pajarito Plateau. There Hewett began numerous excavations in what he claimed, in the time-honored manner of archaeologists, as his private preserve, keeping other potential excavators away.[4]

Hewett had vast ambitions. From this little archaeological fiefdom, he built a cultural empire, bringing guests to his excavations and exchanging prehistoric artifacts dug from his sites for their goodwill and later support. Economically and socially prominent friends could help Hewett achieve his goals. They were conduits to funding and sources of support and defense during the wars for control that so dominated fin de siècle science. At the onset of the new century, Hewett built a constituency in anthropology and archaeology and by 1905 he earned a reputation, albeit not always a positive one, and possessed a cadre of friends who supported him.[5]

Hewett's interest in prehistory was genuine, his empire-building drive innate. He regarded the archaeological record as confirmation of the triumphs of modernity and believed the archaeologist played the role of sage, the transmitter of the wisdom of continuity to a misguided but receptive public. As fin de siècle anxiety gathered momentum, the ability to use science to dissipate cultural tension granted archaeology genuine significance in American society. A certain glory existed in this role, a conceptual myth-making that Hewett embraced. He believed that the "history in storage," as he referred to the contents of the archaeological mounds he sought, held the knowledge that could reconcile the tensions of the modern world, and he worked to communicate that formulation to receptive audiences around the country.[6]

In pursuit of this objective, Hewett initiated the development of a plethora of cultural institutions in northern New Mexico. His exuberant efforts to convey his message and make his mark divided the field of archaeology into a camp that favored him and another that opposed his every effort. Archaeology was a staid profession, and to many, Hewett was a grandiose upstart, an incompetent showman. Despite powerful opponents, Hewett received a Central American fellowship from the Archaeological Institute of America (AIA) in 1905, with the goal of establishing a research center in Mexico similar to the ones the institute sponsored in Athens and Rome. Hewett brought this project, the School of American Archaeology, to Santa Fe. His effort supported AIA leader Francis W. Kelsey's goal of bringing archaeology to a broader public. When Kelsey became president of the institute in 1907, Hewett's most prominent supporter controlled an organization that had been consistently unfriendly to him. The change in leadership provided Hewett an optimal moment to enact his plans; soon after, Santa Fe housed the first permanent school in the Americas funded under the auspices of the AIA.[7]

Hewett now had the context to implement his vision. In 1906 archaeology reached a peak of importance in American consciousness. It could explain the relationship between past and present, mitigate the changes in American society and make them seem part of an orderly, if not always comprehensible process, as nothing else could. In 1906 Congress passed the Antiquities Act and established Mesa Verde National Park.[8] Hewett fused the popular interest in archaeology with the cultural climate in Santa Fe. The School of American Archaeology became the first of many Santa Fe–based institutions that exploited the AT&SF's tourist trade and created the beginning of a marketable cultural heritage.

For Hewett, the school became a springboard to build a western center of culture and to enhance his growing but still dubious reputation as a scientist. Although he lacked formal academic standing until he received a Ph.D. in 1908, he established himself as the premier western archaeologist of the early twentieth century, much to the consternation of many scholars located at the museums and distinguished universities of the eastern seaboard. Before he was through, Hewett founded the Museum of New Mexico and the Museum of Fine Arts in Santa Fe, revived Indian Market and helped organize the Santa Fe Fiesta, orchestrated the establishment of Bandelier National Monument, guided the creation of an informal building code that allowed Santa Fe to retain its pseudohistoric physical facade, developed the archaeological exhibits for the Panama-California Exposition in San Diego in 1915 and 1916, and fashioned Santa Fe into a town where the mythic and real were purposely indistinguishable.[9]

This combination of culture and show transformed Santa Fe and its environs into a place new and different in American society. Santa Fe possessed genuine mystique; it had been the town at the end of the rainbow, a mythic place that had become legend. Its capture during the Mexican War—when conquering general Stephen Watts Kearney promised to protect Santa Fe from raiding Navajos and to apply fair and just law—articulated its role as a dimension of Manifest Destiny. Santa Fe's history as a prerailroad crossroads for trade granted it a certain romanticism. Stories that emanated from nineteenth-century Anglo American observers confirmed that status. Adding romantic science, his descriptions of prehistory as a parable for modern life, Hewett melded these features into an overlay mirroring the one that Clarence Dutton, Charles Lummis, and others invented for the Grand Canyon. Hewett's efforts made Santa Fe comprehensible to the fin de siècle traveling public, creating a place that embraced its closeness to the benefits of industrialization even as it created the illusion of great distance from the mainstream.

Hewett's conceptualization of Santa Fe impressed itself on a real town that had undergone great change. Culture offered solutions to the problems that stemmed from its unsettled status in Americanized New Mexico. By the time Hewett arrived, the leaders of the town were avidly searching for new economic strategies. Hewett's intuitive understanding of the meaning of Santa Fe and his talent for promotion allowed him to cast the area in an intriguing manner. New Mexico's prior image suggested danger and disorder; the story of Billy of the Kid and the Lincoln County war, the murder of Col. Albert Fountain and his son, Henry, the national reporting of the trial and the acquittal of the alleged perpetrators, the Santa Fe Ring of land speculators, and on-going political shenanigans made New Mexico and Santa Fe seem disreputable, unAmerican, part of a cultural Other.[10] Hewett transformed that perceived chaos into a delicious idiosyncracy that fascinated fin de siècle America.

Despite Hewett's contentious personality, Santa Fe's business community recognized his importance. They too attempted to attract tourists, with notably less success than Hewett achieved with his cultural institutions. Focusing on scenery, the dry climate for tuberculars, hunting and other outdoor opportunities in the nearby mountains, and even such alluring appeals as "a city combining romantic and historic interest . . . [a] strong amalgamation of elements, antique and modern," local businesspeople tried to link their town to the myriad AT&SF efforts. The distance from the rail lines inhibited success. Travel to Santa Fe became easier; under territorial governor George Curry, a new road to the town from Albuquerque cut deeply into the steep La Bajada Hill about twenty miles to the south. Previously the road passed through the old mining towns of Cerrillos and New Madrid in a long and circuitous fashion. With more automobiles on the road, and driving becoming more than a fad in American society for men and women, such developments were harbingers of better times. Yet before Hewett, Santa Fe drew only a few tourists. Its reputation as sinful and somehow depraved, a legacy of the more open personal culture that existed during the Santa Fe Trail era, kept people away.[11]

By 1909 civic and economic leaders recognized that despite their often unflattering opinions, Hewett offered a new source of revenue with a strategy that simply required locals to market themselves and their home. The embrace of culture was almost universal within Anglo Santa Fe. The local newspaper, the *Santa Fe New Mexican,* covered archaeology as a local issue, and tourism played an expanding role in the community's view of its attributes. The newspaper marveled at Hewett's ability to find supporters and attract money as he outdistanced his rivals, such as former territorial governor L. Bradford Prince, in what had become a local culture derby. Hewett's status as a professional granted him the authority that made what he said "authentic" in the terms of the time, and in 1912 he found himself, along with his associate Sylvanus G. Morley, appointed to the new Santa Fe City Planning Board, formed to stanch the city's more than thirty-year decline. Although the chamber of commerce's promotional efforts often drew Hewett's ire—in one dramatic instance in 1912, he squashed an effort to claim Santa Fe as the oldest city on the continent after the impecunious chamber paid for large numbers of envelopes and stationary embossed with that slogan—both recognized that culture represented Santa Fe's future. They differed about who would define its representation. The chamber and some of Hewett's staunch opponents maximized control of trade and commerce, but Hewett, known for his insistent need to be in the limelight, remained the most visible figure in the community and the point person in regional cultural and archaeological affairs.[12]

Tourism expanded the economic range of the community, creating an array of opportunities for other entrepreneurs. As these efforts gained momentum, newcomer Dr. John P. Wagner planned a new hotel. Eastern tour syndicates kept Santa Fe off their list of overnight stopping points because its four hotels, the Palace, the Claire, the Coronado, and the Normandie, did not meet their standards. Wagner intended to remedy that. In the manner of newcomers who wish to be liked, he sponsored a contest to name his new hotel. Although sixteen-year-old Anita Baca, a native of Santa Fe, was not the only one to suggest the name De Vargas, she received the cash prize after being judged the applicant who most thoroughly described the importance of Don Diego de Vargas, the leader of the *reconquista* of Santa Fe in 1692.[13] Her selection was instructive. Baca was a native Hispana, a member of the elite of Santa Fe's majority. As the winner, she offered a hint of inclusiveness, of change without consequence. The choice showed Wagner astride a narrow line. He appropriated local people and their symbols in an effort to be accepted; he embraced the Hispano past as a quaint and useful form of public relations. He also valued the special nature of local heritage and wanted to preserve it in an enterprise that embodied transformation of the community.

The neonative Wagner showed an immediate desire to claim Santa Fe as home and heritage, a trait common in generations of Anglo American successors. "I have come to your city to stay," Wagner promised the Santa Fe Commercial Club in July 1909 in classic neonative fashion. "Santa Fe possesses the greatest advantages for a resort city of any city on the American continent if not in the world." He planned to cater to the "men of wealth of the East," a constituency that mirrored the people whom Hewett solicited.[14] Nor did Wagner see his enterprise as a threat to existing hotels. He fashioned his hotel as the catalyst for broadening the market. Wagner embraced neonativity, presenting himself as a native who was simply not born in New Mexico. He brought skills and capital the community lacked, he believed, and all would benefit from his efforts. Hewett's institutions succeeded in attracting outside investment, and Santa Fe would never be the same. As long as the values of the upper classes meshed with the cultural message of archaeology, a sophisticated form of tourism could thrive.

When Wagner spoke to the chamber of commerce, he addressed a different kind of native audience. Early in the century, the chamber served as a gentlemen's club of leaders. By 1900 Anglos predominated, although many spoke Spanish as well as English and a few were Hispano. They were closely tied to the progress-oriented ethic of the age. Addressing them, Wagner spoke to people who believed as he did, who valued what he valued, and who were *muy sympatico*—very sympathetic—to the views he offered. Even Hewett, neonative to the core, agreed with the message of progress. Tourism divided the world into sacred and profane space; sacred space merited preservation, being frozen in a fictive moment in the past, but profane space could be developed so that those who sought sacred space could have their customary comforts.

Following Hewett's pathbreaking work and the message of Wagner and others, the business community developed a parallel strategy for attracting tourists. In 1909 the *New Mexican* pronounced Santa Fe the "best advertised town in the world" as a result of the efforts of the AT&SF. "What a fine foundation for a systematic advertising campaign by the city," the writer continued, challenging local leaders to show the way. Prominent Santa Fe residents, including Wagner and A. H. Broadhead, visited other places that used tourism as an economic strategy. Broadhead focused on Seattle, Washington, location of the Alaska-Yukon-Pacific exposition, as an example for Santa Fe with its growth, diverse industrial base, tall buildings, civic attractions, and other features.[15]

This vision embraced ordinary tourism, a message that could have obliterated Santa Fe's distinctive past in its genuflection to urban technology. This impulse stemmed from the many world's fairs that began with the Centennial Exposition in 1876 and continued until American entry into World War I. A form of boosterism, such sentiment differed from the cultural mecca Hewett envisioned. It promoted the iconography of progress, minimized any relationship to existing cultures in Santa Fe, however altered, and ignored the features that made the community distinctive. Broadhead's vision mimed the norm of the fin de siècle; dozens of small- and medium-sized communities around the nation followed a similar approach. Here was an ordinary framing of Santa Fe's attributes, following fashion too closely and trumpeting the increasingly stale messages of a self-righteous and self-affirming society. If this direction had been followed, a very different kind of Santa Fe would have developed. Facing the power and influence Hewett had amassed, its chances were slim. Hewett's institutions and his very presence often served as a contentious check against wholesale migration toward the norms of the time.

Hewett preserved a special vision for Santa Fe, however different from its past. He used archaeology to carve a liminal place for the community, close to the modern world in technology and amenity but evocative of an identifiably different past that soothed a restless nation. At Hewett's behest, the Santa Fe newspaper touted the value of the cliff dwellings nearby, comparing that relationship to the one between Denver and the ruins at Mesa Verde. Hewett founded the magazine *El Palacio* as another outlet for the stream of information he produced and appointed his friend, banker and former newspaper reporter Paul A. F. Walter, as editor. Hewett even drew sketches of cliff dwellings for a souvenir booklet published by the D&RG Railroad.[16] Santa Fe was distinctive, its attributes unique, Hewett insisted, and over time, he converted most of the business community to his point of view.

Hewett's work helped fashion an overlay similar to the one that developed at the Grand Canyon. He created a context that explained Santa Fe in terms that the traveling public could understand, a veil through which few could see. Empiricism dominated the thinking of the era as did attempts to quantify the mysterious. The explanation of the sublime in romantic yet understandable terms was Hewett's personal forte. His professional writings gleamed with a romance between science and the sublime, uncovering layers of humanity, romanticizing the past and exalting progress. The growing influx of Anglo people and their desire to understand the pre-Anglo world served as proof of the power of Manifest Destiny; the interest in "primitive" and "disappearing" cultures affirmed the triumph of expansion. As had happened at the Grand Canyon, Santa Fe packaged its attributes for the literate public of the early 1900s.

Hewett's Santa Fe offered a special ambience that promoted its intentional distance from the mainstream. The Spanish architecture, small in scale and cut low against the mountains, created a quaint vista. Only the famed Cathedral of St. Francis, built by Archbishop Jean Baptiste Lamy, stood against the sky and mountains. The dust on the plaza, the black rebozos of the women and the men's brightly colored clothing, the sound of the Spanish language, and the Indians who sold jewelry and artifacts in front of the Palace of Governors created an authentic past for the upper-middle class. This was a past elsewhere overwhelmed, the town seemed to say, but here preserved as a pure vision of a preindustrial existence.

To the upper classes, Santa Fe became a revelation. Compared to the soot-choked air of Pittsburgh or the bustle of New York, it seemed sleepy and undisturbed. Spanish flowed softly to Americans, accustomed to harsher-sounding immigrant languages. Burros and shawls, not electric street cars, dominated Santa Fe. To many, this strangely sophisticated town was somehow alluring. It appealed to anyone who had reservations about the pace of the industrialized world.

The overlay Hewett created, the means of translating historic Santa Fe, began in his vision of a premodern town; in its aftermath, only Santa Fe's geographic location and its name retained historic roots. Hewett served as intermediary between the Santa Fe the railroad bypassed and the Santa Fe of myth that so many sought. A parade of Anglo Americans followed, embellishing the conception Hewett initiated. Architects, most notably Isaac Hamilton Rapp and his successor John Gaw Meem, created the Pueblo Revival style, emphasizing traditional northern New Mexican features such as vigas and adobe construction and adding distinctive elements that marked the work as modern but evocative of the past.

Beginning in Trinidad, Colorado, Rapp enjoyed a distinguished career in Colorado and New Mexico. Before coming to Santa Fe, he used the same elements in the design of public buildings in Trinidad as in Colfax, Raton, and Las Vegas, New Mexico. Catron High School, built in 1904, Rapp's first commission in Santa Fe, led him to design public structures such as the New Mexico building at the 1915 California-Pacific Exposition in San Diego. He then received a commission for the Museum of Fine Arts, the Sunmount Sanatorium, and La Fonda, the Inn at the End of the Trail. Meem, who arrived to stay at Sunmount in 1920, became the best-known Pueblo Revival architect. In Santa Fe, the Museum of Fine Arts exemplified the Pueblo Revival, cited even in the work of noted architecture critic Talbot F. Hamlin, whose *American Spirit in Architecture* defined the variations of national style. The combination of architectural design and context turned Santa Fe into the model of a regional style, further articulating its constructed authenticity.[17]

Rapp did not invent the Pueblo Revival; he seems to have snatched from the air one of the prevailing currents of his time. Experimentation with pueblo architectural features appeared across the southwestern landscape, in no small part at the behest of the railroad. Efforts to redesign the University of New Mexico along these lines also occurred between 1905 and 1909. The signs and symbols of southwestern culture pointed in the direction of the style that became the Pueblo Revival. Rapp was merely the most successful of the early architects who sought such commissions.[18]

Nor was the Pueblo Revival a wholly indigenous architectural style. With the New Mexico Building, the form reached an eclectic pinnacle. Rapp, T. Charles Gaastra—who in 1918 moved to Santa Fe and by 1920 had received commissions for Pueblo-style works such as the Cassell Building on the northwest corner of the Santa Fe Plaza—Meem, and their successors remade New Mexico's architecture, using elements from historic structures, melding them, and reshaping them to the size, scale, and taste of the twentieth century. The designs contributed to the definition of a unique New Mexican style, apart from the contemporaneous Mission Revival in California. The Pueblo Revival buildings evoked the New Mexican past but were not of it. They suggested local history yet smoothed its vernacular traits and the idiosyncracy of preindustrial style in favor of an efficiency that never really represented the past. This was even true of the renovation of the Palace of Governors in Santa Fe, accomplished at Hewett's behest. The reconstruction there took the palace back to a mythic historic moment, full of the romance of the fin de siècle, but different from the look of the structure in historic

The Palace of the Governors in 1900, a decade before its restoration. (Photo by Christian G. Kaadt, courtesy of Museum of New Mexico.)

time.[19] Like everything else in Santa Fe, the Palace of Governors was a conceptualization built on a historic foundation. Like the town itself, it blurred the distinction between mythic and actual.

Hewett's ingenuity created the context that transformed Santa Fe from a backwater territorial capital to a place of mystique. He brought cultural institutions, revamped existing buildings and structures and turned them into museums, revived crafts, fairs, and other vestiges of the past and created an intellectual framework to mediate the experience. His town drew designers such as Rapp and Meem and entrepreneurs such as Wagner, who combined to take an ordinary town with mythic symbolism and give that iconography a physical manifestation. As the Pueblo Revival became a distinctive architectural style, it broadened the dimensions of the cultural community that Hewett created, resulting in a wider audience for the idea of Santa Fe well beyond the reach of its historic realities.

This iconographic structuring was a critical addition to the overlay that Hewett initiated. He took Santa Fe from cultural marginality to contrived centrality. The charms of Santa Fe, chronicled widely, passed from the truly different to being contoured by the influences of fin de siècle American society. The descriptions of the 1880s, full of references to the unusual and the quaint, gave way to more stylized and formalized iconographic representations that merged with railroad literature. By the time locals in Santa Fe thought of following the strategies of cities such as Seattle, they had already devised a cultural iconography that had been implemented and widely disseminated.

Santa Fe the icon was possible because the market economy created sufficient wealth and enough discomfort that a place that seemed to shun it had appeal. Locals liked the overlay because their moribund economy needed a jolt. Santa Fe's natural resources could not have supported the kind of growth eventually engendered by the idea of the City Different, an early twentieth-century appellation for the community. In market terms, its environment was more aesthetic than useful, condemning its 1880 residents to a different home, a consumer or market-based economy, or economic disaster. Although Hewett could not have realized the long-term changes he initiated, he quickly grasped that people outside Santa Fe could provide economic resources to transcend the town's typically western problems: a lack of infrastructure, capital, and easily extracted natural resources to attract industry; its foreignness to early twentieth-century Anglo Americans; and the absence of direct transportation. Without a visionary such as Hewett, however autocratic, dogmatic, and unreasonable, the town would today share more with other small western state capitals than the Santa Fe of modern myth.

Santa Fe was different, and Hewett and his successors worked to keep it that way. He could alter its economic and ultimately cultural identity because the main spur of the railroad passed it by. The absence of interest from mainstream America provided the illusion of authenticity, something much in demand as industrial culture and its discontents spread. Hewett created the Santa Fe where Mary Austin and Ansel Adams felt comfortable; he had given a town renowned for its hard-edged commerce, its loose morality—by nineteenth-century standards—and its foreign ways a new ambience that seemed both authentic and unthreatening, quaint yet evocative of a past before machines dominated human endeavor. The fifteen-mile wagon or auto ride from the train station in nearby Lamy became a crucial division between the world of the railroad and that of mythic Santa Fe, a place descended from conquistadores and seemingly frozen in an arbitrary moment in that past. The bumpy ride along an old dirt track became part of the ambience of a romantic niche in the modern world rather than the detriment it had been before culture took the town by storm. Its inconvenience became a symbol; by riding to Santa Fe in a wagon, modern people believed they left their culture of haste behind.

The town's overlay attracted the attention of the national creative community. The region was enchanting, visitors soon proclaimed, and no place was more so than the little village at the foot of the mountains that after 1912 served as the capital of the new state of New Mexico. As Hewett's vision came to physical and psychic fruition, visitors found themselves charmed. The town was both anachronism and trendsetter; by 1915, it possessed the beginnings of the pretensions that have so marked it since. Then as now, a significant number of arrivals announced that although they had never been to New Mexico, they felt they had come home when they stepped out of a conveyance at La Fonda and looked out over the plaza in downtown Santa Fe.

Hewett's Santa Fe superimposed the anxiety of fin de siècle America on the tranquil surface of a town that to Anglo American eyes appeared untouched by modernity. The questions of national identity, the pace of life, and the increasingly visible inequity in American society belied the explanations of Social Darwinists that these inequalities stemmed from a natural order. In their actions, Americans of this era searched for a structure for their society and beyond that, for a liveable rhythm in the face of great change. Although there were many manifestations of this phenomenon, for one segment of American society, ranging from artists and writers to beneficiaries of industrialization disgruntled by its impact, northern New Mexico and especially Santa Fe seemed the solution.[20]

Creating the context for such a structure and rhythm required a subtle process. To preserve Santa Fe's special nature, Hewett had to retain its historic traits while peeling back the facade of the community just enough so that visitors could believe they grasped its essence. The faux fixed moment from the past that survived into the present provided the best framing. Hewett regarded Santa Fe in precisely that manner. As early as 1880 American journalists wrote of a static Santa Fe "hardly altered," according to Ernest Ingersoll of *Harper's Weekly,* "with all the change in its fortunes in the past century." Hewett strove to retain that firm romantic character, to affix the image of a visibly and culturally unchanging place, the "quaint old Santa Fe" to which Charles Lummis referred in *A Tramp Across the Country,* in the mind of the American mainstream.[21] Much of this manipulation was unconscious. Hewett simply believed that progress and the deep past could be fused into a blueprint that could shape not only the American future but also the human one.

Hewett's context required the melding of different influences. A pantheist in interdisciplinary intellectual matters, Hewett enjoyed mixing a variety of dignitaries and officials in his ceremonial endeavors. Typical was the dedication of the Santa Fe Art Museum in November 1917. On its dias at the dedication, Hewett placed state and city officials, scientists from universities and scholarly societies, the governors and other dignitaries from Indian pueblos, and Santa Fe and Taos artists.[22] This configuration brought out what Hewett believed exceptional about the New Mexico experience, a melding of different systems for understanding the world.

Public consensus that favored physical stasis was a dominant feature of Santa Fe. Hewett's 1912 appointment to the planning board resulted in New Old Santa Fe, an exhibit that opened in the Palace of Governors that year. The idea behind it became known as the Plan of 1912, and although never legally binding, it created a consensus about acceptable architectural style that exerted great influence over construction of new buildings. In some instances, style supplanted history as buildings such as the Fine Arts Museum and La Fonda Hotel replaced historic adobe courtyards complexes. Historic design was not only preferred, but a wide range of powerful constituencies demanded it. Advocates of the idea of the City Beautiful Movement, among whom Harry H. Dorman, Hewett's old adversary from the chamber of commerce, was preeminent, made up one powerful group of supporters. Hewett and his friends, the authenticity crowd, were another, as were architects such as Rapp and Meem.[23] This informal but powerful coalition shaped the look of Santa Fe with such comprehensiveness that it persisted through the twentieth century.

The tacit and widespread agreement that New Mexico's capital should include only specific styles of architecture made Hewett's conception of Santa Fe as a place fixed in time part of local thinking and ultimately of local life. In 1880 Santa Fe retained its historic look: "I do not think there is yet a frame building in the place," Ingersoll told his readers. Santa Fe also enjoyed "the singularity of being the only town in the country of 5,000 inhabitants which does not possess a single steam engine of any description." Santa Fe still aspired to a status typical of American cities. Its streets were named for politicians, local leaders, and others: Grant, Garfield, Speigelberg, Johnson, Railroad, and Metropolitan. Aztec and Montezuma Avenues evoked Old Mexico. As the population both declined and became increasingly Anglo American after 1880, this group built many new homes. A percentage of these, especially near the capital building, were frame and constructed in Victorian style. Gables and front porches were out of place in Hewett's Santa Fe; the Plan of 1912 made Euro-American style anachronistic.[24]

This process of defining style as acceptable or otherwise created symbolic and actual change. As early as 1912 Hewett advocated the use of original street names, which mirrored his call for a Pajarito rather than a Cliff Cities national park on the nearby Pajarito Plateau. Hewett's street names included

Paseo Coronado, Paseo Casteñada, Camino de Vargas, Calle Escalante, and even Santa Fe Trail. When Carlos Vierra, a tubercular California native who studied painting and became a skilled photographer, arrived in Santa Fe to stay at a sanatorium in 1904, he made the town his home. Moving from the Santa Fe River basin up to the arid mesa to the southeast in 1918, he initiated not only the geographic expansion of the city but also its intellectual evolution. Vierra built on Telephone Road; after a number of artists followed him there, the street was rechristened Camino del Monte Sol.[25]

More than any other single idea or action, the consensus on architectural style codified the overlay in Santa Fe. It made Hewett's conception dominant as it encouraged the feeling from visitors and locals that modern Santa Fe was genuine and truly a relic of a moment in the past. That psychic location promised authenticity, the reality of a world lost to industrialization. It also made quaintness the dominant architectural quality of Santa Fe, the measure of the scale of the City Different. No matter what went on behind its doors, Santa Fe would always look historic, nestled at the base of the Sangre de Cristo range with the sun leaving its wine-colored hues at the end of the day.

The emphasis on tourism and culture rapidly paid dividends in Santa Fe. The opening of Wagner's De Vargas Hotel was the precursor of further development of the central sector of the town. The School of American Archaeology, renamed the School of American Research in 1917, became a major landowner in Santa Fe. The construction of the Santa Fe Art Museum across the street from the Palace of Governors added another attractive feature, and the Pueblo Revival style came to dominate the plaza. Especially as a result of the Panama-California Exhibition in San Diego in 1915 and 1916, which attracted thousands of Americans from across the nation, more travelers visited the City Different.[26] Hewett designed the New Mexico exhibit for the San Diego exhibition, further enticing visitors with his conception of his adopted state. By 1920 Santa Fe had become a different place, possessed of a clear charter for economic survival.

The change in the town's economic picture was revealed in nearly every facet of regional demography. Ernest Ingersoll was not far from the truth when he described Santa Fe as lacking a single frame building in 1880. Although power had slipped away from the Hispano population in the New Mexico Territory after 1846, Santa Fe remained much as it had been throughout the nineteenth century, a stable, predominantly Hispano place. New Mexico natives constituted about 85 percent of the population, and the vast majority of its residents lived there throughout their lives. A preponderance of those who had never left New Mexico were Hispano. Most of them were engaged in agriculture or ranching or other typical preindustrial endeavors. A few natives of Mexico were present, generally tending stock. Although the railroad recently passed through the region, the population of trained or educated people in white-collar occupations remained small. They largely made up the roughly 15 percent of the New Mexico population born elsewhere in the United States. Many were relatives of merchant families, brought in to run businesses; others came because of the expansion in occupations resulting from the construction of the railroad. Few New Mexican natives, Anglo, Hispano, or Indian, worked in white-collar occupations.[27]

As late as 1880 land in Santa Fe remained predominantly in Hispano hands but at a rate of ownership that was only slightly above the representation of Hispanos in the population as a whole. Hispanos owned about 65 percent of the land in Santa Fe in 1880 and constituted a little more than 60 percent of the population. Although an influx of Anglos had begun first as a result of the Mexican War and then from the construction of the railroad through the New Mexico Territory, in 1880 Hispanos remained firmly in control of land in Santa Fe, sharing it mostly with Archbishop Jean-Baptiste Lamy's diocese, a small cabal of Anglo merchants and attorneys included in the Santa Fe Ring, and Jewish merchant families such as the Speigelbergs, Staabs, and Lehmans. The Anglos who moved into Santa Fe, with the distinct exception of those involved in the Santa Fe Ring, typified rural and small-town people of the time. They too were tied to the earlier antebellum, market revolution ethos. Most possessed general rather than specialized skills and expected to work for a daily wage.[28] They were hardly a threat to Hispano dominance.

By 1910 different patterns of ownership were evident. Twenty percent of the 1880 population had left Santa Fe, the Hispanos who departed typically selling their land to Anglos. Their Hispano neighbors rarely had cash to buy out friends and family. In 1910 Anglo ownership of land in Santa Fe County as a whole reached 65 pecent; in the city, the rate was even higher. The pattern of transfer accelerated as a result of declining economic conditions. Anglo Americans streamed to Santa Fe and brought capital for purchases that could reshape the community. The Hispano hold on this important sector of their homeland diminished. Formerly landed people sold their chief asset and the history it contained and migrated to low-wage, lower status employment.[29]

The people who replaced them were invariably Anglo American, wealthy, from the East, Texas, or California, and often slightly out of touch with the world of their upbringing. The newcomers were searchers, romantic, uncomfortable with the pressure-packed world of industrialization and poorly suited to urban life. Hewett's overlay made New Mexico seem enticing, vibrant, unique, and real in a world that had become mass-produced and seemingly inauthentic. Santa Fe felt preindustrial yet deprived its residents of nothing important. It was remote but not provincial, uncrowded yet hardly dull. Life seemed slow in Santa Fe in comparison to industrial centers. The people were Hispanic; they dressed and acted differently, suggesting a Cervantes novel, and the town retained the warm community traits that the cities of industrial America had long lost. It was also exquisitely beautiful to Americans in search of sublimity and truth. Years of railroad advertising, the emergence of southwestern architectural styles along the AT&SF route and at important stopping places such as the Grand Canyon, and the work of Charles Lummis and other writers influenced the way people interpreted the Southwest. No wonder so many believed they had come home when they first arrived.

New Mexico enjoyed a certain cachet in some circles in American society. In the 1880s it attracted those entrepreneurs who thought that the economic potential of the territory was sufficiently great to relocate there, providing a stab at wealth and power. Most notorious in this respect was Thomas Benton Catron, who forged an economic and political empire and was known as a power in the ubiquitous Santa Fe Ring that dominated territorial politics and whose members amassed great wealth. Others such as a storekeeper/entrepreneur Frank Bond accomplished the economic side of this equation as he acquired considerable local political power. Also typical of these newcomers was Harvey B. Fergusson Sr., an attorney from West Virginia who arrived in New Mexico in 1882 and stayed to forge a political career as a reformer. His children, Erna and Harvey B. Fergusson Jr., became noted writers whose work promoted the Land of Enchantment, as New Mexico was soon labeled. They typified the generation that followed their father's as they extolled the virtues of the unique place that northern New Mexico became in American culture.[30] As New Mexico became a visitation spot, a place apart in an increasingly homogenous society, the promotion of the state and its attributes became an industry of its own. The Fergussons excelled at this sophisticated form of enticement.

Although they were natives, the younger Fergussons were intellectually part of a neonative wave that came especially to Santa Fe and Taos. At Taos, serendipity and the exquisite light brought painters as early as the 1890s. Joseph Henry Sharp came first, and after he shared his vision of Taos with Bert Greer Phillips and Ernest L. Blumenschein, the famed painters' colony began. It reached critical mass with the arrival of five new artists, who joined with the original three to become *Los Ochos Pintores,* the eight painters. But Taos was different, far more remote and exclusive than Hewett's Santa Fe. It was nearly a day's journey by automobile from Santa Fe. With the backdrop of Taos Pueblo, Mabel Dodge Luhan's salon and a place where D. H. Lawrence lived for a number of years, Taos became an elite artist's colony, full of the talk of the moderne, as Santa Fe became a tourist destination for a much broader swath of the public.[31]

Santa Fe required Hewett's overlay to create the intersection of culture and modernity. People who embraced this idea were essential in its rise to prominence. Beginning in 1904 with Vierra and Kenneth Chapman, an Indianan who taught at Hewett's New Mexico Normal School, a parade of artistic and culturally oriented arrivals made Santa Fe home. In June 1909 Jesse Nusbaum, another Hewett protégé who taught at the normal school after Hewett's departure and who owned the first motorcycle in northern New Mexico, joined Chapman and Vierra in assisting in the Hewett-inspired renovation of the Palace of Governors and its transformation into the Museum of New Mexico. The museum and the School of American Archaeology provided an attractive setting for other artists. As the nascent cadre expanded to include Gerald Cassidy, *Los Cinco Pintores,* a group of five painters, Will Shuster, and many others, Hewett's cultural center made the community a destination for a segment of the upper-middle class, a place that served the needs of its visitors above its citizens.[32]

Finding in Hewett's Santa Fe the idyllic preindustrial vision they sought, artists and writers flocked to Santa Fe, in the process transforming the community they embraced. By the late 1910s a varied Anglo American artistic community that attracted the attention of visitors supplanted Santa Fe's primary economic attribute, its status as territorial capital. Government patronage and its attendant corruption, long among the major industries in New Mexico, were dispensed from there. Ashcan School painter Robert Henrí met Hewett in San Diego in 1914 and settled in Santa Fe in 1916; the light attracted him, and when absent he pined for the "sun, the look, the feel of Santa Fe." In 1916 poet Alice Corbin came; by 1925 writer Mary Hunter Austin, an advocate of a romantic vision of the Southwest who first visited Santa Fe in 1918, was firmly entrenched in her Camino del Monte Sol home, *La Casa Querida.* There such guests as Ansel Adams stayed for extended periods. In 1917 Georgia O'Keefe visited Santa Fe briefly and "loved it immediately," she later recounted. "From then on I was always on my way back." During the 1920s she frequently returned. In 1929 she finally moved to New Mexico, sealing its distinctive artistic image. As more affluent and artistic visitors and residents came to Santa Fe, a transformation occurred that homogenized and mythologized the heritage that nineteenth-century Americans found wicked.[33]

Hewett's institution-building was critical to the process of creating a sustainable overlay. The Santa Fe Art Museum was typical. Designed by Rapp and funded by the manipulation of a cabal of Hewett's friends, especially longtime patron Frank L. Springer, who engaged in a number of land deals arranged under the heading of the School of American Research, the museum offered a new means of understanding the town as it captured a more sophisticated constituency. The art museum was designed to provide a venue for the artists Hewett intermittently housed in the Museum of New Mexico. It also authenticated the Pueblo Revival style in art as it played on the intellectual consciousness of the upper-middle class.[34] A home for artists and a place to visit, the Santa Fe Art Museum became the final piece of the first generation of cultural institution-building. It sealed Santa Fe's unique position in the consciousness of American elites.

The new attractiveness became apparent when the results of the 1920 population census became public. That year, 7,236 residents were reported in Santa Fe, a slightly more than 40 percent increase over the 5,072 recorded in 1910. For the first time in four decades, the population of Santa Fe increased, and substantially. The core areas of the city, both south of Paseo de Peralta and east of the plaza, showed most of the growth. Statehood played a role, but to any observer of the state capital, the real action was in arts and increasingly in visitors. Artists, writers, and others attracted by the ambience of such cultural endeavor comprised much of the population increase.[35]

The growth of Santa Fe came from two sources: outsiders moving to town and people from the county who took up residence in the city. In the region, the city of Santa Fe was alone in its growth. The surrounding county increased by less than 300 residents in the decade during which the city added more than 2,000. Surrounding counties such as Sandoval and Rio Arriba showed similar stagnation. Within Santa Fe, growth occurred in the urban precincts; only a few of the rural precincts showed an increase between 1910 and 1920.[36] The template Hewett created proved a draw not only to Anglo Americans but also to Hispanos and Indians from nearby who came in search of work and opportunity.

Even during their initial visits, Austin and O'Keefe saw a Santa Fe that had been refined for their consumption. By 1917 nearly two decades of cultural entrepreneurship transformed the community, creating the overlay through which those schooled in mainstream culture could understand, or perhaps misunderstand, the Southwest. Hewett's various enterprises helped create a class of residents who imbibed culture, and Rapp's buildings added an authentic but quaint feel. The railroad supplied visitors, but the structure of the community denied its importance. The buckboard ride from Lamy soon became a carriage ride, but it continued to mitigate between the industrial world and the idyllic fiction of Santa Fe. The town had become one of those places that everyone wanted to see and even more wanted to be a part of. Art and culture were framed in a romanticized setting. The Museum of New Mexico opened in 1910, and despite American entry into World War I, the Santa Fe Art Museum, which later possessed an outstanding collection of O'Keefe's works, was dedicated in November 1917, just after O'Keefe's initial jaunt. A community of writers and artists settled there, basking in the ambience Hewett created and making it their own in what has been called the golden age of Santa Fe culture.[37]

The preeminent manifestation of the overlay was the creation of the Santa Fe Fiesta, a ritual self-identification celebration that became a tourist event. The roots of the fiesta dated to a proclamation by the Marquis de Peñuela in 1712 that decreed an annual parade in which the statue of La Conquistadora was carried through the streets of Santa Fe to commemorate De Vargas's reconquest of the city in 1692. By the 1890s this tradition had been buried among the myriad cultural changes of the nineteenth century. In its place, military band concerts, held on the bandstand in the plaza, became the chief ceremonial event in Santa Fe. According to tradition, Bertha Staab of the Staab merchant family suggested that the resuscitated event be named the Plaza Fiesta. A young Episcopal minister, James Mythen, who served only a short time, augmented the idea by suggesting a town fiesta. James Seligman, scion of another merchant family, and his wife Ruth, added the idea that the *reconquista*, De Vargas's return to Santa Fe, should be reenacted. In 1910, with the help of Nusbaum and others, the first reenactment occurred; Hispano George Armijo played De Vargas. The De Vargas Pageant and Plaza Fiesta became a local event. In 1912 it was held on July 5 and continued throughout the 1910s, but like many events was slowed and diminished by World War I.[38]

The revival of Fiesta crossed a range of cultural boundaries. The ritual fostered a local identity tied to the past, sustaining and affirming it. Participation made anyone, Anglo, Hispano, or Indian, a native, granting each a part in the cosmology of the rapidly changing town. "Real" Santa Feans defined themselves by their knowledge of community ritual and by their participation in and support of it.[39] Fiesta became a marker of invented community, a way of belonging to the nebulous idea of the authentic and especially a way

The De Vargas Pageant at the Santa Fe Fiesta was part of the process of adapting the past to the needs of the tourist economy. (Courtesy of Museum of New Mexico.)

to differentiate Santa Fe's growing crowd of visitors from the town. When anyone, especially newly arrived Anglo American neonatives, prepared for Fiesta or took part in it, they knew they were more like the people around them—of whatever ethnicity—than like the onlookers.

In the immediate postwar era, the Santa Fe Fiesta flowered into an important event for tourists. The initial conception excited locals and celebrated Santa Fe's heritage; in the aftermath of the war and rising tourism, Hewett's friends took the lead. In 1919 Ralph Emerson Twitchell, a close ally of Hewett's, became director of Fiesta. The staff of Hewett's School of American Research handled the entire festival, from planning to the designation of activities. A mock bullfight was included, emphasizing Spanish heritage and crossing further into the realm of tourist amusement than had most of Hewett's previous efforts. The following year, Paul A. F. Walter, associate director of the Museum of New Mexico and a close friend of Hewett's, was designated as director. When Walter accepted a position at a local bank, he resigned and Hewett took charge. Although Twitchell returned the next year, by then, Fiesta had become Hewett's conception. The addition of the annual burning of Zozobra, Old Man Gloom, each fall further illustrated the mixing of history and modern need. Zozobra, an invention of artists Will Shuster

Zozobra, Old Man Gloom, in the 1930s. Zozobra became an important part of the Santa Fe Fiesta. (Photo by Harold Humes, courtesy of Museum of New Mexico.)

and Gustave Baumann, first appeared in 1926 and became the capstone of Fiesta, further melding cultural forms as it created a script that locals could embrace and that visitors found attractive.[40]

Fiesta fused culture, pageantry, and camp for the audience of the 1920s. Hewett had learned well from the model of the world's fairs of the late nineteenth and early twentieth centuries. He blended the pseudo-authentic, the events and individuals who evoked a rich and perhaps richer-than-real past, with more typical forms of entertainment. Plays and pageants abounded, as did singing performances by Tsianina Blackstone, a famous Cherokee-Creek Indian vocalist, and a Mohawk singer, Oskenonton. One year a Zuñi leader gave a speech in his native language, a stunning moment in an already multicultural display; Col. José D. Sena, acting as majordomo, pretended to translate the speech. Ignorant of the distinctive Zuñi tongue, Sena interpreted the man's words as an offer to set up drinks for the crowd.[41] The real, the sublime, and the merely entertaining fused as the fiesta developed.

The transformation of Fiesta was itself a capstone in the overlay; its very development helped draw a specific kind of people. Fiesta soon became a national event, put on for the media and visitors much more than for locals. It attracted visitors as it mixed Hewett's more serious efforts at education with the popular culture of the era. Charles Wakefield Cadman, a preeminent composer of the 1910s and 1920s, was Tsianina's sponsor. They first played for a Hewett event at the San Diego fair and became regulars in Santa Fe. Cadman successfully joined popular music with Indian themes, bridging not only cultural boundaries but also gaps within the dominant culture. In the process, Hewett's initial vision of the town, its emphasis on cultural redemption through enlightenment, became part of a broader and more generally aimed affected reverence for a quaint and romanticized past. Fiesta moved from a celebration of a significant moment in local history into a party thrown by locals but largely for the edification of visitors. The Santa Feans in costume were actors in the fiesta pageant, but so were the locals who made up the audience.

Though the annual Fiesta celebration was the triumphant moment in the process of making Santa Fe understandable to the American public, it also showed the degree to which the town became something new as a result of Hewett's efforts. Longtime locals certainly recognized the difference. Santa Fe looked much the same, but it felt quite different. "The old Santa Fe of 1891 was entirely unlike the Santa Fe of today," wrote Mary Houghton Harroun, a founder of the 1890s local women's literary group, the Fifteen Club, in 1915. "That Santa Fe was as much a foreign city as if some genii had snatched it out of old Spain and dropped it down here in its valley in the mountains." Although the idea that the Santa Fe of 1891 reflected old Spain and not the New World testified to the new-found aristocratic pretensions of the Hispano community and the racial codes of the early twentieth century, it also demonstrated how dramatically different the invented Santa Fe felt to long-time residents. Harroun remembered herself in 1891 as among those who were "sad and longed intensely for the pleasant things in the homes they had left behind them" in the American East. In 1915 she no longer missed them.[42] The transformation of Santa Fe from a wild, rough town had also planed off many of its most interesting edges.

By the 1920s this contrived cultural community thought of itself as an authentic representation of the pre-railroad, even pre-American past. It manipulated the symbols of the past and carefully organized them in a manner that accentuated the differences between Santa Fe and the rest of modern industrial America. Simultaneously Santa Fe provided the structures of the modern world and as many of its comforts as could be found fifteen miles from a transcontinental railroad. The Santa Fe literary and artistic community that defined the town was largely imported. Before 1927 there had been no bookstore in Santa Fe, but by 1933 two were doing booming business. When *The Turquoise Trail: An Anthology of New Mexico Poetry,* edited by Alice Corbin Henderson, appeared in 1927, just three of its thirty-seven contributors were natives of the state. The only surname that was not Anglo American belonged to dilettante and social promoter Mabel Dodge Luhan, who acquired it when she married Antonio "Tony" Luhan of Taos Pueblo in 1923.[43] The world these culturati fashioned reflected their personal and cultural backgrounds much more than it did the nature of historic New Mexico. Santa Fe's artists and writers turned the community into a backdrop for their neuroses.

Those neuroses had much to do with status and prestige, and in such matters, Mary Austin came to the fore. Austin first visited Santa Fe in 1917 and returned to make it her own in 1924. She became a tireless champion of native cultures, Indian and Hispano, and filtered them through a lens that she created. In the classic neonative formulation, Austin presented herself as a *chisera,* a medicine woman of the Paiute people, a neonative of a different, not mainstream, culture who surely seemed odd to locals but entirely plausible to tourists. She could often be found as Erna Fergusson described her, "crowned with queenly braids, wrapped in a Spanish shawl, enthroned on the bootblack's stand in the [Santa Fe] Chamber of Commerce." Austin collected Hispano arts and crafts, especially *Santos,* the hand-carved figures of saints common in rural New Mexico, and Spanish colonial crafts. When she arrived, the *Santos* were being routinely discarded, while craftspeople were hard-pressed to compete with the mass-produced goods that increasingly dominated the local market. Austin made the preservation of such crafts one of her causes.[44]

This self-defined role as powerful earth mother revealed an equally potent territoriality. Austin and Taos's Mabel Dodge Luhan incessantly battled over preeminence. Dodge arrived in New Mexico first, and her marriage to Tony Luhan gave her access to local life that Austin only intermittently enjoyed; when she did, it resulted from Dodge's generosity. Austin had national prestige as a writer, which helped her advance in the battle for cultural primacy. Mabel Dodge had native access, but Mary Austin had the power to reach thousands. Although the two women were friends, they grappled repeatedly. Dodge's biographer even suggested that Austin chose Santa Fe for her home because she recognized that Taos was too small for both women. Austin's desire for cultural dominance was even more pronounced toward people she perceived as interlopers. Her close friend Willa Cather visited frequently at *La Casa Querida*, writing the final chapters of *Death Comes for the Archbishop* in the study. When the novel was published in 1927 and quickly became a best-seller, the self-protective Austin lambasted it as "a calamity to local culture" for its sympathetic portrayal of the French archbishop Jean-Baptiste Lamy.[45]

Although the calamity Austin resented happened to a local culture that she had helped resuscitate and although her dominance of the local scene was no less colonial than Lamy's, her position as a literary light gave her the ability to define—for an Anglo American audience—the meaning of Santa Fe. The predominantly Hispano community was nowhere in evidence as Austin defended a culture she herself had arrived too late to know in its prerailroad form. The hierarchy of this neonative incarnation of Santa Fe reflected the age-old dilemma of colonial explorers: even in the perspective of one with as an acute sensibility as Mary Austin, the traditional world ended the moment before her arrival. That world, no matter how altered by outside forces, was somehow more pristine than the one the observer inhabited, and its tenets had to be defended against all change.

Austin's sentiments also revealed one of the most common characteristics of the neonative. Having arrived in the community, she sought to pull the door shut behind her, excluding those who followed her. In this she was entirely typical; to maintain the special character of the place, and not incidentally her self-proclaimed special status there, she appointed herself keeper of traditions and arbiter of what was appropriate for the "real" Santa Fe. Here she equaled Hewett's own convictions, even as her views of Santa Fe supplanted his.

Austin and her transplanted friends knew how they wanted their town to be, and they understood power and how to wield it. By 1929 she headed a cadre of writers and artists who had become neonatives and who quickly changed the town to their own satisfaction. They united in support of certain causes that reflected their worldview. Most avidly worked to oppose the Bursum bill of 1922, a measure disguised as an effort to confirm Pueblo Indian land claims that would have legalized much of the Anglo and Hispano encroachment on Pueblo lands that occurred during the territorial period.

Vicious debates over the appropriateness of various cultural constructions also characterized 1920s Santa Fe. From Mary Austin, who embraced neonativity in her adopted home more wholly and rapidly than seemed possible, to the most recently arrived Texans, who sought to impress their own cultural mores, residents old and new grappled for control of the meaning of Santa Fe. In 1926, two years after her arrival, Austin attacked a Texas-inspired Federated Women's Club cultural colony planned for Santa Fe, remarking that the institution was "a pure American product, the outstanding characterization of our naive belief and our superb faith that culture can, like other appurtenances of democracy, proceed by majorities." In another context, she described the people who visited the cultural colony as "yearners," presumably for the self-defined state of grace she inhabited.[46] As Austin tried to pull the door to authenticity shut behind her, as she tried to preserve the transformed community she entered from the ravages of what she labeled Main Street culture, she showed an allegiance to the kind of bottled authenticity, however contrived, that Santa Fe had promoted since Hewett's arrival. His Santa Fe had been transformed into the one Mary Austin embraced; as a neonative, she resisted the Texas invasion with the fervor of a convert, arguing that not her wave, but the next tide of transplants would destroy its unique identity.

The debate revealed the fissures in neonative Santa Fe and the different perspectives of generations of neonatives. Hewett and his friends supported the project; the Republican Old Guard, as they were called, had the deepest Anglo American roots among the elite and the greatest need to make their wealth in Santa Fe. They clung to a vision of Santa Fe as a cultural center that catered to a mainstream audience partly because they were schooled in the cultural context of the fin de siècle and partly because their personal income and community stature depended on growth. Santa Fe enlightened people, and to achieve that end, a continually more diverse group of people had to visit. Broad appeal was the key to economic longevity and cultural change. The addition of the cultural colony was another example of a familiar formula. The opposition stemmed from the generation of neonatives pulled in by Hewett's initial development. With Austin stood the artists and writers who clustered about *La Casa Querida;* the medical community, headed by Dr. Frank Mera of Sunmount Sanitarium; a long-standing conduit of new faces for the artistic and cultural community; and another recent version of the neonative community, the denizens of Bishop's Lodge, a rustic, elegant dude ranch about four miles north of the city.[47] Under the guise of their Old Santa Fe Organization, the vocal Austin and her friends saw the town as unique, a special place that could be corrupted only by the influence of the mainstream. Independently wealthy and despite their denials largely unconcerned with the economic fate of the local population, this group believed that allowing the encroachment of conventional culture would be a death knell for their Santa Fe. Their vociferous opposition succeeded and the plan died. Hewett rescued the city from its doldrums, replacing the existing elite early in the century. Mary Austin and her neonative friends wrested control of the city's direction from him.

Equally significant, Santa Fe's iconography had become important enough to fight over. Described by one reporter as a battle between "progress" and "atmosphere," the conflict exposed the tensions that underlay the transformation of Santa Fe. The meaning of the town that Hewett fashioned changed. This recast conception had to be defended, even if its exemplary identity was a historical fiction. In safeguarding a conception of authenticity, Austin demonstrated her close link to the values of the twentieth century. Santa Fe's difference, however manufactured and packaged, had to be preserved from future intrusion by less culturally sensitive people. From Hewett's perspective, Austin and her friends were a "fanatical group of would-be highbrows" who endangered the town with "a certain supercilious intolerance that is of recent origin." From Austin's point of view, Hewett's efforts would make Santa Fe a common place, "utterly changed and ruined," as Amelia E. White of New York, a Santa Fe devotee, wrote to Paul A. F. Walter, "much like every other American resort."[48] Ironically, the form of the town she embraced as preindustrial existed precisely because of the transportation networks of the industrial age and could be defined as different from the industrialized world only in juxtaposition to fin de siècle society. The distance between Santa Fe and the railroad figuratively and literally seemed great. In reality, it was only a short ride.

By 1930 Santa Fe County experienced substantial growth in white-collar occupations, the census of that year reporting 633 workers in professional and semiprofessional occupations. The state's legal community had many representatives in the state capital, and each of their offices required clerical help. Incoming individuals with assets who required legal and professional advice helped make such occupations more lucrative. Added to the vastly expanded retail sector, which contained almost 600 employees, 80 percent of whom were male, Santa Fe had the makings of a middle class to complement its aristocracy and its growing community of less privileged people.[49] Tourism seemed to create opportunity but only for those of select background and origin.

For most natives and their families, the options remained more limited. By 1930 the city had grown to 11,176 people, and the workforce of the county had reached 6,908. Of those, 1,275 worked in agriculture; the next largest number worked in state government. The two subsequent largest categories of workers reflected the importance of tourism in the local economy. Four hundred eleven women and 216 men worked in domestic and personal service; and hotels, restaurants, and boarding houses employed 152 men and 145 women. With more than 300 workers in construction and the building trades, nearly 20 percent of the Santa Fe workforce in 1930 relied on tourism for an important portion of its income. Most of the jobs it provided offered little opportunity for advancement or substantive increase in income.[50] Local people, especially Hispanos and Indians, were hardly beneficiaries of the change to a tourist-based economy. Typically they found themselves locked near the bottom of the economic ladder.

The increasing emphasis on culture in Santa Fe accentuated the class distinctions of the neonative world. In an artistic town that made its money from visitors, studios and salons became symbols of a kind of preciousness that still permeates Anglo American Santa Fe. There was little room for local residents except as representatives of a mythified past, and in the studios, local people could pose for paintings or photographs or perhaps work on the grounds. Although lionized in the accounts of nearly every writer who came to northern New Mexico and captured for posterity as Eusebio in *Death Comes for the Archbishop*, even Tony Luhan played only a marginal role. He pointed out the sights and explained native culture, but he was never a participant in the rollicking discussions. The hotels were built and owned by corporations or newcomers such as Wagner, who capitalized on the excitement Hewett's overlay created. The process of making the aesthetic virtues of Santa Fe into utilitarian attributes had begun in earnest, Hispanos and Indians serving as props in a consumable culture that differed little from the mainstream. By 1925, because of forward-looking choices by a dynamic if obstreperous institution-builder and his minuscule cabal, Santa Fe became what it is today—a state of mind.

No two places in the West exemplified the transformative process that fin de siècle tourism embodied as thoroughly as the Grand Canyon and Santa Fe. They demonstrated that places with symbolic meaning, though quite different, could be altered by the cultural needs of a society beginning to inspect itself and its motives and by the growing tourism industry. Both locations soon possessed great cultural significance for a nation in search of a reference point. They affirmed the direction of American society for elites, the overwhelming majority of tourists at the time, but in diametrically different ways. The Grand Canyon expressed the grandeur of the continent and the power of the civilization that harnessed its magnificence. Santa Fe's mythic status was enhanced; it had once been a place through which Americans envisioned their cultural and economic future. It also remained the epitome of the American Other, where the trail, at least for Americans, ended; Spanish-speaking traders continued to the end of their trail in Chihuahua beyond the glare of American consciousness. The very name Santa Fe connoted mystery and difference and served as a reminder of the triumph of the idea of Manifest Destiny and of the exotic. It also became a socially viable place to dissent from American society.

Tourism inexorably changed both. The Grand Canyon became convenient as the wealth of industrialization and the cultural needs of the moment shaped a conceptual canyon that visitors could understand. Santa Fe altered its economic and ultimately its cultural identity because the main spur of the east-west railroad passed it by. Its inconvenience became an advantage to a growing group who learned to associate convenience with inauthenticity and banality. They exchanged its nineteenth-century image of wicked and wild for a more benign, romanticized twentieth-century view, a place that tolerated cultural difference and provided a haven for those who sought escape from the pounding rhythms and temporal values of industrial life. The town possessed a cachet that spoke to the disgruntled and discontented among the wealthy, those who embraced the kind of antimodern thinking that characterized the reaction to industrialization. This invented place, organized to the sensibilities of industrial America while purporting to show its visitors a different face, created a mystique that stuck. Ever after, Santa Fe became a place where time stopped—but few people noticed that it stopped at the behest of an Anglo American cultural entrepreneur.

In the organization of iconographically important destinations such as the

Grand Canyon and Santa Fe, the change from local and idiosyncratic definitions to more mainstream articulations of their meaning brought a pacifying and hegemonic message. Even this place could be made tame, experience showed traveling Americans, could be made to conform to the values of the world created by industrialization.[51] Despite their enormous differences, Santa Fe and the Grand Canyon offered remarkably similar messages that affirmed the changes industrialization wrought on the American landscape and social scene.

The system that delivered this message transformed the places and their prior inhabitants. Both soon contained hierarchies typical of fin de siècle America. Perquisites went to the people with capital and connections and not incidentally to those in the local communities who could build ties to outside sources of capital and connection. A transformative process that divested locals of their sense of place, identity, and economic control followed. Most locals were left out of the windfall, offered the opportunity to cooperate in a lesser capacity or squeezed out. Others became less important as the social and cultural conditions around them changed. Local people did enjoy access to a wider range of goods and services, but many of the most attractive of these amenities were beyond their economic reach. The attractive features of industrial culture did much to draw local people into new spheres but little to prepare them for the change in their lives that the embrace of consumer goods and the influx of tourists would effect.

Perhaps most daunting about the transformative nature of tourism was its remarkable malleability. Both the Grand Canyon and Santa Fe quickly passed through several incarnations, each with a constituency that found their replacement vexing at least and more often alienating. The result was a fixed conception of place and rigid hierarchies but a changing on-the-ground reality that caused much consternation. From Elizabeth Compton Hegemann, who saw the Grand Canyon change around her, to Mary Austin, who battled anyone who sought to change the fixed moment her Santa Fe represented, enormous potential for idealistic embrace and subsequent dissatisfaction existed. Controlling the cultural identity of place turned out to be insufficient to prevent change, but few who fought for that control ever grasped how tentative their power was.

Most telling as a measure of the parallels between fin de siècle tourism and other extractive industries, even places that embraced forms of tourism purporting to distance visitors from the modern world marketed the same symbols as places that did not pretend distance. In Santa Fe, economic and cultural entrepreneurs from the outside arrived, bringing different values and shaping local culture to meet the demands of the growing travel constituency from which they sprang.[52] Those who enlisted Santa Fe to serve as a representation of a world gone by rarely understood their participation in its transformation. By the time they arrived, the world they found already had changed in order to cater to their needs. Outside entrepreneurs manufactured the out-of-sync desirability that became emblematic of Santa Fe, allowing visitors to engage their expectations.

By 1920 both the Grand Canyon and Santa Fe had become mainstream American tourist destinations. Both were organized in the hierarchical manner of industrial society and offered levels of amenity commensurate with the expectations of the traveling public. Both places affirmed the American experience, the vision of a Manifest Destiny that so drove nineteenth-century America, the Grand Canyon in an overt way, Santa Fe in an oblique fashion that underlay the critique of mainstream culture espoused by a sizable portion of its neonative artists and writers. Still dominated by railroad visitors, the tourism of hegemony remained a function of class status. It appealed to the tastes and values of the American upper- and upper-middle class, reflected that view of the world, and sold a mythic image of American culture suitable for the exuberant and immature confidence and psychic doldrums that followed World War I.

Despite their seeming differences, the orientation of Santa Fe and the Grand Canyon toward mainstream American culture was quite similar. Neither place was really very far from the industrial world and both depended on it not only for visitors but also for the ongoing stream of capital that kept both places changing within the parameters that prevented rapid ennui. Both were organized in a manner that mirrored the hierarchical nature of early twentieth-century American culture and clearly reflected the values of that time. Together they showed the rapid codification of the nature of tourism. By the mid-1920s two of the most important representations of American myth had been organized to conform to the rules of an industrial market economy and society. Despite the images created for these places and their iconographic meaning, despite the physical and cultural distance between them and the steel mills of Pittsburgh, the banks and brokerages of Wall Street, and other primary representations of industrial society, the Grand Canyon and Santa Fe were a firm part of fin de siècle American culture.

5

Tourism on the Actual Periphery

Archaeology and Dude Ranching

Fin de siècle tourism comprised a dimension that included affirmation of American culture but that thoroughly eschewed the opulence the luxury set demanded as a tribute to their accomplishments. Undertaken partly as a cure for physical or psychosomatic ailment, partly as homage to a mythic way of life passing from the industrial stage, this form built on the conceptualizations of places such as the Grand Canyon and Santa Fe but appealed to specific segments of people within the market for travel. These excursions were expeditions for the hardy, people who wanted more than a train trip dotted with stops at interesting places. These consumers were a small speciality niche, the more adventurous, the more serious, the aficionados, those who did more than pose their distance from the mainstream. The illusion of Santa Fe was a funnel to them, a level to pass through to a deeper plane of truth and understanding, to the mysteries and the meaning held in the prehistoric and historic past. These people recognized that when they pierced the facade of Santa Fe, they encountered not what they deemed real experience but a second facade designed for their comfort.[1] Tearing through this construction was sheer pleasure to such people, proof of their difference from even the most sophisticated and adventurous of their kind. In their estimation, beyond that last cloak was genuine experience, untempered by the amenities of the industrial world.

The people who made up this small but important group were similar to the larger numbers of wealthy travelers who stayed within the constraints of organized travel. They too were typically well-off beneficiaries of industrialization, also most likely to originate in the

Northeast and to have access to the corridors of power. They differed in the way they understood the world; out of step and leaning toward the odd, most of them evinced the traits of the antimoderns who played an important role in the rise of American reform and the transformation of American culture as the twentieth century approached. These out-of-sync individuals were even more conscious of the discord that lay beneath the surface of industrialization, even more repulsed by the official banality of fin de siècle society than were their peers who were attracted to Santa Fe.[2] They were also truth seekers; they believed that in some instance of authenticity, they could seize the meaning of life and convey it to others.

Their authenticity was relative, based in the sense of what was real in the antimodern consciousness. These travelers craved experience but preferred it without the filtering lens of the railroad, although most were not averse to luxury hotel accommodations when possible. They wanted to touch and feel as part of understanding the mythic West and the human past. An unfiltered proximity to what they regarded as nature and the natural world, human as well as physical, made their experience real in their own terms. Their understanding of the world shaped their authenticity. They required a filter but one different from that offered by the railroad's visions and definitions. This crowd needed to be close to the experts, the scientists, paleontologists, archaeologists, anthropologists, linguists, and others who, in the understanding of the antimodern world, possessed the credentials and the knowledge that held the key to truth.

Even more telling, they spread out across the landscape in a fashion that served as precursor of later forms of travel. They rejected the parameters of railroad travel, eschewed the limitations of the "West from a Car Window," as journalist Richard Harding Davis so aptly titled his travel narrative, and used whatever transportation necessary to reach into remote corners of the region. They carried their own baggage, occasionally hunted their own food, and generally scoured up sustenance in distant places. In the form of their travel, although not necessarily in its purpose, they were the forerunners of the automobile tourists. The only boundaries to their experience was self-imposed; the limits came from within, not from railroad brochures and amenities or tour syndicates.

In this respect, these denizens of cultural and heritage tourism initiated the context in which its hegemony collapsed. Although the people who traveled to dude ranches and remote archaeological sites constructed their reality against the form and function of railroad travel, their very method moved beyond its limitations. When they rode in automobiles, when they camped, hunted, broke cattle, or dug in the dirt, they extended the limits of tourist endeavor into experiences that were far more idiosyncratic than anything offered along the rails. Paradoxically, such visitors typically sought a hegemonic result. The truth they craved affirmed the intellectual ethos of fin de siècle American society even as their means of seeking it seemed to refute the dominant notions of the time. In their search, they created a context in which tourism became a pastime for a broader swath of the American public that was not tied to the intellectual formulations of that time.

They could not survive a changing mainstream culture, a tide of popularity that soon enveloped the activities they sought or the decline of resonance for the subjects they held dear. As quickly as it rose in significance, archaeology toppled from its pedestal. Its reign lasted until the initiation of hostilities of World War I, the "quiet afterglow" of the nineteenth century that John Dos Passos so fondly recalled. In post–World War I America, the meaning of archaeology diminished; the preoccupations of the prewar and postwar eras differed greatly. Dude ranching suffered an equally ignominious fate. Begun as a way to refresh the souls and spirits of industrialized beings, it became de rigeur for the American aristocracy, a rite of passage, a ceremonial ritual through which anyone of stature had to pass. As its popularity grew, dude ranching became a shadow of itself, its meaning transformed in the rush of people to an activity that had the life drawn from it by the very demands of those who sought it.

By the early 1900s the people seeking this new dimension were sufficiently wealthy and existed in large enough numbers to sustain divergent forms of mainstream tourism. They stood among those who sought more than a temporary release from the feeling of overcivilization that seemed omnipresent in American society, who craved a preindustrial reality, one closer to nature and tied to village roots. These people were questers, seeking not only escape but reconstitution as they extended the space between themselves and Pittsburgh, Chicago, and even the Grand Canyon and Santa Fe.[3]

Two specific activities dominated this aspect of tourism before the 1930s: the visit to the archaeological site and the trip to the dude ranch. The two excursions shared innumerable characteristics. Both required physical travel from the main rail lines to remote places, and participants lived in less than luxurious circumstances. There was none of the paradox of Santa Fe in archaeological touring and only a little in early dude ranching, none of the purported authenticity laden with amenity that so characterized the development of tourism. Here were activities, the structure and organization of an archaeological camp or a dude ranch seemed to shout, that truly pitted individuals against themselves, people against the rough, cold realities of the American West in a genuine quest for experience and understanding. The fulfillment people experienced served as a direct counter to the public and private crisis of cultural authority, the increasingly slippery legitimacy of the mainstream. In experience aimed at truth lay the opportunity for individual salvation, redemption, and transformation in an industrial society.

A visit to an archaeological site and a trip to a dude ranch also embodied an ideal of enlightenment that the Grand Canyon and Santa Fe could only suggest. At an archaeological site, intrepid travelers could see what they assumed was the real past, uncovered by trowels and shovels before their very eyes. They often lived in tents, the same as the workers who performed the manual labor. Conversations had little to do with banking, commerce, the choice of port or claret, or other features of the life of the wealthy in the industrial age. Instead these strivers used the finds of the day to speculate on the origins of the Anasazi, those who came before the Indian people often working beside them during excavations, to discern the patterns of pre-Columbian life from the artifacts they uncovered. Each tool, each *olla* or pot, each woven basket offered tangible evidence to the searchers but of what? Countless hours by the campfire passed in discussion of such questions, issues that their more stolid relatives would not waste time considering, much less discussing.

People who embraced such an activity consciously gave up the amenities of their time in an effort to comprehend the meaning of the distant past in their search for explanations of the discord that industrialization created. Archaeologists such as Edgar Hewett and Byron Cummings of the University of Arizona welcomed such visitors and incorporated them into their summer excavations. There were pragmatic reasons; the archaeological neophytes who sat by the campfire with summer helpers and seasoned professionals, discussing the state of American prehistory, were almost always wealthy people or their relatives, any of whom could fund future excavation. A week in an archaeological camp was an exhilarating divergence, in the minds of many visitors, truly distant from mainstream life.

Visitors to a dude ranch also experienced this distancing. The prototype of visitor-based dude ranching began in South Dakota and was perfected in the shadow of the Teton Mountains in Jackson Hole, Wyoming. On a working dude ranch, visitors participated in ranch chores and experiences, tending herds and otherwise living as if they were part of the ranch. When ranches first took in visitors, they offered few luxuries, no special favors to alter the camaraderie of the experience. Individuals, always wealthy and usually disaffected, chose to leave their cozy nests on the East Coast and head for the wilds of New Mexico, Arizona, the Dakotas, or Wyoming to live in the American outdoors and experience the proximity of nature. They braved the elements in an evocation of cowboys on the mythic cattle drives of the 1860s and 1870s. Like the visitors to the archaeological sites, they chose to embrace an American creation myth and act it out, using the wealth they gained from decidedly nonmythic sources to create their leisure away from the East.

These participants extended the impulse that made Santa Fe fashionable, creating a distance from modern America greater than that the promoters of the City Different conceived, envisioned, or sought for their town. As the construction of La Fonda Hotel proved, Santa Fe had been scripted to create an ambience of Otherness without eliminating the pleasures industrial life made possible. If the AT&SF could advertise its resplendent trains as the experience of "roughing it in luxury," Santa Fe exemplified roughing it in style. The food and language were different, but the hotel rooms had comfortable beds and the barrooms were stocked with favorite repasts. Santa Fe provided cultural context seen from a drawing room, a world that was different but not so much as to be threatening. If it were, a tourist could always close the figurative shutters.

Archaeological investigation and to a lesser degree dude ranching took the idea of roughing it in style further toward the end of the spectrum that wholeheartedly embraced the concept of the simple life. These activities meant truly roughing it, cushioned ever so slightly by the genteel pretensions of archaeologists and the soft management of dude ranches such as Struthers Burt's Bar BC at the base of the Teton Mountains. There was a slight element of self-flagellation and self-abnegation in the experience. At most dude ranches, the power an individual had at a Wall Street firm had little impact on the ability to ride a horse or work a cow. In archaeology, someone versed in literature or even an individual who had read the formal scholarly reports of the Bureau of American Ethnology and could converse about them at length had never handled a trowel or shovel under the hot southwestern sun. The experience they lacked and craved was sifting the dirt between their fingers. Only the experience, not book learning, not collecting, offered a vision of real life and the legitimation that accompanied it. Organized by class, such distinctions inverted rather than eliminated hierarchy. The mythic art of the nation valued different skills from those on Wall Street but conversely made them attainable.

In these endeavors, the desire for raw experience was paramount to the seekers. Those who joined archaeologists, who braved awful roads and trails, awkward living conditions, bad food, and endless hot and dusty days felt they reached a more primitive and natural state, that they were closer to nature and God, closer to an understanding of the cosmos in all its depth. Dude ranchers swallowed whole the mythology of cattle ranching, the romance of the dime novels, and the feeling, setting, and perspective of the nineteenth-century American West. They converted a mythic past, increasingly distant for both the poor and the well-off who inhabited American cities, into real experience that had meaning, at least to them and their friends. Struthers Burt and the others who worked dude ranches intended to make geographic distance from the modern world into a significant measure of difference, which was more than the hotel keepers of Santa Fe attempted or even wanted to accomplish. The distance became essential to the culture of dude ranching, replete with a hierarchy of behaviors and the resultant pecking order.

Despite their attempts at a manufactured authenticity, these two activities also had traits that affirmed the direction of industrial society, mirroring the hegemony so common in the more systematically organized forms of tourism at the Grand Canyon and elsewhere. More so than the feigned authenticity of Santa Fe, archaeological tourism and dude ranching pitted the civilized of the twentieth century against the world they perceived as natural in a manner that made their success an affirmation of their society. As they experienced what they regarded as the primitive, as they conquered it with their actions and ideas, they reinforced the hierarchical modes of fin de siècle America. Both archaeological tourism and dude ranching simultaneously mirrored the patterns of industrial America while holding out the image of a different life, chock full of the meaning that an industrial economy and a lack of individuality seemed predestined to destroy.

No one epitomized both facets of this ethos more completely than Theodore Roosevelt. No individual embraced its iconographic meaning in as wholehearted a fashion, nor did anyone do more to promote its palliative qualities. An advocate of the strenuous life who hardened himself against physical and psychological frailty in the Dakotas, he became both the archetype and the prototype of the dude rancher. Roosevelt first went west to hunt buffalo, moved to the Dakotas in 1883 after the twin tragedies of the death of his wife and mother in the same house on the same day, and made himself anew against the backdrop of western skies. For Roosevelt, the experience of the rancher and cowman was to be born again, reinvented from the morass of modernity into an independent, intellectually, physically self-sufficient being who had learned to withstand. In this he initially mirrored the needs of the nation, a pattern that continued through his years in the White House. Reinvention was a source of power for this man, often described as having been born with his mind made up, a yardstick of authenticity by which he measured himself and all others.[4]

Roosevelt was sojourner and tourist in the West, a temporary resident who brought resources unavailable to his neighbors and a visitor who found the customs of the region entrancing, yet who changed them by his presence. When he came to the Dakotas, he sought to leave the East behind. He was, he confessed to a companion, Lincoln Lang, "most anxious to get into a buckskin suit" but carried the derisive sobriquet Four Eyes for the initial part of his stay. In a mythic story he retold throughout his life, Roosevelt earned his position in this community of individualists with the power of a right-led combination of punches, learned at Harvard. It made him into Old Four Eyes, a term filled with respect rather than derision. Roosevelt later captured a local badman who had stolen his boat, proving to himself the power of individual action and to his neighbors the substance of this bull-like man.[5]

Throughout his life, Roosevelt epitomized the ethos of the moment in the United States, and his trek on the plains typified his trait of pulling meaning from the air and defining it through his actions. Roosevelt gave the West a meaning more significant than the artists who preceded him. He filled out the heroic form that the dime novel and later that Owen Wister and Frederic Remington cast. As he told the nation of his experiences, he created a trajectory for Americans, a way to embrace their future and past simultaneously. Roosevelt beautifully melded the romantic and the real as he shaped the intellectual tenor of the nation. He "took hold," as he described it, of two cattle ranches on the Little Missouri River, where he "worked under the scorching midsummer sun, when the wide plains shimmered and wavered in the heat; we knew the freezing misery of riding night guard round the cattle in the late fall round-up. In the soft springtime the stars were glorious in our eyes each night before we fell asleep; and in the winter we rode through blinding blizzards, when the driven snow dust burned our faces." Embracing the loneliness of the plains, he made it his own, intending, at least in some interpretations, to become a cowboy for the rest of his life. "We felt the beat of hardy life in our veins," Roosevelt wrote, "and ours was the glory of work and the joy of living."[6]

Roosevelt created a myth. He brought the resources of civilization and his will to bear on what he sympathetically regarded as an uncivilized place. He craved that lack of order but could not resist, indeed was compelled to bring the tools of civilization, the right-led, Harvard-learned combination of punches, the act of will, to the plains. Roosevelt's success was essential to the formulations of early 1900s America. He represented the triumph of culture over a lack of civilization, itself romanticized by the very people who sought to tame and restructure the West along their own lines of thinking. As a new man, made whole on the plains and spreading the virtues of civilization in his wake, he became a representative of the goals of the nation. "I owe more than I can ever express to the West," Roosevelt wrote, echoing a sentiment that pervaded American society.[7]

Roosevelt revered the solitude of the West and recognized that it provided both serenity and terror, that it was to be simultaneously loved and feared. It was genuinely different from his world. In the West, nothing cushioned those who fell, nothing so trite as civilization stood between individuals and their fate. It tested anyone who looked beneath the surface of life for insight and meaning.[8]

As for the changes in the West that followed, ambivalence was simply not part of Roosevelt's repertoire of emotions. Others traveling the path he blazed were less certain. For them the passing of the Great West was tinged not only with the triumph of civilization but also with loss. Perhaps Roosevelt did not recognize such changes. He was an early resident of the Dakota Territory and was able to keep its 1880s condition in his mind's eye for the rest of his life. But others lamented the passing of the frontier, deemed closed by the 1890 Census and codified into national religion in 1893 by the young historian Frederick Jackson Turner, whom Roosevelt himself commended. They saw the pronouncement of the end of the frontier as a kind of closure of a phase in American life and sensed a significant loss.

The impulse to know a place and to embrace its values was precisely the idea that motivated dude ranchers when they followed loosely in Roosevelt's ideological footsteps. As Roosevelt paid for his land with outside capital and absorbed the western spirit during his stay, so did the dude ranchers who followed him, albeit on a lesser scale. Their stays were for months or weeks, not years; they rented their place on the ranch instead of purchasing a spread outright. They achieved their sense of sharing in the values of the mythic West that Roosevelt described, the independence, self-reliance, simplicity, and purity that range life represented to Americans then and now.[9]

Yet Roosevelt, like so many neonatives and tourists, remained tied to the culture from which he sprang. In effect, he impressed the hegemony of eastern values on the West, choosing the aspects of western culture he found laudable and presenting them to the world as virtues and castigating others. He took a decidedly moralistic view of the practices of the nineteenth-century West, decrying in particular the wanton slaughter of animals. To Roosevelt, this behavior could not be rewarded; he had seen the destruction such activity caused in the East and elsewhere in the West, had read James Fenimore Cooper and others who earlier recognized its long-term consequences. Along with the older and more experienced George Bird Grinnell, Roosevelt founded the Boone and Crockett Club, to teach the morality of hunting and to preserve what they regarded as the sporting ethos of big game hunting.[10]

The Boone and Crockett Club was formed in reaction to the declining number of big game animals in the West and as a way to castigate the commercial hunting practices of the era. Grinnell and Roosevelt regarded as appalling wanton hunting, its use of technology, and innovations such as the huge-muzzled punt guns, which allowed the indiscriminate killing of masses of waterfowl. Grinnell previously used his influence for the preservation of the few remaining American Bison, railing against their lack of protection in Yellowstone National Park. Grinnell and Roosevelt used the club and the stature of its members as a tool of moral suasion in their effort to preserve decimated species.[11]

Roosevelt and Grinnell orchestrated a form of cultural hegemony as they persuaded Congress, which consisted largely of other members of their class, to outlaw such hunting practices. Asserting their neonative status, they appropriated the right to pass judgment on the West. Sojourners, they imposed their values on its people and the land. They made moral judgments with economic consequences based on the value systems of their backgrounds, foreshadowing not only the conflicts created by the tourist industry but also its consequences for local people.

There were other members of the privileged classes in American society who influenced life in the West. Before 1900 American science played an important role in shaping the region. Particularly in the Southwest, an unrivaled cultural cachet and mythology developed with both speed and alacrity. The land's rugged and stark beauty, red, gold, and bright instead of green and snowcapped, fascinated observers. They marveled at the spectacular sunsets, the various cultures that inhabited the region, and the different feel life there possessed. Ever tantalizing, the Southwest beckoned.

This special resonance was accentuated by a combination of the efforts of railroads, promoters, and particularly the denizens of the nascent disciplines of anthropology and archaeology. As they had at Yellowstone, railroad operators recognized that tourists provided an additional and important source of revenue. Anthropologists and archaeologists were reconstructing the prehistory of the Southwest, using the region to professionalize their disciplines, and their goals fused with those of the railroads. The scientists wanted professional recognition; the promotional campaigns of the railroads—the illustrations, lantern slides, and mythologized writings—gave the former stature and brought rail, hotel, and other customers.[12] An unlikely marriage of convenience transpired.

This fusion of science, fashion, and economic power illustrated a number of currents in fin de siècle American society. The simultaneous rise of industrial capitalism and Darwinism cast off the doctrinal shackles of the religious past—for better and worse—and resulted in a class of people with the resources to pursue any avocation or idea. Wholesale changes in the world around them inspired numerous members of this class to seek new organizing principles or sets of ideas as a basis for their beliefs. Late nineteenth-century America examined Social Darwinism, but it had only tinny resonance and a short half-life amid the fast-paced changes of industrial life. As challenges to the tenets of this philosophy grew more numerous and more scathing and the inequities of American life became more visible, even the affluent classes looked for new explanations. Americans searched their past for models on which to base their transformed society.[13]

As Edgar L. Hewett's career illustrated, anthropology and archaeology were well suited to fill the ideological vacuum created by Darwinism and the industrial revolution in the United States. Both disciplines spoke to the public in clear, measured, pseudo-objective terms and posited a long view of human society and habitation. The Pueblo rituals and orally transmitted legends fascinated visitors such as Aby M. Warburg, scion of the banking family of Hamburg, Germany, and one of the most influential art historians in early twentieth-century Europe, during his one visit to the Southwest in 1895. The analogy-driven stories of Hewett and his famous predecessor proto-archaeologist Adolphe F. A. Bandelier and the popular efforts of Lummis and other writers had much in common. All followed the hierarchical lines of reasoning of the time and simultaneously held up the superiority, achievements, and hierarchies of industrial capitalism, argued their linkage to the long traditions of native peoples in the New World, and offered a respite from the pace of the modern world. This scripted fiction of relationship gave these disciplines wide currency among the affluent and the literate. The two sciences also created widespread desire to see the relics of this past, the people and places of North American prehistory. Railroads were more than glad to oblige. Science, affirmation of culture, and tourism fused, ostensibly to the benefit of all three.

The roots of anthropology and archaeology were firmly located within the taxonomic tradition that began with Swedish naturalist Carolus Linnaeus. Following his method to classify plants, the *Systema Naturae,* developed in the 1730s, scientists invented similar systems crucial to their understanding of the workings of the natural world, and to a nearly equal degree, its human equivalent. The Enlightenment and oddly Social Darwinism were both based on a view of the human world as a mirror of a static natural one. The Comte Georges de Buffon and Thomas Jefferson offered dueling taxonomies in their intellectual battle over Old and New World natures. Nineteenth-century scientists from Franz Joseph Gall and Cesare Lombroso, who gave the world phrenology and used it to categorize humanity, to Lewis Henry Morgan, responsible for putting into words a hierarchical framework of humanity that reflected the predispositions of the industrial era, created taxonomic structures as they organized the world. When Bandelier rushed down the side of a mesa into Frijoles Canyon in 1881 and inaugurated Southwestern archaeology, he pulled out his staff and measured the height, depth, and width of the cliff dwellings he found. He, too, was heir to this tradition.[14]

In its taxonomic form, science had limited utility for popular discourse in fin de siècle America. Despite an emphasis on rigid styles of education both on the Continent and in the American schools that educated the elites, taxonomic study did not excite the best minds. It lacked connection to the primary values of the time, the Social Darwinist notions of merit, hierarchy, and the means to achievement. Based on a kind of objectivity, it counted and ordered, neither inherently affirming nor denying popular suppositions. After the Civil War, when Americans grappled with the need for new principles to anoint their changing society, taxonomy fell short. It lacked a crucial component, what might be termed a moral parable, to follow its empiricist designations. Most nineteenth-century American scientists, from Othniel C. Marsh to William Henry Holmes, were not prepared to go far beyond the bounds of empirical study to link their observations to the cultural climate.[15]

Writers and scholars who spoke to a wide public translated taxonomy into cultural supposition. Bandelier and Lummis played an enormous role in the popularization of archaeology and anthropology in the United States. In 1883 Bandelier published a novel, *The Delightmakers,* that made human his extensive observational knowledge of prehistory. The novel was a resounding success with the scientific community, for Bandelier made prehistoric people seem real to his audience in a manner that his raw field notes, published with excruciatingly long and unwieldy titles, never could. The indefatigable and narcissistic Lummis wrote voluminous stories about his travels, and the history and prehistory of the Southwest played prominent roles in his accounts of the American scene. He posed in Indian clothing in some instances, gaucho apparel in others, building a myth around himself as he told the American public about the exciting and remote world he encountered. Enthralled by his spellbinding writing and by the whiff of adventure, the public responded to Lummis and his portrayal of the peoples of the Southwest.[16]

At the same time, a government bureau with an intense interest in history and prehistory of native peoples gained power and momentum. The Bureau of Ethnology, renamed the Bureau of American Ethnology in 1894, enjoyed the benefits of a charismatic leader. John Wesley Powell, by the 1880s the triumphant explorer of the West, headed the bureau from its inception. A leading thinker about the consequences of human habitation in arid areas, Powell used his considerable influence to ward off the genuine enemies his often controversial perspectives provoked. Powell's enormous prestige and the excitement that his explorations caused led to multiple avenues of funding for bureau projects. Paralleling Americans' fascination with what seemed to them the "disappearing race" of Native Americans, Powell began an effort to understand the native world on its own terms refracted through a peculiar lens that melded empiricism and romanticism. Scientific desire and popular culture fused in the study of the history and prehistory of native peoples.[17]

Two forms of writing guided the transformation of observational, taxonomic science into the romanticized, affirmative cultural history that cloaked the capitalism and hegemony of southwestern tourism. The brochures of the railroads made the Southwest come alive to the traveling classes. Over time, these brochures changed from the booster style of facts and few illustrations to a form tied to the ideals of consumer culture, emphasizing art and photographs and fewer, more selective words. These brochures advertised not only the destination but also the luxury of the trains and the available amenities. Menus at hotels were printed, as was tour information. Symbols of the railroads, the famous Santa Fe Chief for example, were linked to drawings and photographs of Indian people and artifacts.[18] Instead of persuading an audience with evidence, the later brochures sought to seduce readers by playing to their cultural suppositions.

For the intellectuals of the era, the reports of the Bureau of American Ethnology (BAE) became the linchpin of their understanding and appreciation of prehistory. The bureau initially produced scholarly annual reports in its first year, 1879, and followed those with a publications series in 1887. Both became instrumental in attracting educated and elitist easterners to southwestern prehistory.[19] With the spin that came to characterize Powell's agency, the BAE reports cloaked romantic perception in the guise of taxonomic objectivity.

These two movements created a new cultural history of the Southwest, based in geography, topography, and ethnography. A uniquely American heritage, different from that of Europe and more potent than the nineteenth-century efforts to equate natural formations in the American landscape with the castles and history of Europe, came clear to a believing public. More than "Nature's Nation" in this construction, the American West and the Southwest in particular became an invented geography of conquest and affirmation. The promotional machine fashioned a glorified history as the scenic vistas and deep cañons of the region captivated the public, and the Hispano and Native American people who preceded the arrival of Anglo Americans became an idealized image of themselves. Those who embraced their causes, such as Helen Hunt Jackson, noted that Mexicans had become a "picturesque element" rather than a functioning part of the social and economic structure in the Los Angeles basin by 1885. Writer Mary Austin also noticed and protested the change.[20] A mythologizing process that at once enhanced and diminished the western landscape and its people took root.

This paradox epitomized tourism. The meaning of southwestern locales and their contribution to the view of history promulgated in the confident and optimistic Progressive Era sharply contrasted with the actuality of such places. A tremendous gulf soon existed between the world visitors saw and the world where local people lived. Guided by the values of industrial America, framed by the hierarchical structures of a capital-driven society, visitors created tourism not as the mediation between places but as a cultural commodity to be possessed as if it were a purchased good. Tourism and the visits it included conveyed status, especially as the places involved became part of an iconography of American national prowess.

Tourism also spawned growth and change in the communities where it had an impact. In the early 1890s Richard Wetherill, the man who found the prehistoric ruins that became Mesa Verde National Park, developed a cottage industry in ruins excavation from his home in Mancos, Colorado. Every town near the rock ledges that held Anasazi ruins had their equivalent of Buckskin Joe, an Española, New Mexico, figure who guided visitors from the town to the cliffs of Puye, about nine miles from the rail station. On arrival, noted the journalist Sylvester Baxter, his group fanned out in an orgy of collecting. Burials, pots, and other relics of prehistory were the prizes. As tourists stampeded for their trophies, they overturned 1,000-year-old walls and trampled valuable sites. By 1905 a tour company headquartered in Santa Fe routinely took visitors in its Kruck or Overland touring cars to experience nearby pueblos and archaeological sites. Each tourist paid for these forms of guide service, often staying in a local hotel, eating meals in local restaurants, and buying goods and services. Even the Buckskin Joes of the world contributed to the local economy, and tourism seemed a source of clear benefit to many communities.[21]

Jackson, Wyoming, which became a center of the dude ranching phenomenon, was one such community. Like many places in similar circumstances, the Jackson area came to rely on tourism because locals ignored or passed over strategies that worked in other places. Other efforts to shape an economy generally were not feasible in the Jackson Hole area or were tried there and failed. Before 1850 Jackson Hole acquired mythic cachet as a source of valued beaver pelts; mountain men sought them in regional water courses to meet the demands of London gentlemen, who prized tall, soft hats made from their fur. After the demand for furs and the supply of beaver declined as the 1830s ended, Jackson Hole faded from the American landscape. For more than a generation, the great energy of expansion passed by the region and rarely intruded. Few settlers stayed in the valley at the base of the Tetons. The only Euro-American visitors were surveyors and the military. Passed over when its economic usefulness ended, Jackson Hole became another of the infinite number of western places that lacked the obvious attributes to draw the technologies of the industrial age. As the Indian Wars of the 1870s drew to a close on the northern plains, settlers again made their way to the valley at the base of the Tetons. In 1883 two families of Mormon settlers from Utah and Idaho, who owned more than 100 cattle between them, crossed the Teton Pass and entered what had been wild territory—a haven for hunters, trappers, and fugitives from the law. A stream of new settlers came, increasing population until 1909, when 1,500 people lived in the basin. Nearly all survived by ranching, feeding their animals during the summer in the Gros Ventre Mountains and maintaining them through the winter on wild or cultivated hay.[22]

Location and the choices of communities shaped the direction of Jackson Hole. The first two Mormon families settled in what became Jackson. A spate of government surveys drew the attention of Pres. Chester A. Arthur, who in 1883 visited the region with Gen. Philip Sheridan and a host of other dignitaries. Arthur came west to relax, to acquaint himself with western geography, and to learn more about native peoples. He found excellent trout fishing in Gros Ventre Canyon, succeeding in at least the first of his three goals. Arthur's trip was a banner moment; the five tent camps that the party established in Jackson Hole were a form of authentication. Late nineteenth-century Americans, through their president, took notice. Shortly after, the first homesteaders, mostly converted trappers, filed claims on their lands. Within a few years, Jackson Hole typified hundreds of western communities. A loosely knit network of small towns, without rail access and dependent on the vagaries of local climate, took shape along the base of the mountains.[23]

For most residents, there was little difference between success and stasis in the combination of agriculture, animal husbandry, small-scale mining, and trapping that made up the local economy. In the cold climate and with limited resources at their disposal, people struggled, not to get ahead but to survive. Outside capital, especially federal money, was critical to creating permanence; the differences between Teton County, Wyoming, where Jackson was located, and its counterpart and neighbor, Teton County, Idaho, stemmed precisely from reliance on that all-important source. Before 1900 Teton County, Idaho, embraced reclamation and agriculture as its strategy. Teton County, Wyoming, did not receive its benefits, although by all accounts Wyoming supported the idea of reclamation. As a result, water held behind a dam constructed with federal money on Jackson Lake in Wyoming irrigated sugar beets and potatoes across the state boundary in Idaho, raising the value of land and spawning an irrigated agriculture industry there. Jackson Hole and Teton County, Wyoming, did not receive that water and remained devoted to ranching cattle during its short summer season.[24] This seemingly small decision created separate vectors for the two physiographically and geographically similar counties, divided only by the line on maps.

Lacking the development of irrigation and an agricultural economy, far from the railroad, and blessed only with the spectacular scenery of the Grand Teton Mountains, Jackson Hole possessed little to recommend it to the twentieth century. The attributes modern industrial society demanded, the combination of infrastructure, productive capacity, raw material, and labor, were missing. The cattle industry, the dominant economic source for the region since the 1880s, typified the problems of Jackson Hole. The valley served as a good location for summer grazing, but the short season pressured local ranchers. Worse, the road to market led over the Teton Mountains to the railhead at Victor, Idaho, about seventy-five hard mountain miles distant.[25] Outside the path of the rails, Jackson remained far from the mainstream, even of western life.

Yet the distance that impeded commercial and production-oriented economic endeavor made a significant social point that allowed the development of a new kind of tourism, as it had in Santa Fe. The hard wagon ride from the railroad was essential to the conceptualization of dude ranching. People who chose ranch life as a recreational activity needed to feel more than symbolic distance. Sixteen miles from Lamy to Santa Fe provided symbolic space; seventy-six miles from Victor into Jackson Hole was a distance quite real. That space, the rocking of the wagon, the difficulty of travel, granted the dude ranch its cachet. "It was the remoteness that did it," Nathaniel Burt, the son of dude ranching pioneer Struthers B. Burt, remembered.[26] Solitude spawned an industry based on an activity that was itself a constructed enterprise. More distant from the mainstream and offering fewer amenities than the hotels of Santa Fe, the dude ranches of Jackson Hole were mythic places where ranchers did not engage in any conventional work of significance, save the herding of visitors. While other ranchers hired hands, castrated animals, and conveyed their cattle to the railhead as an integral part of their livelihood, owners of dude ranches offered such activities and pursued the same practices as much for the edification of their visitors as for any market value.

In the lore of the mythic West, dude ranching began in the North Dakota Territory in the 1880s when a visiting easterner, Bert Rumsey, offered to pay Howard, Alden, and Willis Eaton to stay at their Custer Trail Ranch. Accepting a fee of ten dollars per week, the Eatons found themselves with a boarder rather than a visitor, and an industry was born. Rumsey's offer was fortuitous; the Eatons later calculated that before Rumsey made his offer, they had given away more than 2,200 free meals that year alone. As the word of dude ranching spread, the new fee structure created opportunities for ranchers, and by the mid-1880s, ranches that catered to visitors proliferated. At Estes Park, Colorado, Griff Evans and Abner Sprague took guests. The western slope of the Rocky Mountains also sported a number of ranches. Dick Randall, often called the father of Montana dude ranching, owned a string of pack horses and guided hunters by 1887. In 1898, he bought the cabin that became the basis for his famous OTO Ranch, twelve miles from the Gardiner entrance to Yellowstone National Park. Randall guided the wealthy and famous, including Roosevelt, Hartley Dodge of the Remington Arms Company, writer Philip Ashton Rollins, and railroad president Henry Villard. The Burlington Railroad reached Cody, Wyoming, in 1903, and with the road from Cody to Yellowstone, the new forms of access made William F. "Buffalo Bill" Cody's hunting lodges, the Irma in Cody, the Wapiti Lodge, and the Pahaska Teepee, accessible to visitors.[27] Throughout the 1890s dude ranching remained a small industry that mirrored Theodore Roosevelt's experience and catered to a self-selecting segment of an exclusive audience.

The presence of hunting guides offered a major complement to the dude ranching industry. The two activities remained closely linked in early dude ranching, as the men who led pack trips in search of big game for easterners found another way to separate the well-off from a little of their wealth. Some western guides started ranches. Dick Randall provided the classic example. He melded the two activities until after World War I, when dude ranching became dominant. His herd of cattle, favored by the dudes who visited, became a menagerie that included a few lambs and a pet pig as well as red porcupines, badgers, coyotes, and a bear that dudes managed to capture. During his heyday, the dudes nicknamed Randall "the governor"; what a man who had been guiding visitors in Montana for almost forty years thought of his new appellation was not recorded. Randall built his business alone, a point often driven home to him. One summer, a flash flood destroyed his facilities, including the all-important power plant and the bunkhouse, and the guests had to be evacuated. They showed their loyalty not by pitching in to help with the clean-up, but by making their reservations for the next year as they departed, a gesture toward which Randall, amid the wreckage of his life's work, might well have felt ambivalent.[28] Randall at his core was a guide and a stockman, and despite obstacles, his activities were clearly preferred by some westerners and the easterners who formed the heart of the industry.

Stock ranchers often looked askance at dude ranchers, eastern or western. To the men who herded cattle, it seemed that dude-wrangling, as the practice was called, was neither ranching nor work. Such ranchers raised dudes, detractors often remarked, not anything of value. Dude ranching "did not seem a real business" to cattle men, sheep men, or even farmers, Struthers Burt remembered. "There was a tendency to laugh at [the dude wrangler's] products—Easterners."[29] Serving the needs of guests did not appear as substantive and as important as raising beef or wool for market or even growing the potatoes that formed the staple of countless diets. A productive ethos that demanded that people of substance produce something left little room for a service-oriented ideology. Many westerners still thought of their land in its most instrumental terms.

As transportation routes developed in the northern states after 1900, more dude ranches opened for business. Most owners shared similar roots; they began as did Randall, as a local individual leading eastern visitors on hunting expeditions who saw a way to accommodate larger numbers. Pete Karst of Karst's Ranch in Montana's Gallatin Valley was typical. A decade before he started his dude ranch, Karst established a stage line to bring the mail and passengers from the Bozeman area. By 1907 guest cabins welcomed visitors to a beautiful and still largely untrammeled place. Two brothers who came from the Pacific Northwest, Gay and Watson Wyman, followed a similar pattern. After homesteading in 1908, they started a cattle ranch but soon found that visitors were more lucrative. The Trapper Lodge in Shell Canyon, an icon of early twentieth-century dude ranching, resulted.[30] It became part of a string of ranches that stretched through Wyoming and Montana and formed the backbone of the nascent dude ranching industry.

Most early dude ranches operated in similar ways. There were two basic types at which the activities were different but the expectations and processes much the same. At the working stock ranch, where profit from horses and cattle was an important source of revenue, guests generally participated and observed ranching activities, which were limited by the tolerance of the ranch hands and the desire and skills of the guests. The mountain ranches, often labeled lodges, were limited by the high-elevation weather. Year-round stock operations were impossible, and such places typically depended on their breathtaking views as a primary source of revenue. At both types, guests boarded at the proprietors' homes, and the ranch provided lodging, food, and the use of saddle horses.[31]

By 1908, when the first dude ranch opened in Jackson Hole, tourism had made small but important inroads in the economy of the northern-tier mountain states. It offered the beginnings of a shadow economy, a strategy that did not supplant more conventional and time-honored ways of making a living but that added to the regional lifestyle in substantive ways. Tourism and dude ranching rarely received their due from the people of the area. Such endeavor was seen as inferior and even less masculine than conventional stock-raising. To associate with eastern sissies who needed help to find their way in the world, derisive neighbors seemed to say, made any dude rancher, no matter how accomplished at other, more respected western activities, one of them. This sentiment persisted well into the twentieth century.

By 1908 Jackson's dance with tourism had continued for more than twenty-five years. Owen Wister, a friend of Roosevelt, first visited the region in 1887, two years after first being sent West to heal a new malady called the nervous breakdown. Wister hunted the Jackson area every summer between 1888 and 1893, in one instance proving his local guides wrong by following the sound of rushing water to lakes at the base of the Tetons. According to some accounts, he modeled the villain in *The Virginian* after an area badman named Teton Jackson.[32]

Wister inaugurated a growing seasonal migration to Jackson Hole. He and others like him, also from Philadelphia's Main Line, created a cottage industry. Jackson was not a lucrative place to raise cattle, and area people embraced the opportunity to escort visitors for a fee. Hunting, Wister's pastime, became a popular activity, and ranchers guided eastern and European hunters who sought big game. A few became hunting guides to the exclusion of other endeavors. Ben Sheffield, a local man who headquartered an extensive guide service at Moran, about seven miles north of Jackson, and built a wagon road around Jackson Lake to make his clients' trips easier, characterized this cadre.[33] Sheffield's activities and others like him typified this stage of tourism, reminiscent of Captain Hance and the other early prototourist operators at the Grand Canyon. Before 1900 tourism in Jackson Hole had been a local industry that could support only those who combined specialized knowledge with the desire to cater to incoming tenderfoots and greenhorns.

Some of the visitors who came to hunt were so charmed by the region that they purchased summer cabins in the shadow of the mountains. The first of these neonative colonists, easterners Ray Hamilton and John Sargent, built an elegantly furnished ten-room cabin, complete with a classical library, on the north shore of Jackson Lake. Calling their backwoods paradise Merymere, the men entertained their friends in a setting they thought combined old England and the so-called and rapidly disappearing Wild West. After 1900 Wister himself constructed a cabin along the Snake River. Word of the region spread.[34]

In this setting the unconventional and curmudgeonly Jackson Hole native Louis Joy opened his dude ranch, the JY, in summer 1908. While his personal cabin was constructed, Wister stayed there. Aspiring Philadelphia writer and Princeton graduate Struthers Burt followed Wister to the JY, where he learned to rope and ride. Soon Burt became Joy's partner, as they combined Joy's land and knowledge of the Tetons with Burt's connections to the elite. The arrangement linked an easterner and a native, a prerequisite for such an enterprise but a harbinger of an uncomfortable business and often personal relationship.[35] Joy sought profit, Burt experience, making the two a bad match. Burt later dubbed Joy "a financial Blue Beard who inveigled others into intimate business relations and then, when he had derived all the benefit he could from them, got rid of them with infinite subtlety." Within a few years, Burt struck out on his own with Dr. Horace Carncross, an easterner more amenable to Burt's goals, and the two began the famed Bar BC.[36]

The Bar BC typified colonial enterprises in the West. Its owners were eastern, and they did not need to make their living from the ranch itself. Burt hailed from a wealthy family and enjoyed a career as a poet and an author, which provided financial support and the cachet that attracted guests. The

Bar BC served both as a retreat for him and a symbol of his intellectual and emotional aspirations. Struthers Burt, writer, could pull on his boots, carry hay to his horses, and become real, a man of a vigorous nation, not a habitué of studios and salons. The ranch Burt designed incorporated this desire for authenticity in the fin de siècle style; his membership in their class meant he knew his peers. "The dude-wrangler knows that a dude-ranch is not a cow-ranch," Burt wrote, foreshadowing the romantic strains of country musicians Willie Nelson and Waylon Jennings. "He knows that when Eastern damsels put on overalls and wear egregious scarfs they don't look in the least like cow-girls, but he encourages them to do these things because it is good for their souls."[37] The Bar BC was different from the JY; it catered to the demands of people of Burt's background and class. Burt became the quintessential neo-native, perceived as a native by his visitors but not entirely integrated into the local scene. Unlike many who followed, he was aware of the difference.

Burt scripted his public posture as a romantic adventure. "You start something else," he wrote, "and then find yourself in the dude business," not a wholly accurate account. In Burt's formulation, dude ranchers were virtuous, heroic in both traditional and Progressive-Era senses, standing for the right values against the "crooked water-power man, the crooked land-development man." Dude ranchers stood alone against evil and grappled with it even as they allied with the regulated future against the individualist past. Burt manufactured a complicated place between worlds that resonated with the people who read his books. He sounded awkward to many of his neighbors along the Snake River.[38]

Burt's position reflected the difficulties of the dude rancher. Success in the business was predicated on affiliation with the East. Most successful ranchers had eastern roots and ties, which Burt recognized as important. "I know of but one or two successful dude-ranches in which there is not one Easterner at least who is a very important spoke in the wheel," Burt wrote in his semi-autobiographical *Diary of a Dude-Wrangler.* "For all his virtues, the native son does not as a rule know what an Easterner or Middle Westerner wants or why he wants it."[39] This catering to taste was precisely what stock ranchers did not understand and in fact abhorred about dude ranching. Burt's ability to overlook the "egregious scarfs" as he mimicked the social feel of the East gave the Bar BC credence with travelers. A dude ranch, Burt argued, was not simply a ranch; it was a ranch that bent to the needs of its visitors. The best dude ranchers, he believed, were easterners with a great deal of western experience like himself, Theodore Roosevelt, and Owen Wister, to name only the most prominent members of an exclusive club.

The westerner who could negotiate the rules of the East was even more rare. Of the founders of the early dude ranches, only one, Charles C. Moore, was raised in the West. Moore shared a class background with the other ranchers. The son of a U.S. Senate page during the Lincoln administration who had come West to ranch, Moore was schooled at Lawrenceville in New Jersey, and after working as a bronco buster in Buffalo Bill's Wild West Show, graduated from the law school at the University of Michigan. He practiced law in Cheyenne, Wyoming, for one year before he decided to offer pack trips for boys through Yellowstone National Park. The references he offered the parents of prospective campers showed clearly his ties to eastern elites. Owen Wister was chief among them, and professors from the University of Michigan, the governor, and chief justice of the state supreme court of Wyoming rounded out the list.[40] Like many successful entrepreneurs in the early stages of tourism, Moore melded personal desire and connections to forge a position that allowed him to present himself as a westerner with credentials to easterners who sought authentic experience while retaining his western identity in his native region. At a minimum, success in postrailroad dude ranching required Moore's flexibility and unusual combination of skills and connections.

Moore's western roots remained the exception in the dude ranching industry; Burt typified the dominant style of dude ranch owners. His emotional allegiance was to the region as myth, but his intellectual framework embraced national culture. The perspective Burt brought to local issues had its roots in his education in the East, not in his experience in the Tetons. He loved to rope and ride, but he had learned these behaviors; he was not born to them. Burt shared such characteristics with other famous dude ranchers, creating a spectrum within the industry that began near the center of the possible range of experience. People such as Burt replaced the older locals, the heirs to the grubby backwoods types who guided the remittance men of the nineteenth century. There was little room for them in the new industry. Howard Eaton of the Custer Trail Ranch was at one end of the spectrum. He had gone West from Pittsburgh to make his fortune, only to discover the vulnerability of cattle during the vicious winter of 1886–1887. After struggling with a range of other enterprises, he became a "dude-wrangler by chance," starting Eaton's Ranch, near Sheridan, Wyoming, in 1904. Burt was in the middle of the spectrum. Unlike Eaton, he did not need every penny from the operation for his livelihood, but like him, he traded on his eastern credentials and experience. Irving H. (Larry) Larom, a Princetonian, and his friend, Winthrop Brooks, who later headed Brooks Brothers, represented the other extreme. The two started the Valley Ranch in 1915. In 1922 Larom turned it into a college preparatory school; after 1925 the school was one of the three places in the Rocky Mountains where the College Entrance Examination Boards were given. The ranch became a favorite stopping place for eastern friends, but its owners engaged in it as a lifelong hobby rather than as a business.[41]

Dude ranching became a regional industry, but its economic importance in the West was extremely limited. Before 1910 its constituency remained small, and dude ranching shared many of the characteristics of prototourism. A significant portion of visitors were friends of the owners who paid for the privilege of staying awhile. Social contacts and familial ties, not business motives, formed the core of such relationships. But as the industry grew, relationships of class replaced personal ties. Visitors might not be friends of the owners, but they shared the same schools and neighborhoods back East.

Nor did a particular pattern of geographic relationship emerge in the location of the ranches. Dude ranches were scattered along a wide range of paths, not tied to the railroad as were the tourist enterprises of Santa Fe. Some were very remote; the Bar BC was 104 miles from the rail stop at St. Anthony's, Idaho. The dude ranches shared the solitude that Nathaniel Burt described and were typically either self-sufficient or close enough to be provisioned from a nearby town. Characteristically, Struthers Burt kept the larder of the Bar BC well stocked. Although eggs were scarce, he kept an icehouse full of beef, mutton, pork, ham, fruit, and vegetables that could not be grown in the Jackson Hole area. "In early days," he recalled, "food was the cause of more worry than perhaps anything else."[42] Dude ranch proprietors engaged in a balancing act. They provided amenities, but their appeal lay in their remote nature and the varieties of experience for the visitor. The dude ranches sold distance from the mainstream, real distance, hard rides in uncomfortable buckboard wagons from the world of modern technology. The location of ranches remained idiosyncratic, based on the choices of individuals rather than on the patterns that increasingly shaped railroad tourism.

By 1915 tourism in Jackson Hole was on the way to becoming a classic devil's bargain for local people. It grafted on members of a seasonal upper class who mimicked the behaviors of natives but who were not subject to its environmental and economic constraints. These people arrived each year, typically after the long, hard winter, and engaged in shadow activities that paralleled the ones year-round locals relied on for survival. Neonatives waxed eloquent about the region, commenting on its beauty, but they rarely endured its hardship. To the locals in Jackson Hole, their neighbors who ran the dude ranches must have remained perplexing. These neonatives dressed as did local people and engaged in versions of many of the same activities. But they were different; they wrote books and articles, talked about the issues of the nation rather than those of the region, and did not depend on Jackson Hole for their income. The neonatives skimmed the cream off the top of life. They could afford to appreciate the aesthetic magnificence of the Tetons. If locals resented the stream of visitors that grew into a river, it would be hard to blame them.

As was typical of the elites of the fin de siècle, the seasonal newcomers created intellectual parameters, even boundaries, for the region they claimed as their own during the warmer months. Originating in a culture that felt real loss as its people contemplated the end of their frontier past, these neonatives sought to preserve vestiges of that experience. Struthers Burt's son, Nathaniel Burt, wrote of this sense in both a real and romantic way: Jackson Hole and its environs were "beautiful and beneficent, but they were a bit scary too," he recalled. "Dudes who weren't respectful . . . could get into terrible trouble—and served them right. They were drowned in rivers and fell off cliffs and bear and moose mauled them. You didn't fool around with these Presences. Respectful awe was the proper attitude, and you walked softly in Eden."[43]

Nathaniel Burt's evaluation carefully defined the difference between neonative and visitor. Though the younger Burt was not born in Jackson Hole, he mediated its many cultures. To locals, he still smacked of dude, in spite of his experience on his father's ranch. To visitors, he seemed the consummate Wyoming rancher, able to speak clearly for the world the dudes craved in terms they understood. His writing showed that he grasped the multifaceted dimensions of the experience his family marketed. Less self-conscious than his father, the younger Burt embraced the romantic view of the wild as sentient, alive in glorious mythic ways. He also pointed to its reality, the danger of not respecting a harsh natural world. In this Burt, like his father before him, became a new man, a member both of Jackson Hole and the salons of urban America, a hybrid foreshadowed by Theodore Roosevelt and realized in the rare combination of the hardiest and most sophisticated dude wranglers.

To maintain control in the widening cultural gulf, these people needed the scenery and wild nature of the Tetons and its surroundings. The biogeography of the region, the exquisite mountains, steel blue lakes, and bountiful game offered a setting for ritual behavior. The dude wranglers defined themselves and their dudes in juxtaposition to this land. The activities, rituals that offered the form of western endeavor but not its genuine substance, illustrated the importance of relationship to place. The dudes and their wranglers needed Jackson and its environs to remain the same, seemingly if not actually wild and preindustrial.

In this desire the dude wranglers ran counter to the economic interests and the social objectives of most natives of Jackson Hole. A series of disputes, pitting native against neonative, westerner against transplant, began initially over two dams along the Gros Ventre River, Buffalo Fork and Spread Creek, constructed by a company that planned to irrigate poor Wyoming land and that expected to sell its water to Idaho farmers in the aftermath. The fate of the elk herds that migrated to the lower elevations of Jackson Hole during the winter also pitted locals against neonatives. Elk initially migrated to western Wyoming from the plains but with the arrival of Anglo Americans were forced to higher elevations. During fall and winter, early settlers found abundant elk in lower-elevation meadows, where they became easy prey for hunters. Until 1900 poachers decimated the herds; federal and state officials pleaded for protection of the animals, typically by the extension of Yellowstone National Park boundaries to include the wintering area. They succeeded with the 1905 establishment of a 570,000-acre state game preserve north of Moran. In winter 1908–1909, deep snow covered Jackson Hole, threatening the herds with starvation. Elk carcasses littered the countryside, survivors wandered aimlessly, the outline of their ribs poking through their hides, and few local ranchers possessed hay their domestic stock did not need. A local rancher named Stephen Leek captured the scene with a camera, the photographs appeared in magazines, and a cry to save the elk began. Wyoming initiated purchases of hay for winter elk feed in 1910. The federal government followed in 1911. In 1912 and 1913 the federal government set aside the first National Elk Refuge, almost 3,000 acres in size. Although most locals understood the reasons, many would have responded to the crisis in a different way.[44]

Nor were they prepared for subsequent actions that protected elk. Game was important, but not as important as creating settlement. With support from the dude wranglers and visitors, elk protection gained momentum. In 1918 available land in the public domain was removed from entry to expand the elk range. Several subsequent withdrawals eventually inhibited settlement on the east side of the basin north of Jackson. A bill in Congress provided for the addition of a considerable area to the holdings of the U.S. Biological Survey, which took responsibility for the elk herd. The Biological Survey, which did not approve of feed programs for the elk, suggested instead the expansion of the Elk Reserve to maintain the herd under natural conditions at about 20,000 head. By the mid-1920s, cattlemen took animals to higher elevations for summer pasture, only to find the lands reserved for elk. New settlers in search of ranch lands or summer homes found the public domain closed.[45] Locals were aghast at such impinging on their economic prerogatives.

In these scenarios, the people who advocated commercial economic use of land were natives; those who preserved the scenery and fauna were typically neonative. Ranchers, poachers, dam builders, and others had local roots. They lived in a beautiful region, but they knew they could not eat scenery. Neonatives, whose wealth and values came from elsewhere, saw such issues in different terms. "A man seeks seclusion but pretty soon he is surrounded by numerous others of his kind," Struthers Burt wrote wistfully. "The most difficult thing to maintain . . . is a home in loneliness." The preservation of the special nature of Jackson Hole, of the attributes that drew Burt and his kind there, was a prime value, as important if not more so than local livelihood. Burt freely admitted that this sentiment stemmed "partly from clear-sighted selfishness," the fervent desire to preserve the seclusion.[46] The tension between neonative and native grew rife before the latter learned to regard tourism as a source of economic sustenance.

No issue illustrated the difference in views between native and neonative more clearly than did the battle for Grand Teton National Park. When the struggle began in earnest after the creation of the National Park Service in 1916, neonatives such as Burt acquired the status of natives in the eyes of the law. They had become landowners, enjoying the influence that status conferred. Landowners with longer tenure apart from dude ranching had to share their status with neonatives whose rituals they did not understand and whose living was independent of local land. For longtime residents, the situation became a conundrum that made expressing their perspective difficult. To outsiders it seemed that the community of Jackson was split on the issue of a national park; closer scrutiny revealed that the choice of sides correlated closely with the place of origin of the individuals involved.[47]

The battle for the national park also involved two federal agencies, the Forest Service and the Park Service, that collided with growing frequency and intensity throughout the West. The ease with which the Grand Canyon transfer occurred proved an anomaly. More typically, the two agencies grappled for administrative control of western lands, the Forest Service serving as an ally for local control of the resource base for commercial economic use and the Park Service representing a national constituency that sought scenic beauty and cultural uplift. Both reprised these roles to an exponential degree in Jackson Hole, as the Forest Service provided a base for commercial economic activity and the Park Service promised preservation and the development of a tourist industry.[48] Codified in the perspective of the two agencies, the conflicts of the region became institutional.

The affluent and powerful who spent summers in Jackson Hole were among the most ardent supporters of a national park, and they found a few among the community who joined them. An alliance between the dude wranglers and the Park Service formed, a typical relationship for the agency while Stephen T. Mather led it. The classic articulation of the park position occurred in a meeting at the cabin of the eccentric Philadelphian Maud Noble along the banks of the Snake River near Moose on July 26, 1923. Noble, who enjoyed a roaring fire in the fireplace even in the middle of summer—a habit that surely aroused the passions of the locals who cut firewood—Burt, Carncross, businessman Joe Jones, newspaper editor Dick Winger, rancher Jack Aeonian, and Horace Albright, Mather's right-hand man, met to discuss the fate of their valley.[49]

Many residents in the region would not concede that the people in Maud Noble's cabin had the right to call Jackson Hole "their valley." Other economic uses of the valley existed; dude ranching was a specialty industry and an exclusive one at that. The idea advanced by Struthers Burt, that Jackson should become a "museum on the hoof," appealed to dude ranchers and others who catered to visitors. The plan was expensive. It required a fund-raising effort to purchase land north of Jackson, but resentment of the idea forced the activists to work quietly to avoid inflaming their neighbors. The reintroduction of indigenous wild animals, one tenet of the plan, sent chills down the spines of stock ranchers. The elimination of predators across the West had been one of their greatest successes. The cabin group favored leaving the roads of the area unpaved, a joy to a traveler seeking a pristine past but an obstacle to anyone engaged in commerce. A restriction similar to the one in Santa Fe that would have compelled the people of Jackson to build only log homes smacked of paternalism.[50] Despite the good intentions of Albright, Burt, and the others, their proposal was readily construed as self-serving and arrogant.

As the idea of preservation in Jackson Hole gained currency, it also highlighted the tensions created by the internal colonialism of wealthy easterners. Although the meeting led indirectly to the involvement of John D. Rockefeller Jr. in the creation of Grand Teton National Park and Jackson Hole National Monument, which later became a significant and tendentious addition to the park, it also exacerbated tensions between what by 1925 had become two distinctly different kinds of natives of the Jackson area. One group, who made its living from the land, resented restrictions on the commercial economic uses of potentially valuable land; the other, tied directly or indirectly to dude ranches and able to tap economic resources outside the community, sought a preserve that could hold the Jackson Hole area in permanent stasis, not only keeping its aesthetic attributes as they were but also preserving the unique feel of the place.

These newer arrivals had more capital and power than the locals, and despite local and regional animosity and outright resistance, they succeeded. Grand Teton National Park was established in 1929, in no small part to protect the Tetons from the range of ticky-tack structures, including a dance hall, second-rate tourist cabins, a rodeo field, and hot dog stands along the highway, that intruded on the vistas from the valley. Rockefeller spent more than $2 million to purchase land for the park. The preservation movement came largely from the outside, and to a large degree, at the expense of conventional local economic endeavor. Yet development associated with tourism also benefited local ranchers. Roads over the 8,429-foot-high Teton Pass, the 7,921-foot Rim, and Togwotee Pass, at 9,658 feet, and northward into Yellowstone Park were constructed and then improved to facilitate tourists. Stockmen used them to track their cattle, and at the end of the season, to move them to railroads.[51]

Although many area ranchers did not regard the situation in this manner, roads existed not to support the stock industry but to convey tourists to their destinations. Road location demonstrated the importance of tourism. Instead of following along the east side of the basin from Jackson, the main road north began along the east side and cut across to the west side. A ranch road would have followed to the east of the mountains. Roads were a benefit to the recreational and cultural interest in the area, an unforetold advantage that added important infrastructure for Teton County, Wyoming, established in 1922.

Much of the road money came from private or federal sources, not from Wyoming. Rockefeller invested $50,000 in Yellowstone's roads during the 1920s. In the 1930s paving began, stimulated by the increasing number of automobile tourists who left the Tetons for Yellowstone to the north. Even all-year mobility became possible; before the mid-1930s, the only way in or out of Jackson in the winter was by air, a mode of travel far more familiar to Burt's friends and relatives than to most people in Jackson. During winter 1935–1936, the Hoback and Teton Pass roads were kept open for the first time, offering area residents a genuine benefit that they had not anticipated.[52]

The political situation remained tense and confused. In the view of Jackson's population, the basis for the regional economy, ranching, took second place to the unusual pastime of visitors pretending to be cowboys. Federal law and eastern money restricted the expansion of the conventional economy, limiting the land available that could help create a stronger, more populous county. Federal reserves particularly vexed locals; land so designated did not generate property tax, threatening the survival of county institutions. In the view of scholarly observers, dude ranches and tourism crowded out stock-raising, creating an early version of a service economy. Less certain was the sustainability of such an economy. Whether Jackson could survive solely on income from the summer tourists and fall hunters remained the crucial question that would define the future of the region.[53]

By 1930 the dude ranch was firmly ensconced as a western institution. Wyoming dominated this industry with its almost 100 dude ranches. In 1937 the state legislature defined dude ranching in statute as a "ranch offering accommodations, entertainment, and participation in regular ranch activities for a monetary consideration." The JY and Bar BC of Jackson Hole were no longer alone in the region; at least nineteen other dude ranches in the area were open for business during summer 1930. Wickenburg, Arizona, west of Phoenix, developed a thriving trade, as did many other locales in proximity to growing western cities.[54] As its appeal grew, dude ranching became more accommodating. The intellectual advantages of its rough edges diminished, and as it became a way of life rather than a sideline and as a broader, less intellectual, and more effete constituency embraced it, dude ranches reflected Santa Fe in negotiating the distance from the mainstream. Better conveyances picked people up at railheads; faster, smoother vehicles carried them to their dude ranch; and an increasing number of places took on the traits of rustic hotels instead of working ranches. At first distant from the mainstream, dude ranching migrated closer, retaining the perception of difference but becoming more like the Grand Canyon and Santa Fe.

By this point, archaeological tourism and dude ranching had become part of different dimensions of tourism. Archaeological tourism remained a specialty activity that attracted a small, wealthy, and remarkably zealous group. Even in 1930 these people were closely tied to the elites from which they sprang and whom they sought to enlighten. Fewer people participated as archaeology dropped from significant to marginal in a culturally changing America. Archaeological tourists could more correctly be labeled aficionados by 1930. They were hardly tourists; they had become amateur enthusiasts, a much smaller group in numbers but one that still had money to spend and wielded some professional influence. In the places they visited, they were no longer part of an expected constituency of visitors. They had become curiosities.

Dude ranches had grown in size and number, but in the process the experience had been diluted. Early in the new century, dude ranchers understood that they were emulating Theodore Roosevelt; dude ranching was liminal, both mythic and reinvigorating for tired souls. It had been a component of the tourism of hegemony. By 1930 dude ranching had become a common ritual or rite of passage, widely shared among the wealthy and the nearly wealthy. It ceased to mirror Roosevelt and the social and personal objectives he found in the West. Instead, dude ranching evoked the West of popular culture and the incipient western movie, often filmed on one of the dude ranches near Los Angeles. Its roots as a specialty activity, confined to one class, changed as it grew as an industry. It became de rigeur, a moment that members of the elite acknowledged they had experienced as a means of class identification in social settings.

This tourism that pretended to real distance from railroad-inspired hegemony became a precursor not of a unique American type of tourism that resisted the marketplace but of the democratization of travel that accompanied the rise of the automobile. Railroad passengers had been confined to the steel corridors. They were physically, and ultimately intellectually, captives of the railroad. The adventurers who joined an archaeological excavation or took time on a dude ranch were not so bound; once they departed the railroad terminus they were in a world different from the one the railroad constructed. They lived in tents or bunks, camped under the stars or made an evening's bed in a prehistoric cave dwelling. They ate often what they hunted, not what Fred Harvey's chefs concocted. They enjoyed the opportunity to see more widely than did passengers who experienced a largely visual West from their railcar window.

As the cultural meaning of dude ranching and archaeology diverged, the two contributed to the rise of another form of tourism, one with deep roots in the pre-Progressive Era that was to be transformed by the spread of the opportunity for leisure. In the 1920s the United States experienced an ongoing series of cultural sea changes, in which a combination of social values, cultural objectives, technological change, and improved access redefined the basis for travel. The constituency for tourism grew, and the values of the tourism of hegemony appealed to a smaller proportion of travelers. More and more people wanted their travel to include experience, not just the intellectual enlightenment of cultural and heritage tourism. In a society still obsessed with its continent, still proving itself in postadolescent terms, and increasingly equating individual freedom with social good, recreational tourism, participating rather than observing, came to the fore.

6

Intraregional Tourism

Automobiles, Roads, and the National Parks

Despite their intellectual objectives, dude wranglers and archaeological aficionados were the antecedents to a revolution in western tourism made possible by Henry Ford's assembly line and realized by the construction of roads. The devotees of archaeology first recognized this freedom. The automobile took them from the locales overwhelmed by tourism, the railroad depots, the plazas, the towns, the seemingly inauthentic and corrupt places, and transported them to areas where the intrusions of the modern world were limited to the drivers and their vehicles. The technology permitted, even encouraged, the manufacture of the distance that they craved. Wheels gave choices that even the most affluent railroad tourists could not purchase. They allowed travelers to move beyond the corridor the steel rails created, to leave behind a world that catered to the whims of industrial society.

Sometimes that distance could be real. Other times, it could be in the eyes of the travelers, certain that the landscape they viewed remained unchanged from a moment in the far-off past. United States Forest Service ranger David S. Olson noticed this latter phenomenon sometime late in the 1910s; instead of the local sight-seeing traffic to which he was accustomed, a "long black sedan drew up from behind. A liveried chauffeur asked if I wanted a ride," Olson recounted. "I thanked him and said I'd stand on the running board since I only had a short way to go" to the silviculture plots where he had begun the first federal tree farm in the West. "Looking into the car, I saw two elderly ladies sitting in rocking chairs. They smiled and one of them said they were seeing the Wild West for the very first time." In the eyes of tourists who assumed they defined every scene into which they wandered, the forester, whose presence symbolized order, became part of a past that he actually helped bring to an end.[1]

The range of experience allowed by the automobile limited the hegemony of the intellectual message encoded in railroad travel. Rail passengers sought and found the lobbies of hotels such as El Tovar; the automobile traveler, especially the earliest ones, had far less control over the nature of their experience. Yet these experiences became desirable. In 1920 *Art and Archaeology,* a magazine published by the Archaeological Institute of America, described the existing and potential archaeological national monuments of the Southwest. The directions to them could be followed only by driving on the miserable dirt tracks of the region. When Charles L. Bernheimer organized the 1922 expedition that circumvented Navajo Mountain, one of the most remote places on the Navajo reservation, he drove an automobile the ten hours from Flagstaff to Kayenta, Arizona, to John and Louisa Wade Wetherill's trading post. The way hardly resembled a road. He traversed tracks, trails, and paths even before negotiating the slickrock of the Four Corners country. The only other Anglo Americans he encountered were traders at remote outposts. They offered few of the messages of affirmation that so bemused his touring peers at the Grand Canyon.[2]

The change from train to automobile as the dominant mode of travel occurred quickly. In the early 1920s, as railroads restored full service after World War I, travel soared; by the end of the decade, train travel was in a free fall. The number of coach-class travelers dropped dramatically, especially on shorter trips, as Americans learned to drive themselves except when they traveled long distances. The railroads tried to make up the difference with lower fares and more varieties of travel, such as excursions, but the automobile carved a larger share of the travel market in each successive year. The results changed the nature of the tourist experience and every place through which automobile travelers passed.[3]

As automobile ownership spread from the wealthy to a much wider segment of the population, tourism acquired new dimensions to meet the needs of this growing constituency. Municipal automobile campgrounds, typically with communal showers and bathrooms, sprang up across the West. By the early 1920s towns across Kansas, a state through which many auto travelers passed, contained more than 200 overnight municipal campgrounds. Each was stamped with the personality of its place. Visitors who stayed in Wichita's campground experienced different amenities from those who stopped in Kingman, a mere thirty miles distant. The variety even among closely linked communities offered a diversity of experience that entities such as the Harvey Company sought to eliminate.[4]

During the 1920s few such places tried to offer more than creature comforts. Amenities and access to repair facilities dominated the offerings of such enterprises in contrast to the hegemonic treatment of the past, characteristic of the AT&SF or the Great Northern Railway's colonization of Glacier National Park. The railroads guided visitors; automobile travelers, by the 1920s increasingly part of the great middle class, pieced together a West of their own. Conditioned culturally to value the world in terms of mainstream American society, they may have chosen sites that fit earlier conceptions, but unlike railroad passengers, they did not have those sites chosen for them. With the coming of roads, local boosterism and self-aggrandizement replaced the selective promotion of cultural and natural features the railroads practiced. Every town in the West sought to show that its attributes were special.

The cultural terms of the 1920s also altered the terrain of tourism. The 1920s possessed a different cultural feel from the years before World War I. The Jazz Age, as the decade was often called, was defined by divisions: between wets and drys, those who opposed prohibition and those who favored it; between those who embraced the new leisure culture and those, such as the man and woman in Grant Wood's *American Gothic,* who clung to traditional values; and between those who had access to the credit necessary to consume the goods of industrialization and those who did not. The upper-middle-class hegemony of Progressivism became only one of a number of intellectual constructs struggling for dominance during the 1920s. The battle over the teaching of the theory of evolution in public school, waged most prominently in the Scopes Monkey Trial held in Dayton, Tennessee, in 1925, was one manifestation of the close hold the antebellum views of God, nature, and law had on much of the American population. The radio, moving pictures, and the rise of national advertising and mass popular culture contributed to an America that was more capable of acknowledging the diversity of its intellectual parameters. The confidence and the innocence that marked the pre–World War I era were gone, and a cacophony of voices claiming authority followed in the war's wake.

The social values of the era were also different. Instead of the sense of the importance of social goals that dominated the Progressive Era, the 1920s seemed possessed by a rampant and morally seditious individualism. If the Progressive Era stressed collective order, the Jazz Age embodied emotion and individual exploration. The technologies were available; before the end of the decade, researchers in the fictitious Middletown of Muncie, Indiana, learned that young people already embraced a youth-driven culture different from that of their parents, relying on current technologies, especially the automobile, to ensure them the freedom from detection necessitated by the power structure of the day. For most Americans in the 1920s, especially urbanites, veterans, and the young, social objectives fell far behind individual goals.

The automobile epitomized individualism. Its first American users were the wealthy, driven about by chauffeurs. As the automobile became affordable, its constituency changed. Automobile ownership rose dramatically during the 1910s, and that growth increased throughout the 1920s. In 1910, 458,000 automobiles were registered nationwide; by 1920 the number reached 8 million, rising again to 23 million by 1930. The vast increase in the number of drivers presaged a widespread and continuous call for the improvement of roads. As early as 1905, agitation for road construction began in earnest with the See America First movement. The first genuine highway organization, the Lincoln Highway Association, promoted development of a northern route across the plains. The rise of auto camping in the 1920s and federal support for the construction of highways broadened significantly the constituency for leisure-related travel, making lengthy cross-country travel possible for an audience much broader than that riding the luxury trains.[5]

The growing network of roads had tremendous appeal. Not only were they cheaper to travel on, they also seemed to offer an intellectual purpose that mirrored the objectives of the railroad-based cultural and heritage tourism of the elites. The idea of seeing America first became so popular that the railroads embraced it. In 1910, when the Great Northern Railway Company added See America First to its advertising for Glacier National Park, railroads had not yet perceived automobile travel as a threat to their dominance. With only 458,000 automobiles registered in 1910 and less than 10 percent of rural roads paved, the prospect that automobile travel might threaten railroad control seemed remote. The tourism of hegemony appeared secure, and the slogan See America First had wide currency and deep resonance in the formation of American national identity.[6]

The melding of the slogan into one that represented both auto and rail tourism suggested that as travel changed from an elite pastime to one shared more widely among social classes, the distinction between forms of tourism, heritage and cultural in one instance and recreational in the other, similarly blurred. Although visitors who inhabited different social and cultural stations in American life might search out divergent experiences, they did so within the context of the same symbolic rhetoric. As the concept of travel for leisure grew in popularity, the options available to people who chose this new endeavor expanded. The initial difference between auto travelers and train passengers was great; with the growth in the number of people who traveled, that difference diminished each year.

The changes occurred in part because the automobile allowed a broader range of travel than could be accomplished on the rails. Automobile travel revived and attracted new attention for a dimension in western tourism that had been overshadowed since the rise of the railroad. It encouraged the kind of localized tourism that typified the era before widespread railroad travel. Ordinary people could visit places within the limited range of early automobiles and dirt highways. The greatest impact of such visits occurred away from the main trajectories of the railroad lines. Automobile travel initially did not bring significant numbers of visitors to places such as the Grand Canyon, Yellowstone, and Yosemite. The great difficulty reaching such places meant that at first automobiles only trickled in. Instead, local people used the automobile primarily as a way to visit attractions close to home with greater ease than ever before; social travel increased dramatically as the cost and difficulty ceased to be prohibitive. Only after the improvement of roads and automobiles did the number of vehicles arriving at places such as the Grand Canyon begin to soar.[7]

There were significant differences between 1920s auto travelers and their horse-and-buggy predecessors. As Bernheimer illustrated, the travelers of the 1920s had greater geographic range and faced fewer obstacles than did the Radersburg tourists seized by the Nez Perce in Yellowstone National Park in 1877. Bad weather, poor accommodations, frequent need for repairs, and other inconveniences caused interruptions for these later travelers. By the 1920s roads, hotels, restaurants, and other amenities dotted the western landscape, and communities in which to stay and people with whom to interact were common. In addition, migrants were moving throughout the West. They were not vacation travelers but people who stopped and spent money on the way to new destinations, California prominent among them. Their presence initiated another form of economic endeavor that had previously been restricted to the rail corridors. The commercial culture of travel expanded into a broader swath of the West.

The rise of automobile travel played a crucial role in the transformation of western tourism. As automobiles became common possessions of middle-class families and the broader network of roads crisscrossed the nation, the cultural dimensions of tourism shifted from the tastes of the elite, the sometimes cumbersome intellectualizing of places such as the Grand Canyon, and toward the more common tastes of ordinary people, often oriented toward recreation. Experience achieved primacy over enlightenment and insight, and attractions also reflected more clearly class distinctions. The sanctimonious pronouncements of the prewar era seemed naive after World War I. America had lost both adolescence and innocence, maturing in ways that obviated the certainty of the fin de siècle era.

More of the country became available to auto travelers than to people who rode the rails. Automobile travel could be slow and unwieldy, but such endeavors were an entirely different kind of voyage from the railroads and their luxury liners and attendant hotels and restaurants. Railroad vectors were determined by the roadbed on which the track was laid; an automobile driver could go anywhere the combination of imagination, wheels, and a dirt track might lead. These tracks pointed to the wilds of Montana and the rainbow canyons of southern Utah, across the plains and along the coast, into Mexico, and for the brave, into the Rockies. One particular journey from Salt Lake City to the area that became Bryce Canyon National Park, a 270-mile trip, took two-and-one-half days. The last eighteen miles were "only slightly distinguishable from a Paiute Indian Trail," in the words of one observer, typifying both the difficulty of the trip and the driver's ability to compare it to the mythic pioneering experiences of the nineteenth century.[8]

In the West, auto travel added a dimension to local and regional economies. The distances between western communities were vast, and motorists in large numbers purchased food, gasoline, and spent untold amounts of money on auto repair at each stop. They also needed overnight accommodations, showers and restrooms, places to eat, and a range of other services that communities had not previously provided in abundance. Auto travelers became a source of revenue, especially in remote places, and communities offered amenities, from campgrounds to hotels, diners to fashionable restaurants. Arterial highways sprouted new businesses, especially as the construction of major cross-continental highways throughout the West—the famed Route 66 to the south and the Lincoln Highway, Route 50, over the northern plains—began in earnest after 1926.[9]

Strictly tourist-related efforts, such as the national park-to-park highway, a brainchild of Park Service director Stephen T. Mather, also flourished. Conceived in the late 1910s, the park-to-park highway was to link the major national parks, from the Grand Canyon to Glacier and from Rocky Mountain to Yosemite. Travelers were to be able to visit the parks on an extended two-lane, paved-road loop covering more than 2,000 miles. Along the way, gasoline and food would be necessary, and there would also be intermediary lesser national park areas such as the Pipe Spring National Monument, proclaimed in 1923 and located between Zion National Park and the north rim of the Grand Canyon. The highway would provide the typical corridor, creating characteristic opportunities for locals to serve and sometime to prey upon passing travelers.[10]

Such roads also expanded the economic and social impact of tourism. Along the railroad, the places where the trains stopped were affected, and nearby areas were equally altered. A roughly ten-mile corridor on each side of the tracks became transformed, tied to the rails more closely than to the world beyond its influence. The number of visitors and the exposure to different ways of life, not to mention the way in which rail access changed local economies and property values, created new on-the-ground realities everywhere the rails reached. Automobile tourism spread its impact among many communities, as smaller numbers of visitors reached infinite places, lingered longer than most rail travelers, sometimes by accident as well as by design, and learned more about the places from the wider range of interaction offered in a local diner instead of in a railroad dining car or a Harvey Company restaurant.

The combination of technology and ongoing migration gave rise to new kinds of tourism. With a larger local and area population to serve, western communities developed recreational opportunities located within easy reach of area residents. These forms encouraged a kind of tourism that was different from the heritage-dominated tourism promoted by the railroads in two important ways: it served a predominantly local and regional overnight and day-use audience, and those constituencies sought recreation and experience rather than the enlightenment and cultural message promoted in fin de siècle national parks and monuments. A clear class difference existed between the people who traveled the rails in splendid sleeping cars and those who slogged through the mud and experienced the frequent flat tires and other motoring problems common along rutted western roads. Tailored to local taste and made possible by roads, expanded rail service to remote communities, and the growing affluence of a burgeoning population, this intraregional tourism reflected both the beginning of a revolution in values and a similar change in the audience for mainstream tourism.

Recreational tourism embodied a more personal set of values instead of the broad and community-defined ones of the earlier era when tourism functioned as a part of a national affirmation. Visitors of the 1920s began a recognizable modern trend: they traveled primarily to see different things but also to escape the pace of their life in the industrial world. Rather than an intellectual experience, they craved difference—new sports, new activities, seeing new places and doing new things. Travel was not designed to make them better, wiser, or more prepared; it merely restored them to their native condition, the way they had been before the rigors of urban civilized life wore them down. To the middle class of the era, travel did not have to mean anything more than an opportunity to get away.

Tourism as recreation was not new in American society, but the end of World War I and the freedom the automobile offered made it dominant. Since the 1880s Americans had experimented with recreation as a form of tourism, the rise of the back-to-nature movement giving a great boost to outdoor activity. John Muir, the most ardent outdoorsman of his time, noted the increase in popularity. The "scenery habit," as he called it, seemed to him a precursor of a stronger environmental ethic.[11] Early recreational travel did belong within the constructs of the tourism of hegemony, but it remained for the automobile to liberate it from the control of the elites.

Recreational tourism came to embody the changing American value system of the 1920s. In the Jazz Age, the combination of urbanization and economic prosperity created a remarkably individualist climate. The tenets of the Progressive Era and the conditions of World War I required sacrifices for the good of the community, and in its aftermath, the nation erupted in a frenzy of individualism. The kinds of values Americans read into the Grand Canyon and Santa Fe or saw expressed in the great fairs and expositions of the pre–World War I era seemed trite in the era of prohibition, speakeasies, radio, silent movies, and fictional heroes such as F. Scott Fitzgerald's Jay Gatsby. The new values emphasized individuals and their attainments over the concept of community.[12]

This new attitude responded to and anticipated changing national culture. As the ethic of the new urban America took hold, as style replaced substance and image became more important, recreational tourism offered a personal proving ground. While some people bought raccoon coats and swallowed goldfish, others framed themselves above the mass by embracing a remnant of the tourism of hegemony, the idea of individual self-worth earned through challenge. Tourists who sought these activities independent of the structured market but quite susceptible to more localized sociocultural scripting found a kind of freedom with the automobile that railroad travel did not offer. Automobile travel liberated them from the shackles of their society, the hegemony of the railroads, the forms and structures of their world.

From this freedom grew the order and form of a recreational tourism that retained elements of the tourism of hegemony but that moved into a realm defined by experience. Early automobile travelers viewed their surroundings without many of the filters common to their time. As late as 1915, someone who drove the narrow, winding roads between Missoula and Spokane experienced a voyage through a world that seemed primeval. Despite centuries of Native American habitation and as much as a generation of sedentary American life, observers routinely perceived this world as untrammeled. Within a decade, such an illusion was impossible. In that brief time, "The automobile has revolutionized the average American's vacation," wrote Frank Brunner in *Outlook* magazine. "It has brought about a renaissance of the outdoors and it has firmly planted a brand-new outdoor sport," auto touring.[13] With the codification of the Lincoln Highway, Route 66, and the National Park-to-Park Highway, the patterns of hegemonic tourism shifted to a tourism based in experience.

The national parks served as the transitional stage between the old and new forms of tourism. In some ways, they mirrored the themes and terms of fin de siècle tourism; in others, the arrival of automobile travelers proclaimed the individualism and free-spirited nature of an age that measured itself by freedom and new experience. When people visited the Grand Canyon, they were awed by the vistas. Disembarking from a train configured those views. People were spectators before an enormous and living canvas of nature, separate from the world from which they disembarked. Wheeling up, covered with dust, wearing goggles and scarves, automobile tourists experienced an entirely different meaning. Drivers and their passengers were participants in the difficult endeavor of reaching the canyon. Approaching the rim was a symbol of personal and cultural conquest, attained not in the hush of a museum but with the ebullience of accomplishment, the camaraderie and expressions of disbelief of those who achieve the impossible. The canyon remained the same. The prism through which people interpreted it was entirely different.

The patterns of roads offered new opportunities to create national parks and to visit them. A plethora of places became national park areas, many as a result of the peripatetic wanderings of Mather and his assistant and alter ego, Horace Albright. Throughout the 1920s the two men engaged in a mission of their agency's development that involved a certain imperialism regarding the holdings of other federal agencies. East of the Mississippi River, national parks such as Great Smoky Mountains and Shenandoah were fashioned from tracts of private land. Mather and Albright envisioned a national park system that followed specific dictates. Huge natural areas were to be the

Auto travelers could feel they reached the ends of the earth, as this photo of Pipe Springs, on the Arizona-Utah border in the early 1920s, reveals. (Courtesy of National Archives.)

cornerstones, linked by roads that traversed smaller areas, some of which were added to the national park system, and before 1933, designated national monuments. Pipe Spring was only the most obvious of such locations. When Mather arranged to have Cong. Louis Cramton, chair of the House Appropriations Committee, travel from Zion National Park to Mesa Verde National Park via Pipe Spring so that he could assess its importance as a stopping point at the edge of a desert, he codified a long-standing practice that made convenient sites with some significance more valuable than their attributes alone warranted.[14]

The automobile and the tourists it brought altered the meaning of the national parks and simultaneously facilitated the expansion of the system and its managing agency into a powerful federal entity. Mather's conception of national parks remained narrow, derived from the late nineteenth-century California milieu from which he came. Like John Muir and Josiah Whitney, Mather valued the spectacular mountaintop parks. He saw pristine nature in the nineteenth-century conception of wilderness, places that people could not reach to defile. These monumental parks tugged at the heartstrings of fin de siècle America, but in the roiling Jazz Age they presented severe limitations to the growth of the park system. Horace Albright, Mather's junior by a generation, felt none of the strictures of his mentor. He instead envisioned a multitiered park system, one that included expansive national parks but also smaller areas, scientific resources, and other features, including the history of the American Republic. By the mid-1920s the park system extended to the eastern half of the nation; by the end of the decade Albright helped fashion the system into a national entity with national reach. In his own account he had already planned to capture battlefields, forts, and other historical places for the park system. The automobile encouraged Albright to create a park system that met the needs of a middle-class audience and those of its elite counterpart.[15]

The new and broader national park system no longer held a few spectacular mountaintop parks and the bizarre array of national monuments presidents proclaimed; instead, it included a range of places, easily accessible by highway, that contained a far broader series of messages for the American public. By the end of the 1920s Americans could visit recreation-oriented national parks and monuments and scenic ones, a few historic places, archaeological ruins, and a range of natural areas where the kind of physical experience that became faddish during the 1920s was primary. The hegemonic message of fin de siècle parks was muted in the 1920s, mixed with a variety of other messages that offered the growing convenience of American society, the experiential freedom and challenge that young Americans especially craved as a rite of passage, and the sense of power that came from navigating the roads, trails, and paths of the American West. This broadening of national park holdings and the new means to reach them were instrumental in the emergence of recreational tourism.

Nowhere was this growing distinction more evident than in the efforts of the Park Service to explain—"interpret" in agency parlance—the meaning of the national parks. As the 1920s ended, the agency invested heavily in creating an educational division to interpret the scenic national parks. As some people within the Park Service, especially Frank Pinkley of the Southwestern National Monuments group, pointed out, intellectualizing the emotional impact of national parks did little to further social objectives. Turning the vistas of the Grand Canyon into a taxonomic tour of plant life hardly persuaded first-time visitors of the special meaning of the national parks or the American experience. Until the system acquired historic sites during the 1930s, education in the national parks lacked direction; only at Pinkley's archaeological national monuments did the concept make sense.[16]

The emphasis on education revealed an important fault line in tourism that even the flexible and adaptable Park Service found difficult to negotiate. Its leaders aspired to attract the elites, and the agency continued to offer the affirmation of the fin de siècle in a reflexive manner to the middle-class automobile travelers of the 1920s. As they strategized, Park Service leaders recognized that this audience differed from those who rode the trains. The former possessed a set of values that granted primacy to the individual. Park officials sought to educate people who simply wanted experience, who valued the automobile trip as much as the destination. The early problems of the Educational Division stemmed at least as much from this misreading of audience as they did from turf wars within the agency.

The depression and the New Deal rescued the Park Service from the fate of anachronistic interpretation. The depression challenged American institutions and values. In a 1932 summer train trip to see the parks, a habit of early directors, Albright was astonished at the depth of resentment toward the Hoover administration and the lack of respect for what he considered American values. After Albright's famous ride with Franklin D. Roosevelt in the first days of his administration and the pivotal role of the Park Service in early New Deal programming, the agency's focus included Albright's broader plans for the park system.[17] Also encoded in that new conceptualization was a need once again for affirmation.

One dimension of this need encouraged the Park Service to use its broadened mission to convey a positive social message. Its officials needed little encouragement; Mather and Albright shared the values of American elites, and Albright's successor, the often ineffectual Arno B. Cammerer, followed their lead. The depression decade was hard on the American sense of self. One disheartening event, such as the emigration of 200,000 Americans to the Soviet Union in search of work, followed another. Confidence in American institutions stood at all-time lows. In Roosevelt's government, with the old Bull Moose Republican Harold Ickes at the helm in the Department of the Interior, the idea of an affirmative function for national parks did not seem unusual.[18]

Yet the history the park system contained and the areas the Park Service acquired under the reorganization of 1933 did only a little to support a meaningful affirmative function. Most were battlefields, episodes in Civil War or Revolutionary War history that had great emotional power but little depth in national consciousness. Gettysburg had enormous significance, but its struggles seemed idiosyncratic, out of step with the civilian adventure called into question by the New Deal. Such places spoke to specific moments in the American past, not to its grand sweep.

In 1935 no federally managed historic place articulated the broad contours of American history. Unlike the natural wonders that so enthralled the late nineteenth- and early twentieth-century public, historical places were part of a continuum of human experience that required explanation. These were stories that had to be told, not felt, and they were messages that the nation direly needed. With New Deal resources at their disposal, federal officials conceived of a monument to the historic past, one that could equate the problems of the present with the obstacles that Americans had overcome in their past. This unprecedented invention of meaning found expression in the Jefferson National Expansion Memorial (JNEM) in St. Louis, where the Park Service and its academic consultants reaffirmed the vision of westward expansion as a way to counter the cultural gloom of the 1930s.

Americans in that decade needed accessible affirmation of a national cause, and the message of the site aimed at a hegemonic value system, expressing the ideals of the American quest from its roots in the idea of a city on a hill to its fruition in the conquest of the continent. JNEM was invented to convey precisely this story. From its inception, the scope of JNEM covered more ideological territory than any other park area; by building from the ground up, its planners could shape an intellectual construction with genuine social value. The charge to create the memorial encouraged such thinking. In early 1935 Roosevelt authorized the U.S. Territorial Expansion Memorial Committee to formulate "plans for designing and constructing a permanent memorial on the Mississippi River, at St. Louis, Missouri, to Thomas Jefferson, the Louisiana Purchase, the Lewis and Clark Expedition and other important movements in the achievements connected therewith in the Mississippi Valley or elsewhere in the United States."[19]

If the government planned to spend money to shore up sinking spirits, it could do worse than construct a monument to American expansionism. The gateway to the West, the portal through which much of nineteenth-century America passed on its way West, St. Louis remained the midpoint of the nation. It was also a logical location from which to portray the breadth of westward expansion. JNEM represented the moment when the United States first felt its substance, a frame of reference worth recapturing in the dark 1930s. It offered an overview of American experience, linking discrete events in a chronological structure that elevated the disparate achievements of eighteenth- and nineteenth-century America to the status of myth. The Territorial Expansion Memorial Committee created a site with extraordinary cultural significance.

Compared to other historic preservation efforts, the scope of JNEM was unequaled; even the Rockefeller-funded restoration work at Williamsburg did not compare. The restoration of Williamsburg preceded the depression and the collapse of American institutions, and it lacked an explicit cultural message. JNEM was designed to articulate the glory of the American past and to link it to the future of the nation. At Williamsburg, physical structures were restored; the Jefferson National Expansion Memorial rehabilitated ideas, giving them new vitality.

Roosevelt backed this psychosocial quest with federal money. On December 21, 1935, he signed Executive Order 7253, authorizing the memorial and allocating $6.75 million from the Emergency Relief Appropriations funds for 1935. The city of St. Louis also contributed to the project, bringing the total funding to $9 million.[20] The National Park Service acquired land for the memorial under the Historic Sites and Buildings Act of August 21, 1935.[21] The constellation of forces aiming to resurrect history in support of contemporary social objectives took shape.

A $9 million expenditure to create a historic site articulated a new primacy for an affirmative, red-white-and-blue history that seemed anachronistic; only the circumstances of the depression decade kept this from being an elite folly. The vast sum of money created numerous jobs, and as JNEM took shape, it became a beacon to a society in turmoil. The designers recognized this need. In 1937 a subcommittee of the Advisory Board of the National Parks, Historic Sites, Buildings and Monuments composed of museum expert Hermon C. Bumpus, historian Herbert Bolton, and Archibald McCrea reported that the initial plans for the memorial needed modification. The three wanted the site to "signify the realization on the part of the nation, in its early youth, that it was destined to occupy an important position in the family of nations, and that . . . it was justified in trying to arrange its estate according to [a] conception of its ultimate maturity. It was a national realization calling for national action."[22] The experts envisioned a place that linked the events portrayed at other sites into a cohesive ideology.

No further rationalization for the emphasis on this one area ever became necessary. Located at the gateway to the West, JNEM became the figurative connection between the Civil War and the Oregon Trail, between the Big Horn battlefield and Bunker Hill. The memorial became the emblem of Manifest Destiny in a time when the optimism of that idea shored up failing national spirit. The specialists saw their conception as a symbol for a nation muddling through the greatest tests its institutional structure had ever faced. Faux history for a weakened nation provided a way to hold up the values of a distant, glorious, and mythic past and to cast it upon the future. Part crystal ball and part backbrace, the Jefferson National Expansion Memorial was designed to put the fortitude of the past into the crisis of the present. The mood of the young United States was to be recaptured in the rejuvenation of an economy gone sour.

In this conception, JNEM served as a microcosm of the American experience. It existed to validate the achievements of nineteenth-century Americans and to lead their descendants to a potent heritage, transformed to suit current goals and purposes. The essential purpose of the memorial, Bumpus, Bolton, and McCrea believed, was "to record and explain the series of important events incident to the growth and maturity of the nation. . . . [It] would become an inspiring volume rather than a highly interesting chapter."[23] JNEM became a living lesson in American values for the traveling public. Here was a successful America, quite different from that of the 1930s, held up to reveal a path lost along the way.

Historic sites became part of a tourism of hegemony but in a more desperate, less confident fashion than at the turn of the century. The history constructed at JNEM was politicized to its core, especially during the 1930s. The scenic wonders of the fin de siècle had artfully masked that dimension. JNEM and other historic places served as an elaborate and seemingly objective civics lesson, a psychological tonic for the socioeconomic ailments of the nation. They inspired pride and persistence and guided Americans toward a lost ingenuity and resourcefulness. As Americans wheeled up in their automobiles, they were encouraged to feel that they shared a link to the national past. They too were adventurers, they too were strong enough to overcome hardship.

In this redefinition of significance, automobiles changed the hierarchy within the park system. During the railroad era, the great western parks, Yellowstone, Yosemite, Glacier, the Grand Canyon, Rocky Mountain, and Mesa Verde, dominated. Their superintendencies pointed toward agency leadership positions in Washington, DC, a salient feature of the early Park Service.[24] Roads and the changing values of visitors granted new significance to a range of areas. From JNEM to Shenandoah National Park, from Dinosaur National Monument on the Utah-Colorado border to Homestead National Monument in Nebraska, most did not fall in the large mountaintop national park category.

Travelers now brought expectations that differed from their elite, railroad-bound predecessors. Park officials had to accommodate what one travel writer, Hildegarde Flanner, called the "strangeness made homelike by the sight of campers and their tents" in almost every national park. Automobiles rendered the older divisions of class and status in accommodations, perfected at the Grand Canyon, Yellowstone, Zion, and Yosemite, obsolete. Whatever their differences, auto campers seemed of the same class and certainly shared experience. The national parks seemed more democratic.[25]

Even support operations used the automobile to transform experience. Beginning in 1926 the Harvey Company offered Indian Detours, single- and multiday trips around northern New Mexico, from its headquarters in Santa Fe. The first two cars left the Casteñada Hotel in Las Vegas, New Mexico, in May 1926 with four passengers, a driver, and a guide in each. They toured northern New Mexico for three days, staying two nights at La Fonda in Santa Fe and one in Albuquerque. As the Harvey Company had at the Grand Canyon, it soon monopolized the touring-car market in Santa Fe, which had been the province of local operators since early in the century. Erna Fergusson trained guides, "the daughters of senators," advertisements attested, for the Indian Detours. After R. Hunter Clarkson, an Englishman who was the son-in-law of AT&SF official Arthur G. Wells, purchased the operation from the Harvey Company, service became even better. The guides wore the hand-hammered concho belts and squash-blossom necklaces of the Southwest as they took visitors wherever a trail led for $100 a day.[26]

During the late 1920s, the Indian Detours maintained the elite, hegemonizing message in the form of its travel even as it used the freedom the automobile provided to expand the range of sites tourists could see. By 1927 the Indian Detours added service to Mesa Verde National Park; by 1930, when La Posada Hotel in Winslow opened, the detours had an important Arizona base. Building off the railroad routes, the Indian Detours provided an alternative reality to that of the rails. After Clarkson bought the company and renamed it in 1931, he served the more than 47,000 passengers.[27] Figurative and literal distance from the railroad grew, as auto touring in northern new Mexico manifested the change in the significance of travel. The road from Bernheimer's idiosyncratic adventures to the railroad-controlled Indian Detours to Clarkson's CourierCars spoke volumes about the changes in the structure and meaning of auto travel.

Tourist destinations devoid of railroad influence also appeared as the automobile gained position and place in American society. The new mode of travel made far-away places attractive, many of them national monuments and other designated sites and others simply locally controlled or regionally owned. The automobile could reach such places, could negotiate narrow tracks and trails to places that railroad passengers could only dream of. The automobile altered tourist destinations for the public of the 1920s.

No place served as a better example of this process than Carlsbad Cav-

Typical of the vehicles that carried tourists during the 1920s and 1930s, this Clarkson Bus was one of the mainstays of the famed Indian Detours. (Courtesy of National Archives.)

erns National Park, which catapulted to prominence during this era. Anglo Americans had been aware of the enormous network of caves beneath a portion of the Permian Uplift in southeastern New Mexico since before the turn of the century. An industry that took bat guano from the caves and shipped it to southern California for use as fertilizer in orange groves helped create a regional economy in southeastern New Mexico, but only in 1924, when Dr. Willis T. Lee and *National Geographic* first described the caves, did this unique feature attract public attention. Stunning increases in visitation followed, from about 1,280 in 1923 and 1924, the year Carlsbad Cave National Monument was established, to 10,904 in 1925 and 1926 and a remarkable 76,822 in 1928 and 1929.[28] Under the leadership of Col. Thomas Boles, who thought no promotional stunt beneath him, the monument flourished.

Carlsbad Caverns became the first area to force itself into the national park category with automobile visitation. Its evolution from monument to park followed a tried-and-true pattern within the park system, but no other park changed status for the same reasons. Zion National Park acquired its status because of Mather's appreciation for its scenic beauty, Grand Canyon for its iconographic significance. Only Acadia National Park in Maine became a park because of increased visitation, and in the late 1910s and 1920s, its growth came from trains.[29] From the moment of its establishment, Carlsbad Caverns National Park served as a prototype of the new parks that automobile travelers demanded.

Carlsbad Caverns differed from the great scenic parks in almost every respect. Its discovery by the nation resulted from a scientific endeavor, and the publicity reflected science and romanticism. It was small in comparison to even the smallest of the mountaintop parks, and its main feature was underground and required a guided tour. Although the interior of the cavern was amazing, unlike El Capitan in Yosemite or Mather Point at the Grand Canyon, the place was a curiosity. From the moment an elevator replaced a pulley and bucket rig and an underground lunch counter opened in 1927 on the cavern floor, 750 feet below the surface, Carlsbad Caverns was tuned to the increasing emphasis on convenience in modern America instead of to the older, more reverential notions of the meaning of nature. The people who visited the caverns were awed but not overwhelmed as were visitors to the Grand Canyon.

Accommodation to the demands of the new marked Carlsbad Caverns as different from the Grand Canyon and every other place shaped to reflect the values of fin de siècle America. Humans were intruders at the Grand Canyon or Yellowstone; at Carlsbad Caverns, the Park Service made people feel at home. They could eat, walk around with a guide, and generally feel part of the place. Carlsbad inspired emotions similar to the great natural parks, but it seemed somehow more tame, more supple to the touch of humanity, less a reflection of the great contest between humans and nature on the American continent. Instead of compelling visitors to think of a wild nature of the past, Carlsbad provoked questions about how science modified nature, a point driven home by the many magazine articles about the caverns. *Popular Mechanics* especially illustrated this relationship; a 1939 article averred that "nature, the greatest showman of them all, outdid herself on Carlsbad Caverns . . . but it remained for modern science to make it accessible and convert it into the most dramatic natural phenomenon in the world."[30]

Carlsbad was always promoted in a manner that was inherently different than the other national parks. Jim White, a cowboy who mythologized himself with a story so successful that many credit him as the modern discoverer of the caverns, popularized the area even before *National Geographic* crews arrived. Boles, from 1928 the superintendent for twenty years, had his own agenda. Among the activities he initiated was the Rock of Ages ceremony. The ranger leading the guided tour would bring his group to a stunning stone formation in the Big Room of the cavern. There he extinguished the lights, asked for silence, and as one writer recalled, "and got it," and in the

A postcard of the lunchroom in Carlsbad Caverns National Park, 750 feet below ground. The lunchroom was a great attraction for the auto travelers of the 1920s and 1930s. (Collection of the author.)

absolute darkness, "Rock of Ages" was played. The moment had tremendous emotional power. Audiences were routinely reduced to tears, and for many visitors, the Rock of Ages ceremony was the most memorable event of a trip to Carlsbad Caverns.[31]

The caverns provided an experience different from seeing over Mather Point, watching Old Faithful erupt, viewing Tower Falls, or even gazing at El Capitan in Yosemite National Park. For the many people who protested the surreptitious end of the Rock of Ages ceremony in 1944, the ceremony, not the cavern itself, was the most powerful memory of their experience.[32] Here was nature subordinate to human imagination and manipulation, a wondrous place made understandable by brazen and direct orchestration that appealed to the most meaningful and to the most contrived emotions Americans possessed. Clearly tourism aimed at automobile travelers presented intellectual conceptualizations that travelers on fin de siècle luxury trains would have found base.

In this redefinition of the meaning of nature, the visitors who sought Carlsbad Caverns moved toward a recreational ideal. Nature no longer evoked thoughts about culture and society; it was a curiosity, a wonder. It no longer overpowered, as did Yosemite, Yellowstone, or the Grand Canyon. It could be made friendly, turned on and off as individuals needed. Instead of subsuming the individual in the setting, this new nature was organized to cater to the individual. Its impact scripted, its importance secondary to that of individual experience, the nature revealed at Carlsbad Caverns stood beyond the collective awe of the fin de siècle and foreshadowed the personal challenge embodied in the activities of recreational tourism.

The new automobile travelers also moved the focus of the identity tourism fostered from the national onto a long path toward the personal. The Grand Canyon had a collective purpose, an affirmation of national objectives, but Carlsbad Caverns melded that aspect with much more personal dimensions. Even the Rock of Ages ceremony, as contrived as it was, attempted to move viewers from the personal to universal goals. It demonstrated that automobile visitors responded to cues different from those of their railroad-based counterparts. Diffuse, and in the late 1920s, largely originating in Texas, a state with an identity and self-image large enough to fill the caverns, automobile visitors at Carlsbad Caverns reflected the change in the meaning and constituency of tourism.

These automotive arrivals also created new vectors of visitor service. Before the automobile became important, concessions and accommodations in national parks had been captive to train audiences. Location was critical. The Park Service enjoyed great control over these operations, assisting the ones its officials thought served visitors in the appropriate fashion and refusing its services to business that did not conform. This symbiosis had been an important goal of Mather's, and his decade at the helm solidified it as agency practice.[33] Carlsbad Caverns defeated this stratagem, proving that national parks reached by automobile depended less on the Park Service and more on the road.

The development of White's City, named not for explorer Jim White but for C. L. (Charlie) White, who homesteaded the tract astride the road that led to the caverns, illustrated another of the ways in which automobile tourism broadened the conventions of travel. When Charlie and Emma White arrived in southeast New Mexico from Kentucky in 1909, the approach road to the cavern entrance served only the guano industry. White came to New Mexico for the dry air; like many arrivals since the turn of the century, he initially worried less about how to make a living than about the air he breathed. White taught school at Francis, New Mexico, herded sheep, served as cashier in a bank he tried to start, and installed the first gasoline pumps at Loving, New Mexico. In a chance meeting in 1926, he encountered Jim White, and on hearing of the caverns and Jim White's promotional efforts, Charlie White

White's City was typical of the tourist accommodations just beyond the boundaries of national parks. (Postcard collection of the author.)

rushed to Carlsbad to file a homestead claim on one-half section, 320 acres, that straddled the road at the turn-off. He had never even seen the land.[34]

In 1926 automobile visitors had yet to reach the caverns in huge numbers, but White, a seasoned entrepreneur, anticipated that a deluge would not be far behind. Like Ralph Henry Cameron at the Grand Canyon, he owned his land, putting him beyond the reach of federal officials. White built a Texaco station, a little cafe, and put up ten tents. Despite struggling to acquire water, he found himself in control of a precious resource, the only stop with food, gasoline, and overnight accommodations between the town of Carlsbad, twenty miles down the road, and the caverns. A tireless worker, White developed the area; by 1940 not only did White's City sport a post office, but it also offered more than 300 rooms that were typically filled each night during the summer season.[35]

Like many early tourism entrepreneurs, White was a character who did anything he could to attract visitors and entice them to stay. More than thirty billboards dotted the roads to White's City, each announcing a different attraction there. White opened the Million Dollar Museum, full of hundreds of butter molds, typewriters, bear traps, roller skates, buttons, shoes, postcards, and other implements of daily life. The rattles of almost 100 rattlesnakes stood beside animal horns and heads, doll houses, and other curiosities. A two-headed rattlesnake and a two-headed turtle once graced the museum, and the head of the twelfth largest moose ever shot in Wyoming remains. Kiss-o-meters, an arcade device that used an individual's handshake to rate their puckering style and ability, offered a diversion.[36] Road travelers might not be awed by White's City, but they were likely to be amused.

White's City posed some problems for the Park Service. Like Cameron's hotel and the Kolb brothers' studio, it was outside their reach, but it played an important role in shaping how people regarded the caverns. The fact that White shared the same last name as the unrelated Jim White, who served as ranger at the caverns until the 1940s, also hindered the Park Service's efforts to create a respectable image for Carlsbad Caverns. The collection of kitsch outside the park somehow intimated that what was inside it was no more sacred. The lunchroom on the floor of the cavern, while convenient, also accentuated the sense of the caves as profane space, as part of the modern world. Even Superintendent Boles's showmanship, designed only to attract attention to the park, often compromised it. His hucksterlike approach helped draw a line between Carlsbad Caverns and the scenic national parks.

The relationship between White's City and Carlsbad Caverns illustrated an always-problematic situation for the Park Service after automobiles became a primary means of conveyance: how to ensure the quality of experience when the agency did not control the people and facilities that offered service. At the Grand Canyon, control had been accomplished by moving the train depot closer to the appropriate facilities, but that was when rail passengers made up the overwhelming majority of visitors. With automobiles and roads, parks such as the Grand Canyon experienced the same situation as did Carlsbad. With myriad ways to approach the park and many choices among places to stop on the way, visitors could be subjected to influences that combined to undermine the impact of the park's message.[37] At Zion and Grand Teton, a plethora of businesses, dance halls, gasoline pumps, and cafes opened along the boundaries of the park, depending on the park but somehow diminishing it as well. This broader market was far more difficult to manage.

National park amenities differed from those of the roads. Most parks, such as Glacier, had the roots of their services in the railroads. Mt. Rainier, proximate to Seattle and Tacoma, relied on the regional business community. People of the same class as Mather ran such operations, and camaraderie between Park Service leaders and these local elites developed easily and lasted.[38] Operators such as Charlie White or the Kolb brothers were different; they had little allegiance to the Park Service, a need to maximize their own investments, and often, little sense or appreciation of the larger objectives of park leaders. When Mather went to Chester Thorne, general manager of the Rainier National Park Company, to discuss business, he usually encountered a more receptive audience than he might have with Charlie White or other independent operators.

The regulated monopolies the Park Service established also codified the hierarchical structure of capital that preceded national parks in western communities. The Park Service selected local elites, ensuring that under its control, economic success and its own version of appropriate service would be intertwined. These elites operated from positions of power within communities and typically did not share its perquisites. The hierarchical nature of local communities was transferred to park operations, which remained overwhelmingly seasonal, ensuring that its benefits accrued narrowly within the social spectrum. Only outside entrepreneurs such as Charlie White could counter this intrinsic effect, and as such people succeeded they developed their own hierarchical view. Although the Park Service slowed the ingress of outside power in places such as Carlsbad Caverns, it did not help change the often unequal structure of local economic relations.

Yet automobile travel did provide ways for local businesspeople to resist change. Its popularity meant that more visitors came not only to Carlsbad Caverns but also to nearly every other attraction, auto camp, and gasoline station. Businesses that fared poorly with the national parks had only to set up shop outside the park boundary, at a nearby crossroads, or in a nearby town, where they could sell or say whatever they wanted. Some of the examples of this strategy annoyed national park advocates. John D. Rockefeller purchased much of the land in Jackson Hole to prevent common intrusions such as dance halls and gasoline stations from marring the vista of the Grand Tetons. Approved and unapproved businesses had plenty of customers, and the control of the Park Service remained limited. Local businesses could resist, could control local government, and could battle the Park Service because the automobile offered such an open form of transportation.

Despite myriad efforts to influence concessions outside parks and to alter the messages offered by small-time operators, the Park Service never successfully controlled activities outside park boundaries. The combination of local animosity, hostile congressional representatives, antigovernment sentiment, and the older ideas of states' rights and individualism limited any authority that the Park Service could exert. As a result, park officials concentrated on activities within park boundaries, as at Mount Rainier, where a local camping club that had run an operation within the park found its right to transport campers to the park in jeopardy.[39] This control strengthened a psychic line drawn between land outside the park boundary and the special, sacred space within.

The clarification of this distinction further separated the older hegemonic tourism from the automobile-based recreational tourism that included national parks and so much else. Railroad tourists alighted from evidently modern space into a transition zone when they reached the amenities of the south rim of the Grand Canyon. The sacred space of the canyon stood beyond them. Automobile travelers who reached Yellowstone crossed miles of terrain outside the park identical to that located within park boundaries. Only the guard's box and perhaps a marker delineated the difference. In places such as Carlsbad Caverns, the lunchroom on the cavern floor further muddled the perception of distinctiveness. A ride to Carlsbad Caverns in an automobile offered few of the distinct demarcations of a train ride to Yellowstone.

Consequently, the conceptualization of the specialness of travel was reinvented in a manner that mirrored the rise of recreational tourism. As the challenge to the individual replaced the message of cultural affirmation, auto travelers became the center of their own story, the trip itself part of the experience. This necessarily diminished the destination and changed the tourist's relationship to it. The hardships and travails of the road taught as much as did the inn at its end, and instead of being a separate part of the journey, as was a train trip, the road and the goal merged into one continuous narrative.

From these new circumstances grew a tradition in American society, travel as a rite of passage toward self-fulfillment. Deeply rooted in national myth and existing in many forms before the 1920s, this need took a new shape with the automobile. Automobile tourists inspired others, and a generation of travelers followed. For innumerable reasons the automobile came to represent independence and freedom. From this grew a tradition in which the automobile served as the means of escape. Haydie and Ted Yates served as prototypes; one night in 1927, as they arrived home from a summer in Europe, they spontaneously decided to flee New York, where she worked at the *New Yorker* and he in real estate. "We resigned our jobs, listed our apartment . . . cashed in all our savings," Haydie Yates wrote, and they were on their way to Wyoming, to them a place both mythic and real. They had met there, he rescuing her from an unwise marriage to a dude rancher and hunter, and they retained an abiding affection for the place. The West made them whole, represented all that was free about the world and about their love for one another. The six-day automobile trip, made in their "unkempt but fashionable foreign clothes," served as the ticket to their freedom, the transition zone between past and exciting future.[40] As it had for post–Civil War migrants heading West, the trip encouraged the process of reinvention that enabled the couple to come out whole at the end.

Although there were other more famous versions of this story of reinvention, no more perfectly whole recitation of the myth existed until Jack Kerouac came along in the 1950s. *On the Road,* the classic American novel of the Beat generation, recapitulates the Yates's story in an urban setting. It is also the wild and spontaneous abandonment of New York and the East, also of reinvention in the West—in Denver, ironically—also about finding truth and meaning and casting off banality and becoming whole.[41] In this sense, automobile travel foreshadowed far more than the end of the tourism of hegemony. Kerouac's journey also presaged the obsession with individual freedom that engulfed the nation in the second half of the twentieth century.

Recreational tourism offered many manifestations of individualism, of the pitting of the self against the world. Although the very mobility of the automobile seemed to make controlling a tourist industry impossible, these other forms used the principles of recreational tourism and offered its message, further promoting the diversion from historical standards. In a changing America, first in the Jazz Age and later during the depression and the New Deal years, even winter sports, essentially the skills of survival for rural winter life, became part of the cosmology of individual achievement.

7

From Steamboat Springs to Sun Valley

Regional and Nationally Marketed Skiing

The automobile gave travelers freedom of movement and a broader range of experience than did railroad tourism, but it did not always offer them a feeling of personal satisfaction derived from accomplishment. Although drivers and passengers might appear enthusiastic when they arrived on the rim of the Grand Canyon, their triumph was tempered by their dependence on the very technology that their travels attempted to escape. They too were spectators, watching from an automobile window closer to the world than the railroad car offered but still not entirely of it. In this sense, the freedom of the automobile, though temporal, became intellectually bittersweet. Automobiles provided excitement, but thousands of miles of bad roads, uncomfortable beds, stale food, and consistent breakdowns and repairs curbed its power. The freedom that the people of the 1920s sought came from other sources.

Skiing offered a way to personally achieve the strong sense of individual control over raw nature that American travelers craved. It also maintained important class distinctions. In harmony with the tone of the 1920s, an individual sport such as skiing required none of the cooperation and interdependence that typified the Progressive Era and World War I. Even the dominant team sport of the 1920s, baseball, possessed overwhelmingly individualist dimensions. Unlike other team sports, which required continuous cooperation among players, baseball was a series of individual confrontations punctuated by vignettes of cooperation. Skiing offered similar individualism. It provided a confrontation with nature and gravity; it represented a kind of freedom, a feeling of sheer exhilaration combined with exercise that manifested the exuberance of the 1920s. Skiing also hinted at the triumph of technology, embodied in the process of getting to the top of a mountain in relative comfort. Yet such a recognition was too profound for many people in an era bent on shedding the restraints of the past in a quest for independence.

The messages and experiences of skiing and recreational tourism differed completely from those of the tourism of hegemony. Outdoor experience, camping, fishing, skiing, and the like, offered real and unavoidable contact with nature. In comparison, the tourism of hegemony merely allowed the existence of such relationships. A fisherman in a western stream stood in hip-deep icy water; visitors to the rim of the Grand Canyon or at a hotel in Yellowstone or Glacier had to choose to experience that cold, that motion, the sheer exhilaration of that moment from a menu of other options, dictated by their culture or the railroad. Even leaving the hotel for a day- or week-long adventure in the wild was still somehow different than engaging in the same activity without railroads and hotels to cushion the experience.

Among these outdoor activities, skiing provided the clearest view of the changing nature of the meaning and practice of tourism. It started as a specialty sport in the 1920s and 1930s, difficult and expensive, limited to the upper classes and regional audiences, but definitive in the West. Extralocal visitors to the mountains gave up the freedom the automobile offered to enjoy the exhilaration and independence of the winter outdoors. Trains, the most controlled form of hegemonic transportation, conveyed enthusiasts to base points, from which skiers departed over a managed and sometimes unmanaged landscape. In this construct, not significantly different from the Indian Detours of Santa Fe or a nature walk at the Grand Canyon, industrial society provided the context—the train tracks, the amenities, and the opportunity—in which experience could occur, but the experience itself highlighted individual aspirations and emotions and not the dominant goals or values of American society.

In the West, skiing began as a local and regional activity but before World War II had become a national activity marketed to a national audience. In places such as Steamboat Springs, skiing began as a symbol of community unity and became something more; at Sun Valley, it emerged as a form of national popular culture. The transition from local to national presaged dramatic changes in communities that harbored the new sport and augured the invention of the form and context of postwar recreational tourism. Through skiing, recreational tourism moved from local to national, from parochial to central in the iconography of American society.

Like many other recreational activities in American society, skiing began as necessity. Its transformation moved it from a reflection of skill to an activity that defined high-elevation snowy regions, such as the Steamboat Springs, Colorado, area, to a sport for the wealthy, who saw the activity as part of a social rather than an economic regime. In this transformation, skiing took its place among the desirable and exclusive pastimes available in the West. As it acquired cachet, the sport anticipated a more affluent, more mobile future, one in which communities were reinvented as ski towns, or in some instances were started from nothing, for the sole purpose of recreation. In the typical pattern, locals conceived of using skiing as an economic strategy; but outside capital, in the form of Union Pacific money at Sun Valley in the 1930s, was essential if skiing were to fulfill such dreams. When outside capital came in and success followed, the patterns of neonativity, outside control, limited opportunity for locals, and a hierarchy that displaced them followed.

Before recreational tourism, the history of skiing in the American West followed typically utilitarian patterns. It long provided essential transportation for people at higher elevations and in snow-filled climates; Native Americans fashioned snow-travel instruments even before coming across the Bering Straits. Trappers and other explorers depended on similar conveyances during winter or bad weather expeditions. Beginning in the gold rush of 1848, which attracted sizable numbers of Scandinavian and Swiss immigrants, skiing took on European traits. Proto–cross-country skis, "snowshoes," became essential for winter transportation. These eight- to twelve-foot-long slats of white pine or spruce were cut to a four- to six-inch width and one-inch thickness. Doctors traveled to patients on these long and clumsy boards; midwives used them to reach expectant mothers. The mail arrived in snowbound and mountain communities by ski. Some itinerant preachers used skis to reach remote congregations. Even census takers had to ski. It was the only dependable form of winter transportation, although the dangers from overexposure, cold, avalanche, and injury were very real. The story of a skiing mailman, who in 1880 lost nine toes to frostbite, was typical; the death on skis of a frozen Per Hansa in O. E. Rolvaag's *Giants in the Earth* was an extreme example of the hazards of winter travel. For those who lived at high elevations, the ability to ski was essential, its necessity tempered by the inherent risk.[1]

As the population grew and Americans transformed activities that had been necessary for survival two generations earlier into recreation, skiing became a substantive local and regional industry. Winter meant drudgery

Steamboat Springs in the 1890s, before skiing, before the Winter Carnival. (Photo courtesy of the Tread of the Pioneers Museum, Steamboat Springs, Colorado.)

in western mountain communities, especially on remote farms and ranches. Travel became impossible and people felt trapped, experiencing the unwelcome, unbalanced feeling of cabin fever. As a counter, westerners who habitually skied created competitions that exalted the skills necessary to survive high-altitude winters. These events initially offered locals the means to test their skills and provided a community ritual to anticipate during the inevitable whiteness of winter. Ski competitions mirrored the famed turkey shoots and no-holds-barred wrestling contests of Daniel Boone and his peers in the Ohio Valley. These rituals ranked people within the hierarchy of the community and formalized bonds among its members. Soon the level of expertise attracted a few hardy visitors, and a new source of revenue emerged for towns that offered such events and were easily accessible.

Steamboat Springs, Colorado, led such communities. Located in the Yampa Valley in Routt County in the north-central part of the state, the community carved an economic identity for itself before the advent of recreational skiing. Rabbit Ears Pass, a summit beyond the mountains east of town, prevented contact with the outside world each winter. In a place where people measured the severity of the winter by the number of strands of barbed wire, each ten inches apart, covered on a fence by snowpack—the famed four-wire winter of local legend—the people of Routt County fended for themselves. Only between the heaviest snows could mail and supplies arrive by sled, snowshoe, and ski. With peak snowfall topping 260 inches, sixteen feet of snow atop the mountains, and as much as four feet consistently on the ground in town in an average year, Steamboat Springs seemed destined to winter isolation.[2]

Early in the twentieth century, Steamboat Springs offered a model of diversified economy in the typically one-industry West. Raising stock was a primary regional economic activity, and the remarkable water-glass-sized Remington strawberries that thrived in the soil and climate of the region provided a brief moment of agricultural prosperity. Summer tourism became one of the first industries to augment agriculture and ranching. Featuring fishing, hunting, and "delightful scenery and cool breezes," the small community fashioned itself an "inter-mountain resort" and experienced a surge in summer visitation during the 1890s. But tourism attracted only a small number of visitors, a small segment of the wealthy travelers who dotted the western landscape. Limited access to the mountains and the competition from other communities that offered similar amenities combined to keep profits small. Tourism remained a sideline for the community, seasonal and undependable. Characteristic western sources of revenue sustained Steamboat Springs. Sheep and cattle provided a solid ranching industry. Strawberries offered a future until 1917, when the industry collapsed. Steamboat Springs's diverse economy became monodimensional, and the community searched for a new source.[3]

One possibility was the mineral springs trade, made viable when the Denver and Salt Lake & Pacific Railroad—the Moffat Road—reached Steamboat Springs through the mountain passes in 1909. This seasonally dependable way to reach the region provided a consistent tourist trade. The town had much to offer; it received its name because early arrivals thought that the bubbling of its springs sounded much like an arriving steamboat. The 150 springs in the area promised a trade similar to that of Idaho Springs and Hot Sulphur Springs. With the completion of the Moffat Road, Steamboat Springs more aggressively courted the mineral springs trade, a practice it shared with numerous places with similar amenities. Charting a future in summer tourism presented real difficulties, and Steamboat Springs sought a niche. In 1910 the Cabin Hotel, containing 100 steam-heated rooms, opened. The waters there were purported to cure all kinds of ailments, one pamphlet noted, "especially rheumatism, kidney and bladder troubles." Another seasonal economy, limited in scope and reach, held out promise.[4]

The most telling feature of each effort in Steamboat Springs was its dependence on the short summer. The abbreviated season was the stuff of local lore. Some wags referred to the supposed thirty-one-day length of the growing season. One old-time joke had a grizzled local responding to a newcomer's questions about summer by saying, "I don't know about it. I've only been here ten or twelve years and we haven't had one yet." The cool breezes and warm sunshine of August quickly turned to ice, snow, and harsh winter winds, and the regional economy depended on the variable summer season. In the winter the community simply closed its doors. Families with automobiles put them up on blocks until spring. Transportation ceased. Even the railroad could not guarantee regular service. Tracks crossing the 11,000-foot-high Corona Pass were often snowed under, and plowing roads to isolated communities was expensive, often impossible, and rarely undertaken early in the twentieth century.[5]

By 1915 technology played a major role in the economy of Steamboat Springs and Routt County, but its impact remained seasonal. The railroad provided a dependable source of transportation but only during seven months of the year. In the winter, those who could went "outside," local slang for leaving the community until spring. There was little to do in an agricultural and livestock-based economy in the deep snow. The best technologies of the early twentieth century did not yet offer stable and consistent access in the interior of the Rockies.

During the winter the people of Steamboat Springs got around on skis. Skiing was birthright and obligation in Routt County. Everyone in town, boys and girls alike, were raised on skis. "I learned so early I have no recollection of it," Carol Rickus, who was born in Steamboat Springs in 1918, asserted. All were proficient by the age of seven, and many depended on their skis for communication during the long winters. Locals became expert practitioners. In one instance, Marjorie Perry, the iconoclastic daughter of a family with considerable coal and railroad interests, made skiing into an obsession. She was renowned for skiing to Denver and back, a 320-mile round trip.[6]

In an effort to liven up the winter, in 1913 Steamboat Springs planned a winter festival that highlighted skiing. In doing so the town followed an old American tradition; it celebrated prowess in an activity essential to its survival. This ritual accentuated the meaning of community and the sense of togetherness critical in remote communities. As people shared activities such

Children in Steamboat Springs often could ski as soon as they could walk. (Photo courtesy of the Tread of the Pioneers Museum, Steamboat Springs, Colorado.)

as long-distance ski racing, sprints, and shooting matches from skis, they felt the bonds that held them together. The festival catered to a predominantly local audience, keeping spirits up during the long winter.[7]

After a chance meeting, the Flying Norseman Carl Howelsen, an international ski jump champion and an attraction in the Barnum and Bailey Circus, became part of the Steamboat Springs festival. The pivotal figure in the popularization of skiing as a sport in the United States, Howelsen immigrated to America in 1905 and worked as a stonemason in Chicago, became a founding member of the Norge Ski Club of Chicago within months of his arrival, and was quickly recognized as an exceptional skier by his peers. He designed a ski jump at Cary, Illinois, the first of its kind in the country, and found his place in history by adapting a carnival attraction, the "shoot-the-chute," a ninety-foot tower with a chute that dropped into a pool of water, for skis. In his first attempt, Howelsen shot almost 100 feet out of the chute and into the water. Later, he again adapted the chute, building a ramp at the bottom that gave him a lift of as much as sixty feet in the air. This sight of this lone man arcing through the air on Chicago mornings drew crowds that grew

Carl Howelsen and his friends in Steamboat Springs. Howelsen greatly contributed to the special identity of the town. (Photo courtesy of the Tread of the Pioneers Museum, Steamboat Springs, Colorado.)

and grew; he became a local celebrity. Barnum and Bailey's Greatest Show on Earth recruited Howelsen, and in 1907, for the unheard-of sum of $200 per week, the Norwegian immigrant with the unique talent joined the circus. He traveled the country, jumping in front of more than 1 million people, but departed and returned to Chicago and resumed working as a stonemason. His brief circus career was over, but ski jumping gave him near celebrity status.[8]

Howelsen's move to Denver in 1909 precipitated the first winter carnivals in Colorado. After settling in Denver, Howelsen became involved in the nascent Swiss and Scandinavian skiing community there. A Swiss named John Peyer heard Howelsen's tales of the ski festivals of his youth and borrowed the concept, assembling a winter carnival in Hot Sulphur Springs, about ninety miles west of Denver, as 1911 ended. The winter carnival was an extension of the county fairs and other forms of social get-togethers typical in rural parts of the nation. What set them apart was the time of year they took place—winter—and the activities featured in them. As these immigrant westerners exalted the skills necessary for their survival, they broke new ground and repeated time-honored patterns of American and European life. These events simultaneously showcased local ability and spoke volumes about the technological successes of the industrial age. Even in lower-elevation mountain towns such as Hot Sulphur Springs, skiing remained an important skill. In a town that depended on a summer trade, a winter activity that brought some paying customers was a virtue. Without a railroad, the people of Denver could not have enjoyed Carl Howelsen's skiing exhibition.[9]

The winter carnival at Hot Sulphur Springs became an annual event. The first one served as a prelude to another later the same winter, 1911–1912. Hot Sulphur Springs, which had used its mineral waters to fashion a summer economy based on visitors, seemed likely to develop winter trade as well. The combination of accessibility and amenity increased its popularity. A moving picture company planned to film the carnival, and the townspeople believed they had created a special niche that would sustain their community better than the ranching, mining, and other unorganized extractive activities. Hot Sulphur Springs was one of many possibilities in the summer. The winter carnival depended on the same transportation routes as the mineral springs trade, but it enjoyed a significant advantage: in the winter, the amenities Hot Sulphur Springs offered were unique. A kind of protorecreational tourism, combining mineral springs and skiing, appeared to be in the ascent there.[10]

The intrepid Marjorie Perry changed that. She recruited Howelsen to Steamboat Springs, farther into the mountains. On his first visit, Howelsen fell in love with the area and settled in the community. He provided a tremendous impetus for the start of winter activities, and in 1914, copying Howelsen's idea, Steamboat Springs debuted its initial full-fledged winter carnival. The two-day affair featured racing and jumping for men and women, amateur and professional, capped by the pinnacle of the competition, the grand professional jump. Howelsen won the professional competition, pocketing a sizable cash prize.[11]

Although competition was inevitable, each town's identity stamped its carnival. Easily reached by rail, Hot Sulphur Springs created its event for tourists. With Howelsen, the premier name in American skiing, Steamboat Springs offered far better attractions, but the question of reaching the town always posed problems. Before the completion of the Moffat Tunnel in 1927, which gave the nation a central rail route through the Rockies, the largest audience remained local; when the train could make it through the pass, an outside audience sometimes arrived. Even when visitors came, they were few in number and generally avid ski enthusiasts who easily fit into a community where skiing was a way of life. At the first carnival, twenty residents of Den-

The ski jump was the highlight of the early winter carnivals. (Photo courtesy of the Tread of the Pioneers Museum, Steamboat Springs, Colorado.)

ver were counted among the 1,500 to 2,000 spectators. Locals and nearby ranch families constituted the crowd. With the exception of Howelsen's ski jumping, most activities and festivities aimed at local audiences. The crowning of the first Borean Queen, Ruler Supreme of the Slaves of Snowland, in Steamboat Springs in 1916 illustrated the importance of local audiences. Selected from among the young women of the area, the queen received fifty dollars in gold and a fifty-dollar certificate from a Denver dry goods store for a ceremonial gown, a meaningful prize for a young woman from a small town. Forty-two entrants from nine Yampa Valley towns responded; the winner was crowned in the Cabin Hotel and led a carnival parade down Lincoln Avenue, the main street in town. This festivity both entertained locals and bound them even more closely together. Despite the presence of Howelsen, the limitations of existing transportation networks ensured that well into the 1920s, Winter Carnival remained a local and regional event aimed at an audience of peers.[12]

As late as 1927 Winter Carnival remained a distraction, not a source of revenue. Its audience remained Yampa Valley people and its events reflected local tastes. Few outsiders arrived for the festival; when they did, they entered a place that seemed engrossed in the kind of ritual that anthropologists sought to record elsewhere around the globe. The people in the streets hailed from Routt County, and they understood its signs and symbols. Outsiders must have felt the distinction in a place where everyone knew everyone else by name. The county fair mentality remained untainted. Affluent visitors did not purchase homes and stores, seek their favorite meals in restaurants, and otherwise impinge upon the town. At the Winter Carnival, the people of the Yampa Valley celebrated the skills, the courage, and the sense of community and self they needed to survive in the snowy mountains. They knew little of the desires of visitors.

Two features of the carnival did have the potential to attract outsiders: Howelsen's ski jump, completed in 1915, and the practice of "ski-jöring," a race where skiers were pulled through town by horses. Both events excited audiences. Howelsen's prominence and his design of the slope on the south edge of town attracted other professional ski jumpers. Ski-jöring was useful as a form of transportation. After the founding of the Steamboat Springs Winter Sports Club in 1915, a promotional entity for the carnival came into being. Not only did the club encourage local youth to ski, but it also helped promote the community to ski enthusiasts elsewhere in the region energized by a boom in winter sports activities on the front range of the Rocky Mountains.[13]

During the 1910s winter sports became a fashion in urban areas in Colorado. This interest, which reflected the changing lifestyles and habits of urban Americans and the back-to-nature cult of the era, created a broader audience for outdoor winter activity. Far more so than the people of Steamboat Springs who participated in the winter carnival as a celebration of essential activity, Denverites who embraced winter sports in the aftermath of a major snowstorm on December 4, 1913, engaged in a form of recreation. When, in response to the storm, residents poured into the streets and undertook a range of outdoor activities, they did not plan to use skis, skates, and sleds as regular means of transportation. The falling powder that triggered outdoor sports meant regular transportation would not function. Traffic tie-ups, streetcars and trains that did not run on time or at all, and other impediments to movement were an aberration. In Denver, skiing to work was truly an exhilarating, once-in-a-lifetime experience that accentuated its residents' sense of identity.[14]

Denver residents were hardly connoisseurs of outdoor experience. Accustomed to limited winter mobility, they found conditions in nearby mountains sufficient for sport. They did not envision vacations there; they merely sought invigorating exercise or an opportunity to see the splendor of new-fallen snow. They were not skilled in outdoor winter sports, nor did they typically need to be. Limited winter transportation possibilities created barriers, especially for skiing. The nearby peaks of the front range were too far to travel for recreation in adverse winter weather. Enthusiasts faced a paradox: the snow that enabled outdoor sport also made the potentially best places for such activity much harder to reach.

The December 1913 storm was inspirational, and in its aftermath groups formed to promote outdoor winter activity. Organized by enthusiasts in 1912, the Colorado Mountain Club conducted its first annual ski outing in Rocky Mountain National Park in 1915. Soon after, companion clubs formed in Boulder, Colorado Springs, and Estes Park, and subgroups within each club promoted skiing at different locations. The Genessee Winter Sports Club organized immediately after the December 1913 storm. One month later the Denver Ski Club, sometimes called the Denver–Rocky Mountain Ski Club, formed; by 1928 it had become the largest club west of the Mississippi River. In 1924 the many local clubs joined in a statewide organization, the Colorado State Ski Association. Renamed the U.S. Western Ski Association in 1927, the organization and its powerful first president, C. W. Broomell, brought a national ski championship competition to Colorado that year. The snow-clad Rockies, previously worthless for commercial economic purposes in the winter, developed a new kind of value.[15]

But the mountains were still distant, and the solution to the problem of access was the development of winter sports aimed primarily at regional audiences. By the 1920s in Denver, a local ski industry developed. Skiing became a sport Coloradans could embrace. In 1919 Denver's Colorado Arlberg Club built a 1,000-foot ski jump on Genessee Mountain, just outside of Denver. Rilliet Park, also on Genessee Mountain, attracted the local social set, and the Rilliet Hill Club, an offshoot of the Colorado Mountain Club headed by socialite Lucretia Vaille, set the tone for society skiing. Proximity, easy access to the mountain, and the exclusivity of a sport that required expensive equipment made skiing popular among the affluent. Skiing as recreational sport in the West gained momentum, but its scope remained extremely limited.[16]

The opening of the Moffat Tunnel solved the problem of access. It provided a year-round link between the intermountain area and the front range, giving Steamboat Springs and other towns consistent and easy rail access to Denver. For fifteen years, the people of Steamboat Springs held their winter carnival for themselves. The Moffat Tunnel changed that; instead of being for a purely local audience, the event soon aimed at visitors as much as locals.

The intermountain communities enjoyed a ready constituency, the people in front range communities who experimented with skiing. As a direct result of the opening of the tunnel, the popularity of Steamboat Springs dramatically increased. Instead of remaining a distant local attraction, its Winter Carnival became a day trip for the people of Denver.[17]

The Moffat Tunnel also created new, easily accessible places to ski, some of which were more challenging and at higher elevations than the Denver area locations. The Colorado Arlberg Club cut its own ski trails at West Portal, where the tunnel opened on the western side of the Continental Divide. Construction cabins became skiers' huts, providing a resting place and occasional overnight housing for enthusiasts. The Winter Park ski area came together under the watchful eye of Graeme McGowan, who founded the Arlberg Club. As a recreational activity, skiing developed a structure, albeit a rudimentary and local one.

The transformation of skiing from cross-country style to downhill also increased the constituency for the sport. Downhill skiing, with the wind whipping as a skier accelerated, was almost as exciting as Howelsen-style ski jumping. But it also depended on getting to the top of a hill with a trail to ski down. Downhill allowed relative novices most of the thrill of the ski jump without requiring the expertise. The traditional cross-country skiing was hard, physical work; the new activity was fun. In Steamboat Springs, people were so ensconced in their way of skiing that when McGowan arrived in town in 1931 and taught the "Kristiana turn," the slalom racing turn, two years passed before a Steamboater placed in the new downhill races at the carnival.[18] The revolution had begun, and the downhill skier, whose skill had far less practical application, soon replaced the cross-country skier who previously typified Routt County and the high-elevation rural West.

The constituency for this new recreational activity remained largely regional. Skiing was an enthusiast's game. Denverites who took the initiative and enjoyed the leisure time and money traveled the farthest to ski. Few travelers from the East planned vacations to ski the slopes outside of Denver; on a Colorado slope, such people were experienced ski enthusiasts or visitors to the region trying out an activity popular with their local friends. Colorado skiing largely served Coloradans, as did other similar local ski areas throughout the West.

The popularity of skiing grew even during the depression decade. At Mt. Rainier National Park, a day-use ski area opened early in the 1930s, serving the people of Seattle, Tacoma, and the coastal Northwest. In a decision typical of the time, the National Park Service encouraged the concept. At

Timberline Lodge on Mt. Hood, Oregon, a similar endeavor serving Portland began. At Yosemite National Park, the first winter carnival was held in 1931; by December 1935, a lodge and ski runs greeted winter visitors. In the early 1930s, the Denver and Rio Grande Western Railroad (D&RGW) operated a ski train from Salt Lake City to Gogorza on the Park City, Utah, line. On February 9, 1936, the first Denver and Salt Lake Railroad "snow train," sponsored by the *Rocky Mountain News,* left urban Colorado for the mountains. That year, Hot Sulphur Springs was the primary destination as Coloradans received the opportunity to "see what the real 'snow country' looks like in its majestic beauty." The first trains coincided with the winter carnivals. Subsequently, trains regularly left for weekend and week-long excursions to ski areas throughout Colorado. By 1938 nearly every accessible place to ski enjoyed train service, and trains carried more than 2,000 skiers to nearby slopes.[19]

New access encouraged widespread development of skiing as a commercial activity. The throngs who filled the ski trains encouraged the individuals who envisioned an economic future in the sport. Long-term success in skiing depended on proximity to a large urban area and dependable transportation. All along the front range of Colorado and well into the mountains, communities sought this new economy. In 1937 Berthoud Pass, near the western opening of the Moffat Tunnel, commenced operations and quickly became the best known ski area in the state. In Creede, Leadville, Telluride, Colorado Springs, and other places, ski trails dotted the sides of mountains. A European count taught skiing to locals on the slopes of Pike's Peak, volunteers used their own axes to clear skiways at Arapahoe, and the recreational club of the Climax Molybdenum Corporation groomed the slopes at Leadville and paid for lighting. One newspaper, the *Leadville Herald Democrat,* asserted that skiing could revive old mining towns, but this remained wishful thinking. The nascent ski industry still served a small and mostly local constituency, hardly the impetus for the full-fledged economic transformation of remote towns.[20]

Recreational skiing in the West still experienced one primary problem: physical access. The sport demanded deep snow, steep slopes, and difficult terrain, but the infrastructure and technology to deliver people to such places in inclement weather remained limited. Nor were the systems to support skiing well developed. Since the advent of downhill skiing, skiers needed more than open, snow-covered terrain. To ski down, they had to get to the top of good skiing mountains. Few people would climb a hill merely to ski down. Many ski centers lacked even rudimentary rope tows, relying instead on boats or pontoons pulled by tractors to bring skiers to the hilltop. Most skiers considered two runs from top to bottom in a day the maximum. Skiers were hearty, genuine enthusiasts, atypical of tourists in their search for rigorous activity. They were also a minority, too small in number to sustain an industry. In Colorado, access to first-rate ski terrain existed, but the amenities that could turn a backwoods experience into the "roughing it in style" that Americans travelers expected was expensive, time-consuming, and hardly the goal of the enthusiasts who dominated the local scene.

Skiing as a recreational activity ran against the dominant trends in the western tourist industry. Since the 1860s, western tourism had offered higher levels of amenities to travelers who sought the comforts of home in different settings. From the Hotel del Coronado outside of San Diego to El Tovar at the Grand Canyon, visitors dined and relaxed in luxury that equaled any city in the nation. Even the self-consciously primitive dimensions of Santa Fe's tourist trade offered upscale amenities. The luxury of the Inn at the End of the Trail, La Fonda, was a welcome sight for many who rode the buckboard from the train station at Lamy. "Roughing it," code words for leaving the well-worn paths of tourist travel, involved some diminishment but hardly the abandonment of luxury. Only the back-to-nature movement early in the century and the rise of the automobile countermanded the upper-class features of tourism.

Hard, outdoor exercise and the values of the wealthy of the 1920s and 1930s did not mesh well, removing skiing from the realm of typical travel by the elites. During the Jazz Age, the culture of the nation followed a different orientation. The 1920s embodied frenzied abandon, the kind of wanton behavior so common in the works of authors such as F. Scott Fitzgerald. The rigors of skiing provided the antithesis of such sentiments. Nor were outdoor winter activities fashionable. The abundance of wealth in cold northern cities and the sophisticated travel infrastructure, advertising industry, and climate made Florida a major destination. Industrialists, civic leaders, and gangsters spent winters in Miami, leading to a huge resort industry there and a cultural iconography that isolated western skiing as a local phenomenon.[21]

Yet visionaries who recognized that they stood on the cusp of a popular form of recreation developed ski resorts. One group attempted a full-fledged resort near the old mining town of Aspen, Colorado. Aspen had been in decline since the silver panic of 1893, and its leaders sought a revival. During the 1920s they advertised Aspen as a summer vacationland, an economical playground where visitors could see "the majestic wonders of our ageless sentinels." The Forest Service established a primitive area, its wilderness designation during the 1920s, in the nearby mountains.[22]

Summer tourism alone failed to develop the local economy. Still, the D&RGW sought a major attraction in Colorado. The railroad refurbished its nineteenth-century tracks to Aspen, first constructed to capitalize on a late 1880s mining boom and to preempt the efforts of competitors. The initial resort featured four modest cabins and a lodge, housing about fifty guests. Although the D&RGW's effort featured a horse-drawn sleigh, it did not compare to the opulence of competing resorts.[23]

The nascent effort in the mountains attracted other entrepreneurs. Attempting to capitalize on the potential of the Aspen area, Thomas Flynn, a pioneer in the Roaring Fork Valley where Aspen was located, William L. (Billy) Fiske III, an Olympic bobsled champion and scion of a New York banking family, Robert Rowan, a Los Angeles real estate magnate, and Ted Ryan, a New Yorker with inherited money, hired Swiss avalanche expert Andre Roch to design a ski trail at Highland Slopes, halfway between Aspen and Ashcroft, about twelve miles apart. Predicated on the belief that streamliners, the new railroad cars of the 1930s, would make Aspen an overnight trip from Chicago, the men named their prospective hotel the Highland-Bavarian Lodge, installed a 1,600-foot tow rope, and planned a tramway, a "teleferique," to the top of Mt. Hayden. From there, the visitors were to ski down into Ashcroft.[24]

The project faced many obstacles. The infrastructure upon which Flynn and his friends depended remained tenuous, and despite their wealth, the partnership experienced trouble raising funds. Fiske financed the early stages of development, but he and the other partners left much of the work to Flynn, their local manager. Flynn spent two years in search of funding. Though he enjoyed some success, he could not raise enough for a large-scale project. Yet the partners remained optimistic.

The group's dreams obscured their understanding of the situation. They misread the audience for skiing, planning ski runs for experts and ignoring the need for a broad constituency. They also linked their success to the tramway alone, seeking a wealthy clientele and discouraging visitors until they could offer extraordinary skiing and top-flight service. The partners never recognized that their competitors offered lower-cost accommodations to bring in the middle class as well as an exclusive clientele. In one instance, despite borrowed capital that required interest payments, a small lodge to fill, and ski trails deemed among the best in the world by their publicity material, Flynn discouraged a prospective client by explaining that until the tramway opened, the area had "just ordinary terrain to offer." At the same time, local newspapers touted the development as a new destination.[25] The choice was a calculated gamble. In Flynn's view, if he and his friends could not offer extraordinary skiing, they had little claim on skiers who reached more easily accessible locales. But the partners failed to realize that for many people, what an expert would call ordinary skiing to them meant a pleasant vacation in the mountains.

A potential constituency for Aspen existed. Skiers in Colorado sought remote or unique places. The Exposition Flyer reached Glenwood Springs, reducing the difficulty of getting to the Aspen area to a forty-one-mile drive, and the Highland-Bavarian Lodge offered a carrying service that met people at the train station in a "heated station-wagon."[26] For the exuberant, Aspen was a genuine possibility. The popularity of other areas, particularly those along the train lines, created a constituency in search of a less crowded, more individualistic experience. The equivalent of the cultural tourists who sought out Santa Fe from the railroad station in Lamy, they craved the pristine and the pure.

The growth of the local ski industry and the involvement of local government changed the economic terrain in which Flynn and his partners operated. George Cranmer, manager of the Denver Department of Parks and Improvements, spearheaded a drive that developed West Portal, the old trail at the western end of the Moffat Tunnel, into the Denver Winter Sports Park, commonly known as Winter Park. Cranmer and Howelsen developed a friendship during the 1910s, and as parks manager, Cranmer crafted a coalition in favor of the project despite its seventy-mile distance from Denver. Opponents suggested that Cranmer indulged his rich friends with the project, but he secured funding that included Public Works Administration (PWA) funds and an additional $30,000 to build a one-half-mile rope tow. Designed as a recreational area for Denver and owned by the city, Winter Park blossomed after opening in 1940. The park featured intermediate ski trails that most skiers easily navigated. Its older neighbor, Berthoud Pass, offered good skiing and also was within easy reach of Denver. The two areas became the primary regional ski areas for the front range.[27]

Cranmer's development dimmed the chances for success in outlying areas that competed with the city-sponsored project. The opening of the Berthoud Pass resort cut the chances of rescuing Flynn's Ashcroft endeavor through the middle-class constituency that the partnership previously overlooked. It also coincided with the last Hot Sulphur Springs Winter Carnival, an event rendered irrelevant by the opening of the new park. Funding for the Aspen venture became more tenuous as investors lost interest in a remote ski location. After Flynn discovered that with Cranmer's support, the Berthoud Pass–West Portal ski area received a federal grant that ensured its construction, he too pursued New Deal money, but to no avail. When financing for the tramway fell through, the partnership collapsed.[28]

Despite having a vision of a first-class ski area, the Aspenites marketed their town before the infrastructure necessary for their endeavor existed. Tourists could reach Denver by train, but getting from there to the Aspen area remained a chore; ski areas closer to Denver were far more accessible. Flynn and his friends could have marketed their enterprise with greater zeal, but their genuine constituency represented a fringe group within the skiing community. The remote situation suggested that the chances of economic success remained marginal. Although Aspen capitalized on Roch's presence and hosted the 1941 National Downhill and Slalom Races, it lacked the features of a national tourist destination.

Lacking dependable transportation, the Aspen venture was doomed. Skiing in Colorado still was primarily a local habit; in many places hiking up the mountain was the only way to get to ski down. Despite the more than 70,000 people who skied in Colorado in 1938 and 1939 and a boom in ski areas between 1939 and 1942 when Monarch, Winter Park, Wolf Creek, Ski Cooper, and Pioneer opened, without the power of a major corporation Aspen lacked the necessary components to survive. It was on the wrong side of the mountains, too far from populations that could ski closer to home. Flynn and his partners correctly recognized that Aspen needed a national constituency. They simply lacked the means to ensure that those people arrived at their mountain in a timely, comfortable manner.[29]

The economic impact of local and regional skiing remained limited. Given the difficulty of attracting visitors from afar, the relatively few who could afford to make daily outings into week-long journeys, the limited transportation and accommodations, and other similar obstacles, skiing as tourism seemed designed to fill a minuscule niche in the regional economy. Unlike summer travel, which was transformed by automobiles, roads, and the national parks and monuments set up to accommodate visitors, skiing remained confined to the intraregional level. Locals made up the bulk of the market. Enthusiasts from all over the country might occasionally arrive, but they were too few in number to foster economic growth. Skiing seemed destined to remain a local activity, supported by local tax dollars for the benefit of a regional audience, and administered as much for fun as for profit.

The limitations of skiing as a sport were those of the scope, scale, capability, and vision of its promoters and the technological restrictions of the early twentieth-century West. Cranmer and others had goals, but they served a regional, day-use population. The visionaries at Ashcroft possessed grandiose objectives but lacked sufficient common sense, capital, infrastructure, and marketing experience. The winter itself was a deterrent to travel. It ruled out the automobile, greatly shrinking the market. Nor were amenities available in any consistent fashion. Although some ski areas enjoyed first-rate, nearby accommodations, most offered more haphazard services. Western skiing for a national audience awaited someone who could consistently deliver the experience of skiing to a national audience on the terms it expected. Skiing was a sport; national consumable skiing, a form that linked experience with symbols, required much more.

National rail lines, the dollars that supported them, and the history of a class-based tourism offered the means to transcend the limits of regional skiing. Having the resources of a major economic force in the American marketplace, W. Averell Harriman, owner of the Union Pacific (UP) Railroad, created a national attraction with western skiing. Harriman understood the relationship between status, cultural cachet, and sport. Less a skiing enthusiast than a businessman, Harriman sought increased passenger traffic on his rail line during the depression. The surge of interest in skiing following the 1932 Winter Olympics at Lake Placid, New York, attracted his attention. In places such as Killington in Vermont the popularity of skiing grew, even after the icy experiences of Lake Placid, but Harriman's rail lines were closer to western slopes than the already crowded hills of the East. Harriman sought a place that was far enough from western cities and close enough to the main line of his railroad to ensure a healthy passenger trade in the winter. He wanted to invent everything about such a place, from its location and amenities to the transportation networks that would deliver his visitors.

Harriman offered a broader conceptualization of the economic and cultural value of skiing than previously existed elsewhere in the United States. Extant ski resorts in the nation catered to a remarkably narrow constituency; enthusiasts from nearby cities made up the skiers on the slopes of Stowe, Vermont, as completely as they did at Yosemite National Park or Mt. Rainier. The combination of cost and skill, limited access, and the expensive accommodations kept the ranks of skiers to two basic categories of people: the wealthy and the die-hard aficionados. Harriman added a new dimension. He intended to make skiing into a vacation pastime by increasing its profile with the American public and associating the activity with status and celebrity.

His plan turned skiing into a national activity enjoyed by the people whom Americans idolized, the stars of the silver screen who so dominated American vistas in the pit of the depression. Harriman simply needed the right place, one that only his railroad could reach.

To find this Shangri-la, Harriman selected an Austrian who possessed considerable experience with European resorts, Count Felix Schaffgotsch, to travel the West and assess various areas. In some ways, this was a quixotic quest that evoked memories of nineteenth-century Europeans who explored the West for specific purposes. Like Prince Maximilian of Wied, Karl Bodmer, Charles Drummond Stewart, and Baron Heinrich von Möllhausen, the count took his instructions as personal purpose. In professional and personal affairs, Schaffgotsch was something of a raconteur, but according to Harriman, the count knew tourists. Staying close to the UP's main tracks, Schaffgotsch evaluated more than a dozen locations before 1935 ended. In some places the count found excellent skiing, but most were too close to cities. Potential Union Pacific passengers could either use other rail lines, or in some instances, could reach the location by automobile. Places near Seattle, such as the Mt. Rainier slope, or Salt Lake City, such as Alta, were too close to population centers and too competitive to risk the investment a new resort required. Others, such as Jackson, Wyoming, and Enterprise and Joseph in Wallowa County, Oregon, were too far from the main track or were too steep for the novices and average skiers Harriman understood were his market. Local legend in Wallowa County offered a different version; in the story, one man refused to sell the land above Wallowa Lake to the railroad, eliminating it from consideration. Aspen, at an elevation of almost 8,000 feet, was too high for the count. In his estimation, ski areas should be no higher than 6,000 feet. With increasing doubts about success, he combed the intermountain region.[30]

Schaffgotsch spent weeks exploring, but the hunt for an extraordinary ski area to match those of the Alps reached a dead end in the American West. After a final week of futile search in Idaho, the count left for the Brown Palace Hotel in Denver, and his companion for his trips in Idaho, UP area representative William J. Hynes, retreated to a Boise establishment, the Locker Club. Over a scotch and soda with Joseph Simmer, the Idaho director of highways, Hynes described the many trips. Simmer asked if Hynes had toured the Hailey and Ketchum area. "By God, no," Hynes responded, in a mythic version of the encounter. "I forgot." He wired Schaffgotsch, who returned to Idaho, and in December 1935 the two proceeded to the Ketchum area.[31]

Reaching Ketchum in the winter remained an arduous task. The railroad ran to Shoshone, about forty-five miles away, but no consistent form of winter access continued past that point. Local residents recognized the problem; those who could, in their parlance, "went out," departed the region for the winter, most to lower-elevation Jerome, Idaho, a considerable distance from Ketchum. The roads were snowpacked, making automobile travel impractical. Hynes prevailed upon Simmer to get him and the count through. "You got me into this mess," Hynes purportedly told Simmer in a heated telephone conversation. "Now get me out." The district engineer drove a bus full of people taking advantage of the unforeseen opportunity. In the deep snow, the bus got stuck, and because of Simmer's ties to the highway division, a snowplow arrived to ram through to Hailey and Ketchum ahead of the bus. The only real hill dropped into the Wood River Valley, and outside of Ketchum, the bus skidded off the road into a snowbank. There Schaffgotsch got out of the bus and looked around. What he saw reminded him of a small village in the Alps dominated by a huge mountain and smaller hills around it. Although the valley was too wide for a resort near Hailey, the count could see genuine promise.[32]

At the base of the Sawtooth Mountains in the Wood River Valley, Ketchum had no economic future when Schaffgotsch arrived. During the 1880s silver mining created a brief heyday. With thirteen saloons and a general store, the town's population had reached 2,000, dwindling for the following fifty years to the approximately 270 who remained in the 1930s. Freight reached the nearly abandoned town on the old Oregon Short Line, built to carry silver. Passenger service could be found only at the rail stop at Shoshone. To Dorice Taylor, who later became a local legend during her twenty-five years as the head of the Publicity Department for the Union Pacific in Sun Valley, Ketchum was "just a wide spot in the road." It was a cold, poor area, especially during the 1930s. The growing season was always short and animal husbandry difficult; one resident recalled regularly keeping stock alive by carrying cottonseed cakes to them during the winter.[33]

Schaffgotsch looked through a different lens when he saw the Wood River Valley. From his perspective, the isolated community had one unsurpassed attribute for a ski area: a small, open valley, less than a mile from Ketchum's Main Street, protected from fierce north winds, and surrounded by treeless slopes on the mountains at its edges. Schaffgotsch's excitement was palpable; the valley looked more like a European ski area than any other place he had visited. It afforded an ideal location for Harriman's resort. Even better, the only way to reach it in the winter was on the Union Pacific line. Schaffgotsch was smitten. Locals suspiciously eyed his clothes and thought his European manner effete, and local entrepreneur Jack Lane, who wintered in Jerome, advised friends not to cash the count's checks unless the Union Pacific guaranteed them. Schaffgotsch spent three or four days cross-country skiing with a local youth. The two traversed the mountains from top to bottom, crossing hundreds of acres of pristine powder that seemed perfect for alpine downhill skiing. Schaffgotsch envisioned a resort in this remote place.[34]

In the apocryphal version of the story that Harriman frequently told, Schaffgotsch could not restrain himself. As soon as he could, the Austrian cabled him, extolling the virtues of the Wood River Valley: "I've found it! Come and see for yourself! . . . It contains more delightful features than any other place I have seen in the U.S., Switzerland, or Austria for a winter sports center."[35] A new economic purpose for the defunct mining town had been conceived. The question of its implementation depended on factors outside the region.

Harriman possessed the capital, vision, and control of the access; his willingness to invest remained the only intangible. The resort had been his idea in the first place, and with the positive recommendation from Schaffgotsch, Harriman was excited, and as he later recalled, also "skeptical but interested." He invited his friends William Paley, chairman of the Columbia Broadcasting System, and Paley's wife Dorothy to join him for a trip to Wood River Valley in Harriman's personal railroad car. Harriman's daughter, Mary, and two Austrian skiers accompanied the travelers. Within days, the entourage reached central Idaho, finding an idyllic winter wonderland. Hynes rigged up a covered wagon with a stove, and the group traveled by day and returned to cabins on Bald Mountain overlooking the valley at night. For Harriman, the trip was instructive. As he traveled the valley jostled about in the covered wagon, he realized he had found what he sought: the place really was perfect for a ski resort.[36]

Harriman's visit illustrated the elements necessary to create a full-scale tourist industry. As had the arrival of the AT&SF at Grand Canyon, Harriman's trip inaugurated new ways of framing the meaning of the Wood River Valley. Like Santa Fe, Ketchum had a coded value, revealed only through a different vision of its attributes, the application of technology, and a level of capital investment impossible from within the region. Harriman's arrival in the Idaho mountains was a catalytic moment in recreational tourism that fused place and image.

Once Harriman agreed to the conception, the process of transforming the Wood River Valley began in earnest. Land for the resort became the immediate need. The legal department of the UP descended upon Ernest Brass, a rancher who had lost his cattle to poisonous larkspur weeds and his sheep to the plummeting prices of the depression and whose daughters, Roberta and Marjorie, served as guides for the Austrians who assessed the region. Harriman paid $4,000, a little more than one dollar per acre for 3,881 acres. The daughters even contributed to the selection of the location of the lodge. Roberta Brass pointed out to the count the place in the valley where the cows huddled on the coldest winter days. Schaffgotsch selected it for the lodge; the congregating cattle proved it the warmest part.[37] The mixture of local knowledge and outside capital seemed a potent combination.

Harriman set out to create a national image. He hired a public relations specialist, Steve Hannagan, a man who hated winter and could not conceive of the pleasure of skiing but whose previous accomplishment was the creation of Miami Beach for the northeastern public. On a spectacular sunny March day in 1936, Hannagan found himself sweating in the snow of Ketchum and promptly named the resort Sun Valley. The new moniker reflected a vision different from the name Wood River Valley. Harriman planned a medium-sized hotel, but Hannagan returned to New York bursting with plans for a $1 million luxury hotel where the famous and wealthy would become part of the spectacle. He bombarded Americans with the image of a young man, muscular, handsome, and stripped to the waist, skiing through the powdery snow of Sun Valley. Although the advertisement was photographed in a Manhattan studio, it represented the ambience that Hannagan promoted as Sun Valley. Regional newspapers quickly picked up on the development. Reporters were fed press releases from Hannagan's publicity machine, and sensing the economic importance of the venture in the depression-ridden state, they eagerly anticipated the opening.[38]

As the gala planned for New Year's Eve, 1936, drew near, the excitement became national in scope. The 250-room lodge, built to rival the chalets of the Swiss Alps, filled for the grand opening. Errol Flynn, Robert Young, Melvyn Douglas, Claudette Colbert, David O. Selznick, and numerous other celebrities attended the affair, dining on an exquisite meal of Brioche au Caviar, Supreme of Sole au Champagne, and Tournedos Saute Chatelaine. A lack of snow almost made the festivities pointless, but when it fell on New Year's Eve, Sun Valley became the St. Moritz of the United States, a place with far more glamour and more exciting skiing than anywhere in North America. "The whole country was crazy about skiing and where skiing was concerned, Sun Valley was IT," Dorice Taylor recalled much later. "If you had the money to ski, you came here." Hannagan took the notion of roughing it in style, crucial to the development of tourist amenities in the West, and raised the stakes. He made Sun Valley a place where guests could "rough it in luxury," a concept that extended the definition of amenities beyond existing limits and made no illusions about creating cultural distance from the mainstream. Sun Valley glorified celebrity from its inception; its image created new excitement that embraced wealth, unlike Santa Fe, where manufacturing a distance from Main Street culture attracted an economically similar but culturally distinct constituency.[39]

Sun Valley was popular from the outset. People flocked to the resort in the winter, basking in the reflected glare of the many celebrities who came to enjoy the ambience. Being seen in Sun Valley in the late 1930s was truly being seen; it added cachet even to the lives of the wealthy. The resort publicly connected them to Hollywood stars, creating an iconography of proximity to the idols of the moment. On the slopes and in the restaurants and bars of Sun Valley, photographers captured a seductive intimacy. Recognizable public figures and their less well-known friends found themselves gracing the pages of national newspapers. Print, film, and radio media readily accepted Sun Valley's iconographic meaning, and Harriman and his railroad basked in the concentric rings of glory that surrounded their endeavor.[40]

The winter trade possessed genuine importance, but it hardly justified the Union Pacific's expenditure. Nor would an astute business executive such as Harriman tolerate an expensive investment standing empty for more than half the year. To increase the return, Harriman conceived of a crucial strategy that, if he succeeded, would catapult Sun Valley to the highest echelon of resorts. He wanted it to become a year-round resort, one that attracted visitors not only for the prime ski season but also for summer vacations, hunting season in the fall, and at any other time. Beginning as the snow melted after the first winter, when visitation dropped, the Union Pacific publicity machine spread the word. Regional newspapers carried stories about the summer attributes of the region and promotions of planned events such as rodeos and races. The second annual Sun Valley rodeo, held in summer 1938, included 113 participants. They came to what the program touted as "America's foremost year 'round sports center," boasting fishing, hunting, tennis, golf, riding, hiking, and swimming. "Gentle ponies and modern playgrounds" for children were in evidence. By summer 1938, Sun Valley offered the features to support an all-year constituency.[41]

Sun Valley's image as a year-round resort received crucial authentication with the appearance of Ernest Hemingway. He arrived in September 1939 with his companion Martha Gellhorn, staying two months and returning in the subsequent two years to hunt and fish. Harriman recognized the importance of Hemingway for Sun Valley's image. Sun Valley was the place to be during the winter. Hemingway accorded it the same cachet during the rest of the year. When he moved from a suite at the main lodge to the less expensive Challenger Inn at the start of the 1939 ski season, Harriman brought him back at no charge to the suite with the patio where Hemingway reviewed the galleys of *For Whom the Bell Tolls.* The image stuck, perfect for the multifaceted tourism that Harriman sought; three generations later people still spoke of Hemingway on the patio reading his pages as the people around him enjoyed themselves.[42]

During the 1940s all-year tourism at Sun Valley developed, but it never attained the level to which Harriman aspired. Steve Hannagan, who continued to hate winter, fished the Sun Valley area with friends and clients during the summer, but even his remarkable promotional skill failed to attract a wide constituency. Though winters featured an array of wealthy individuals and celebrities such as Daryl Zanuck, Ina Claire Wallace, Gary Cooper, and in 1941 the Texas A&M football team on its way to the Cotton Bowl to play the University of Alabama, the rest of the year remained more tenuous. Sun Valley closed for recreational activities during the war, but even afterward it did not attract a summer constituency that paralleled its winter prestige. After World War II, organizations such as the Split Pea Soup Association and the National Selected Morticians vied for the use of facilities during the off-season. Most of these organizations were regional; the Idaho Coal Dealers Association and the Idaho Optometric Association were typical. They were hardly the same constituency as the winter guests.[43]

The Union Pacific continued to promote spring, summer, and fall activities. Sun Valley served as the summer training camp for the Brooklyn Dodgers and the Baltimore Colts of the All-America Football Conference, which began in 1946 and merged with the National Football League in 1950. Trapshooting became another activity for the off-season. Joe Burgy, the director of Outdoor Activities, placed nationally in a range of shooting contests. The Union Pacific sponsored two trophies, one for shooting and the second for rodeo competition, named after railroad president George F. Ashby; still, the resort attracted only a specialized off-season trade. A basis for a mainstream summer trade did not materialize.[44]

Though the mountains at Sun Valley made its skiing extraordinary, its hunting, fishing, and other amenities were quite ordinary. The snow, slopes, and ambience of the winter became a campground for rich friends and clients of Harriman, Hannagan, and the Union Pacific in the summer. The winter charm of the resort was unique, but its summer offerings could be matched elsewhere. Its iconographic cachet extended only over part of the year, leaving glorious Sun Valley running a deficit in the postwar era.

The opportunities that came coupled with the resort were an integral part of the devil's bargain of tourism. The rails did create access to the town in the winter, did bringing paying customers to moribund Ketchum. But the visitors who arrived bypassed the town and headed straight for the resort. The rules of life in Wood River Valley changed as greatly as had the name, and locals adjusted their dreams to fit the new realities of the town. As in every similar situation, they embraced the opportunities but failed to calculate the cost of the changes in the way they ordered the world.

The resort and the rail spur raised the stakes in the Wood River Valley. The resort obliterated the economy of scale that existed before the railroad. Instead of merchants and ranchers who owned large holdings at the pinnacle, a new standard, based in the world of glitz and glamour and measured by the values and mores of Harriman's wealthy friends, applied. The change from the Wood River Valley to Sun Valley meant more than a transformation of economic base; it created a new hierarchy that altered the symbols and scope of local life.

Local merchants experienced both sides of these transformations. They benefited from the changes by access to a larger potential clientele, but the greatest advantages of the change remained more elusive. Jack Lane, one of the most powerful men in the area before the founding of Sun Valley and owner of Lane's Mercantile, one of the primary businesses in Ketchum, felt the limits of the new regime. Although Lane's Mercantile had been the headquarters for railroad men, contractors, architects, and engineers during the construction of the resort, when the postconstruction plums were handed out, Lane received none. The ski shop in the Sun Valley Lodge, the top-of-the-line hotel in the resort, was initially run by Saks Fifth Avenue and later by a French designer of women's ski clothes, Henrí Picard, a clear marker of the difference between local people and the status essential to Sun Valley's image. Only when the Challenger Inn, with its more modest accommodations and clientele, opened one year later, did Lane receive a ski shop contract.[45] This scripting of prerogative reflected the iconography of the new resort, the realities of the distribution of the economic benefits of its appearance, and the pretensions to status crucial to its high tone. It also clearly showed how power had shifted from locals. Passing over Jack Lane spoke volumes about the relative importance of activities in Sun Valley. Even the most powerful locals, those who had participated in setting up the resort, who had transferred at least some dimension of their allegiance to the incoming powers, were part of an era swiftly and dramatically brought to a close. They became suppliers of materials—if they were fortunate—as the decisions about the community emanated from Harriman's people. Sun Valley functioned with a different set of symbols and meanings than did the Wood River Valley, and nearly every decision made by the Union Pacific reflected that reality.

In employment, a superstructure that elevated specialized expertise at the expense of local knowledge and custom became a consistent feature. Even though locals who stayed in the valley through the winter were excellent skiers, incoming Europeans hired by the railroad laughed at their homemade equipment and denigrated their skills. Designed for durability and transport rather than fast alpine runs, local equipment seemed antique. The condescending Europeans thought that people who used such equipment, Americans at that, could not possibly be their equals on the slopes. Nor did local people have the cultural cachet of foreigners; to Americans who sought skiing as status, a French, Austrian, or Swiss instructor was far more chic than one from Idaho. For the ski school and other skiing amenities, the resort imported Europeans. Hans Hauser, an Austrian ski champion, his "corps of bronzed young Tyrolese instructors," and other expatriate Europeans dominated skiing at Sun Valley. Instructors included Florian (Flokie) Haemmerle, a Bavarian who doubled as an artist and local philosopher; Freidl Pfeifer, an Austrian who later brought nationally marketed skiing to Aspen; and Sepp Froelich, another Austrian ski racer who married Natalie Rogers of the Warburg banking family.[46]

The hotel itself reflected this new ethos. The chefs in the hotel were French, the waiters German; the local women worked as chambermaids. Another German, Frederich Blechmann, ran room service and later became captain of the dining room. Such opportunities were available to those who fit the image of Harriman's resort. Local people, no matter how skilled or subservient, could reach only a limited portion of the Sun Valley myth and its attendant opportunities.[47]

Outsiders, European and American, quickly scooped up most of the economic advantages offered by the new resort. Even organized crime captured a piece of the local action. George Weinbrenner of the Detroit Purple Gang was the reputed owner of the fashionable gambling establishment in Ketchum, the Christianna Club. Dorice Taylor herself played a part in the transformation. She and her husband, Everett "Phez" Taylor, an Ivy League–trained lawyer, embraced the community. He joined a local law firm, specializing in what was then the province of the rich—divorce—and she took over the publicity division at the resort.[48]

Through these movements of individuals, the transformation of the economy clearly emerged. The Wood River Valley needed Jack Lane and his store. As a conduit of information, a source of credit, and a buyer of local and regional products, he attained ongoing significance. Sun Valley rendered Lane irrelevant, importing its own class system and hierarchy, providing its own capital, and maintaining its supply link with the outside by rail. Phez Taylor's kind of service law, unshackling the unhappy rich from their personal mistakes, had greater resonance in the resort economy than did Lane's store.

The advent of the resort quickly altered the demography of Blaine County, where Sun Valley was located. The county was unique in rural Idaho because its sources of income, occupational structure, growth of population, and the chronological distribution of its foreign-born residents became distinctive after the opening of the resort. By 1940 5,295 people lived in Blaine County, up from 3,768 in 1930, a 40 percent increase that exceeded any other rural Idaho county during the same time period. In 1920 and 1930 less than 10 percent of the population of Blaine County was foreign-born. In 1930, 298 Blaine County residents were born outside the United States; most were nineteenth-century immigrants. Of these, 137 were fifty-five years and older, and another sixty-nine were between the ages of forty-five and fifty-four. Although the percentage of foreign-born residents shrunk as a result of the growth in population that followed the opening of the resort, their demography revealed changes in occupational structure in the county. By 1940 the foreign-born population was dramatically younger, as they played an important role at the ski resort. One hundred seven of the foreign-born residents were between the ages of twenty and forty-five, up from the thirty-eight recorded in the 1930 census who would have been part of the twenty to forty-five age group in 1940.[49]

The agricultural economy, the mainstay of the county, also showed changes resulting from the resort's presence. People quickly switched from agriculture. In 1935, 1,647 people lived on farms in Blaine County, roughly 40 percent of the population of the county. By 1939 farm income had dropped significantly in every category of production, from livestock to crops, at a rate faster than that of comparably sized counties in the state. Adjacent Camas and Butte Counties, one to the east and one to the west, showed income drops typical of agriculture in rural northern states during the depression decade, but Blaine County doubled those declines. Replacing this income in what was a modestly more prosperous county than it had been in 1935 were 284 hotel and lodge workers at Sun Valley, making up more than 17 percent of the 1,839 workers in the county. In Idaho, only Ada County, which included the state capital of Boise, had more hotel workers, but more than half of these workers were women. At Sun Valley, 210 of the 284 hotel workers were men, reflecting the predominance of resort workers in the county economy.[50] A new economic niche in rural Idaho had opened up with different gender segmentation than was common elsewhere in the state.

In 1930 Blaine County mirrored other predominantly rural counties in Idaho, but by 1940 the growth of the population and its distribution by age, place of birth, and occupation had become significantly different. Besides showing unparalleled growth during the 1930s among rural counties in Idaho, Blaine County developed entirely new segments in the labor force. No other rural counties included a significant percentage of service occupations, nor did they show as high a percentage of renters of land and housing. The percentage of farmers in the county population declined from about one-half to one-third of the total, but the number of people who lived on farms remained constant. The resort quickly transformed the economic and demographic structure of the entire county.

This economic structure excluded most natives from the opportunities skiing brought. Most people who left the area farms were marginal candidates for permanent employment at the resort. Their primary economic resource became the land they owned, not their labor. Local landowners found that their property had renewed value, yet unless they were young and willing to work in service occupations, there was little for them to do. Most sold their property for what they considered exorbitant prices, only to find that same land selling for thousands of times more within a very few years. Their initial elation turned to dismay as the scope and scale of the resort dwarfed the icons of their earlier world.

From the opening of the lodge, Sun Valley embodied a caste system. At its peak were the guests drawn by the mystique of the place, those who could afford the most expensive accommodations and could match the stars in wealth if not celebrity. After the opening of the Challenger Inn in 1938, a second tier of visitors followed, those who could afford Sun Valley but could only gawk at the stars and their companions. Beneath them, at the bottom of the newly invented social order, were the remaining local people. Most worked in service occupations or owned small businesses in Ketchum. They experienced little benefit from the coming of the resort except for improved transportation. No longer cut off in the winter, most locals remained wage workers who lived in small homes while the rich and famous played at nearby lodges.

This transformation attracted a different constituency, the first of many generations of neonatives to Sun Valley. Dorice and Phez Taylor were prototypical; they were the first incarnation of Sun Valley in the same manner that the Lanes represented pre–Sun Valley Ketchum. Dorice Taylor had grown up in DuBois, Pennsylvania, skiing straight downhill. A teacher at a fashionable New York day school, she first discovered Sun Valley in the window of Sak's Fifth Avenue in New York City. As Sak's prepared to open the ski shop in Sun Valley, they arranged a borax-and-flannel ski chute in the New York store. Dorice Taylor craved skiing, but two winters of limited snow in succession in the East had discouraged her. Her husband arranged for a Sun Valley trip, and they were the first guests to register in the Challenger Inn. Although they actually left Sun Valley after a first and second trip, in Dorice Taylor's account, in their minds, they never left. "To hell with this city," Phez Taylor announced in their sweltering New York apartment one summer day in 1940, "we're going to Sun Valley."[51]

The Taylors were the first of many who abandoned promising careers elsewhere for the combination of greater psychic and smaller monetary rewards of resorts such as Sun Valley. In her memoir, Dorice Taylor remarked that she and her husband were always shocked when they heard of people making such a decision, until they remembered that long ago they had chosen the same route. In this embrace of the shaped identity of the place, they became the archetypical neonatives. Their Sun Valley was that of the Union Pacific Railroad; they took its values and institutions as their own. Dorice Taylor's position as publicity agent for the resort and her social stature as the dowager queen of Sun Valley, a sort of local celebrity who told the tales of the town, reflected that embrace.

Outsiders themselves, the Taylors' tenure depended on the largesse of other outsiders. As long as the Union Pacific ran the resort, their positions, status, and indeed cosmology were safe. Despite his law practice, the couple needed the protectorate created there by the Union Pacific. Natives after a fashion, they were tuned to the rhythms of Harriman and Hannagan's place, citizens of the Union Pacific's regime. They secured their status simply by arriving ahead of the postwar horde, before living in Sun Valley became an attractive prospect even to a minuscule portion of the American public.

The geographical reach of the Union Pacific's Sun Valley was acute within its boundaries but small in the hinterlands around it. Sun Valley was an island; it transformed adjacent Ketchum but before 1960 had relatively little impact on Hailey or other communities in the vicinity of the Sawtooth Mountains. The rails reached Sun Valley alone, and particularly in the summers, visitors traversed the region, but they did not stay and settle. Most merely passed through, engaging in transient activity but causing few permanent changes outside of Sun Valley and Ketchum.

After the war, people came to Sun Valley to enjoy the life it represented. Before the war, Sun Valley had been first in linking celebrity with outdoor sports, the pinnacle of an image of fun and carefree relaxation. Postwar people sought to escape the turmoil, to leave mainstream society behind. Sun Valley offered an unparalleled opportunity, and the original ski bums, who came for the pleasures of the region, claimed the town as their own. Working in service industries, they skied when they could and stayed to enjoy the perquisites of a resort town during the seasons when it was only lightly used. The result was a prototype of a lifestyle peculiar to resort towns, where people took jobs below their social, economic, and skill level to live in the community and enjoy its amenities. Sun Valley developed a personality that would later be mirrored in places such as Aspen, Jackson, and dozens of other desirable locations.

As this second generation of neonatives arrived, embraced the Union Pacific protectorate, and put their own stamp on the place, Sun Valley acquired an enticing feel. "There was a great sense of informality," Jack Hemingway remembered, describing a place where the "help mingled with the high and mighty." Larger-than-life personalities dominated the horizon, from Pat (Pappy) Rogers, who managed the resort for the railroad from 1938 to 1952, to celebrities such as Louis Armstrong and Ann Sothern, one of the first celebrity homeowners to come from outside the region. Residents of the time remembered the place as egalitarian, fun, and surprising. Skiing down the mountain with a dishwasher, in the words of long-time resident Johnny Lister, one might discover that the person "had a doctorate from MIT." A charismatic openness existed that encouraged people to be themselves, and residents and visitors of the time fondly recalled that quality.[52]

This view of a halcyon era exists in almost every resort community. It often coincides with carefree or seminal times in the lives of the people who recount such moments and even more frequently mirrors the time when respondents entered such communities. They and the community they joined were younger, freer, somehow less tainted or jaded. Part nostalgia, part memory of a more innocent time in life, and part resistance to change, such attitudes permeated local perceptions of life in a tourist community. People with such views often saw the world in antimodern terms, seizing on a perfect moment in the past and seeing a fallen world in the changes since. Such a view often reflected changing values in the community and frequently appeared as a result of growth and expansion of resort amenities.[53] Yet such perceptions, real or not, offered an important perspective in tourism-based communities.

Besides visitors, postwar Sun Valley attracted two distinctly different categories of people. One large contingent was similar to the Taylors and Johnny Lister; like these transplanted easterners, such arrivals came from the world of the visitors, shared its assumptions and values, and found in the experience of living in Sun Valley a pleasant diversion from typical upper-middle-class American life. The second group, people from the surrounding region, were drawn by the economic opportunities the industry offered. For many in this agriculture- and ranching-based part of the West, where the economy had been weak throughout the twentieth century, the chance at even seasonal employment offered a potential solution to the economic problems of rural life. Still, the advantages of the resort economy almost always carried social and psychic costs.

The invasion of skiing offered economic opportunities that effectively changed the scope and scale of the regional employment picture. Before Sun Valley, little market existed for hunting and fishing guides and snow-removal workers. Under the Union Pacific, resort officials spent much time drumming up summer business, transforming the meaning of local skills from subsistence to market value. During the 1950s, writer John Rember's father served as a hunting and fishing guide during summers in the Sawtooth Valley, about sixty miles from Stanley, itself an hour north of Sun Valley. In the winter, he drove a ski bus at the resort while his wife worked as a nurse. The family catered to a constant stream of visitors to the house during the summer; after the road through the valley was paved in 1957, 4:00 A.M. arrivals for "sourdough pancakes and strong black coffee" before a day of fishing or hunting were common in the Rember household. "It was a kind of paradise we lived in," Rember recalled. "By winter, our southern freezer was full of venison and elk and the french-bread shapes of salmon, and you only had to look at your plate to realize where you were based, where your sustenance lay."[54]

The kind of sustenance that Rember recalled was both illusory and insular. Tourists provided most of the family income. Rember's parents both worked in the industry. Their livelihood required the uprooting of the family twice a year—once to move to the Sawtooths and then back to Sun Valley for the winter season. It was a migratory existence, offering a child a wonderful view of the world but exacting a toll on parents. Though they enjoyed a kind of independence, the Rembers had little opportunity either for upward mobility or for anything more than an illusory sense of rootedness. The insistence on the importance of place in John Rember's writing was one likely offshoot of this complicated relationship to home. Living as much as 100 miles from Sun Valley, the Rembers were bound to it by a web of connections that determined where and when they lived in various locations and that created a conversely rooted transience in their family. They were as much a part of the Union Pacific's structure as were the Taylors, albeit less directly.

This world had clear limits in time. Internal rhythms did not drive its transformation; the larger world beyond the borders of Idaho dictated its changes. Although the young John Rember enjoyed his "paradise," however much it was created by the Union Pacific's resort, myriad forces propelled its transformation. The world he fondly recalled "lasted long enough for me to be raised in it," Rember wrote, its transformation resulting from the stronger links of access between the world and Sun Valley and the resort community and the hinterland beyond.[55] The railroad was augmented by the paved road from Stanley in the 1950s, and these connections brought the Rembers and the stream of executives who envied them at the breakfast table in ever closer contact. Those ties played an essential role in transforming the greater region.

Rember, Taylor, and Lister combined elements of nostalgia for a disappearing way of life as they were directly affected by changes that swirled around them but over which they no control. Rember's childhood, Taylor's move to Sun Valley, and even Lister's fond remembrance revealed a vision of place intertwined with the formative experiences that shape identity. These individuals had grown up, had become new versions of themselves, in this variegated place, were shaped by it and had deep emotional ties to it. Changes, even ones that possibly had economically positive dimensions, also had the potential to disrupt these carefully constructed worlds.

Such bifurcated qualities, the showy, celebrity-filled winters and the genial, community-oriented summers, became the hallmark of this prototype of western resort communities. Between the founding of the resort in the late 1930s and the early 1950s, Sun Valley was unique, not only in the American West but in the nation as a whole. It had become a national tourist destination while other ski areas retained largely regional constituencies; it had assumed the ethos of celebrity ahead of the remainder of American society. Funded by a major national corporation, promoted by a public relations wizard, and staffed by a constituency generally from the same background as the people they served, the resort became exceptional. Sun Valley was a far cry from the winter carnival in Steamboat Springs.

In a figurative instant, outside capital, entrepreneurial vision, and changing cultural fashion replaced a defunct economy and transformed a moribund community into a status-conscious, tiered phenomenon marketed to the public through the most sophisticated techniques of the day. With the stars on its slopes covered by national magazines, newspapers, and newsreels, Sun Valley developed powerful influence over American consumers. It acquired a meaning that surpassed that of any similar resort. The sleepy Wood River Valley of the years between 1880 and 1935 had been replaced by a new incarnation tied to the dominant currents of midcentury.

Sun Valley revealed the characteristics of modern tourist economies. It served visitors ahead of residents, attracted neonatives who embraced its transformed ethos, grafted a new power structure onto the community, relegated most locals to the lower levels of the economic ladder, and linked the resort more closely to the nation than to its surroundings. After Sun Valley, the Wood River Valley enjoyed a place in national popular culture at the expense of its relationship to the surrounding region and the people who lived there.

The massive influx of outside capital directed at one purpose set a new standard in travel accommodation in the West. The earlier western resorts, the great hotels of the nineteenth century, among them the Hotel del Coronado on Coronado Island outside of San Diego, the Spring at Manitou, the Cliff House at San Francisco, and El Tovar at the Grand Canyon, preceded the era of media-made celebrity. Their constituency had been tuned to a different kind of rhythm, the stylish, ornate, immediate post-Victorianism of upper-class America.[56] Sun Valley offered a more understated, rustic veneer that masked the true heat of its celebrity constituency. The Colberts, the Selznicks, and their compatriots provided cachet that equaled that of the spectacular architecture of the old hotels. Their showiness highlighted the special nature of the resort and its package of amenities, making it different from any place in the West.

Sun Valley was a prototype, a concept that others struggled to imitate. It fused capital and culture in a manner directed at the mainstream American audience by intimating that Sun Valley and skiing were fashionable and indeed sexy. Being first created a mystique about Sun Valley that lasted for a generation. Between 1936 and 1960, the race was on to equal Sun Valley, but the Idaho community remained the pinnacle of American chic and outdoor activity.

8

The Spread of Recreational Tourism

Skiing in the Postwar West

The importance of the tourist industry dramatically increased in the American West following World War II. During the war, the West's population grew substantially as it became the locus of a range of war-related industries, including the Basic Magnesium plant outside the newly founded town of Henderson, Nevada, halfway between Hoover Dam and Las Vegas; the California shipyards; the Washington and Kansas aircraft factories; and the Kaiser Steel Works at Fontana, California. The region became a magnet for workers in search of high-paying jobs. These migrants transformed much of the region, populating areas that had been sparsely inhabited. A consequence of the spreading modern infrastructure, they also served as its conduits.[1]

The aftereffects of the war prompted postwar travel in a number of ways. Wartime restrictions deprived Americans of most opportunities for nonmilitary travel even as it allowed them to improve their financial status. During the war, few opportunities to spend the money saved from industrial jobs existed, and with rationing of commodities such as gasoline and rubber, most Americans enjoyed only limited chances to see the continent. At Navajo National Monument in Arizona, always a remote destination, custodian James L. Brewer reported one visitor in July 1942; only half joking, he told an archaeologist that he planned to put up a sign on a nearby road offering a free set of dishes to all visitors in an effort to assuage his loneliness. After the war, more widespread distribution of wealth in American society gave greater numbers of people the means to travel, and previously inaccessible places were more easily reached because of new and better roads, often built to facilitate wartime activities. The Grand Canyon experienced this change when visitation totals reached new highs each month in fall 1945, as discharged military personnel and departing war-industry workers returned to the places they left when the war began. Sensing that this might be their only chance to see the country, many stopped at the great icons of the American West, the Grand Canyon, the Grand Tetons, and Yellowstone. The increase in visitors continued throughout 1946 as the stream of workers heading home became a feature of western highways.[2] This movement served both as a precursor and a catalyst of an increase in tourism in the West.

After World War II the traveling public expanded in numbers and breadth, and its expectations reflected a different ethos. The prosperity generated by the war gave more Americans a chance at the perquisites of the good life, and the constituency for vacation travel grew immensely. Within a few years of the war's end, most Americans enjoyed greater disposable income and more vacation time. A combination of affluence, pent-up demand for leisure after more than a fifteen-year lean period, and new fashions that stressed access to a wider intellectual and conceptual world as part of the pleasures of middle-class life heightened the importance of tourism.[3]

Much of this travel occurred by automobile, with its promise of individual freedom and authentic experience. Automobiles had been instrumental in slicing the meaning of tourism in new ways, in taking the narrow vectors of the hegemonic cultural and heritage tourism of the fin de siècle and broadening them for an audience with different leisure objectives. After the war automobile ownership became a badge of middle-class status, and the annual two-week auto vacation in the summer became first a requirement of middle-class life and then a caricature of itself. The demand for recreation in national parks and forests soared so that neither the Park Service nor the Forest Service could keep pace; not only were available campsites as rare as the American bald eagle, but the existing campgrounds were covered with uncollected garbage, timber illegally cut for firewood, and other eyesores. Bernard DeVoto even recommended closing the national parks if they could not be better managed. Automobile ownership changed western tourism, but in the postwar period it also strained the limits of federal and private systems.[4]

Automobile tourism typically took place between Memorial Day in late May and Labor Day in early September, the boundaries of the classic and idealized summer, when children were out of school, the weather was warm, and families could spend time together. Auto travel maintained many of the same geographic characteristics of the 1920s: tourists went everywhere and anywhere, purchased enormous quantities of food, gasoline, and other staples, filled motels and hotels, and generally kept moving, staying only an insignificant length of time in all but one or two of their stops. A chaos of auto travel existed, tourists traveling the mythic landscapes of the West, staying where they landed at the end of a day. Two days before Memorial Day weekend, tourist camps and motels were vacant; two days after Labor Day, the cacophony subsided and they returned to silence. The chaos seemed to suggest the features of vacationing that emerged in television cartoons such as *Yogi Bear,* a madcap bear inhabiting Jellystone Park whose adventures gave both the mythic Ranger Smith and visitors fits.

Automobile tourism simultaneously centralized this chaos of travel and promoted individual experience. Postwar American society craved both mobility and its psychic history, and travel to national parks amply filled that longing. A visit to the Grand Canyon or Yellowstone conferred validation, a sense of belonging to a successful society that reflected one dimension of the message of late nineteenth-century tourism. Yet the postwar middle class sought individual affirmation rather than its social counterpart. Like railroad travel of the late nineteenth century, travel to western national parks created intellectual and physical paths that the overwhelming majority of visitors followed. These corridors spawned their own world, different from the realities a few miles away. Instead of barns, pastures, and grain elevators, the paths to the parks were dominated by gasoline stations, motels, and souvenir shops. These places created a message of their own, a tale of convenience that spoke to the new, postwar America, not of the historic West typically beyond the corridors highways created. The middle class embraced travel as a reflection of themselves, as individual affirmation.

Other dimensions of tourism grew in the postwar era. A combination of wealth and exposure to the sport helped skiing emerge in the postwar West. Before the war it followed either the local model of Steamboat Springs or the luxury formulation of Sun Valley. Its popularity was limited to these circles; nationwide, only about 10,000 Americans could call themselves avid skiers in 1935, and most of them lived in the East. The small clusters of individuals at the Winter Sports Park outside Denver or at the Timberline Lodge at Mt. Hood in Oregon typified western skiers. The sport ranged no deeper into the western populace than this rock-solid core of enthusiasts. The war provided a catalyst for expanded interest in the sport. Through the military, more than 200,000 people nationwide had experienced skiing by 1945. Coupled with the growing emphasis on leisure and vacation in the immediate postwar era, the very trend that catapulted the western national parks to a central position on the American recreational stage, skiing seemed poised to transcend the limitations of places such as Sun Valley. In the postwar era, easier and less expensive ways to reach ski areas than by rail changed the sport's constituency.

New amenities facilitated the public's growing interest. For the first time, almost anyone could learn to ski in the West. The Tenth Mountain Division, the cadre of American ski troops that trained at Camp Hale, Colorado, about two hours drive from the old mining town of Aspen, produced as many as 2,000 new postwar ski instructors. Finns on skis resisted the Soviet invasion in 1939, earning the admiration of many people who channeled their enthusiasm into the sport. One veteran of the ski corps, Frank Bulkley, returned from military service to restart his Eskimo Ski Club in Denver, teaching ten- to sixteen-year-olds the fundamentals of skiing; he became the best known of a burgeoning group who trained novices. Surplus military equipment made skiing affordable and the industry boomed, albeit in the reversible olive drab/white parkas of the military. By 1953 Colorado alone sported more than 200,000 skiers at its nine resorts, a tremendous increase from the minuscule numbers of the prewar era.[5]

At the end of the war, skiing presented problems for potential entrepreneurs. The sport depended on inclement weather; required access to mountaintops, a large investment of capital, and usually land leased from the Forest Service; and was limited at best to six months of the year. As a seasonal industry, it reflected historic problems in both tourism and the western economy. Temporal conditions limited the sustenance skiing could provide. Building an economy on a seasonal industry, particularly one dependent on the vagaries of the weather, remained as difficult a task in 1950 as it had been in 1875. Only Sun Valley solved this problem before 1950, but after the war its luster faded.

Skiing then developed a new form in the postwar era, not because of its innate appeal or growing claim on the American public but because of an entrepreneurial businessman with a quixotic desire to reform American culture. Chicago industrialist Walter P. Paepcke, head of the Container Corporation of America and a leader in bringing together American intellectuals and business leaders, provided the impetus that altered the moribund mining town of Aspen, Colorado. An enlightened business leader, Paepcke joined with a group from the University of Chicago, including its president Robert M. Hutchins and philosopher Mortimer J. Adler, to offer a critique of American society that would promote cultural reform. Central to this idea was the dissemination of a Great Books course offered to business and civic leaders. Paepcke's introduction to the group came through this course. First the industrialist merely sent a check and affirmed his support for the mission of educating Chicago's business community. When prodded by Hutchins, who offered to return Paepcke's money if the businessman did not want to attend, Paepcke and his wife, Elizabeth Nitze Paepcke, came and stayed. Their reaction was common; the course became a huge success with business leaders. It also spurred one of the most impressive efforts at adult education ever attempted.[6]

Included in this attempt at cultural reform was the idea of an institute for humanistic studies. In actualizing this idea, the Paepckes played the leading role, discovering a lost Aspen and creating a modern resort. Elizabeth Paepcke first visited the area in 1939; driven from the train station at Glenwood Springs, about forty miles away, she arrived in the 800-person town after dark and found only one electric light bulb illuminating the place. This incident was transformed into the myth of the town with only one electric light, greatly exaggerating Aspen's condition in 1939. Although watching the sheep come through town remained a favorite autumn pastime, Aspenites possessed a vibrant local life even at the town's nadir.[7] It had the problems of rural and small-town America: limited infrastructure, population decline, and lack of an economic future.

Paepcke's decision to locate the institute in Aspen instantly resolved the town's problems of capital and access. It also combined features of recreational and heritage tourism at the precise moment that the popularity of skiing mushroomed. The venture embodied the traits of twentieth-century tourism: an entrepreneurial visionary with capital who saw that the place could be marketed to a segment of the public who could afford travel, an area with particular appeal, and the intellectual and cultural construction of a new identity for the town that resonated in the nation but confounded longtime locals. Midcentury Aspen combined these traits, and Paepcke provided any others that were lacking.

Since its days as the Crystal City of the Rockies, a silver-producing center during a brief era of remarkable prosperity that preceded the demonetization of silver in 1893, Aspen greatly declined in population and stature. A typically rural, high-elevation regime followed, in which small mining operations paired with local agriculture and animal husbandry to sustain the community. Dependent on the railroad, the community was transformed from a predominantly male mining community in the late nineteenth century to a more typical family distribution, with men and women constituting roughly 50 per cent of the population in 1920. Farms grew in number and size throughout this period as mining precipitously declined. The community became a relic of itself, its beautiful but largely unused and increasingly debilitated Victorian structures, its central business district, and other impressive buildings such as the old opera house recalling a more vibrant and elegant past. When Elizabeth Paepcke first saw the town in 1939, she remembered thinking, "If a place looked like Sleeping Beauty awaiting Prince Charming's kiss, this was it." Persuading her husband was far more difficult.[8]

Six years later, as World War II wound down, Walter Paepcke shared his wife's infatuation with the little mining town. He invited some friends from Chicago along on a Memorial Day excursion to the mountain community. Elizabeth Paepcke was surprised and delighted by her husband's seemingly sudden interest; unknown to her, he had initiated a series of secret inquiries, gathering information about the little town in the mountains. Among his objectives was to entice his new friend, the Bauhaus School painter and graphic artist Herbert Bayer, who had assisted in the conceptualization of a recent Container Corporation of America exhibit at the Chicago Art Institute, to settle in a place that he would find congenial. Aspen fit. Bayer was homesick for his native Austrian Alps and was a skilled outdoorsman and accomplished skier. For him, Aspen offered a faux Europe.[9]

Paepcke's motives typified the man. Aspen allowed him to accomplish his primary objectives. He could pursue social goals such as education and cultural reform as he helped bring the people he felt the nation needed, such as Bayer, to places where they would be comfortable. These personal concerns fused with a professional strategy. Paepcke loved raw entrepreneurship, the sheer excitement of a new venture, and Aspen offered a perfect situation. The idea of transforming a moribund mining town into a cultural center was vintage Paepcke, known for far-sighted thinking and the willingness to risk ventures with unlikely prospects of economic reward but grand potential for psychic and social benefit. An institution builder at heart, he found the pleasure and simultaneously the challenge of a lifetime.[10]

Within two days of their arrival in Aspen, Paepcke initiated an intricate series of purchases of lots and properties in the town. Judge William Shaw of the Pitkin County Court served as his agent, concealing Paepcke's carefully constructed plans. Two weeks after his arrival, his first purchase, the Lamb house, an elegant Victorian that had once belonged to Aspen's druggist, was made public. By then he had negotiated the purchase of hundreds of lots, a number of commercial properties, homes, and the Jerome Hotel. The transformation of Aspen was under way, but only Paepcke was quite sure why.[11]

Paepcke's venture and its implications served as an archetype for the beginning of tourism in the post–World War II American West. Aspen began as a one-owner resort, the crown jewel of a powerful figure's career. The visionary Paepcke saw in the declining town a spectrum of possibilities that were barely evident to others and that only he had the capital and range of connections to develop successfully. He found an insider, a native of standing, to support his cause. A local civic leader, Judge Shaw saw the value of Paepcke's efforts, telling the Chicagoan that he was delighted "for all the residents of Aspen that they had fallen heir to an angel." Paepcke recruited his friends, ostensibly to maintain his interests but also to further his hegemonizing impulses. His favorite architect, Walter Frazier, was asked to consider the prospect of rehabilitating the entire town. Paepcke recruited Floyd N. Gibbs, a hotelier acquaintance from Illinois, to stay rent-free in the Lamb House if Gibbs would keep track of the properties and pursue the acquisition of the Jerome Hotel. Paepcke also brought in ski enthusiasts, bon vivants, intellectuals, and cultural leaders, in his words, to "become fellow Aspenites." A revolution began, but with the exception of Shaw and Tom Sardy, a native of Ouray, Colorado, who owned the local hardware store and mortuary, separated by a curtain, it started without the cooperation or even the participation of the local community.[12]

In essence, Paepcke's vision for Aspen mirrored the elitism of the time. Paepcke came from the class that possessed resources to create change, and in Aspen he could make anything happen. His strategy aimed not at making the community accessible to the growing middle class. A closer parallel was the mythic colonial island paradise, where outsiders came in, ran the community as they saw fit, and enjoyed their secluded lives there as docile locals worked in service positions. What Paepcke brought was exactly what all colonizers brought—access to goods and the amenities of the modern world, the potential to acquire wealth, and a new vision of place. The people who lived in Aspen faced the characteristic two choices as old as colonialism and just as deeply embedded in tourist development: they could embrace the changes and accept the diminished roles offered them, or they could actively or passively resist change. Each strategy had advantages and drawbacks. The choice ultimately became personal, determined by the individual's beliefs.

Paepcke worked to persuade Aspen of his good intentions and to illustrate the benefits of his and his friends' presence. He quickly became a quintessential neonative, embracing the community and explaining his intentions as soon as it became clear that changes were in the works. Locals, especially so-called old-timers, people who had been in Aspen since silver and later zinc dominated the local economy, resisted the onslaught, preferring to believe that mining would someday return and rescue the town. Paepcke astutely cultivated local leaders, and they lent him their prestige. After a trip to the offices of the *Aspen Times*, a typically prodevelopment small-town paper, Paepcke enlisted its editor. The newspaper praised Paepcke's integrity. He paid a fair price for the property he purchased, its editorial emphasized, marking him as a man of judgment and character. The newcomer wanted a typical resort no more than locals did.[13]

This moment of explanation defined neonative status. Like Wagner in Santa Fe, Paepcke sought local acceptance for his actions, presenting his idea of Aspen to a public he fully expected to be receptive and engaging in strategies that minimized the differences between the Chicago industrialist and the town he adopted. Paepcke used the public pathways of small-town America to reach his audience. He aimed to be local as he explained himself, revealing the ways in which he desired to connect with the place he had come to see as his Magic Mountain. Amid some muted local grumbling, Paepcke made himself and his friends into Aspenites, in the process radically changing the meaning of the designation.

As he became more established, Paepcke grappled with old-timers for control of the meaning of the idea of Aspen. As a neonative, his ability to charm had limits; in 1946 he offered free paint to residents for their houses, but his insistence that Herbert Bayer choose the colors prickled even the most sympathetic of locals. Paepcke's twenty-year lease on the Jerome Hotel, the almost $100,000 he spent on its renovation, and the imported chefs and the labeling of local dishes such as trout with fancy names inspired disdain. A long-term lease of the burned opera house invited more criticism of his motives, but nothing riled locals as much as the establishment of the Four Seasons, a private club that Paepcke created from two remodeled homes southwest of Aspen. Paepcke sought exclusive fishing rights for nearby Castle Creek, and the local community was insulted. To many locals accustomed to a different concept of community, it seemed that Paepcke truly sought a kingdom of his own in their mountains.[14]

Paepcke's brand of neonativity transformed instead of adapted. When accused of taking over the opera house for his own purposes, Paepcke threatened to leave the town to the typical predatory tourist trade, tacky and insignificant, "a mammoth amusement park, [in which] I have not the least interest but which might pay promoters well in hard cash while ruining, to my way of thinking, the entire charm of a potentially most beautiful community." In some instances he was conciliatory; as he bought property in town, he allowed locals to purchase the long-standing vacant lots that harbored gardens and livestock.[15] Yet his persona was domineering, his control comprehensive, and such gestures were designed to appease public opinion much more than to reflect a softer policy. Longtime residents easily resented this dynamic entrepreneur.

Paepcke offered people a choice. Change was coming to Aspen. They could choose between elitist but structured control of that change or risk any foolish operation that might come down the road. As did many neonatives facing local resistance, Paepcke presented himself as a mediator. He was new to town but willing to throw the force of his personality, energy, wealth, and connections between it and the onslaught of mass culture. He might not preserve every aspect of prewar Aspen, but he seemed sensitive to it. Paepcke's approach typified the combination of enlightenment and blackmail that so characterized the devil's bargain of tourism. Locals were, as always, asked to choose between the devil they knew and the devil they did not, with no hope of returning to the ways they had known and to which they periodically wished to return.

Paepcke remained a shrewd businessman tuned to the possibilities of profit. His actions drove the price of local real estate upward. As this occurred, he let the local grapevine know that he was through buying property. Prices returned to the torpor from which he had awakened them. Paepcke brought in a quiet and unassuming attorney from his Chicago firm to handle all future negotiations, continuing to buy properties that his pronouncement had artificially deflated.[16] He loved the idea of Aspen as a cultural resort and the raw art of entrepreneurship equally well. His actions in building the community clearly demonstrated the close linkage of these two concepts in the mind of this man some affectionately called the "prosaic boxmaker."

Paepcke's desire for a cultural community won out over his commercial instincts. Unable to own the entire town, he instead aimed to control its destiny. One strategy involved running candidates for local office. Wisely, Paepcke abandoned the idea; its potential for permanently dividing the newcomers from the existing community was unparalleled. Instead he brought in Walter Gropius, the Bauhaus architect, to design a master plan for the community. Expecting the spare German modernist to be repelled by the ornate Victorianism of the town, Paepcke was surprised that Gropius advocated a program that took into account local traditions, social composition, institutions, geography, climate, and the concerns of the existing community. His one piece of advice that smacked of modernist sensibility was to restore the old but to build new. This, Gropius believed, would prevent the restored community from becoming a trite anachronism. Although no formal master plan developed from Gropius's visit, a tradition of resistance to uncontrolled growth began that subsequently came to mark the community and define its parameters.[17]

About the time of Paepcke's arrival, another group first regarded Aspen as attractive. Immediately after the war, veterans of the Tenth Mountain Division, including Peter Siebert and Steven Knowlton, who later emerged as leaders of the Colorado ski industry, became ski bums in Aspen. As soldiers at nearby Camp Hale, they had been acquainted with Aspen and the Roaring Fork Valley. Although they lacked capital for development, they did enjoy a skier's paradise all to themselves for a brief moment. These "strangers," as Judge Shaw referred to them, were sufficiently numerous to attract attention as they scoured the area for cabin sites.[18]

Two disparate sources of energy on the Aspen horizon foreshadowed later conflicts in the community. Although the Paepckes were skiers, their primary interest was Aspen's potential as a summer institute for studies in music, literature, and the arts. Winter recreation was interesting, but it remained secondary. Paepcke's Aspen personified high culture. Knowlton and the other ski bums cared little for that. The freedom of the mountain air and the thrill of the sport attracted them. They sought experience, not enlightenment, physical stimulation and the rush of athletic endeavor, not intellectual stimulation. These two different spirits were uncomfortably intertwined in Aspen from its inception as a resort.

Paepcke understood the value of winter sports. With $100,000 invested in the Jerome Hotel alone, he always needed paying customers. Aspen's greatest attribute was its beautiful powdered snow. As the community took shape, Paepcke divided it three ways: he took charge of business and the mind, Elizabeth Paepcke was in charge of taste and culture, and his brother-in-law, Paul Nitze, was in charge of the body, which in Aspen meant skiing. At the urging of Freidl Pfeifer, the Austrian who had been the assistant manager of the Sun Valley Ski School and had helped train the Tenth Mountain Division, and with Nitze's help, Paepcke funded a ski resort. Pfeifer brought more Tenth Mountain Division veterans, and in 1946 the funds he and Paepcke raised strung the first chair lifts on Ajax Mountain. By 1947 the longest chairlift in the world, two sections that covered 14,000 feet, operated, and Paepcke's Aspen Ski Company formed. The company seemed unlikely to make anyone rich.[19]

The investors in the ski company reflected the increasing interest in skiing as a sport. Paepcke and Nitze together put up more than one-third of the $300,000 that started the project; Nitze added $75,000 and became the single largest investor. Other Paepcke friends such as Eugene Lilly became investors, as did Joseph Binns of the Hilton Hotel chain. A few Aspenites, including David R. C. (Darcy) Brown, a landowner descended from a prominent nineteenth-century Aspen family, also became part of the group, as did Minot Dole, the originator of the Tenth Mountain Division, and Ted Ryan, who had invested in the failed endeavor at Ashcroft.[20] Money for skiing came both from hard-core ski enthusiasts and Paepcke's cultural friends.

The idea of a year-round resort in the mountains, offering different possibilities during different seasons, was a far-sighted counter to the long-standing problem of northern tourist destinations: the winter. Just as the experiences at the Grand Canyon and Sun Valley demonstrated, conquering the seasonal dimensions of tourism posed major problems. Even in the early 1940s, Aspenites understood the need for twelve-month recreation. The 1940–1941 Pitkin County brochure touted "year-round recreation" for the first time but emphasized skiing over summer recreation. The transition from summer to winter tourism appeared easier than its reverse. The summer visitors to Aspen seemed secure; then the growth of skiing after the war ensured a year-round tourist-based economy in the revived town.[21]

Paepcke's role in securing this year-round trade remained both catalytic and pivotal. He cautioned Nitze against aiming exclusively for profit with the ski resort, stressing that his goal for Aspen was for it to be an exclusive vacation community that also turned a small profit. A "mass skiing center," as Paepcke described the worst possible outcome of his development to Nitze, was not the objective. "I would like to see us avoid the tourist trippers who litter the scenery with orange peelings and sardine cans," Paepcke told the Associated Press in 1947, instead preferring to create the "Athens of the Rockies." His emphasis on intellectual endeavor accomplished for Aspen exactly what Edgar Hewett's focus on cultural tourism managed in Santa Fe. Aspen was remade unique; there were hundreds of similarly elegant summer mountain resorts in the nation, but only Aspen was clearly tied to the arts and the sophisticated circles of Euro-American cultural elites and enlightened American business leaders.

A barrage of attention from the cultural community, including Harold Ross of the *New Yorker* magazine, an Aspen native, made the town seem desirable to a small segment of the moderne crowd, and the mainstream press followed the lead of the culturati. *Life, Reader's Digest,* and other similar publications touted the Aspen revival as early as 1946. When Paepcke's summer institute opened with a commemoration and celebration of the 200th anniversary of the birth of Johann Wolfgang von Goethe in 1949, an event that University of Chicago president Robert M. Hutchins called "the greatest cultural festival of its kind ever held in our country," the community had a firmly shaped and suave identity. Lectures by Albert Schweitzer, Jóse Ortega y Gasset, and Thornton Wilder and music by Arthur Rubinstein and Gregor Piatagorsky highlighted the Goethe celebration, exemplifying the arts and sophistication in what was soon labeled Paepcke's *Kulturstaat,* a civilized community organized around culture and sustained by it.[22]

There was a certain amount of sophistry and wishful thinking in the idea of Aspen as a *Kulturstaat.* Paepcke possessed a utopian vision of and for the community, but it was not a view of paradise widely shared in American society. "There are too few communities which offer good opportunities for combining work, play, and culture," Paepcke commented. In Aspen, he tried to fashion a place where people could live a "happier and more complete life." Even before the advent of television, this definition of happiness had only a small constituency in the post–World War II United States. Despite the importance of the Goethe festival, which appeared to raise the level of awareness about the German intellectual at least in Colorado and spurred the idea of an Aspen University, the audience for this endeavor remained small. Nor did the cultural side of Aspen offer significant opportunities for profit. Paepcke poured most of his own money into the Aspen revival, investing more than $200,000 in the physical redevelopment of the community by 1947, and the expenditure drained his resources.[23] But the endeavor still needed an economic backbone. Without a consistent source of funding, the cultural miracle Paepcke believed in might never occur.

Winter activity held the real economic future of the resort. The opening of the lift on Ajax Mountain attracted much attention, and the ski slopes of Aspen, not its nascent cultural revival, caught the attention of the public. *The March of Time,* the newsreel sequence that transmitted so much of the visual information that Americans received before television, featured Aspen, albeit in a manner Paepcke disliked. The show contained too much revelry, he wrote in an apologetic note to ski company shareholders. But even Paepcke's dynamism could not slow the trend toward recreational tourism in Aspen. Although initial media reports focused on the revival of community and its cultural attributes, by 1949 their tone changed. *Look* magazine's approach typified the newest accounts; it packaged the skiing conditions with the "gingerbread architecture," a damning with faint praise in the minds of Bayer, Gropius, and others, and highlighted the longest ski lift and other recreational assets in eight pages of photographs. A clear impression of the institute and the cultural dimension of the community was missing. Recreation received another boost as journalist Lowell Thomas became a devotee of Aspen, recounting its charms in his broadcasts. Aspen hosted the World Ski championships in 1950, the second time for Aspen and an indication of impending transformation.[24] Although the ski company initially lost money until 1951, everyone understood that recreation had to support culture if Aspen were to retain both features of its amazing revival and the year-round economy that came with them.

Paepcke stumbled across one of the fault lines of American cultural experience in the postwar era. The kind of cultural tourism he fashioned would have been remarkably successful early in the twentieth century, but by mid-century the tastes of the public and the segments of it who traveled changed dramatically. As had Santa Fe and the Grand Canyon, a cultural center such as Paepcke envisioned would have appealed to the traveling classes of the fin de sìecle, secure in their hegemonic control of the question of taste in American society and endowed with the capital to support their views. By 1950, with the spread of wealth that resulted from World War II, the earlier rise of the automobile, the advent of the paid vacation for employees, the culture of physical experience that became commonplace, and the subsuming of exclusivity in common experience, the cultural mecca that Paepcke envisioned was an economic anachronism, a province of the few in a rapidly changing society that slowly but inexorably began to take its cues from popular culture instead of from the elites. The few culturati could not foot Aspen's costs, and only a minuscule slice of the larger public showed any interest. Cultural Aspen needed sustenance. That the town Paepcke selected for his dream happened to be blessed with extraordinary mountain terrain at the moment that skiing became fashionable and accessible was more than coincidence. It was a remarkably fortuitous occurrence that rescued the brilliant career and personal fortune of one of the nation's most innovative businessmen.

With his characteristic feel for the cultural climate, Paepcke fused two distinctly different ethics of tourism: the older heritage-cultural metier transformed for the postwar era and the exercise- and experience-oriented dimension of the immediate pre–World War II era. In Paepcke's Aspen, the two coexisted easily although not simultaneously, in effect solving the problem of differing ideologies by sharing the year. The sequencing left a down time, a period when people who lived and worked in the community and those who had long resided there could come out and enjoy the beauty, serenity, and camaraderie of a small service-oriented town. These moments provided a balance that encouraged old-timers willing to remain in a transformed community, their grumbling muted, and made underemployment at high altitude worth the sacrifices for a generation of incoming neonatives.

Throughout the 1950s Aspen enjoyed an attractive flavor, and people from all over the country arrived to share in its distinctive cultural milieu. Some were simply eccentric hedonists, such as the individual who liked his little trailer so much he built a $100,000 party house around it. He continued to live in the trailer but threw grandiose parties in the house. More typical of this breed was pianist and writer Bruce Berger, who, like many early Aspenites, grew up in the suburbs of Chicago. The Aspen where he arrived in 1952 at the age of seventeen for a spring vacation was "less a town than a conspiracy," he fondly remembered, an esoteric collection of characters that deviated from the mainstream. The teen-aged Berger, who in his own words "converted to Aspen," was inspired. He returned to stay after a stint in college when his sister secured the right of first refusal on a log cabin on a one-acre plot. Berger became ensconced in Paepcke's Aspen, an eccentric citizen of the *Kulturstaat* who defined himself by refusing to ski. He recognized the shared sense of community Paepcke sought, using Kurt Vonnegut's description of a *karass,* a psychic brotherhood, to describe Aspen. Peggy Clifford, a long-time *Aspen Times* columnist who lived there from 1953 to 1979, first heard of Aspen in 1949 from a professor who told her of its charms. Four years later, on a train west, she stopped in Denver and had drinks with Luke Short, the western writer who also wrote for the *Saturday Evening Post* and the movies and was known as Fred Glidden in Aspen. Short told her she would like "the fine quirky" Aspen. When Clifford first saw the town, she too was charmed. Aspen was "as wonderful and mysterious as the mountains." She found authenticity in Tomkins Hardware, the tall and white-haired Mr. Tomkins presiding; the store and its proprietor seemed a relic of an earlier time. "Truth with a capital T," Clifford decided, could be found in both the Museum of Modern Art and in the hardware store, but in Aspen, "it was more accessible," she wrote. Clifford found a job in the Berko-Henry photography studio, itself a neonative enterprise, and Aspen acquired another neonative who sought its idiosyncratic comforts and its feigned distance from the mainstream.[25]

Berger and Clifford typified the 1950s wave of neonatives who came and stayed. They embraced Paepcke's Aspen, its eccentricity, emphasis on culture, and seeming distance from the mainstream, and were willing to stay in relatively low-paying jobs to remain in the town where they had invested their identity. They had, Clifford wrote much later with more than a little sarcasm, "exorcized [their] material lusts and achieved a fine purity."[26] These neonatives were integral to the formation of postwar Aspen. As did newcomers in Santa Fe and Sun Valley, they embraced a notion of culture and place that had been defined and created just before their arrival. They too saw their community as authentic, meaningful, traditional, and deep-rooted. They also changed the town, bemoaning the impact of successive waves of visitors often without recognizing their own effect on the place.

From the prewar local community of miners, ranchers, and farmers, Aspen developed not one but two distinct neonative communities with claims on the place and on its future. Both were essential despite the difference in their interests, values, and finances. The conflicts that would have been inevitable if skiers and intellectuals simultaneously had inhabited Aspen were muted because of the seasonal preeminence of each. As Paepcke's scripting reconceived the community, each of the new activities, thinking and skiing, became a dimension of local culture.

The emphasis on ideas and discussion that made Aspen the "benchmark for deep thinking in high places" also differentiated its neonative communities from its only peer in this regard, Sun Valley. The Idaho resort contained none of the intellectual breadth of Aspen; no one in Sun Valley ever thought of trying to start a Sun Valley University. Even when Hemingway located there, the cachet that developed was not because of his literary skill but because of his celebrity. Sun Valley's neonatives came for recreation and relaxation. When they engaged in other activities in the summer, their purpose was the same.

The commonality of values in Sun Valley belied the complicated interclass relations of the neonative community in Aspen. By the early 1950s the winter crowd and the summer crowd were distinct. The summer people were affluent, educated, and cultured, the daredevil carefree skiers of the winters protohedonistic. These athletic iconoclasts "reigned four months of the year," Peggy Clifford remembered. "When the lifts closed, they became carpenters, bartenders, and real estate salesmen, unheralded through the spring, summer, and fall."[27] While the culturati reigned, the skiers' identity remained a secret, known only to other year-round residents. Aspen had not one but two class systems; status in one did not necessarily confer status in the other. An all-for-one, one-for-all spirit dominated the town, but tenuous bonds formed from necessity anchored it.

During the early 1950s being a neonative in Aspen offered a taste of the idyllic. "No one was getting rich," Clifford remembered, "but tourists in adequate numbers both winter and summer supported the pastoral pretensions of the residents, and the off-seasons were long and luxurious." Culturally distant from the mainstream, albeit sustained by the fortunes of Walter Paepcke and Paul Nitze, Aspen developed an arrogance about its cultural superiority, fostered by Paepcke's *Kulturstaat.* Aspen's script gave its actors a sense of being real. "We were a special and consecrated breed," Clifford mused, inhabiting "the best of all possible worlds, unspoiled by excess, spacious, open, and tranquil."[28] This conception fostered a singular moment, equivalent to a similar epoch in Sun Valley, characteristic of tourist towns and of the memories of the neonatives who inhabit them. This was their moment, skiers and cultural aficionados could say with certainty, and they could only hope Walter Paepcke could keep it from changing.

Between Aspen's two cultures and not always thrilled with the changes around them stood the local community. Many of these people had psychic investment in the way Aspen had been since the decline of mining, the small, quiet town the world had passed by. Native Aspenites, Clifford noted, "resided somewhere between the menials and the leaders." They had endured difficult lives, and many were "hard, suspicious people who saw the revival simultaneously as one last chance to make it and a rich man's trick." This was their home, and they lived what they regarded as real lives there. "In their stores," Clifford wrote, "one found nuts and bolts instead of Venini glass and Irish sweaters," a marker of the growing class differences in Aspen. Some locals, Hal Boyle of the *Associated Press* noted, could not "quite see a ski chair as progress." According to Luke Short, others "longed passionately to see Aspen's skies murky with the smoke of a mill or smelter, and to them, a new shaft house is a far nobler work of man than the cunning architecture of a symphony." They laughed at newcomers, such as the one who renovated an old mansion and moved in with his family, unaware that the structure had been the premier brothel in town in times past. The renovator "sure did put in a nicer sounding piano," one sly and unreconstructed old-timer drawled, capturing the intricate tension that underlay the transformation.[29]

Some locals found opportunity in the changed town, but new options were generally limited in scope and scale. The Aspen Ski Corporation provided most of the employment. Beginning in 1946 with the construction of the ski mountain, locals worked in unskilled and skilled labor positions. They put in the lifts, built water diversion tunnels, and otherwise transformed the mountain for its new purpose. Neonatives initially departed in search of work in the summers, but a few found local jobs. Dick Wright, one of the first postwar ski instructors, worked as a carpenter. Another instructor, Jim Snobble, sold bottle caps; more worked as plumbers, painters, or at other occupations. Locals also retained positions after the resort opened. They sold lift tickets, operated the ski lifts and grooming equipment, and generally filled the typical role assigned to locals in the tourist industry: performing hourly wage labor and experiencing little opportunity for upward mobility. Red Rowland, son of a turn-of-the-century mining engineer, was the exception. His previous experience as a foreman in mines and on road crews won him the position of assistant manager of the ski company when it opened in 1946. He retained the position until his retirement in 1977, advancing in pay, title, and certainly veneration during the ensuing thirty years but finding his authority curtailed.[30] Despite its local flavor, the power in the ski company emanated from outside Aspen.

Throughout the 1950s the community remained bifurcated. It was as if Aspen were two different places: the up-and-coming skiing center that, despite Paepcke's insistence on cultural reform and enlightenment, increasingly attracted widespread public attention, and the cultural institute where the best minds of the modern era discussed great ideas. Each "town" possessed a distinct personality, each dominated one season of the year, leaving the off-season, spring and fall, for locals and neonatives. Summers in Aspen saw an upper-class, highly cultured audience discussing ideas and artistic matters in the brilliant light and cool breezes; the winters were more egalitarian, featuring a rough-and-ready crowd catapulting down the mountains at breakneck speed and reveling into the early hours of the morning. The difference between the famed Aspen "executive seminars" and the athletic crowd of the ski races could not have been more pronounced.[31] A tension but also a symmetry existed between the two. The overlap of people was limited to Paepcke's intellectual friends who also skied, but both groups offered a dynamism that completed the awakening of the town.

Businesses responded to the bifurcated economic and cultural climate. The Bookshop typified the successful strategies employed by the commercial community. In the "profound summer-seminar time," as *Ski Country* magazine called it, the store stocked the great books popular with the intellectual crowd. The works of Voltaire, Kant, Matthew Arnold, and others graced the shop. During the winter, the intellectual material came down from the shelves, replaced by books about skiing and the mountains. Restaurants and lodges had little difficulty with the change in seasons, although in 1951 two-year-resident Jack dePagter, a bartender at the Hotel Jerome, sought to increase Aspen's winter popularity. He initiated Winterskól, Aspen's version of the classic winter carnival begun earlier at Hot Sulphur Springs and Steamboat Springs, and another neonative adaptation to the new tenor of the town. Both the winter and summer crowds required their specific offerings, and the range of available amenities greatly expanded. By the 1950s accommodations and meals were a far cry from the six dollars a night columnist Jack Foster paid for the best room in the Jerome Hotel in 1940.[32]

Aspen also developed fashionable dimensions as entrepreneurs capitalized on the ski crowd. Outside capital, much of it from Los Angeles, colonized the community. The construction of Shadow Hill Lodge by film director Frank Myers, who shot the feature film *Devil's Doorway* in the area, was typical. When the lodge opened for business in 1950, it joined a growing number of accommodations built by outsiders who wanted to make Aspen their home. The New Norway Lodge, the project of University of Colorado graduates Les and Jean Gaylord, was another example. Newcomer Edith Rader of Edie's Restaurant managed to cross the most difficult of boundaries; her home-style cooking appealed even to Aspen old-timers. Paepcke had indeed created a place that outsiders wanted to believe was their own.[33]

The problems of the influx of capital were indicative of the transformation process. The capital was colonial in nature but intraregional. It came from California and from the front range, and it imported people who exercised influence over the direction of the community simply because they began important commercial concerns. These people, movie directors and state university graduates alike, possessed a different vision of Aspen from that of longtime residents. They also acquired more influence than the old-timers, who had only the length of their tenure to call on as a mark of their belonging. After Paepcke, most of the old-timers had already been divested of their greatest resource—the ownership of property. Their status was increasingly marginal in the town that had been their birthright. A tension that would be replayed time and again in western tourism took shape.

The emergence of a small celebrity contingent became another measure of change. The town's most significant celebrity in the 1940s was Gary Cooper. At Paepcke's behest, Cooper came to Aspen to ski in 1948, bought thirty acres of land, and constructed a home. He, his wife Rocky, and their daughter caught the attention of the media and were featured in national news magazines.[34] Paepcke had his Hemingway, someone famous with enormous cultural cachet, who had made the entrepreneur's town his own.

A professional class sought Aspen as a place to find their way in the world. Such people "were bound to be unusual," Peggy Clifford noted, "as life in Aspen offered neither much money nor many challenges." A small cadre of physicians, attorneys, and others gradually migrated to the town throughout the late 1940s and 1950s, establishing another dimension among the neo-native communities. Robert (Bugsy) Barnard, a physician from California, defined the breed; loud and opinionated, he "dressed like a rich rancher, had the vocabulary of a hipster," collected antique cars and drove sports cars, and made himself a visible figure in town. But his role differed from that of a professional person in most communities, and Barnard and others like him reveled in the difference. Although Aspen counted about 2,000 residents in 1960, its social structure was considerably more complex than a typical town of that size. Aspen was one of the few towns in the Rockies that boasted a newspaper operated from the kitchen of a wealthy man with a Harvard degree who rented rooms to boarders.[35]

As skiing developed in the 1950s, the community faced more of the problems of rapid growth. Paepcke's oversight mitigated many such issues but also inspired an increasing amount of grumbling directed at his ideas and plans. In 1954 one manifestation surfaced in a battle of "music versus manure," as the Denver papers called it. A group of sportsmen wanted to form a roping club; at a cost of almost $12,000 they planned to renovate ten acres of land, adding calf pens and bleachers and creating an Aspen rodeo. Paepcke was livid. This summer activity detracted from the Aspen Institute. The community had never provided such a sum to support Paepcke's activities. According to one account, Paepcke forbade the community to have the rodeo. It clashed with his script for the town. The summer audience was his, he insisted, and he would not have them exposed to "common rodeo entertainment." A clash of cultures and of control ensued. Ultimately, the local community won, although some accounts credit the victory to Paepcke's magnanimity. Herbert Bayer purportedly told Paepcke to practice what he preached, and in this version of the story Paepcke assented. During the same year, a rift between Paepcke and Richard Leach, vice-president of the institute and manager of the summer program, led to the severing of music from the other summer programs. Paepcke's characteristic demand that people do things his way or without his backing brought about the formation of Music Associates of Aspen. The organization took over the music program and developed an association with the Julliard School of Music in New York.[36]

Throughout the 1950s, the heyday of the Aspen Institute, Paepcke's dream flourished. Although the wrangles with locals and among factions in the cultural community remained a constant, the ski area finally turned a profit. An idyllic little invented community that, like Santa Fe, served its visitors ahead of its residents, and like Sun Valley, depended on the goodwill and capital of one entity, took shape. The 1949 celebration created incredible cachet, and the founding of the Aspen Institute gave the community a special feeling. Paepcke's scripted *Kulturstaat* was as close to existing as it ever came.

Yet the native community experienced growing alienation as their town was overwhelmed. Paepcke's energetic style included a healthy dose of arrogance, and in some respects he regarded the community as his own rather than as an experience he shared with its earlier residents. In his mind, the summer institute and its needs took precedence, but few locals agreed. The businesses that capitalized on growth were typically started by outsiders, in particular the first generation of ski bums such as Federation Internationale de Ski (FIS) team member Steven Knowlton, who developed ventures that catered to skiing enthusiasts. By 1950 he had purchased the Golden Horn corner and started a ski shop on the first floor; the basement held a bar and restaurant. Even Werner Kuster, the legendary owner of the famed Red Onion, was a neonative. A Swiss émigré who had grown up in a family that ran a resort, he came to Aspen as a cook and eventually took over the ownership of the legendary bar. Possessed of different skills and interests from those of the old-timers, these outsiders capitalized on their specific niche, in the process giving the town its first neonative identity. Locals in hardware, construction, and even sporting goods found opportunities, but they were often overshadowed by newcomers. Paepcke's Aspen Lumber and Supply Company was the first division of his enterprise to turn a profit, but this business competed with locals. The ongoing construction Paepcke and his friends instigated typically went to his companies. Locals still inhabited the same places in Aspen, but they seemed frozen both by intent and circumstance in a limited realm; the action that drove Aspen occurred beyond their reach.[37]

During the 1950s skiing grew significantly in Aspen. By 1954 it was a skiing center, replete with the kind of kitsch that Paepcke assiduously had avoided. A hot-dog stand in a covered wagon sat at the base of Aspen Mountain; parties and other revelries were a constant. The breadth of the summer institute showed that culture had a place in the community but largely during the short summers. The long winters were conducive to profit and sport. According to Bill Brenneman of the *Rocky Mountain News,* everyone in town had taken up skiing. Culture might be the forte in Aspen, but in 1954 skiing paid the bills. The mines were "gone," Pitkin county clerk Bill Stapleton noted. "Not a single man in Aspen is on a mine payroll now . . . even the farming and ranching is about shot." Despite the fears of Stapleton and others, skiing became the economic basis of the community. In 1959 the *Denver Post* announced that skiing and tourism were "responsible for a good deal of [Aspen's] growth."[38]

Aspen passed its first zoning ordinance in 1955, a reaction to the rapid transformation of the community. It codified the town's existing structure, compelling spatial relationships and construction to reflect that nature. Tourist accommodations could be built only in areas where such facilities already existed. Future construction in the West End, with its larger yards, had to be on equally large lots, and businesses were restricted to the four-square-block business district. The ordinance was designed to preserve the status quo, forcing the appearance of the town to belie its changes.[39]

Despite Paepcke's support, the ordinance contravened Gropius's injunction to retain the identity of the town. The structural restrictions shaped the rigid boundaries of the community, effectively freezing it in a moment in time that was pseudohistoric. This move was a form of the kitsch that Paepcke and Gropius eschewed, a step that mirrored the nearly simultaneous codification of adobe in Santa Fe in 1957. Designed to preserve the historic character and relationships of towns, such ordinances became integral parts of the process of transformation.

They also showed that the transformation of community affected even the individuals who thought they drove the process. The embrace of the ordinance by Paepcke, Bayer, and Fritz Benedict demonstrated that by 1955 the magic mountain no longer belonged entirely to the entrepreneur who had created it. Paepcke needed the ordinance because he did not own the entire town, and the people who owned the rest did not respect his sense of aesthetic relationships. Paepcke still held the power in Aspen, but his hold was weakening. Along with local elites, he faced displacement by fresh outside capital with different values. Even for Walter Paepcke, tourism could be a devil's bargain.

Another transformative dimension of Aspen's spreading neonative character first appeared in the 1950s: the construction of elegant and expensive second homes by Paepcke's associates and the small but growing professional class. The ski bums dominated the winter, but the cultural reform summer crowd made its mark on the community. Building $30,000 to $75,000 homes, extraordinary sums for the 1950s, that were typically "more modern and more expensive" than the owner's first residence, these newcomers changed the topography of the town and its demography.

Usually hailing from Denver, Texas, or Illinois, they brought not only financial resources but also distinct ways of thinking along with their own vision of Aspen. As part-time residents, not visitors, they enjoyed a much greater stake in the community and acted accordingly. Henry L. Stein, chief executive of Inland Steel Corporation and a close associate of Paepcke's, built an "imposing home" that overlooked the Roaring Fork River, where he planned an innovative irrigation system for the mesa above him and bottled water from the spring on his property for sale in the town. Courtlandt Barnes, a former partner in the Wall Street investment firm of H. N. Whitney, Goadby, and Company, resided in Aspen three months of the year and became chairman of the Music Associates of Aspen. Reginald Kell, the eminent clarinetist, and Nate Feinsinger, a University of Michigan law professor and a well-known labor negotiator, together became the full membership of the BBC, the Below Basalt Club, named for the streams that ran below the nearby town of Basalt. The two were avid anglers who firmly guarded their favorite spots, mimicking a long-standing local pastime and turning fishing into a full-blown recreational activity.[40]

The rush to build new second homes both accelerated change in Aspen and supported the status quo in Paepcke's *Kulturstaat.* Some of the owners were close to Paepcke, and their presence accentuated his power and influence; others were independent of the cultural community and became a potential threat. Each of these new part-time residents spent money in the town, added to its tax base, and as newspapers noted as early as 1959, created more opportunities in lower-wage occupations. More construction workers, waiters and waitresses, clerks, and storekeepers were necessary to meet the needs of new residents and visitors. The newcomers also had no qualms about showing longtime Aspenites what they considered better ways of doing things. But by building their own homes, extravagant by local standards, they inadvertently supported the status quo in the town. The nature of their construction and the use of previously undeveloped hillside and mountainside land meant that this wave of construction initially had little impact on the price or availability of housing for lower-wage workers. The two neonative communities of the 1950s, the winter and summer crowds, were also delineated by their accommodations. The denizens of Paepcke's cultural mecca resided in newly constructed, lavish homes that followed Walter Gropius's admonition to build new. The homes of the mining era stayed in longtime local hands or passed by sale or rental to the winter crowd, the typically impecunious ski enthusiasts.[41]

Throughout the 1950s the transformation of Aspen continued. The 800 full-year residents of 1940 became 1,200 in 1950 and 1,800 in 1959. By 1959 at least 200 part-time residents joined the year-round crowd. Aspen became known for its combination of lectures, music, and skiing, and as the decade progressed and Americans became more interested in leisure, technology made the slopes more accessible and the equipment to use them lighter in weight and less expensive. As popular culture communicated the joys of skiing to a wider, more affluent swath of the public, winter sports became increasingly dominant. By 1954 Aspen was so enamored of skiing that its leaders sought the 1960 Winter Olympics for the town. The fact that the little community in the Rockies, so recently moribund, was a serious contender reflected the transformation wrought by Paepcke and his successors.

The growth masked turmoil. Despite the efforts and wealth of Paepcke and his friends, Aspen became more oriented toward its winter activities than toward the culture that had launched it. Paepcke grappled with the town over a range of issues. Most prominent was the battle that created Music Associates, a supposedly amicable split but one that left the innovative entrepreneur shaken. The Aspen Institute continuously lost money; between 1955 and 1957 the loss averaged almost $100,000 annually, disheartening Paepcke and contributing to the strain on his finances. On a vacation in Europe in 1954, his first visit to the Continent since before World War II, he found a new diversion: the smell of pulp processing inspired a new division of the Container Corporation of America, Europa Carton. Inevitably this new venture consumed him as much as Aspen once had. In 1957, partly as a result of the 1956–1957 recession, Paepcke turned the institute over to oilman Robert O. Anderson, a devotee of Paepcke's ideas who had the connections and resources to lead it. A surprising rebirth of Aspen as a possible center for uranium mining gave heart to those who had never accommodated the transformation to tourism. Kennecott Mining Corporation and the federal government explored the area throughout the early 1950s, and in 1955 the Ski-Hi Uranium Corporation, with Edward Smart of Aspen as president, formed and filed thirty-three claims within twenty miles of the town. Paepcke's vision once had been the only hope for Aspen. But with the challenges from within the cultural community and opportunities apparently outside its boundaries, neonatives, seasonal residents, and old-timers alike looked beyond Paepcke. Paepcke's hegemony broke down. Like Socrates, he saw his Athens transformed.[42]

Although Aspen lost out on the Winter Olympics to Squaw Valley in California, it thrived as a winter resort. The nation's cultural direction headed toward the individualist affluence embodied in skiing in fashionable Aspen and away from the endeavors of the institute. "Today skiing in the mountain states has become big business," the *Overland News* reported in January 1958.

"Thousands of dollars are spent annually for skis of wood, metal, or plastic or combinations of the three; ski boots, bindings, etc. The amount spent on transportation to and from ski areas, food, and lodging, is impossible to estimate." Twenty-five thousand skiers resided in the Rocky Mountain states, and thousands more availed themselves of the railways, highways, and increasingly the airways to ski in Colorado and the West. With the expansion of the sport, Aspen, with its "very latest skiing facilities and superfine accommodations," became one of its focal points.[43] The recreation that Paepcke thought would pay for his cultural endeavor was well on the way to overwhelming its founder's desire.

Paepcke's health failed toward the end of the 1950s, but he barely noticed. He was diagnosed with bone and lung cancer during fall 1959, although knowing his penchant for disparaging the medical profession, Elizabeth Paepcke kept the news from him. For a few months he continued his active, vigorous lifestyle, but early in 1960 the disease took a toll. By February Paepcke was bedridden, and on April 13, 1960, he died. Although the Aspen Institute continued under Anderson's able leadership, the passing of the powerful founder left a vacancy in vision that even the prescient Anderson did not entirely fill. Aspen had been Paepcke's dream; without him it was different.[44]

In his elitist construction of a cultural Aspen to be subsidized by winter activities, Paepcke inadvertently presaged the structure of modern resorts. The most important trait was the year-round activity; by 1958 observers understood the centrality of this dimension. "Communities which at one time were forced to depend only on summer trade have now discovered the skier and balanced their seasonal business," the *Overland News* announced in 1958 in a direct reference to Aspen. "Is it any wonder that has proved to be a second bonanza for many a deteriorating mining town or summer resort?"[45] Although he framed skiing as an afterthought for economic purposes, Paepcke revealed a strategy that entrepreneurs more concerned with economic profit would embrace. One season had to be subsidized by the other, but as Sun Valley proved, the off-season was necessary to ensure that the profits of winter created a positive ledger.

The Aspen that Paepcke fashioned had the same impact on locals as did Edgar Hewett's Santa Fe and Averell Harriman's Sun Valley. In each, the new configuration changed the balance of power, granting incoming neonatives a greater say in the direction of the town than its longtime residents possessed. The process alienated locals, many of whom did not understand and few of whom could participate in the changes. The neonatives who were attracted to these transformed places soon recast them as reflections of their values. Visitors perceived the neonatives as natives, and a social and economic hierarchy that solidified change took shape. In a one-owner resort such as Paepcke's Aspen, the power that stemmed from the one source of capital drove the community. Resistance existed, but it was typically fragmented, and the Aspen of 1960 no more resembled the town of 1940 than Sun Valley did Ketchum.

Paepcke's experiment in idiosyncratic enlightened capitalism proved to be a pivotal moment in the evolution of tourism in the twentieth-century West, a bridge between a more elitist past and a future of mass culture. Paepcke's Aspen reflected earlier endeavors such as Hewett's Santa Fe, which sought a combination of distance and proximity to mainstream culture. Indeed, Hewett's Santa Fe offered a palliative similar to the cultural reform Paepcke envisioned growing from his *Kulturstaat;* both men saw their mission as a way to fix the woes of American culture. Paepcke's Aspen also melded the characteristics of Harriman's Sun Valley resort, the emphasis on skiing, outdoor activity, and the recreation-based neonative culture, even as it straddled the fault line between the fading domination of the culturati and the rising youth-oriented popular culture. Aspen presaged future trends, especially in patterns of home ownership, income distribution, demography, and the distribution of wealth. After Paepcke, neither tourism nor culture were ever quite the same.

Residence-based Resorts

Second Homes and Outside Influence

Walter Paepcke was the last of one kind of entrepreneur in western tourism, the individual who sought the intangible benefits of cultural uplift, not just monetary profit. He represented the aspirations of a generation of enlightened capitalists who saw social improvement in their endeavor. Paepcke fashioned Aspen as a center for understanding and ideas and for transmitting values and meaning in a rapidly changing time. Paepcke's Aspen served as an antidote to change, a place that expressed values to soothe social and cultural ills. It celebrated humanism, and as long as he lived and maintained control of the Aspen Institute, the town remained "the benchmark for deep thought in high places." But culture was expensive; even with Paepcke's backing, profit was important. The trend toward skiing, recreation, and increasingly, hedonism accelerated. By the early 1960s, the *Kulturstaat* was disappearing. Aspen and its skiing had become fashionable.

Popularity held its own devil's bargains for communities like Aspen, caught between different worlds and previously isolated from the mainstream. The success and camaraderie of 1950s Aspen resulted from its arguably autocratic leadership combined with the specialized interest in skiing. Aspen anticipated the future of American culture, its dreams and desires, but in a fashion that was not yet self-conscious. When the barriers that kept Aspen physically, intellectually, and attitudinally separate fell, the town was ripe for more than transformation. It stood the chance of being overrun, with only its fragile institutions to mitigate against change.

Aspen's new cachet stemmed from a number of sources. Its seemingly idyllic life, replete with Kerouac-like restlessness, transience, growing hedonism, and mobility and with its anti-Kerouac emphasis on an extravagant "good life," possessed a kind of meaning that resembled Sun Valley's. The town acquired its image of high culture from the Aspen Institute, but skiing benefited from its association with wealth and celebrity. Just as the spread of the automobile changed the profile of visitors to the Grand Canyon during the 1920s, the combination of changing culture, more wealth, and easier access made skiing a far more democratic endeavor than it had been in the 1930s. Like Sun Valley in the 1930s, Aspen became chic because it had a certain luster newly associated with skiing in American culture.

The presidential election year of 1960 was a watershed for skiing in the American West. The Winter Olympics that year at Squaw Valley near Lake Tahoe in California catapulted the sport to a new kind of prominence. The nation watched on television as skiers whizzed down the Sierra Nevada, whetting the appetite of an increasingly prosperous nation and notably expanding the audience for the sport. The impact was so great that a number of the hotels and restaurants around Squaw Valley became year-round operations. The Sunnyside Inn, once the private residence of one Captain Kendrick, who owned the Schlage Lock Company, became a summer resort in 1946; after Squaw Valley, it offered a twelve-month season.[1] Skiing became more visible, better understood, and more socially and culturally attractive after the Winter Olympics.

The NCAA's annual ski championship provided one measure of the sport's wider audience. Throughout the 1930s Dartmouth University, in Hanover, New Hampshire, with its famous coach Otto Schneibs, consistently won the national collegiate championship. By the 1950s Western State College, a small state school in Gunnison, Colorado, labeled "Wasted State," emerged as a powerhouse. This college lacked the serious academic reputation of Dartmouth, was in a remote part of the state, and mirrored the situation of other small state schools, such as Adams State College in Alamosa, Colorado. But skiers at Western State hailed from the mountain towns of Colorado and Utah and had grown up on skis; they were not the children of the wealthy who learned to ski on vacation in Vermont. The ascendance of Western State and later of the University of Utah demonstrated that skiers no longer came exclusively from the most affluent groups in American society. Small towns such as Steamboat Springs produced their own champions, individuals such as Gordon Wren, who became the first American to qualify in four Olympic events in 1948 and who placed fifth in the special jump, and Wallace J. (Buddy) Werner, America's leading skier in the 1950s. These natives of small-town working families were the vanguard as skiing spread to a multiclass, national audience.[2]

The development of new resorts and the expansion of existing ones kept pace with the growth of the industry. Throughout the late 1950s, older ski areas upgraded their lifts, accommodating the growing number of people with the wealth, leisure, and inclination to ski. Especially after 1960 the numbers rose significantly in the United States, from 1,584,250 skiers in 1960 to 2,448,000 by 1963 and 1964. In Colorado in 1964 and 1965, 1,102,690 skier visits took place, with 393,296 occurring in the mountain destination resorts. By 1967 and 1968 the numbers in the mountain resorts nearly doubled, to 749,719. The consistent growth created the opportunity to develop new resorts—under the right conditions.[3]

Singular in its importance among this new generation of resorts was Vail, in Eagle County, Colorado, which opened for business in 1962 in the geographic center of what had become the ski corridor in the state. Another offshoot of the Tenth Mountain Division, Vail was more than a mere ski resort. Designed to become a premier year-round outdoor recreation resort, Vail aspired to be a place apart from the rest of the nation, retaining all the amenities of prosperity. Its audience expected first class; Vail intended to provide it.[4] If Aspen reveled in its difference, Vail planed off the edges and made that idiosyncracy suburban.

Peter Siebert, a ski corps veteran wounded in the war, founded Vail. He moved to Aspen after the war, served as head of the ski patrol, and became a member of the 1950 U.S. ski team. Anticipating the future of the industry, he studied hotel management in Switzerland and after graduation returned to Colorado to manage the booming Loveland Basin ski resort. Siebert planned his own resort; he simply acquired the experience he knew he needed. While he was at Loveland Basin, he searched for the right mountain, an objective requiring a certain amount of self-confidence, indeed brashness.[5] In the mid-1950s the market for Colorado skiing showed the beginnings of saturation. Regional skiing had grown, but the national market remained limited. Sun Valley and Aspen still dominated; both were perfect locations for skiing, mountains that in the view of the time could not be equaled. Despite its distance from Denver, Aspen was significant. It had been a leading candidate to host the 1960 Winter Olympics. Resorts blossomed in California, further dividing the market. Any new resort faced competition. Surpassing the existing hierarchy posed problems, no matter how spectacular the scenery and the skiing. To dream of creating a new resort required both considerable nerve and great faith in the sport and its growth.

Siebert's opportunity came in 1956, when Earl Eaton, a ski patrolman who prospected for uranium in the mountains during the off-seasons, told the budding entrepreneur of a potential ski mountain. Located on the west side of Vail Pass on U.S. Highway 6 between Denver and Grand Junction, Colorado, the long ridge of excellent north-facing terrain hid a series of grand, south-facing treeless bowls with nearly 2,000 vertical feet of powder, prime downhill skiing territory. Siebert's faith was repaid; a new and better place to ski in the Colorado Rockies did exist. Even more promising, skiing the bowls at Vail required far less skill than the steep slopes of Aspen. From the moment Siebert first saw the location, he recognized that it had a quality no other place could match. Its slopes could accommodate beginners and less accomplished skiers, and its scenery equaled or surpassed other resorts.[6] With easy slopes, Vail offered the chance to attract an even broader cross-section of the American public.

In the small, crowded, and close-knit skiing industry of 1950s Colorado, the project had to remain a secret. Siebert, Eaton, and four associates, including another veteran of the Tenth Mountain Division, John Tweedy, purchased the 500-acre Hansen ranch at the base of Vail Mountain for $55,000. They put the word out that they planned a hunting and fishing club, going so far as to name themselves the Trans Montane Rod and Gun Club to deceive anyone who suspected another purpose. The roughly $110 per acre they paid was as much as the group could afford. Their secret held, and in 1960 they were able to complete their predevelopment holdings unnoticed with the purchase of another property, the 500-acre Katsos Ranch.[7]

Acquiring the land was the first step, but getting the financing and the permits for such a project posed a far more difficult task. New resorts opened annually in the immediate postwar era, and older ones were renovated. By the mid-1950s Colorado bankers and investors feared overbuilding. After being repeatedly asked why the state needed another ski area when it had Aspen, Siebert purportedly coined what might be the tourism entrepreneur's mantra: "To hell with them; we'll do it anyway." In 1959 the Forest Service offered a thirty-year conditional-use permit for the project, provided that the Vail Corporation possessed $1.5 million in available capital, the first $1 million in cash and $.5 million in guaranteed borrowed funds. Traveling with George Caulkins, a Denver oilman, Siebert sold limited partnership shares in the project. Each of the 100 available shares cost $10,000 and included four lifetime ski passes, with one acre of land in the development included for an additional $250. The $1 million seemed like a small sum for such a project, but even that was hard to raise.[8]

Like Sun Valley, Vail was a new resort that had to be created, not built from the ruins of an older economic tradition. Unlike the earlier ski resorts, there was no previous Anglo American settlement to function as a physical base for the community, no neighboring town such as Ketchum, no mining town like Aspen. Everything had to be built. It could be scripted in accordance with Vail Corporation's desires. Late in 1962 a $1 million lodge, upper and lower terminals to provide food and warming facilities, and a gondola and two chair lifts had been constructed. Nine buildings along Bridge Street made up the commercial community.[9] By the slated grand opening on December 17, 1962, a new resort had been constructed where a meadow had been and plans laid for more than $20 million of development in a six-year period. Vail had no previous identity; even its name was new and different. It was a precursor of future changes in the nature of resort communities.

Vail focused on two specific constituencies, the affluent and families. Its advertising aimed at higher-than-average income groups, the people who read the *New Yorker* or *National Geographic.* This audience required sophisticated nightclubs and fine bistros, nightlife and entertainment. Yet skiing enjoyed a wholesome image, and Vail possessed soft, sloping terrain to attract families. In contrast to the more aggressively male images of skiing that emanated from Aspen or Sun Valley, Vail appealed to parents who sought an activity they could enjoy with their children.[10] This carefully managed but seemingly contradictory vision of wholesome nightlife and sophisticated but clean fun illustrated how thoroughly Vail Associates defined its audience and the niche that made them comfortable.

Although the initial development was entirely company-controlled, subsequent development used other sources of capital. In 1963 three lodges and three condominiums were completed, a liquor store, service station, ski shop, restaurant, drug store, and beauty shop opened, and the meadow had become a town. The first homes were constructed on the lots optioned with the investment package the same year. Most were in the $15,000 to $25,000 range, substantially less expensive than the ones built around the increasingly swank Aspen. The Architectural Control Committee enforced a broad building code that emphasized faux European styles; second-home owners competed to have the most authentic-looking Swiss architecture. Vail found or perhaps created a niche, catering to a combination of upper-middle-class second-home owners, day users from Denver whose access was enhanced by the 1966 extension of Interstate 70 through Vail Pass and Eagle County, and lodge- and hotel-based visitors who responded to the resort's massive advertising campaigns. By the ski season of 1967 and 1968, Vail's new idiom within regional tourism was firmly established.[11]

Vail also became an important fulcrum for business within Colorado's ski corridor. The combination of easy highway access, moderately difficult skiing, and a vast investment in advertising brought success in this competitive industry. Vail boomed. It attracted entrepreneurs and salespeople, those who sought to take a risk on what appeared to be a nineteenth-century-style boomtown. Rapid growth followed; from 1963 to 1967 more than $4 million worth of construction occurred each summer. By 1967 Vail had 3,500 beds and the lift capacity to transport 8,400 skiers per hour. Expansion resulted in the investment of $21 million in the regional economy and the expenditure of as much as $34 million. During 1967 and 1968, 290,000 skiers visited Vail, about 70 percent of whom were from outside Colorado's boundaries. Visitors spent more than $7 million at the resort alone. Vail had become not only an important destination but also an integral part of the Colorado ski economy.[12]

In its demography, Vail resembled Aspen more than Steamboat Springs but was decidedly different. Like Aspen's, Vail's constituency came from outside Colorado, but the clientele was different from the effete culturati and the restless ski bums who came to Aspen. Vail offered mass-marketed skiing, affordable experience and amenities, hotels and second homes aimed at the broad segment of the public that could almost afford the pleasures of the rich. It tempted everyone who enjoyed status by association. Vail was skiing democratized but made to appear a beacon of affluence; few idiosyncracies existed in the planned community. Sun Valley, Aspen and Steamboat Springs had distinct yet different personalities determined by local characteristics. Vail lacked such traits, but as Peter Siebert observed, "Mass follows class," and the resort soon typified mainstream 1960s culture.

Vail followed the script of one-owner resorts. Conceived as a complete leisure experience, the town filled its visitors' needs. It was run by one entity, Vail Associates, formed in 1966 as a publicly held successor to Vail Corporation. Siebert and his people used their experience in the ski industry to script what they believed was the perfect ski community, a faux alpine village complete with the crooked and winding streets that Americans associated with such places. Vail Associates created a paradoxically antiurban urbanism in their village; architects could place amenities where they were needed since there were no historical patterns of community life to consider.[13] Vail was not really a community but a script, a collection of buildings designed for the comfort of transient visitors. It elevated to new heights the concept of serving visitors first.

In the late 1960s such service was a decisive and important choice that inadvertently increased Vail's popularity. The nation seemed divided, at war with itself over Vietnam and the changing conceptions of morality that stemmed from popular culture. Antiheroes replaced heroes in the American pantheon, and an oppositional culture that challenged the values of the postwar era took shape. In the resulting dissension, Vail posed itself as an island of tranquillity. One of its marketing techniques was to show that the resort offered distance from the chaos of the era.[14]

The ownership of Vail broke away from the pattern that seemingly characterized one-developer resorts. Vail remained in the hands of a small group of ski enthusiasts, many of whom enjoyed personal and social ties. Because Siebert and his friends sneaked up on the skiing industry, they obviated the immediate need for large amounts of capital, which would have minimized their expertise and input in design and made them dependent on large metropolitan banks or similar funding sources. By raising capital privately and quietly, by knowing the industry well enough to recognize their discovery, they kept control among a small group of aficionados until their development became financially secure. When that finally occurred, they took a marketable commodity public while maintaining ownership of a majority of its stock.[15]

There was a new twist introduced at Vail that resulted from the drive to raise funds for construction. The original $10,000 fee per share was small enough to include ordinary investors. Consequently, people of relatively modest means owned the lots in the development, which showed in the construction of dwellings in the community. Instead of the luxury homes of the wealthy, Vail soon sported both condominiums and more modest second homes. The need for a permanent resident population in Vail, the opportunity of early investors to buy land, and the sale of land as another source of cash flow and profit for Vail Associates contributed to this innovation. But the construction of medium-priced second homes became a catalytic decision that transformed the nature of ski resorts in the American West.

The new construction at Vail initiated a pattern of development in which resorts that had catered to exclusive constituencies, both in wealth and skiing ability, lowered their sights and courted the upper-middle class, somewhat affluent and typically inexperienced at skiing. This innovation was driven partly by the rising cost of land near resorts and equally by the saturation of the market for the truly wealthy. By subdividing desirable acreage, developers could reap a much larger profit than they could from selling one-acre or larger lots to individuals for expensive homes. With the attraction of less difficult skiin, Vail enjoyed instant cachet with this less wealthy constituency, and its members came to the new resort in droves. In Vail's third season, it began to top the skier-visit numbers of its most direct rivals; by its fifth season the number of skiers reached 250 percent of original projections.[16] In the process, the demography of skiing dramatically changed.

Vail Associates also initiated another important change in the western resort industry. Before Vail, ski towns and skiing had been closely intertwined but not indistinguishable. In Ketchum, Lane's store remained open for the local trade; in Aspen, numerous businesses were not part of the cultural or recreational regimes. But Vail was different. It was an invention where everything depended on the resort and consequently on Vail Associates. This measure of control was desirable for the developers because they could more completely control their visitors' experiences.

Such control had been a hallmark of the most successful postwar skiing resorts. La Grande Plagne near Savoy, France, was perhaps the best known example. Founded in 1961 as an economic solution to declining agriculture and extractive industries, La Grande Plagne developed from the actions of five communes in the Isere Valley. They built an access road to the area, but a regional development company failed. It was replaced by a consortium of Paris banks, which established a development company, Société d'Aménagement de La Plagne (SAP), that took control of the region. By 1968 more than 5,000 beds were available, mostly in condominiums, and the SAP controlled shops, hotels, and movie houses. As at Vail, the operators at La Plagne calculated the capacity of ski lifts and coordinated business with the available overnight accommodations. This planning and the prominent role of the consortium of banks made the site attractive to investors, and SAP rapidly turned a profit. Selling apartments, condominiums, and other facilities provided short-term profit, which SAP used to develop three satellites. By 1974 more than 14,000 beds were available at this preeminent ski resort.[17]

Contemporaneous with La Grande Plagne, Vail was the first truly one-developer, integrated resort in postwar western skiing. Aspen shared many of the characteristics of such places, but it also contained a range of variations. Paepcke's interest in cultural reform, less a tourist theme than a class-driven one, and the institutions he established to support it provided a range of experience and reflected a breadth of values atypical in one-developer resorts. The original community of Aspen itself also attenuated the patterns of control. Ketchum played a similar role at Sun Valley. In the West, Vail alone had one set of developers and one distinct purpose: to create an environment where people could enjoy the experience of skiing while the company and the many entrepreneurs who flocked to the town made outstanding profits.

Unlike Aspen and Ketchum–Sun Valley, where skiing first enticed and then dislocated local residents, the initial residents of Vail were seasonal service workers. The people who worked there in 1962 were part of a self-described elect. They chose skiing and work in resorts as had Aspen's ski bums of the 1950s; they understood that part of their bargain required that they smile and be courteous at all times. Their accommodations were typical of those for seasonal workers. Some lived down the road in Mintern. A range of same-sex communal living arrangements, dormitories and barracks, housed others. With the construction of condominiums and second-home developments, better living arrangements became possible, but workers often most needed such accommodations at exactly the same time that the owners wanted to use their high-elevation retreats. Although workers in ski towns that stemmed from existing communities were relegated to the worst structures available, they at least could expect private sleeping quarters and facilities. In early Vail, most workers shared not only rooms but also showers and bathrooms. Early construction established the hierarchical pattern of resort accommodations at Vail. Visitors found nice rooms, and workers experienced the living conditions of military conscripts.

By the early 1970s class disparity and a lack of attention to the needs of workers created a backlash. Employees became fed up with Vail's low wages and poor living conditions and with the autocratic attitudes of management toward employee prerogative. Vail workers were like serfs; even recreational amenities in the area were geared to the needs of visitors over residents. During the 1960s the company forbade employees to sport beards. Al Hills, a local iconoclast who briefly edited an alternative newspaper, noted that this edict rendered Vail "off-limits to Jesus Christ, Abraham Lincoln, and other Subversive Employees." As Vail became desirable, its cost of living rose and low wages did not suffice. Permanent employees were forced to live out of town, "down valley" in local parlance, and commute; temporary employees had no incentive even to consider a permanent career.[18] Vail's quality of life was exceptional for second-home residents and visitors, but life as an employee became progressively less desirable. The class system at the core of resorts was exposed, illustrating another of the devil's bargains of tourism.

The rapid pace of growth affected everyone in town, even its financial beneficiaries. The ever-optimistic editor of the *Vail Trail*, George Knox, wondered whether Vail "could become a monster." He spoke for a growing number of local business and home owners, most of whom first came to Vail for economic opportunity but who had come to regard the town as their home. In their view it was under siege by development. Paragons of the business community such as Joe Stauffer, who came as the resort opened in 1962 and later managed and owned lodges and other businesses, became a particularly vocal opponent of unbridled growth. Stauffer made Vail his home and fought to protect it.[19] Development for profit alone threatened him and other residents as much as it did hourly-wage employees.

Even the faux alpine character of the town came under siege. A battle over an authorized Holiday Inn sign defined the parameters of aesthetic conflict. In 1967 Kemmons Wilson and the Holiday Inn Corporation agreed to build its Vail hotel in pseudoalpine style, but it refused to relent on its trademark sign. Although Siebert originally informed the corporation that neon was inappropriate in Vail, the Holiday Inn was too great a prize to reject, and eventually Vail Associates granted permission. Despite widespread local opposition, the sign stayed, rending the veil of isolation that the resort touted.[20] With its Holiday Inn road sign, Vail lost a little of its claim to being unique.

The conflict over the sign illustrated the devil's bargain of rapid growth. Even in ostensibly highly controlled Vail, the issue of expansion pitted different elements of the community against one another. The Architectural Control Committee became a focal point of dissent. It seemed determined not to protect the character of Vail but to alter it. Beyond Vail Associate's Town of Vail, the limits of control were particularly apparent. Conventional sprawl in the valley replaced the quaint feel of a small town. Even in the village, the need for amenities spurred rapid change, and Vail Associates' chronic shortage of available funds weakened the resolve to hold the line against profitable albeit sometimes questionable development. The opening of the Crossroads at Vail, a seven-story shopping center, served notice that the town would never again be small and quaint. An eight-story tower at the lodge further altered the town's scale. The 1969 opening of LionsHead, a prefabricated and architecturally bland second village and ski area that sought to redistribute some of the skiers whose presence had made Vail a success, illustrated yet another devil's bargain. Everyone was making money, but many people found that the town that made it for them was not their own any more. By 1969, when the Night Latch dormitory was torn down to accommodate the new Mountain Haus condominiums, clear lines between past and present had been cast.[21] Advocates of growth could no longer claim that they represented the interests of the entire community; many of their neighbors opposed any decisions that altered the aesthetics and the feel of their town. A wedge between elements of the community became apparent and grew larger.

Despite such problems, Vail opened a plethora of new possibilities for resort developers. It fused the managerial ethic of the postwar era with the skiing industry and the idea of a year-round haven for leisure, adding efficiency and organization to the idiosyncratic autocracy that Paepcke had promoted in Aspen. Vail embellished the pattern of control that the AT&SF, the Union Pacific, and Paepcke previously established. The earlier concerns dominated the economics of possibilities in the resort, and as a result, the range of experience. But in Vail, even the physical order of the resort was planned from above. Devoid of the pretext of cultural values that characterized the packaging of the Grand Canyon, Santa Fe, and Aspen, Vail was like Sun Valley in its obsession with skiing and like Aspen in the structure of its dominant organization. This fusion of managerial capitalism and recreational sport had great power during the 1960s. Vail was a precursor of a more sophisticated form of organization among western tourist destinations. Its model could be followed; it could be recast into an entirely new mode of resort development.

Relying on this new model, William Janss of the Janss Corporation became the catalyst in the transformation of western resorts and the communities that surrounded them. A cattle rancher and construction magnate, Janss was the son of Peter Janss, a physician from Nebraska who became a real estate developer at the turn of the century and developed the area of Westwood and the University of California, Los Angeles. A talented skier who was named to the U.S. Olympic team in 1940, an experienced developer, and a member of the board of the Aspen Institute during the 1950s, Bill Janss had an entirely new conception of what a resort should and could be. His vision shaped the post-1970 resort West.[22]

Janss took the skills and practices learned as an important California developer and made them the preeminent pattern in western mountain resorts. Under his control, the Janss Corporation had been instrumental in the creation of Thousand Oaks, California, a 45,000-person planned community in Ventura County in greater Los Angeles. Using this experience, he designed Snowmass, outside Aspen, along the pattern established at Vail, and in 1964 he purchased Sun Valley, forging a "new vision" that came to typify western resorts. Janss derived his insight from the Vail project. He envisioned the creation of a second-home market in what had previously been hotel room–based resorts. Janss's resorts expanded from the room rental business into more comprehensive development, structuring every aspect of the communities he built or bought. He initiated a new stage of development, characterized by condominiums and second homes, that became standard in the resort industry.

The Janss developments created a primacy for the one-developer resort, the ordered, structured location that functioned as a result of predetermined precepts and that followed the patterns of planned communities. This highly structured and controlled environment, company-owned or tightly zoned elsewhere, served as a precursor of later housing developments across the West. Janss took patterns common in California and spread them throughout the region. He brought a script with two clear consequences for his resorts: they would put the visitors first but in a way that they would be unaware of their primacy, and they devalued the importance of local people except in service capacities. Janss recapitulated and formalized the colonialism of extractive industries and the devil's bargains of tourism faced by so many communities.

Impressing this grid on the seemingly spacious resorts of the western mountains seemed incongruous, but it had a basis in the spacial realities of mountain communities. The planned community, the restricted private space ethic, developed in the Los Angeles basin, where space was at a premium; mountain development faced equal constraints. Federal land dominated the mountain West. Most ski communities abutted the holdings of one of the many federal land management agencies. The narrow mountain valleys dictated that although expansive vistas surrounded people, only small parcels of land were available for development. Federal land was typically inaccessible to private developers; much land was on slopes too steep for safe construction or that would be extremely expensive to provide with utility services and adequate roads. Ever more crowded communities crammed into the bottom of mountain valleys typified the problems of life in mountain resorts. The order that Janss impressed on his developments shielded them from the dense living of some urban areas.

Janss's arrival was also a harbinger of significant cultural change. His purchase and subsequent transformation of Sun Valley inexorably altered the resort. From New Year's Eve 1936 until 1964, Sun Valley had remained a Union Pacific resort. It had a checkered history within the company, for after Gov. C. A. Robins cracked down on gambling in the state in 1945, Sun Valley remained prestigious but was a consistent drain on UP finances. In the postwar era, the railroad shifted its focus from passengers to freight. These circumstances combined to decrease Sun Valley's importance. The opening of newer and more easily accessible ski areas throughout the West and the advent of air travel made Sun Valley's preeminence even more tenuous. Vail developed the most sophisticated marketing scheme in the industry, David R. C. Brown's leadership of the Aspen Ski Company catapulted Aspen to the forefront of skiing, but Sun Valley remained as it had been.

After W. Averell Harriman ceased his day-to-day management of the railroad, Union Pacific officials could no longer reconcile the meaning of the resort with the red ink. It had been Harriman's pet project; without his support, it floundered. Sun Valley lost some of its appeal to the traveling public. Although both Ketchum and Sun Valley were incorporated as villages in 1947, between 1940 and 1950 population growth slowed in the county to 1.7 percent, and a precipitious decline followed. By 1960 the population of Blaine County fell more than 14 percent from its 1950 level to 4,598. In the words of one observer, Sun Valley had "gotten kind of old and stodgy." UP president Arthur Stoddard long supported the resort and in 1964 sought refurbishing ideas. He hired the Janss Company, which suggested a $6 million facelift. Aghast at the sum, Stoddard decided to sell.[23]

After Janss and his partners purchased Sun Valley in 1964, they envisioned a resort that differed from the Union Pacific's. Despite the survey that discouraged the railroad, Janss believed his company could refurbish the old resort and reinvent it. Sun Valley was "run down" when he purchased it, Janss recalled, and was no longer fashionable, but it offered a better overall situation for tourism than existed even in Colorado. Stating his philosophy that the critical aspect of ski area management was to own enough land to "preserve options for future development," Janss planned to become, in the words of journalist/writer Philip Fradkin, "the Henry Ford of ski developers, with overtones of Cadillac styling and Pentagon computer techniques."[24]

Janss's ideas for Sun Valley differed from those of the Union Pacific. Inspecting the physical plant on his first postpurchase tour, Janss looked into a cavernous basement area that had once been the boiler room and announced that it would become the resort's new discotheque, the Boiler Room. Such instinctive decision making was Janss's signature. He was a canny individual with an understanding of how to please the public. Janss also upgraded the facilities. The original Challenger Inn had been built on European lines, with multiple rooms sharing one bathroom down the hall. By the 1960s such accommodations were unacceptable to American travelers. Janss ordered every other wall torn out and bathrooms installed for each room. By the completion of the renovation, he spent much more than the $6 million he estimated.[25]

Janss also invested heavily in a twelve-month tourist season for Sun Valley. Despite its efforts, the Union Pacific never succeeded in making summers as attractive as winters. Janss believed this failure resulted from a lack of facilities. Three asphalt tennis courts and seats for watching skaters on the rink had been the only summer amenities. The asphalt courts were "like not having a court at all," Janss, a sports enthusiast, remarked, and eight new courts, an Olympic-sized swimming pool, and a shopping mall that connected the Sun Valley Lodge and the Challenger Inn were constructed. Later Janss added to the horseback and skeet-shooting facilities and improved the golf course. The course was in "very sad shape," Janss remembered, "it was narrow and the rough was rocks." He made it into a championship golf course.[26] In Janss's Sun Valley, summer activity meant more than hunting and fishing. As with almost everything else he did, Janss catered to people of wealth and taste, people who could be said to initiate rather than follow trends in midcentury society and culture.

The development program also focused on the slopes themselves. An expert skier, Janss wanted the slopes to be a challenge, always a risky strategy and one that flew in the face of the logic that propelled Vail to prominence. Sun Valley possessed the steepest slopes in the industry. In Janss's estimation, the only problem before his purchase of the resort was poor maintenance of the slopes. "When it got icy," Janss told reporters, "you just skied on ice." Investment in snow-grooming equipment made the slopes better for expert and beginning skiers alike.[27]

Janss ran a risk he might not have grasped. His model could succeed only if the number of avid, skilled skiers increased sufficiently and only if Sun Valley retained enough of its earlier cachet to attract a constituency that might ski poorly but would embrace the social life that Janss provided. With this formula, he changed the terms of the resort; the draw became the entire Sun Valley package, not merely the skiing. Janss's brash confidence, his string of successes, and his own status possibly blinded him to the risks.

Janss's Sun Valley looked different from the Union Pacific's resort. Condominiums, another innovation that was so new in Idaho that it required a change in law to be legal, changed the physical layout of the community. One hundred twenty-eight small studio apartments were part of the initial construction, as were a number of two-bedroom units. "It was my concept," Janss remembered, "and they sold out before we could finish them." Some of the condos, particularly near the upscale lodge, were attractive, but the second and third developments were prefabricated and ordinary. One of the complexes earned the sobriquet Camp Janss. Janss himself even referred to them as "cookie-cutter houses," but they helped create a more permanent market for Sun Valley.[28] People who owned them, owned shares in them, or who leased them came back each year, filling the coffers of the community in other ways.

As was common among one-owner resorts, Janss sold land and made arrangements that gave him other sources of profit besides the lodges and the ski slopes. Land sales and home and condominium construction were most lucrative. The profits from land sales offset interest or paid down debt, were pumped back into the resort, or paid out to shareholders. Nor did the sale of land in any way proffer control. Janss held tight to his prerogatives. Sun Valley was still his place, and he decided which lands would be developed and which would not.

Condos became big business in Sun Valley. Late in 1967 new projects opened, housing more than 100 families, "several of them Idahoans," according to one newspaper account. Built by Boise-Cascade, an Idaho-based company, and the Janss Company and located between Dollar Mountain and the Challenger Inn, these "ateliers" were modular units, which helped lower the extraordinarily expensive nineteen dollar per square foot average cost to a more reasonable fourteen dollars. This inexpensive construction and plans for developments such as the 3,000-bed Elkhorn Village prompted a regional construction boom that altered the face of the community and the surrounding region.[29]

Upscale houses followed the condos. Along Trail Creek and the golf course, luxurious homes belonging to the wealthy and famous sprouted. Russell Stewart, senior vice-president of Field Enterprises and a devotee of cooking, built a house with five kitchens; Walter Annenberg built along the golf course. Steve McQueen, Tom Hormel of Hormel's Meats and his wife Janet Leigh, and William W. and Mignon Winan added their personal touch as they built an enclave of homes that reflected sheer wealth and the revived mystique of Sun Valley. By 1970 Janss's resort had regained its glamour; even the *New York Times* pronounced Sun Valley "neat again."[30]

But Janss's Sun Valley was not the same as the Union Pacific's. Although it contained the same primary attractions, spectacular skiing and the aura of wealth and fame, a different set of economic and cultural premises governed it. Sun Valley remained the "social center of the ski world," but the rules and relationships set up under UP administration and nurtured by its benign neglect no longer held. Instead a more bottom line institutional structure, rigidly controlled from the top, prevailed. Janss's developments at both Sun Valley and Snowmass were "Southern California come to the Rockies," Fradkin noted. "The two lifestyles meet, and the resulting compromise preserves little of the two components."[31]

This shift dislocated even the most loyal Sun Valley neonative, the venerable Dorice Taylor. In her memoir, the chapter describing the sale to Janss is titled, "We Are Dumped." Her identification with Sun Valley suggested the depth of neonative proprietary feeling; her clear ties to the UP's Sun Valley indicated the degree of alienation she felt in the transition. Taylor's memoir reads as if she believed the railroad had no right to sell the resort. Even though she retained her position as publicity director, the new Sun Valley felt different to her and other longtime locals. Janss's plans disrupted the status quo and upset existing convention, angering some people in the town who gave "loud yowls of grief" every time a new condominium project went up. The population grew dramatically between 1960 and 1970; 5,749 people were recorded in the 1970 census, a 25 percent increase from the 1960 total, and they crowded the resort and the surrounding area. One resident, John E. P. Morgan, immortalized the changes in verse: "The mountains are now like a city; with pandemoniums [condominiums] at prices pretty." Innovations such as the Janss-initiated Sun Valley Center for the Arts and Humanities, an Aspen Institute knock-off with art displays, workshops in literature, and programs such as glassblowing and ceramics, reflected a broadened sense of the resort's possibilities. The 8,000 available beds in 1976, including bed space in condominiums, up from the 800 available when Janss purchased the resort, illustrated the sweep of the change.[32]

By 1970 Janss's efforts accelerated patterns of change in the distribution of occupations in Sun Valley and Blaine County. The number of farmers fell from 1,647 in 1935 to 1,312 in 1950, to 1,166 in 1960, and to 877 in 1970. At the same time, the percentage of hotel and other service workers increased. Of 2,295 workers in 1950, 481 were identified as participating in service occupations. Forty-two percent of female workers in the county labored in such capacities, the highest recorded percentage for female workers to that time. The gender segmentation became more typical of resorts as growth created employment for women in positions such as maids at a much faster rate than predominantly male ski instructors were hired. Even at the nadir of development in 1960, fully 15 percent of male employees and 34 percent of female employees in Blaine County worked in the service industry. The initial years of the Janss era masked the growth in service as a percentage of the workforce since construction jobs made up a large percentage of job growth in the late 1960s. Subtracting construction employment above the level of 1960, the early years show an increase to almost 25 percent of male workers in the county in service occupations, female service workers remaining constant as a percentage of female employment, and a dramatic increase in self-employed individuals.[33] Janss created a structurally and economically different community that, like Santa Fe and Aspen before it, catered to outsiders more than to locals.

A backlash against Janss's activities accelerated in the mid-1970s. The extensive Sun Valley building boom spilled over to nearby Ketchum and Hailey, extending the tentacles of the resort and with them its transformative impact. A master plan for the region was under way, linking in ordinance the resort with the surrounding communities that were still dominated by longtime locals. The changes inspired an outcry. Some longtime visitors to Sun Valley felt that the quantity and quality of development threatened the community, and many locals agreed. A questionnaire about development in Ketchum circulated to residents, who expressed clear dislike for those responsible for the changes. Antidevelopment and antioutsider rhetoric dominated responses. One protest advocated "no more developers, no more condos, just private homes," a reflection of the altered demography of the resort. "Stop advertising Idaho," read another. A third bemoaned the fate of the creek in which he fished as a child, muddied by debris from upstream construction.[34] The feelings of the neonative elite were common across a broad spectrum of the local population.

Far from capitulating, Taylor, Morgan, and the others who objected to Janss's changes engaged in a negotiation with new realities. Under the Union Pacific, they felt themselves part of a community and a place that, although designed for visitors, also sheltered them and not incidentally granted them special status. Janss's changes fundamentally altered their situation; he fashioned a different town with its own self-contained importance. Janss brought his own people and placed them in positions of leadership and power. Even those whom he retained, such as Dorice Taylor, found their responsibilities altered, their decision making curtailed, and their status lessened. Located in Sun Valley and with little desire to leave, the first generation of neonatives had to reach accommodation with new forces that inadvertently or intentionally devalued their presence. The many newcomers who followed Janss to Sun Valley made accommodation even more difficult. Grumbling disguised as social critique accompanied neonatives' reluctant participation in the new situation.

The results of Janss's plan were even more pronounced at Snowmass. Quietly completing the purchase of 3,400 acres of land in Brushy Creek outside Aspen at about $500 per acre in 1961, Janss fashioned a community where first the upper class and then the middle and upper-middle class could buy a second home and enjoy the recreational opportunities nearby. Snow-cat skiing tours started in 1962, and the 5,000 people who took them offered ideas about how and where the ski runs should be located. Kingsbury Pitcher, a grandson of Colorado pioneer Otto Mears and a childhood friend of Janss's from Pasadena who lived in Aspen, was hired to survey the mountains from a treacherous old military-issue weasel. After his hard work, he was supplanted by the Aspen Ski Company, which ran the resort for Janss. The Forest Service granted permits in 1964, Janss sold part of the development to the American Cement Company for $4.5 million, and the resort took shape.[35]

Janss followed the time-honored practice of incoming entrepreneurs: he used local talent, in this case, local legends, to design the new resort that would take Aspen further from the direction a solid core of its citizens desired. This approach created a fracture between the first generation of neonatives, who accommodated growth, and their successors, who regarded Aspen as a tightly knit community. Pitcher and the Aspen Ski Corporation supplied the expertise in skiing and recreational management. Aspen legend Fritz Benedict, an architect who had served with the Tenth Mountain Division, worked with Herbert Bayer, and married Bayer's wife's sister, became Janss's principal designer. Some segments of cultural Aspen were aghast. A beacon of the age of cultural reform, an exemplum of the first generation of Aspen neonatives, joined the commercial development crowd. Benedict's assignment was simple: in the words of Peggy Clifford, he was to "design a village that would serve the needs of skiers at a cost-profit ratio that the computer approved." Such caustic commentary reflected the tension in the changing community. In Clifford's view, Janss talked a great deal about Thoreau while on the board of the Aspen Institute, but at Snowmass his "version of Walden Pond wasn't particularly Thoreauvian."[36] An ideological fault line appeared, pitting proponents of growth against people who wanted to keep Aspen pure, and acrimonious debate replaced camaraderie.

The Snowmass development was expensive and multifaceted. The Aspen Skiing Corporation started a wholly owned subsidiary, the Snowmass Skiing Corporation, to build the lifts at Snowmass and to administer the skiing. The Janss Colorado Corporation, an arm of the Janss Investment Corporation, and the American Cement Company handled both real estate sales and resort development. The three firms invested as much as $10 million in the resort, altering the economies of scale in the Roaring Fork Valley.

When Snowmass opened in December 1967, it was a complete community. Five lodges, one hundred twenty condominiums, twelve private residences, a conference center, an Olympic-sized swimming pool and three smaller ones, and a range of other amenities graced the Brushy Creek Valley.[37]

Janss adopted the new structure that had been invented at Vail and that gave developers greater control over the ski communities they owned. In comparison to Snowmass, Vail was an amateurish operation that exerted a number of forms of de facto control over the nature of the development but that lacked the comprehensive control of a master-planned resort. Vail Associates remained shy of capital even after it went public. Siebert and Caulkins's tour for investors raised less money than one phone call by Bill Janss. Vail allowed a tremendous range of diversity in enterprise. Janss perfected the corporate model of ski resorts, with all its advantages and disadvantages. Everything at Snowmass, from restaurants to lodges, had to pass Janss's review. The control he established through landownership at Sun Valley was even more comprehensive when he built Snowmass.

Janss aimed Snowmass at a relatively new market for skiing. Unlike Sun Valley or Aspen, Snowmass targeted the same segment of the upper-middle class as did Vail. It was a large market, expanded greatly by postwar prosperity and the growing premium on recreational experience. Snowmass not only allowed people to enjoy outdoor sport, but it also defined their place in the American hierarchy of status.

The initial development at Snowmass, West Village, targeted an affluent constituency. "At last you see the village," a reporter wrote, confirming the image Janss coveted. "Unexpected. Compact. Intimate. Honey colored windows beckon through the night." Janss's developments, from Westwood and Thousand Oaks in California to Sun Valley, always bore this imprimatur; they were distinctive, signature properties, architecturally and in status "better" than the norm. At Snowmass as elsewhere, Janss aimed to provoke envy. Its residential lots selling for $10,000 to $30,000 and its apartments costing in the $45,000 range, West Village offered the aura of Sun Valley and gentrified Aspen with the amenities of modern suburbia. Janss paid $250,000 to bury the utility lines, following a pattern perfected in Scottsdale, Arizona, where even signage was regulated. He understood that his script had to eliminate the banal and the cultural cusp. To protect the desired ambience, Janss declined offers from both the Playboy Club and Howard Johnson's, opposite ends of the cultural spectrum. Snowmass marketing manager John Cooley, a member of a southern California shopping center development family, best expressed the sentiment: "We want the effect [of the resort] to be one of total harmony."[38]

Flushed with success, Janss broadened the audience that Snowmass targeted. A second community there aimed at enticing ordinary suburbanites to invest in a second home or a time-share, a purchase of a property for a fixed amount of time during any given year. "Superb Snowmass homesites especially designed for middle income families," an advertising brochure proclaimed. Owners could enjoy a vacation home on weekends and could stay for extended periods, "with Dad joining them on the weekends. Many offer their property for rent when they aren't using it." With lots starting as low as $6,000 at Meadow Ranch and $7,000 at Country Club, less than half the initial price of lots in the Phase I development at West Village, and with condos built in a style identical to the Elkhorn development adjacent to Sun Valley, Snowmass II was genuinely affordable for the middle class.[39]

Janss placed himself in the vanguard of the skiing revolution. In the West, skiing had long been too important to leave to the locals. Only small ski areas, typically out of the way or adjacent to the larger Aspen resort structure, could survive. One instance of the latter was Aspen Highlands, run by Whipple Van Ness (Whip) Jones, an Ivy League–educated iconoclast who came to Aspen at Paepcke's behest. Outside capital and in many cases the experience of entrepreneurial innovators elsewhere were crucial to success in the competitive ski industry. Janss borrowed from the various models—the total control of land and construction from the ground up at Vail, the one-owner domination of Sun Valley, and the idea of sophisticated amenities that Paepcke's Aspen demanded—and added his experience in community development. The result was a new script for resort communities with greater levels of structure, organization, and control. Businesses entered Janss's Snowmass because he wanted them, not because the resort needed their fees.

Business ownership at Snowmass followed a pattern that by the 1960s typified resorts. One restaurant, Cyrano's, was imported in its entirety from Sunset Strip in Los Angeles. Southern Californians John Cooley and project manager Roland Herberg enjoyed management positions. Norwegian Stein Eriksen, a holdover from a 1950s Norwegian invasion of Aspen skiing, ran the lucrative ski school. Most of the bars, restaurants, and lodges were owned by outside capital. Even locals who ran lodges were transplants. Arthur Preusch, owner of the Norway Lodge in Aspen and the forty-five unit Snowmass Inn, first moved to Aspen in 1965. Jack Kemp, the quarterback-later-turned-politician, and Phillip Battaglia, California governor Ronald

Reagan's chief assistant, invested in other properties. Locals were relegated to service and menial employment at the resort.[40]

Janss's developments were transformative and clearly delineated generations within resort communities. Before his arrival, both Aspen and Sun Valley had been hotel-based resort communities, visitors coming to stay only for a short time. In Sun Valley, vacation homes were exclusive; Aspen attracted Paepcke's affluent friends, who built extraordinary houses there. The older homes in both towns rarely attracted the eye of wealthy transplants. They were too small, not contemporary enough, or too tawdry or rundown. Into the 1960s, most of these in Aspen were owned by people who, wealthy or not, resided there most of the year.[41]

With Snowmass, Janss created a new constituency for second homes in the greater Aspen area. Unlike the prototrophy homes of the wealthy, these more modest structures could be marketed to a mass audience. They were also interchangeable. Built as modifications on a minute number of floor plans, fundamentally they looked the same. This plan made them more affordable, posing a kind of threat to places that claimed if not economic exclusivity, at least its psychic equivalent. Even more challenging to the idiosyncratic culture of such locales, planned developments raised the profile of the communities in question, increased local population, and set the stage for clearly distinguished hierarchies.

Janss's developments threatened nearly everyone who inhabited a resort community and felt at home there. The influx of people who were neither wealthy and famous nor committed to the concept of a skiing community changed the nature of the place for the residents, ski bum and business magnate alike. Flocks of people who did not respect the town's past, did not understand its intricate hierarchical structure came and effectively staked a claim to the town as their own. To them, the annual picture taken on the Aspen rugby field where people stood by the markers that denoted the year of their arrival was a detail to circumvent rather than a marker of local status. The new climate fused together everyone who preceded the development of second homes, even the newest of the new. These circumstances created a premium on belonging to a fictitious authentic world, any moment that predated the arrival of Janss and the condo community.[42]

Defining the parameters of that moment before modern mass culture tourism arrived became a function of the ownership of space. When anyone could own a middle-class, cookie-cutter condo or second home, the Victorian homes in Aspen and the more modest and sometimes ramshackle homes in Ketchum acquired a new significance. They were unique, at least in comparison with modern homes. Instead of escaping attention and remaining the province of older local families, they became a desired acquisition for people who saw their homes as an expression of their individuality, of their longtime resident status in a community threatened by the next wave of trendsetting, and consequently of their claims to authenticity. History, especially personal tenure reflected by location and property, was important as a mode of self-definition as local identity changed. Personal identity marked by membership in place could be defined only externally, by ownership that proved position and place.

Even more telling, in both Snowmass and Sun Valley, the availability of middle-class homes and "pandemoniums" changed the character of the local population. Instead of the Annenbergs and other moguls, more affordable vacation homes brought ordinary people seeking status by association. A fierce new demand for existing local residential structures, the plums of local real estate, and for newly built condos and homes followed. The new-found desirability of existing homes spurred rapid rises in the cost of real estate. Advertisements for residential properties in the Aspen area showed approximately 12 percent annual increases in asking price between 1964 and 1968, topped by increases in the 20 percent range in 1969 and 1970. Beginning early in the 1970s, Sun Valley real estate prices soared as local population doubled to nearly 3,000 people. By the mid-1970s in Sun Valley, average home prices ranged from $129,000 to $320,000, with a few homes in the $.5 million range. One-half- to three-quarter-acre homesites ranged between $35,000 and $120,000. By 1976 Sun Valley had once again become, in the words of a financial reporter, the "hottest and most high-priced land development spot in the Northwest."[43]

Proximate and quaint, older homes in such towns acquired an iconographic meaning that belied their size, location, and level of amenities. Ownership of an older house in a town given over to tourists conferred de facto old-timer status, granting owners a claim to a neonative pioneer station in the rapidly changing resort community. As prices rose, a frighteningly rapid inflation of real estate values in western resort towns occurred. Combined with the zoning of such communities and the tax hikes that paid for needed infrastructural improvements and amenities, the increase in property cost drove some older families from their homes and placed most property out of reach of longtime local residents and the average resort worker.

Janss developed an understandably proprietary sense toward his communities that earlier residents simultaneously appreciated and resented. When asked about homes built on Sun Valley hillsides before his era he announced, "There won't be any more of that."[44] This autocratic sense of ownership offended locals such as Dorice Taylor, who felt the community was hers as much as Janss's, but she and others like her appreciated that he preserved the vistas of the community. Janss created a typical predicament for locals, faced with a powerful force that dictated terms to them. They understood and appreciated the effort but wished for the greater input that they remembered, accurately or otherwise, from the days of the Union Pacific.

In his autocratic traits, Janss mirrored Paepcke, but he had different goals. They shared a sense of defining how and in what ways their communities would grow and change. Paepcke, whom Peggy Clifford referred to as "the ultimate innocent . . . in a town of innocents," wanted Aspen to enlighten the nation's business leaders and reform American culture; Janss had good skiing, good times, and profit as his goals. Achieving Janss's goals was far less complicated than fulfilling Paepcke's elusive dream.

Janss's objectives meant another wholesale transformation for Sun Valley and Snowmass. "Aspen will be one of the great skiing cities," he predicted in newspapers as he prepared to open Snowmass. "It will never return to being [a] pleasant small skiing town." To the residents of both places, Janss declared war, a threat to their way of life. People who had preceded Paepcke in Aspen wondered how their town ever became a small skiing city. It certainly seemed large enough to them. Such a declaration meant that the captive constituency who chose these locations as home and provided service work would also have to adjust to new realities. Janss implemented the same rigid control of development in Sun Valley, creating what one newspaper reporter in 1976 called its "enviable position." By then, Janss had master-planned and zoned his community, advocating "slow orderly growth" limited to about fifty condominiums a year. Only 15 percent of the land Janss held was scheduled for eventual development. The rest was to remain open space. The people outside the area he owned looked to his operation to provide a healthy portion of their yearly income. The buffer zone he owned around the resort ensured that he could implement his vision; the surrounding region's economic dependence on Sun Valley guaranteed reluctant compliance.[45] But Sun Valley was no longer the place that the devotees of the Union Pacific era remembered, and the new Aspen, with Snowmass, continued its transition from cultural center with skiing attached to a ski town playground of the rich and famous.

In Sun Valley, even direct beneficiaries of the changes revealed considerable ambivalence. Howard Richards, a broker for Ketchum Realty, reported increases in the cost of housing that averaged 6 to 10 percent annually throughout the early 1970s. Although clearly prospering as a result, Richards reported "mixed feelings" about the area's growth during his eight years in Sun Valley. He was "a little fearful" about its consequences but thought it brought advantages. "When I first came here there were hardly any permanent residents. It was a transient population," he reported. "Now people are staying and buying their own homes." To Richards, this trend suggested permanence, despite the reality that more than 70 percent of homes were occupied seasonally.[46]

Although beneficiaries could see positive change from development, Janss's vision was the subject of scathing critiques from people with psychic investment in a different kind of community. Prominent among them was Peggy Clifford. At Brushy Creek, where the Snowmass development was located, "mountains, men, and machines came together in a very sophisticated way," Clifford wrote. In her view, Snowmass "exemplified qualities that Aspen had itself eschewed—large scale, efficiency, group think, and a no-nonsense cost-profit ratio. It was an anomaly in the landscape . . . [that] looked not unlike a prison." Culturally, it promoted "endless fun, comfort, and surprises that were uniformly pleasant. . . . It was not a town but a good-times machine, and the good times were organized and codified. They were also unreal."[47]

Like Dorice Taylor in Sun Valley, Clifford represented an earlier neo-native generation of greater Aspen. Her ideal was the antithesis of the Snowmass development so widely praised in business circles, but with resignation she recognized the inevitability of the transformation. Her community had "turned its back" on America in the postwar years, "celebrating art and sport over money and goods," and later it mocked the nation when elsewhere Americans took their country seriously. Aspen had been proudly different, attractive in an intangible way. But for Clifford, and others of her generation such as Bruce Berger, the Janss development left Aspen culturally common. "The eccentric's hideout was becoming affluent America's playground," Clifford mused. "We hated and feared America, but it was still in love with us, for we were everything it was not." Berger became so alienated that he began to spend his winters, still the prime season in Aspen, in Phoenix.[48]

But words were the only weapons that Janss's detractors found available. His philosophy generated a maximum level of control, and only businesses and even employees in line with his views could find a place in these systematized organizations. To Janss, people such as Dorice Taylor and Peggy

Clifford provided local color. They were eccentrics whose stories entertained visitors, overwhelmed anachronisms that could barely slow the steamroller of growth. Yet these recalcitrant voices spoke for local sentiment, and many people who held such beliefs did not leave. During the 1960s and 1970s they fashioned political, social, and cultural responses to the processes that dwarfed them.

10

"Powder Aplenty for Native and Guest Alike"

From Community to Corporate Control

The Grenoble Winter Olympics in 1968 elevated skiing another notch in the American recreational cosmology. Again television showed sleek athletes whizzing down spectacular slopes, this time in the French Alps. Skiing no longer seemed a remote pastime of the wealthy but a legitimate sport for anyone of means. It was exciting; sun- and windburnt faces, the racoon eyes left by goggles evinced health, vigor, and sexual charisma. People flocked to the slopes. Jean-Claude Killy, the French Olympic champion of 1968, gave skiing an even more glamorous face. His charismatic presence and radiant sensuousness made him a star on the promotional circuit. A string of auto shows, trade shows, many in tandem with Heisman Trophy–winner O. J. Simpson, and ski resort openings blended together, exhausting Killy but marketing his persona.[1] In Colorado alone, the number of skiers increased by 42 percent the following season. Skiing meant freedom, luxury, and tantalizing personal transformation, an attractive combination at any time but especially so during the height of the Great Aberration, the period between 1945 and 1974 when more Americans achieved greater economic success than at any time before or since.

The appeal of skiing was not lost on the business community. Multinational corporations, reveling in unparalleled profits and aware of the need to put a face on their products for the consumer market, looked to integrate their operations in ways that would please the public and provide more profit. Skiing had positive cachet; it offered a way to put a company's best image forward even as it added to the bottom line. After Squaw Valley and Grenoble, skiing was well positioned in American society. In an era when image became ever more important, ski resorts attracted the attention of powerful sources of capital.

Corporations eyeing ski resorts knew what they observed. During the 1960s and 1970s, the industry grew at a phenomenal rate. The transformation of Sun Valley and the construction of Snowmass were still prototypical. Janss knew skiing and engaged in its development as much from love of the sport as for the profits. He led; others followed as he astutely recognized that vast new audiences possessing both time and money could be converted to his favorite activity. Fusing this insight with his corporate experience in development, he created resorts that attracted a broad array of enthusiasts, novices, and hangers-on. Squaw Valley and Jean-Claude Killy linked skiing with the good life. Janss and others made it accessible to the upper-middle class.

The new audience radically transformed the identity of skiers and assaulted the places they lived with numbers, capital, and new value systems. Following World War II, ski communities had become small, tightly knit places with one core obsession: how to get enough money to eat and sleep comfortably while skiing as many days as possible. Business development took place within a narrow spectrum. Ski shops predominated. Aspen became part of a sort of American underground, where the living was easy and nonconformist. It stood alone before the 1960s in its emphasis on cultural and intellectual transformation. A distinct feel permeated Aspen and other ski towns, a shared set of objectives that typically, at least before Janss, had little to do with profit. The small-town roots of these places held solidly through the first generation of neonatives.

These communities also had entrenched elites, people to whom the place had meanings other than those of the neonatives. Local oligarchies, business owners, newspaper editors, bankers, and wealthy old-timers who perceived advantage in stasis ran ski towns as they did other small towns. Although such coalitions were also fragile—business owners in particular saw growth as necessary—its leaders knew each other well and governed by cabal. If they could agree among themselves, they could implement their typically limited agendas. As long as they did so gently, as long as nothing intruded upon their paradise, they could continue without challenge. Such communities possessed many of the traits of small European villages; everyone knew his place, there was little to be gained from upsetting the prevailing order, and the people who might do so were content simply to ski all day.

Rapid growth such as Janss created and the changes it caused weakened the existing ties in skiing communities and in some cases threatened their very identity. Internecine struggles developed, pitting new against old, old against older, and every other convoluted combination of natives, neo-natives, and new residents in a struggle to define their place in the community and to accentuate the features of their town that they believed made it special. For each, those features were different, sometimes even diametrically opposed. The struggles that resulted and the tension that such conditions fostered did much to ruin the idyllic self-image of ski towns and drive residents away. In an articulation of the tension and its consequences, one political campaign in Aspen in 1970 used the slogan, "When will Aspen become the place you left?"[2]

The increased importance of skiing changed the structure in which both local elites and communities functioned. Bill Janss served as a precursor. His developments, the improved transportation to resorts, the growing profits that could be realized, and other cultural factors attracted the interest of emerging multinational corporations. When CEOs noted that between the 1967–1968 and the 1970–1971 ski seasons, average pretax profits at ski resorts grew from 1.2 percent to 10.5 percent, they sought to join the expansion.[3] As in other forms of tourism, the rise of skiing made the sport too lucrative to be left to locals or idiosyncratic private entrepreneurs. Ski resorts could become part of a corporation's image, a way to meld its many assets with a high-status capstone that served as a magnet for consumers.

Beginning in the late 1960s these multinationals and other corporations previously uninvolved in winter recreation purchased ski resorts and transformed them. The pattern began even before Janss, but it became an art form as LTV Incorporated, a Japanese-American conglomerate, purchased Werner Mountain, the resort outside the boundaries of Steamboat Springs, in 1969. Twentieth-Century Fox bought the Aspen Ski Company in 1978, and Dutch oil trader John Duess purchased Teton Village in Jackson, Wyoming, in 1987. These purchases were often highly leveraged, accumulating great debt for the parent company and requiring reorganization of the resort, and as a result, of local life.

The conditions that so aggravated Dorice Taylor in Sun Valley in 1964 were exacerbated by the corporate ownership of ski resorts. The little upward mobility within communities that previously existed was lost as corporations brought in professional managers with an eye often exclusively on the bottom line. Categories of employment became discrete, with company leadership and financial management operations more closely tied to corporate headquarters than to the resort and typically staffed from afar. Managing skiing, once perceived as a whole, became a dead-end. Lodge and resort operations were also separate from other factions, managers sometimes meeting only at the corporate CEO's office. The integrated nature of resorts, the commonality of experience, was refashioned as various tracks and employment opportunities changed dramatically. There were fewer and fewer stories of people who had come to town broke and one, two, or five years later found themselves owning businesses, running an operation of significance in the resort, or advancing to a higher level within the operation. A freewheeling place such as Vail or Aspen became, in the phrase of Peggy Clifford, "a free-for-all."[4]

The impact of transformation was quickly obvious within such communities. Native young people and the first generation of neonatives found the conventional avenues of upward mobility blocked. Corporate ownership attracted new kinds of residents, as had the operations of Bill Janss, but they came in larger numbers and were further removed from the prevailing ethos of each place. Though upward mobility had been clogged under Janss and by the remarkable control and profitability of the Aspen Ski Company, under corporate regimes a veritable caste system developed that was reflected in the increasing wealth of patrons and the ponderous stasis of most locals. If Janss brought dislocation in his wake, corporate takeover foretold displacement.

Corporate control and increased demand for the lodges, slopes, and lifts of ski communities exacerbated tensions that existed from earlier transformations. Luke Short wrote of "a nightmare in lace pants" in 1950s Aspen, and Dorice Taylor had felt dumped with Janss's arrival. The new increase in scale pitted at least three figurative local generations against each other. The people who preceded Walter Paepcke in Aspen, the development of skiing in Jackson, and the construction of the resort at Mt. Werner outside Steamboat found their objectives different from those of the people who embraced each successor regime. But the successor regimes lost their power to the representatives of corporations, who answered to shareholders far away and were concerned with mass experience rather than with the idiosyncracies of little ski towns. A new wave of change atop a previous round of alteration to which locals had not yet entirely adjusted stirred the first rumblings of widespread discontent. The alienation that followed was infectious. Locals departed, for personal and equally often economic reasons, longtime residents became disgruntled, and the very character of these communities changed.

Steamboat Springs, long protected by its remote location and by a firm regional agricultural and ranching economy, was the first Colorado resort to be purchased by large-scale outside corporate interests. After the heyday of the ski trains during the 1930s, Steamboat Springs slipped back into obscurity, a town where skiing was a local activity and pastime, both utilitarian and recreational. The Routt Valley produced a string of great skiers who represented the town. As some small towns cherished their high school sports teams, the heroes of Steamboat Springs were its locally born-and-bred skiers. The town enjoyed a personality and an identity, and skiing was an integral part of its sense of self.

After Winter Carnival began in the 1910s, Howelsen Hill, located against the mountain at the southern end of town, became the centerpiece of local skiing. The distance-jumping competition took place there, and other events, such as ski-jöring, involved cross-country skiing and framed it as transportation rather than as recreation. A 110-yard downhill slalom course opened in 1933, followed by a longer run, but these remained the extent of alpine or downhill skiing.[5] Despite a generation of ski champions, Steamboat Springs still primarily regarded skiing as a winter necessity and not a sport.

The real growth in importance of alpine skiing in Steamboat Springs followed World War II. In the immediate postwar period, city revenue bonds converted Howelsen Hill to a predominantly downhill slope. Gordy Wren supervised the creation of a new downhill trail in 1950, and another was developed on nearby Emerald Mountain. But Howelsen Hill was a small local area, and with it as the primary attraction, Steamboat Springs had little appeal in the commercial skiing world. Its ski-jumping competition lost out to downhill skiing, and more people wanted to experience the sport and not merely observe it at the Winter Carnival. Nor did Howelsen Hill challenge increasingly skilled and extremely aggressive local skiers such as Buddy Werner.

There were places near town where these aggressive young people could practice. One local rancher, James Wood Temple, envisioned Storm Mountain, just outside the city limits to the east, as the ultimate skiing experience. In 1956 the twenty-nine-year-old Temple debuted a plan for a resort; he was already experienced both in business and skiing. After serving as assistant head of the ski patrol and as avalanche forecaster at Sun Valley from 1952 to 1954, he returned to Steamboat to develop a new resort. Temple faced a mixed reception in the community. Downtown merchants cared little for the possibility of a new slope outside of town, but the Winter Sports Club, a mainstay of local life in Steamboat Springs, expressed interest. The club members and Temple worked together, surveying possible routes, assessing the advantages of each location, and engaging in an all-for-one, one-for-all spirit. With Temple as a spearhead, a local project shaped by local experience and attitudes took shape.[6]

As in many such ventures, Temple used his own and his family's money. He sold his part of the ranch to his parents and bought land. Temple founded the Storm Mountain Corporation in 1958, and between 1958 and 1961 it took options on 827 acres of meadowland at the base of the mountain. These acquisitions, not all of them successful, gave Temple a degree of control to which many developers could only aspire. After securing an agreement with the Forest Service for use of the mountainsides, Temple had the land he needed to execute the plans he first made public in 1956: a $1 million ski area with a $.6 million tram to carry passengers in the first steel and plexiglass-enclosed cable cars in the country, six electric lifts that could serve 3,000 skiers, and more than twenty miles of ski trails.[7]

Temple followed the typical pattern in the development of tourism. Like Edgar Hewett, Struthers Burt, Walter Paepcke, and countless others, he was a visionary; he had clear objectives and ways to move toward achieving them. In the tight-knit Routt Valley, his status as a local and the fanatical affection for skiing eased his task. Temple could count on locals, in no small part because he was one of them, and the people of the community provided moral support for the endeavor.

The financial problems that the Storm Mountain Corporation faced were equally typical in tourism development. By the time the company printed its first brochure in 1959, it had accumulated more than $80,000 in debt, most of it to directors and officers of the company. A subsidiary, Storm Mountain Ski Corporation, offered stock for the first time in November 1960, and although the Securities and Exchange Commission allowed a $750,000 stock offering, only $80,000 actually sold. With the demand for equipment and other necessities accelerating and the typical local entrepreneur's cash flow problem, Storm Mountain opened on December 22, 1961, with one small lift, a Cub Claw, typically used for beginners. The lift sustained the area for the first season, which recorded $1,123.70 in income from lift tickets and only $948.23 in expenses. The $265.47 profit, a pittance when stacked against the facilities that needed to be built and the equipment, materials, and labor that needed to be paid for, was still, in local eyes, a remarkable achievement. The idea of turning even a minuscule profit from the Cub Claw alone and before the road to the lift was completed offered tantalizing promise.[8]

As was almost always the case in the mountain West, local capital was insufficient. Despite Temple's best efforts, his position soon became untenable. A reorganization in 1961 turned the Storm Mountain Ski Corporation, more than $500,000 in arrears and facing more than $200,000 of necessary new expenditures, into the Steamboat Partnership. Two new principals, both tied to the world of finance, joined the board of directors. Henry (Hank) Perry, a thirty-three-year-old investment broker for Bosworth, Sullivan, and Company, and forty-seven-year-old John McCready, an experienced mortgage banker, played increasingly prominent roles. In exchange for a promise to keep the resort open for the 1962–1963 winter and to complete the construction of the Bear Claw lift, long a problem for the Storm Mountain Ski Corporation, Perry received control of Temple's stock in the corporation for eight years. With this, Perry acquired control of the ski company and used his position to secure funds to keep the operation afloat.[9]

Once again the devil's bargain of tourist enterprises entered local life. Temple was the visionary with the knowledge and the skills to build the resort. He dreamed big dreams but could not raise the capital and probably lacked the experience to achieve his goals. The search for capital and professional management ultimately cost Temple control of his company. By 1966 he and his family had moved to Boulder, Colorado, where they operated a dry cleaners and a laundromat.[10] Like the old-timers at the Grand Canyon and Thomas Flynn and his compatriots at Aspen, the locals with the idea gave way to outsiders who could capitalize on a vision that locals could not quite afford and probably did not entirely understand.

The principals who replaced Temple also faced significant financial and structural problems. After the death of Buddy Werner in an avalanche outside Saint Moritz in April 1964, Storm Mountain was renamed in his honor. By the time the ceremony took place at the Winter Carnival in 1965, Perry had waved "a magic wand of greenbacks over the mountain's slopes," pumping more than $1.7 million into the project. People poured into Steamboat Springs in increasing numbers each winter during the late 1960s, and more development capital was necessary. Small business administration loans played a role, as did developers, and the borrowing was expensive. Almost $2 million in outside development capital supported motels, the resort, and other facilities in 1967, but despite vastly larger numbers of skiers, returns for the Mt. Werner Company remained slim. Indebtedness ate away at profitability.[11]

The first inklings of problems with growth emerged. One-hour lift lines were common. The need for capital pressed the limits of the company's borrowing power. Although the signs at Steamboat Springs and Mt. Werner were promising, the resources supporting the endeavor were too small. Rapid growth had a price. When mountain manager Gordy Wren announced to the stockholders' meeting in 1968 that Steamboat had "grown up and [was] rapidly closing in on the big boys such as Vail, Aspen, and Snowmass," he was also tacitly acknowledging that the existing leadership group was likely to be replaced soon.[12]

After the buyout of Temple, locals disappeared from leadership in the company, but their replacements were made honorary members of the community. The capital that people such as Perry raised made them popular; everyone could see that these outsiders had the power to bring to fruition a local dream that would benefit everyone. No one expected that success would rapidly change these first neonatives into anachronisms, but once again another of the devil's bargains of success vexed local decision making. Success begat new needs, and the people responsible could not always fulfill them. As did many similar enterprises, Steamboat Springs grew so much and so quickly that it attracted the attention of larger entities.

In an age of business expansion and corporate diversification, a popular industry such as skiing, which by 1968 grossed more than $1 billion each year, attracted the large corporations so powerful in the American economy. American Cement Company, which had been partners with Bill Janss at Snowmass and then bought him out, was only the most visible of many others. By 1968 Ralston-Purina owned half the Keystone resort outside Dillon, Colorado, and Leander-McCormick owned 17 percent of Copper Mountain.[13] These new sources of power in ski towns radically changed the assumptions of local life. Corporations pursued objectives that differed from those of Bill Janss. Janss envisioned a holistic environment managed for the simultaneous benefit of the skier and the shareholder, but corporate ownership offered a more bland level of amenity and paid much greater attention to profits. Janss enjoyed a reputation for snap decisions. A corporate regime required layers of management, cost-benefit analysis from accountants, and typically, a board meeting to finalize any plan. Less adventurous and devoutly attentive to the whims of a broad swath of potential visitors, the corporations packaged skiing in ways that even Janss could not have imagined.

Steamboat Springs continued to struggle, and within a very few years corporate interests took control. In September 1969, LTV Aerospace Corporation, a subsidiary of Ling-Temco-Vought of Dallas, Texas, paid the Perry group $4 million for the Mt. Werner resort, a sizable profit for stockholders in the enterprise. A rumor that the purchase was prompted by LTV chairman James J. Ling's inability to obtain last-minute reservations at either Aspen or Vail at Christmas 1968 suggested a level of caprice in the purchase that belied the importance of a share of the $1.1 billion skiing market. Like many other corporations, LTV sought to diversify into a growing industry. But also like many of its peers, LTV had much capital and little expertise in its new acquisition. The line of LTV executives from Texas who descended on the ski school, ski tips pointed together in the beginner's snowplow, proved as much.[14]

This lack of expertise left a niche for locals, but it was specialized and small and had little impact on the direction of the resort or the community. The only people in the new arrangement who possessed expertise in skiing were locals. American Olympian Billy Kidd became LTV's director of skiing, and Loris Werner, Buddy Werner's youngest brother and twice National Collegiate Ski Champion at Western State College, took charge of the ski school.[15] LTV traded on local expertise by hiring nationally known local heroes for the public side of its operations. It made skiing into service at Steamboat Springs. Locals could use their skills and mastery of the slopes while corporate officials in Texas ran the finances.

LTV Recreation Development, the subsidiary created to manage the resort, envisioned a different, more dramatic Steamboat Springs that appealed to a broader audience than did the old resort. In a June 1970 public meeting at the high school auditorium, the company presented its grand aspirations, the investment of more than $60 million over a ten-year period, a total more than ten times larger than that invested by previous operators. LTV proposed a name change for the resort, giving up any ties to local mythology and history and naming the place simply Steamboat. A red, white, and blue logo that suggested the all-American nature of the town was part of the package, as was a massive advertising campaign that cautioned potential visitors: "Don't miss the 'boat!" A semicircular development with underground parking was planned and an eighteen-hole golf course and a convention center. A gondola was added to the slopes to make skiing more attractive and accessible. At the behest of a Minneapolis advertising agency, filmmaker Dick Wilson and songwriter Steve Griak produced four films for LTV that promoted the friendly western atmosphere of the area.[16] The company constructed an image of Steamboat Springs especially for outside consumption as a place that mirrored the attributes of the locals' town but refracted the values of tourists back to them.

LTV's well-intended development directly challenged everything that locals valued about their town. Until the plan, locals had always been able to integrate resort development with their sense of place. LTV's $10 million investment in the community in 1969 and 1970 affected the social and cultural structure of the community. Steamboat Springs had always been the town that skied. As local writer John Rolfe Burroughs wrote, it was a place where skiing was not born, "it just grow'd."[17] Locals filled the slopes not only of Howelsen Hill but also of Mt. Werner. LTV recruited another constituency of destination visitors, a young, largely male, wealthy group typically from Texas or the East or West Coasts, who brought a vision of skiing as a gung-ho, macho activity. LTV's amenities catered to them, not to the local and regional skiers whose parents had come on the ski trains of the 1930s.

The result was a place in flux, with changes happening at an astonishing pace. In the first five years of LTV's ownership, Routt County's population jumped from 6,170 to 8,060, a 30 percent increase. Most of the newcomers were better educated and more affluent than typical Routt County residents, providing obvious advantages. The popularity of the resort helped. Skier visits and bank deposits in Routt County nearly tripled between 1968 and 1974, and taxable retail sales doubled. Land with subdivision potential increased in cost from roughly $100 per acre to almost $1,000. By every economic measure, the community seemed better off.[18]

Yet the changes that accompanied this increased prosperity had considerable negative impact on segments of the Routt County population. Growth was alienating. Subdividing ranches set off a debate within the community about land-use planning. Many people advocated some form of zoning or another planning mechanism as a way to protect existing residents from the negative consequences of change.[19] Despite its support from Gordy Wren and others, the idea of zoning was threatening. It seemed to draw a stark line between past and present. With laws that governed problem-solving, the friendly western town where people settled their disputes by talking to each other would be gone forever, replaced by a world of rules and the bureaucrats, albeit local, who made them. The freedom inherent in Routt County could be curtailed. If no regulations were instituted, Steamboat Springs risked inundation by outsiders who did not respect local custom and culture or the historic patterns of the place. This dilemma plagued similar communities throughout the West. The choice was a devil's bargain: fight to maintain identity and risk the very fabric of the town or accept the new power and its money and acquiesce in the transformation.

When Mayor Marvin Elkins accepted a place on LTV's payroll as a community relations consultant, the decision was made. Steamboat Springs gave itself over to outside money. Some residents regarded the mayor's decision as perfidy, others interpreted it as a way of further linking growth to the structure of the community. Dividing lines were drawn. Old-timers retreated, warning of con artists and fraudulent deals; newcomers found law enforcement too harsh, especially regarding long-haired youth. Steamboat Springs's first neonative community took up residence, and clashes between them and native culture were under way.[20]

The loudest objections came from the ranching community. Long the mainstay of the regional economy and the group who considered skiing chiefly as transportation, ranchers saw the changes on Werner Mountain through the most skeptical eyes. "There's a new breed of people here," observed rancher Vernon Summer, a few years after the LTV purchase. Steamboat had become, in his estimation, "not hardly a Colorado ski area." Summer's community changed around him. To this area native and his lifelong friends, their town seemed to belong to others.[21]

Economic change played a large role in their discomfort. Ranchers and miners predominated in Routt County, but few were wealthy. The high altitude and short growing season made prosperity the exception in regional history. Mostly locals struggled to survive, secure in the knowledge that their neighbors and friends struggled equally hard. LTV's purchase created a rift in this set of socioeconomic arrangements. Developers who subdivided ranchland for housing tracts and estates eyed ranches near the community and inflated their value. The upward spiral in land prices forced assessments up, and an increase in tax liability based on the value of ranchland as subdivided real estate followed. Although a survey showed that per capita costs decreased following 1968, this fact provided little solace for locals. Few had substantial resources, and in the new circumstances they needed new ways to earn money. Some Routt County ranchers took second jobs in area mines. Few families could afford to stake their children to ranch life in the increasingly expensive climate. The result was a decline in agriculture and ranching as a percentage of the workforce between 1970 and 1980 and the transformation of numerous ranches into subdivisions.[22] Roughly the same number of ranching and agricultural jobs that existed a decade earlier made up a much smaller percentage of the local workforce, resembling the transformation that occurred in Sun Valley between 1960 and 1970. New workers in construction and service added a broad demography not only to workplace statistics but also to the community itself.

Newcomers brought new values in a pattern of change that served as an archetype of the impact of tourism on communities. As people came to capitalize on the ski boom, local culture reflected the presence of transplanted urbanites. Some outsiders such as Denver stockbroker John Worchester invested heavily in local businesses like bars and restaurants. Others moved to town, bringing different social values. The change was quickly apparent among the young. In the early 1970s, the local high school was divided between "freaks," long-haired individuals who espoused the culture of urban and suburban youth of the day, which included smoking marijuana, ingesting other drugs, and claiming an antiauthoritarian view of the world, and "stomps," young people tied to the ranch ethic that was symbolized by wearing the oversized cowboy hats common on the area range. By the end of the 1970s the stomps had disappeared, suggesting that ranch families had declined in number and those who remained had children who embraced the vision of newcomers instead of the older traditions.[23] The end of a clearly defined ranch-based identity meant the end of the old Steamboat, the town that skied with its pantheon of heroes such as Gordy Wren, Buddy Werner, and Billy Kidd. Only Werner, dead well before his time, remained untarnished by participation in the transformation. The others found themselves in a liminal position, working for LTV but remaining essential parts of the iconography of a place that no longer existed.

The growth of the resort also skewed regional economic demography. By the early 1980s skiing supplanted ranching and agriculture in the local economy; winter generated more than 60 percent of sales tax revenue. In summer, construction provided much of the employment that drove the local economy, and many winter employees took construction jobs. Few permanent jobs with benefits existed. Most work was seasonal, low-wage, and aimed at young and often transient individuals who might spend a few years in Steamboat but were unlikely to settle permanently. Change threatened the older, rooted culture of the region.[24]

Greater stratification in the workforce followed. Incoming ski bums competed with locals for jobs at the resort. The distinction of being from a place that had commodified localism was no longer an advantage. Locals knew the slopes, but they were real natives, socially different, a little fierce and a little awkward in comparison to their smoother city-raised peers. As Steamboat's cachet increased, the resort became a more desirable destination, a better place to spend the winter working and skiing. This popularity contributed to a rivalry between ski bums and local youth for the menial positions in the tourist workforce. The mines and construction of the resort offered the best pay, in the mid-1970s in the nine- to ten-dollar-an-hour range; agriculture and ranching, dependent on seasonal labor, could offer only three to four dollars an hour. When construction slowed, the competition for lucrative employment grew intense.

The combination of stagnant or falling wages and increased land values affected the demography of the area. Natives of Steamboat Springs could no

Storm Mountain circa 1984. Development at the base of the mountain grew greatly in the fifteen years following the corporate takeover. (Jim Steinberg/The Portfolio Collection 1998.)

longer afford to stay in town; young people who grew up in the community lacked the resources to buy the rapidly appreciating homes in the valley. Many left for urban areas in search of opportunity. Ranch families often found that they were compelled to sell off their land in pieces. The typical 300-to-400-acre spread that remained could barely sustain a family and was far too small to allow parents to bring in an adult child with a family into the business. Instead of being passed from generation to generation, ranches were sold when the parents reached retirement. With the influx of outsiders, local people acquired a taste for amenities that a ranch income could not sustain. The land brought good money but at the cost of social and community continuity and of regional identity.

By 1982, when researcher Thompson R. Smith studied the area, Steamboat Springs was no longer the town that skied. The local community was demographically and culturally different; neonatives with capital or ties to the resort industry played prominent roles in local decision making, and some longtime residents felt pushed from the center of local life. Ranchers especially felt the changes, grousing about the shallow nature of the new resort as others made the real profits. Regional identity had been subsumed by the larger world outside. Ranching suffered severe economic decline and its culture appeared under siege. Steamboat Springs had become a resort town with many of the pretensions of such places. In little more than a decade, an identity forged in 100 years of winter camaraderie had been buried under the onslaught of the resort industry.

With the development of Snowmass and the change from hotel-based to residence-based resort as backdrop, Aspen faced many of these same predicaments but on a more cosmic scale. Paepcke's vision for the town inspired great dreams and created real comfort for many people, and after his death a battle for succession—not only in cultural affairs but also for community leadership—ensued. Combined with the national discovery of Aspen as a special place, particularly by eccentric celebrities such as Hunter S. Thompson, this struggle defined the community's parameters as it found various aspects of the mainstream seeking to expropriate its essence. The Aspen Ski Company, the economic mainstay of the town as the Aspen Institute slipped from preeminence, had become extremely profitable. The 1960s became a difficult and pivotal decade as Aspen had to reinvent its social and cultural values.

Paepcke's *Kulturstaat* had been a benevolent dictatorship, run by a charismatic figure widely trusted by the neonatives his regime attracted. Even the locals grew accustomed to Paepcke's Aspen, although whether they entirely embraced it remains unclear. People such as Tom Sardy, who jointly owned the local lumber company with Paepcke, typified the local perspective. They were not entirely sure about culture, but as long as it was lucrative, they listened. Paepcke's Aspen was comfortable and enjoyable and for most of the people it attracted, wealthy, intellectual, or ski aficionado, it seemed an idyllic spot in industrial, conformity-mad America.

Aspen's placid exterior shielded fierce internal rivalries for control of the place. The institute brought one kind of resident, wealthy, socially concerned, and self-described as enlightened. During Paepcke's life, these people led the community. The ski community had its own representatives, as did local business. Nor were the neonatives alone in Aspen. Longer-term residents, who predated Paepcke's arrival, still constituted a sizable and viable constituency. With Paepcke's tacit approval, locals such as Sardy controlled the politics that existed, as long as they followed the general trajectories Paepcke envisioned for the town. After his death, these rivalries, muted by his power and presence during his life, surfaced with a vengeance.

Following Paepcke's death, the rules that governed Aspen abruptly ended.

Robert O. Anderson, the heir apparent at the Aspen Institute, took the lead but remained more aloof than Paepcke in local politics. Aspen was Paepcke's passion; for Anderson, it was only one of many places. The absence of a dominant local force left a vacuum, and competing interests hurried to fill it. One group, led by the tall and lean Harold (Shorty) Pabst, an heir to the Pabst Brewing Company fortune and a longtime member of the board of the Aspen Institute, engineered a sweep of local elections in 1962. Pabst became mayor on this Clean Sweep ticket, and local physician Robert (Bugsy) Barnard, who moved to town in the immediate postwar era and made himself a force in local politics, two other newcomers, and a young native took seats on the council.[25] By displacing the older natives, who under Paepcke at least maintained the illusion of control, Pabst and his friends effectively took Aspen from the previously enforced consensus to wide-open internecine conflict over both the petty and the significant.

Social affairs in the community exacerbated growing political tensions. By 1960 the first generation of neonatives and locals learned to get along well, owning the town in its entirety when the Aspen Institute was not holding events. Institute functions typically occurred during the summer, leaving the ski season to neonatives, locals, and visiting enthusiasts. A sense of skiing as a birthright existed in this incarnation of Aspen; children's all-day lift passes cost seventy-five cents, enabling a madcap egalitarianism on the slopes. But as Aspen became a place that more people had to visit, as the combination of its cultural cachet and the desirability of skiing increased its psychic value, some of those visitors stayed. They upset a delicate balance, for they purchased property, which out-of-town developers promptly made available. Condominiums, the scourge of content resort communities, appeared in Aspen.[26]

As in Sun Valley, condominiums symbolized a piercing of the armor. They made a place common. Aspenites were confident about their place in the world; the people who lived there knew they held something special. They did. Their carefree way of life in an era of conformity, of mindless attention to structure and profit, was in vogue. Consequently, others who did not share the cultural values of Aspen but who possessed the wealth to transform the community joined the village in the mountains.

Condominiums aggravated the increasingly tense local climate because the people who purchased them did not seem to understand the psychic cost of their presence. To its residents Aspen had unique qualities, but to developers who sought to profit from its culture, the town was, in the words of Peggy Clifford, "merely a rich market." Land remained cheap by resort standards, and as Aspen's cachet increased, more people sought membership in the exclusive club that it had become. Developers accommodated them, lining their own pockets and building stark and unattractive "giant kitsch-Swiss chalets, ersatz-Bauhaus boxes, and ponderous edifices of timber and stone," Clifford observed, as community members quibbled among themselves about the efficacy of the idea.[27]

Their dilemma resulted from fundamental divisions within the community. As new buildings and rows of condominiums created barriers to the visual past, Aspenites fashioned a response. The town was an odd place. Residents of all vintages had as much allegiance to a place in their mind as to any physical reality, and Aspen's sociocultural and political organization depended on that mythic perception. "Condoization" was genuine; as did countless similar kinds of growth, it fractured old alliances. The very construction of condominiums diminished the distinctions between neonative and local. Both opposed development, yet many also felt that they could exercise more control over change by being part of the process. In effect, they tacitly accepted development and accommodated it. The social reconfiguration of the community matched its physical changes, depriving the older Aspen of powerful community leadership at the moment it needed it most.

The newcomers who bought the condominiums clearly did not understand that their presence violated existing norms. To someone who had recently left Chicago, Texas, or either coast for Aspen, a few condos did little to mar its pristine nature. Maroon Bells still overlooked the town, Smuggler Mountain still sported careening youngsters skiing full-tilt downhill, crime was not even an issue, and traffic barely existed. To anyone accustomed to life amid the growth of American cities in the postwar era, Aspen seemed serene, with or without condominiums.

But these were economies of scale, and locals could perceive a difference. The downtown, once the province of locals, became home to transient newcomers as local building owners participated in the change by evicting residents, refurbishing, and selling or leasing for exorbitant sums. Locals, who included the first generation of neonatives, replaced by the incoming condo-buyers, typically moved from the upper floors of downtown businesses to the peripheries of town or beyond to the smaller communities such as Basalt that dotted the Roaring Fork Valley. The result was the rapid transformation of downtown from a place for residents, affluent and less affluent alike, to a place for visitors who could afford the increasingly expensive fare. To call this change the death of Aspen would dramatically overstate the case, but to the people of the time, there was a clear difference, and many—even most—

liked Aspen better before the arrival of the condominiums. Their town was no longer their own, and they felt it.

The ingress and egress of capital illustrated the transformation. Before his death, Paepcke and his friends were the major source of building money in the community. A zoning ordinance written in 1955 reflected their priorities, but with material difficult to attain and the only local source of lumber and other construction materials the Aspen Lumber Company, maintaining control not only of what was built but also of who built it was relatively easy. But as land values and house and condo prices rose, the market opened to a wider range of developers, many of whom hailed from other places. Some were hit-and-run builders, who slapped together new construction, took their profits, and headed for the next town.[28] Others aimed at a sustained relationship with Aspen, but not with the town of Paepcke's era. Their profits were tied to the growing number of people of means who wanted a second home there.

Clearly there was more at stake in Aspen, financially and ideologically, after the arrival of the condominiums. Without Paepcke's leadership and control, Aspen was different from other resort towns only in the allegiance of many of its citizens to the ideals of his regime. When local people participated in the transformation — County Commissioner Orest Gerbaz sold part of his ranch to investors who built a trailer park and former mayor Mike Garish sold his family's home to a supermarket chain and moved across the river — it frayed the ties that determined local identity, threatening the significance of the local voice in Aspen's future.[29]

In an idealistic community confronted with outside money and the use of raw economic power, the logical response was to turn to politics. As prices skyrocketed in town, as Bill Janss's community at Snowmass attracted the ordinary upper-middle class, as the community divided on how to respond to the changes, participatory politics became the battleground of conscience in Aspen. Enervated and passionate, Aspen politics most resembled those of a college campus, with the resulting level of emotion and the permanent fractures in relationships. Aspen's many layers of residents, tied to various intellectual conceptualizations and excited about its future, stood willing, for personal and community reasons, to engage in political debate. Politics promised salvation; chaos seemed equally likely.

The intensity of Aspen politics in the mid-1960s was diametrically opposed to the politics during Paepcke's era. Despite his egalitarian charm, Paepcke was a benefactor who regulated the community in a manner that obviated the need for vibrant local politics. The community agreed with him or at least accepted his vision; his changes drew them there, as Bruce Berger's presence demonstrated. Those who did not like Paepcke's Aspen often financially benefited from it. They might grouse, but the work on the construction of new houses, the appearance of new businesses that might hire locals, and other opportunities kept the complaining to a muted undercurrent. The condo revolution brought unconnected capital and people to a place with a strong sense of community. Those who fought to maintain such ties no longer had their benevolent benefactor. They entered the public arena, bringing the out-of-sync metier of Aspen into American popular culture.

The political culture of mid-1960s Aspen remained complicated as the old sources of power in town dissipated and new sources appeared that could claims parts of the whole but had little interest in its entirety. The Aspen Institute remained a figurehead; after Paepcke's death, its real power drifted away. Issues of succession dogged the institute, and Robert O. Anderson was not interested in a benevolent and expensive protectorate.[30] The institute turned inward, a foretelling of its increasing marginality in a changing Aspen.

The only other source of real power in town was the Aspen Ski Company, and its influence was economic. After Paepcke asked his brother-in-law Paul Nitze to run skiing in the late 1940s, the company became the economic center of the community. Under the leadership of Denver attorney and ski enthusiast William Hodges, the company grew in a community-friendly way throughout the 1950s. It embarked on a construction program to alleviate crowding on the slopes; new lifts eased the two-hour wait at the existing lifts, and by the end of the decade, the company boasted of a maximum wait of ten minutes. Nor did the company dominate local skiing. As the demand for less competitive skiing grew, Freidl Pfeifer, still head of the ski school for Aspen Ski Company, and local rancher Art Pfister opened nearby Buttermilk Mountain, which catered to beginners and intermediate skiers.[31]

When David R. C. (Darcy) Brown succeeded Hodges in 1958, a new era in skiing in Aspen began. Brown was typical of the professional entrepreneurs who soon replaced the aficionados and enthusiasts who ran the postwar industry except that he was familiar to Aspenites. His father struck it rich in the silver boom in nineteenth-century Aspen and remained its most powerful man until his death in 1930, but Darcy Brown was born in San Francisco and schooled at Yale. "Well-bred, Eastern-educated, autocratic, and stern," in the words of an approving newspaper reporter, Brown led Aspen to unparalleled levels of economic prosperity during his twenty-year tenure at the head of the company. By 1962 Aspen Ski Company consolidated its position at the top of the ski industry there. Brown purchased Buttermilk, leaving only Aspen Highlands, owned by Whip Jones, out of the company's reach. Between 1965 and 1970 alone, the Aspen Ski Company maintained a growth rate of 145.26 percent per annum. This kind of professional management, though extremely profitable for shareholders, required a focus on the bottom line that did little for community harmony or to increase the popularity of the Aspen Ski Company. It simultaneously renounced Paepcke's vision as it affirmed the paternalism he had created for his *Kulturstaat*.[32] Like many local institutions, the Aspen Ski Company had been perceived as benevolent. As its policies changed, the company came to symbolize corporate mentality, the values that inspired a revolution in local politics.

Much of the community resisted the centralization of power in the ski company almost from the outset. Spurring the transformation of skiing from an avocation into an industry, the company made decisions that seemed designed to rile Aspenites. When the company raised the cost of local children's lift tickets from the traditional seventy-five cents to two dollars in the early 1960s, mothers tried to persuade the board to rescind the increase. The board demurred, pointing out its fiduciary responsibility to its shareholders and suggesting that Aspen's children, known for their speed on skis and their antics with visitors, might not be Aspen's most desirable representatives. Rebuffed, the women organized a Mother's March through downtown Aspen that culminated with the burning in effigy of a dummy labeled D. R. C. Hodges, after the two presidents of the ski company.[33] Children carrying rude placards outnumbered mothers, giving the protest the feel of a 1960s student demonstration.

The resistance to the increase in prices clearly illustrated the battle lines in 1960s Aspen. The mothers and their children sought a community ski slope, a place where natives outnumbered visitors and local custom held. In this formulation, skiing skill and experience and local residency took precedence over visitors and their money. The ski company sought to make the mountain safe for visitors, to curtail the skilled and sometimes dangerous enthusiasm of locals, and to create a climate, both physical and psychic, that made Aspen desirable to visitors. The local model, the community that skied, had once enjoyed its moment, but from the perspective of Darcy Brown, that moment was over.[34]

Relations between the ski company and the community deteriorated throughout the 1960s. The children's ticket issue was the inaugural salvo in the war between the new power source in Aspen and the neonative community. Brown practiced the adage of baseball manager Leo Durocher, "Nice guys finish last." He did not believe that residents enjoyed the special privilege of guaranteed access to Aspen Mountain; in some instances he told locals they were unwelcome at the resort. "As not everyone can afford to drive a Cadillac," Brown often said, "not everyone can afford to ski in Aspen." Although he later relented with "host passes," which funneled locals away from the touristed Aspen Mountain to other area slopes, class warfare joined neonative-corporate tension as dominant features of the landscape.[35]

Aspenites, local and neonative alike, disagreed with Brown. They believed they held a proprietary right not only on the mountain but especially in the community. The immediate postwar generation, those attracted to the little town they helped turn into a resort, also believed that they were entitled to a voice in its future. Between 1960 and 1965, Aspen's population rose by more than 40 percent, most people coming for the combination of ambience and skiing that characterized the 1950s. Included in this group were journalist Hunter S. Thompson and his wife, Sandy.[36] Of all groups, these "newest-comers" were the least enthusiastic about the increasingly corporate structure of the ski company and about the very growth of which they were part. They embraced a mythic Aspen, one that probably never existed, but they were sure that their efforts to save the community were right. They also saw protest about change as an entry into local society, a way to prove their right to local or at least to neonative status paradoxically by closing the doors behind them.

Translated into local politics, the tension irrevocably altered the existing landscape. The old guard, Sardy and Gerbaz, had become dinosaurs; their replacement, Shorty Pabst, was irrelevant as the power shifted from the institute and toward the ski company. As his mayoral term ended, Pabst focused on the morality of the community, claiming that the high school was filled with drug dealers and the community with immoral people. District Attorney John Wendt impaneled a grand jury, which heard testimony from terrorized teenagers but turned up no evidence of illegal activity. The grand jury set a new and decidedly unpleasant tone in Aspen; it pitted local officials against the town in the most polarizing way. The family of one girl who was subpoenaed to testify, typically described as "leading citizens, people of substance," moved away after the inquiry. The old commonality that accorded all Aspenites the benefit of the doubt disappeared. New issues, fraught with friction, assailed the community, and many voices influenced its direction.

The mayoral election of 1965 offered real evidence that tears in the fabric were real. In a fierce campaign, Bugsy Barnard defeated Pabst. Barnard, who had always fashioned himself a man of the people, now assumed the uncomfortable task of representing them. For the next four years, his combative style defined Aspen's politics, exacerbating tensions. Barnard was both a member of the elite and a representative of the people. Like many Aspenites, he idealized the *Kulturstaat* and claimed to seek to restore it. His actions as mayor were far more complicated. He seemed to want Aspen to stay small and to develop. Though professing civil rights, he engineered a crackdown on long-hairs, further eroding the core of civility and community that had characterized Aspen. By the time Barnard left office in 1969, he too had fallen victim to his own aspirations. Following Paepcke's footsteps was no easier for him than it had been for Pabst.

The abdication of true leadership in a community accustomed to a strong, benevolent figure simply pushed more power toward Darcy Brown. Like a croupier in a crap game, he pulled it in, shaping the community toward his goals. Aspen was in disarray, lacking leadership and often a clear sense of who was allied with whom. The ski company experienced its most rapid growth during this time, capitalizing on internecine struggles to transform Aspen Mountain and its environs into a tourist resort. Brown and his company quietly filled the vacuum the squabbling created. The community saw Brown as the villain; it reacted vigorously to the company's actions, missing the way that Brown centralized power in himself.

In the process, local politics, the icon of the rationalistic, town hall democracy that Paepcke's Aspen espoused, became more volatile as its importance turned from actual to symbolic. With rapid transformation, the question shifted from whether to grow to how to grow. Brown's absolute control of the ski company gave him carte blanche regarding development. As the company attracted more skiers, the town became crowded, houses and condos became more expensive, more hotel and motel rooms were constructed, and more restaurants, bars, and other ancillary operations for the enjoyment of visitors opened. Local politics engaged the question of whether to grow at the moment it became irrelevant, but it aroused considerable passion. A form of guerrilla theater masquerading as politics reigned.

Hunter S. Thompson's campaign for sheriff of Pitkin County in 1970 epitomized the symbolic politics of the town. Reflecting Paepcke's concerns with the grand questions, Thompson framed his campaign in the most cosmic of terms. Writing in *Rolling Stone,* Thompson announced that his campaign would test his theories of antipolitics. A combination of theater of the absurd, challenge to the local establishment, and gonzo journalism, the campaign both polarized and provided levity to assuage the increasing tension of local life. Thompson's programs included ripping up all city streets and replacing them with sod, changing the name of Aspen to Fat City, requiring

Aspen's politics were exclusive to the town, but with Hunter S. Thompson as a candidate, they attracted national attention. (Photo courtesy of the Aspen Historical Society.)

transportation only by foot or bicycle, and installing a platform and stocks in which dishonest drug dealers were displayed on the courthouse lawn.[37] He offered no explicit provisions for the punishment of honest drug dealers.

Thompson's campaign verged on the absurd, but it had a dimension of genuine foresight that offered wide appeal. He advocated a massive drug information program for Aspen's schools and the establishment of seven "action units" within the sheriff's office to handle everything from citizens' complaints to public information.[38] Although not an expert in police practice or procedure, Thompson conceived of a sheriff's department that was more than fast cars and big guns. His program anticipated the development of "community policing," officers working within the communities they serve, a strategy later devised by the African American police chief of Charleston, South Carolina, Reuben M. Greenberg. Murky and often hard to understand, Thompson's program offered a different vision of police protection than did his competitors for office.

The sheriff's race became a generational battle. Thompson represented a new Aspen, one that resented the normalization of the town, its transformation from a special place to just another resort. The resistance he represented appealed to the first generation of neonatives and a few of the old-timers. Incumbent sheriff Carroll Whitmire and challenger Glenn Ricks, a former deputy sheriff, were traditional lawmen in the mythic western mode, natives whose limited view of the world granted tacit approval to the changes that occurred. They never understood what the sheriff's race had to do with social issues. In their cowboy boots and hats and mirrored sunglasses characteristic of rural western law enforcement officials, the two showed a clear idea of what to do as sheriff but little conception of how to grapple with the bizarre Thompson. The journalist's issues were cosmic; they dealt with the change in the valley from the most neonative perspective. Here was a simultaneously cynical and idealistic newcomer who expected to find Shangri-la and was disappointed by a transformation that was well under way before his arrival and of which he was an important part. "And now we are reaping the whirlwind," Thompson told an audience in one particularly memorable speech:

> Big-city problems too malignant for small-town solutions. Chicago-style traffic in a town without stoplights. Oakland-style drug busts continually bungled by simple cowboy cops who see nothing wrong with kicking handcuffed prisoners in the ribs while the sheriff stands by watching, seeing nothing wrong with it either. While the ranchers howl about zoning, New York stockbrokers and art hustlers sell this valley out from under them. The county commissioners are crude dim-wit lackeys for every big-city dealer who wants a piece of the action. These rapists should be dealt with as harshly as any other criminal. This is 1970—not 1870. The powers of the sheriff's office can be focused in this direction.[39]

Typical of the people and values of pre-Paepcke Aspen, Whitmire and Ricks merely wanted the power that came with putting criminals in jail. Thompson mystified them.

Thompson lost the election, but the questions he raised stayed front and center not only in Aspen but also on the national cultural agenda. The national press was enthralled with the politics of Aspen, seeing it simultaneously as the ritual of an unusual tribe and a model for the future of participatory politics in a time of consolidation of power and wealth. Thompson's campaign teased the press and with it, an American public searching for answers to the hard questions of the age. Although Thompson played to the national media, his real concern was with the distribution of power at the local level. Ultimately, the most significant and vituperative questions he asked were of local, not national, import.

Thompson's run created the context for Aspen in the 1970s. Eve Homeyer, who won the mayoral race over no-growth advocate Joe Edwards, a twenty-nine-year-old attorney from Texas, was an advocate of growth, but the anti-growth faction gained enough power to limit her options. Behind the scenes, the Aspen Ski Company amassed more power, but the value of it was in its perception. The attempt to use power revealed its limits. As Denver negotiated to bring the 1976 Winter Olympics to Colorado, the ski company secretly offered Aspen as a location for the alpine events. Brown and the leadership were sure they could deliver the community, but they seriously miscalculated. From locals to neonatives, most people vehemently opposed the Olympics. It would ruin the town, they thought. Elizabeth Paepcke, overlooked by the new Aspen, spoke eloquently against the Olympics. Even Homeyer, typically an ardent proponent of growth, vowed to defeat the idea although soon after, she capitulated. The mayhem served its purpose. The Denver Olympic Committee eliminated Aspen before taking the idea to a state referendum. The voters of the state rejected the Olympics, creating a political career for Richard Lamm, who later became governor of the state and mounted a half-hearted challenge to Ross Perot for the Reform party nomination in 1996.[40] The rejection also vindicated the perspective of "true" Aspenites and repudiated the ski company, sending precisely the kind of symbolic message for which Aspen became famous.

The struggle proved that Aspen had become a different place. Despite the election of progressive leadership in the early 1970s, Aspen already had acquired new traits. National attention meant attracting more people, some of whom stayed. By the mid-1970s Colorado provided only 7.5 percent of skiers on Aspen slopes. Four states, Illinois, New York, California, and Michigan, provided larger percentage totals. As bizarre an array of celebrities as could be imagined trooped to the town; instead of Gary Cooper, 1970s Aspen claimed Claudine Longet and skier Spider Sabich, who died under mysterious circumstances and for whose death Longet was tried and convicted in a media circus. Singer John Denver made Aspen his home, and his ode to the town, "Rocky Mountain High," further transformed its iconography and made it popular in the most obsequious of ways. Don Henley of the Eagles rock group bought a home in Woody Creek near Hunter Thompson and the estate of the Hobby family, characteristic summer residents from Texas who owned the *Houston Post.* Henley's appearance in Aspen, along with Jack Nicholson's and Steve Martin's, signified the meeting of popular culture and

American elites. Even serial killer Ted Bundy was drawn to the town, committed a murder there for which he was jailed, and escaped from the notoriously lax Pitkin County jail. Aspen no longer had meaning; it was another stop on the underground railway of the 1970s, places where lost individuals went to make themselves feel important, to breathe the elixir of faux freedom brought by wealth and status.[41]

Brown's ski company and its vision of place triumphed in Aspen. Paepcke had fashioned culture and meaning; Brown cut recreation and pleasure into the snow with the edges of an ever-growing number of skis. Aspen still retained cachet, but it was not the same. No longer associated with cultural reform and the arts, Aspen instead became a playground for the wealthy, the disoriented, and people who aspired to put their name in the lights of the late twentieth century. There were few places where finding Andy Warhol's fifteen seconds of fame happened with more regularity than post-1970 Aspen. It also became more exclusive. In 1975 more than 25 percent of Aspen visitors reported incomes of over $50,000 per year, a figure that placed them among the wealthiest 10 percent of Americans. They outnumbered the cultural reformers or people who envisioned Aspen as a place apart. Slowly but with regularity, neonatives packed up and left. Peggy Clifford, who had invested much of her life in the town, returned to her hometown of Philadelphia. Bruce Berger became so alienated that he spent his winters in Phoenix. Even Whip Jones, the curmudgeonly founder of Aspen Highlands, the local resort known for difficult skiing and wobbly infrastructure, departed for Las Vegas, where he could play golf throughout the year. Some said he left to avoid paying personal income tax in Colorado.[42] Aspen truly became another place.

That new, more popular, less elite but still chic Aspen possessed great appeal in the business world. Darcy Brown made the bottom line more than respectable, and the increasing popularity of the community and its growing number of celebrities turned the town into an alluring conquest in an ongoing era of corporate takeover. The changes, even the chaotic politics, softened the community for outside takeover. After the 1970 elections and the Olympic controversy, the differences between outsiders and Aspenites seemed diminished. The transformations that the ski company wrought while the community argued over principles attracted corporations in search of gemlike additions. Brown changed not only the image of the town; he also brought it toward the mainstream of American society and popular culture just as that vector sought out Aspen. He also made the profile of the corporation more attractive to larger corporations. In 1975 Aspen Skiing Corporation (ASC) became half-owner of Fortress Mountain, a resort outside Calgary, Canada. With the principals in Fortress Mountain, ASC developed a new ski area called Blackcomb in Whistler, British Columbia. The ski company increasingly looked like a multinational and caught the eye of other corporations. In 1978, following on the heels of an almost snowless winter that threatened the entire Colorado ski industry, Twentieth-Century Fox purchased the Aspen Ski Corporation.[43]

For Brown, the sale was a logical step in an increasingly competitive market. Before the sale, Aspen Ski Corporation had valuable properties and the ability to grow but lacked the resources to compete in what had become a wholly corporate endeavor. The 1977–1978 winter hurt the Colorado ski industry; little snow fell and business contracted. Accidents on the slopes, including one at Vail, tarnished skiing. The market also changed. Vail became a threat to Aspen's dominance. By 1977 Vail superseded Aspen's total of skier visits per annum, putting economic rather than cultural pressure on ASC. Vail's rise was another impetus to sell; Vail had resources and the potential to overtake Aspen, and the two resorts shared an overlapping constituency. By the time of the sale, Brown recognized that unrestricted growth was not the best goal for places such as Aspen, but he was unsure how to mitigate it. In his view, Twentieth-Century Fox showed a willingness to maintain the highest level of service and facilities in Aspen. Perceiving a tightened market, Brown believed he had transferred Aspen to responsible stewards.[44]

The purchase of the ski company culminated the existing trends in Aspen and exacerbated the problems of the Brown regime. During twenty years at the helm, Brown made the company profitable, eliminated local idiosyncracies, fostered expansion that increased access to the market, and engaged in the combination of profitable and paternalistic practices that typified company towns. His saving graces in a fractious community were his blunt outspokenness and his familial ties to Aspen. Though he exasperated neonatives as he obliterated the *Kulturstaat,* he also relied on the old-timers to admire his straight-shooting style and on occasion to claim him as their own. Brown was a local with outside training and an agenda. Aspen recognized him even when they disagreed with and sometimes despised his actions.

Twentieth-Century Fox had no such cachet. A major film company, located in Los Angeles, it lacked prior experience in the ski industry. Like LTV, corporate synergy motivated its move. Twentieth-Century Fox capitalized on the growing identification of Aspen with celebrity as a way to link its films and stars with this chic aspect of American society. As in most takeovers at the time, corporate headquarters did not replace on-the-ground managers. It simply required that the same managers respond to different constraints.

The result was another eerie shift for locals. Aspen still looked like Aspen, sometimes even still felt like Aspen, but there was something distinctly different about it. The old leaders, to some the old villains, were diminished as a new corporate regime, far away and out of reach of locals, set the parameters.

The takeover solidified the process of stratification that Brown's actions set in motion. Aspen became sandwiched between two large constituencies, the growing horde of more affluent visitors and the consistent crowd of arrivals who expected Aspen to have remained a place apart from the mainstream or who simply wanted to ski. Aspen became another of the places where people would accept remarkable levels of underemployment to stay in town. It was as if the magic of the name were sufficient pay. The chamber of commerce even warned prospective job applicants that employment was seasonal and "wages [were] minimal." The takeover started to change that desirability. Newspaper reporter Alan Gersten observed just after the Twentieth-Century Fox purchase that there were two kinds of signs in Aspen: No Vacancy and Help Wanted. The former attested to Aspen's popularity, the latter to the fading sense of identity that made people willing to bus or wait tables in order to call this once-special place their own.

The buyout also illustrated how rapidly tourism could change shape and how dependent the industry remained on the perspective of the visionaries who preceded it. Aspen developed a tradition of strongmen, individuals who by a combination of charisma, money, and power, ruled the community although each had different goals. Paepcke's town was a respite from modern America, a place to think and work, to come to grips with forces larger than the self and more substantial than the temporal. In Brown's Aspen, hedonism and pleasure ranked above enlightenment, and the exploration of meaning gave way to the desire to be noticed. While Paepcke's Aspen offered a palliative to modernity, Brown's embraced it in its modernist emphasis on the self. The script Brown wrote for Aspen was attractive during the 1960s and 1970s, and corporate attention followed. Despite local protests, Twentieth-Century Fox made Aspen a premier resort, but one that was just like all the others.

This transformative pattern pervaded the skiing industry. As skiing gained popularity in American society, resorts passed to corporate ownership. Corporations were hardly innovators; their forte was to bring enormous amounts of capital to develop the programs their predecessors had begun. They also standardized amenities and increased the emphasis on the bottom line. With decisions made beyond the sociocultural boundaries of resort communities and often with little interest in local conditions, corporate takeover simultaneously secured the economic future of places and accelerated patterns of transformation that were already in progress.

Jackson, Wyoming, followed a similar pattern, its players tied to the region. It was not important enough to attract multinational attention as a ski resort, but its skiing facilities were essential to a healthy regional economy. Winter had always been an obstacle. A summer recreational area with a history that stretched back to dude ranching, the Hole, as the area was often called, simply shut down during the winter before the 1960s. Everyone who remained waited out the winter with a variety of diversions. Drinking became winter sport, the sole pastime in the town; writer Donald Hough explained that the cocktail hour in Jackson began when the tourists left on Labor Day and lasted six months. The drinking habits and health of a 300-pound local man were major concerns during the winter, Hough reported. The town cemetery was located on the side of a mountain, and the local funeral parlor had no vehicle that could climb the frozen mountainside. If the man died, his friends would have to carry him to the cemetery, a prospect that left everyone toasting his health and long life. Local sports included betting on the day the ice floated on Jackson Lake and watching the road for shipments of salable goods.[45]

Hough's portrait of 1950s Jackson showed a community of contented if slightly alcoholic locals who rented their town out during the summers and reclaimed it after Labor Day. Everyone knew everyone by name, and they congregated to pass the time as did small-town people across the nation. If they were a little sodden, their winter accounted for it, and perhaps even the service nature of their occupations contributed to their need. Yet locals were in control, were in the distinct majority, at least throughout the winter, and the community ran in a manner they found acceptable. In Hough's portrait, locals endured the summer and the profits it brought to rediscover the essence of their town and themselves during the long, cold, and thoroughly unattractive winters.[46]

Content to make their living off the summer, the people of Jackson skied as a diversion. In the late 1930s, locals constructed a rope tow to ascend Snow King Mountain. Skiing was not yet in fashion. "There were only about six people in town who could ski down Snow King," Neil Rafferty, who constructed the rope tow, remembered. The cable had been salvaged from an old oil-drilling rig, old car tire rims kept the cable from dragging in the snow, and metal clamps were attached to the eighteen people the lift could transport at any one time. A season pass cost ten dollars in 1939. Skiing became popular, and locals added a building at the foot of Snow King Mountain, locally called the ski shelter, where they could warm themselves after a run. In 1946 the Jackson Hole Winter Sports Association raised $40,000 to build a chairlift, and again Rafferty constructed it.[47] After its completion, Jackson offered a typical ski area. Locally owned, it aimed at locals as would a shooting range or a skating rink.

Skiing continued as a winter diversion until the hard-driving Paul McCollister, a California advertising executive who first visited Jackson during the 1940s, became a regular summer visitor beginning in 1946. He built a house on twenty acres in 1952 and explored the possibilities for taking the area to the next level. When he sold his business and retired to Jackson in 1957 at the age of forty-two, McCollister sought a project in skiing. He initially thought of California, but that same year, when a group of Utah businessmen approached him about a resort in Jackson, he was swayed. Within a few years, McCollister found a property for his idea, 166 acres located at the base of Rendezvous Mountain northwest of town. A neonative with more experience in business than anyone in Teton County, McCollister pursued his resort like a professional, forming the Jackson Hole Ski Corporation in 1963. He sold his option on the 166 acres to the company and became its president at a salary of $10,000 per year. McCollister, vice-president and secretary Alex Morley, and treasurer Gordon A. Graham, a business associate from California, raised funds for the project.[48]

McCollister typified the catalytic figures in the development of tourism in the twentieth-century American West. He perceived Jackson differently from its residents. Like Edgar L. Hewett, he became a resident and the chief promoter of an idea; like Walter Paepcke, he had a vision, capital and access to more, and a sense of what he believed the place and the nation needed. Unlike the winter drinkers or even the local skiers, McCollister envisioned winter recreation in Jackson on a level that had never before been imagined.

Funding remained the critical issue. McCollister and his friends were wealthy, but by the 1960s few could finance a ski resort from their own resources. A stock offering was a disaster. An attempt to raise $1 million netted only $50,000 and from almost 100 investors. Jackson's economy remained seasonal; nonexistent best described the economic climate during the long, cold winters. As a result, the community was eligible for low-cost government loans that supported urban renewal throughout the United States. In 1963 Sen. Gale McGee announced that the resort would receive $975,000 from the federal Area Redevelopment Administration and another $150,000 from the Wyoming Farm Loan Board. With $1 million in government capital, raising other money became easier. The Teton Investment Company added $300,000, the Wyoming Natural Resources Board $150,000, and the Jackson Hole Ski Corporation contributed $75,000.[49]

Crucial to the conception was the construction of an aerial tramway to the top of the Teton Range. The two-and-one-half-mile ride offered spectacular vistas to skiers and summer visitors alike and a new and exciting way to bring skiers from the new Teton Village at the base of the mountain to the six square miles of outstanding skiing above. With a thirty-year lease for 2,500 acres of ski slopes from the Forest Service in hand, the project forged ahead. The Jackson Hole Ski Area opened to skiers for the 1965–1966 season, and the tram debuted in July 1966. McCollister had his resort.[50]

The new Jackson Hole Ski Area had much to recommend it. Jackson enjoyed established cachet as a summer resort, and in the early 1960s the town was featured in a string of magazine articles promoting its virtues. The tram offered a diversion, and with the development of skiing as an industry and the selection of Gordy Wren to oversee the ski complex and of Buddy Werner to head the ski school, McCollister's resort was well positioned. In 1969 a full-page feature story in the *New York Times* confirmed the importance of the Jackson area as a winter destination.[51]

Suited to dominance by temperament and inclination, McCollister fashioned a classic one-developer resort. He and his partners controlled the base and the mountain and could take advantage of the nearby airport in Grand Teton National Park, which first opened in 1955, as a way to bring customers. They did not have to contend with competition; Snow King had grown, but it remained local, lacking cachet or stature. McCollister was a forceful individual who demanded absolute control. One by one his close associates fell from favor. Graham left first, shortly after the resort opened, and Morley lasted into the 1970s, when he lost a proxy fight that would have forced McCollister to pursue broader avenues of financing.[52] McCollister's vision made him a powerful leader, but his approach limited the resort.

The Jackson Hole Ski Area experienced little of the growth that characterized Aspen, Vail, and Steamboat Springs during the 1970s. Part of the problem remained access to Jackson; McCollister had to arrange personally for commercial air service to Jackson in the mid-1970s. The weather in the Jackson area was another liability. The northerly location and the high elevation meant that Jackson and the surrounding environs got cold early in the winter and stayed that way for a long time. Few skiers were willing to run the risk of day after day of extreme cold when the chances of more favorable weather at other resorts were far greater. McCollister's management also limited the growth of the resort and the company; consequently, the company ran short of funds. In 1987, after more than twenty years of operation, it had never paid a dividend to its stockholders, a marked contrast from the Aspen Ski Company.[53] McCollister's independence and iconoclasm kept the Jackson Hole Ski Area apart from the corporate revolution that swept the industry in the 1970s and 1980s.

The downside of that independence locked the Jackson Hole Ski Area into a pattern of slow growth and slower replacement of facilities and equipment. Like Darcy Brown at Aspen, McCollister did little to cultivate the local community. The people who brought new ideas often moved on, leaving McCollister with a 1960s-style philosophy in the economic climate of the 1980s. The bad relations that characterized the departure of shareholders such as Graham exposed the operation's weakness. Although McCollister owned controlling interest, large blocks of stock that belonged to people who avidly disliked him could be purchased.

During the 1980s corporate takeovers, especially hostile ones, dominated the business landscape. Armed with so-called junk bond funding, corporate raiders targeted companies with potential, low debt, and a lack of resources either to grow or to defend themselves. Arranged by financial gurus Michael Milken and Ivan Boesky, both of whom later went to jail for securities fraud, such loans engineered the buyout of major corporations such as RJR-Nabisco and made the careers of investors such as Ronald Perelman. They also saddled companies with immense debt, brought in new managers who cared little for corporate culture, and in other ways radically changed operations.

On a small scale, the Jackson Hole Ski Area was ripe for such a takeover. McCollister always needed money, and as Jackson's cachet increased, a wide array of the rich and famous settled there. A second-home industry took shape, and many well-known newcomers chose Jackson for that purpose. In an innocent gesture, McCollister picked up the telephone in December 1986 and called one such newcomer, Dutch oil trader John Duess, and solicited an investment. In May 1987 Duess purchased 24 percent of the ski company for $3.6 million, providing that the company divested itself of its real estate holdings.[54]

Although Duess's investment was hardly a corporate takeover, McCollister's call to him typified the process by which locals and neonatives lost control of tourism and watched it transform. The principal in Transworld Oil, one of the largest oil trading firms in the world, Duess was a shrewd businessman; and to him, the sums at stake were small. Typical of the idiosyncratic way he did business, McCollister made a number of rash promises that Duess expected him to fulfill. Almost instantly, the territorial McCollister regretted the decision to invite the oil trader's investment. Hoping to retain his control, he tried to limit Duess's influence but keep his money. Duess balked and a lawsuit resulted.[55]

The struggle occurred against a backdrop of an increasingly polarized Jackson. By the late 1980s the quaint town that Donald Hough described during the 1950s no longer existed, replaced by a community in which outsiders were the mainstays, from Wyoming natives and former secretary of interior James Watt and secretary of defense Richard Cheney to people like Duess. The construction of the tram in 1965 had been one dividing line; the second occurred as Jackson became fashionable in the 1980s and more of the "superrich," as *Jackson Hole News* editor Angus Thuermer Jr. referred to them, called it home. So did seismic survey teams, or "juggies," mobile oil exploration teams displaying the social characteristics of oil field roustabouts whose activities were funded by the high price of oil and the Carter-era windfall profits tax. In taking these jobs they were much like the native peoples of the Amazon, such as the Quchua and the Huaorani of Ecuador, who accepted survey employment from the oil companies drilling their homelands. The combination of the wealthy and wild superimposed a heady drug culture on the alcohol that had always fueled Jackson. With the continued decline of ranching and the rising cost of raw land and property, locals found Jackson less familiar and a great deal more oppressive. In his mystery *Murder in Jackson Hole,* local J. Royal Horton described his protagonist's cabin in nearby Wilson, Wyoming, as sitting "in the middle of a cul-de-sac, next to the big log homes of doctors, shrinks, and airline pilots." This juxtaposition described an innocence lost in transformation. Though Jackson remained small, to locals its small-town feel eroded.[56]

McCollister was by no means uniformly popular in Jackson. He initiated the process that displaced locals, that spread the community's influence over a much larger swath of the region, and that ultimately turned downtown Jackson into a place that catered to the whims of tourists. The ski resort had an important consequence for the community; as long as Snow King was the only downhill ski area, tourism stopped at Labor Day and the locals reclaimed their town. Teton Village, the development near McCollister's ski area, brought year-round tourism, itself a factor in changing the community. With his mercurial temper and general orneriness, McCollister was regarded as the catalyst who displaced locals but also as the person who brought innumerable dollars and people into the community. When the difficult issues had to be decided in Jackson, McCollister could count on little more than ambivalence from the community.

McCollister's problems stemmed from his desire to retain control of the company at the same time he desperately needed outside funds. When he called Duess for money, the ski corp showed a loss of more than $3.3 million; the infusion of capital prevented disaster, but it came at a high price. Duess dictated terms that favored him, but as the financial picture cleared, McCollister aimed to regain the advantage. In the view of one observer, McCollister would have still been "running the resort if he hadn't gotten himself into financial problems." In summer 1987 McCollister requested restructuring of the arrangement; in February 1988 he said he would pay back the investment but could not do so immediately. Duess filed suit, and in court the following month, McCollister asked that the agreement be abrogated because it did not say what he intended. He had reason to worry; under the terms of the agreement, 1988, the ski corp's best year, gave Duess a 49 percent stake in the company, negating McCollister's control. In 1989 the court granted a summary judgment in favor of Duess, which McCollister appealed, the federal district court turned back, and which was reinstated by an eleventh-hour stay. Although the court order returned McCollister's control temporarily, Duess's resources far outstripped McCollister's. At one point, Duess purchased an additional 12 percent that had initially belonged to Gordon Graham, giving Duess an even larger stake. The legal proceedings dragged into 1992, when the resort was sold to a third party, a company formed by John L. Kemmerer III of a prominent Wyoming family and by John Resor, a neighbor of Teton Village who was also a member of the largest landowning family in Teton County, for approximately $19.7 million. The deal closed in a New York City hotel room graced with a bottle of Dom Perignon on ice. Only the sale of the corporation determined how much McCollister and Duess owned. The *Jackson Hole News* estimated that at the time of the sale, McCollister owned 35.28 percent of the company, which was worth roughly $6.96 million. Duess received his $3.6 million from the proceeds of the sale as part of the $10 million the 50.72 percent he owned generated. He also received another $1.2 million for the additional 12 percent his holding company owned.[57]

The Jackson Hole Ski Area had come full circle. After the transaction, it belonged to a wealthy local and a wealthy Wyoming family. The ski resort had more regional control than had any tourist operation in Jackson since the arrival of Struthers Burt early in the century. Duess's involvement was that of an aficionado or a wealthy neonative. At one point during the negotiations, Resor later remarked, it was "difficult to get Duess's attention." The oil trader had a $20 billion deal with Chevron in the former Soviet Union in the works. In a strange way, Duess's gesture was equally the patriotism of a neo-native and a profit-making venture. When McCollister called, Duess helped save the local ski resort. The endeavor turned nasty only when McCollister realized what he had legally given away and tried to reclaim it. Even during the negotiations to sell what must have been an annoyance to a man engaged in much larger projects, according to John Resor, "Duess didn't want to sell unless he felt the ski area was in good hands."[58] The sale kept the resort in local or at least in regional hands, allowing the illusion that Jackson remained as it had been: a local place for local people.

Some truth remained in this idea, but the real story was far more complicated. A multinational did not purchase the resort because it was not large enough or sufficiently profitable. Skiing in Jackson remained too small for corporate interest. The real tourist trade in Jackson remained the summers. People built summer homes, not winter ones, and summer tourism remained a more difficult economic proposition. Though skiers stayed a week and paid premium prices for every service, the vast majority of summer visitors arrived in automobiles and could come and go as they pleased. By the mid-1990s the area around Jackson, especially in the little fingers of land that faced the Tetons but were surrounded by Grand Teton National Park, had become prime second-home territory. Peter Gabelli of the Gabelli Mutual Fund family owned a house there, as did many other wealthy people and celebrities, their capacious dwellings earning the sobriquet trophy homes. Located among them was former University of Wyoming history professor Robert W. Righter. In the late 1970s and early 1980s, Righter wrote a history of Grand Teton National Park, in the process spending much time in the Jackson area and purchasing a plot of land that faced Grand Teton Mountain. After he and his wife, historian Sherry Smith, constructed a modest house on the land, people of wealth and stature coveted similar properties and many moved into their neighborhood. Describing the situation, Righter remarked with his typical wit: "I can hear my house appreciating in my sleep."[59]

The attractiveness of Jackson brought newspaper editor Thuermer's superrich in droves, and they further changed the community. The old family stores on the town square that catered to locals were replaced by national resort chains, the Banana Republics and Eddie Bauers. The Silver Dollar Bar in the Wort Hotel, the scene of much of Donald Hough's *The Cocktail Hour in Jackson Hole,* became a tourist trap. The pleasant if slightly demonic drinking of Hough's novel became the Alcoholics Anonymous meetings that permeate J. Royal Horton's contribution to local literature. Whether from frustration or circumstance, the quaint and happy town of the 1950s had given way to a new and different place.

Although Jackson was not owned by a multinational or other corporation, it experienced changes remarkably similar to those of communities whose resorts were purchased by big money. At different paces and at different times, Steamboat Springs, Aspen, Jackson, and Sun Valley underwent similar transformations. Local ownership and leadership gave way to outside money, bringing neonatives tied to the new regimes with values that were different from those of the people they supplanted. Locals faced the classic devil's bargain of tourism. When they acquiesced, they found themselves displaced; they could neither afford to live in the new circumstances nor did they necessarily enjoy them. Their labor had no more meaning in the new circumstances than it had in the old, yet the climate they worked in looked the same but felt different. They engaged in myriad forms of resistance but typically found that local business, usually synonymous with local leadership, supported the changes because they significantly improved the bottom line for landowners. The result was a process typical of colonialism in American history. Local elites found their interests most closely tied to incoming power. In the process of allying with newcomers, they severed ties with the rest of the community and created a new one made up of outsiders who sought local acceptance.

By the time the ski areas became corporate-owned resorts, tourism itself in the West had become a corporate endeavor. In all its facets, large-scale control dominated the industry. In heritage and cultural tourism, the least lucrative and the hardest to own, the National Park Service emerged as a dominant entity. Underpinning it were AMFAC, Aramark, the Curry Company, and other large concessionaires who held contracts at multiple parks. In the skiing industry, local and area ownership passed to corporations that saw the sport as an adjunct. Entertainment tourism, the most lucrative of the three, had corporate roots in places such as Disneyland. Elsewhere, a corporate revolution was taking place that put the stamp of the postindustrial world first on Las Vegas, Nevada, and later on the rest of the nation.

11

Entertainment Tourism

Making Experience Malleable

The most important event in the history of modern Las Vegas was not the advent of Benjamin (Bugsy) Siegel, the mobster and sometime impresario who arrived in 1945 and transformed the city's regional-themed gambling industry into a gaming-resort spectacle that captured the imagination of the American and international public. Far more significant was the passage of the revised Corporate Gaming Act in 1969 that changed the laws concerning licensing for casino owners. Between 1955 and 1969, every owner of a casino had to undergo the Nevada Gaming Commission's investigation. The regulation of this period effectively eliminated the possibility that large publicly held corporations, with their thousands of shareholders, could participate in the lucrative gaming industry. It also institutionalized the idiosyncratic role of organized crime in the casinos of Nevada and ensured that investment capital, which had always been in short supply in the Silver State, remained difficult to secure.[1]

The 1969 act proved a pivotal moment in the history of Las Vegas, a town that by the 1960s people around the world equated with fun, excitement, and a little bit of danger. The largest city in the only state in the nation that permitted casino gaming, Las Vegas developed a reputation as a town conceived, designed, and built to facilitate the pleasures of the high rollers on whom its prosperity depended. Yet a significant stigma remained attached to gaming even in a culturally liberalizing American society, limiting the sources of capital available to casino operators. A generation removed from the crusty iconoclasts of the 1930s, who fancied themselves participants in an institution-free world that mirrored the qualities of the mythic Wild West, Las Vegas casino operators in the 1950s and 1960s were professional gamblers with close attachments to the underworld. Their career choices were legal only in Nevada. With conventional sources of investment capital such as Wall Street loath to back gaming, mob money, directly or indirectly, was the only funding operators could find. Las Vegas had a Stepford Wives quality to it: it appeared normal, but the community's energy and its substantial postwar growth were fundamentally out of sync with the rest of the nation.[2]

In this malleable deviance, Las Vegas became the perfect incubator for the culmination of the historic trends of tourism. It provided the most dramatic example of entertainment tourism, the form that both succeeded and enveloped heritage and recreational tourism, including their virtues and shortcomings. At the same time, it foreshadowed the transformation of industrial capitalism and its emergence in a postindustrial form. Because of the glaring absence of other economic—and as a result, cultural and social—features, Las Vegas and indeed Nevada required a specific niche in order to survive. In the scorching desert of southern Nevada, sheep and cows could not graze; nor was there water or rich soil for crops. Las Vegas acquired its staples from the outside, and that acquisition depended on what it could offer in return.

In fits and starts, Las Vegas became the prototype for entertainment tourism, the process in which communities and their residents cease to educate, enlighten, or even provide inspirational outdoor experience and instead refracted back on to visitors what they most want. Aspen and Sun Valley possessed identities that locals guarded. The National Park Service preserved values at the Grand Canyon, Grand Teton, and the entire plethora of national park areas. Santa Fe codified its manufactured identity in 1957 with the formalization in law of the practice of only constructing adobe or adobe-imitation or -style buildings in the town. Such places sold visitors a vision of better social and cultural status. Las Vegas offered the promise of individual aggrandizement, of fulfilling everyone's needs. It simply asked visitors what they could pay for what they wanted. Understanding the fragility of their position, Las Vegans made their past, present, and future malleable, reflecting what the world saw in the mirror called Las Vegas.

That malleability became the most critical feature of entertainment tourism. It permitted Las Vegas to reinvent itself time and again, to respond to changing trends in American society, to anticipate individual needs in ways that icons such as Santa Fe and Sun Valley could not. Despite its template, Santa Fe purported to be about the authentic; Sun Valley promised rejuvenation through skiing. Las Vegas merely offered affirmation of the self, packaged to the tastes of the moment. Nothing about Las Vegas, not its past, present, or future, was permanent. Malleability was the key to its survival.

This flexibility was characteristic of colonies. In material terms, Las Vegas had little to offer industrial America. During the 1940s and 1950s it defined itself as the town where the people from the places central to national life could cast off their shackles and let down their guard. In this colonial formulation crystallized the most regressive form of taxation, gaming, which routinely took from the poor and gave to the rich. The niche that Las Vegas claimed was perfect for peripheral places. Nevadans not only legalized but they also embraced a stigmatized activity to claim and secure a place in American society. In the process, they remade tourism. Going beyond the elitist roots of tourist travel in the late nineteenth century and the democratized travel made possible by the automobile, Las Vegas turned gaming into an offering of all things to all people. In the process, it set a tone for tourism without deep meaning. It was neither to inform daily life, nor to promote physical strength and prowess; it was merely to occupy, distract, and arguably to pacify its audience.

From this script came other forms of entertainment tourism, long regarded as more benign. Preceded by Coney Island, Atlantic City, and other earlier distractions, Las Vegas anticipated the context in which places such as Disneyland, Knott's Berry Farm, Six Flags, and others evolved. Although Walt Disney took the conceptualization of his park from the great fairs of the fin de siècle, Disneyland reached for the public in the same manner as did Las Vegas. Disneyland and its followers placed the visitor at the center of the story in a manner eerily reflective of Las Vegas; they promised complete experience, as did Las Vegas, but especially before the 1980s each had an infinitely stronger claim on marketing good clean fun. What Las Vegas gave adults, these other places gave children and with a wink and a nod, adults.

In this respect, Las Vegas and Disneyland shared enormous parallels. Founded in 1954, Disneyland became the epitome of entertainment tourism at a time when Las Vegas could not compete in the mainstream marketplace. Disneyland offered the same sort of refraction of experience as did Las Vegas but through a lens focused directly on the heart of the baby boom generation. Disneyland offered a form of cultural and heritage tourism—some said indoctrination—along with its scripted entertainment. Like Santa Fe and Aspen, Disneyland created an identity; it became static and immutable in a way that Las Vegas could not afford to be. Disneyland invented faster rides. Las Vegas reinvented itself time and again.[3]

In Las Vegas, the combination of malleability, legalized activity at odds with national norms, and the stigma attached to it created a town more mythic than real, one that catered to tourists in a broad sense but focused its efforts on one extremely specialized segment of the market: the serious gamblers, or high rollers. In this respect, Las Vegas of the 1950s and 1960s resembled Edgar Hewett's Santa Fe more than Mary Austin's or Walter Paepcke's Aspen more than the mass ski center that followed. Las Vegas too was a specialty taste, but its guests were not tuned to the highbrow. It was a tourist town but in an odd sense; the people most at home in Las Vegas understood the signs and symbols of the netherworld of illegal gaming. Whether visitor or resident, they were the insiders who fashioned this desert outpost, created its norms, and conversely made the town exciting. Like the veterans of the Tenth Mountain Division in Aspen, these gamblers, driven by intensely American values, speaking a cultural language of their own, and offering a romanticized vision of the nature of their world, defined the parameters of the Las Vegas scene.

In the mid-1960s Las Vegas became the first city in the nation to embrace a service economy, albeit an idiosyncratic one, as its dominant formulation. While Detroit built cars, Bethlehem, Pennsylvania, made steel, and southern California and the Sun Belt embraced the defense and entertainment industries, Las Vegas locked itself into tourism and gaming. The limitations of climate and infrastructure dictated the choice. Few efforts to manufacture in the archetypal American way occurred in the desert of southern Nevada. Agriculture and ranching remained fantasy, the town offered little to industry, and few of the characteristic features of midcentury economic organization existed in Las Vegas. Instead the city and surrounding Clark County made its money as did colonies and peripheries: it offered people of the core areas pleasures that they could acquire at home only with the risk of embarrassment, stigma, and sometimes arrest. For many people who sampled the opportunities of Las Vegas, the budding resort in the Mojave Desert served as a time-out from daily life. They could be respectable in Sausalito, Ventura, or Davenport, but when they came to Las Vegas to cut loose, all bets were off. For Nevadans, this situation was merely a way of life.

The basic realities of Nevada drove its unique economic formulation. Even in the 1950s Nevada remained a colony of the rest of the nation, especially of California. The Hoover Dam typified the state's predicament; in 1997 vehicles inscribed with the insignia of the Los Angeles Municipal Water District sported Nevada license plates. Lake Mead was Los Angeles's reservoir, located in Nevada. Founded as a result of the Comstock Lode and the need for another state in the Union to guarantee Abraham Lincoln's reelection in

1864, desolate Nevada survived by catering to the needs of people outside the state, particularly Californians. From the mining industry, called extractive for a reason, that dominated the nineteenth and early twentieth centuries to the development of divorce and gaming as bases of the state economy, Nevada derived its sustenance by trading raw materials—gold, silver, and the possibility of quick freedom in personal or economic terms—for the finished products of American society. Nevadans fashioned a world apart in an effort to attract their neighbors' interest and to sustain themselves.

In Nevada, as in other colonies, the relationship between core areas and their peripheries dominated life. The economic structure of a colony differed from that of a core area; the colony depended on a core for much and often all of its sustenance. In industrial economies, core areas produced goods that were marketed in both cores and peripheries, but colonies only received expensive finished goods in exchange for much less expensive raw materials. Colonies shipped out their raw materials until the source was exhausted, but the appetite for finished products on the periphery remained insatiable. The accoutrements of the core had great symbolic power on the periphery. After the demise of traditional extractive commodities in the West, successful colonies faced clear and striking choices: market other amenities or decline. One sure way to survive was to provide services that the core culture eschewed, scorned, or did not permit but that its people coveted. In the case of Las Vegas, that lure of fun, excitement, and a little bit of danger created an economy that allowed the distribution of the finished goods signifying the veneer of modernity and civilization in an outpost. Nearly everything that sustained the institutions of dominant culture societies on a colonial periphery came from outside. In Nevada, its power, water, food, economy, and raison d'etre as an independent entity came from beyond its boundaries. Nevada imported almost everything.

Nevada in general and southern Nevada in particular became the first American state to embrace the ethic of the future, the concepts, emotions, and packaging that became entertainment tourism. This outcome hardly resulted from prescience; instead a combination of serendipity, colonial history, and unadulterated good fortune propelled Las Vegas from a regionally themed gambling resort to a malleable pinnacle of the power and concomitant shallowness of the postwar era and later the postmodern and postindustrial worlds. The process began as a result of the aftermath of World War II when Americans enjoyed more disposable income and more vacation time, and visitation to the West increased.[4]

Initially, Las Vegas owed its growth to federal spending. In 1910, only a few years after the arrival of the railroad, its population reached 945. But in 1927 Las Vegas lost its role as division point and regional center for the railroad to nearby Caliente as punishment for the support locals offered the national railroad strike in 1922. Without its railroad shop, Las Vegas became another of the innumerable towns along western railroads that consistently struggled. The passage of the Boulder Dam Act in 1928 rescued the town, leading to a six-fold increase in population by 1930. The combination of the dam project and the subsequent embrace of gaming changed the community's orientation. In 1933 alone, more than 200,000 visitors combined a trip to see the dam with a visit to Las Vegas. The Nevada divorce industry offered lucrative economic possibilities, requiring only a six-week residency before a person could file. In February 1931 the Nevada state legislature relegalized gambling; although illegal from statehood in 1864 until 1869, the activity had been legal until the 1910s, when Progressive Era efforts to legislate morality put the state in compliance with the rest of the nation. Relegalization was a return to a state norm rather than an innovation, and gambling attracted outsiders to southern Nevada.[5] Las Vegans learned to see visitors as a basis of the local economy.

The completion of the dam in 1935 presented the town with a problem of immense proportions. Accustomed to the impact of the construction workers' salaries on the local economy, Las Vegas had to find a new source of revenue. Visitors seemed one likely remedy. The dam remained the best feature southern Nevada offered, far superior to other amenities such as Pueblo Grande de Nevada, the Lost City that was partially inundated as Lake Mead filled. In a typical formulation of local attributes, Las Vegans saw their town as the Gateway to the World's Greatest Engineering Project. They exalted the accomplishments of their culture, embracing the conquest of nature by industry and technology. Incongruously, Las Vegans also saw themselves as a symbol of the wide-open life. In a place that conceived of itself as "still a frontier town," in the phrase of the chamber of commerce, western festivals, horsemen in the streets, and miners and their mules in hotel lobbies reflected an image of a prerailroad past that accentuated traditional western values. Gambling was part of the matrix but not always one of its central features.[6]

Even supported by gaming, mid-1930s tourism in Las Vegas typified the small-town West. The place possessed nothing special: a few hotels, a road to a major technological accomplishment in an era when marketing the sublime, the empirical, and the powerful retained meaning, the promise of attaining a quick divorce with no stigma, the option to purchase sexual liaisons, and the opportunity legally to risk wages. Only the lack of legally defined social constraints made the town different. Las Vegas remained ordinary, stuck in a rut.

Typically, growth on the periphery depended on change at the core. Municipal reform in Los Angeles spurred the importance of gambling in southern Nevada. In the late 1930s Mayor Fletcher Bowron forced Los Angeles gambling underground, and some of its operators relocated across the mountains in southern Nevada. They included a former Los Angeles Police Department Vice Division captain-turned-gambling entrepreneur, Guy McAfee, and gambler Tony Cornero, who ran "floating casinos" off the coast of California until Bowron shut them down. The operators provided critical expertise that expanded gaming in Las Vegas. Only illegal operators possessed the requisite knowledge, and they brought not only skills but also different conceptions. Their arrival served as a precursor to change in Las Vegas.[7]

The first resort hotel in Las Vegas was another harbinger. Lured by developer Robert Griffith and car dealer James Cashman, Californian Thomas Hull added a new hotel to his holdings, which included the Bellview in San Francisco, the Mayfair in Los Angeles, and the El Rancho chain. Designed by Los Angeles architect Wayne McAllister, the El Rancho had expansive gardens and a large swimming pool, a rustic-looking casino and restaurant, the Opera House Showroom, and a few shops when it opened in April 1941. The resort offered Las Vegas its initial opportunity to draw the clientele that came naturally to places such as Sun Valley.[8]

Hull also added one little twist to his new resort; he built it beyond the city limits in an area that Guy McAfee labeled the Strip, after his beloved Sunset Strip in Los Angeles. Hull wanted more space than he would pay for within the city limits and also wanted to be free of what he regarded as an onerous local tax burden. Breaking the pattern of downtown Las Vegas, Hull fashioned a resort rather than a hotel, convincing others to follow him onto the highway south of town. In 1942 the Last Frontier opened about one mile south of the El Rancho; in 1947 it added the Last Frontier Village, a historic re-creation of the western past a full decade before Disneyland and Knott's Berry Farm experimented with such concepts.

Despite resort development, the theming of Las Vegas remained an afterthought. Locals and outside entrepreneurs who brought capital simply followed existing patterns. The El Rancho, the Last Frontier, and most of the hotels built downtown during the 1940s continued the Wild West imagery. Locals were so content with this ersatz frontier conception that in 1944 civic

Fremont Street in Las Vegas in the early 1950s. Gaming was a way of life. (Photo courtesy of Special Collections, James L. Dickinson Library, University of Nevada, Las Vegas.)

leaders sought legislation to ensure the conformity of all future construction. The western theme was safe; it served as a mask for gambling, increasingly the dominant activity, and played to American cultural iconography. Las Vegans retained a continuing ambivalence toward gambling as their primary attraction; the growing numbers of visitors clearly did not share their sentiment.[9]

After the war, the potential of Las Vegas became apparent. It seemed an easy place to make money, although not by sitting at the tables and betting on cards, and for a while, Las Vegans expected that outside capital might build their town. Wealthy visitors often remarked that they, too, would build a hotel. Among those who considered it were Mae West and Frank Sinatra, part of a consortium that planned a resort with its own radio station. Others included aggressive entrepreneurs such as Billy Wilkerson, founder of the *Hollywood Reporter* and a Los Angeles restaurant impresario, and Wilbur Clark, who left his Illinois home as a young man, went to California, and worked at menial jobs in southern California before coming to Nevada to open the Desert Inn. Even Roy Rogers wanted to be part of the exciting new town. In keeping with the typical prewar themes of Las Vegas, he planned a dude ranch.[10]

The components were in place before Bugsy Siegel fashioned them into a resort with national appeal. The extension of gambling beyond the city limits, the idea of resort hotels, and the desire to appeal to a wealthy clientele existed before his Flamingo Hotel. Missing was the vision of a national constituency, access to the capital to support comprehensive development, and the concept of a place that transcended regional themes. Siegel's hotel resolved these issues by creating a resort that aimed at the modern luxury traveler.

When Siegel took over the Flamingo, he was an established figure in Nevada. In 1945 he and a group of associates that included Arizona bookmaker Gus Greenbaum, Willie Alderman and David and Charles (Chickie) Berman from Minneapolis, and Moe Sedway from Los Angeles purchased the El Cortez on Fremont Street. Vaunted underworld figure Meyer Lansky held a 10 percent share. The group ran the hotel for six months and sold it, turning a 27 percent profit. Siegel reinvested in the booming industry and seized on the Flamingo Hotel, the brainchild of Billy Wilkerson, who envisioned Las Vegas as Beverly Hills in the desert. Wilkerson planned a swank and elegant resort that appealed to a fashionable crowd in ways that the sawdust-covered floors and cowboy boots of the western casinos could not. Wilkerson's project faced a typical problem in the development of Las Vegas: his plans outstripped his resources, and with little capital in the state and less chance to borrow from conventional sources, Wilkerson searched for investors. Siegel and his friends bought two-thirds of the project for $650,000. Using his own money and raising more from associates in $50,000 shares, Siegel took over the project, broadening even Wilkerson's concept of glamour.[11]

This "sportsman," in the parlance of the time, envisioned a place that would impress even Cecil B. DeMille. In the words of Meyer Lansky, he took a "dinky, horrible, little oasis town . . . [and built] the greatest, most luxurious hotel casino in the world." With underworld financing, Las Vegas could transcend its inherent limitations. When the Flamingo opened in half-finished form in December 1946, it instantly became the finest place in town. "You never saw so many black-chip [$100-chip] gamblers in your life," Siegel's attorney, Louis Wiener, a Las Vegas fixture, remembered. The resort clearly set a new standard in Las Vegas. Its architecture mirrored the modern styles developing in Los Angeles. The casino embodied the opulence of

Monte Carlo, and the hotel, which first opened in March 1947, resembled the style of Miami Beach. The 105 rooms were lavish, the grounds contained a three-story waterfall and beautiful landscaping replete with exotic trees, and the staff was clad in tuxedos. The building was even air-conditioned, although in the casino it was often hard to tell. The technology to air-condition large spaces successfully did not exist until 1951. Jimmy Durante headed the first opening night bill; Abbott and Costello opened the completed hotel the following spring.[12] National celebrities had never before played the dusty, dirty desert town.

The combination of capital and vision was more prescient than even Siegel realized. Although Las Vegas clearly evolved from rest stop to destination on the Los Angeles highway, in reality, a greater transformation was in the works. Automobiles initiated the process as Las Vegas distilled postwar California culture for the rest of the nation, the combination of speed embodied in a McDonald's meal and the recreational pleasure of surfing that became cornerstones of the postwar California dream. It also developed a broad cultural meaning, creating a national base that grew when air travel could whisk visitors to new worlds of leisure. As Las Vegas evolved, it increasingly offered a middle-class clientele the potential of a luxury experience.

Finding the capital to support this process remained arduous. Nevada lacked indigenous capital. Sporting an industry that repulsed most investors, the state resorted to unorthodox financial venues. The consistent need for resources created a series of dependent capital regimes, periods of time when the dominant source of capital shaped the direction not only of the gaming industry but of the sociocultural conditions of Las Vegas. It also helped define whom southern Nevada attracted, the kind of ancillary industries that came to the rapidly growing region, and the nature of available employment opportunities.

As in most western states, the tale of where the money came from began with the federal government. Before 1930, southern Nevada's economy was at best precarious. The turn-of-the-century mining booms in places such as Rhyolite, Goldfield, Tonopah, and Bullfrog had ended after World War I. The sale of the San Pedro, Los Angeles, and Salt Lake Railroad to the Union Pacific created another link in the seemingly endless series of colonial relationships that dominated this periphery. After the Union Pacific left Las Vegas, town leaders feared that they would be unable to sustain a future. Las Vegas remained a dusty little town with no distinct identity or purpose and no claim on the nation.[13]

Federal spending prompted a rebirth of colonial Las Vegas, as two events led the way: the construction of the Boulder Dam (now Hoover Dam), beginning in 1929, and the New Deal with its development programs. In southern Nevada alone, the federal government invested $70 million between 1929 and 1939, $19 million on the dam alone. The nearly 5,000 workers lived in Boulder City, a few miles from the Colorado River canyons where the dam rose. Las Vegans recognized that the workers sought amenities and distractions, alcohol and prostitutes chief among them, that Boulder City's small business district did not offer. They anticipated that the flow of visitors passing through southern Nevada during the dam's construction would continue after its completion. Their money, combined with federal support for the many people who came to Las Vegas in search of work but failed to find it, provided southern Nevada with a new lifeline that replaced mining and the railroad.[14]

This first capital regime, federal funding, only made Las Vegas typical of many western locales. During the 1930s federal projects became the dominant economic source throughout the nation, especially in the West, and many towns shared the circumstances Las Vegas experienced. This dependence on federal spending began earlier in southern Nevada because the dam preceded the New Deal, but in many ways 1930s southern Nevada served as a prototype of the West and the nation.[15]

One major difference set Las Vegas apart so that its 1930s experience was both deviant and ultimately central to the United States. The relegalization of gaming in 1931 followed the pattern the state had previously taken with its liberal prostitution, marriage, and divorce laws and its characteristic disregard of prohibition. With gambling, Nevada offered an activity that could augment, redirect, and ultimately supplant federal capital. Especially when the dollars from the dam dried up after 1936, this source of revenue proved increasingly important.[16]

This first modern capital regime illustrated the perils of colonial existence. Lacking industry or infrastructure, Las Vegas depended primarily on money provided by the federal government. Almost as an afterthought, the state permitted activities that were seen as scandalous at best in an effort to create an ongoing economy. Southern Nevadans especially recognized the perils of dependence. A change in federal policy could eliminate not only individual livelihood but also the economic viability of the region. Before air-conditioning, attracting newcomers to a town where summer temperatures routinely topped 110° Fahrenheit was a difficult task without the lure of easy prosperity.

Las Vegas shaped itself to the needs of the outside. In the 1930s and 1940s in the West, this approach was not unusual. It was as true of Los Alamos,

New Mexico, and Richmond, California, as it was of Las Vegas. The difference was that Las Vegans recognized that their opportunity to capitalize was time-bound and that other strategies were essential for long-term sustenance. Perhaps the much touted Nevada individualism promoted a climate that encouraged augmenting federal largesse; perhaps federal dollars seemed one more panacea in the long line that had come and gone. Southern Nevada especially welcomed the federal money and engaged in strategies to encourage those dollars to stay in the area even as its people looked for new ways to diversify their income base.

Throughout the 1930s and World War II, federal money remained the dominant source of outside capital in the region. The dam project ended, and Nevadans cast about for a new strategy. Tourism and divorce in the 1930s filled a gap, but the prosperity of the dam years did not return. Only the response to Pearl Harbor rescued Las Vegas from postdam doldrums as the federal government again located important projects in southern Nevada. An air base north of town was commandeered by the federal government, which ultimately spent more than $25 million on the construction of facilities there. The Las Vegas Gunnery School, as the installation became known, supplied the Pacific theater with gunners, graduating 4,000 every six weeks by 1942. The Basic Magnesium Incorporated (BMI) factory in the newly founded town of Henderson, between Las Vegas and Boulder City on the Boulder Highway, supported by federal dollars, was another manifestation.[17] By 1945 Las Vegas was accustomed to a two-pronged economy: federal dollars that drove the local economy and catering to the needs of people who sought personal freedom through divorce or who enjoyed gambling.

Federal dollars dominated, driving local decision making. Access to the federal money in the form of construction contracts, service work, or the opportunity to liberate dollars from the pockets of workers were charters for economic success. Federal dollars were so crucial that the community gave in to certain demands: in 1942 Las Vegas closed its red-light district to oblige the military, and after November of that year bars and casinos were closed from 2:00 A.M. to 10:00 A.M., exceptional for southern Nevada. But closure was worthwhile if the consequence of failing to comply meant designation as off-limits to military personnel.[18] Nevada's colonial nature was once again made clear. As it once catered to the mining industry and the railroad, it catered to the demands of the federal government.

Bugsy Siegel's arrival inaugurated the second capital regime in modern Las Vegas. Lansky and his associates had an eye on Las Vegas as early as 1941, but in most accounts it is Siegel who receives credit for envisioning the complicated relationship between gaming and status that made the Flamingo a world-class location. Siegel transformed Las Vegas from a western, institution-free center of vice into a world-renowned spectacle of gambling, entertainment, and fun by melding the themes of Monte Carlo, Miami Beach, and Havana with the resortlike character of the clubs that preceded the Flamingo on Highway 91 south of town. In the process, he launched an era in which the capital to fund gaming resorts, soon the dominant industry in Las Vegas, came first from the pockets of organized crime and later from legitimate money the mob could control. The second capital regime was born.[19]

Locals did not object to this seemingly nefarious involvement in what had not yet become the primary local industry. Even the strait-laced southern Nevada Church of Jesus Christ of Latter Day Saints (Mormon) culture welcomed these newcomers. They had cash and lots of it, essential to any periphery. Siegel's arrival opened a new pipeline to the capital for which Las Vegans thirsted. Even the mobster's association with Murder Inc. did not deter locals who were so desperate for capital that they embraced anyone who had money to invest.[20]

Initially, organized crime's investment was masked by local involvement. When Siegel purchased the El Cortez in 1945, his investors included locals as well as Lansky, Greenbaum, the Berman brothers, Alderman, and Sedway. The El Cortez initiated a pattern; in virtually every subsequent purchase or development of a resort on the Strip, participation by "connected" illegal gamblers whom Nevada legalized was evident. This visible relationship between locals and newcomers linked outside capital with local respectability. Locals who could pass Gaming Board inspections usually found an individual with ties to organized crime but with no criminal record to speak of holding a significant percentage of a new casino. Most of these "owners" apparently had recently come into money and had expertise useful in the casino business. Who truly owned their percentage was not a good question to ask.

The story of the funding of the Flamingo Hotel illustrated the point. The construction of the Flamingo went well over budget. The initial estimate of $1.5 million ballooned to almost $6 million, aggravated by expenses such as the $1 million that Siegel's insistence on providing a private sewer line to each room added to the cost. In 1946, when Siegel tried to extort $2 million from the Chicago mob to complete construction, he had $1 million of his own money in the project and $3 million that his connected friends had invested in $50,000 blocks of stock. Not a dime of legitimate money financed the Flamingo after Siegel took it over from Billy Wilkerson.[21]

This pattern typified the funding of Las Vegas casinos into the mid-1950s. Even resorts with legitimate origins, such as Wilbur Clark's Desert Inn, became part of vast organized crime networks. Clark, his brother, and two investors began the Desert Inn in 1947 with $250,000. They soon ran out of money, and for nearly two years the framed structure sat in the hot desert sun, looking more like an ancient ruin than a nascent casino. At one point, Clark even approached the New Deal–era Reconstruction Finance Corporation (RFC) for money. In 1949 Clark met Morris B. (Moe) Dalitz, and within a few months, Dalitz and his partners in the notorious Cleveland Mayfield Road gang contributed $1.3 million in capital and owned 75 percent of the project. The mix led to an exquisite future. When Wilbur Clark's Desert Inn opened in April 1950, local residents called it "the most brilliant social event in the history of the Strip." Clark soon became a glorified front man at the resort that bore his name, reduced to ensuring that "Wilbur Clark" preceded the words "Desert Inn" on souvenirs. The Desert Inn opened a pipeline of money from similar points of origin, and hotels such as the Sands, completed in 1952, the Riviera in 1955, the Tropicana in 1957, and the Stardust in 1958 soon followed similar financing patterns.[22]

This second capital regime fed the roots of the world of mythic Las Vegas, the seedy mob town that still had enough cachet to pull in growing numbers of Americans. Las Vegas became a world of individual investment, sometimes hidden and consequently untaxed, with consistent deliveries of paper bags and briefcases full of money to individual mobsters in distant cities. These figures held "points" in Las Vegas, percentage investments that were concealed but that returned monthly profits skimmed from the casino's profits and never recorded in their ledgers. Insidious and nefarious to be sure, most of these were also small-time, accruing as little as a few thousand dollars a month in profit. Jack Entratter, the ostensible head of the Sands in the early 1960s, held twelve points in the operation. A former headwaiter at the Copacabana in Miami Beach who became a player and philanthropist in Las Vegas—the social hall in the oldest synagogue in town, Temple Beth Sholom, was constructed with his donation and named for him—Entratter owned two of those points himself. The other ten he held for various people, including the real power at the Sands, an old associate of Lansky's named Vincent (Jimmy Blue Eyes) Alo.[23] The mythic Las Vegas was a personal world where everyone knew everyone else and also knew who buttered their bread.

There was much to celebrate in this world for the people who came to Las Vegas in an effort to legitimize their lifestyle in the postwar period. After the

Flamingo opened, the town became a magnet for every gambler, hood, and small-time entrepreneur. In every other state, the activities that Las Vegas allowed regularly landed people in jail. Most were relieved to live where their activities were legal, and they came by the thousands, swelling the population of the city and creating a company town by professing allegiance to the quirky set of practices that defined 1950s and 1960s Las Vegas. Even local political culture was transformed, as politicians found gamblers to be the only major source of campaign contributions. Las Vegas became one big carpet joint, a place where the mores of illegal gaming culture became the norm and where the only casinos that lost money, after Siegel's initial fiasco at the Flamingo, were run by people who did not understand the rules of this imported culture.[24]

For the people who preceded mob-financed gaming in Las Vegas, these changes embodied the disenfranchisement that local residents typically experienced with the rise of tourism in other locales. After the founding of the Flamingo, connected individuals ran the important hotels and casinos. As hotel-casino combinations opened on the Strip throughout the 1950s, a coterie of associates arrived to run them. Many were from Chicago, but their geographic and ethnic backgrounds varied. They shared filial ties to the owners. These "hoods," as the daughter of one referred to her father and his associates, filled the best jobs, hiring other outsiders for positions as dealers. Local people were consigned to their usual rung near the bottom of the economic ladder. Even locals with experience in the gaming industry before 1945 found that they lacked the right kind of experience. As elsewhere in the tourist industry, newcomers linked to the source of capital held the best positions.[25]

In the comfortable political and cultural climate of southern Nevada, Las Vegas became the center of gaming in the Western Hemisphere. Gaming masked its social cost; despite the reality that many casino employees spent equal time on both sides of the tables, most of the money the casinos won came from visitors, not from local residents. This obviated the problems associated with the redistribution of wealth that accompanied gambling by residents and gave the industry a positive impact on the state economy's bottom line. Political change elsewhere guaranteed Nevada's preeminence. After Castro closed the Havana casinos, only one location in North America offered legal big-time gambling and made its operators legitimate. Combined with technological improvements such as the expansion of McCarran Airport in 1963, the "dinky horrible little oasis town" that Lansky and Siegel

The expanded McCarran Airport in Las Vegas, circa 1963. The new airport changed the demography of visitation in Sin City. (Photo courtesy of Eric A. Taylor Collection, James L. Dickinson Library, University of Nevada, Las Vegas.)

first saw stood poised to take advantage of widespread wealth and changing cultural mores. Las Vegas claimed a double-edged position of prominence in the worlds of recreation and organized crime.[26]

One key to this new significance was the jet airplane. Particularly before World War II, propeller planes provided a dependable if ponderous mode of transportation. The frequent stops required by such aircraft made communities such as Columbus, Oklahoma City, and Wichita central in air travel; post-1960 jet travel obliterated that centrality. More densely seated and more numerous, passengers from everywhere crowded flights to Las Vegas. Individual hotel owners first recognized the opportunity. Warren (Doc) Bayley, a farmer from Platteville, Wisconsin, who built the Hacienda Hotel, locally known as Hayseed Heaven, owned eight airplanes that ferried 150,000 visitors from New York, Detroit, Chicago, St. Louis, Los Angeles, and San Francisco in 1962 alone before federal authorities determined he was running an airline without a license and shut him down.[27] As streamlined trains brought visitors to the slopes of Colorado and Idaho overnight, jets put Las Vegas within the reach of millions. People from throughout the country and the world could enjoy this city of illusions.

This new form of accessibility changed the demography of visitation to Las Vegas. Before 1960 Californians predominated, making up between 65 percent and 75 percent of visitation. The opening of the new domed terminal at McCarran Airport reflected the impact of jet travel and highlighted the broadened geographic reach of Las Vegas. Although California and the West dominated auto travel, ranging from a high of 90.3 percent in 1963 to a more typical 58 percent in 1978 and 60 percent in 1980, as a percentage of visitation to Las Vegas Californians peaked in the late 1950s. Auto travelers also declined as a percentage of the total; more visitors came by air. By the 1970s midwesterners dominated visitation, with California slipping to as little as 30 percent. The appeal of Las Vegas became truly national.[28]

Serving this broadening constituency accelerated the demand for capital and brought about obvious changes in operations. Until 1963, when the Fremont Casino skimming scandal was exposed by illegal Federal Bureau of Investigation (FBI) wiretaps, Las Vegas was a small-time operator's paradise.[29] It functioned as had illegal gambling all over the country, run by the experienced gamblers who flocked there. Accustomed to seeing their occupation as a risk, these individuals operated their casinos as fly-by-nights. They looked at the short-term profit they could pocket as the best profit, almost instinctively feeling that although they were legal in Nevada, the idyllic environment could not last. They believed that like any gambler's streak, their run of good fortune would end.[30] But with growing interest in recreation, gambling was seen less as a moral violation and increasingly as a legitimate recreational pastime, and operators catered to a more general audience. To do so required different values in management and a lot more money.

The limitations of the individual capital phase of mob rule were evidenced in the physical layout of the city. After the spate of hotel construction during the 1950s—which included the Tropicana, where the gaming take was found on a piece of paper in mob boss Frank Costello's pocket after a 1957 attempt on his life in New York—that ended with the completion of the Stardust in 1958, no new Strip hotels were constructed until 1966. A nongaming resort, the Tally-Ho, built by New York stockbroker Edwin Lowe, was completed, but without the casino that Lowe eschewed, the endeavor soon ended in bankruptcy. The limitations of small-time mob rule and the capital to which it had access slowed growth. Siegel, Dalitz, and the other early mob entrepreneurs dug into their own pockets and went to their friends for capital, but as the market expanded and the amount of capital necessary to build a competitive resort increased, the sources that had previously funded growth fell short. Nor would the financial markets support gaming resorts; the only such source in southern Nevada was a local bank, the Bank of Las Vegas, founded in 1954 and reorganized as the Valley Bank in 1964. Although most of the bank's capital came from outside Nevada, its status as a conduit for outside money helped legitimize the financing of the gaming industry. Among its first projects in the 1950s was the development or expansion of the Fremont, the Sands, the Desert Inn, the Dunes, the Stardust, the Riviera, and the Thunderbird.[31] Despite the immense significance of this local source of capital and its leading banker, E. Parry Thomas, who was instrumental in financing and handling transactions, the growth of the resort corridor outstripped local funding. The capital necessary to turn Las Vegas from a huge carpet joint into a resort had to come from somewhere else.

The money was easy to obtain. The visionaries in organized crime looked for large sources of money that they could control. The most significant became the Teamsters Central States, Southeast and Southwest Areas Pension Fund, run by Allan Dorfman, the stepson of a mobster and an associate of the Chicago mob. Attorney Morris Shenker, a confidant of Teamsters president Jimmy Hoffa who served as counsel to a small Texas insurance company, American National Insurance Corporation, became the initial conduit. Through the Bank of Las Vegas, American National funded casinos, and Shenker soon held a stake in a number of them. Thomas received a $5 million loan from American National, which facilitated the building of an economic empire; it also helped open the door for the Pension Fund. By 1963 the sixteen-person board that administered the fund possessed more than $167 million in assets. Hoffa clearly influenced the investing patterns of the board; in 1963 more than 60 percent of its funds were invested in real estate, compared to the 2.3 percent typical of similar consortiums.[32]

The pattern of real estate financing began in 1956, before Hoffa and Dorfman turned their attention to Las Vegas. The first such loan was a $1 million, ten-year mortgage at 6 percent interest to Cleveland Raceways, which Bill Presser, a Hoffa ally and the Teamsters boss of Ohio, had encouraged. It was quickly paid back in 1958 after the passage of the Landrum-Griffin Act of that year spurred an investigation by Robert F. Kennedy, who aspired to clean up the union movement by outright assault on its ties to organized crime. In 1957 a series of new loans followed on similar terms. One financed the Castaways Motel in Miami, Florida; another went to longtime Hoffa friend Benjamin Dranow, who owned a department store and was mired in a difficult labor negotiation with another union. As became common, the loan to

Sunrise Hospital in Las Vegas, funded by the Teamsters Pension Fund, helped the town maintain the illusion of being normal in the late 1950s and early 1960s. (Photo courtesy of Dorothy Dorothy Collection, James L. Dickinson Library, University of Nevada, Las Vegas.)

Dranow had to be written off. By 1961 the Pension Fund was out $766,000 of the $1 million original loan.[33] Under Dorfman, the Pension Fund consistently made atypical loans that turned out to be losers.

Early Teamsters Pension Fund forays into Las Vegas had little to do with gaming. In 1958 *Las Vegas Sun* publisher Herman (Hank) Greenspun, one of the few Americans to challenge Sen. Joseph McCarthy, had loudly criticized the mob, later calling his memoir *Where I Stand: The Record of a Reckless Man.* Greenspun received $250,000 to finance a golf course. If there was any anticipation that this gesture would silence him, it was entirely wrongheaded; he continued to speak out against hypocrisy and corruption. On April 14, 1959, the 100-bed Sunrise Hospital opened, built by the Paradise Development Company, whose officers included Moe Dalitz, casino executive Allard Roen, who had been indicted in the United Dye and Chemical stock fraud case along with bookmaker Chickie Berman, and two young Las Vegas businessmen, Irwin Molasky and Mervin Adelson. The Paradise Development Company needed capital, and the Pension Fund provided it,

Hoffa ensuring its profitability by delivering the Teamsters Union health care to the new hospital. Although the arrangement showed characteristics of a front for organized crime and developed more after the hospital opened, it also provided a genuine benefit. The population of Las Vegas welcomed it as a step toward the advantages locals craved.[34]

Subsequent construction, especially the 1967 Boulevard Mall, also drew accolades from the community. With its unique local access to capital for development other than casinos and resorts, the Paradise Development Company effectively planned the future of nonresort Las Vegas. It turned Maryland Parkway, a two-lane road that paralleled the Strip about two miles to the east, into the main commercial thoroughfare for the growing city. Las Vegans, from worker to executive, lived in the neighborhoods east of the new commercial center.[35] The enclosed Boulevard Mall, the first modern shopping center in Las Vegas, became the capstone. With its completion, Las Vegans could believe that their city had the amenities to match their resort.

The selective embrace of capital was the most complicated dimension of mob rule in southern Nevada. In a colony that lacked sources of indigenous capital, that was in the middle of substantive growth, and that was dominated by an industry not supported by mainstream backing, fresh capital was lifeblood. No matter what its origins, people embraced it. Teamsters Pension Fund investments in social projects, albeit profitable ones such as the hospital and mall, made that infusion of capital even more important. To most of the population of greater Las Vegas, which had grown from roughly 8,000 in 1940 to 269,000 in 1967 and was increasingly composed of casino service workers who considered legalized gaming as the solution to their woes, the hospital and mall were community assets, the source of their financing and their profits to be expected. The hospital, the mall, and other similar developments normalized Las Vegas, investing its people with a sense of their own typicality that had been obviously fiction before the 1960s. For that, Las Vegans were grateful and were usually willing to overlook any machinations in the sources of their normalcy.

As Las Vegas acquired the amenities of a typical American town, its neonative gaming-based community forged its own identity. The Strip and local life became separate; although the world continued to see Las Vegas as merely the Strip and downtown, locals perceived their town as different from the visitors' destination. Las Vegas in their view was a conservative company town with a twist, full of amenities for children such as Little League and the Girl Scouts, with high rates of church and synagogue attendance. A duality lay at the core of legitimization. It made hardened hoods yearn for the respectability that accompanied legal standing, that allowed a man such as Davy Berman, one of the principles at the Flamingo and later the Tropicana, to have a rising star named Elvis Presley wish his daughter a happy twelfth birthday.[36] Others were thrilled to give their daughters a gift of cash at their weddings—the only difference was that the cash came in Las Vegas money, $100 bills, and was often skimmed from the counting rooms of casinos. Normalcy was easier to sustain in 1960s Las Vegas, but it still masked a complicated reality. The town and its facade were closely linked, but scratching the surface often showed a core at great variance from American norms.

From that problematic normalcy grew the support for the basketball teams coached by Jerry Tarkanian at the University of Nevada, Las Vegas, the primary marker of identification for Las Vegans. From the moment the brash and outspoken, and charmingly roguish Tarkanian arrived in 1972, he embodied Las Vegas for locals. Like the town, he was an upstart who called 'em like he saw 'em and damn the consequences. Even better, he was a winner. By 1977, when he took his first team to the NCAA Final Four, support of UNLV basketball was a local ritual and an important way one real Las Vegan could identify another. Allegiance to a school sport promised a normal town. Tarkanian was so like the people who followed his team that a generation of Las Vegans, the children of the mob era, grew up in close proximity to the Tarkanian family, thinking of them as their ambassadors to the outside world. Even in Tarkanian's ongoing troubles with the NCAA, the locals identified with him. It was easy to draw a parallel between the persecution of Tarkanian and the stigma that attached to gaming and the primary community that offered it. Las Vegans held their ritual forms of identity even more closely as growth transformed their town.

Pension Fund money that built a hospital for these locals also led to the development of distinctive new hotels after 1966. Foremost was Caesars Palace, financed by the Pension Fund and run by Jay Sarno, an eccentric but brilliant entrepreneur. In the late 1950s Sarno first borrowed from the fund to finance hotel projects in Atlanta and Dallas for his national Cabana chain. By the time he conceived of Caesars Palace, he had the combination of vision and access that allowed him to dream of even more grandiose projects. Sarno envisioned a new level of distinction in the casino industry, building the quintessential "high-class joint." Its $19 million price tag was the most money ever spent on a Las Vegas resort, and the hotel reflected Sarno's idiosyncracies. The casino was elliptical, following the hotelier's belief that egg-shaped structures relaxed people. A frieze showing the battle of the Etruscan Hills graced the wall next to the Noshorium Coffee Shop, itself a play on the Yiddish "nosh" for snack and the "orium" that in American popular culture indicated Roman origin. Romanesque fountains and statues covered the property; eighteen huge fountains bordered the 135-foot driveway. An 800-seat Circus Maximus Theatre, patterned after the Colosseum in Rome, hosted only the top acts of the day. Frank Sinatra and Barbara Streisand headed the opening bill.[37]

During the 1960s Pension Fund money also financed other, less distinctive new resorts. The fund granted loans that supported the Landmark Hotel, the Four Queens, the Aladdin, and Circus Circus, another of Sarno's idiosyncratic innovations, an almost kinky casino with a circus theme but no hotel. The Landmark began as the project of wealthy Kansas City, Missouri, developer John Carroll, who started construction with $3.3 million in funding from the Appliance Buyers Credit Corporation, a subsidiary of Whirlpool. Lacking the additional $10 million his plans demanded, Carroll built apartments and a small shopping center while searching for additional funding. In the typical partnership between unknowing legitimate front man and mob-controlled money, the Central States Pension Fund came up with a $6 million loan in August 1966, offering Carroll the opportunity to build his resort.[38]

By the time Carroll received the loan for the Landmark in 1966, the Pension Fund was the dominant source of capital in southern Nevada. The growing cost of resort development, particularly after Caesars Palace, made the intraorganization funds that supported early development insufficient. With the exception of Valley Bank, local funds were scarce and, compared to the needs of the growing industry, which required upward of $100 million in development capital between 1960 and 1965 alone, wholly inadequate. Despite instances such as the stock offer by the Golden Nugget in the late 1940s, the traditional avenues of capital formation, such as stock offerings and bond financing, were blocked. Wall Street was not ready to take a chance on gaming, leaving its potentially lucrative rewards to the Pension Fund and the organized crime bosses who ran it. This situation made southern Nevada dependent on any source of capital that could support its growth. It also contributed to Nevada's colonial status, but in a dangerous way. By the 1960s Las Vegas was beholden not to industrial America but to the parasitic forces that preyed upon it, and because the people who were attracted to gaming were not bothered by the prospect of silent and powerful control, the situation seemed entirely ordinary. The veneer of typicality was quite thin in the Las Vegas of the 1960s. Las Vegans argued that behind the glitz, they lived in a "normal" town, but their definition of normal was quite at odds with the one held by the rest of the nation.

Nevada's gaming laws contributed to its unique form of well-paid colonial status. To counter what state authorities perceived as the organized crime "menace," state-level regulation of gaming began during the mid-1940s. Before then, counties and their sheriffs licensed, collected taxes, and administered the industry. The 1947 murder of Siegel contributed to new statutes, which gave the Nevada Tax Commission the power to investigate, license, and monitor gaming licenses. This remedy hardly succeeded. Following in the tradition of Sen. Joseph McCarthy, Sen. Estes Kefauver held public hearings into organized crime in the early 1950s that seemed designed to ferret out its reach. Many Las Vegans, and many others they knew, were interrogated on television and made to look foolish or humiliated. Clark County commissioner Harley Harmon complained during the 1952 hearings concerning the license of Sands entertainment director Jack Entratter that the tax commission "has let every syndicate in the country into Las Vegas." Subsequently, the Nevada Gaming Control Board and the state gaming control commission were created to administer the gaming industry. But even the establishment of a list of people barred from casinos in 1960, the so-called Black Book, formally known as the List of Excluded Persons after 1976, amounted to little more than a public relations ploy.[39]

Beginning in 1955, one cardinal state regulation determined the pattern of the gaming industry: every stockholder of a gaming establishment had to be licensed by the board. Although the legalization act in 1931 permitted corporate ownership of casinos, the 1955 regulation effectively eliminated that prospect. Ostensibly the regulation ensured that undesirable elements could not control casinos and that the state would receive its tax revenue, but the statute had other ramifications. One major consequence was that it effectively barred large, publicly held corporations from owning stock in the gaming industry.[40] Qualifying the seemingly infinite number of stockholders in any major publicly traded corporation was a daunting if not impossible task. In an era when Wall Street shied away from Las Vegas, this restriction did not pose a problem. As American culture liberalized during the 1960s and some of the stigma associated with gaming diminished, Nevada law blocked the most important source of legitimate capital for the expansion of gaming.

The process had a dramatic unintended consequence. Instead of freeing the gaming industry from the influence of organized crime, the Nevada statute enshrined that dimension. The law made the Teamsters Pension Fund the only source of capital upon which Las Vegas could rely, achieving exactly the opposite of its framers' intentions. When organized crime provided the only source of capital and southern Nevada needed it, the county commission and other civic leaders recognized that they needed the mob as much as the mob needed them. Nineteen sixties Las Vegas became a partnership between local interests that needed capital and mobsters who were its only source. The stigma of gaming and Nevada statute combined to deny legitimate capital to the gaming industry when it needed it most.

Two events changed this situation, leading to the transformation of Las Vegas from a mob-dominated gambling town to a corporate-owned modern resort. The first was the return of reclusive billionaire Howard R. Hughes to a suite in the Desert Inn in Las Vegas on Thanksgiving Eve, 1966. After a few weeks, the management sought to persuade Hughes to leave so they could return the suite to the use of the high rollers on whom the casino depended. Hughes paid approximately $13 million for the resort instead of leaving his suite and remained for four years. His choice of Las Vegas initiated a buying spree that included the Frontier, for which he paid approximately $14 million, the Sands for $14.6 million, Castaways for $3 million, and the Silver Slipper. He also bought a television station, airlines, small airport facilities, and much undeveloped land. Hughes made overtures to purchase Caesars Palace, the Riviera, and the Dunes in Las Vegas and Harrah's in Reno and Lake Tahoe, but an antitrust suit halted negotiations. Even before the Nixon administration overruled the Justice Department's objections to the purchase of the famous Harold's Club in Reno and the Landmark Hotel, just off the Strip, in a maneuver that was later exposed as resulting from a bribe, Hughes controlled about one-seventh of the state's gaming revenue, one-quarter of that in Las Vegas, and more than one-third generated on the Strip.[41] Hughes's entrance changed the face of the gaming industry.

Although he knew nothing about casinos and his operations sometimes lost money, Hughes was a public-relations dream for the besieged state of Nevada and its most important industry. In 1966 another in the seemingly endless series of skimming scandals broke wide open, pitting the state against the FBI and the federal government. The FBI engaged in a series of illegal wiretaps of casino offices, and the information from them appeared in newspapers such as the *Chicago Sun-Times.* When the state initiated its own investigation, the FBI refused to allow state officials access to the information gathered through the wiretaps. This denial enraged Nevada, where the doctrine of individual rights was firmly entrenched, and it impugned the integrity of state oversight of gaming. It also made the public suspicious that something was amiss in Las Vegas. Hughes's reputation as a brilliant entrepreneur who would not invest in anything that was not a genuine moneymaker removed some of the tarnish that had spread across Nevada gaming.[42]

Hughes's entrance into the gaming industry was pivotal. He was part of the old and a harbinger of the new. Hughes was the first wealthy entrepreneur with the resources and the desire to compete with organized crime, the first set of truly deep pockets to seek to make Las Vegas his own. He arrived at the perfect moment for a new entrepreneur, exactly as his predecessors in the industry gave way. The first generation of mob impresarios, men such as Meyer Lansky and Jimmy Alo, had aged, had grown tired of the constant federal surveillance that they endured. Selling out to Hughes, whom they regarded as a quintessential sucker, seemed a good idea. They took their profit and largely left the field.[43]

Hughes shared as much with the gangsters he replaced as with the corporate America that revered him. Gaming was a natural for Hughes; he was the sole stockholder of Hughes Tool Company, meaning that only he had to pass licensing investigations. A man of his stature and wealth had little problem stalling state regulatory bodies. Hughes also held enough cash to finance any deal he wanted. Like the development of the first hotels on the strip, the source of capital Hughes relied on was private and personal. The reclusive billionaire was different because his vast empire had no public taint of organized crime associated with it. He was a forerunner of the new Las Vegas, and his interest helped legitimize investment in the gaming industry.

The second event to bring change made the mobsters who sold out look like geniuses. In 1967 at the behest of Howard Hughes, William F. Harrah of Harrah's, a northern Nevada gaming enterprise, and Baron and Conrad Hilton of the Hilton Hotel chain and with the support of Nevada governor Paul Laxalt, the state passed the Corporate Gaming Act, which changed the rules that governed casino ownership. After 1969, when the law was revised, corporations could invest in casinos without each stockholder passing a Gaming Control Board background check.[44] Publicly held corporations, previously eliminated from the casino industry, now had an opening. In the liberalizing cultural climate and following corporate consolidation in the 1960s, large corporations with related specialties eyed Las Vegas. If gaming was good enough for Howard Hughes, it was certainly good enough for the Hilton, Holiday Inn, and Ramada corporations.

The first purchases by major multinational hotel chains followed quickly on the heels of the new law. In 1970 the Hilton chain purchased the Flamingo and the International from Kirk Kerkorian, a self-made multimillionaire who also sought to make Las Vegas his own. Kerkorian had a dream of a new, world-class resort, which he intended to call the MGM Hotel; selling the two hotels moved him closer to his goal. The sale fully inaugurated the new capital regime. After the arrival of the Hilton Corporation and its enormous success in Las Vegas—by 1976, 43 percent of the gross revenues of the 163-hotel chain came from its operations there—new and legitimate capital was available as it had never before been. Holiday Inn followed in 1972 with the 1,000-room Holiday Hotel next to the Flamingo, Ramada purchased the Tropicana in 1979, and a new form of financing supported the development of Las Vegas.[45]

The innovation solved two major problems in southern Nevada; it created easily accessible sources of capital that permitted investment, and it limited the need for organized crime's money. Wall Street routinely invested enormous sums far larger than organized crime ever could. The $269 million the Teamsters Pension invested in Las Vegas in the late 1960s might have remained the largest single source of capital in southern Nevada, but it ceased to represent the dominant vector of investment. The passage of the revised Corporate Gaming Act redirected power in Nevada away from Teamsters capital and toward Wall Street and corporate America.

The consequence of this change in the law was great. The Corporate Gaming Act took Las Vegas along the same path that the skiing resorts followed; it too passed from specialized and often local ownership and into the realm of corporate commodity. When the Hilton chain came to town on the heels of Hughes and Kerkorian, it brought a stamp of legitimacy in a changing culture along with vast capital resources. Although it took a long time for the mob town to disappear, the passage of the Corporate Gaming Act sealed its fate. As the 1970s dawned, Las Vegas was poised to leave its unique position on the fringe of American society for a place much closer to the heart of the national mainstream.

12

Purifying the Wages of Sin

Corporate Las Vegas

The transformation of Las Vegas from idiosyncratic gaming town to themed destination resort took shape, accelerated, and was completed between the 1970s and the 1990s. Las Vegas became more like the rest of the nation as the nation became more like Las Vegas. Despite the city's characteristic dominant industry, gaming, and its attendant tourism, the patterns of local life came to mirror those of the American mainstream. The wide-open feeling that made Nevada special still existed, but it was tempered by the realities of late twentieth-century capitalism. The stigma attached to Las Vegas diminished as cultural changes, affluence, and access allowed more people to enjoy its amenities. Under corporate control, the city gave up its peculiar social, economic, and power structure and operated under the same kinds of business and later cultural rules as the rest of the nation. Howard Hughes, Kirk Kerkorian, and later Steve Wynn, the impresario who carved a new niche for Las Vegas in the American consciousness beginning in the late 1970s, operated their businesses with only a nod to the older ways of the gambler's town. Few of the shenanigans that so distinctively marked the mob era survived. As the nation shifted toward a postindustrial, service-oriented economy, Las Vegas's dominant industry, once thought deviant in American culture, became an essential segment. In 1996 more than 30 million people passed through the 100,000 hotel and motel rooms in Clark County, leaving a profit of more than $15 billion for the gaming and tourism industry and not incidentally sustaining the state during its wildest period of growth.

Clark County itself also grew tremendously during these twenty-five years. In 1970, 273,288 people lived in the county. In 1980 the population reached 463,087; by 1990 it had risen again to 770,280; and by 1995, to 1,016,177. Most growth resulted from migration; 82.3 percent of the more than 400,000 new residents in Clark County between 1980 and 1992 came from other places. The high birthrate of a young and rapidly expanding city accounted for the rest.[1] No other standard metropolitan statistical area (SMSA) could claim a similar growth rate in the post war United States. Las Vegas's growth was simply unparalleled.

The expansion of the city was driven first by corporate power and later by advantageous economic conditions. Nevada weathered the recession that pounded California and hurt the rest of the nation during the early 1990s. Not only did the population of Las Vegas increase dramatically, but its demographic structure was also altered. As the 270,000 or so people of 1970 became 1 million by 1995, an upper-middle class that was only indirectly dependent on the tourism and gaming industry grafted itself onto the town. The community developed a visible white-collar population, a professional class that remained proportionately small in 1996 but that had gained significantly in numbers and influence and seemed poised to refract the locals' Las Vegas in new and different ways. They represented one dimension of the wave of neonatives that followed the emergence of corporate Las Vegas. Others included retirees and people attracted to the opportunity for blue-collar prosperity, the $30,000 or more in annual income that successful dealers and others in the gaming industry routinely earned in a time when a growing percentage of unskilled Americans spent their days in convenience stores stocking bottles for minimum wage. With these changes, Las Vegas ceased to be a large company town and became the Last Detroit, the last place in the nation where relatively unskilled workers could find a job after high school, earn a middle-class wage, and expect to remain with the company for their entire working life.

To many people, Las Vegas perfected the service economy, the model for the resurrection of dormant economies elsewhere in the nation. The prototype of the colony becoming colonizer was Atlantic City, New Jersey, which was redesigned around gaming during the 1970s and became the second major American city to bet its future on games of chance. By the mid-1980s, legalized betting spread to most of the nation. A growing number of states, faced with the decline of industrial economies, as was Illinois, or tired of per capita income at the bottom of the fifty states, as was Mississippi, embraced gaming. They patterned themselves on Las Vegas, and many states engaged in partnerships with Las Vegas corporations to run their casinos, but they were not Las Vegas. They were unable to mirror the fluidity of that city, and in each instance, gaming created social pathologies that stemmed from grafting a volatile industry onto places with prior economic structural problems. Las Vegas itself developed an enviable record: higher employment rates than national norms, lower unemployment rates, consistently rising per capita income, and with more than 20 percent of the population in the county self-identifying as retired, more than 60 percent of the people in the county were employed or self-employed on a full-time basis.[2] The spread of gaming actually accelerated the growth of Las Vegas; after gambling on a river boat in the Mississippi River, people believed that they truly had to go to the desert town where it all began. Instead of hurting that town, the increase in gaming venues created many minor league diversions filled with people who aspired for their moment in the neon of Las Vegas.

The desert town might have appeared the same, despite all the construction. But it too was in the middle of a transformation that preserved its illusion of being a place where the rules did not apply but that made its structure like that of any other American city. Labor-management relations in Las Vegas had always been peculiar; during the mob era, the workers and the owners of the town were really of a piece, sharing a view of the world and bound by their roots in illegal gaming. With the rise of corporate power, labor-management interaction took on the traits of the rest of the country, albeit at the moment that those relationships broke down elsewhere with the advent first of cutbacks in unionized, working-class jobs and later with the widespread elimination of their white-collar counterparts in the phenomenon of downsizing. After a bitter 1984 labor battle in which corporate casino owners sought to destroy Las Vegas's unions, the latter gained strength as a result of a split between older casino families and the new corporate regime.[3] After the strike, with the notable exception of the Culinary Union strike at the Frontier Hotel that started in 1991 and became the longest-running labor dispute in American history, labor relations tended to be harmonious. The economic pie grew, and the issue was simple: how to distribute the benefits of growth. In a changing American economy, this was a form of labor negotiation that the more troubled industrial sectors of the economy fondly remembered and wished would return.

Throughout this transformation, Las Vegas came to represent the America that people believed was disappearing elsewhere. The strong union presence on the heels of the corporate takeover of the gaming industry in the 1970s created formalized stability. Casinos reflected the hierarchy of corporations at the same time that jobs in Las Vegas, unionized and otherwise, offered one of the few remaining opportunities in the United States for semi-skilled workers to enter an industry, earn a middle-class income, and lead a middle-class life, artificially subsidized by tourists and the competition among homebuilders in particular. Yet corporatization created an intrinsic dilemma: workers who started at the lowest levels could not expect to go far into management in the course of a career. No longer did Twenty-one dealers rise above the level of pit bosses as had routinely occurred under the mob regime. The employment structure of casinos became stratified. Genuine management jobs were reserved for those with the proper credentials, graduates of business and hotel schools who learned to gauge the behavior of consumers from books rather than from experience. Although Las Vegas hotel workers were far better paid than employees elsewhere in the same hotel corporations, they faced a glass ceiling defined less by race or gender than by credentials and relationships. Trapped by the very prosperity these hard-to-find, well-paying jobs offered, veterans of entertainment tourism found themselves in a bind. Their jobs offered little emotional or personal satisfaction, but no matter what other aspirations they held, they were hard-pressed to find other employment that paid as well.[4]

One consequence of this transformation was a decline in multigenerational gaming families, a phenomenon that made work in the industry less idiosyncratic and more traditionally blue-collar. During the era of the mob-run casinos, employees were treated like relatives in a family business. They could expect lifetime employment and concomitant perquisites as well as opportunity for their children and any other family members who might stray through town. Corporate gaming ended such practices, alienating many people who previously made a career of the casinos. Such people found themselves disaffected and discouraged their children from entering the tourist industry. Resort employment became a transitional step to white-collar status much as had the industrial jobs of the generations before. Poor, uneducated people, immigrants, and others followed a route through the gaming industry that eventually led them to send their children away to school, and if the children aspired to a career in the gaming industry, to return with credentials that would get them off the casino floor and into management suites.

Las Vegas developed a different feel under corporate control. Neonatives tied to the mob era felt out of place in the new Las Vegas. The personal relationships that had characterized that world became corporate. On the Strip, dealers and croupiers no longer knew their customers by name, and Las Vegas followed the rest of the nation into an impersonal world. The response of neonatives was typical: "Las Vegas was better when the mob ran it." And old-timers claimed, "In those days you could leave a thousand-dollar bill in the middle of the Strip and no one would touch it." Hyperbole, certainly, but such sentiments showed a less positive view of the changes that corporate ownership brought.

Of all the tourist towns, Las Vegas stood alone with a market sufficiently large and segmented to accommodate neonatives who felt displaced. The expansion of off-Strip casinos made the local market much more competitive, and corporations like the Station Casinos and the Boyd Group, which owned Sam's Town, found themselves locked in competition not only with one another but also with many newcomers. Station Casinos' response was an Initial Public Offering (IPO) that gave them capital for expansion and a television advertisement that extolled its psychic ties to Las Vegas's past. "This is how Las Vegas used to be," comic-turned-pitchman Joe Piscopo, by 1997 a handsome middle-aged man who exuded a charisma that the firm hoped Las Vegans would take as their own self-image, affirmed for the Palace Station, the flagship in the chain, "before the pyramid [at the Luxor, a Circus Circus project that opened in the mid-1990s], before volcanoes," such as impresario Steve Wynn placed in front of his Mirage Hotel. This play to neonatives showed the struggle for market share and Las Vegas's changing nature. The Palace Station was off-Strip, across Interstate 15; the commercial encouraged neonative resentment that the Strip had shifted from a playground for locals and tourists to a place where locals worked and visitors played. The local casinos aimed for the earlier feel, when everyone was in it together.

The town also drew thousands upon thousands of new residents. The glitter and the lights of the gaming industry attracted many. Others were lured by the opportunity in a state where housing prices were low and taxes, except for the sales tax and other regressive forms, were nonexistent. Nevadans paid no state income tax, and property taxes remained low. In the late 1980s, a four-bedroom, 2,000-square-foot new home in a respectable neighborhood sold for about $110,000, about one-third the price of a similar home in southern California. With housing prices well below those in Seattle and urban California and even Portland, Las Vegas became a mecca for three different groups: retirees, working-class refugees, especially from California, and people who saw the business climate in Nevada as more desirable than in their home state. In the late 1980s and early 1990s, an average of 6,000 people each month traded in driver's licenses to the Nevada Department of Motor Vehicles (DMV). As many as two-thirds of these came from California, a dominance increasingly reflected in the culture of Las Vegas. One new resident in the line at the DMV station on Sahara Avenue in 1992 was asked where he came from. When he replied "Kansas," the questioner asked: "Where in California is that?"[5]

By the mid-1990s, retirees made up 20 percent of the population of Clark County. Clustered increasingly in two Del Webb developments, Sun City in the Summerlin area in the northwest part of the city, and Sun City-McDonald Ranch in the Green Valley section of Henderson, southeast of the Strip, retirees fashioned a community that mirrored retirement villages all over the country amid the topsy-turvy growth of Las Vegas. Southern Nevada was tremendously desirable. Besides low costs and taxes, there was much to do besides gambling; and the climate, though overpowering in the summer, was more than temperate the rest of the year. Working-class retirees from the Rust Belt could take their pensions to a tax-free environment and never see snow again except on television or visits back home. These incentives pumped a steady stream of retirees into the local mix and over time gave seniors a disproportionate influence in local affairs.

Las Vegas also became a haven for lower-middle-class southern Californians, whose access to their perceived birthright of the American dream was limited by escalating costs of living and diminished employment in the aerospace and defense industries. They flocked to southern Nevada; in the late 1980s and early 1990s, it seemed to southern Nevadans that the entire Los Angeles basin picked up and moved in next door. Some were the fortunate, who sold 1,200-square foot homes in the Los Angeles area for $280,000 or more and came to southern Nevada, where considerably less money bought 3,500 square feet of living space. Others were excised, downsized, or simply fired and came in search of work, with a stake perhaps not as large as the homeowners but sufficiently sizable to help them relocate. Still others were families, some teachers or other professionals but mostly semiskilled, who perceived a shorter route to a home in the suburbs and a middle class life in Nevada than they had in California. Well represented among this group were the grandchildren of the Okie migration to California during the depression. In introductory history lecture sections at the University of Nevada, Las Vegas, between 1992 and 1996, of the white students who identified themselves as graduating from a California high school, fully two-thirds kept their hands up when asked if their antecedents had come from Oklahoma or the Midwest during the Dust Bowl.[6]

Another group was also overrepresented in this late twentieth-century migration to the desert. As the California economic climate worsened, more businesses moved to Nevada to take advantage of what could be termed libertarian business conditions. Nevadans prided themselves on individual freedom, and their state imposed regulations reluctantly. Again, lower costs and flimsy state tax structure encouraged business development. As a result, Las Vegas developed a range of small business and industry that was not directly tied to gaming or to the other mainstay of the region, the Nevada Test Site. These newcomers were idiosyncratic, most closely tuned to a mythic, wide-open Nevada of the past but ironically anachronistic in the corporate town that Las Vegas became. Their rhetoric appealed to the self-image of many Nevadans, old and new, and they became another vocal constituency in local affairs.

The massive growth contributed to the changing demography of southern Nevada. In the postwar era, Las Vegas had been a company town, a working-class place populated by working-class people. An ever-present shortage of professionals, physicians, lawyers, architects, and teachers, persisted, and recruiting new professionals remained difficult. Nor did pre-1980s Las Vegans accord their professional community much respect. Status in 1950s Las Vegas meant going elsewhere for medical care, a habit many longtime Las Vegans retained in the 1990s. This behavior reinforced the limited desirability of the town as a home for professionals before the 1980s.

Growth spawned incredible economic opportunity and options for professionals at a time when it diminished elsewhere, and Las Vegas became attractive to the upper-middle class. In southern Nevada, a physician, lawyer, or architect could earn much money; the community was skilled at keeping desirable people by compensating them at levels that other places could not match. Opportunity abounded. Las Vegas law firms hired scores of new associates, and any qualified graduate of the education school at the university easily found a job in the Clark County Independent School District. A different demography resulted. By 1995 Clark County exceeded the national average for college graduates by almost 3 percent. Historically, the region reflected the lower middle-class origins of many of its inhabitants.[7] An imported upper-middle class emerged and then during the 1980s and early 1990s grew significantly, giving Las Vegas a dimension that most other resort towns did not share. This group had different expectations from the people who lived in the mob's Las Vegas, and they slowly asserted themselves in local and regional culture, changing the face of the community. Yet as the 1990s ended, that class was strangely silent in politics, typically limited to one-issue campaigns and not at all well represented in local government.

In the early 1990s Las Vegas became an economically and culturally heterogeneous place that resembled the rest of the nation. Competing interest groups grappled for dominance of local politics and with it the direction of the county. Seniors exerted their influence and extraordinary ability to organize and deliver the vote, turning back a school bond issue in 1994 that would have added a mere $39 of tax per year to the average $100,000 home. The 22 percent of the population who identified as retired combined with antigovernment and antitax factions to defeat a measure that the grafted suburban upper-middle class heavily favored. In a subsequent bond issue in the 1996 general election, advocates were better organized and won a 63 percent majority to build the schools essential to the needs of the community. As if to heal the rift caused by the failure of the earlier bond issue, senior coalitions made a public point of supporting the new bond issue.

Las Vegans themselves took pride in their miracle in the desert. Even as the population of Clark County swelled to more than 1 million, they regarded its growth as testimony to the vindication of the idea of a state economy built on providing various forms of entertainment to visitors. More than elsewhere, Las Vegans remained optimistic about growth as it consumed them; historically and in the present they saw expansion in the terms of the Manifest Destiny of the nineteenth century. In this view, their dance with tourism and gaming provided only benefits to their city. People who worked as Blackjack dealers and waiters sent their children to college and professional school. Shelly Berkeley, a University of Nevada System Regent and 1998 candidate for the U.S. House of Representatives, was an acclaimed example. Other residents pointed to the gaming industry as a place to begin a career. Las Vegas was "a rising tide that raises all ships," remarked Phyllis Darling, a former Clark County School District administrator and principal of the Hebrew Academy, one of the growing number of private schools that catered to upper-middle-class suburbanites, as she recounted her family's history in the town.[8]

The malleability of Las Vegas, its ability to reinvent itself time and again, made possible such transformations. Of all American cities, Las Vegas most clearly recognized its cultural transience. Each of its incarnations reflected the changing mores, values, and perceptions of the nation more than did any other resort. The changes in Aspen or Sun Valley were as tied to the ownership regime as they were to national culture; only in Las Vegas did local economic health and indeed its future depend on an accurate analysis of the mood of the nation. The mob-era Las Vegas was predicated on the rigid morality of midcentury culture. When grandstanding politicians such as Estes Kefauver held hearings to attack gaming and found themselves on the television news, when Elvis Presley could be shown only from the waist up on television because of his gyrations, and a few years later, when the Rolling Stones were required to change the lyrics of one of their songs, "Let's Spend the Night Together," to perform on the *Ed Sullivan Show*, a town that let down barriers occupied a unique station. It became the place to indulge, to cast off sins in a socially sanctioned manner. Following the OPEC oil embargo and post–Vietnam War inflation, when the industrial economy began a rapid decline and cultural mores had already changed, Las Vegas followed those trends, too. By the 1990s, massive theme parks were tacked onto billion-dollar casinos. Las Vegas became mainstream entertainment offered by the purveyors of American popular culture to its consumers.

The people of Las Vegas understood their role in these transformations better than did residents of any other tourist town and especially better than did people in towns with self-images tied to dominant tourist activities such as Santa Fe and Aspen. Las Vegans recognized that they were merely purveyors of amenity. What they gave was inherently what visitors wanted and were willing to pay for, and in most circumstances they freely admitted these realities. Such an honesty was absent in places like Santa Fe and Aspen; Las Vegans lacked the need for the overlay so essential to communicate the virtues of heritage and cultural tourism and to a lesser degree its recreational counterpart. Americans needed only the tools they brought with them to understand this desert metropolis: it was them. Las Vegas knew exactly what it was. Santa Fe, Aspen, and similar places engaged in a range of delusionary pretension.

This fundamental clarity of vision made the transition of regimes in Las Vegas a much less traumatic process than it had been in Sun Valley or Aspen. Like colonial people all over the globe, Las Vegans assessed the strength of the corporate newcomers against the power of the existing mob regime, found the newcomers offered more and different benefits in exchange for their cooperation, and shifted their allegiance to the new. They did not turn their backs on the mob and its casinos and operators, betray them, or abandon them, as popular culture accounts suggest. Slowly, gradually, often imperceptibly, they simply moved away from their dependence on the mob and joined forces with the corporations that pumped new money into their town. By the mid-1970s, the $250 million that the mob had invested in Las Vegas ceased to be as important as the roughly $75 million corporations invested. The deeper pockets of corporate America clearly held the future. Ever malleable, Las Vegans understood how to capitalize on an opportunity when it appeared.

Against this backdrop, Las Vegas once again reinvented itself as it had with the arrival of Siegel and the mob. By the mid-1970s Las Vegas enjoyed

The Las Vegas Strip in the early 1970s, before corporate investment changed the scope and scale. (Photo courtesy of Las Vegas Sun Collection, James L. Dickinson Library, University of Nevada, Las Vegas.)

another of its periodic shifts and spasms. Kerkorian's International Hotel, on Paradise Avenue parallel to the Strip, opened in 1969, inaugurated an era of behemoth hotels that included the first MGM Grand, a twenty-six-story structure completed in 1973, and additions to numerous Strip and downtown hotels.[9] Early in the 1970s, the Hilton Corporation purchased the International and the Flamingo, and the new corporate Las Vegas, with its larger and more expensive hotels, took shape. With the millions of corporate dollars flooding the town, the mountain of Teamsters Pension Fund dollars diminished in significance, and the power shifted from a set of rules defined within the world of organized crime to one that took on the concerns of image and standing that dominated the corporate world.

This change in source of capital and attendant transfer of power set the stage for the best-known of Las Vegas's modern scandals, the Argent Corporation fiasco of the mid-1970s. In 1974 Allen R. Glick, a largely unknown San Diego businessman, received a $62.7 million loan from the Teamsters Pension Fund to purchase Recrion Corporation, which owned the Stardust, the Fremont, and the Marina hotels. Glick was a Vietnam veteran who had earned a Bronze Star as a helicopter pilot; he was also a hard-nosed enterprising businessman who worked in real estate. A partner directed him toward Las Vegas, and Glick bought the bankrupt Hacienda Hotel and Casino at the southern end of the Strip. Glick's takeover of another bankrupt casino in Lake Tahoe brought him into the orbit of the Teamsters Pension Fund. Soon after, he pounced on an opportunity to purchase Recrion and needed money fast. After efforts to raise it elsewhere, he came to the Teamsters at almost the same time they sought him out for his clean-cut image. It was a marriage seemingly made in heaven. What followed was entirely predictable. Involved were Frank "Lefty" Rosenthal, the mob's representative in the casino and chairman of the executive committee of Glick's Argent Corporation, utilizing the skills of famed slot cheat–turned–counting room boss Jay Vandermark, and enforcer Anthony (Tony the Ant) Spilotro. Under their watchful eyes, a 1950s-style mob skimming operation at the Stardust took place.[10]

The corporate hotels rising in the background revealed the Stardust to be an anachronism. During the 1950s hotels such as the Desert Inn, the Sands, the Dunes, the Riviera, the Tropicana, the Stardust, and the Flamingo were owned by the mob and run according to their codes. Each of these casinos had ostensible owners and each had a mob front placed in a position of power within the casino to oversee the "proper" distribution of profits, the one-for-us, three-for-the-hotel, one-for-the-government formula that has been codified into legend. In the most well-known example, Jack Entratter played that role at the Sands, recruiting the famed Rat Pack at the same time he oversaw the finances. Skimming was part of their game, part of repaying the hidden money that financed construction and of offering tribute to the hierarchies of organized crime. By the mid-1970s, other sources of capital to support the tourism and gaming industry became extremely appealing, and Nevada authorities and indeed citizens neither needed nor chose to look the other way when connected casino operators and employees reverted to type. Rosenthal found himself playing a role from another era to unappreciative audiences.

Bound by its fealty to a time gone by, the Stardust experienced severe problems almost from the beginning of the Glick-Rosenthal regime. Unlike the Hilton-owned hotel-casinos or Kerkorian's, a whiff of illegitimacy wafted from the Stardust. The 1975 murder of Tamara Rand, a San Diego woman tied to Allen Glick's real estate endeavors there, sounded an alarm. This inexplicable crime, which occurred at Mrs. Rand's kitchen table, drew attention to the earlier murder of a Caesars Palace employee with known mob ties who had had an altercation with Glick one week before his execution-style killing in the parking lot. In another suspicious move, Rosenthal received a ten-year, $250,000 per year contract from Glick the week before his gaming board licensing hearing. The contract stipulated that Rosenthal would be paid whether or not he received a gaming license. In January 1976 the Gaming Control Board informed Glick that Rosenthal, a gambler since his youth, could not be licensed to run casinos. Yet after his subsequent ouster from the CEO position at the Stardust, Rosenthal received his $250,000 annual salary from Argent to serve as its entertainment director. He hosted a weekly television show, to prove to the world that he truly was a legitimate player in the entertainment business and to vindicate himself after the board's denial of his license. Rosenthal looked silly in this capacity, and by all accounts and despite a parade of celebrity guests, the television show acquired the reputation as one of the worst ever to air. Still, it proved that he worked for his salary while he fought for licensing. The show became a cult classic on local television, so bizarre that it acquired a following in a manner similar to that of *The Rocky Horror Picture Show* and other camp classics of the era.

Rosenthal clearly did not understand the changes that had occurred in Las Vegas as he fought for his "right" to be a mob conduit. The scope and scale of the corporate revolution was so vast that it dwarfed existing mob holdings. Kerkorian's International Hotel, which soon became the Las Vegas Hilton, was the largest hotel in the free world when it opened. Its 1,500 rooms, 30,000-square-foot casino, and $60 million price tag were harbingers of a future in which the Stardust and its comparatively small-time operators did not share. Rosenthal operated within a niche, but his window was closing. He fought back, in a desperate move, taking his case to the Nevada Supreme Court. There he challenged the state's right to regulate his ability to work in the gaming industry and with it, the state's right to regulate the industry at all. Rosenthal's defense was the stale but time-honored argument that legalized gambling devolved from illegal gambling and that he, like everyone else in the industry, had "all had run-ins with the law." On the steps of the state supreme court after the decision went against him, Rosenthal argued that the issue was constitutional and informed the press he intended to pursue it. Perhaps naive, certainly megalomaniacal, Rosenthal fully expected to have his license restored at a 1979 hearing.[11]

The Stardust faced other problems. Despite Vandermark's expertise, a May 1976 Gaming Control Board raid on the hotel's counting room uncovered a skim in process that was later thought to total more than $7 million from slot machines alone in the space of one year. The amount skimmed from the table games could not be discerned, but speculation suggested that it at least equaled the take from the slots. Vandermark fled to Mexico, and Glick and Rosenthal blamed him for the operation; the public remained suspicious.[12] Such allegations jeopardized the enormous stream of incoming capital, threatening the increasingly complacent sense of legitimacy and normality that Las Vegans embraced. The Stardust was Las Vegas's past, and in a community that prided itself on malleability, history, even in its romanticized form, was not a priority. Las Vegas had set its eyes on the future, and in economic terms that future included a lot of corporate money and very little from the Teamsters Pension Fund and other similar sources.

The 1979 Gaming Control Board hearing in which Frank Rosenthal's license was permanently denied clearly illustrated this change. By 1979 Rosenthal had become a problem. His battle with the state attracted considerable attention, and even mobsters who supported him recognized that the U.S. Constitution contained no such guarantees. The television show raised his profile, and the mob bosses in Chicago and Kansas City grew uncomfortable with his celebrity status. In their world, flamboyance meant prison or death, and the public status of their front man, even in a town that lived off gaming and once embraced its organized crime ties, made them uneasy. Their histories in hiding their accomplishments and the wealth it provided made them strangely circumspect. In some ways, they still could not believe that Las Vegas was real, that the police would not swoop down on the edifice they had created and simply put them out of business. Rosenthal seemed determined to tell the world about their scam. As a front man he could put himself forward, but his behavior could endanger behind-the-scenes operatives. Rosenthal sat atop a house of cards, but in the opinion of mob leaders, he failed to understand the precariousness of his position.

The proceedings showed Rosenthal at his worst as they illustrated the new climate for gaming in Nevada. The hearing, recorded in the documentary *Mob on the Run,* a project of Channel 8 television investigative reporter Ned Day, was brief, and Rosenthal felt he had been cheated. Sporting a yellow porkpie hat placed at a jaunty angle, a yellow suit, an off-yellow necktie, and an Ascot, Rosenthal accused Gaming Commission chairman Harry Reid, who later became a U.S. senator from Nevada, of a range of duplicity. Rosenthal played to the camera, swearing and threatening not only the commission but a county commissioner, members of the governor's staff, and members of the press. He regarded the action as evidence of the "hypocrisy" of a state that permitted gaming but did not want a professional gambler to run a casino. When a reporter queried the embarrassed and clearly ruffled Reid about the allegations, Rosenthal interrupted with a question of his own designed not to incriminate Reid, as had the reporter's question, but to force the chairman to rescind his characterization of Rosenthal as a liar. Vain, arrogant, and clearly wounded by the decision, Rosenthal cared only about vindication, not about exposing any manifestations of the corruption he alleged. "You're all so self-righteous," he snapped at the press as he departed, transferring a characteristic he evinced in quantity to the people who reported the events of the day to the society Rosenthal so disdained.[13]

Most important about the situation was not its drama or Rosenthal's vehemence but that the Gaming Commission rendered such a decision at all. The commission's new posture revealed the flexibility in standards of suitability for licensing, as a pattern of normalizing the casino industry and the state took shape. The burden of proof of suitability fell on the applicant for a gaming license; the acknowledgment of suitability demonstrated community standards. By the 1970s, Las Vegas's standards had changed. Throughout the 1950s and 1960s, gaming regulators beginning with the Nevada Tax Commission routinely licensed a range of thugs to run casinos. During the Kefauver hearings a line of casino owners and operators paraded to the witness stand, the committee implying if not accusing the industry of being owned by organized crime. During the 1950s Joseph (Doc) Stacher ran the Sands; Stacher's arrest record dated from the 1920s and included New York and Nevada convictions during the 1950s and a grand jury appearance in Los Angeles in 1962. Stacher's preeminence in gaming testified to the ineffectiveness of regulation. L. B. (Benny) Binion arrived in Las Vegas in 1946 with an arrest record in his hometown of Dallas, Texas, that began in 1923; in 1951 he received a gaming license. Listed hotel owners in 1963 included Moe Dalitz, Ruby Kolod, Morris Kleinman, and Sam Tucker at the Desert Inn, Edward Levinson, Meyer Lansky's known front man, at the Fremont and the Horseshoe Club, Ben Goffstein and the Gus Greenbaum estate at the Riviera, and Jack Entratter at the Sands. These legal listings were the tip of an iceberg, and in the 1960s the questionable assortment of people licensed to own and work in casinos continued.[14]

With such precedents, the Rosenthal case clearly demonstrated change in Las Vegas. The most important source of capital in the 1960s, the Teamsters fund, still had immense sums invested in the late 1970s, but that money no longer drove the town, determined its directions, dominated its rule making, and allowed the exercise of sufficient influence to sway either local politics or the gaming board. The new standards applied to Rosenthal, whose worst known crime was unethical illegal gambling, held the gaming profession to a corporate conception. No one among the first generation of Las Vegas gamers could have passed these standards without the application of considerable political influence. The case revealed that the allegiance to sources of power had shifted to the latest capital-endowed benefactors. The county commission did not get even, as Nicholas Pillegi's book and Martin Scorsese's 1994 film *Casino* suggests; they had no such pretension. They simply moved on from that source of capital and power to the next and far more powerful source. In the process, they used political power to redirect gaming away from career gamers and tainted Teamsters capital and toward conventional sources that typically funded development in American society.[15]

Access to conventional capital for casino development in Las Vegas still posed problems. Throughout the 1970s large national banks shied away from Las Vegas, despite the Hilton Corporation's purchasing the Flamingo and Kerkorian's building the MGM Grand after taking over MGM Studios in California. Even in a liberalized nation, where older standards of morality were in flux, Nevada retained a stigma that was too great for national financial markets. Only the legalization of casino gambling in Atlantic City and large profits that investors raked in persuaded East Coast and California banks that Las Vegas might be legitimate. When Las Vegas ceased to be unique in the nation, funding the city became plausible. After the successes of Atlantic City, the bankers were more willing. Through the auspices of the Del Webb Company, the Sahara received $135 million from New York banks for improvements. The sum was $10 million greater than the company requested, testifying to the new perception that casinos were as appropriate as they were lucrative. Around the same time, Aetna Insurance Company loaned Caesars World, the parent corporation of Caesars Palace, $60 million. Soon after, First Interstate Bank developed a sizeable casino and gaming loan portfolio. By 1980 the dominant gaming organizations in Nevada, Harrah's, Del Webb, the Hilton, and Caesars World, were publicly held.[16]

Corporate influence was staid and stolid, profiting without offending, and early 1980s Las Vegas revealed a lack of imagination. After a disastrous fire at the original MGM in November 1980 in which eighty-four people died and more than seven hundred were injured, and another at the Las Vegas Hilton, the city slumped. The nadir of modern Las Vegas followed; the city entered an era of bland architecture. Undistinguished structures such as the seventeen-story tower added to the Dunes or the four look-alike towers at the Flamingo that cast Bugsy Siegel's palm-lined pool in shadows from sunrise to sunset characterized this version of growth.[17] Corporations possessed vast amounts of capital, but design by committee with overwhelming attention to the bottom line shaved away the flair that made the place special. Corporate capital's fundamental lack of imagination threatened Las Vegas.

In this new context, with the possibility of the unlimited capital that public financing could generate, Las Vegas again reinvented itself. A visionary entrepreneur, Steve Wynn, who raised the ante of casino theming and financing, and a challenger for that crown, Kirk Kerkorian, who sold his interests and left Las Vegas in the mid-1980s but returned with greater grandeur a few years later, laid the basis for the reinvention of a new and presumably competition-proof Las Vegas, funded by corporate America, stock offerings, and Wall Street. Wynn's genius lay in seeing the possibilities that the broadening of access to capital provided and envisioning what visitors to Las Vegas sought. Large-scale funding meant that Las Vegas could be more than the mecca of glitz and excess; as its capital came from the mainstream, its attractions could be shaped to the tastes of that audience. The gradual easing of the stigma associated with gaming and the willingness to combine it with conventional postwar attractions on the scale of Disneyland meant broader reach for Las Vegas. Not only did people who wanted to gamble come to the transformed desert town, so did people who wanted to enjoy the spectacle and have a vacation in a classic but updated sense of the word. Sin City became more palatable and perhaps even less sinful.

Wynn, Kerkorian, and their enterprises represented the changes in the gaming-as-entertainment industry. The initial, western-themed casinos belonged to crusty iconoclasts, individualists who were themselves participants in their industry. Steve Wynn, in contrast, often quipped, "The only way to make money in a casino is to own one." Some of the originators built empires; others just ran their one hotel and casino. Many operators did not look at the long term, and most of these did not survive. By the 1950s western tourism as a whole had taken on corporate and institutional characteristics; gaming followed by 1970. The successful gaming entrepreneurs of the first half of the century grew old or died—at least one prematurely in a hail of gunfire—and the business became too lucrative to be left to mere entrepreneurs. The construction of interstate highways during the Eisenhower era added to the mosaic, increasing access to some places, bypassing others, and generally encouraging further travel.[18] As in other industries that developed from local, regional, or idiosyncratic roots, the western tourism industry was co-opted. After a certain point, the people who marketed it spent more time guessing what the public wanted and invested less time in retaining the special character of what they presented.

Wynn especially typified the breed of entrepreneurs who made Las Vegas unique. As the apocryphal story goes, Wynn, a protégé of banker E. Parry Thomas, parlayed a small share of a casino and a liquor distributorship into the purchase of the only piece of land that Howard Hughes ever sold, a parking lot across the street from Caesars Palace. Wynn sold the property, netting a $766,000 profit, allowing him to buy a large enough stake in the downtown Golden Nugget that he developed controlling interest; by June 1973 he ran it. In 1978 he bought into Atlantic City, securing the backing of financier and later convicted felon Michael Milken and his Wall Street firm of Drexel Burnham Lambert. Before the decade ended, Wynn's casino became the most profitable in Atlantic City. His ties with a major source of development capital were secure. Wynn also built a tower on the Golden Nugget in Las Vegas and planned to make the hotel upscale.[19]

Wynn was a visionary, among the first in Las Vegas to see long-term possibilities instead of the short-term profits that had limited the horizons of the 1960s gamblers. He melded Las Vegas's past with its future. He understood what people wanted, applied Wall Street capital, corporate methods, and accountability and added new dimensions to the amenities people expected from Las Vegas. Wynn could feel the pulse of the nation's desires, and in creating them, he redefined Las Vegas once again.

The opening of the $637 million Mirage resort in 1989 was the pinnacle of that redefinition, the inauguration of a new era. The Mirage reinvented the theming of Las Vegas resorts. Before the Mirage, resorts were tied to places or ideas—the original Flamingo mimicked Miami and Monte Carlo; the Tropicana mirrored Cuba; the Sands, the Sahara, and the Dunes had desert themes; and Caesars Palace took a visitor back to ancient Rome. The Mirage marketed fantasy and illusion, wry conceptions in a town based on straightforward and shameless moneymaking. Visitors enjoyed a level of amenity that left other hotels far behind. Wynn was a perfectionist; everything in his hotel had to be just right. He took excellent care of his employees. Under the Treasure Island, which opened in 1993, was a mirror universe, a network of shops, restaurants, and other amenities exclusively for the workers. Their loyalty was unmatched, and service at the Mirage and other Wynn properties was the best in town. The Mirage lifted the expectations of Las Vegas. It became an overwhelming success, placing immense pressure on other resorts to follow suit.

When it opened, the Mirage was the most expensive property ever to grace the Strip, adding the dimension of fantasy in a new and spectacular way at a cost of $500 million more than any previous casino resort. The

$637 million came from the only source of funding of that scale in the mid-1980s: the lucrative junk bond market. With a relationship that began with Wynn's entry into Atlantic City, Michael Milken was the obvious source of capital. Through Milken and Drexel, Burnham, Lambert, Incorporated, the parent company of Wynn's enterprises, Golden Nugget Incorporated, borrowed $535.1 million to finance the Mirage in what observers of the financial markets called "a work of art," money from junk bonds. Wynn's equity came from the sale of the Golden Nugget in Atlantic City. With "fantasy become reality" as a theme and a volcano cooled by water in a desert locale, the Mirage embodied the essence of Las Vegas: a reality that only rarely required the suspension of disbelief. Siegfried and Roy and their famed white tigers were part of this ambience, as were dolphins, and later, the nouvelle circus, Cirque du Soleil.

In the process, Drexel, Burnham, Lambert became the dominant financial force in Nevada gaming. The $2.57 billion invested through it in the Silver State represented at least 100,000 new Nevada jobs during the 1980s. No less a financial luminary than E. Parry Thomas recognized the impact; in 1989 he told a reporter that "Milken has been the primary mover [in Nevada] for the last several years." In a nod to the difficulties of acquiring capital before corporate gaming, Wynn referred to Milken's influence as equaling that of Thomas during the 1960s and 1970s.[20]

Kerkorian followed Wynn's lead with his plans for the second MGM Grand Hotel and theme park, complete with an Emerald City and Wizard of Oz motif, that he first announced in the late 1980s. The 1980 fire at his MGM prompted Kerkorian to leave the industry, but after selling out to Bally's in 1985, he contemplated a return to Nevada gaming. His $594 million arrangement with Bally's forbade him to use the MGM name in Nevada for three years. In 1987 Kerkorian bought the Sands and Desert Inn hotels from Summa Corporation, and in early 1988 the Sands became the MGM Sands. Within one year Kerkorian sold the hotel to casino impresario Henri Lewin, by some accounts doubling his investment. By 1989 he planned the financing for a new resort of unparalleled proportions. When he sold MGM-UA to Turner Communications, run by Atlanta billionaire media mogul Ted Turner, for $1.5 billion, Kerkorian possessed the resources to finance his newest endeavor. A sale of $140 million of stock in his parent MGM Grand, Incorporated, reduced his holding in the company from 98 percent to 72 percent and allowed the construction of what became the new MGM Grand, on the northeast corner of Tropicana and the Strip. By the time the hotel was completed, the largest in the world with 5,005 rooms, its cost approached $1 billion.[21]

As gaming spread, Wynn, Kerkorian, William Bennett of Circus Circus, and others in Las Vegas recast the town as a first-class entertainment resort, replete with options for every member of the family. The exotic themes of earlier resorts were supplanted by an iconography derived from popular culture and directed at younger people. The opening of the Grand Slam Canyon at Circus Circus, the Luxor, an immense Egyptian pyramid, Wynn's Treasure Island resort, and the MGM Grand in 1993 signaled a new Las Vegas, appealing to adults and young people alike and eagerly continuing the adaptable traditions of its past. "This is part of a major metamorphosis in Las Vegas," Mayor Jan Laverty Jones said as the MGM plan debuted. "Las Vegas is changing from just adult entertainment to a resort destination." [22] Steven Spielberg located his DIVE! Restaurant in Las Vegas; Planet Hollywood followed, first with a restaurant and later with plans for a hotel. The Hard Rock Cafe added a hotel and casino, aiming at the Rock 'n' Roll generation. Sin City was hardly sinful anymore. Once again it obliterated its past in its ongoing search to fill the desires of the American and international public. Its unparalleled malleability made it timeless, always chameleon-like and supple, always prepared to reinvent itself as it catered to a broader and different audience.

The roots of this transformation had begun as early as the 1970s, when impresarios of the industry offered innovations to attract a broader audience. Circus Circus became the first such resort, but its origins were more eccentric. When the $15 million Circus Circus Casino opened in 1968, it raised an emphasis on entertainment for a young adult crowd to an unabashedly hedonistic level. Circus Circus needed a strong drawing card; it was a freestanding casino, with no hotel to house its visitors. Its ticket to success became a combination of camp and sexiness, a wild and unfettered place tuned to the cultural rhythms of the late 1960s. When Hunter Thompson saw this early incarnation of Circus Circus, he called it the "Sixth Reich," noting that it was "what the whole hep world would be doing on Saturday night if the Nazis won the war." Initially, the ambience had such appeal that the casino charged an admission fee. All but locals paid to enter. The lack of a hotel was unwieldy, and the initial owner, Jay Sarno, lost money, but the place had flair. A baby elephant walked the aisles, pulling slot machine levers for customers. Slides and fire poles took customers from the Midway, where orangutan acts were among the attractions, to the casino floor. One former employee remembered that keeping the smell of the orangutans out of the hallways was a major problem at the casino.[23] Circus Circus fit its time, but in its initial incarnation, the casino was too idiosyncratic to turn a consistent profit.

When Sarno sold the operation in 1974 its new owners, William Bennett and William Pennington, recognized the appeal of a family vacation resort with gambling. Retaining the big-top theme, Circus Circus changed from a "playhouse for adults" to a "themed destination resort for families," pulling a different audience to the myriad attractions of Las Vegas. Sarno built a hotel in 1972, and the new owners expanded, adding a new tower. Bennett and Pennington identified a niche in the market, a middle-class constituency that differed from the suave high rollers. Circus Circus's clientele arrived in Winnebagos and station wagons, ate at the cheap buffet, which served more meals than any restaurant in the world, and stayed in inexpensive rooms. Bennett and Pennington decided that they would make their profits through volume and succeeded wildly. The occupancy rate at Circus Circus continuously topped 99 percent; during holidays and peak weekends, the rate exceeds 100 percent, as the hotel resells rooms that are prepaid and nonrefundable when people do not arrive in time to claim them.[24]

The idea of a family vacation resort played an important part in opening up Las Vegas to a middle-class constituency and burying the last vestiges of stigma attached to the town. Circus Circus was a little tawdry, but it replaced fancy showgirls with circus acts that children could enjoy while their parents played the slot machines below. Gone were the fire poles and the acrobats, the barely controlled mayhem and camp that characterized Sarno's vision. As corporate capital moved into Las Vegas and expanded the audience of the community, Bennett and Pennington discovered a recipe for success that was often imitated.

In the late 1980s the spread of gaming to other locales and the decline of the California economy threatened the hegemony that Las Vegas enjoyed over this important form of tourism. The renovation of Atlantic City as a gaming resort in the late 1970s began the challenge and was bolstered by the popularity of dog tracks, horse racing, Jai Alai, state lotteries, and other forms of wagering. Gambling ceased to be considered a moral deficiency as destitute state and local governments saw the industry as a source of revenue. The Indian Gaming Regulatory Act of 1988 allowed Native Americans to operate casinos in a variety of settings, providing another potential competitor for Las Vegas and independent sources of revenue in states with constant or declining tax bases. As casinos appeared in places such as Davenport, Iowa, and Tunica, Mississippi, the leaders of Las Vegas recognized both an opportunity and a threat to their dominance of the industry.[25]

In this changing economic climate, the colony became the colonizer. From 1931 to the 1980s, Las Vegas survived because no other American locale was sufficiently desperate to stoop to reap the financial rewards of gaming. In the postindustrial climate, and especially during the rocky economic times of the late Reagan and Bush years, when the amount of wealth possessed by the top quartile of American society grew significantly as that of the rest of the nation fell, gaming offered a panacea to declining and decrepit communities and to individuals who had lost track of the conventional American dream. Las Vegas corporations were in demand from London to Australia and especially among poorer states and other places in the nation where old economic structures were failing and prospects were limited. Without the cultural stigma and with the rise of Indian gaming, casinos became just another industry, another source of jobs, and Las Vegas owned the expertise to sell. Nevada corporations soon ran gaming enterprises in numerous states; as travelers passed through the security check to the A and B gates at Las Vegas's McCarran International Airport in 1997, a map of Harrah's resorts served as advertisement above their heads. Adelaide, Australia, Joliet, Illinois, and Biloxi, Mississippi, were among Harrah's operations. The same corporate names that graced Nevada neon were obvious everywhere in the United States that permitted gaming.

Although some observers predicted the demise of Las Vegas with the expansion of gaming, they underestimated both the malleability of the desert community and its vast cultural cachet. Las Vegas was a myth, an icon of excess, a place to which people aspired. Sitting at a Twenty-one table in Tunica, Mississippi, or San Felipe, New Mexico, did not feel the same as it did at Caesars Palace. No place could match the edifice of Las Vegas, which in the 1990s would require more than $140 billion to construct. Only Branson, Missouri, thought that it could, but it rarely reached the amenity level of even the mid-range Las Vegas experience. Las Vegas remained the standard by which the gaming and entertainment tourism experience was measured. In the quest for postmodern authenticity, the idea of genuine experience in an inauthentic world that was deeply ingrained in entertainment tourism but paradoxically was exactly what that form of tourism could not provide, casinos in other places fell short; people could gamble there, but they were not sated. Other casinos were pale imitations, not quite the fantasy they were in Las Vegas. Such places lacked the feel, the glitz, the ambience. Las Vegas was experience, a postmodern definition of real. No other place compared.

The growth of legalized gaming served as a feeder system for Las Vegas. After 1989 the city grew at a phenomenal rate. Visitation almost doubled in a ten-year period, by 1996 topping 30 million annually. As one local joke went, the official bird of southern Nevada became the crane, the machine used to build skyscrapers. In an eighteen-month period in 1993 and 1994, more than 20,000 new hotel rooms opened; almost every hotel on the Strip had plans for a major expansion. The investment seemed likely to be justified. Between 1993 and 1996, three old hotels on or near the Strip were imploded. The implosion of the Dunes was a Wynn project that became a local event. Hundreds of thousands lined the Strip to watch, and Wynn provided a show replete with fireworks that seemed designed to bring down the curtain on the old Las Vegas once and for all. The scene appeared in the film *Casino,* as Robert DeNiro's voiceover told of how the city changed. The Landmark was imploded early in the morning with little fanfare, but the Hacienda came down in a New Year's Eve implosion that coincided with the dropping of the ball in Times Square in New York, the timing of which made New York newspapers complain that Las Vegas coveted the Big Apple's thunder. Las Vegas could even market the destruction of its past. When the Sands, home to the antics of the Rat Pack, was destroyed, its fate was part of the set of *ConAir,* a 1997 action film that left the tail of an aircraft protruding from the wreckage of the once preeminent hotel. From the debris sprang the Venetian, a $1 billion extravaganza with over 6,000 rooms designed to outdo Wynn's Bellagio, built with its own lake on the location of the Dunes, and Kerkorian's MGM.

Other markets supported this growth. An immense convention trade, highlighted by the annual Comdex computer gathering of over 200,000, provided the basis for consistent growth, as did the remarkable publicity that saturated the nation and indeed the world. Las Vegas's malleability also contributed. If the Mexican boxer Julio Cesar Chavez was scheduled to fight, Las Vegas turned Mexican; when the National Finals Rodeo arrived each December, the community went cowboy. Classic black English taxicabs in London during summer 1996 sported advertisements for Las Vegas hotels. Early in 1997, with the opening of New York, New York Casino and Hotel, Las Vegas became the first American city to top 100,000 hotel rooms. By 1997 there was talk of hosting a national political convention there. The niche that Las Vegas had carved in an era when people regarded it as Sin City became legal and then desirable all over the world.

By the mid-1990s Las Vegas had perfected the service economy and become the last Detroit, the last place in the United States where relatively unskilled workers could find a job out of high school, earn a middle-class wage, and expect to remain with the company for their entire working life. In 1995 service workers, most of whom were in the tourism and gaming industry, made up more than 47 percent of the workers in Las Vegas. The 254,200 service workers more than doubled any other category of worker, with the vague category of trade employing 107,400, followed by government with 54,100. Construction, the only other significantly sized percentage of the employment market, reached 45,500, many of whom were employed on large projects on the Strip and other places where casino and hotel expansion and growth took place.[26] With the relatively low cost of living and especially of housing in southern Nevada, industry workers expected to live a comfortable life. Unionization in the industry kept wages high. Circus Circus, the Mirage, and other large organizations worked with the unions to ensure that wages and benefits remained competitive. Even non-union casinos paid well to keep the unions out. Only occasional renegades, such as the Elardi family, the owners of the Frontier Hotel, which engaged in a protracted labor dispute with the Culinary Union, and the powerful Sheldon Adelson of the Venetian, marred the labor harmony in Las Vegas. The Elardis were so poorly regarded within the gaming community that on one Labor Day, other gaming corporations publicly paid for food and refreshments delivered to strikers to show their support.[27] Added to the wages was the opportunity to have income augmented by the "toke," local parlance for the tip, ever the elixir of life in Las Vegas. The combination of wage and toke made positions in the gaming industry a far better employment opportunity than remained in much of the Rust Belt or in many open shop Sun Belt states. Certainly Las Vegas workers in hotel chains made considerably more money than their counterparts in other cities.

Although Las Vegas perfected the service economy, its mode of operation was discrete, not transferrable to places that sought to imitate it. Gaming itself could be lucrative, but it could also be pathetic on Indian reservations and in poor states. It functioned as a regressive form of taxation, typically taking from the poor and giving to the rich. In places such as New Mexico, it complicated an already tense ethnic climate, primarily redistributing money from the Hispano poor to Indian communities, reversing a process of divestiture that began with Coronado in 1542, as it slowed the flow into state revenue coffers. Gaming brought a range of pathologies to places that grafted it upon an existing structure; pressured by a changing world, people looked only at the benefits and saw little of the dislocation the industry could cause. Las Vegas could perfect service because at its core it was malleable. There was only a fluidity there, no rock solid definition of local identity as in Santa Fe and Aspen. Las Vegas had been founded to be a colony, to serve the demands of the outside, and because it was first and in many ways best, it stood alone and at the top. The essence of Las Vegas perfectly mirrored that of the world of late capitalism, a world where people increasingly made their living visiting each other.

Las Vegas possessed a special place in American society, a unique meaning that no imitator could match. Other places, with deep fidelity to the idea of themselves as places that produced, had trouble with the ephemerality of gaming and tourism. Although Las Vegas had a kind of integrity about it—in Las Vegas it was *always* about money—other places had pretensions about their involvement in gaming. It was only a temporary remedy, they seemed to say, while they awaited a more respectable solution. Even the best of the new casinos, Foxwoods in Connecticut, run by the reconstructed Pequot tribe, was not Las Vegas, regardless of the shows and amenities it offered. No one ever went to Las Vegas and thought afterward that they must try Foxwoods.

In a 1994 cover story, *Time* magazine declared that Las Vegas had become an all-American city, the new American hometown. The rest of the nation had become more like its capital of sin, writers for the magazine averred, arguing for a convergence of the aberration that had been Las Vegas and the rest of the nation and granting the city a leading role in the service economy that has become, for better and worse, the future of the nation.[28] What this glitzy and superficial analysis failed to note was that at the same time the rest of the nation had become more like Las Vegas, it had become more like the rest of the nation. As the nation moved toward service economy, the advantages of Las Vegas seemed increasingly apparent. In this mecca of gaming, unskilled individuals with high school educations could still earn a middle-class income. Las Vegas provided solid pay for unspecialized work; for anyone with a modicum of skill and grace, it was an easy place to do well in service positions.

The transformation was completed by the way that the Las Vegas experience became ordinary. By the 1990s ITT–Sheraton, Hilton, and other major hotel chains owned major casino-hotels. Graduates of Wharton Business School made the decisions. They sought to follow the lead of the brilliant Wynn, himself trapped by the enormous corporate money and power that imitated his every move. At the debut of the $1 billion Venetian, a Sands Corporation marketer was asked who composed the target audience for the hotel. "We just hope Steve Wynn has his market research right," was his response. The gaming industry had developed a hierarchy that resembled the army in that special training was essential to receive the opportunity to lead. There was even a glass ceiling in gaming. No longer could dealers work their way off the floor to management positions. In the large resorts, the upward mobility of organized crime's days disappeared. Pit boss was as high as a dealer or floor worker could expect to go. Background and connections limited upward mobility for workers, and the profits from the industry went into the pockets of outside investors who recognized opportunity and seized it. Workers remained workers throughout their careers even though they could earn a middle-class wage, which created a paradox for many. The money they made trapped them in an industry they came to resent. The management positions were filled by MBAs, professional businesspeople who did not repeat the mistakes that caused Howard Hughes to lose money as a casino operator but who also did not truly understand the gaming industry. The personal side of gaming, the floor manager who recognized patrons, diminished as gaming came to resemble every other industry.

Still a colony in many ways but well on the way to creating its own form, Las Vegas shared greater commonality with the rest of the nation. It depended on the same sources of capital as other communities and became subject to many of the same rules and regulations. It was not simply that the rest of the nation had normalized the behaviors of Las Vegas, had become more like the center of gaming, cheap sex, and easy living; in the locations of its power, in its hierarchy and distribution of wealth and status, in the stratification of its labor force, Las Vegas had become more like the rest of the nation. The transformation of gaming into entertainment tourism had truly become a two-way street.

13

The Mélange of Postmodern Tourism

The transformation of Las Vegas typified the changes in western tourism after 1970. Consolidation occurred throughout the industry as corporations competed to acquire the valuable marketing resources and profits that tourist destinations represented. Besides the potential to generate enormous cash flow, such destinations conveyed cachet and hipness in postindustrial, postmodern culture, driven by the media and marketed through a range of outlets—television, CDs, home computers and the images downloaded from the Internet—to the sycophantic portrayal of the wealthy and the famous as icons of an era that clogged the television airwaves. In the process, the intellectual vestiges of cultural and heritage tourism melded with the image of skiing and the recreational experience of hunting and fishing to create a form of entertainment tourism that so thoroughly blurred the lines between the actual and its imitation that basic activities were rendered anachronistic and others transmuted into different forms of entertainment.

The travel public still distinguished between authentic and inauthentic. It no longer understood why authentic was more significant. In Japan indoor beaches and faux skiing mountains replaced the real ones, an admittedly invented reality but one to which people flocked. The Japanese even embraced a new and entirely postmodern form of the travelogue, using real people to show them foreign lands replete with art, activities, foods, and smells without leaving Japan. In Las Vegas the Luxor offered a ride down the Nile; Grand Slam Canyon attempted to take the place of the real one; New York, New York offered the Big Apple of *Singing in the Rain* and Frank

Sinatra, with change carts painted in yellow and black checkerboard like taxicabs. Local wags anticipated the opening of Las Vegas, Las Vegas, which, as the joke went, would have a cut-down faux Strip inside a hotel along the Strip. Outside national parks such as Zion, IMAX theaters offered sixty-foot-high screens that showed the most spectacular of the features of the park from viewing points that most visitors lacked the time, determination, or skill to reach. Even Caesars Palace in Las Vegas offered an IMAX feature that in 1994 showed Yellowstone National Park, further blurring any remaining distinctions between differing forms of experience.

For the iconographical places of an earlier generation, the new rules meant significant changes in status. Annual visitation at Carlsbad Caverns, New Mexico, once a destination for a generation of Americans, continued a twenty-year slide that began during the American Bicentennial of 1976. Over 200 miles from Interstate 40 and over 100 in the opposite direction from the airport in El Paso, Texas, the caverns did not fit the pattern of convenience and experience-on-demand, faux or otherwise, that drove postmodern tourism. Its caves were remarkable, but they offered none of the glitz and glitter that came to mark the tourist experience. People could walk through the caves or ride the 750 feet to the bottom in an elevator, but in the parlance of post-1970 America, there was "nothing to do" there. Eating lunch 750 feet below ground was hardly the thrill it had been to the visitors of the 1920s and 1930s. Even more telling, caverns similar to those at Carlsbad could be experienced in an IMAX theater from a better perspective at less expense in a shorter time. By the mid-1990s visitors to Carlsbad Caverns represented specialized intraregional tourism rather than the national model that succeeded it. They were old and young and came on two-lane highways from around the Southwest, or they were spelunking enthusiasts. Entertainment tourism swallowed the previous forms, integrating them into a mass market form that in itself was authentic to people who had never experienced any other kind.

Tourism also became a growing and increasingly important part of the economy, an endeavor well positioned to capitalize on any trend in American society or culture. As service economies eclipsed manufacturing and agriculture, the importance of Las Vegas as an economic and ultimately cultural model for American society grew. Changes in the national and global economy also enhanced the significance of tourism as a premier manifestation of the service economy. It grew as traditional economic forms shed workers, increasing its importance as American business downsized both blue-collar and white-collar workers. As American society passed from its obsession with the consumption of things into a growing preoccupation with status, tourism, exclusively defined, became an even more important indicator of standing.

Acquiring image took on a meaning it had never before had; since the iconographic revolution of the 1920s, when commercial imagery became symbolic, the importance of image had grown substantially in American society. In post-Watergate, postmodern America, image was paramount. In its amalgamated form, tourism was sufficiently flexible and segmented to provide the correct experience of status for every group of people. The entirely fraudulent creation of the concept of ecotourism, a description of a historic pattern of visitation that crossed the globe, served as the classic example, from safaris in Africa to climbing the peaks of the Himalayas to hiking the natural area of national parks and their exquisite backcountries. Ecotourists regarded their visits as more than recreation or entertainment precisely because someone defined it for them in a manner that affirmed their beliefs: that they helped the planet when they traveled. But their impact was the same as anyone else's. They too flew in jets, burning fossil fuels; they too traveled on roads hacked through the jungle, stayed in rooms laden with amenities where locals worked in menial positions for a pittance, and they too purchased supposedly "green" goods from authorized gift shops that put money in the pockets of international entrepreneurs, not in local hands. The link between such travelers and the environment, which they supposed differentiated them from the other tourists, was entirely a figment of their imaginations. Ecotourists for all the hullabaloo were no better nor worse than any other tourists. A global economy marketed experience to them that masqueraded as genuine because it appealed to their sense of what was right in the world. In this they were no different from the railroad travelers of the fin de siècle, who received their own affirmation through precisely the same kind of overlay.

The amalgamation of tourism into one overarching form with many manifestations created a mélange of postmodern tourism that was self-referential and trend-driven. Entertainment tourism survived by being quintessentially malleable, by responding to every passing fad with either a cosmetic or a fundamental redesign of its attributes in the race to reflect to the public what it already believed. Even Disneyland's Electric Light Parade was reengineered to stimulate new generations; despite its immense popularity, its script was changed to avoid becoming anachronistic. The decision pitted the comfort of Disneyland's past against the hipness Walt Disney Company sought for its future. Corporations, accustomed to marketing their products in this climate, easily adjusted their resorts to fit passing trends. For the other forms of tourism that were incorporated into entertainment tourism as popular culture and mass media set the trends in American society, this mutability was problematic. Making resorts designed in other contexts malleable meant challenging the premises of the people who lived there and ultimately destroying the self-defined self-image at their core.

As the ethos of Las Vegas spread, its ability to transform itself to fit people's desires on demand became crucial to the expectations of tourists. Places such as Aspen that once had clear identities found those conceptualizations entirely changed from the outside instead of from within. As local author Peggy Clifford feared, Aspen became a giant cash register, tuned to the vagaries of the market, not to its own special qualities that set it apart before skiing took the town by storm. Walter Paepcke's vision became a distant memory in the minds of people who had experienced the town then. Real Aspen became a haven for celebrities, the superrich, the trendy, a place where people went to be seen rather than to ski, where newspapers around the country reported the arrivals and departures of the famous, the near famous, the wealthy, and the hangers-on who aspired to that status. Places such as Telluride, Colorado, had their fifteen minutes of fame as resorts. Santa Fe went through another of its many transformations as it too became self-referential, no longer valued for the overlay of its history and culture but for its ties to New Age spirituality, alternative lifestyles, and a range of other consistently shifting ways of living. Jackson, Wyoming, for so long too cold for winter recreation, became a desired place, and real estate prices rose beyond the conception of anyone who saw the valley before 1950. Snowmobiles played a role in this transformation, making winter less a threat and giving the hardy a summerlike accessibility. Locals who once thought of the winter as their own, and even after the rise of winter visitation thought of outdoor winter activity as their own, found themselves inundated with visitors. In Colorado, as corporate moguls began to play "musical chairlifts," in the phrase of *Newsweek*, a range of ski areas merged. Vail Resorts, which already controlled Vail and Beaver Creek, added two resorts, Keystone and Breckinridge. Only Copper Mountain, Arapahoe Basin, and Loveland along the I-70 corridor through the central Rocky Mountains remained free of the dominance of Vail, clearly making it the power in this twenty-five mile stretch of the Rockies.[1] The individuality of place disappeared as corporations that regarded identity as a selling point took control and developers with cookie-cutter plans followed.

Las Vegas's fundamental and inherent malleability suited it to this process of reinvention, but in Aspen, Steamboat Springs, Santa Fe, and Jackson, where identities were formed across the boundaries of dominant regimes, the change was far more dislocating. To people who came to Aspen in the 1960s for a new culture, its transformation into a playground for the superrich was disconcerting. To those who remembered the earlier incarnations of Jackson as a summer resort crammed with dude ranches, its role as summer resort of the chic, enhanced greatly by the summer visits of Pres. Bill Clinton and his family in 1995 and 1996 tore at the local fabric. The layering of entertainment tourism on previous regimes that ran sometimes five levels deep greatly affected the people who had come earlier. The neonatives who had once alienated locals found themselves overwhelmed by the latest invasion, struggling to hold their places in these shifting communities.

The superrich changed the scope and scale of resort communities such as Aspen and Jackson. The homes they built, the causes they supported, even their idea of fun was different. "I tell you, the rich are coming out of the closet, like gays," Mary Eshbaugh Hayes, a thirty-eight-year veteran of Aspen who wrote the society column for the *Aspen Times*, remarked in 1988. More of the new residents were the "type to give a million, to back a whole performing-arts center," instead of merely offering $50,000 gifts, a genuine advantage for the development of cultural affairs in the community. Like any such change, the new scale put pressure on Aspen in different ways and had an impact on its freewheeling, hedonistic culture. According to Walter Ganz, in 1985 a twelve-year resident of Aspen, fund raising had replaced skiing and sex as the new pursuit of the status-conscious in Aspen. This generosity reflected the invasion of old money, not the disaffected scions of the elite or the committed activists of earlier generations. But that money came with strings attached, as people who gave increasingly influenced the community. People such as Donald Trump, Prince Bandar of Saudi Arabia, or the wealthy Palestinian developer Mohammed Hadid lived on a larger scale than did Aspen's existing wealthy. Starwood, the subdivision that housed John Denver, was no longer sufficient. The flamboyance of the newest newcomers prompted the already established wealthy to show off, and as author Ted Conover noted in 1988, "Ostentation was on the rise."[2]

Yet the neonatives who found themselves faced with the changes in such places were different from the locals they once displaced. Many had upper-middle-class roots and experiences; a significant number arrived with political experience, college degrees, and access to capital. In towns such as Aspen, they could build on a twenty-year history of activism and a local culture that embraced it, thanks to Walter Paepcke. In Steamboat Springs, a powerful local business community often sided with locals against outside capital.

Local businesspeople had to live in the community beside their neighbors, and that investment often dictated their political and to a lesser degree their economic action. In Santa Fe, the entrenched power structure often welcomed wanton growth, which typically came at the expense of the Hispano population. Hispano resentment teemed throughout the 1980s and 1990s, exemplified by a Hispano Santa Fe native who remarked that the town had become a haven for "Californians, Texans, New Yorkers, [homosexuals,] and every other kind of weirdo on the planet."[3] This sentiment was exceptional only in its vituperativeness and the broad brush of its resentment.

The association with celebrity had much to do with placing such locales in the middle of mainstream, postindustrial popular culture. Ever since Hemingway came to Sun Valley in 1939, celebrities flocked to resorts to avoid the public and to be seen in the right places. Aspen was one of the first. By the 1970s it had become so fashionable that a procession of celebrities claimed it as home, beginning with John Denver, who was, as his most popular song claimed, "coming home to a place he'd never been before." In the 1980s, with Hunter S. Thompson as its local pet, the cachet of the community grew. Successive individuals claimed it, including Donald Trump, who sought to make the place his own. Other places flirted with celebrity. Former U.S. president Gerald R. Ford owned a condo at Vail. Tom Cruise and Nicole Kidman married at Telluride, and *Megatrends* author John Naisbitt had a house there. Shirley MacLaine owned a house in the hills above Santa Fe, and the townspeople resented the way her place blocked their view of the mountains. By the mid-1990s, a seat at the Silver Dollar Bar in Jackson meant a license to celebrity-watch. Donald Hough, author of *The Cocktail Hour in Jackson Hole,* would not have recognized the people around him from his old perch.[4]

Following the model of Las Vegas, each of these places became extra-specially ordinary. Beginning with firm roots in idiosyncracy and retaining a rock-hard and increasingly disgruntled core, they too became malleable as much as a result of outside cultural influence as of incoming capital. Soon there was little local about such places except the cachet of their name; local life in the historic sense was consigned to private homes and the shadows of local social life. By the mid-1990s the stores in each were the same; the Nature Company, Eddie Bauer, and countless similar concerns offering the same kind of chic as did the places themselves. Gone were the locally owned businesses and national chains catering to locals that once surrounded the plaza in Santa Fe and the town square in Jackson, gone were the opportunities in Aspen to live there in the conventional sense. By the mid-1990s only Woolworth's remained as a local venue in the heart of Santa Fe. Upscale chains and innumerable small businesses, many poorly positioned in the market, replaced them. Even longstanding neonative businesses such as the Santa Fe Bookseller, a local institution tied to the neonative community by its specialization in art books, sold out and were replaced by tony tourist chains. Though the activities that attracted tourists to these places might differ, the range of surrounding experience and the names and nature of the amenities became remarkably similar. Companies prided themselves on being represented in all the best resorts, and hotels and other service entities transferred its employees from one resort to another. Any independent identity became buried in the McDonald's-like emphasis on standardization. The embrace of tourism and its promise of prosperity overwhelmed the individual character of resorts.

A manufactured individualism remained. Resort communities possessed innumerable restaurants and shops designed to look fashionable and locally owned—in a word, unique. Close inspection revealed that many were part of chains that followed a formula but fashioned their enterprises as discrete. The lack of familiarity with the name and the tony local trappings were the draw; this status-conscious audience found even Eddie Bauer's too common, much less McDonald's. In such stores, there was no way to differentiate from the same store at home. Faux chains, with their tremendous emphasis on formalized service and goods in distinct environments, met that need.

For the people who worked in these towns, the consequences of change were vast. Most tourist destinations typically had been seasonal, in the words of John Rember, creating a niche for the people who made up "the essential skeleton of maids, cooks, bartenders, ski patrolmen and women, cat drivers, lift operators, waitresses, and life guards." These people found the place special and were willing to stay there, underemployed, to enjoy its virtues during the off-season. Such places pretended to egalitarianism. In the old Sun Valley, dishwashers with MIT Ph.D.'s supposedly skied down the slopes next to aristocrats. In 1988 Aspen's Mellow Yellow taxi company included a San Francisco debutante and diplomat's daughter, a former pilot for Pan American Airlines, a disillusioned psychiatrist, a woman who had been associated with the Chicago Seven, and a former Playboy bunny.[5] In Aspen, longevity rather than wealth or station in the community conferred a certain status. The annual photograph of residents standing on the rugby field near the marker that designated the year of their arrival to prove their position in the community illustrated the importance of extended neonativity. Lining up at a marker labeled with the year of their arrival, people proved their claim to Aspen by being able to say they were there when. Locals were not transient in

The Mellow Yellow Taxi Company typified both the idiosyncracies of the town and its limited employment opportunities. (Photo courtesy of the Aspen Historical Society.)

this formulation. They chose to stay when their skills would clearly be worth more elsewhere. That investment of self in place gave them a currency in the town they owned, a proprietary sense about what happened to their place but one they had to share, by choice and under duress, with the wealthy who came to visit and with the people who bought or built second homes there.

This ritual of self-definition that denoted community values and sometimes solidarity was most prominent in Aspen. It sometimes took the form of bumper stickers expressing a message that offered allegiance to a vision of local community; Colorado Native was a marker of that and more. At Telluride, the local Free Box, a place where people left things they did not need and picked up things they did, all for no cost, helped define the local community. Begun in 1975 by a woman who left clothes with a sign that said "Free, take whatever you want," the Free Box became a local tradition that defined the spirit of preresort Telluride. According to legend, someone once left a BMW and its keys and registration, a telltale sign of changing economic demography. In other instances such rituals were identified by locals who understood insider status. Jackson gadfly Tim Sandlin, whose book-jacket

A winter sled near Jackson in the early 1990s. Such amenities helped expand the tourist trade in many northern-tier towns. (Photo courtesy of Angus Thuermer Jr.)

blurb described him as someone who for over twenty years had held every "entry-level, demeaning job known to the tourist industry," invented fictional characters, the Pym family, who practiced the rites of self-definition by recounting the memory of places lost. Aspen's more formal process reflected the enormous status longevity in the town conveyed. Standing by the marker on the rugby field proved legitimacy, no matter how many times the Aspen Ski Company changed hands, no matter how many developers built ritzy resorts or 20,000-square-foot homes. Here was a status that affirmed an older sense of community, and no amount of new money could buy it. It promised solidarity among the people who counted, who remembered Paepcke's *Kulturstaat* and who epitomized the town's soul. The photo offered a hierarchy based on commitment to the community demonstrated across time. Even the home someone owned, the redesigned faux Victorian that once had been the primary claim of nativity, could not transcend the reality of a 1995 designation on the rugby field. The ritual provided a form of authentication and psychic sustenance for increasingly beleaguered neonatives.[6]

Tourist towns were seductive even to natives. John Rember, a native of the Sawtooth Valley in Idaho, had always believed that locals were superior to tourists because of their close ties to place, but a junket to Sun Valley resulted in another view. "I found that it was perfectly possible and fun to be a tourist in your own town," Rember observed. Riding in a sleigh along the Warm Springs golf course on the way to a Mongolian yurt for dinner and seeing into the homes that wealthy people built along the course, Rember "began to think that some tourists—people of taste and discretion, not tied to any geographical area, never subject to invasion by franchise owners—were a higher form of life than locals." Privilege had hegemonizing influence. The amenities were also alluring. "Dinner in the yurt was quite possibly the best meal I've ever had in the Wood River Valley," Rember wrote. "I would say this even if the cook hadn't tended bar with me at Elkhorn ten years earlier."

Neonatives, expecting to scorn the subject of their study, could also succumb to tourist towns. Ted Conover, whose *Whiteout* chronicled two years he spent in Aspen in the late 1980s, arrived with "some ill intent" toward Aspen. "Not a grudge, really," he explained, "but a bad feeling, let's call it, about the town and what it represented. To be skeptical about Aspen was to take a position against hype and elitism . . . to endorse traditional values like neighborliness and a dislike of pretension, and to eschew trendiness, in-crowds, and the influence of cities like New York and Los Angeles." After only one year there, he too had been pulled in. Wearing teal-colored NIKE cycling shorts, cross-trainers with a strip of fluorescent sewed in, and sunglasses pushed up on his head, he was accused by a friend of having gone Aspen: "You've been infected," his friend gleefully observed. "Aspen's gotcha. You thought you'd just study it, but Aspen has you in its *grip*." Conover's relations with the outside world proved the observation. He saw a friend of his father's, an important Denver attorney, in a lift line. "I felt almost sorry for [him]. . . . He was wearing blockish outmoded glasses and a long nylon parka, belted in the 60s style." In Conover's view, the man might have been important in Denver, but "Aspen had a way of demoting the fashion retro; why would he choose to come up here, I wondered, and embarrass himself?" Nor were Conover's favorite restaurants in Denver sufficiently interesting; the trendy had possessed him. His Aspen-induced arrogance was even directed at his own family. Conover's father had long considered buying a place in Aspen but was unwilling to pay the exorbitant prices. Conover asserted that a certain price qualified individuals to play in certain leagues. "I saw the hurt in their eyes," he recounted, "but didn't realize why until months later, when my stepmother told me I had made them feel timid, like hicks, failures."[7] If Rember could be persuaded that some wealthy guests were higher on the evolutionary scale than the locals he prized, and if Conover could swallow whole the Aspen of the superrich, it meant the charms of such resorts were

Aspen in the summer, when there was still an off-season. (Postcard collection of the author.)

not only difficult to resist but also seductive. To sensibilities that looked down on modern popular culture, they were corrupting.

By the mid-1980s the bonds that held resorts together as communities showed considerable fraying. Tourism had become a year-round occupation, exactly as so many entrepreneurs and corporate leaders wished, and the valued off-season disappeared. Winter resorts developed summer programs, descended in one way or another from Paepcke's summer festivals but thoroughly revamped for mainstream consumption. A parade of music programs, film festivals like the enormously successful one at Telluride, bluegrass concerts, and opera filled the ski towns in summer. Ski resorts invested heavily in snow-making equipment, ensuring that even when winter offered little snowfall, as occurred during the disastrous 1977–1978 season, they could accommodate the visitors who paid the bills. Local response to the new situation revealed the colonial core of tourist communities.

The changes inspired an endemic alienation, part and parcel of the process of self-selection that led people to the inherent powerlessness of neonative status in a community dependent on cheap labor and outside dollars. The greatest advantage to living in a resort town and being underemployed was the time when there were few visitors. Successful year-round tourism brought that to an end. Bring Back Off-Season read the bumper stickers on cars in Jackson with Teton County license plates and on the never-ending line of vehicles headed downvalley each afternoon from Aspen. Bring Back Slack became the slogan in Sun Valley.[8] No longer did the window of time in which locals took possession of their town exist; nor did the people who sacrificed because they believed in the ideal of the place have the moment when the town again belonged to them. Instead a constant stream of visitors and the need to cater to second-home owners and the resident rich made people who believed that their choices were choices into full-time wage slaves.

Some made compromises to stay; many others, idealistic but now older, fled for places where they could earn a living and maintain their dignity. Remarkably, the ski bum, the devoted enthusiast icon of the early ski industry, all but disappeared. Those who remained in changing communities worked long days and had little time left for skiing, increasingly priced beyond their economic reach. The demography of resorts changed dramatically as corporate control accentuated new sets of priorities and these changes inspired an endemic alienation.

John Rember has best captured the character of the "Post-Ironic Recreational West," as he calls it, with its substitution of wealth for human spirit and narcissism for human relationships. Writing of the fictional town of Gomorrah in the shadow of Mount Mammon, a thinly disguised version of Sun Valley, Rember chronicles refugees from life who seek solace in hedonism and meaning in the most bleak of gestures. Consumed by their search for humanity, they represent the social and ultimately the personal powerlessness of people who cannot muster the energy to defend what they find meaningful. Extensions of activists such as Dorice Taylor, who could fight back and negotiate accommodation, Rember's protagonists, the fictional cheerleaders from Gomorrah in the Lycra Archipelago, drift along from meaningless pleasure to subsequent encounter.[9]

The corporations that owned most resorts were not sorry to see powerful local figures acquiesce or depart. From Bill Janss to Darcy Brown, industry leaders had done their utmost to marginalize vocal elements concerned with local culture and values that were not part of their bottom line. Brown typically ran roughshod over his opponents; Janss turned them into quaint anachronisms since such neonatives were a genuine threat to the hegemony upon which corporate owners insisted. Educated and concerned, these leaders embraced their investment in the place and routinely challenged the dominance of corporations. Their acquiescence, abdication, or departure contributed to the transience of the community, depriving it of familiar leadership and continuity and also creating a shortage of labor. Myles Rademan, the experienced planner and the director of public affairs in Park Ciy, Utah, widely known as the Prophet of Boom, attributed the absence of leadership to a combination of the massive growth in the ski and resort industries, the departure of older ski bums, and the unwillingness of the so-called Generation Xers to fill the gaps. In 1994 more than 6,000 tourist jobs remained unfilled in five Colorado ski counties. The departing neonatives were replaced with foreign workers, sometimes illegal, from Central America, Mexico, and in some instances, Africa, who performed as corporate leaders thought resort menials should. They worked long hard hours for low wages and were far less likely to complain than American workers. One American business owner explained his preference for Mexican workers succinctly: "Most Americans are lazy. . . . That's why we hire Mexicans."[10]

The growing predominance of Hispanic workers in resort communities became a public issue the week before Labor Day, 1996, when federal agents and local police raided Jackson, Wyoming, and arrested over 150 undocumented workers. Of these, two were from England and the rest Hispanic and overwhelmingly Mexican. Authorities estimated that the arrestees represented about 15 percent of Jackson's Hispanic population of around 1,000; the next day more than 120 were deported to Mexico. One worker rode handcuffed all the way to Mexico in a bus, spent a few hours in a Ciudad Juarez jail, got in a car with some friends, headed for the Arizona border, and made his way back to Jackson. Within one week of the police raid, all but four of the arrested workers, including those deported, were back on the job.[11]

The situation in Jackson illustrated the dependence of resorts on Hispanic labor. Restaurants closed for lack of kitchen help, motel owners made their own beds, and the laundry services were so short-staffed that owners worked sixteen-hour days. One disgruntled hotelier called Jackson's chief of police and asked him if the police intended to help him make the beds. The disappearance of the ski bums, the middle- and upper-middle-class white college-age students who had been the stalwarts of the ski industry since the 1950s, made Hispano labor into the backbone of the industry. For Mexican workers, the conditions that Americans disdained were often appealing. Accustomed to wages of two to three dollars per day at home, the six dollar per hour of the resort industry offered a pathway to a better life.[12] As in agribusiness, the needs of the resort industry and those of the workers coincided, making the work of law enforcement officials futile and often foolish in the face of the enormous power of tourism and a general willingness in that industry to ignore American labor law.

Another side to the story existed, best expressed by officials with broad views of social change. As Jackson police chief David Cameron explained,

Tourism in the 1990s came to rely on illegal workers. This sweep of Hispanic workers in Jackson, Wyoming, paralyzed the tourist trade. (Photo courtesy of Angus Thuermer Jr.)

people who hired illegal workers competed unfairly. They paid a lower wage, depressing the local wage scale. Illegal workers accepted that wage, contributing to the depressed scale. They also made it harder for legal residents to find affordable housing, contributing to the social stratification that in resort towns increasingly was manifested in the perception of Hispanic workers as criminals. The workers contributed only to their own welfare and to the bottom lines of corporations, but their presence set in motion a range of social accommodations for which they did not pay and to which they were not entitled under law.[13] In this view, illegal workers were a stop-gap, a short-term solution with many long-term ramifications that no one assessed.

This increasingly Hispanic labor force served an overwhelmingly white constituency, introducing race and reintroducing a dimension of class into tourism that had been in abeyance since the days of fin de siècle tourism and almost totally absent as tourism became democratized during the post–World War II era. Some resort towns suggested South Africa before the end of apartheid, with white visitors and guests and nonwhite behind-the-scenes workers. Even in Santa Fe, with a strong claim as the multicultural capital of the nation, race and class lines were clear. Hispanos worked in the shops, Indians sold jewelry in front of the Palace of the Governors on the plaza, and the shoppers were overwhelmingly white. During a four-day, summer 1994 stay in Aspen, an observer saw only two African Americans who were not working, one a recognizable celebrity, and no Hispanics except in restaurant kitchens, laundry rooms, and behind clean-up carts. The jugglers and street-corner performers, even those who played rap music as background, were white, as were the shoppers who sported license plates from around the country. Public Aspen was white, not by mechanisms of racism but by cultural values. Behind-the-scenes Aspen, in its demography, skin color, and the expectations of its workforce, increasingly resembled a colonial outpost of the nineteenth century.

Las Vegas transcended that class-based whiteness; here there was room for everyone. Casinos had a peculiar effect on people. They created a shared space that came from the expectations of visitors. To some players, the "something-for-nothing" crowd, the casino held the answer, the chance of a lifetime. Along with the traffic jam, which ground a Mercedes to a halt as it did a GEO Storm, the casino stood as one of the few remaining egalitarian features in American life. Everyone was on the same side there; everyone's values were parallel. No matter who people were or what they looked like, everyone in a casino celebrated the attention-grabbing clang of coins into a slot machine tray. Someone else's victory only anticipated your own.

Concerned predominantly with the bottom line, corporations elsewhere encouraged these new dimensions of class and race, showing little sense of the loss of integrity or identity of the place they now owned. Not only did the situation weaken local opposition to corporate goals, but it also furthered the increasingly exclusive image of resorts. In effect resort communities built on an idea that had characterized 1960s Las Vegas; they offered a middle-class constituency a luxury experience, enhanced by the curious who came to such towns to catch a glimpse of celebrities. The more labor became extra-local and foreign, the easier it became to maintain the illusion of exclusivity at a more profitable bottom line.

Indian vendors selling goods to tourists under the restored facade of the Palace of the Governors during the 1950s. (Photo by Tyler Dingee, courtesy of Museum of New Mexico.)

A pattern of cultural homogenization seemed to occur hand-in-hand with the development of economically successful tourism. Places such as Aspen, Santa Fe, Jackson, and especially Steamboat Springs revealed regional variation. They possessed specific ways of life and even language and expressions that were native to their area. With small-scale tourism, those variations persisted. As tourism grew and became attractive to outside corporations and innumerable visitors, the differences in the communities were shaved off in pursuit of the widest popularity. Places that looked the same but felt different became common; they also inspired local and neonative resentment and response.

As in all contentious places, the local response to efforts to homogenize these communities not only racially but also culturally and economically was complex. As had happened in each change of ownership or identity, some neonatives acquiesced in the changes, believing that this particular tide would raise their fortunes. Others felt resistance to change was futile, and still others simply did not identify with any sense of "the way things ought to be" enough to care. By the 1980s corporate control was so complete in places such as Sun Valley and Vail that many of the earlier generations of neonatives lost their standing as dissenters in any viable way. Older, tired, and increasingly outnumbered by a docile foreign workforce, by younger corporate managers who could see only dollar signs in the resort, and by the transient wealthy, many neonatives simply stepped back from public life.

For different reasons the same situation resulted in less thoroughly organized places such as Santa Fe, Jackson, and Steamboat Springs. Throughout the 1980s and 1990s similar issues arose in response to growth and change. The intrusions on the historic character of Santa Fe—from the construction of the immense El Pueblo Grande Hotel built by New York developer William Zeckendorf that overshadowed downtown to the rapid growth of the area—pitted Anglo American neonatives against other Anglo Americans against the backdrop of Hispano and Indian culture. The success of Santa Fe's artist community made southwestern style fashionable in food, clothing, furniture, and architecture. National developers followed closely behind. In Jackson, the transfer of the ski resort reflected the increased interest of the superrich, which was further heightened by the technology of the snowmobile. Even Steamboat Springs fought internal battles over growth that pitted the owners of the resort against the community in its effort to avoid the constellation of social, spatial, and environmental problems that its residents called Aspenization.[14]

Aspen itself became the outstanding exception in resisting the dislocating cultural invasion of new money. It was wealthier than most similar towns, and its history of community activism, though not strong enough to prevent corporate and then superrich takeover, was sufficiently durable to resist it in myriad ways. Aspenites were bemused more than impressed with the celebrities among them, and many residents professed embarrassment at what their town had become. Only Steamboat Springs, always at variance with typical ski towns because of its history as "the town that skied," joined Aspen in organized resistance to growth through political, legal, and social channels. In Sun Valley, Jackson, Telluride, and other places, the resistance was individual, episodic, somewhat haphazard, and closely involved with self-identification rituals, strategies that typically did not lead to significant results.

The rapid growth throughout the region did little to help people who engaged in the ongoing negotiation with power that marked the transformation of tourist communities. The rich and, as the ability to telecommute increased, the upper-middle class came in growing numbers, smothering local voices and changing not only the demography of communities but also their physical layout, iconography, and identity. Communities such as Park City, Utah, home of journalist Raye Ringholz, "a little more than a V-slash in the mountains" in 1974, doubled in population and doubled again, spreading the tentacles of subdivisions outward from the old community core toward the once-distant interstate highway. "Even the country roads were being widened," Ringholz lamented, "to accommodate roaring traffic." The downtown became the province of tourists in such places, with locals relegated to the physical peripheries in a version of what visionary urban theorist Joel Garreau has called "edge cities."[15]

Nowhere was this change more evident than in Santa Fe, where the downtown and the east side, the area north and east of the state capital, underwent an ethnic transformation. Hispano families, many of whom traced their roots to the *reconquista* and before and who lived in multigenerational units divided among two or three houses within one walled compound, historically dominated this area, at least into the 1960s. Anglos typically lived west of the plaza and south of the state capital in the anomalous Victorian-style homes they constructed before the 1920s, when artists' colonies spread to Canyon Road to the southeast of the plaza and significant numbers of Anglos embraced the Pueblo Revival ethic. Then, as the town became first a destination resort for oil-rich Texans and later for Californians and New Yorkers who came to experience the mystique of the desert, these Hispano properties were targeted by newcomers who desperately wanted to belong to this self-styled multicultural oasis. Tempted by the large sums offered them for old family compounds, local Hispanos took the money and moved to the west side of town, where they participated in the greatest faux adobe construction in history. There, street after street of adobe-style concrete block structures covered with chicken wire, sprayed with styrofoam, and painted brown, tan, or peach so as to keep the entire city in compliance with the restrictive code that became law in 1957 sprouted and multiplied. A new Santa Fe, tied to mainstream American popular culture by television, popular music, film, and other mass media, came to fruition, represented with the opening of the Villa Linda shopping mall far south of the Plaza near Interstate 25 in 1985.

An entirely new shopping district for the locals who could no longer find what they needed on the historic plaza suggested that Santa Fe had become two different towns, one Anglo and New Age, enthralled with the overlay of historic Indian and Hispano culture, the other predominantly Hispano, embracing the material opportunities of middle-class American life. Newcomers craved authentic culture, and the people who seemingly possessed it were glad to relinquish it for a place in the American amalgamation.

In Santa Fe, where the availability of land created ethnically segregated but proximate suburbs, the appearance of the newest generation of neonatives altered only the community; in the small mountain towns of the ski industry and in places such as Jackson, the consequences were greater. Land was at a premium in such communities, so much so that "teardowns," homes purchased so that the new owners could bulldoze existing structures and replace them with custom-designed homes, typified Aspen and other resort communities. Teardowns also represented a cultural shift from embracing the values of the town as it existed, from dress to architecture, and toward a redefinition of the place in the terms of the two coasts that drove American culture. Extant homes no longer conveyed cachet in the minds of the wealthy. Instead their location was the currency of the local real estate market. Home construction changed dramatically, as more homes of extraordinary size, wryly labeled "starter castles," graced the greater Aspen skyline. In response to an epidemic of 20,000-square-foot and larger homes, Aspen limited the size of new home construction to 15,000 square feet, easily a palace anywhere in the country. Still, some people chafed. One enterprising individual defied the ban by putting 15,000 square feet above ground over a basement of more than 10,000 square feet.

Decisions such as the ban on jumbo homes created a kind of stratification among the most recent residents of the town who were culturally and economically similar. The size of a wealthy person's new home offered a de facto identity, a link to the time of arrival. For the wealthy who could afford monster trophy homes but could not build them because of legal restrictions, the law marked them as new arrivals among their neonative peers. The passage of the ordinance became a demarcation line in longevity in Aspen, much as the markers on the town rugby field did for previous generations. More than ever, first in time meant first in right and conveyed the privilege of an authoritative voice in local affairs.

Aspen split along two lines, one defined by politics and power and the other by money. Those who held power in politics typically had arrived in the 1960s and 1970s and were determined to create a small-town normalcy through ordinance and law. Those who arrived later and had primarily second homes there used their money to address the problems a sometimes rigid governmental structure presented them. In some ways, the situation reprised the traits of the old tourist town, where locals kept the place in a way that visitors loved. In this formulation, locals made sure that Aspen remained a place that second-home owners could love even if, from time to time, it impinged on their personal pronouncements of status and wealth.

For the newest wave of neonatives, sacrificing even the slightest prerogative of wealth gave them, in their own view, standing in the community.

The consequence of the competition for space reverberated throughout the mountain West. Unlike in Santa Fe, where an entirely new community sprang up adjacent to the tourist town, the mountain towns lacked cheap and easily available space as a pressure valve; the attraction of the superrich put a premium on any existing space, and real estate values continued to soar in an essentially thirty-year rise. Wealthy families bought existing space, and hotel developers also added pressure on the local housing market. The old Aspen was a state of mind; people in psychic Aspen lived throughout the valley as temporal Aspen became an exclusive suburb that unwillingly grandfathered in a few preexisting anachronisms. As the price and the property taxes of Aspen increased, fewer neonatives and locals could afford to stay. As a result, workers almost uniformly lived elsewhere, and commuting became a necessity. The symbol of this daily movement was the endless line of traffic headed downvalley toward Glenwood Springs on Highway 82 from Aspen each afternoon, and it illustrated the class structure of Aspen. The exorbitant cost of housing forced not only workers but much of the middle class from the town. Long-distance winter commuters, who in 1985 included the director of the Aspen Chamber of Commerce, Carol Kiesinger, dotted the highways of Colorado, driving long distances across snow- and ice-covered roads to work in service jobs with limited pay and little chance for advancement.

Even service professionals could not afford the cost of resort communities. In 1995 thirty-nine of Vail's forty-eight-person police and fire departments could not afford to live in the town. The consequences of winter commuting were sometimes tragic. An accountant for the Mellow Yellow taxi company in Aspen was seriously injured during a winter commute in the later 1980s, a service worker who later became a reporter for the *High Country News* was injured in another accident, and accidents that resulted from fatigue or impossible driving conditions became a common feature in the local news. Highway 82 acquired the moniker Killer 82. One satirical songwriter became a local celebrity with a song, the "Downvalley Shuffle," that chronicled the predicament of Aspen's commuters. In Sun Valley, commuters came from as far away as the Sawtooth Mountains, seventy-five miles distant, to work each day. Even transplants such as the French waiter from a restaurant in Los Angeles, whom John Rember met at a new Sun Valley area restaurant where the chamber of commerce wanted the reporters it hosted to eat, lived elsewhere. In Jackson, first Wilson and then other nearby towns were colonized by people who could no longer afford to live in Jackson and

Trailers of Aspen and Vail workers in Peach Valley, Colorado. These people do the downvalley shuffle every day. (Photo courtesy of Andrew Gulliford.)

by those who could but just wanted to get away. Within a few years after Jackson became chic, people commuted from as far away as Driggs, Idaho, seventy-six miles over a mountain pass through the snow and ice of the northern Rockies. The regional situation had become "basic serfdom," one Aspen area motel manager observed.[16]

The structure of commuting revealed a dimension of race and class. By the late 1980s the number of ski bums decreased as working conditions worsened, and a growing segment of the people who did menial work were nonwhite and Spanish-speaking. In the mid-1990s African and Filipino workers were prevalent, sometimes living in rare but crowded quarters or in trailer park ghettos in Aspen but, like Hispanics, generally living downvalley. Their jobs were essential; without cooks, maids, catering workers, busboys, janitors, and other behind-the-scenes workers, the resort could not exist. As with most temporary labor, such employment, typically in the six-to-seven-dollar per hour range, was too low to allow workers to live in Aspen. Nonwhite workers constituted a disproportionate percentage of the commuters. The community remained overwhelmingly white, as it had been in the 1930s. Then its sole black residents had been Hannibal Brown and his wife Willie Mae, noted for their Hudson automobile, his dabbling in the bootlegging business, and his general conviviality.[17]

For workers who lived in the resort community, conditions were bad. Crowded condos and trailer park ghettos housed most local service workers, highlighting the class distinction. During the 1994–1995 winter, one twenty-three-year-old Anglo worker slept under a bridge; he could not afford an apartment on the $8.75 per hour salary he received for driving a bus. Later he and a friend moved into a van that they kept underground in the lower level of the town's parking garage in an area reserved for maintenance. It was the only place they could find where they were not "hassled." As a cabbie in the late 1980s, Ted Conover knew the four or five condos where Mexicans lived in Aspen; every couple of days, a young Mexican man would hop into his cab about 3:00 A.M. for a ride home after working two shifts. Another Hispanic, Pedro Lopez, became an entrepreneur by saving money to buy the beat-up mobile home where he lived in Avon, near Vail, and renting space in it to seven other workers. The men slept and worked in staggered shifts. But even though Lopez owned the trailer, Vail Associates bought the land underneath it and planned a development. The residents of the trailer park were able to wrangle a $4,000 per household compensation package, but the purchase meant that many of them had to tow their trailers more than forty miles to the Leadville area, a place a newspaper reporter called the "working-class side of the high [mountain] passes," and become commuters.[18]

Although Hispanic and sometimes African workers were often men alone, living as cheaply as possible and sending money home, Anglo American families who worked in the service industry faced working poverty. At the bottom of the skills ladder, employment remained seasonal, typically six months on, six months off, and generally lacked benefits. Nor were amenities such as day care available at affordable prices. For people from the region, with extended networks upon which to rely, family support helped address child care and other issues. For others without local or regional roots, the work scene remained more problematic. Many workers seemed one step away from economic collapse; without benefits, any personal, familial, or other catastrophe meant certain impoverishment. One thirty-four-year-old mother began the 1994–1995 ski season living in a tent with her three children, one a seven-month-old baby, on national forest land. Another who had begun working at the age of twelve lamented that she had never had a childhood.[19] The glint of the sun off the immense picture windows of expensive vacation homes with their exquisite views, managed by a caretaker and lived in typically six weeks each year, exacerbated the grind of poverty.

Although by the early 1990s regional newspapers such as the *High Country News* championed the cause of workers, the rising value of each square inch of land in places such as Aspen suggested that the problem of limited space and unlimited popularity had yet to be solved. Too many people wanted to be part of places like Aspen and Jackson, more than their geography could hold in any comfortable way. A competition for living space resulted, with costs rising perennially and exorbitantly. The situation forced a two-tiered society, workers commuting or living in meager and crowded quarters in town and the wealthy and guests staying in the expensive comfort that marked the resort experience. Once again, the hallmark of tourist towns was clear; they served their guests well ahead of their residents.

Corporate control also changed the demography of labor in the mountain towns. Downsizing took place in the resort industry long before the term became fashionable. In the 1970s and 1980s, in a move that presaged a similar late 1980s shift in the corporate world, ski resorts across the West expanded their services to meet the growing demand and, instead of hiring permanent employees, used temporary labor to fill even midlevel managerial positions. This move helped the bottom line but cut into the special feel of ski resorts. Visitors dealt with a seasonal employee at the counter, as the counterperson's supervisor, and often in the manager's office. An evident decline in the caliber of service followed since even in managerial positions, employees had little investment in their jobs. As in corporate Las Vegas, people complained of the decline in service and lamented the loss, not only nostalgically but also as a claim on the standing that a long personal history there conveyed.

In places such as Durango, Colorado, in the midst of the move toward a tourist-dominated economy, these new practices altered the character of the regional economy and the demography of the region. Durango endured a series of temporarily or marginally successful economies, the most recent of which, the development of energy resources, came during the 1940s and 1950s. After their demise, the area faced long-term recession and economic irrelevance. Marketing itself offered a time-honored and potentially lucrative way to cast off economic blues, and with nearby Mesa Verde National Park little more than one-half hour's drive to the west, Durango possessed the ingredients to be a stop on the summer excursion route for vacationers. In 1954 the town's chamber of commerce summarized its growing promotional sentiment with its jingle, "Come to play, you'll want to stay."[20]

By 1965 tourism emerged as the replacement for extractive natural resource industries in the Durango area. Summer activities played an important role, especially after the opening of the narrow gauge railway to Silverton, but the future was in winter recreation. The expansion of the lodge at the nearby Purgatory ski area in 1969 set off a minirush to Durango. In 1971 and

1972 the number of lift tickets sold there nearly doubled the 39,666 of 1968–1969. Before 1988 the ski area had become the leading employer in the area. Even the summer resort, Tamarron, employed a larger staff than the local school district. Fun-seeking students attracted to local Ft. Lewis College by the opportunity to ski 120 days a year made up an important segment of the workforce. They also nearly tripled enrollment at the college in a fifteen-year period.[21]

As skiing transformed communities in the 1980s, these principles of growth held. Telluride in southwestern Colorado succeeded with an all-year program that combined skiing in the winter with bluegrass and film festivals in the summers. A mining town that peaked early in the century and faced its demise a number of times in the 1950s and 1960s, Telluride was reinvented as a remote counterculture neoresort where skiing was a right instead of a privilege. By the mid-1970s, it had become a haven for people who avoided what they perceived as the excesses of modernity; such were the founders of the Free Box. Telluride's existing slopes were too easy or too difficult for the intermediate skiers who made up the most profitable segment of the ski industry, and the nearest airport was over a ninety-minute drive away in Montrose. Remote location sheltered Telluride's culture.

The community remained isolated until 1985, when the Telluride Regional Airport opened. Easy air access created rapid transformation, including the construction of the new, upscale $75 million Doral Telluride Resort and Spa and a steep increase in the cost of local property. A consistent lament from longtime residents that the changes were for the worse followed. The influx of wealth threatened the sense of community that Telluride had cultivated; some of the newcomers even complained that the Free Box had become, in the words of journalist Deborah Frazier, "an unsightly downtown dump" in a town thirty miles from a conventional dump and more than fifty from the nearest Salvation Army or Goodwill operation. Telluride cemented its fashionable status in 1989, when actors Tom Cruise and Nicole Kidman picked it as the location for their marriage, and the community aspired to become the new Aspen for those who missed the old one. Labeled an "Upper West Side [of Manhattan Island] with ski lifts," Telluride became a first-class resort, its access and celebrity bestowing the advantages and disadvantages of the presence of international jet setters and celebrities and the lack of places for local service workers to live.[22]

The new resorts faced a series of constraints that their predecessors had not. Celebrities packed the initial opening at Sun Valley because there was no comparable place, but with the rise of Aspen and the subsequent resorts that challenged for iconographical supremacy, the terrain was ever after contested. In that ongoing striving for preeminence, certain traits and especially certain people contributed to the sense that a place was special. The salmon had to be the freshest, the caviar, champagne, and cocaine the most exquisite, the models the most tantalizing, the people the most wealthy and famous. In their efforts, resorts spared no expense in offering their guests the best. This opulence came at the cost of a sense of community that included workers and contributed mightily to growing class distinctions. People who worked in the industry and played at the resort in their spare time and those who stayed as guests or second-home residents embraced different values that never interacted.

As the transition to a temporary workforce grew pronounced, one casualty was an icon of the slopes, the ski bum. Since the late 1940s ski bums had decorated ski resorts and become a backbone of the industry. Unlike the local people displaced by skiing, these beneficiaries of the affluence of American society selected this experience as a second career or as an interlude in their lives. Often they were between college and graduate school or their first job, exploring life for the first time. As outsiders they brought capital and attitudes that locals and even neonatives did not share, and they limited the upward mobility of local people who depended on the ski industry for their livelihood. They also added a kind of zest for life to ski resorts that became an important part of the oeuvre of ski towns.[23]

Ski bums, once essential to the industry, nearly disappeared under corporate control. Some selected other options in a changing cultural climate, once the ski towns lost some of their charm and the bottom line became the dominant local goal. But the new practices of the corporate leaders, the minuscule wages, and the increasing cost of living made a year as a ski bum a chore instead of a pleasurable respite from ordinary life. The work conditions worsened under corporate ownership and camaraderie diminished. As the cost of living rose exorbitantly in nearly every ski community, even the long-term ski bums, the adult professional ski workers who served as an alternative icon for younger aspirants in the manner that a real hobo did for displaced young during the Great Depression, left in disgust. Their replacements felt temporary; they did not belong to the places they worked. Ted Conover described the sense of alienation from living in a town devoted to other people's fun. As he bent over the frozen fender to check the oil on the cab he drove on the night shift, "The snow fell. The wind blew. Gusts from over the frozen hedge carried the sounds of people having fun and the smell of a hot tub. Young men made jokes and young women laughed; all I could see over the hedge was steam rising through a spotlight. But I could imagine them, naked, surrounded by bubbles, perspiration, warm except for the wind on their faces and the beer in their hands." Their frisbee got away from them. "Hey bro'!" one shouted. "Can you toss us the Frisbee?" As Conover stood blowing on his hands in an effort to warm them from the touch of the cold metal, he considered his options. The line was clear: "Young white people, on vacation. You worked for them, and were best off to remember it."[24]

Although the alienation was consistent, individuals handled it in different ways. Jackson resident Tim Sandlin, whose writing reflected the nature of self-definition rituals in communities that lacked organized resistance to growth and change, used his fictional Pyms to satirize the Teton Valley's journey through various incarnations of tourist development. His characters decry the replacement of business that served locals in the downtown area with trendy shops that cater to tourists. "Jackson hasn't been a hometown kind of place since Benson closed the hardware store," one character announces in the midst of an argument over who has the longest and most authentic claim on being a real local. Echoing the eternal tourist town refrain that nothing is the way it used to be, the story accentuates the way change alters meaning for local residents who, by choice or design, remain outside the local power structure. When ritual is most clearly depicted in the work of local writers, it suggests shortcomings in resistance and negotiation with the forces of change.[25]

John Rember ponders the consequences of skiing: "Just as the West is covered by piles of mined-out and slightly toxic tailings, might it not someday be covered by Sun Valleyed valleys, notable for their floodplains packed full of Gothic-rustic mansions and log-walled K-Marts? Senile real estate agents will tell tales of open fields and empty highways and of a time before snowmaking, when a drought could delay the natural course of urban development three, four, even five years."[26] Rember's combination of poignancy and irony provides a whimsical version of a typical response. The optimism and ebullience of resort communities had become a relic, replaced by professional serving classes and people who loved their place but hated what it had become.

Tourist-based transformation drove wedges into communities; some benefited, others were hurt, and hardly any relationships, either among residents or with the place, remained the same. The feel of communities changed. Struthers Burt's Jackson Hole was a charming place, peopled by elegant easterners and taciturn but warm cowboys. Even Donald Hough in his paean to alcohol describes a heavy-drinking town where people remain in control; they use alcohol to cushion themselves against the elements, not against each other. The protagonist of J. Royal Horton's *Murder in Jackson Hole,* local sheriff's deputy Tommy Thompson, is an alcoholic struggling to stay sober with the help of Alcoholics Anonymous. Set in the 1990s, the novel shows a community of alcoholics or recovering alcoholics who drink to help them deal with the changes that surround them. Locals have lost their place in Horton's Jackson, replaced by wealthy outsiders.[27] What was once their respite has become personal affliction. The transition from elegance to conviviality to alcoholism suggests the transformation of resort communities from the perspective of the people who lived there. They were trapped in a world they could not control and in which they had little say.

The communities devising the most successful strategies to address the changes that tourism and its attendant growth brought were Steamboat Springs and Aspen, bipolar opposites that shared a rock-solid core for different reasons. At its heart, Steamboat Springs was a real place where people lived, a town that had a history, an identity, and a clear sense of its purpose. With its huge mountain strawberries among its unique features of the early twentieth century, Steamboat Springs understood how it differed from places that lacked a multigenerational resident population. As late as 1960, natives of Steamboat Springs remained among the best skiers in the world. Here was a town that embraced skiing as its local sport. Unlike Vail, it had not begun as a sheep ranch that catered to the upper-middle class. Even the Steamboat Mountain resort just outside town could not impinge on its identity; Steamboat was a local's town where the residents were generous enough to share with visitors.

Steamboat residents fought hard to maintain the qualities they regarded as special, and in the mid-1990s it still retained a sense of being distinct. There were few of the fancy hotels and pretensions that seemed so common elsewhere, few of the chains that signified tourist chic. It was as if there were two Steamboats, the town and the other, the resort mountain. Visitors to the resort stayed there except for nightlife and occasional jaunts to town; visitors to town went to the resort only to ski. Many more were cross-country ski enthusiasts who needed no mountain; others were content to use Howelsen Hill, abutting the town to the south. The community invested heavily in studies that were designed to show its leaders how to prevent Aspenization, and a valiant local effort brought a planned ski and summer development called Lake Catamount to a grinding halt in June 1995.[28] Steamboat compromised in certain ways, but its core, the legacy of people such as skiing champion Buddy Werner, remained intact.

Aspen's resilience came from its first and second generations of neo-natives, the people who arrived during Paepcke's time and those who followed soon after. Many of them possessed an activist background and an interest, if not in history, in politics. They used local power, alliances formed over two decades, and the experiences of local campaigns such as Hunter S. Thompson's run for sheriff as they battled the influx of the rich and superrich. When they grasped the levers of power, they possessed the skill, opportunity, and ideology to use government to achieve their ends. It was an odd position for these veterans of the 1960s, a strange legacy for people who once wholeheartedly fought the system.[29]

Opponents of growth did much to slow the encroachment of the superrich in Aspen, only to find that they had closed the door too late. This treehouse effect, or pulling up the ladder after climbing up, meant that the loudest proponents of slow or no growth were the recent arrivals. Antigrowth forces also grandfathered an element of the superrich into their community; the rules they passed were typically reactive, not proactive, and were responses to actions already taken and to on-the-ground realities. The result was a flawed defense so that any savvy entrepreneur could get around the rules.

Yet another backlash against tourism and neonative economic dominance emerged in Santa Fe. After more than two decades of turmoil associated with growth, Santa Feans elected Hispana Debbie Jaramillo as mayor in a divisive 1994 campaign that saw a record voter turnout of 59 percent, which carried her to victory by a plurality. In her six years on the city council, Jaramillo established a track record in supporting the idea that growth should be connected to opportunity for longtime residents. "My victory meant so much to the *viejos* [old ones or elders]," Jaramillo commented. "They have watched the town they love slowly disintegrate from greed and misuse of power. Some of them had given up hope." The business community, thriving on "inflated real estate, resort hotels, and coyote kitsch," as *High Country News* reporter Bruce Selcraig characterized it, regarded her election as a disaster. They blamed her policies for a cyclical falloff in tourism that paralleled her first two years in office. Empty tables at fancy restaurants and shuttered stores on the plaza, where rents rivaled the ninety dollar per square foot that typified Manhattan, illustrated the problems. A fifty-merchant indoor market, the Santa Fe Mercado, closed in summer 1995. In the first half of that year, real estate sales fell 35 percent from the same period in 1994, the upper end of market homes, between $300,000 and $750,000, becoming the slowest segment of the market. The hotel and motel occupancy rate fell from 87 percent to about 82 percent, exacerbated by the opening of as many as 1,000 rooms at about seventy dollars per night, nearly half the average room rate in town. Although Santa Fe had experienced similar downturns in the past, the most recent in the mid-1980s, Jaramillo's outspoken manner made her a likely target. She advocated taking Santa Fe to the world instead of bringing the world to Santa Fe, a strategy that involved exporting Santa Fe products rather than enticing visitors. Implementing this idea meant a change in the way Santa Fe operated since the turn of the century.[30]

Jaramillo's indifference and at times outright hostility to tourism and the inequality it bred sparked much opposition. Newspapers quoted her as saying that she would not be "pitching tacos on Kathie Lee," a reference to the promotional strategy of her predecessor, Sam Pick. In an act that angered both Art Bouffard, the director of the New Mexico Hotel and Motel Association, and Don Baxter, the director of the Santa Fe Lodgers Association, Jaramillo refused to spend $1.2 million from the city's lodger tax on tourism promotion. "Santa Fe is a community, not a playground," she remarked in response to criticism. Nor was Jaramillo willing to play the typical role in colonized tourist towns and cater to newcomers. "They bring their culture, their values, and we are supposed to assimilate," she once remarked. "That has got to change." With a strong focus on community and on what Wallace Stegner once called "stickers," Jaramillo tried to move Santa Fe away from its traditional reliance on tourism and state government and toward a more interactive economic and social model that included affordable housing, education, job training, and a range of other programs designed to put the longtime community's interests ahead of visitors and the business community dependent upon them. As 1996 ended, Jaramillo's tenure remained stormy and her prospects for reelection uncertain.[31] Challenging the power of tourist economies was not easy, even in places with other powerful economic forces and with extant communities that received little of tourism's benefits.

Jaramillo's objections to tourism illustrated two of its major problems: the way it pinched local life and the impact of outside wealth on the functioning of a community. Baxter and Bouffard advocated expanding the base for tourism in Santa Fe by recruiting the middle class or by seeking out wealthy Canadians and Japanese, but Jaramillo stood by her convictions. "We can remain popular by being ourselves," she noted, highlighting one of the recurrent devil's bargains of tourism. By being itself, Santa Fe reached the limits of its market; only if it embraced malleability could that market grow. But malleability meant offering modern visitors what they wanted to see, not hewing to the historic overlay that had generated Santa Fe's appeal. Although observers argued that Santa Fe had long since assumed malleability, Jaramillo recognized that the core of the city she knew as a child was threatened by the unceasing growth of tourism and by pandering to the taste of audiences who defined that growth. She entered at some point on a continuum, but that point had tremendous significance to her and to her generation. To someone from an earlier time, Jaramillo's resistance could easily seem to exemplify closing the barnyard gate long after the animals departed. But for many people in modern Santa Fe, Jaramillo stood vigil to ensure the viability of the traditions of their city.

From a financial perspective, the progrowth forces made considerable sense. Since the 1920s tourism had been the driving force in Santa Fe's economy. It had taken on many forms, beginning with the artists' colony symbolized by Mary Austin's *La Casa Querida* and later including a broadening swath of the American public. From the point of view of the managers of tourism, responding to changing trends was critical. If Santa Fe remained as it had been, its base audience would reflect that. If it stayed where it was, then in the world driven by popular culture, its hipness would disappear, and with it, the dollars that supported the city's growth.

Jaramillo correctly noted evident consequences of tourism. The disfranchisement of Santa Fe's middle class, hastened by their move to the west side and by a growing resentment of the privileged, meant that the town's demography increasingly mirrored that of places such as Aspen and Sun Valley. Santa Fe was on the road to becoming a place where the wealthy and the people who served them lived among the stream of visitors, all of whom, it often seemed, wanted to make the town their home. The old model of the Santa Fe neonative, the Texans who had once been "poor, poor, poor, poor, poor," as one old dowager maintained, but who had made their money with the discovery of oil, was supplanted by coastal people from New York or Los Angeles or by Europeans, who did not come to absorb the special essence of Santa Fe but to remake the town into a place that reflected their values.

Santa Fe's desirability drove the prices of real estate so high that few natives of the community could stay. Housing became so expensive—in winter 1996 a three-bedroom, three-bath, 2,635-square-foot adobe house had been marked down $90,000 to $345,000—that only people with resources from elsewhere could buy there. Civil servants, children who had grown up in town, married, and wanted to stay, and the rest of Santa Fe's middle class simply could not afford the town. In 1994 the median home price reached $200,000; the average annual wage remained at about $16,000. "Our children face a future of waiting on tables and cleaning toilets," Jaramillo noted. "They won't be able to live here." Locals were being forced out, replaced by outside money and people who were willing to be underemployed, indeed poor, to live in Santa Fe. The stratification also spread to the Anglo world. "I'm not sure I can name one person in town who has a liveable-wage job with a promising career track in front of them," observed city council member and Green Party activist Cris Moore in 1996. Typical hotel industry wages ran between five and eight dollars per hour, yet according to data compiled by the Hotel Employees and Restaurant Employees International Union, who sought to organize labor in Santa Fe, $12.60 per hour was the minimum living wage in the region. Nor was advancement possible for a maid. The middle sector of the local economy was missing.[32] Santa Fe was well on its way to a stratified profile in which only the rich and the poor lived in town. Jaramillo correctly recognized that such a profile would have a tremendous impact on the community she called home.

Ultimately, tourism in the American West and in the world manifests the changes in the boundaries of human experience. Travelers became tourists when they could travel and experience on the terms of their own culture or their own niche within their culture, when they had to make a conscious choice and a concerted effort to shed the advantages of the world from which they came, the world that provided the wealth and leisure time to make their travel possible. In the twentieth century, tourism turned into a bona fide industry in the same manner as did advertising. Tourism became pervasive because growing numbers of people possessed the wealth and time to travel and because that travel acquired significance and cachet in most cultures. Tourist travel helped people define themselves as special—as experienced, as knowledgeable, as adventurous, as wealthy, and in myriad other ways. Its growth also resulted from technological innovations, the very grouping of phenomena that led Marshall McLuhan to label the world a "global village." Not only did technological advancement allow people to be aware of more places, it also permitted them to reach them. The ability to see and to experience brought a kind of superiority. The extent of their travel and tourism measured their status in the modern and postmodern world. The experiences contained within, often defined by the context of amenity that surrounded them, became the prize.

This form of consumption, acquiring the intangible of experience, became emblematic of American society. Possessing ceased to be sufficient to give Americans what they needed; even in a culture given to ostentatious displays of wealth, simply buying became gauche. Experience, especially in luxury, could be new every time, in every place. It renewed the soul by reflecting to the world the wealth, presumably paired with the prowess, of the individual purchaser. The key to the success of tourism as status was to offer the most lavish accommodations and amenities. People experienced the new within the context of the familiar, an idea that dated back at least to the operations of the Fred Harvey Company and clearly well before. The amalgamation of the new and the familiar promised fresh experience without making it uncomfortable and gave it meaning and status.

As with many other cultural innovations in an oddly democratized but fundamentally top-down culture such as that of the United States, tourism spread throughout American society. From the automobile vacations of the 1940s and 1950s to the Lear jet trips to Telluride and similar places in the 1980s and 1990s, the participation in tourism affirmed what was American about each successive generation: their sharing in the life and times of their society. Just as movies, television, and the fashion trends set by stars and athletes did, tourism allowed people to belong to what they believed was best about their culture. In this context, it hardly represented a decline from a state of grace, as many locals clearly thought, for there had never been such a state. The visitors of the nineteenth century had been as manipulated as those of the twentieth, but in different ways. Their nineteenth-century definitions of authentic were not shared by their great grandchildren; the ideas and places that attracted those earlier travelers became passé to the generations that followed.

The democratization of tourism accelerated the move toward self-definition that tourism embodied. In the post-1945 world, the tourist market became segmented; in the American West, nearly every resort and most major national parks had options to suit almost any budget, especially in the places where an off-season remained. As more locales embraced tourism, the market in each became segmented. Hotels such as the California in downtown Las Vegas, struggling to compete with the glittery Strip to its south, found their niche catering to Hawaiian visitors; Parker, Arizona, in the words of one local resident, became a haven for "the Los Angeles civil servant class." These variations magnified longstanding niches largely beneath the radar of corporate tourism, sufficiently lucrative to sustain small companies and small towns but lacking the potential to attract the interest of multinational corporations.

In the places where tourism became an important part of the local and regional economy, an evident pattern appeared and persisted. Generally, tourism served as a replacement economy; it was added on, sometimes with embarrassment, after the demise or decline of another economy, usually by someone from elsewhere who could redefine the place in national or at least in extralocal terms. Individuals and communities greatly underestimated its impact and transformative power. By the way it drew people to visit or live, it altered the meaning of local life, the very soul of the places it touched. Although appearing to be an unskilled profession, tourism in fact required specific traits that neonatives were far more likely to possess than were prior residents of transformed towns. Places evolved into caricatures of their original identities, passing from inarticulate reflection and affirmation of the unique heritage of the dominant culture to colorful backdrop for a script in which visitors tacitly understood themselves to be the principal characters, self-consciously moving among the sights and sounds, natural and cultural, around them. Tourism did not really destroy; it created the new, promised fresh myths, responded to the poignant pleas of a changing culture, in the process making towns that looked the same, as John Rember notes, but felt different.

The sleight-of-hand that allowed tourism to offer such promises was both self-induced and self-made. Tourists, called fish at the Grand Canyon because of the way they gape at its awesome vistas, were both the target of mockery and essential to the survival of national parks, ski resorts, and especially entertainment tourism. As the industry reflected to visitors more of what they wanted to be, it changed the people of those places even more. In this aspect, the devil's bargain became most apparent. In the 1990s the West built casinos, theme parks, and prisons. Westerners sold the riches in their land or their identity, both forms of the raw material of the colony, often to the denizens of western cities. This internal colonialism masked harsh choices for residents, obscured the pace of change, overshadowed the ways that the opportunity to develop fractured the fiction of community in so many places. It also threw the question of what was real up for grabs. As one businessman noted, "Montana is the Last Best Place — Incorporated. And everywhere else in the West, if you don't like rubber tomahawks, what's left?"[33]

Stephen Morath's painting *Where the Wild West Went* answers the same questions I ask in this book with a great deal more verve and in a considerably more succinct fashion. Although Morath's baseline is a conception of a once and somehow real Wild West, he paints where it has gone—to the kitsch of popular culture, the drive-in screen, the boots of a faux cowboy, an airstream roaring by with a Sinclair dinosaur sign in the background—to the land of mythic meaning. Morath depicts a West stripped of identity and history, packaged to outside taste, and repeated ad nauseam. The road from Interstate 15 to Zion National Park is no different. The over twenty-mile jaunt begins in the modern Old West. Solid ranch homes and trailers, pickup trucks and hay movers, horses and cows appear along the road. About seven miles from the park, its corridor of influence begins. Feed stores disappear, replaced by bed and breakfasts in quaint little Victorians (I never got out of the car to see if they were ersatz). By the time Springdale beckons, the highway has become a path through visitor service from lodging to kitsch. The IMAX Theater at the park boundary sums up the experience: convenience über alles.

*

In a crowded Safeway on a summer Sunday afternoon in King's Beach, California, on the shores of Lake Tahoe, the checkout lines feel endless. My wife and I stand in line with our six- and two-year-olds. Scanning the crowd, I see sun-tanned faces, supple muscle, the casual wear of resort towns. They look like the Park Service crowd I once worked and ran with, young, excited, and poor, loading up on groceries for a week of serving visitors. In the manner of small towns, people recognize friends and stop to chat. It is reassuring; maybe this is a real place. After forever, we reach the checkout counter. I can't resist: "Locals stocking up for the week?" I ask, ever the intrepid researcher. My wife rolls her eyes; here he goes again. A look of disdain on the cashier's face is masked in an instant. "No locals here," she says with a wink. "They know better." Just the weeklong visitors like us, creating around us exactly what we left behind.

*

On a recent Los Angeles Saturday night, Michael Duchemin, the curator of Western History at the Autry Museum of Western Heritage, and his wife,

Paivi Hoikkala, took me to see CityWalk, which they considered one of the highlights of Los Angeles tourism. An early 1980s John Jerde design, CityWalk serves as an urban promenade that in its initial incarnation was to create a new space of memory, a place apart from that invaded by the culture of the street. CityWalk was supposed to evoke Los Angeles's past, as *Singing in the Rain* does for a glorious but long-gone New York. It would create a faux Los Angeles, a place that planed off the rough edges of a city that once promised much but had grown scary. Its Web page, at www.mca.com/citywalk, promotes precisely this idea, of space for visitors to relax, to dig their toes into the sand of an ersatz beach bar, but this illusion lasts only until dark. On this summer night, CityWalk's eight blocks were filled elbow-to-elbow with the culture of the street, urban youth in their astonishing variety of hairstyles and clothing. Belly rings were hardly outrageous here. The upper level, off the promenade, hid the tourists. At one end stood a small carnival, suggesting nothing so much as a county fair. Jerde is known for creating caricaturelike urban spaces in which he stacks mock replicas of all the places any metropolis has in cartoon dimensions. He believes that visitors want the sites of a city gathered in one place, the real and the replica indistinguishable, as in one of his recent and most stunning efforts, the Fremont Street Experience in downtown Las Vegas. According to critics, the excitement Jerde's kitsch generates quickly wears off. Tourists do want to see the real thing, and they stay away, leaving a niche that is soon filled by variations of local culture, an observation echoed by Michael Duchemin's surprise at the changes that had taken place since his last visit two years before. Adjacent Universal Studios, with its tall, iron gates, locked at night, was where the tourists could be found, at $37.50 a head, ruling out the minimum-wage crowd. Here is one future of tourism, not as experience people pay to receive but as space they pay to enter.

*

Founded as a sin city for nearby Kennecott around the turn of the century, McCarthy, Alaska, long served as a refuge. Dwindling to a few residents, the town slumbered; but gradually, after about 1960, a few people straggled in, seeking a different life. McCarthy's modern population self-selected for their remote paradise, away from the clamor of the modern world.

The people who lived there treasured that blending of wilderness and town and fought to preserve it. In remote Alaska, access determined all; although most travel was by air, roads were the greatest vectors of change. McCarthy was connected to the Alaska highway system by a sixty-mile, "narrow, washboarded fair-weather" gravel road, Bill Sherwont of *Alaska Maga-*

zine wrote, along the old railroad bed. The rickety Kuskulana Bridge threatened peril. Under the best of conditions, the sixty-mile trip from Chitina took more than four hours. Even at the end, the trip discouraged visitors, to understate the case; a hand-pulled cable-car tram was the only way across the rapid Kennicott River.

Four miles from town stood the skeleton of the Kennecott Copper Mine, and with the Alaskan National Interest Lands Conservation Act of 1980, a national monument that soon became Wrangell–St. Elias National Park came into being. The people of McCarthy still sought to keep the outside world away, but the national park changed their prospects. Its designation meant that one day, sooner or later, that world would arrive on their doorstep. Bob Jacobs, owner of St. Elias Alpine Guides, came to the region in 1970s. Back then, there was "little difference between McCarthy and the wilderness," he told Sherwont. "The boundary wasn't distinct." As late as 1984, he had the only business in McCarthy or Kennicott. In 1985 the Kennicott Lodge reopened, run by Rich Kirkwood, but little was there to attract the run-of-the-mill visitor.

The national park served as the catalyst for change. It attracted more visitors — Americans love their national parks — and brought improvements, most significantly to the road. In the mid-1980s, the state widened it, graded it, and built a new Kuskulana Bridge. New models replaced the old cable cars. The sixty-mile trip soon averaged a little over two hours, and the hardest part of crossing the river in the summer was waiting in line with all the visitors.

Although the 5,000 or so people who visited McCarthy in 1988 seemed like a crowd, they were only a vanguard. The national park and the tourism it spawned brought new realities, businesses downtown and lines of visitors waiting to cross the Kennicott River on the hand-operated tram. By 1992 the number topped 20,000, and the entire community felt the pressure. To some people, the Park Service was the enemy; to others, the sheer numbers posed a threat. The community began to fracture as some residents benefited from tourism and others felt its impact on the place they cherished. They pointed fingers at one another. Renowned glaciologist Ed LaChapelle noted, "There's a fear of getting run over by outside forces." Rich Kirkwood and the Kennicott Glacier Lodge took much of the venom; to some residents, Kirkwood seemed like a traitor. Kirkwood has "helped destroy the community he wanted to save," Jacobs averred. "Now we sit around and moan about the good old days," as tourists clamber over the town.

The state planned to widen the McCarthy road, and the prospect of eventual paving hung like an albatross around the necks of the old-timers. To many, their special place was gone; even at the end of a wide gravel road, tourists and neonatives could create irrevocable change.

*

In Showcase on the Las Vegas Strip on a Saturday night, SKG Gameworks is jammed with young people, teenagers and young adults alike. The massive collection of arcade games, virtual reality rides, competitive state-of-the-art shooting games and rides, three-dimensional graphics, motion simulators, and even one-of-a-kind games such as Vertical Reality, a competitive high-tech visual motion ride in which participants are suspended from ropes and shoot at each other's image with laser guns, rising and falling in height with each hit or miss, creates a paradise for postindustrial, television-bred youth. Billiards and darts entertain the more sedate in an elegant but nearly empty barroom, indicating just how young the crowd is. Skateboarding and other games cater to the preteen crowd. Surge Rock, the faux climbing rock, is the centerpiece. The crowd mixes tourist kids and locals, wearing the same clothes, listening to the same music, and eyeballing each other. It's good clean fun for the 1990s, surreal and virtual and charged with the sexual tension of youth, loaded onto Gameworks cards that take the place of coins. Exit surveys from the first year of operation show that Gameworks has been the answer to the need of traveling parents: a safe, wholesome, and hip place for their kids while they enjoy the illusion of Las Vegas. The Showcase was a prototype but one most likely to be imitated. Caesar's Forum could claim comparison, but only at first blush. Even with its exciting expansion, Atlantis, which debuted in fall 1997, the Forum remained a retail endeavor, offering shopping, not entertainment. Significantly, Gameworks and the adjacent Coca-Cola and All-Star Cafe sold enormous quantities of logo merchandise to the tourists of the future; brand identification conveyed status, even one replicated everywhere. Somehow a Showcase jacket or a Gameworks T-shirt projects an image of hipness, of prosperity.

*

The stark, rusting shell of the federal prison on Alcatraz Island, a mile from shore in San Francisco Bay, remains a potent symbol of fear and hope, of justice and injustice. Americans flock to it. Once a forbidding military fortress, it was the site of the nation's highest security prison. At one point after that it was occupied by Native American people drawing attention to their claims to land taken from their ancestors. They planned to initiate Thunderbird University there, an all-Indian learning institution and cultural center. The Rock speaks to the American soul. Here were housed Al Capone, Alvin Karpis, George "Machine Gun" Kelly, and Robert "the Birdman of Alcatraz"

Stroud; they were cloaked in prison-mandated silence, so eerie it was deafening. Released convicts complained that the silence made them crazy. By the time Alcatraz was incorporated in Golden Gate National Recreational Area in 1972, it housed only that silence. The clang of a cell door by a Park Service interpreter reverberated through the crumbling halls. The awesome quiet spoke for itself, mute testimony to an intriguing past. As the Park Service handled growing numbers of visitors, guided tours gave way to self-guided tours delivered on radio headsets. The excellent program was a favorite with visitors; tuned to their headsets, they jostled each other for position to better hear the words, the recorded clang of jailhouse doors, and the silence of the airwaves in their ears. Their excuse mes as they maneuvered for better radio reception echoed where silence once reigned.

*

> It proved once again the basic futility of seizing turf you can't control. The pattern never varies; a low-rent area blooms new and loose and human—and then fashionable . . . expense account tastes drive local rents and street prices out of the reach of the original settlers . . . who are forced once again to move on.

Hunter S. Thompson was describing Haight-Ashbury, but his words express one kind of neonative frustration with the transformation of tourism. A combination of observer and participant, Thompson illustrates one point on the spectrum of neonativity. He is, as always, angry—at change, at social structure, at life—but here his focus is sharper, more direct. Change has uprooted Thompson but he refuses to accept his fate, sees it as parable and cautionary tale. Elsewhere on this spectrum lies Elizabeth Compton Hegemann, writing near the end of her life, recalling a special moment of discovery in her youth at the Grand Canyon. Understanding is internal, not external; wonder, not anger, is the dominant emotion, and memories of community mark her thoughts:

> After the travelers had departed on the evening Pullmans or had fallen stiff and exhausted into bed after a trail trip, we could drop our cloak of professional hospitality and relax in the routine of our own local activities. These consisted of endless committee meetings and "auction" bridge parties where we laughed and talked between hands while consuming huge slabs of homemade cakes and cups of coffee. Afterwards while we stumbled home in single file behind the beam of a wavering flashlight, we could sense the silent void of the Canyon depths close by.

> No one could possibly live on the Rim and be oblivious to the Canyon, so beautiful and majestic in all moods, nor to the feeling of what little consequence our life might be when compared to the Canyon's millions of years of existence.

Struthers Burt of the Bar BC took another neonative stance. He was the teacher, the conduit through which visitors could understand a purer world: "No man should be judged by what he doesn't know, he should be judged only by how quickly and sensibly he assumes his new duties." Burt offered the keys to transformation to a generation of upper-class travelers, posing himself on the very line between them and the neighbors he purported to represent. To the visitors, he was a man of the West. He offered them what they craved, a reality scripted for them that promised spiritual renewal, cultural affirmation, and genuine experience in an otherwise banal existence. To his neighbors, Burt raised a strange crop, generally useless until the harvest produced sufficient numbers to create a tourist town. Out the other end came satirist Tim Sandlin, whose fictional characters made a mockery of any meaning left in Jackson.

John Rember offers a fifth position, wry postirony in the face of change in both his memoirs and fiction. The Sawtooth Valley where he was raised is gone, and he grudgingly grants virtue of a sort to its successor regimes. Recognizing the way his world is scripted, he seeks a place on its pages but not in a typical role. Thompson offers revolution, Hegemann nostalgia, Burt insight, and Sandlin satire, but Rember becomes the community's conscience, a check against selling out, a claim on the ephemeral real. This position produces tension in the writer and in his work, between himself and his community. Rember's reflections about place always test the individual, challenging assumptions and premises.

Nativity too posed its problems. "What is my place in all this?" pondered J. Royal Horton's protagonist in *Murder in Jackson Hole,* Tommy Thompson.

> What did it mean to be a native of the state, to be as deeply embedded in the Mountain West as he was? Did it have any real value in and of itself? Or did it mean nothing more than its worth in the cheap oneupmanship that was typical of Jackson Hole—"How long have *you* been in Jackson? *I've* been here over ten years." "Me? Oh my family came out here in the forties (pause) the *eighteen* forties." A cheap game to play, but fun to see the look on some faces. They knew they had missed it and it was something they could not buy, no matter how much else they had.

They will never see it the way we saw it, he said to himself. For some reason that gave him a sense of deep satisfaction.

*

Around a kitchen table at a garden party in the upper-middle-class urban West: "You should look at this!" one woman nearly shouts. "Can you believe how cheap Mammoth is? Less than $300,000 for 2,800 square feet just off the slopes. Why pay for Park City?" For once, I keep my mouth shut. "If they get that airport in there, these places will be worth a fortune." A developer demurs, recognizing the flaw in the logic. If they get the airport, the houses won't be $300,000 anymore, but in the California mountains, the combination of local power, state law, and special interests makes a new airport less than unlikely. It would be a $300,000 investment on a wing and a prayer, five hours by car from the nearest megalopolis and more than two from an accessible airport. "I just don't understand those damn environmentalists," the woman continues. "None of the businesses up there make it. Every year there are new restaurants." You don't understand, I think to myself; the only people who want those restaurants to make it are people like you, and the people up there don't much like your kind.

*

When Edward Abbey pulled up the road-marker stakes in Arches National Monument, he had to know that he was merely a pimple on the backside of progress. He offered chewing gum in the cracks, a ritual form of resistance to industrial tourism but one that did nothing to slow its march. Like Mary Austin and so many others, Abbey drew an arbitrary line; on one side stood virtue, not incidentally that included himself, on the other corruption in the shape of Bureau of Public Roads officials and their stakes. Abbey's romantic resistance confronted a harsh truth: all tourism was industrial tourism, made possible by the same system that built the car that brought the officials and generated the desire for the road. Abbey, anticipating martyrdom, correctly identified the problem that vexed the residents of the American West throughout the twentieth century. Sadly his response was sophomoric, available only to militant few, ready to sacrifice all in opposition to existing power. Biting the hand that fed also had consequences.

*

We are all industrial tourists. Physically we can take only pictures and leave only footprints. Psychically, socially, culturally, economically, and environmentally, we inexorably change all we touch.

NOTES

1. INTRODUCTION

1. John R. Logan and Harvey L. Molotch, *Urban Fortunes: The Political Economy of Place* (Berkeley: University of California Press, 1987); Karl Kim, "Tourism on Our Terms: Tourism Planning in Hawaii," report, Western Governors' Association, 1991, 14.
2. Dean McCannell, *The Tourist: A New Theory of the Leisure Class* (New York: Schocken Books, 1976), 91–98.
3. I owe the concept of scripted space to Norman M. Klein, "The Politics of Scripted Space: [Las] Vegas and Reno," Keynote Address, Nevada Historical Society Fifth Biennial Conference on Nevada History, May 20, 1997; Cynthia Weiss, conversation, February 1993; Mike Davis, *City of Quartz: Excavating the Future in Los Angeles* (New York: Verso, 1991).
4. Edward Abbey, *Desert Solitaire* (Tucson: University of Arizona Press, 1968, 1988), 54–70.
5. I attended this party; many thanks to Michael P. Cohen's unpacking the paradigm of climbing gyms as he explained his paper, "The Climbing Gym : An Environmental History."
6. Jon Krakauer, *Into Thin Air: A Personal Account of the Mt. Everest Disaster* (New York: Villard, 1997).
7. Pauline Maier, *American Scripture: Making the Declaration of Independence* (New York: Alfred A. Knopf, 1997); Alan Taylor, "Pluribus," *New Republic*, June 30, 1997, 34–38.
8. William Kittredge and Annick Smith, eds., *The Last Best Place* (Seattle: University of Washington Press, 1991); David Wrobel, *The End of American Exceptionalism* (Lawrence: University Press of Kansas, 1994).
9. Kim, "Tourism on Our Terms," 8–9.
10. William Dean Howells, "The Problem of the Summer," *In Literature and Life* (New York: Harper Brothers, 1902), 216–17; Gary S. Becker, *Accounting for Tastes* (Cambridge: Harvard University Press, 1996); Patrick Long, *Win, Lose, or Draw?: Gambling with America's Small Towns* (Washington, DC: Aspen Institution, c. 1994).
11. Daniel T. Rodgers, *The Work Ethic in Industrial America, 1850–1920* (Chicago: University of Chicago Press, 1978); William Leach, *Land of Desire: Merchants, Power, and the Rise of a New American Culture* (New York: Random House, 1993); T. J. Jackson Lears, *Fables of Abundance: A Cultural History of Advertising in America* (New York: Basic Books, 1996).
12. Leach, *Land of Desire;* Stuart Ewen, *Captains of Consciousness: Advertising and the Social Roots of Consumer Culture* (New York: McGraw-Hill, 1976); Tom Wolfe, "The Me Decade and the Third Great Awakening," in *Mauve Gloves and Madmen, Clutter and Vine and Other Stories, Sketches, and Essays* (New York: Farrar, Straus, and Giroux, 1976), 3–14; David Halberstam, *The Fifties* (New York: Villard Books, 1993).
13. Christopher Lasch, *The Revolt of the Elites: And the Betrayal of Democracy* (New York: W. W. Norton, 1995).
14. Mark Edmundson, "On the Uses of a Liberal Education: As Lite Entertainment for Bored College Students," *Harper's*, September 1997, 40–41.

15. Sunnyside Inn 50th Anniversary Menu, Lake Tahoe, summer 1997; n.a., T S Restaurants, Hawaii and California, copy in possession of the author.
16. John Rember, "On Going Back to Sawtooth Valley," in *Where the Morning Light's Still Blue: Personal Essays About Idaho,* ed. William Studebaker and Rick Ardinger (Moscow, ID: University of Idaho Press, 1994), 88; on the problems of the idea of authenticity, see James Clifford, *The Predicament of Culture: Twentieth-Century Ethnography, Literature, and Art* (Cambridge: Harvard University Press, 1988), and James Clifford, *Routes: Travel and Translation in the Late Twentieth Century* (Cambridge: Harvard University Press, 1997).
17. William Cronon, *Nature's Metropolis: Chicago and the Great West, 1848–1900* (New York: W. W. Norton, 1991); xvii, 56–57.
18. Ibid., 265–67.
19. Douglas C. Comer, *Ritual Ground: Bent's Old Fort, World Formation, and the Annexation of the Southwest* (Berkeley: University of California Press, 1996); Andrés Résendez, "Caught Between Profit and Ritual" (Ph.D. diss., University of Chicago, 1997). Many thanks to Tom Latousek for alerting me to the existence of this ritual. Palace Station commercial aired on Las Vegas local television, January–April 1997.

2. TOURISM AND THE FRAMING OF A CULTURE

1. Edward Relph, *Place and Placelessness* (London: Pion, 1976), 83; John A. Jakle, *The Tourist: Travel in Twentieth-Century North America* (Lincoln: University of Nebraska Press, 1985), 3–4.
2. Gary S. Becker, *Accounting for Tastes* (Cambridge: Harvard University Press, 1996), 3–6, 12–16.
3. Peter Hopkirk, *The Great Game: The Struggle for Empire in Central Asia* (New York: Kodansha America, 1992), 123–31.
4. Charles Sellers, *The Market Revolution: Jacksonian America, 1815–1846* (New York: Oxford University Press, 1991); Ronald G. Walters, *American Reformers, 1815–1860* (New York: Hill and Wang, 1978); T. J. Jackson Lears, *No Place of Grace: Antimodernism and the Transformation of American Culture, 1880–1920* (New York: Pantheon, 1981).
5. Jakle, *The Tourist,* xii, 1–3; Becker, *Accounting for Tastes,* 7–11, 17–21; Douglas Pearce, *Tourist Development,* 2d ed. (New York: John Wiley and Sons, 1989), 2, 25–32.
6. Dona Brown, *Inventing New England: Regional Tourism in the Nineteenth Century* (Washington, DC: Smithsonian Institution Press, 1996), 2–5; C. Brenden Martin, "From Trails to Rails to Roads: Tourism and Accessibility in the Mountain South," paper presented to the Society for the History of Technology, London, August 1996.
7. Howard Mumford Jones, *O Strange New World: American Culture, The Formative Years* (New York: Viking, 1952), 344–62; Thomas Jefferson, *Notes on the State of Virginia* (New York: Harper and Row, Harper Torchbook Edition, 1964); Merle Curti, *The Growth of American Democratic Thought* (New York: Harper and Brothers, 1943), 245–65; Ralph Henry Gabriel, *The Course of American Democratic Thought,* 2d ed. (New York: Ronald Press, 1956), 21.
8. Brown, *Inventing New England,* 44–46; Barbara Novak, *Nature and Culture: American Landscape and Painting, 1825–1875* (New York: Oxford University Press, 1980); James Fenimore Cooper, *The Pioneers or Sources of the Susquehanna* (D. Appleton and Company, 1885); Charles Brockden Brown, *Wieland, or the Transformation* (Garden City, NY: Dolphin Books, 1962).
9. C. Brenden Martin, "Selling the Southern Highlands: Tourism and Community De-

velopment in the Mountain South" (Ph.D. diss., University of Tennessee, 1997); Earl Pomeroy, *In Search of the Golden West: The Tourist in Western America* (Lincoln: University of Nebraska Press, 1957), 9; Peter Wood, *Black Majority: Negroes in South Carolina from 1670 Through the Stono Rebellion* (New York: Alfred A. Knopf, 1974).

10. Henry Marie Brackenridge, *Journal of a Voyage up the River Missouri in Eighteen Hundred and Eleven,* in *Early Western Travels, 1748–1846,* ed. Reuben Gold Thwaites, vol. 6 (Cleveland: Arthur H. Clark Company, 1906); Maximilian, Alexander Philip (Prince of Wied Neuwied), *Travels in the Interior of North America,* in Thwaites, ed., *Early Western Travels, 1748–1846,* vols. 12–14 (1906–7); William H. Goetzmann and William N. Goetzmann, *The West of the Imagination* (New York: W. W. Norton, 1986), 51–61; Pomeroy, *In Search of the Golden West,* xv–xviii.
11. Richard Grove, *Green Imperialism: Colonial Expansion, Tropical Island Edens, and the Origins of Environmentalism, 1600–1860* (Cambridge: Cambridge University Press, 1995); Mae Reed Porter, Foreword, in Bernard DeVoto, *Across the Wide Missouri* (Boston: Houghton Mifflin, 1947), xvi–xviii; Goetzmann and Goetzmann, *The West of the Imagination,* 61; John Hemming, *The Conquest of the Amazon: The Defeat of the Brazilian Indians* (Cambridge: Harvard University Press, 1987); Caoimhín P. Ó Fearghil, "*Fatum Manifestus:* Botanical Taxonomy in the American West," seminar paper, University of Nevada, Las Vegas, 1996; William H. Goetzmann, *New Lands, New Men: The Second Great Age of Discovery* (New York: Alfred A. Knopf, 1992).
12. Herman Melville, *Typee: A Peep at Polynesian Life* (Evanston: Northwestern University Press, 1968).
13. Goetzmann and Goetzmann, *The West of the Imagination,* 60–61, 65; Robert G. Athearn, *High Country Empire: The High Plains and the Rockies* (New York: McGraw-Hill, 1960), 38–40.
14. Jules Verne, *Around the World in Eighty Days,* trans. George M. Towle (New York: Dodd, Meade, and Company, 1956), 1–35.
15. Albro Martin, *Railroads Triumphant: The Growth, Rejection, and Rebirth of a Vital American Force* (New York: Oxford University Press, 1992), 35.
16. Martin, *Railroads Triumphant,* 42–43; L. L. Waters, *Steel Trails to Santa Fe* (Lawrence: University Press of Kansas, 1950), 261–63; Pomeroy, *In Search of the Golden West,* 9. Paul Theroux, *The Old Patagonian Express* (New York: Penguin Books, 1979), demonstrates clearly the difference between train travel and other forms of travel.
17. Martin, *Railroads Triumphant,* 45–54; Waters, *Steel Rails to Santa Fe,* 262–70; Keith L. Bryant Jr., *History of the Atchison, Topeka, and Santa Fe Railway* (Lincoln: University of Nebraska Press, 1974), 108–13; Pomeroy, *In Search of the Golden West,* 7, 29–30.
18. Pomeroy, *In Search of the Golden West,* 34–35; Curtis M. Hinsley and David Wilcox, eds., *The Southwest of the American Imagination: The Writings of Sylvester Baxter, 1881–1889* (Tucson: University of Arizona Press, 1996), 21–33; see also Sylvester Baxter, "Around Santa Fe: The Natural Attractions as a Summer Resort," *Boston Herald,* June 29, 1881; Sylvester Baxter, "Zuñi Revisited," *American Architect and Building News* 13 (March 17, 1883): 124–26; and Birge Harrison, "Española and Its Environs," *Harper's Magazine,* May 1885, 17.
19. Jakle, *The Tourist,* 86.
20. Alfred Runte, *National Parks: The American Experience,* 2d ed. (Lincoln: University of Nebraska Press, 1987); Pomeroy, *In Search of the Golden West,* 34; Joseph J. Ellis, *American Sphinx: The Character of Thomas Jefferson* (New York: Alfred A. Knopf, 1996), 83–84; Alfred W. Crosby, *Germs, Seeds, and Animals: Studies in Ecological History* (Armonk, NY: M. E. Sharpe, 1994), 141.

21. William H. Goetzmann, *Exploration and Empire: The Explorer and the Scientist in the Winning of the American West* (New York: Alfred A. Knopf, 1967); Goetzmann and Goetzmann, *The West of the Imagination;* William H. Goetzmann and Joseph Porter, *The West as Romantic Horizon: Selections from the Collection of the InterNorth Art Foundation* (Omaha: Joslyn Art Museum, 1981); Goetzmann, *New Men, New Lands;* Novak, *Nature and Culture;* Richard A. Bartlett, *Yellowstone: A Wilderness Besieged* (Tucson: University of Arizona Press, 1985); Alfred Runte, *Yosemite: The Embattled Wilderness* (Lincoln: University of Nebraska Press, 1990); Michael Cohen, *The Pathless Way: John Muir and American Wilderness* (Madison: University of Wisconsin Press, 1984); James P. Ronda, *Lewis and Clark Among the Indians* (Lincoln: University of Nebraska Press, 1984).
22. Goetzmann, *Exploration and Empire;* Novak, *Nature and Culture;* David Nye, *American Technological Sublime* (Cambridge: MIT Press, 1994); Bartlett, *Yellowstone;* Runte, *Yosemite;* Cohen, *The Pathless Way;* Peter B. Hales, *William Henry Jackson and the Transformation of the American Landscape* (Philadelphia: Temple University Press, 1988).
23. Dan Flores, "Place: An Argument for Bioregional History, *Environmental History Review* 18, no. 4 (winter 1994): 1–18.
24. Mark David Spence, "Crown of the Continent, Backbone of the World: The American Wilderness Ideal and Blackfeet Exclusion from Glacier National Park," *Environmental History* 1, no. 3 (July 1996): 29–49; Mark David Spence, "Dispossessing the Wilderness: Yosemite Indians and the National Park Ideal," *Pacific Historical Review* 65, no. 1 (February 1996): 27–60; Dee Brown, *Bury My Heart at Wounded Knee: An Indian History of the American West* (New York: Holt, Rinehart, and Winston, 1970).
25. Morse Peckham, *The Triumph of Romanticism: Collected Essays* (Columbia: University of South Carolina Press, 1970); Stephen J. Pyne, *Dutton's Point: An Intellectual History of the Grand Canyon* (Grand Canyon, AZ: Grand Canyon Natural History Association, 1982); see also Runte, *National Parks.*
26. Martin, *Railroads Triumphant;* Maury Klein, *Union Pacific* (Garden City, NY: Doubleday, 1987), vols. 1 and 2; Paxton P. Price, "The Railroad, Rincon, and the River," *New Mexico Historical Review* 65, no. 4 (October 1990); 437–54; Hal Rothman, "Slide and Tape Interpretation Packet," Adobe House Museum, Hillsboro, KS, ca. 1990, copy in possession of the author; Pomeroy, *In Search of the Golden West,* 7–24.
27. Cronon, *Nature's Metropolis;* Eugene Moehring, "The Comstock Urban Network," *Pacific Historical Review* (Autumn 1997): 337–62.
28. William Cronon, "Kennecott Journey: The Paths Out of Town," in *Under an Open Sky: Rethinking America's Western Past,* ed. Cronon, George Miles, and Jay Gitlin (New York: W. W. Norton, 1992), 28–51; Malcolm J. Rohrbaugh, *Aspen: The History of a Silver Mining Town, 1879–1893* (New York: Oxford, 1986); Rodman W. Paul, *The Mining Frontiers of the Far West, 1848–1880* (New York: Holt, Rinehart, and Winston, 1963).
29. Bartlett, *Yellowstone,* 14–16, 43–44.
30. Ibid., 22–23; H. Duane Hampton, *How the U.S. Cavalry Saved Our National Parks* (Bloomington: Indiana University Press, 1971), 32–52.
31. Carroll Van West, *Capitalism on the Frontier: Billings and the Yellowstone Valley in the Nineteenth Century* (Lincoln: University of Nebraska Press, 1993), 112–61.
32. William Wykoff and Katherine Hansen, "Settlement, Livestock Grazing, and Environmental Change in Southwest Montana," *Environmental History Review* 15, no. 4 (winter 1991): 45–71; James B. Hedges, *Henry Villard and the Railways of the Northwest* (New York: Russell and Russell, 1965).

33. Bartlett, *Yellowstone,* 44; Pomeroy, *In Search of the Golden West,* 9.
34. Pomeroy, *In Search of the Golden West,* 19; for more on the intellectual and cultural development of California in the late nineteenth century, see Kevin Starr, *Americans and the California Dream, 1850–1915* (New York: Oxford University Press, 1973), and William Deverell, *Railroad Crossing: Californians and the Railroad, 1850–1910* (Berkeley: University of California Press, 1994).
35. Pomeroy, *In Search of the Golden West,* 20–21.
36. Mark Twain, *The Innocents Abroad* (New York: Hippocrene Books, 1989).
37. Pomeroy, *In Search of the Golden West,* 22.
38. Ibid., 20–25; Runte, *Yosemite,* 105; Alfred Runte, *Trains of Discovery: Western Railroads and the National Parks* (Flagstaff, AZ: Northland Press, 1984), 60–76; Billy M. Jones, *Health Seekers in the Southwest 1817–1900* (Norman: University of Oklahoma Press, 1967), 150–73.

3. THE TOURISM OF HEGEMONY I

1. Stephen Pyne, *Dutton's Point: An Intellectual History of the Grand Canyon* (Grand Canyon, AZ: Grand Canyon Natural History Association, 1982), 3–13; William H. Goetzmann, *New Lands, New Men: The Second Great Age of Discovery* (New York: Alfred A. Knopf, 1992).
2. Pyne, *Dutton's Point,* 33–38; Wallace Stegner, *Beyond the Hundredth Meridian: John Wesley Powell and the Second Opening of the West* (Boston: Houghton Mifflin, 1954), 243–50.
3. Pyne, *Dutton's Point,* 33–38; Goetzmann, *New Lands, New Men,* 404–16; Curtis M. Hinsley, *Savages and Scientists: The Smithsonian Institution and the Development of American Anthropology, 1846–1910* (Washington, DC: Smithsonian Institution Press, 1981), does the best job of detailing the growing relationship between science and Manifest Destiny; see also Caoimhín Ó Fearghail, "*Fatum Manifestus:* Biological Taxonomy in the American West," seminar paper, University of Nevada, Las Vegas, 1996, who illustrates the pervasiveness of Manifest Destiny in even remote realms of American science and shows clearly its ties to the cult of individualism.
4. Al Richmond, *Cowboys, Miners, Presidents and Kings: The Story of the Grand Canyon Railway* (Flagstaff, AZ: Grand Canyon Pioneers Society, 1985), 1–3; Douglas H. Strong, "Ralph H. Cameron and the Grand Canyon (Part I)," *Arizona and the West* 20, no. 1 (spring 1978); 43.
5. J. Donald Hughes, *In the House of Stone and Light: A Human History of the Grand Canyon* (Grand Canyon, AZ: Grand Canyon Natural History Association, 1978), 47–52.
6. Geographers who study tourism would refer to this scenario as "spontaneous development," the neochaos that results from unplanned localized involvement in the industry when visitors seek a place before or in absence of a developed structure; see Douglas Pearce, *Tourism Development,* 2d ed. (New York: John Wiley and Sons, 1989), 58–59 and Barbaza, "Trois Types d'intervention de tourisme dans l'organization de l'escape littoral," *Annales de Geographie* (1970): 446–69.
7. "Notice of Location" (mining claim), April 23, 1890; "Mining Claim Notice," April 21, 1893, Grand Canyon Research Library, Grand Canyon National Park, Grand Canyon, AZ; Hughes, *In the House of Stone and Light,* 54; Doug Strong, "Ralph H. Cameron and the Grand Canyon" (Tucson: Arizona and the West, 1978), 43–44.
8. W. W. Bass to P. D. Berry, August 22, 1891; Peter D. Berry, "Always Bring This Book," diary dated May 24, 1892–July 20, 1892; time book, Last Chance Mine, 1891–1892;

time book, Grandview Trail, July–December 1892; Ralph H. Cameron to Peter D. Berry, April 20, 1897; Ed Gale to P. D. Berry, December 5, 1900, Ed Gale to P. D. Berry, December 23, 1900, and Ralph H. Cameron to Peter D. Berry, December 5, 1900; Ralph H. Cameron to "Boys," February 26, 1896, Ralph H. Cameron to P. D. Berry and N. J. Cameron, May 17, 1896, Grand Canyon Research Library. In the entire correspondence between Cameron and Berry, in only one of the more than 300 letters Cameron is not dictating terms to Berry; see Cameron to Berry, September 10, 1897, Grand Canyon Research Library. Strong, "Ralph H. Cameron and the Grand Canyon," 45, suggests that Berry was a good businessman, but Berry's records, part of the collection at Grand Canyon National Park, do not bear this out; see especially Statement for $552.85 to Mr. E. B. Davison from P. D. Berry, February 21, 1889; J. R. Lowry to P. D. Berry, September 27, 1891; Louis Zapp and Co. to P. D. Berry, March 29, 1892, Grand Canyon Research Library.

9. Charles F. Lummis, *A Tramp Across the Continent* (New York: Charles Scribner's Sons, 1892), 244; Pyne, *Dutton's Point,* 38–41.
10. Though it is hard to imagine that the sheer beauty of the canyon could not affect any arrival on its rim, the extensive correspondence between Cameron and Berry shows no evidence that the men at the mine appreciated the power of the place. In more than 200 letters, there is absolutely no reference to the canyon in any but the most instrumental terms; in their letters, it is a place from which to derive a living. By about 1895, the letters clearly show that the men believe they can gain economic advantage from the scenery of the canyon, but not one sentence refers to its beauty, magnificence, or awe-inspiring vistas. Berry frequently remarks on the cold at the canyon in letters to his son and in one instance, a December 6, 1899 letter, comments on its depth but never mentions the vista from Grandview, which is spectacular. Perhaps familiarity does breed contempt, or at least ennui. For the ennui of the fin de siècle, see T. J. Jackson Lears, *No Place of Grace: Antimodernism and the Transformation of American Culture, 1880–1920* (Chicago: University of Chicago Press, 1994); for Lummis, see Edwin R. Bingham, *Charles F. Lummis: Editor of the Southwest* (San Marino, CA: Huntington Library, 1955), 7–10, and Dudley Gordon, *Charles F. Lummis: Crusader in Corduroy* (Los Angeles: Cultural Assets Press, 1972), 99–109.
11. Peter D. Berry to Ralph Berry, August 24, 1896; Hughes, *In the House of Stone and Light,* 50; Byrd H. Granger, ed., *Will C. Barnes' Arizona Place Names* (Tucson: University of Arizona Press, 1960), 145; Lummis, *A Tramp Across the Continent* (Albuquerque: Calvin Horn, 1969), 9; John Muir, "The Wild Parks and Forest Reservations of the West," *Atlantic Monthly* 81 (January 1898): 28; John Burroughs, "The Divine Abyss," in *The Writings of John Burroughs,* vol. 14, *Time and Change* (Boston: Houghton Mifflin, 1912), 49; Lears, *No Place of Grace;* David Shi, *The Simple Life: Plain Living and High Thinking in American Culture* (New York: Oxford University Press, 1985).
12. John F. Sears, *Sacred Places: American Tourist Attractions in the Nineteenth Century* (New York: Oxford University Press, 1989); Hughes, *In the House of Stone and Light;* Al Richmond, *Cowboys, Miners, Presidents and Kings* (Grand Canyon Pioneer Society, 1985); Robert H. Wiebe, *The Search for Order, 1877–1920* (rept.; New York: Hill and Wang, 1995).
13. George U. Young to Commissioner of the General Land Office, January 13, 1898, Records of the General Land Office, Grand Canyon File Box 59, Div. R, NFF, RG 48(?), National Archives; Richmond, *Cowboys, Miners, Presidents, and Kings,* 3–14; Strong, "Ralph H. Cameron and the Grand Canyon," 51.
14. Keith L. Bryant Jr., *History of the Atchison, Topeka, and Santa Fe Railway* (Lincoln:

University of Nebraska Press, 1974), 106–9; see also Leah Dilworth, *Imagining Indians in the Southwest: Persistent Visions of a Primitive Past* (Washington, DC: Smithsonian Institution Press, 1996).

15. Richmond, *Cowboys, Miners, Presidents, and Kings,* 4–5, 28–44; Hughes, *In the House of Stone and Light,* 62; Strong, "Ralph H. Cameron and the Grand Canyon," 49–50; Pearce, *Tourist Development,* 61–78. The AT&SF gained control of the rail spur to the canyon as an undercapitalized local railroad succumbed to bankruptcy, a captive to bonds held by Ripley and the AT&SF. Although it offered service beginning on March 15, 1900, reaching Anita Junction, about forty-five miles from Williams, progress after that was slow and laborious. The operation came apart, and on September 5, 1900, the company went into receivership. The AT&SF purchased the line for $150,000, well below its capitalization.
16. Bryant, *History of the Atchison, Topeka, and Santa Fe Railway,* 106–11; Lesley Poling-Kempes, *The Harvey Girls: Women Who Opened the West* (New York: Paragon House, 1989), 29–47.
17. The issue of the transformation of place by outside forces is crucial to the understanding of the processes of tourism. See Immanuel M. Wallerstein, *The Modern World-System: Capitalist Agriculture and the Origins of the European World-Economy in the Sixteenth Century* (New York: Academic Press, 1974); Immanuel M. Wallerstein, *The Modern World-System II: Mercantilism and the Consolidation of the European World-Economy, 1600–1750* (New York: Academic Press, 1980); Urs Bitterli, trans. Ritchie Robertson, *Cultures in Conflict: Encounters Between European and Non-European Cultures, 1492–1800* (Stanford: Stanford University Press, 1988); David J. Weber, ed., *Foreigners in Their Native Land: Historical Roots of the Mexican Americans* (Albuquerque: University of New Mexico Press, 1973); Leonard Pitt, *The Decline of the Californios: A Social History of the Spanish-Speaking Californians, 1846–1890* (Berkeley: University of California Press, 1966); and Richard White, *The Roots of Dependency: Subsistence, Environment, and Social Change Among the Choctaws, Pawnees, and Navajos* (Lincoln: University of Nebraska Press, 1984), for examples of this process. My argument here is that the application of industrial technology to preindustrial people of the same culture has a markedly similar impact.
18. Ralph H. Cameron to P. D. Berry, June 17, 1897, Grand Canyon Research Library; Strong, "Ralph Henry Cameron and the Grand Canyon," 49; on 46, Strong indicates that "control of the [Bright Angel] trail became the key to controlling the canyon's development." In fact, Cameron could only use the trail to block the efforts of others, and for more than two decades after 1905, he fought a defensive war. But he could hardly control the development of the canyon as much as he would have liked to; the best he could do was to be an enormous headache and temporarily to slow efforts.
19. Harold K. Steen, *The United States Forest Service: A History* (Seattle: University of Washington Press, 1976), 28–32; John Ise, *Our National Park Policy: A Critical History* (Baltimore: Johns Hopkins University Press, 1961), 230–32; Thomas R. Cox, Robert S. Maxwell, Phillip Drennon Thomas, and Joseph J. Malone, *This Well-Wooded Land: Americans and Their Forests from Colonial Times to the Present* (Lincoln: University of Nebraska Press, 1985), 175–83; Edwin Tucker and David Gillio, eds., "The Early Days: A Sourcebook of Southwestern Region History Book 1" (Albuquerque: USDA Forest Service, 1989), Cultural Resources Management Report no. 7, 3; Strong, "Ralph H. Cameron and the Grand Canyon," 51; Ralph H. Cameron to Peter B. Berry, June 17, 1897; Cameron to Berry, November 17, 1897, Grand Canyon Research Library.
20. Cameron to Berry, November 17, 1897, Grand Canyon Research Library; Serge Taylor,

Making Bureaucracies Think: The Environmental Impact Statement Strategy of Administrative Reform (Stanford: Stanford University Press, 1984); Paul J. Culhane, *Public Lands Politics: Interest Group Influence on the Forest Service and the Bureau of Land Management* (Washington, DC: Resources for the Future, 1981); Daniel McCool, *Command of the Waters: Iron Triangles, Federal Water Development and Indian Water* (Berkeley: University of California Press, 1987).

21. Fred Harvey to Peter D. Berry, May 14, 1900; E. B. Gage to P. D. Berry, October 14, 1900; G. S. Peabody to Peter D. Berry, September 11, 1903; J. L. Hibbard to P. D. Berry, June 28, 1902, Grand Canyon Research Library.
22. P. C. Bicknell to Ralph Henry Cameron, June 4, 1901; Putnam and Valentine to P. D. Berry, June 25, 1901; Putnam and Valentine to P. D. Berry, August 20, 1901, Grand Canyon Research Library; Hughes, *In the Canyon of Stone and Light,* 53; Strong, "Ralph H. Cameron and the Grand Canyon," 52–53.
23. Major John R. White, telegram to Stephen T. Mather, December 13, 1921, Records of the National Park Service, Series 6, Grand Canyon National Park, RG 79, National Archives; James D. Henderson, *Meals by Fred Harvey: A Phenomenon of the American West* (Fort Worth: Texas Christian University Press, 1969); Poling-Kempes, *The Harvey Girls,* 167–69; Bryant, *History of the Atchison, Topeka, and Santa Fe Railway,* 120–21, 186; John Willy, "Fred Harvey's Facilities and Service at the Grand Canyon," *Santa Fe Magazine,* December 1928, Atchison, Topeka, and Santa Fe Railroad Collection, Kansas State Historical Society, Topeka; Elizabeth Compton Hegemann, *Navajo Trading Days* (Albuquerque: University of New Mexico Press, 1963), 5–6. George Wharton James, *The Grand Canyon of Arizona* (Boston; Little, Brown 1910), describes the coming of the railroad to the area. Though the consensus is that AT&SF rail service to the Grand Canyon began in 1904, Gordon Strachan, "Arizona: Jewel in the Crown," *Santa Fe Magazine,* August 1948, 14, gives July 1, 1907, as the date; the *Santa Fe Magazine,* December 1929, 38, shows a photo of the first train to Grand Canyon, dated September 18, 1901. This photo is surely of the abortive Grand Canyon Railway Line, swallowed up by the AT&SF. Though train service certainly operated to the canyon before 1907, Strachan's assertion suggests that the AT&SF did not formally take over this line until 1907; according to Richmond, *Cowboys, Miners, Presidents and Kings,* the line was held in AT&SF–controlled receivership from 1901 to 1907.
24. W. M. Davis to P. D. Berry, March 28, 1901; W. M. Davis to P. D. Berry, April 28, 1901; John Chetwood to "Dear Sir," March [19], 1902; John Chetwood to "Dear Sir," April 3, 1902; Peter D. Berry to John Chetwood, April 12, 1902; P. D. Berry to H. K. Gregory, April 14, 1902, Grand Canyon Research Library; Strong, "Ralph H. Cameron and the Grand Canyon," 44–45.
25. Ralph H. Cameron, "A Word to the Tourist," n.d. (ca. 1905), Grand Canyon Research Library; Strong, "Ralph H. Cameron and the Grand Canyon," 45, 53.
26. Ralph H. Cameron to Peter D. Berry, February 14, 1910, January 2, 1914, and April 10, 1909, Grand Canyon Research Library; Strong, "Ralph H. Cameron and the Grand Canyon," 50 and 45–50; Margaret M. Verkamp, "History of Grand Canyon National Park" (Master's thesis, University of Arizona, 1940). Cameron's legal maneuvering fills boxes in RG 79 of the National Archives; the best summary of the legal situation prior to 1906 is Gifford Pinchot to William Loeb Jr., May 12, 1906, Grand Canyon Research Library; the best post-1915 summaries are Frank Pinkley to Director, National Park Service, March 3, 1919; Bob [Robert S. Yard] to Steve [Stephen T. Mather], October 10, 1919; Hubert Work to Attorney General, February 28, 1924; and H. C. Bryant to

F. H. Barnard, April 4, 1924, Series 6, Box 50, Private Land Claims, Cameron, Grand Canyon National Park, RG 79, National Archives.

27. *United States Statutes at Large*, L. 27, Stat. 1064 (1893), created the Grand Canyon Forest Reserve; *United States Statutes at Large*, L. 34, Stat. 607, and L. 34, Stat. 3263 (1906) replaced the forest reserve with a game reserve.
28. *United States Statutes at Large*, L. 35, Stat. 2175 (1908), established the national monument; *United States Statutes at Large*, L. 40, Stat. 1175 (1919), established the national park; Hughes, *In the House of Stone and Light*, 78.
29. W. R. Mattoon, "A Working Plan for Grand Canyon National Monument," June 28, 1909, Grand Canyon Research Library; Robert Shankland, *Steve Mather of the National Parks*, 3d ed. (New York: Alfred A. Knopf, 1970), 227; Hughes, *In the House of Stone and Light*.
30. Mattoon, "A Working Plan for Grand Canyon National Monument," 1–5; Steen, *The United States Forest Service;* David Clary, *Timber and the Forest Service* (Lawrence: University Press of Kansas, 1986); Gifford Pinchot, *Breaking New Ground* (New York: Harcourt Brace, 1947).
31. Mattoon, "A Working Plan for the Grand Canyon"; for more on the early Forest Service, see Hal K. Rothman, ed., *"I'll Never Fight Fire with My Bare Hands Again": Recollections of the First Foresters of the Inland Northwest* (Lawrence: University Press of Kansas, 1994), 3–17.
32. Don P. Johnston and Aldo Leopold, "Grand Canyon Working Plan: Uses, Information, Recreational Development," April 9, 1917, Grand Canyon Research Library; Frank A. Waugh, "A Plan for Development of the Village of Grand Canyon, Arizona," U.S. Department of Agriculture, 1918, Grand Canyon Research Library; Hughes, *In the House of Stone and Light*, 57, 70–71.
33. Hughes, *In the House of Stone and Light*, 72; Timothy Manns, *A Guide to the Grand Canyon Village Historic District* (Grand Canyon, AZ: Grand Canyon Natural History Association, n.d.), 7; Shankland, *Steve Mather of the National Parks*, 143; Karen L. Taylor, *Grand Canyon's Long-Eared Taxi* (Grand Canyon, AZ: Grand Canyon Natural History Association, 1992), 21.
34. Johnston and Leopold, "Grand Canyon Working Plan"; Taylor, *Grand Canyon's Long-Eared Taxi*, 21; Hughes, *In the House of Stone and Light*, 71–72; Manns, *A Guide to the Grand Canyon Village Historic District*, 9; Rothman, ed., *I'll Never Fight Fire with My Bare Hands Again*, 3–17; Ellsworth Kolb, *Through the Grand Canyon from Wyoming to Mexico* (New York: Macmillan Company, 1914). The author owns a copy of the thirty-second edition of Ellsworth Kolb's *Through the Grand Canyon from Wyoming to Mexico* (Tucson: University of Arizona Press, 1989), autographed in 1969 by eighty-eight-year-old Emory Kolb.
35. Johnston and Leopold, "Grand Canyon Working Plan"; Hughes, *In the House of Stone and Light*, 53.
36. Johnston and Leopold, "Grand Canyon Working Plan"; Pyne, *Dutton's Point*, 27–36.
37. Frank A. Waugh, "A Plan for the Development of the Village of Grand Canyon, Arizona," USDA, 1918, Grand Canyon Research Library.
38. Henry Graves to W. B. Acker, March 2, 1915; Henry Graves to Stephen T. Mather, March 17, 1915; Mark Daniels to Stephen T. Mather, April 8, 1915; M. W. Edy, assistant to the forester to Horace M. Albright, April 28, 1915; Sen. Marcus A. Smith of Arizona to Secretary of the Interior [Franklin K. Lane], December 6, 1915; Arizona Good Roads Association resolution, January 1916; Yavapai County Chamber of Commerce

resolution, January 15, 1916; E. P. Ripley, letter to the editor, *Chicago Tribune,* February 21, 1916; Stephen T. Mather to Edward Chambers, June 25, 1915; Chambers to Mather, February 10, 1916; Mather to Chambers, February 12, 1916; Sec. of Agriculture D. F. Houston to Secretary of the Interior [Franklin K. Lane], n.d. (ca. October 1915); Mather to Houston, October 23, 1915; *Forest Notes* (USDA publication), April 20, 1916; A. F. "Bertie" Potter to Mather, February 8, 1916; O. F. Andrews, "U.S. Bureaus Clash on National Parks," *Chicago Examiner,* October 16, 1916; Albright to Mather, telegram, December 6, 1916; Albright to F. W. Griffith, Chief Clerk, NPS, June 29, 1917, Grand Canyon, Series 6, Pt. 1, Box 54, RG 79, National Archives.

39. Charles F. Punchard Jr., Landscape Engineer, to Stephen T. Mather, September 3, 1919; D. L. Reaburn, Superintendent, Grand Canyon, to Mather, December 1, 1920; Mather to Reaburn, March 15, 1921; Reaburn to Mather, July 12, 1921; Arno B. Cammerer to Reaburn, July 19, 1921, Records of the National Park Service, Grand Canyon, Series 6, Buildings, Pt. 1, RG 79, National Archives. For the Park Service–Forest Service dispute, see Hal Rothman, "'A Regular Ding-Dong Fight': Agency Culture and Evolution in the NPS–USFS Dispute, 1916–1937," *Western Historical Quarterly* 20 (May 1989): 141–61.
40. H. V. Kaltenborn to Stephen T. Mather, May 26, 1920; H. V. Kaltenborn to Stephen T. Mather, June 3, 1920; Stephen T. Mather to H. V. Kaltenborn, June 7, 1920; H. V. Kaltenborn to Stephen T. Mather, June 10, 1920, Grand Canyon, Series 6, Pt. 1, Box 46, RG 79, National Archives; Horace M. Albright as told to Robert Cahn, *The Birth of the National Park Service: The Founding Years, 1913–1933* (Salt Lake City: Howe Brothers Press, 1986); Shankland, *Steve Mather of the National Parks;* for the Forest Service strategy, see Rothman, ed., "*I'll Never Fight Fire with my Bare Hands Again,*" 3–17, and Rothman, "'A Regular Ding-Dong Fight,'" 141–61.
41. Shankland, *Steve Mather of the National Parks,* 70–71, 120–27, 179–83; Ise, *Our National Park Policy,* 233–37.
42. W. H. Hopkins to [National Park Service], July 22, 1920; Ned Johnson to Department of National Parks (*sic*), July 28, 1920; Mrs. Henry B. Sacks to Department of National Parks (*sic*), October 15, 1920; Secretary of Agriculture to National Park Service, January 3, 1921; R. L. Johnson to National Park Service, June 30, 1921, Grand Canyon, Series 6, Pt. 1, Box 46, RG 79, National Archives.
43. Reaburn to Stephen T. Mather, June 21, 1921; R. Hunter Clarkson to Arno B. Cammerer, June 5, 1923; E. K. Sykes to National Park Service, June 16, 1923, Grand Canyon, Series 6, Pt. 1., Box 46, RG 79, National Archives; Hegemann, *Navaho Trading Days,* 5.
44. Josephine Henson to Stephen T. Mather, April 24, 1924, Grand Canyon, Series 6, Pt. 1., Box 46, RG 79, National Archives.
45. Arno B. Cammerer to Charles Punchard, July 31, 1920, Grand Canyon, Series 6, Pt. 1, Box 46, Buildings, RG 79, National Archives; Albright as told to Cahn, *The National Park Service: The Founding Years.*
46. Laura Thompson, *Culture in Crisis: A Study of the Hopi Indians* (New York: Harper and Brothers, 1949), 51; Walter Collins O'Kane, *Sun in the Sky* (Norman: University of Oklahoma Press, 1950), 116–17; Peter M. Whiteley, *Deliberate Acts: Changing Hopi Culture Through the Oraibi Split* (Tucson: University of Arizona Press, 1988), 13–42; Scott Rushforth and Steadman Upham, *A Hopi Social History: Anthropological Perspectives on Sociocultural Persistence and Change* (Austin: University of Texas Press, 1992), 97–148. Richard O. Clemmer, *Roads in the Sky: The Hopi Indians in a Century of Change* (Boulder, CO: Westview Press, 1995), 3, indicates that Hopi aboriginal claims total more than 13 million acres, including all of the Grand Canyon, the San Francisco

Peaks, all of Black Mesa, and a large area south of today's Interstate 40; he locates religious shrines in the Grand Canyon and in the San Francisco mountains (16); for an estimate of the length of interruption of the salt trips to the Grand Canyon, see 197.

47. Clemmer, *Roads in the Sky,* 99, 288–89; Robert W. Rydell, *All the World's a Fair: Visions of Empire at American International Expositions, 1876–1916* (Chicago: University of Chicago Press, 1984), 38–72; Virginia L. Gratton, *Mary Colter: Builder upon the Red Earth* (Grand Canyon, AZ: Grand Canyon Natural History Association, 1992), 10; see also Hinsley, *Savages and Scientists.*
48. Johnston and Leopold, "Grand Canyon Working Plan"; Gratton, *Mary Colter,* 14–19; Manns, *A Guide to Grand Canyon Village Historic District,* 19.
49. Clemmer, *Roads in the Sky,* 53–55, 65–66; Diana F. Pardue and Kathleen L. Howard, "Making Art, Making Money: The Fred Harvey Company and the Indian Artisan," in *The Great Southwest of the Fred Harvey Company and the Santa Fe Railway,* ed. Marta Weigle and Barbara A. Babcock (Phoenix: Heard Museum, 1996), 171–73.
50. Hegemann, *Navaho Trading Days,* 1, 4–5, 10, 35; Rosemary Nusbaum, *Tierra Dulce: Reminiscences from the Jesse Nusbaum Papers* (Santa Fe: Sunstone Press, 1980), 53; Hughes, *In the House of Stone and Light,* 86–87, 97.
51. Hegemann, *Navaho Trading Days,* 35; Hughes, *In the House of Stone and Light,* 50.
52. Warren A. Beck and Ynez D. Haase, *Historical Atlas of the American West* (Norman: University of Oklahoma Press, 1989), 51; Gratton, *Mary Colter,* 19; Emily Benedek, *The Wind Won't Know Me: A History of the Navajo-Hopi Land Dispute* (New York: Vintage Books, 1992), 25–57; McLuhan, T. C. *Dream Tracks: The Railroad and the American Indian, 1890–1930* (New York: Abrams, 1985), 67; Clemmer, *Roads in the Sky,* 289.
53. Leslie Spier, *Havasupai Ethnography* (New York: American Museum of Natural History, 1928), 91, 101–17; Steven A. Weber and P. David Seaman, eds., *Havasupai Habitat: A. F. Whiting's Ethnography of a Traditional Indian Culture* (Tucson: University of Arizona Press, 1985), 3–15; Juan Sinyella, interview by J. Donald Hughes and John Motherhead, August 10, 1964, transcription available at Grand Canyon Research Library, 17–18; Hegemann, *Navaho Trading Days,* 6.
54. Spier, *Havasupai Ethnography,* 101–16; Hughes, *In the House of Stone and Light,* 88–89.
55. Hegemann, *Navaho Trading Days,* 10; Spier, *Havasupai Ethnography,* 91; Sinyella, "Havasupai History," 23–24; Hughes, *In the House of Stone and Light,* 77–78.
56. Louise M. Hinchcliffe, "Origin and Development of Supai Camp (South Rim, Grand Canyon)," report, 1976, Grand Canyon Research Library; Jacilee Wray, "Havasupai Ethnohistory on the South Rim of Grand Canyon National Park: A Case Study for Cultural Resource Management in the National Park Service" (Master's thesis, Northern Arizona University, 1990).
57. *Report of the Director of the National Park Service for Fiscal Year Ended June 30, 1931* (Washington, DC: Government Printing Office, 1932); H. B. Hommon, "Report on Havasupai Indian Colony at the South Rim, Grand Canyon National Park," May 14, 1938, Grand Canyon Research Library; Hegemann, *Navaho Trading Days,* 8; Hinchcliffe, "Origin and Development of Supai Camp"; Wray, "Havasupai Ethnohistory on the South Rim of Grand Canyon National Park."
58. Hommon, "Report on Havasupai Indian Colony at the South Rim, Grand Canyon National Park"; Hinchcliffe, "Origin and Development of Supai Camp"; Wray, "Havasupai Ethnohistory on the South Rim of Grand Canyon National Park."
59. M. R. Tillotson, "The Problem of the Havasupai Camp Near Grand Canyon Village in Grand Canyon National Park," June 18, 1936, Grand Canyon Research Library; Arno B. Cammerer to M. R. Tillotson, July 22, 1936, Grand Canyon Research Library;

Hommon, "Report on Havasupai Indian Colony at the South Rim, Grand Canyon National Park"; Hinchcliffe, "Origin and Development of Supai Camp"; Wray, "Havasupai Ethnohistory on the South Rim of Grand Canyon National Park."

60. Alfred C. Kuehl, "Technical Comment—Landscape," November 4, 1936; J. V. Lloyd, "Memorandum to Superintendent Tillotson," November 29, 1937; John Herrick to Guy Hobgood, January 27, 1938; Guy Hobgood to John Herrick, May 16, 1938; J. G. Townsend to J. V. Lloyd, July 6, 1938; M. R. Tillotson to J. G. Townsend, July 12, 1938; A. E. Demaray, "Memorandum for Commissioner Collier, Office of Indian Affairs," August 22, 1938; M. R. Tillotson, "Memorandum for the Director," September 8, 1938; A. E. Demaray, "Memorandum for Acting Superintendent [H. C.] Bryant," March 17, 1939; H. C. Bryant to C. F. Shaffer, April 14, 1939; H. C. Bryant, "Memorandum for the Director," April 21, 1939; J. V. Lloyd, "Memorandum for Acting Superintendent Bryant," April 29, 1939; H. C. Bryant, "Memorandum for the Director," May 2, 1939, Grand Canyon Research Library.

61. The literature of the New Western History is rife with examples. Richard White, *It's Your Misfortune and None of My Own: A New History of the American West* (Norman: University of Oklahoma Press, 1991), 236–97, presents an overview of this issue. Numerous case studies support this hypothesis: Donald Worster, *Dust Bowl: The Southern Plains in the 1930s* (New York: Oxford University Press, 1979); Albert Camarillo, *Chicanos in a Changing Society: From Mexican Pueblos to American Barrios in Santa Barbara and Southern California, 1848–1930* (Cambridge: Harvard University Press, 1979); Sarah Duestch, *No Separate Refuge: Culture, Class, and Gender on an Anglo-Hispanic Frontier in the American Southwest, 1880–1940* (New York: Oxford University Press, 1987); William G. Robbins, *Hard Times in Paradise: Coos Bay, Oregon, 1850–1986* (Seattle: University of Washington Press, 1989); William E. deBuys, *Enchantment and Exploitation: The Life and Hard Times of a New Mexico Mountain Range* (Albuquerque: University of New Mexico Press, 1985); and Hal K. Rothman, *On Rims and Ridges: The Las Alamos Area Since 1880* (Lincoln: University of Nebraska Press, 1992), offer prominent examples. The vagaries of the rural economy in the inland Northwest are presented in n.a., *Early Days in the Forest Service* (Missoula, MT: United States Forest Service, 1944), a collection of letters from turn-of-the-century foresters in the inland Northwest, and Edwin A. Tucker and David A. Gillio, eds., *The Early Days: A Sourcebook of Southwest Region History* (Albuquerque: USDA Forest Service, 1989–1991), vols. 1–3, a collection of oral histories with southwestern foresters. Richard White, *The Middle Ground: Indians, Empires, and Republics in the Great Lakes Region, 1650–1815* (Cambridge: Cambridge University Press, 1991), shows the process through which these choices evolve.

62. Poling-Kempes, *The Harvey Girls*, 170–72; Bryant, *Atchison, Topeka, and Santa Fe Railway*, 106–22; "The Harvey System," *Santa Fe Magazine*, July 1907, 271–78; John Willy, "Dropping in on Fred Harvey from the Cañon to Chicago," *Santa Fe Magazine*, January 1929, 43–48.

63. Shankland, *Steve Mather of the National Parks*, 225–42; Rothman, " 'A Regular Ding-Dong Fight,' " 150–52; Ise, *Our National Park Policy*, 235–38; Edwin Corle, *Listen Bright Angel* (New York: Duell, Sloan, and Pierce, 1946), 206–10; Albright as told to Cahn, *The Birth of the National Park Service*, 169–86; see *Report of the Director of the National Park Service, 1919* (Washington, DC: Government Printing Office, 1919), 365–69, for the text of the commissioner of the General Land Office's final decree in the Cameron mineral cases; for Rowe, see Hegemann, *Navaho Trading Days*, 39; for Boone, see John

Mack Faragher, *Daniel Boone: The Life and Legend of an American Pioneer* (New York: Henry Holt, 1992).

64. Hegemann, *Navaho Trading Days*, 3.
65. Ibid., 6–7.
66. Ibid., 8–10.
67. Ibid., 13; C. J. Birchfield, "First Airplane Landing at Bottom of the Grand Cañon," *Santa Fe Magazine*, October 1922, 17–20; "Fred Harvey Coat Rule Upheld by Oklahoma Supreme Court," *Santa Fe Magazine*, October 1922, 29–32; Frank McNitt, *The Indian Traders* (Norman: University of Oklahoma Press, 1962), 265–70.

4. THE TOURISM OF HEGEMONY II

1. John A. Gjerve, *Chili Line: The Narrow Rail Trail to Santa Fe* (Española, NM: Rio Grande Sun Press, 1969); Jerry I. Williams and Paul E. McAllister, *New Mexico in Maps* (Albuquerque: Technology Application Center, University of New Mexico, 1979), 104, provide population information for late nineteenth- and early twentieth-century Santa Fe; Oakah L. Jones, *Los Paisanos: Spanish Settlers on the Northern Frontier of New Spain* (Norman: University of Oklahoma Press, 1979), 117–29, provides earlier population figures. According to these sources, the 6,728 people in Santa Fe in 1817 roughly equaled the 1880 population of 6,635 but outnumbered the population of 1900, 5,603, and that of 1910, 5,072.
2. Malcolm Ebright, *Land Grants and Lawsuits in Northern New Mexico* (Albuquerque: University of New Mexico Press, 1994); John R. Van Ness, *Hispanos in Northern New Mexico: The Development of Corporate Community and Multicommunity* (New York: AMS Press, 1991); Alvar W. Carlson, *The Hispano Homeland: Four Centuries in New Mexico's Río Arriba* (Baltimore: Johns Hopkins University Press, 1991), 73; David J. Weber, "Spanish Fur Trade from New Mexico, 1540–1821," *Americas* 24 (1967): 122–36; Floyd S. Fierman, *Guts and Ruts: The Jewish Pioneer on the Trail in the American Southwest* (New York: KTAV Publishing, 1985), 7–48; Floyd S. Fierman, "The Speigelbergs of New Mexico: Merchants and Bankers, 1844–1893," *Southwestern Studies* 1, no. 4 (winter 1964): 3–48; Hal K. Rothman, *On Rims and Ridges: The Las Alamos Area Since 1880* (Lincoln: University of Nebraska Press, 1992); and William DeBuys, *Enchantment and Exploitation: The Life and Hard Times of a New Mexico Mountain Range* (Albuquerque: University of New Mexico Press, 1985).
3. "Historic Santa Fe," *Santa Fe New Mexican*, July 9, 1898, and rerun a number of times; Billy Mac Jones, *Health Seekers in the Southwest, 1817–1900* (Norman: University of Oklahoma Press, 1967); deBuys, *Enchantment and Exploitation*, 245–59; Hal Rothman, "Cultural and Environmental Change on the Pajarito Plateau, 1880–1910," *New Mexico Historical Review* 64, no. 2 (April 1989): 185–212; Robert MacCameron, "Environmental Change in Colonial New Mexico," *Environmental History Review* 18, no. 2 (summer 1994): 17–40; Craig D. Allen, "Changes in the Landscape of the Jemez Mountains, New Mexico" (Ph.D. diss., University of California, Berkeley, 1989); Sarah Duestch, *No Separate Refuge: Culture, Class, and Gender on an Anglo-Hispanic Frontier in the American Southwest, 1880–1940* (New York: Oxford University Press, 1987); and Suzanne Forrest, *Preservation of the Village* (Albuquerque: University of New Mexico Press, 1989).
4. Rothman, *On Rims and Ridges*, 39–83; C. W. Ceram, *The First American: A Story of North American Archaeology* (New York: Harcourt Brace Jovanovich, 1971), 100–120.
5. "Exploring the Cliff Dwellings," *Santa Fe New Mexican*, October 5, 1907; "It Is Blessed

to Give," *Santa Fe New Mexican,* January 25, 1910; "Many Lectures at School," *Santa Fe New Mexican,* July 19, 1910.

6. Edgar L. Hewett, *The Pajarito Plateau and Its Ancient People* (Indianapolis: Bobbs-Merrill, 1930); Rothman, *On Rims and Ridges;* see also Curtis M. Hinsley, *Savages and Scientists: The Smithsonian Institution and the Development of American Anthropology, 1846–1910* (Washington, DC: Smithsonian Institution Press, 1981), for an analysis of the role of archaeology in the early twentieth-century United States.
7. Rothman, *On Rims and Ridges,* 83–91.
8. Hal K. Rothman, *Preserving Different Pasts* (Urbana: University of Illinois Press, 1989), 25–45.
9. The Edgar L. Hewett Papers, Box 22, Museum of New Mexico History Library, contain much of Hewett's correspondence on these matters; "Only School of Its Kind in the Entire World," *Santa Fe New Mexican,* January 14, 1909; "Public Pride Aroused at Archaeological Lecture," *Santa Fe New Mexican,* February 3, 1909; "Important and Salutary Measures Placed on the Statute Books," *Santa Fe New Mexican,* March 19, 1909; "Museum Board Holds Its First Meeting," *Santa Fe New Mexican,* April 6, 1909; see also Chris Wilson, *The Myth of Santa Fe: Creating a Modern Regional Tradition* (Albuquerque: University of New Mexico Press, 1997), 117–21; Curtis M. Hinsley Jr., "Edgar L. Hewett and the School of American Research in Santa Fe, 1906–1912," in *American Archaeology Past and Future: A Celebration of the Society for American Archaeology, 1935–1985,* ed. David J. Meltzer, Don D. Fowler, and Jeremy Sabloff (Washington, DC: Smithsonian Institution Press, 1986), 217–32; Beatrice Chauvenet, *Hewett and Friends: A Biography of Santa Fe's Vibrant Era* (Santa Fe: Museum of New Mexico Press, 1983), 63–174; Arrel M. Gibson, *Santa Fe and Taos Colonies: Age of the Muses, 1900–1942* (Norman: University of Oklahoma Press, 1983), 30–49; Keith L. Bryant Jr., "The Atchison, Topeka, and Santa Fe Railway and the Development of the Santa Fe and Taos Art Colonies," *Western Historical Quarterly* 9 (October 1968): 437–54; Rothman, *On Rims and Ridges,* 84–89, 95–104, 117–30, 150–52, for more on Hewett's personality and role in the cultural history of Santa Fe in the early twentieth century.
10. H. B. Hening, ed., *George Curry, 1861–1947: An Autobiography* (Albuquerque: University of New Mexico Press, 1958), 80–119; Ebright, *Land Grants and Lawsuits in Northern New Mexico,* 43–45.
11. "Historic Santa Fe," *Santa Fe New Mexican,* July 8, 1898; "Boosting Santa Fe's Attractions," *Santa Fe New Mexican,* July 13, 1909; Hening, ed., *George Curry,* 223; Virginia Scharff, *Taking the Wheel: Women and the Coming of the Motor Age* (New York: Free Press, 1991).
12. "Historic Santa Fe," *Santa Fe New Mexican,* July 8, 1898; "Only School of Its Kind in the Entire World," *Santa Fe New Mexican,* January 14, 1909; "Ancient, Quaint, and Progressive," *Santa Fe New Mexican,* January 25, 1909, 3; "Public Pride Aroused at Archaeological Lecture," *Santa Fe New Mexican,* February 3, 1909; "Boosting Santa Fe's Attractions," *Santa Fe New Mexican,* July 13, 1909; "What Is Santa Fe Doing for the Tourist?" *Santa Fe New Mexican,* July 26, 1909; "Lively Board of Trade Meeting," *Santa Fe New Mexican,* September 11, 1909; "Splendid Work," *Santa Fe New Mexican,* October 15, 1909; "Interest in Archaeological Work," *Santa Fe New Mexican,* October 26, 1909; "Special Exhibit Each Week," *Santa Fe New Mexican,* May 7, 1910; Wilson, *The Myth of Santa Fe,* 122–25; Rothman, *On Rims and Ridges,* 110–11; Chauvenet, *Hewett and Friends,* 109–13.
13. "Building a Tourist City," *Santa Fe New Mexican,* July 11, 1909.

14. "A Fond Dream Coming True," *Santa Fe New Mexican,* April 10, 1909; "Hotel De Vargas It Will Be," *Santa Fe New Mexican,* June 12, 1909.
15. "The Best Advertised Town in the World," *Santa Fe New Mexican,* April 27, 1909; A. H. Broadhead, "From Santa Fe to Seattle," *Santa Fe New Mexican,* June 29, 1909; "Santa Fe's Advantages Need to Be Outlined," *Santa Fe New Mexican,* January 17, 1910.
16. "Begin Campaign of Advertising," *Santa Fe New Mexican,* May 22, 1907; "Hundreds Visit Pajarito Ruins," *Santa Fe New Mexican,* May 22, 1907; Edgar L. Hewett, *Ancient Ruins of the Southwest* (Denver: Denver, Rio Grande, and Western Railroad, 1909); "Ancient Wonders of the Pajarito Cliff Dwellings," *Santa Fe New Mexican,* June 17, 1909; "Cliff Dwellings as Tourist Attractions," *Santa Fe New Mexican,* July 8, 1909; "Work of American Institute of Archaeology," *Santa Fe New Mexican,* July 12, 1910; "Good Advertising for Santa Fe," *Santa Fe New Mexican,* May 20, 1910. These are among dozens of examples that attest not only to Hewett's vision of tourism in Santa Fe but also to his influence on the local media and in local culture. See also Wilson, *The Myth of Santa Fe,* 122.
17. Carl D. Sheppard, *Creator of the Santa Fe Style: Isaac Hamilton Rapp, Architect* (Albuquerque: University of New Mexico Press, 1988), 3–16, 81, 94–97, 111–15; Talbot F. Hamlin, *The American Spirit in Architecture* (New Haven: Yale University Press, 1926); Chauvenet, *Hewett and Friends,* 124–27; Wilson, *The Myth of Santa Fe,* 76–78, 131–40.
18. Sheppard, *Creator of the Santa Fe Style;* E. Dana Johnson, "A University Pueblo," *World's Work* 14 (October 1907): 9468–74; "A Revival of Old Pueblo Architecture," *Architects and Builders Magazine* 10 (1908–1909): 282–85; "Pueblo Architecture Adapted to Modern Needs in New Mexico," *Craftsman* 19, no. 4 (1909): 404–6.
19. Wilson, *The Myth of Santa Fe,* 125–29.
20. T. J. Jackson Lears, *No Place of Grace: Antimodernism and the Transformation of American Culture, 1880–1920* (Chicago: University of Chicago Press, 1994); David Shi, *The Simple Life: Plain Living and High Thinking in American Culture* (New York: Oxford University Press, 1985); Robert Wiebe, *The Search for Order, 1877–1920* (New York: Hill and Wang, 1967); Hinsley, *Savages and Scientists;* Robert Rydell, *All the World's a Fair: Visions of Empire at American International Expositions, 1876–1916* (Chicago: University of Chicago Press, 1984).
21. Ernest Ingersoll, "La Villa Real de Santa Fe," in *New Mexico 100 Years Ago,* ed. Skip Whitson (Albuquerque: Sun Publishing Company, 1977), 17; Charles F. Lummis, *A Tramp Across the Continent* (Albuquerque: Calvin Horn, 1969), 99.
22. Chauvenet, *Hewett and Friends,* 129–31.
23. Wilson, *The Myth of Santa Fe,* 236–37; Chauvenet, *Hewett and Friends,* 138–41, 175–77.
24. *Daily New Mexican,* April 5, 1881; N. L. King, "Map of the City of Santa Fe, New Mexico, Showing Street, Park, and River Improvements Proposed by the City Planning Board," Santa Fe Planning Board, 1912; see also Christopher Wilson, "The Santa Fe, New Mexico, Plaza: Architectural and Cultural History, 1610-1921" (Master's thesis, University of New Mexico, 1981).
25. Wilson, *The Myth of Santa Fe,* 122–23; Chauvenet, *Hewett and Friends,* 125–27; James H. Purdy, "The Carlos Vierra House," *Bulletin of the Historic Santa Fe Foundation* 5, no. 1 (January 1979): 3–14.
26. Wilson, *The Myth of Santa Fe,* 125–34.
27. Steven Ruggles and Matthew Sobek, *Integrated Public Use Microdata Series: Version 1.0* (Minneapolis: Social History Research Laboratory, University of Minnesota, 1995), hereafter referred to as IPUMS. This is data from the 1880 IPUMS; Standard Eco-

nomic Area (SEA) 274 for the Santa Fe area; data derived from a 1 percent sample of 391 people; cross tabulations of place of birth (POB), M/F POB, Age, OCC1950, OCC.

28. Linda Tigges, "Santa Fe Landownership in the 1880s," *New Mexico Historical Review* 68, no. 2 (April 1993): 153–80; Paul Horgan, *Lamy of Santa Fe: His Life and Times* (New York: Farrar, Straus, Giroux, 1975), 114–16; Fierman, *Guts and Ruts*, 7–49; Fierman, "The Speigelbergs of New Mexico: Merchants and Bankers, 1844–1893," 3–48.
29. Ruggles and Sobek, *1910 IPUMS;* SEA 274; data derived from a 1 percent sample of 259 people; cross tabulations of POB, M/F POB, OCC1950, OWNERSHIP, MORTGAGE; Carlson, *The Hispano Homeland*, 67–87; Richard L. Nostrand, "The Century of Hispano Expansion," *New Mexico Historical Review* 62 (October 1987): 361–86.
30. Victor Westphall, *Thomas Benton Catron and His Era* (Tucson: University of Arizona Press, 1973); Rothman, *On Rims and Ridges*, 128–201; Calvin A. Roberts, "H. B. Fergusson, 1848–1915: New Mexico Spokesman for Political Reform," *New Mexico Historical Review* 57, no. 3 (July 1982): 237–56; Erna Fergusson, *New Mexico: A Pageant of Three Peoples* (New York: Alfred A. Knopf, 1951).
31. Arrel M. Gibson, *Santa Fe and Taos Colonies: Age of the Muses, 1900–1942* (Norman: University of Oklahoma Press, 1983), 50–68; Marta Weigle and Kyle Fiore, *Santa Fe and Taos: The Writer's Era, 1916–1941* (Santa Fe: Ancient City Press, 1984), 3–69. Sylvia Rodriquez, "Art, Tourism, and Race Relations in Taos: Toward a Sociology of the Art Colony," *Journal of Anthropological Research* 45, no. 1 (spring 1989): 77–100; Lois Palken Rudnick, *Mabel Dodge Luhan: New Woman, New Worlds* (Albuquerque: University of New Mexico Press, 1984); Robert M. Crunden, *American Salons: Encounters with European Modernism, 1885–1917* (New York: Oxford University Press, 1993), 383–408.
32. "Staff of the New Museum," *Santa Fe New Mexican*, April 9, 1909, 6; Rosemary Nusbaum, *Tierra Dulce: Reminiscences from the Jesse Nusbaum Papers* (Santa Fe: Sunstone Press, 1980), 9–11; Edna Robertson and Sarah Nestor, *Artists of the Canyons and Caminos: Santa Fe, the Early Years* (Salt Lake City: Peregrine Smith Books, 1976), 39–40; Howard R. Lamar, *The Far Southwest 1846–1912: A Territorial History* (New Haven: Yale University Press, 1970), 136–201; Gibson, *The Santa Fe and Taos Colonies*, 24–38; *The WPA Guide to 1930s New Mexico* (Tucson: University of Arizona Press, 1989), 167; Fergusson, *New Mexico*, 366–81; Chauvenet, *Hewett and Friends*, 104–9; Earl Pomeroy, *In Search of the Golden West: The Tourist in Western America* (Lincoln: University of Nebraska Press, 1985), 37.
33. "Staff of the New Museum," *Santa Fe New Mexican*, April 9, 1909, 6; Lois Palken Rudnick, *Mabel Dodge Luhan: New Woman, New Worlds* (Albuquerque: University of New Mexico Press, 1984), 236–237; Robertson and Nestor, *Artists of the Canyons and Caminos*, 39–40; Lamar, *The Far Southwest 1846–1912*, 136–201; Laurie Lisle, *Portrait of an Artist: A Biography of Georgia O'Keefe* (New York: Simon and Schuster, 1980), 111; Gibson, *The Santa Fe and Taos Colonies*, 34, 69–86, 199–217; Fergusson, *New Mexico*, 366–81; Chauvenet, *Hewett and Friends*, 104–9; Pomeroy, *In Search of the Golden West*, 37. For an instructive view of the way many nineteenth-century Americans viewed Santa Fe, see Richard Allan Baker, *Conservation Politics: The Senate Career of Clinton P. Anderson* (Albuquerque: University of New Mexico Press, 1985), 15.
34. Chauvenet, *Hewett and Friends*, 124–26; Nusbaum, *Tierra Dulce*, 54, 60–64.
35. *Fourteenth Census of the United States: 1920, vol. 1, Population* (Washington, DC: Government Printing Office, 1923), 3: 667–70; Robert Larson, *New Mexico's Quest for Statehood, 1846–1912* (Albuquerque: University of New Mexico Press, 1968).

36. *Fourteenth Census of the United States Taken in the Year 1920*, vol. 1, *Population 1920* (Washington, DC: Government Printing Office, 1921), 527–29.
37. Gibson, *The Santa Fe and Taos Colonies*, 41–49, 69–86; Chauvenet, *Hewett and Friends*, 121–35.
38. Wilson, *The Myth of Santa Fe*, 181–205, 213–15; Chauvenet, *Hewett and Friends*, 147–51; Henry J. Tobias, *History of the Jews of New Mexico* (Albuquerque: University of New Mexico Press, 1992), 113–14.
39. Douglas C. Comer, *Ritual Ground: Bent's Old Fort, World Formation, and the Annexation of the Southwest* (Berkeley: University of California Press, 1996).
40. Wilson, *The Myth of Santa Fe*, 205–21; Chauvenet, *Hewett and Friends*, 151–53.
41. Chauvenet, *Hewett and Friends*, 152–59.
42. Weigle and Fiore, *Santa Fe and Taos*, 7.
43. Ibid., 23–24.
44. Rudnick, *Mabel Dodge Luhan*, 169–71; Fergusson, *New Mexico*, 371.
45. Gibson, *The Santa Fe and Taos Colonies*, 199–217; Weigle and Fiore, *Santa Fe and Taos*, 25; Esther F. Stineman, *Mary Austin: Song of a Maverick* (New Haven: Yale University Press, 1989).
46. Mary Austin, "The Town That Doesn't Want a Chautauqua," *New Republic*, July 1926, 195; Kyle S. Crichton, "Philistine and Artist Clash in the Battle of Santa Fe," *New York World*, June 27, 1926; Weigle and Fiore, *Santa Fe and Taos*, 18–19; Kenneth Philp, "Albert B. Fall and the Protest from the Pueblos, 1921–1923, *Arizona and the West* 12, no. 3 (1970): 242; Marc Simmons, "History of the Pueblos Since 1821," in *Handbook of North American Indians 9 Southwest*, ed. Alfonso Ortiz (Washington, DC: Smithsonian Institution, 1979), 215; see Chauvenet, *Hewett and Friends*, 171–204, for a blow-by-blow account of the cultural controversies of the 1920s.
47. Chauvenet, *Hewett and Friends*, 177–86.
48. Amelia E. White to Paul A. F. Walter, May 8, 1926, Edgar L. Hewett Collection, Museum of New Mexico History Library, Santa Fe; Gibson, *The Santa Fe and Taos Colonies*, 256–58; Weigle and Fiore, *Santa Fe and Taos*, 20–21.
49. *Fifteenth Census of the United States: 1930, Population*, vol. 3, pt. 2 (Washington, DC: Government Printing Office, 1932), 247.
50. Ibid.
51. Edward Said, *Orientalism* (New York: Pantheon Books, 1978), coined the idea of the "Other." See also Dean MacCannell, *The Tourist: A New Theory of the Leisure Class* (New York: Schocken Books, 1976), who argues that tourist settings, a category he describes as places where there is no evidence that the "show" is for the sightseers, are "copies that are presented as disclosing more about the real thing than the real thing itself discloses" (102). In many ways the fin de siècle Grand Canyon did exactly that.
52. Douglas Pearce, *Tourist Development*, 2d ed. (New York: John Wiley and Sons, 1989), 1–77.

5. TOURISM ON THE ACTUAL PERIPHERY

1. Dean MacCannell, *The Tourist: A New Theory of the Leisure Class* (New York: Schocken Books, 1976), 100–102, describes this phase as stage three of six he defines as characteristic of the tourist setting.
2. T. J. Jackson Lears, *No Place of Grace: Antimodernism and the Transformation of American Culture, 1880–1920* (Chicago: University of Chicago Press, 1994), 7–25.
3. Ibid., 4–7; Hinsley, *Savages and Scientists*.

4. Edmund Morris, *The Rise of Theodore Roosevelt* (New York: Coward, McCann, and Geoghegan, 1979).
5. Theodore Roosevelt with Wayne Andrews, ed., *The Autobiography of Theodore Roosevelt* (New York: Scribners, 1958), 58–59, 65, 79–80; Hermann Hagedorn, *Roosevelt in the Badlands* (Boston: Houghton, Mifflin, 1921).
6. Roosevelt with Andrews, ed., *Autobiography*, 58–59.
7. Ibid., 76.
8. G. Edward White, *The Eastern Establishment and the Western Experience: The West of Frederic Remington, Theodore Roosevelt, and Owen Wister* (New Haven: Yale University Press, 1968), 79–93; see also Carleton Putnam, *Theodore Roosevelt*, vol. 1, *The Formative Years* (New York: Scribners, 1958), 198–595, for detailed coverage.
9. Theodore Roosevelt, *Ranch Life and the Hunting Trail* (New York: Century Company, 1888); recent popular culture articulations of this myth include the film *City Slickers* (1991) and its sequel, the less persuasive *City Slickers II.*
10. John F. Reiger, *American Sportsmen and the Origins of Conservation*, rev. ed. (Norman: University of Oklahoma Press, 1986), 99–102.
11. Ibid.
12. T. C. McLuhan, *Dream Tracks: The Railroad and the American Indian, 1890–1930* (New York: Abrams, 1985); Keith L. Bryant Jr., *History of the Atchison, Topeka, and the Santa Fe Railway* (Lincoln: University of Nebraska Press, 1974); L. L. Waters, *Steel Trains to Santa Fe* (Lawrence: University Press of Kansas, 1950).
13. Richard Hofstadter, *Social Darwinism in American Thought* (Philadelphia: University of Pennsylvania Press, 1944); Lears, *No Place of Grace;* George Forgie, *Patricide in the House Divided: A Psychological Interpretation of Lincoln and His Age* (New York: W. W. Norton and Company, 1979).
14. Donald Worster, *Nature's Economy: A History of Ecological Ideas* (New York: Sierra Club Books, 1977), 131–38; Thomas Jefferson, *Notes on the State of Virginia* (New York: Harper Torchbooks, 1964), 22–71; Comte Georges de Buffon, *Natural History: General and Particular*, trans. William Smellie (London: A. Straham and T. Cadell, 1791); Alfred W. Crosby Jr., *The Columbian Exchange: The Biological and Cultural Consequences of 1492* (Westport, CT: Greenwood Press, 1972), 20–21; Charles H. Lange and Carroll L. Riley, *The Southwestern Journals of Adolphe F. Bandelier, 1880–1882* (Albuquerque: University of New Mexico Press, 1966), 165; Robert E. Beider, *Science Encounters the Indian, 1820–1880: The Early Years of American Ethnology* (Norman: University of Oklahoma Press, 1986), 60–80.
15. Hinsley, *Savages and Scientists;* Keir Sterling, "Naturalists of the Southwest at the Turn of the Century," *Environmental Review* 3, no. 1 (fall 1978): 20–33.
16. "Charles F. Lummis Tells of the Cliff Dwellings," *Santa Fe New Mexican*, August 20, 1909; Charles F. Lummis, *A Tramp Across the Continent* (Albuquerque: Calvin Horn, 1969); Adolphe F. Bandelier, *The Delightmakers* (New York: Dodd and Mead, 1918); C. W. Ceran, *The First American: A Story of North American Archaeology* (New York: Harcourt, Brace, Jovanovich, 1971; Tracy Brady, paper, Pacific Coast Branch of the American Historical Association Annual Meeting, San Francisco, August 1996.
17. Neil M. Judd, *The Bureau of American Ethnology: A Partial History* (Norman: University of Oklahoma Press, 1967), 1–5; Brian Dippie, *The Vanishing American: White Attitudes and U.S. Indian Policy* (Lawrence: University Press of Kansas, 1991); Ceran, *The First American;* Earl S. Pomeroy, *In Search of the Golden West: The Tourist in Western America* (New York: Knopf, 1957), 9–11; Alfred Runte, *Trains of Discovery: Western Railroads and the National Parks* (Flagstaff, AZ: Northland Press, 1984); Billy Mac

Jones, *Health-Seekers in the Southwest, 1817–1900* (Norman: University of Oklahoma Press, 1967), 155–81; Richard Bartlett, *Yellowstone: A Wilderness Besieged* (Tucson: University of Arizona Press, 1985).

18. Leah Dilworth, *Imagining Indians in the Southwest* (Washington, DC: Smithsonian Institution Press, 1996), 78–83; Chris Wilson, *The Myth of Santa Fe: Creating a Modern Regional Tradition* (Albuquerque: University of New Mexico Press, 1997), 89–92.
19. Judd, *The Bureau of American Ethnology*, 78–115; Hinsley, *Savages and Scientists.*
20. Esther Stineman, *Mary Austin: Song of a Maverick* (New Haven: Yale University Press, 1989); Helen Hunt Jackson, *A Century of Dishonor: A Sketch of the United States Government's Dealings with Some of the Indian Tribes* (Boston: Roberts Brothers, 1885).
21. Frank McNitt, *Richard Wetherill: Anasazi* (Albuquerque: University of New Mexico Press, 1957); Hal K. Rothman, *On Rims and Ridges: The Las Alamos Area Since 1880* (Lincoln: University of Nebraska Press, 1992).
22. David Wishart, *The Fur Trade of the American West, 1807–1840: A Geographical Synthesis* (Lincoln: University of Nebraska Press, 1979); Irving Stone, *Men to Match My Mountains: The Opening of the Far West, 1840–1900* (Garden City, NY: Doubleday, 1956); Frederick Merk, *History of the Westward Movement* (New York: Alfred A. Knopf, 1978), 252–55; Preston L. James, "Regional Planning in the Jackson Hole Country," *Geographical Review* 26, no. 3 (July 1936): 442.
23. David J. Saylor, *Jackson Hole, Wyoming: In the Shadow of the Tetons* (Norman: University of Oklahoma Press, 1970), 114–18.
24. Robert Righter, *Crucible for Conservation: The Creation of Grand Teton National Park* (Niwot, CO: Colorado Associated University Press, 1983), 9–10; T. A. Larson, *History of Wyoming* (Lincoln: University of Nebraska Press, 1965), 355–57; Robert Athearn, *High Country Empire* (New York: McGraw-Hill, 1960), 282.
25. Saylor, *Jackson Hole*, 149–53.
26. Nathaniel Burt, *Jackson Hole Journal* (Norman: University of Oklahoma Press, 1983), 10.
27. Lawrence R. Borne, *Dude Ranching: A Complete History* (Albuquerque: University of New Mexico Press, 1983), 1–46; Elizabeth Clair Flood, *Old-Time Dude Ranches Out West: Authentic Ranches for Modern-Day Dudes* (Salt Lake City: Gibbs-Smith, 1995), 8–11.
28. Borne, *Dude Ranching*, 44–45.
29. Struthers Burt, *The Diary of a Dude Wrangler* (New York: Charles Scribners, 1924), 49.
30. Borne, *Dude Ranching*, 30–33.
31. Ibid., 37–39.
32. Saylor, *Jackson Hole*, 125–27.
33. Ibid.; Burt, *Jackson Hole Journal*, 188–94; Owen Wister, *The Virginian: A Horseman of the Plains* (New York: Grosset and Dunlap, 1904), 304–5.
34. Saylor, *Jackson Hole*, 149–50.
35. Borne, *Dude Ranching*, 37–38.
36. Burt, *The Diary of a Dude Wrangler*, 65; Borne, *Dude Ranching*, 38; Burt, *Jackson Hole Journal*, 6, 9.
37. Burt, *The Diary of a Dude Wrangler*, 50; see also Willie Nelson, "Mama, Don't Let Your Babies Grow up to Be Cowboys," as recorded on *Wanted: The Outlaws* (EMI, 1976).
38. Burt, *The Diary of a Dude Wrangler*, 48–50, 60.
39. Ibid., 49.
40. Borne, *Dude Ranching*, 35–36.
41. Ibid., 33–38, 44–45; Burt, *The Diary of a Dude Wrangler*, 61–62.

42. Borne, *Dude Ranching*, 33–34; Flood, *Old-Time Dude Ranches*, 95; Burt, *Diary of a Dude Wrangler*, 88.
43. Burt, *Jackson Hole Journal*, 22.
44. James, "Regional Planning in the Jackson Hole Country," 443; Saylor, *Jackson Hole*, 156–62; Righter, *Crucible for Conservation*, 10–17.
45. H. P. Sheldon, O. J. Murie, and W. E. Crouch, "The Present Plight of the Jackson Hole Elk," U.S. Department of Agriculture, Bureau of Biological Survey, Wildlife Research and Management Leaflet, BS-12, 1935.
46. Burt, *Diary of a Dude Wrangler*, 3–4, 49.
47. Righter, *Crucible for Conservation*, 17–21.
48. Hal K. Rothman, "A Regular Ding-Dong Fight: Agency Culture and Evolution in the NPS-USFS Dispute, 1916–1937," *Western Historical Quarterly* 2 (May 1989): 141–61; Righter, *Crucible for Conservation*, 18–21.
49. Righter, *Crucible for Conservation*, 33.
50. Thomas R. Dunlap, *Saving America's Wildlife* (Princeton: Princeton University Press, 1988); Righter, *Crucible for Conservation*, 34–35.
51. James, "Regional Planning in the Jackson Hole Country," 444–45.
52. Ibid., 445–46; Righter, *Crucible for Conservation*, 45.
53. James, "Regional Planning in the Jackson Hole Country," 448–51.
54. Rocky Mountain Motorists, *Official Travel Directory of Wyoming 1930* (Denver: Rocky Mountain Motorists, 1930), 8–9; American Heritage Center, Laramie, Wyoming; "Dude Ranches Excluded from Unemployment Compensation Contributions in Wyoming," *Dude Rancher* 7, no. 1 (January 1939); 2; Borne, *Dude Ranching*, 5.

6. INTRAREGIONAL TOURISM

1. Hal K. Rothman, ed., *"I'll Never Fight Fire With My Bare Hands Again": Recollections of the First Foresters of the Inland Northwest* (Lawrence: University Press of Kansas, 1994), 263; Ivan Doig, *Dancing at the Rascal Fair* (New York: Atheneum, 1987); Karl Hess, "A West Without Heroes," *Environmental History* 2, no. 1 (January 1997): 1–34.
2. *Art and Archaeology* 10, nos. 1–2 (August 1920); Charles L. Bernheimer, *Rainbow Bridge: Circling Navajo Mountain and Explorations in the Bad Lands of Southern Utah and Northern Arizona* (Garden City, NJ: Doubleday, Page, and Company, 1924), 1–5, 21; Francis Gillmor and Louisa Wade Wetherill, *Traders to the Navajo: The Story of the Wetherills of Kayenta* (Boston: Houghton, Mifflin, 1934).
3. Earl S. Pomeroy, *In Search of the Golden West: The Tourist in Western America* (New York: Knopf, 1957), 127–29.
4. John A. Jakle, *The Tourist: Travel in Twentieth-Century North America* (Lincoln: University of Nebraska Press, 1985); "Municipal Campgrounds in Kansas," Tourism, Kansas State Historical Society, History Research Room.
5. Jakle, *The Tourist in Twentieth-Century America*, 123–26; Marguerite S. Shaffer, "See America First: Tourism and National Identity" (Ph.D. diss., Harvard University, 1994), 1–26; Warren Belasco, *Americans on the Road: From Autocamp to Motel, 1910–1945*, (Boston: MIT Press, 1979).
6. Shaffer, "See America First," 1–4.
7. Jakle, *The Tourist*, 126–33; Belasco, *Americans on the Road*.
8. Robert Shankland, *Steve Mather of the National Parks*, 3d ed. (New York: Knopf, 1970), 136–38.
9. Belasco, *Americans on the Road;* Shaffer, "See America First"; *Annual Report of the*

Director of the National Park Service for 1919 (Washington, DC: Government Printing Office, 1920), 64.

10. *Annual Report of the Director of the National Park Service for 1919;* Hal K. Rothman, *Preserving Different Pasts* (Urbana: University of Illinois Press, 1989); John Ise, *Our National Park Policy* (New York: Arno Press, 1979); Shaffer, "See America First"; Michael Wallis, *Route 66: The Mother Road* (New York: St. Martin's Press, 1990); Quinta Scott and Susan Croce Kelly, *Route 66: The Highway and Its People* (Norman: University of Oklahoma Press, 1988).
11. Pomeroy, *In Search of the Golden West,* 139–47; Michael Cohen, Michael P., *The Pathless Way: John Muir and American Wilderness* (Madison: University of Wisconsin Press, 1984); Roderick Nash, "The American Cult of the Primitive," *American Quarterly* 18 (1966); 517–37.
12. Robert M. Crunden, *From Self to Society, 1919–1941* (Englewood Cliff, NJ: Prentice-Hall, 1972); Robert Rydell, *All the World's a Fair: Visions of Empire at American International Expositions, 1876–1916* (Chicago: University of Chicago Press, 1984).
13. Frank Brunner, "Autocamping—The Fastest Growing Sport," *Outlook* 87 (July 16, 1924); 437; Pomeroy, *In Search of the Golden West,* 146.
14. Rothman, *Preserving Different Pasts,* 102–3.
15. Ibid., 188–90; Ronald Foresta, *America's National Parks and Their Keepers* (Washington, DC: Resources for the Future, 1984), 19–21, 30–32; Horace Albright, *The Origins of National Park Service Administration of Historic Places* (Philadelphia: Eastern National Park and Monument Association, 1971), 13; Horace Albright, as told to Robert Cahn, *The Birth of the National Park Service: The Founding Years, 1913–1933* (Salt Lake City: Howe Brothers Press, 1986), 234–47.
16. Rothman, *Preserving Different Pasts,* 172–78; Hal Rothman, "Forged by One Man's Will: Frank Pinkley and the Administration of the Southwestern National Monuments, 1923–1932," *Public Historian* 8, no. 2 (spring 1986): 83–100.
17. Rothman, *Preserving Different Pasts;* Ise, *Our National Park Policy,* 349–58; Foresta, *America's National Parks and Their Keepers,* 40–46.
18. Rothman, *Preserving Different Pasts,* 162–64; Ise, *Our National Park Policy,* 358–59; Foresta, *America's National Parks and Their Keepers,* 129–32; Albright as told to Kahn, *The National Park Service,* 215–32.
19. Jefferson National Expansion Memorial File, Office Files of Arno B. Cammerer, Series 18, RG 79, National Archives.
20. Executive Order no. 7253, December 21, 1935.
21. Jefferson National Expansion Memorial File, Report 3, Office Files of Arno B. Cammerer, Series 18, RG 79, National Archives.
22. Hermon C. Bumpus, Herbert E. Bolton, and Archibald M. McCrea to Arno B. Cammerer, September 2, 1937, Office Files of Arno B. Cammerer, Series 18, Jefferson National Expansion Memorial File, RG 79, National Archives.
23. Ibid.
24. Rothman, *Preserving Different Pasts.*
25. Hildegarde Flanner, "Geological Fantasia: Through the Carlsbad Caverns of New Mexico—A Pageant of the Earth's Hidden Curiosities," *Travel* 62, no. 4 (February 1924): 16; Ise, *Our National Park Policy,* 209–12, 241–44; Shankland, *Steve Mather of the National Parks,* 129–34; Belasco, *Americans on the Road.*
26. Hal K. Rothman, *On Rims and Ridges: The Las Alamos Area Since 1880* (Lincoln: University of Nebraska Press, 1992), 186–191; Diana H. Thomas, *The Southwestern Indian*

Detours: The Story of the Fred Harvey/Santa Fe Railway Experiment in "Detourism" (Phoenix: Hunter, 1978), 117–21; Marta Weigle, "Insisted on Authenticity: Harveycar Indian Detours, 1925–1931," in *The Great Southwest of the Fred Harvey Company and the Santa Fe Railroad*, ed. Weigle and Barbara A. Babcock (Phoenix: Heard Museum, 1996), 47–59.

27. Weigle, "Insisted on Authenticity," 50.
28. Rothman, *Preserving Different Pasts*, 132–36; Ise, *Our National Park Policy*, 328–31.
29. Hal Rothman, "Second Class Sites: The National Monuments and the Growth of the Park System, *Environmental Review* 10, no. 1 (spring 1986); 45–57.
30. "Greatest Show Under the Earth," *Popular Mechanics* 72 (July 1939): 50–54.
31. Kenneth L. Dixon, "Ban on Rock of Ages Ceremony Still Brings Protests," *El Paso Times*, June 1, 1946; Edwin C. Alberts to Thomas R. Boles, June 25, 1944; Minor R. Tillotson, Memorandum for the Director, August 26, 1944; Newton R. Drury, Memorandum for the Regional Director, September 12, 1944, Series 7, 201, Carlsbad Caverns, RG 79, National Archives; Robert Nymeyer and William R. Halliday, *Carlsbad Caverns: The Early Years* (Carlsbad, NM; Carlsbad Caverns–Guadalupe Mountains Association, 1991), 35–46, 114–35.
32. B. J. Lynch to Director, National Park Service, February 7, 1945; Jay F. Strawiniski to Thomas R. Boles, March 28, 1945; Thomas R. Boles to Jay F. Strawiniski, April 7, 1945; Rev. James D. Wiliford to Harold L. Ickes, April 18, 1945; Mrs. John C. Koster to U.S. Sen. Dennis Chavez, February 26, 1945; Mrs. John C. Koster to U.S. Sen. Carl Hatch, March 7, 1945; Kenneth L. Dixon, "Ban on Rock of Ages Ceremony Still Brings Protests," *El Paso Times*, June 1, 1946, Series 7, 201, Carlsbad Caverns, RG 79, National Archives.
33. Ise, *Our National Park Policy*.
34. Bart Ripp, "Greetings from White's City," *Albuquerque Living*, March 1984, 70–71; Billy Mac Jones, *Health-Seekers in the Southwest, 1817–1900* (Norman: University of Oklahoma Press, 1967), 175–98; *White's City Gazette* and Souvenir Menu, n.d.
35. Ripp, "Greetings from White's City," 70; Robert Bryant, "Cashing in on the Caves," *New Mexico Business Journal* 9, no. 11 (November 1985): 53–55.
36. Bryant, "Cashing in on the Caves," 54–56; Ripp, "Greetings from White's City," 71.
37. Rydell, *All the World's a Fair*.
38. Theodore Catton, *Wonderland: An Administrative History of Mount Rainier National Park* (Seattle: National Park Service, 1996), 247–89.
39. Catton, *Wonderland*, 260–67.
40. Haydie Yates, *70 Miles from a Lemon* (Boston: Houghton Mifflin, 1947), 1–12.
41. Jack Kerouac, *On the Road* (New York: Viking, 1957).

7. FROM STEAMBOAT SPRINGS TO SUN VALLEY

1. Charlie Meyers, *Colorado Ski Country* (Helena and Billings, MT: Falcon Press, 1987), Colorado Geographic Series no. 4, 49–50; Sureva Towler, *The History of Skiing at Steamboat Springs* (Steamboat Springs, CO: Sureva Towler, 1987), 48–49; O. E. Rolvaag, *Giants in the Earth* (New York: Harper, 1927), 447–53. There is no comprehensive history of the ski industry to date; for the closest, see E. John B. Allen, *From Skisport to Skiing: One Hundred Years of an American Sport* (Amherst: University of Massachussetts Press, 1993); see also J. S. Holliday, *The World Rushed In: The California Gold Rush Experience* (New York: Simon and Schuster, 1981), 296–310, who discusses the difficulty of winter travel, and John A. Hawgood, *America's Western Frontiers: The Story of the Explorers and Settlers Who Opened up the Trans-Mississippi West* (New

York; Knopf, 1967), 234–65, who discusses the evolution of western transportation. Abbott Fay, *Ski Tracks in the Rockies: A Century of Colorado Skiing* (Denver: Cordillera Press, 1984), 3–8; Duncan Craighead, "Skiing the Way We Were," *Three Wire Winter* 6 (fall 1977); 7–10.

2. Jean Wren, *Steamboat Springs and the Treacherous and Speedy Skee: An Album* (Steamboat Springs: *Steamboat Pilot,* 1972), 1–3; Towler, *The History of Skiing at Steamboat Springs,* 47–51.
3. Margaret Duncan Brown, *Shepherdess of Elk River Valley* (Denver: Golden Bell Press, 1982); *Denver Times,* August 24, 1899; Rick Tibbetts and Bethany Craighead, "The Remington Berry: Steamboat's First Boom," *Three Wire Winter* 1 (winter 1976); 61–72, Vertical File, Routt County Collection, Bud Werner Memorial Library, Steamboat Springs, Colorado.
4. Towler, *A History of Skiing at Steamboat Springs,* 50; *Colorado Business Directory, 1913.*
5. Jeanne Varnell, "Skis Were Transportation in Snowbound Steamboat Springs," *Sentinel Avenues,* February 13, 1986, 17; Wren, *Steamboat Springs,* 1–3.
6. Varnell, "Skis Were Transportation," 17; Fay, *Ski Tracks in the Rockies,* 9; Towler, *The History of Skiing at Steamboat Springs,* 52, 54–55.
7. Elliott J. Gorn, "Gouge and Bite, Pull Hair and Scratch": The Social Significance of Fighting in the Southern Backcountry," *American Historical Review* 90, no. 1 (February 1985): 18–44; Elliott J. Gorn, "Eye-Gouging in the Backwoods," *Harper's,* August 1985, 32–35; John Mack Faragher, *Daniel Boone: The Life and Legend of an American Pioneer* (New York: Holt, 1992); Allan W. Eckert, *Wilderness Empire: A Narrative* (Boston: Little Brown, 1969); Allan W. Eckert, *The Frontiersman;* Wren, *Steamboat Springs,* 17.
8. Leif Hovelsen, *The Flying Norseman* (Ishpeming, MI: National Ski Hall of Fame Press, 1983), 22–34.
9. Hovelsen, *The Flying Norseman,* 37–39; Meyers, *Colorado Ski Country,* 14, 49–50; *Denver Times,* August 24, 1899; *Denver Republican,* January 26, 1912; Cal Queal, "Steamboat Springs Winter Carnival Rates the Best," *Denver Post,* February 21, 1956; "50th Carnival Golden Success," *Steamboat Pilot,* February 14, 1963; "Winter Carnival Arrives," *Steamboat Pilot,* February 8, 1973, 1. There is considerable discrepancy about the year the winter carnival began. The years 1912, 1913, 1914, and 1918 are the most commonly cited, with the preponderance of evidence supporting 1913 and the first full-scale carnival taking place in 1914. Steve Patterson and Kenton Forrest, *Rio Grande Ski Train* (Denver: Tramway Press, 1984), have the Denver–Rocky Mountain Ski Club sponsoring the 1914 Steamboat Springs carnival (14). Hovelsen, *The Flying Norseman,* 37–39.
10. Hovelsen, *The Flying Norseman,* 42.
11. Ibid., 51–57; "Steamboat Will Hold a Two-Day Ski Tournament," *Steamboat Pilot,* January 21, 1914; "Midwinter Sport Will Attract Large Crowds," *Steamboat Pilot,* December 9, 1914; "Omtvedt, World Champion, Will Come to Steamboat," *Steamboat Pilot,* January 31, 1915; Cal Queal, "Steamboat Springs Winter Carnival Rates the Best," *Denver Post,* February 21, 1956; "50th Carnival Golden Success," *Steamboat Pilot,* February 14, 1963; "Winter Carnival Arrives," *Steamboat Pilot,* February 8, 1973, 1; John Rolfe Burroughs, "Ski Town, U.S.A.: Rapid Developments Bid Fair to Make Steamboat Springs, Colorado, the St. Moritz of the Rockies" (Steamboat Springs: Steamboat Springs Winter Sports Club, 1962), 1–3.
12. Wren, *Steamboat Springs,* 14, 21–22.
13. Ibid., 23–28.

14. "The Ski Riders of Genesee," *Municipal Facts,* February 1922; Roderick Nash, "The American Cult of the Primitive," *American Quarterly* 18 (1966); 517–37; Fay, *Ski Tracks in the Rockies,* 16; Hovelsen, *The Flying Norseman,* 43; Patterson and Forrest, *Rio Grande Ski Train,* 8; Stephen J. Leonard and Thomas J. Noel, *Denver: Mining Camp to Metropolis* (Niwot: University Press of Colorado, 1990), 153–54.
15. "Steamboat Has Been Leader in Winter Sports," *Steamboat Pilot,* January 6, 1928; Fay, *Ski Tracks in the Rockies,* 13–16; Alfred Runte, *National Parks: The American Experience,* 2d ed. (Lincoln: University of Nebraska Press, 1987), 48–64; for similar endeavors in outdoor activity in the summer, see Michael P. Cohen, *The History of the Sierra Club, 1892–1970* (San Francisco: Sierra Club Books, 1988), 57–71.
16. Helen Eastom, "Denver Social Set Finds Pleasure on Ski Course: Local Skiing Attracts Social Set on Rilliet Park on Genessee Mountain," *Denver Post,* December 1, 1929, 1; Fay, *Ski Tracks in the Rockies,* 16.
17. Patterson and Forrest, *Rio Grande Ski Train,* 15; Charles Albi and Kenton Forrest, *The Moffat Tunnel* (Golden, CO: Colorado Railroad Museum, 1978).
18. Wren, *Steamboat Springs,* 34–37.
19. "Big Rush Is on for Snow Train to Steamboat," *Rocky Mountain News,* February 15, 1936; Wildred S. Davis, "Many Ski Areas Located in Arapahoe National Forest," *Rocky Mountain News;* "News Started Excursions," *Rocky Mountain News,* December 18, 1938; Alfred Runte, *Yosemite: The Embattled Wilderness* (Lincoln: University of Nebraska Press, 1990), 152–53; Patterson and Forrest, *Rio Grande Ski Train,* 18; for Mt. Rainier, see Theodore Catton, *Wonderland: An Administrative History of Mount Rainier National Park* (Seattle: National Park Service, 1996), 300–311.
20. "Ski Run Is Being Built at Creede," *Silverton Standard,* November 26, 1937; "Telluride Ski Course Assured," *Silverton Standard,* December 8, 1939; "European Nobleman to Teach Skiing in Springs District," *Pueblo Star Journal and Chieftain,* November 7, 1937; "Skiing Revives Mining Towns," *Leadville Herald Democrat,* March 26, 1938; "Arapahoe Ski Tow Nears Completion," *Leadville Herald Democrat,* October 26, 1939; Joseph T. Radel, "Leadville Ski Facilities Expanded," *Rocky Mountain News,* December 18, 1938; "Routt National Forest, Colorado" (Denver: United States Forest Service, 1941); Meyers, *Colorado Ski Country,* 13.
21. John A. Jakle, *The Tourist: Travel in Twentieth-Century North America* (Lincoln: University of Nebraska Press, 1985), 59–61; Horace Sutton, *Travelers: The American Tourist from Stagecoach to Space Shuttle* (New York: William Morrow and Company, 1980), 225–28; Polly Redford, *Billion-Dollar Sandbar: A Biography of Miami Beach* (New York: E. P. Dutton, 1970); National Park Service, "Park Conservation: A Report on Park and Outdoor Recreational Resources in the United States for the Secretary of the Interior," January 28, 1946, confidential, declassified by Assistant Director Hillory A. Tolson, December 11, 1947, copy in possession of the author, 40–41.
22. "Spend Your Vacation in Colorful Aspen Colorado," promotional brochure, ca. 1927, Aspen File Clippings 1920–1929, Western History Department, Denver Public Library; Harold K. Steen, *The United States Forest Service: A History* (Seattle: University of Washington Press, 1976), 153–56, 158–59; Donald C. Swain, *Federal Conservation Policy, 1921–1933* (Berkeley: University of California Press, 1963), 137–38; for a history of the mining boom in Aspen, see Malcolm J. Rohrbough, *Aspen: The History of a Silver Mining Town, 1879–1893* (New York: Oxford University Press, 1986).
23. Robert Benchley, "How to Ski Aspen," Aspen, Clippings 1930–1939, Subject File, Denver Public Library; "Aspen Will Have Snow Trains This Year on D.&R.G.W.," *Gunnison News-Champion,* December 2, 1937; Robert Athearn, *The Denver and Rio Grande*

Western: Rebel of the Rockies, 1st Bison Books ed. (Lincoln: University of Nebraska Press, 1977), 158–64; James Sloan Allen, *The Romance of Commerce and Culture: Capitalism, Modernism, and the Chicago-Aspen Crusade for Cultural Reform* (Chicago: University of Chicago Press, 1983), 122–24.

24. F. Martin Brown, "Let's Aspen," n.d., F1, Thomas Flynn Collection, Denver Public Library; C. L. Parsons, "Aspen Boomed as Ski Spot," *Denver Post*, April 4, 1937; *Aspen Times*, April 14, 1938; for the history of streamliners, see Jeffrey L. Meikle, *Twentieth-Century Limited: Industrial Design in America, 1925–1939* (Philadelphia: Temple University Press, 1979).
25. Thomas Flynn to W. C. Tagert, January 14, 1936(?); Flynn to Tagert, June 5, 1938; Flynn to K. G. Fuller, December 8, 1938; Flynn to Capt. William S. Biddle, December 12, 1938, Thomas Flynn Collection FF24, Denver Public Library; "Colorado Rockies Unsurpassed as Skiing Territory," *Western Nyheter*, December 21, 1939.
26. "Highland-Bavarian Lodge, Highland, Colorado," Thomas Flynn Papers, F1, Western History Department, Denver Public Library.
27. "Berthoud Pass–West Portal Development Assured by $17,360.00 P.W.A. Grant," *Rocky Mountain Winter Sports News*, December 15, 1938; Meyers, *Colorado Ski Country*, 13, 54; Patterson and Forrest, *Rio Grande Ski Train*, 25.
28. "Berthoud Pass–West Portal Development Assured by $17,360.00 P.W.A. Grant," *Rocky Mountain Winter Sports News*, December 15, 1938; "Seek Additional Funds to Finish Ski Course Work," *Aspen Times*, April 6, 1939; Meyers, *Colorado Ski Country*, 13, 54; Verna Noel Jones, "Downhill in Colorado," *Rocky Mountain News Sunday Magazine*, November 13, 1988, 17 M; Patterson and Forrest, *Rio Grande Ski Train*, 25.
29. "Arapaho Ski Tow Nears Completion," *Leadville Herald Democrat*, October 26, 1939; Jones, "Downhill in Colorado," *Rocky Mountain News Sunday Magazine*, November 13, 1988, 17 M–19 M.
30. W. Averell Harriman, Foreword, in Doug Oppenheimer and Jim Poore, *Sun Valley: A Biography* (Boise, ID: Beatty Books, 1976), 8, 21–23; Peter Donovan to Hal Rothman, September 7, 1994.
31. Oppenheimer and Poore, *Sun Valley*, 24–27; Dorice Taylor, *Sun Valley* (Sun Valley, ID: Ex Libris Sun Valley, 1980), 13–16.
32. Oppenheimer and Poore, *Sun Valley*, 26–27; Taylor, *Sun Valley*, 15.
33. Rudy Abramson, *Spanning the Century: The Life of W. Averell Harriman, 1891–1986* (New York: William Morrow and Company, 1992), 221–33; Carlos A. Schwantes, *In Mountain Shadows: A History of Idaho* (Lincoln: University of Nebraska Press, 1991), 210–14; Rodman W. Paul, *Mining Frontiers of the Far West, 1840–1880* (New York: Holt, Rinehart, and Winston, 1963), 144–49.
34. Oppenheimer and Poore, *Sun Valley*, 28–32.
35. Ibid., 29–31.
36. Ibid., 31.
37. Ibid., 31–33, 46–49.
38. "Tell the World All About Sun Valley Ski Paradise in Shelter of the Sawtooths," *Hailey Times*, August 27, 1936; "Idaho's Winter Sports Mecca," *Idaho Sunday Statesman*, August 30, 1936; "World to Learn of Idaho: Union Pacific Plans Extensive Advertising Campaign Telling About Recreational Advantages of State and Nature of Famous Primitive Area," *Idaho Statesman*, September 2, 1936; Dick d'Easum, *Sawtooth Tales* (Caldwell, ID: Claxton Printers, 1977), 30–41, 97–100; Taylor, *Sun Valley*, 39–52.
39. "East Goes West to Idaho's Sun Valley, Society's Newest Winter Playground," *Life*, March 8, 1937, 20–27; Sun Valley Celebrates 50th Anniversary," *Rocky Mountain News*,

February 9, 1986, 72; Abramson, *Spanning the Century,* 222–30; "Sun Valley, Winter Sports Capital, Ready to Open Monday," *Boise Capitol News,* December 19, 1936; "First Pictures at Sun Valley Since Snow Covered Sawtooths," *Idaho Statesman,* January 2, 1937; Taylor, *Sun Valley,* 45–46; A. Scott Berg, *Goldwyn: A Biography* (New York: Alfred A. Knopf, 1991), 287; Irene Link, "Early Arrival at the Inn," *Twin Falls Times-News,* April 2, 1980.

40. For examples of major newspaper and magazine articles extolling the virtues of Sun Valley, see John Price, "Idaho's New Bonanza," *Travel,* February 1939, 32–33, 55–58, and "Sun Valley: The American St. Moritz," *Reader's Digest,* February 1939, 55–58; see also Peter J. Ognibee, "At the First Ski Spa, Stars Outshone the Sun and Snow," *Smithsonian,* December 1984, 108–20.
41. "Reveal Plan for New Summer, Winter Resort at Sun Valley," *Boise Capitol News,* March 15, 1937; Sun Valley Rodeo Committee, "Second Annual Sun Valley Rodeo, Staged at the 'Gateway of America's Last Wilderness,'" August 12–14, 1938, Vertical File, Sun Valley, History, Idaho State History Library.
42. Lloyd R. Arnold, *Hemingway: High on the Wild* (New York: Grosset and Dunlap, 1968), 1–33; Abramson, *Spanning the Century,* 225–30; John Rember, "My Life as a Tourist," *Idaho Ski Guide 95/96,* 6.
43. Neil T. Regan, "New Year's Celebration," *Valley Sun,* January 5, 1940; *Valley Sun,* December 15, 1941; "6000 to Convene Here," *Valley Sun,* Spring Time, 1947; Dorice Taylor, "per-SUN-als," *Valley Sun,* July 16, 1947.
44. "Reveal Plan for New Summer, Winter Resort at Sun Valley," *Boise Capitol News,* March 15, 1937; "Second Annual Sun Valley Rodeo, Staged at the 'Gateway to America's Last Wilderness,'" August 12–14, 1938; "Idaho State Trapshoot to Highlight July 4th Weekend," *Valley Sun,* June 1947; Dorice Taylor, "Per-SUN-als"; "Big League Football Comes to Sun Valley," *Valley Sun,* July 23, 1947; "Ashby Trophy Won by Manuel Enos of Fort Worth," *Valley Sun,* September 10, 1947. The *Valley Sun* was a Union Pacific promotional newspaper printed from about 1940 to 1964. Dorice Taylor frequently wrote for the paper.
45. Taylor, *Sun Valley,* 40; "Owner of Sun Valley Ski Shop, John Pete Lane, 60, Dies," *Idaho Statesman,* March 19, 1980.
46. Taylor, *Sun Valley,* 40–42; Oppenheimer and Poore, *Sun Valley,* 45–47.
47. Oppenheimer and Poore, *Sun Valley,* 48.
48. Taylor, *Sun Valley,* 57–59, 69, 73, 115–21; Abramson, *Spanning the Century,* 228; "The Valley of Sun and Snow," *Saturday Evening Post,* n.d. (ca. 1937); Meyers, *Colorado Ski Country,* 38, 43.
49. *Fifteenth Census of the United States: 1930,* vol. 3, pt. 1 (Washington, DC: United States Government Printing Office, 1932), 562; *Sixteenth Census of the United States: 1940, Population vol. 2* (Washington, DC: United States Government Printing Office, 1943), 415–30; *Census of the Population: 1950, vol. 2, Characteristics of the Population,* Pt. 12, *Idaho* (Washington, DC: United States Government Printing Office, 1952), 12–12; the 1930 numbers list twelve Chinese, down from forty-three in 1910, thirteen Mexicans, and no Japanese living in Blaine County. Presumably the vast majority of remaining foreign-born individuals were European in origin, and a large percentage of those were most likely Basque.
50. *United States Census of Agriculture, 1935,* vol. 2 (Washington, DC: United States Government Printing Office, 1936), 815–30; *Sixteenth Census of the United States: 1940, Agriculture,* vol. 2 (Washington, DC: United States Government Printing Office,

1942), 44–76; *Sixteenth Census of the United States: 1940, Population,* vol. 2 (Washington, DC: United States Government Printing Office, 1943), 432, 441.

51. Taylor, *Sun Valley,* 53–79.
52. Oppenheimer and Poore, *Sun Valley;* Taylor, *Sun Valley,* 97–105.
53. T. J. Jackson Lears, *No Place of Grace: Antimodernism and the Transformation of American Culture, 1880–1920* (Chicago: University of Chicago Press, 1994); Raye Ringholz, *Little Town Blues: Voices from a Changing West* (Salt Lake City: Peregrine Smith Books, 1992), provides an example of the kinds of sentiments locals express about change; see also Douglas Pearce, *Tourist Development* (New York: Longman, 1981), 183–243, for an analysis of the impact of tourism in aggregate form.
54. John Rember, "On Going Back to Sawtooth Valley," in *Where the Morning Light's Still Blue: Personal Essays About Idaho,* ed. William Studebaker and Rick Ardinger (Moscow: University of Idaho Press, 1994), 84.
55. Ibid., 85.
56. Earl S. Pomeroy, *In Search of the Golden West: The Tourist in Western America* (New York: Knopf, 1957), 19–25.

8. THE SPREAD OF RECREATIONAL TOURISM

1. Gerald D. Nash, *World War II and the West: Reshaping the Economy* (Lincoln: University of Nebraska Press, 1990), gives the most comprehensive look at the impact of World War II on the West; for an account of the people who came West and the way the war transformed them, see Dan Morgan, *Rising in the West: The True Story of an "Okie" Family in Search of the American Dream* (New York: Alfred A. Knopf, 1992).
2. James L. Brewer to Byron Cummings, August 14, 1942, Byron Cummings Collection, Arizona Historical Society; Monthly Report, Grand Canyon National Park, August 1945, September, 1945, and October 1945, Series 7, Grand Canyon, RG 79, National Archives; Eugene P. Moehring, *Resort City in the Sun Belt: Las Vegas, 1930–1970* (Reno: University of Nevada Press, 1989).
3. Eric Goldman, *The Crucial Decade—and After: America, 1945–1960* (New York: Random House, 1960), 4–5, 12–15; John A. Jakle, *The Tourist: Travel in Twentieth-Century North America* (Lincoln: University of Nebraska Press, 1985); Bernard DeVoto, "The National Parks," *Fortune,* September 1947, 120–21; Bernard DeVoto, "Let's Close the National Parks," *Harper's,* October 1953, 49–52; Robert D. Baker, Robert S. Maxwell, Victor H. Treat, and Henry C. Dethloff, *Timeless Heritage: A History of the Forest Service in the Southwest* (Washington, DC: Intaglie Press, 1988), 59–68, 131–33; Ronald A. Foresta, *America's National Parks and Their Keepers* (Washington, DC: Johns Hopkins University Press, 1984), 50–55.
4. DeVoto, "Let's Close the National Parks"; David A. Clary, *Timber and the Forest Service* (Lawrence: University Press of Kansas, 1986); Clary, *Timber and the Forest Service;* Jakle, *The Tourist.*
5. H. Benjamin Duke Jr., "Skiing Soldiers to Skiing Entrepreneurs: Development of the Western Ski Industry," typescript, H. Benjamin Duke Jr., Vail Associates Collection, Denver Public Library, 8–9; *Ski News,* December 1, 1945; Verna Noel Jones, "Downhill in Colorado," *Rocky Mountain News Sunday Magazine,* November 13, 1988, 17 M; "Skiing Then and Now," *Overland News* 1, no. 6 (January 1958); Alfred Runte, *National Parks: The American Experience* (Lincoln: University of Nebraska Press, 1987), 156–77; Earl S. Pomeroy, *In Search of the Golden West: The Tourist in Western America* (New York: Knopf, 1957), 123–30, 145–51; John M. Findlay, *Magic Lands: Western Cityscapes*

and American Culture After 1940 (Berkeley: University of California Press, 1992), 14–33; Nash, *World War II and the West;* Carl Abbott, *The Metropolitan Frontier: Cities in the Modern American West* (Tucson: University of Arizona Press, 1993), 3–31.

6. James S. Allen, *The Romance of Commerce and Culture: Capitalism, Modernism, and the Chicago-Aspen Crusade for Cultural Reform* (Chicago: University of Chicago Press, 1983), xi–xv, 100–102.
7. Allen, *The Romance of Commerce and Culture,* 113–15; Anne M. Gilbert, "Re-creation Through Recreation: Aspen Skiing from 1870–1970," (Aspen Historical Society, 1995), 49–50; Anne Gilbert Coleman, "A Hell of a Time All the Time: Farmers, Ranchers, and the Roaring Fork Valley During the Quiet Years," *Montana: The Magazine of Western History* 47, no. 1 (spring 1997); 32–45; Mary Eshbaugh Hayes, "Changes Still Coming to the Old West," *Aspen Times,* October 28, 1982.
8. Anne M. Gilbert, "Rural People with Connections: Farm and Ranch Families in the Roaring Fork Valley, Colorado" (Master's thesis, University of Colorado, 1992), 1–18; Malcolm J. Rohrbough, *Aspen: The History of a Silver-Mining Town, 1879–1893* (New York: Oxford University Press, 1986); Allen, *The Romance of Commerce and Culture,* 113–15.
9. Jack Foster, "Hard Work Gives Mining Town New Look: It Could Only Happen in Aspen," *Rocky Mountain News,* January 2, 1954, 26; Jack Foster, "Aspen—Before and After Paepcke: A Ghost Town Risen," *Rocky Mountain News,* April 17, 1960, 37; Allen, *The Romance of Commerce and Culture,* 125–27; Mary Eshbaugh Hayes, "The Way It Was . . . and the Way It Is," *Aspen Times,* August 21, 1975.
10. Allen, *The Romance of Commerce and Culture,* 126–30.
11. Ibid., 130–31.
12. Mary Eshbaugh Hayes, "Tom Sardy's Vision Created the Airport," *Aspen Times,* October 24, 1991; Allen, *The Romance of Commerce and Culture,* 132–33; Douglas G. Pearce, *Tourist Development* (New York: Longman, 1981).
13. *Aspen Times,* June 12, 1945.
14. Hal Boyle, "A Mining Town Is Reborn: Aspen May Become Athens of the Rockies," *Denver Post,* January 15, 1947, 10C; Allen, *The Romance of Commerce and Culture,* 140–42.
15. Walter Paul Paepcke to V. E. Ringle, June 11, 1946, Walter Paul Paepcke Archives, Chicago; Allen, *The Romance of Commerce and Culture,* 141–42; Gilbert, "Re-creation Through Recreation," 51.
16. Allen, *The Romance of Commerce and Culture,* 132–33.
17. Ibid., 132–34.
18. Duke, "Skiing Soldiers," 10–12; Jones, "Downhill in Colorado," 17 M; "Skiing Then and Now," *Overland News;* Allen, *The Romance of Commerce and Culture,* 134.
19. Mary E. Hayes, "Freidl Pfeifer: Ski Pioneer of Aspen," *Aspen Times,* March 28, 1991, May 30–31, 1992; Duke, "Skiing Soldiers," 9; Bill Sonn, "The Life and Times of Aspen," *Colorful Colorado Magazine* 12, no. 5 (March/April 1977): 6–10, 72–73; Allen, *The Romance of Commerce and Culture,* 140–43.
20. Gilbert, "Re-creation Through Recreation," 54; "Historical Dates on Aspen's Ski History, 1935–1946," typescript, Aspen Historical Society, 1987.
21. "Pitkin County: Year-Round Playground," promotional brochure, 1940, Aspen, Clippings File, 1940–1949, Western History Department, Denver Public Library.
22. Aspen Chamber of Commerce, "Beethoven, the Brown Hackle, and the Schuss," promotional brochure, 1949, Aspen, Clippings File, 1940–1949, Western History De-

partment, Denver Public Library; Hal Boyle, "A Mining Town Is Reborn: Aspen May Become Athens of the Rockies, *Denver Post*, January 15, 1947, 10C; "Paepcke's Aspen Grew Out of Picnic," *Pueblo Chieftain*, February 4, 1968, 5C, 1–5; Mary Eshbaugh Hayes, "Profile: Hometown Boy Makes Good," *Aspen Times*, December 20, 1973; Allen, *The Romance of Commerce and Culture*, 144–50, 174–94.

23. Boyle, "A Mining Town Is Reborn; Allen, *The Romance of Commerce and Culture*, 142–43, 146.
24. Patricia Coffin, "Aspen," *Look*, November 8, 1949, 23–27; "*Look* Turns Spotlight on Aspen Attractions," *Denver Post*, October 25, 1949; Meyers, *Colorado Ski Country*, 38; Jones, "Downhill in Colorado," 18M–19M; Luke Short, "Nightmare in Lace Pants," *Denver Post Empire Magazine*, October 22, 1950; Duke, "Skiing Soldiers," 10; Allen, *The Romance of Commerce and Culture*, 143–44.
25. Bruce Berger, *Notes of a Half-Aspenite* (Aspen, CO: Ashley and Associates, 1987), 1–6; Peggy Clifford, *To Aspen and Back Again: An American Journey* (New York: St. Martin's Press, 1979), 7–10, 28–29; Bill Brenneman, "Aspen—The Zaniest Town in the Whole U.S.A.," *Rocky Mountain News*, December 31, 1953; Mary Eshbaugh Hayes, "Westerns: Can They Tell Us Something?" *Aspen Times*, May 24, 1973; Mary Eshbaugh Hayes, "Berko Photographed Aspen in 1949," *Aspen Times*, June 22, 1989.
26. Clifford, *To Aspen and Back Again*, 50.
27. Ibid., 40–41.
28. Ibid., 49.
29. Boyle, "A Mining Town Is Reborn"; Luke Short, "Nightmare in Lace Pants"; Clifford, *To Aspen and Back*, 46.
30. Gilbert, "Re-creation Through Recreation," 66–67; Kathleen Daily and Gaylord T. Gueninm, *Aspen: The Quiet Years* (Aspen, CO: Red Ink Incorporated, 1994), 415–16; Mary Eshbaugh Hayes, "The Way It Was in Ski School," *Aspen Magazine*, February/ March 1975, 2–5.
31. Sidney Hyman, *The Aspen Idea* (Norman: University of Oklahoma Press, 1975), 106–20; Sloan, *The Romance of Commerce and Culture*, 226–43.
32. Tom Nagel, "Good News from Aspen," *Ski Country*, December 1, 1950; Foster, "Aspen—Before and After Paepcke"; Gilbert, "Re-creation Through Recreation," 68–69.
33. Nagel, "Good News from Aspen."
34. Allen, *The Romance of Commerce and Culture*, 145.
35. Clifford, *To Aspen and Back*, 47–48, 52–53.
36. Brenneman, "Aspen: The Zaniest Town in the Whole U.S.A."; Hyman, *The Aspen Idea*, 102–3, 132–34; Sonn, "The Life and Times of Aspen"; Allen, *The Romance of Commerce and Culture*, 264–65; Clifford, *To Aspen and Back*, 55–56.
37. Nagel, "Good News from Aspen"; Mary Eshbaugh Hayes, "The Town's Not the Same but the Old Bar Is," *Aspen Times*, October 2, 1975; Mary Eshbaugh Hayes, "The Old Golden Horn," *Aspen Times*, September 6, 1979; Allen, *The Romance of Commerce and Culture*, 143; Duke, "Skiing Soldiers," 10; Clifford, *To Aspen and Back Again*, 59–60.
38. Bill Brenneman, "Hard Work Gives Mining Town New Look," *Rocky Mountain News*, January 2, 1954; "Aspen Sprucing Up for Biggest Season," *Rocky Mountain News*, May 22, 1955; "Booming Aspen Looks to Big Sports Year," *Rocky Mountain News*, October 19, 1955; Duke, "Skiing Soldiers"; Sonn, "The Life and Times of Aspen"; Mary Eshbaugh Hayes, "Aspen Caught on During the 1950s," *Aspen Times*, October 15, 1987. Gilbert, "Re-creation Through Recreation," 56–66, discusses the growth of skiing.
39. Clifford, *To Aspen and Back Again*, 63–64.

40. Jack Foster, "A Village Reborn to a New Purpose," *Rocky Mountain News,* June 1, 1957; Bob Tonsing, "Mountains, Culture, 'Spirit' Have Roles in Aspen's Boom," *Denver Post,* April 5, 1959; Allen, *The Romance of Commerce and Culture,* 264–65.
41. Tonsing, "Mountains, Culture, 'Spirit' Have Roles in Aspen's Boom." Tonsing's article does not present the creation of lower-wage jobs pejoratively as later writers do, both because the community still viewed any growth of employment as good and also because the cultural trend that challenged the noblesse oblige hegemony of the wealthy in the American cultural revolution of the 1960s was in its infancy.
42. "Aspen Becoming Booming Town," *Rocky Mountain News,* September 26, 1954; Allen, *The Romance of Commerce and Culture,* 258, 265; Hyman, *The Aspen Idea,* 121–38.
43. "Skiing Then and Now."
44. Allen, *The Romance of Commerce and Culture,* 258–60; Hyman, *The Aspen Idea,* 143–50.
45. "Skiing Then and Now."

9. RESIDENCE-BASED RESORTS

1. "Sunnyside Inn 50th Anniversary Menu, Summer 1997," tells this story (Sunnyside Inn, Squaw Valley, California).
2. H. Benjamin Duke Jr., "Skiing Soldiers to Skiing Entrepreneurs: Development of the Western Ski Industry," typescript, H. Benjamin Duke Jr., Vail Associates Collection, Denver Public Library, 2; C. L. Parsons, "Aspen Boomed as Ski Spot," *Denver Post,* April 4, 1937; Sureva Towler, *The History of Skiing at Steamboat Springs* (Steamboat Springs, CO: Sureva Towler, 1987), 35–37; John B. Allen, *From Skisport to Skiing : One Hundred Years of an American Sport, 1840–1940* (Amherst: University of Massachusetts Press, 1993), 75–79, 117–29; Abbot Fay, *Ski Tracks in the Rockies: A Century of Colorado Skiing* (Denver: Cordillera Press, 1984), 55–58.
3. Colorado Ski Country USA, "Colorado Ski Industry Statistics: Skier Visits"; Fay, *Ski Tracks in the Rockies,* 50–53; Peggy Clifford and John M. Smith, *Aspen/Dreams and Dilemmas: Love Letter to a Small Town* (Chicago: Swallow Press, 1970).
4. William Philpott, "Visions of a Changing Vail: Fast-Growth Fallout in a Colorado Resort Town" (Master's thesis: University of Wisconsin, 1994), 20–25, 48–50. Philpott offers the most comprehensive look at the development of Vail to date.
5. Stacy Standley III, *The Impact of the Vail Ski Resort: An Input-Output Analysis* (Boulder, CO: Business Research Center, University of Colorado, 1971), 4; Bernard Udis et al., *An Analysis of the Economy of the Upper Main Stem Sub-Basin of the Colorado River Drainage Basin in 1960 with Emphasis on Heavy Water-Using Industries* (Boulder, CO: Bureau of Economic Research, 1967), 17; Duke, "Skiing Soldiers," 10–11.
6. Philpott, "Visions of a Changing Vail," 29–34; Fay, *Ski Tracks in the Rockies,* 49.
7. Philpott, "Visions of a Changing Vail," 32; Charlie Meyers, *Colorado Ski Country* (Helena and Billings, MT: Falcon Press, 1987), Colorado Geographic Series no. 4, 31–32; Standley, *The Impact of the Vail Ski Resort,* 5; Duke, "Skiing Soldiers," 10–11.
8. Philpott, "Visions of a Changing Vail," viii; Standley, *The Impact of the Vail Ski Resort,* 5; David Lissy, *Colorado Ski: Vail Special Edition* (Englewood, CO: Westcliffe Publishers, 1989), 2–5. In 1986 the last original lot in Vail sold for $675,000.
9. Standley, *The Impact of the Vail Ski Resort,* 36.
10. Philpott, "Visions of a Changing Vail," 49–55.
11. Standley, *The Impact of the Vail Ski Resort,* 36; Philpott, "Visions of a Changing Vail," 42–44.

12. Standley, *The Impact of the Vail Ski Resort*, 50–54; Philpott, "Visions of a Changing Vail," 76–83.
13. Douglas G. Pearce, *Tourist Development* (New York: Longman, 1981), 67–69; Philpott, "Visions of a Changing Vail," 34–47.
14. Philpott, "Visions of a Changing Vail," 53–59.
15. Douglas G. Pearce, "Tourist Development: Two Processes," *Travel Research Journal* (1978); 43–51; G. Cumin, "Les stations intégrée," *Urbanisme* 116 (1970): 50–53. The community-owned Green Bay Packers provide a similar model of ownership in professional football.
16. Philpott, "Visions of a Changing Vail," 69; Colorado Ski Country USA, "Colorado Ski Industry Statistics."
17. Pearce, "Tourist Development: Two Processes," 43–51.
18. Philpott, "Visions of a Changing Vail," 92–96.
19. Ibid., 87–88.
20. Ibid., 98–99; David Halberstam, *The Fifties* (New York: Villard Books, 1993), discusses Wilson and the rise of Holiday Inn.
21. Philpott, "Visions of a Changing Vail," 100–101, 115–20.
22. *Los Angeles Times*, May 30, 1971; "Dr. Peter Janss Dies," *Los Angeles Times*, March 6, 1972; Doug Oppenheimer and Jim Poore, *Sun Valley: A Biography* (Boise, ID: Beatty Books, 1976), 174–75; Hyman, *The Aspen Idea*, 149.
23. *U.S. Census of Population: 1950, Idaho* (Washington, DC: Government Printing Office, 1952), 12–62; *1960 Census of Population, vol. 1, Characteristics of the Population*, Part 14, *Idaho* (Washington, DC: U.S. Government Printing Office, 1963), 14–23; Oppenheimer and Poore, *Sun Valley*, 165–69; Dorice Taylor, *Sun Valley* (Sun Valley: Ex Libris Sun Valley, 1980), 243–47; Leonard J. Arrington, *History of Idaho*, 2 vols. (Moscow, ID: University of Idaho Press, 1994), 2: 203–4; Maury Klein, *Union Pacific* (Garden City, New York: Doubleday, 1987), 490–92.
24. Philip Fradkin, "King of the Mountains," *Los Angeles Times West Magazine*, January 29, 1968, 7–10; "Janss Corporation Buys Sun Valley," *Northwest Skier* 7, no. 2 (October 16, 1964): 1; Paul Andersen, "Laying a Foundation for Snowmass," *Aspen Times*, January 29, 1967; Oppenheimer and Poore, *Sun Valley*, 176.
25. Oppenheimer and Poore, *Sun Valley*, 177; Taylor, *Sun Valley*, 244.
26. Oppenheimer and Poore, *Sun Valley*, 177–78.
27. Ibid., 184.
28. Taylor, *Sun Valley*, 244–48; Oppenheimer and Poore, *Sun Valley*, 177.
29. Dorice Taylor, "No Growing Pains for Sun Valley as 100 New Families Move In," *Idaho Sunday Statesman*, November 26, 1967; Steve Ahrens, "Imagination, Skill, Know-How Join Forces to Produce Sun Valley Ateliers," *Idaho Daily Statesman*, January 2, 1968; O. A. Kelker, "Ketchum Area's $6 Million Building Boom Is Really Something to Behold," *Twin Falls Times-News*, September 14, 1969; "Sun Valley Council Hears Plan for Elkhorn Village," *Wood River Journal*, December 16, 1971.
30. Martin Arnold, "To the Rich Who Ski by Day and Party at Night, Sun Valley's Neat Again," *New York Times*, January 18, 1970, 38L; Taylor, *Sun Valley*, 244.
31. Fradkin, "King of the Mountains," 7–10; Steven Birmingham, "The Sun Valley Set," *Holiday*, November 1967, 62–66, 133–36.
32. *1970 Census of the Population, vol. 1, Characteristics of the Population*, Part 14, *Idaho* (Washington, DC: U.S. Government Printing Office, 1973), 14–13; Oppenheimer and Poore, *Sun Valley*, 178; Taylor, *Sun Valley*, 245–48.

33. *U.S. Census of Population: 1950, Idaho,* 12–63, 12–75; *Census of Population: 1960, Idaho,* 14–129, 14–149; *Census of Population: 1970, Idaho,* 14–13, 14–238, 14–242.
34. Shannon Besoyan, "Ketchum Questionnaires Find Dislike for Developers, Population Growth," *Idaho Daily Statesman,* April 10, 1973; Oppenheimer and Poore, *Sun Valley,* 177–78.
35. Fradkin, "King of the Mountains," 7–10; "Snowmass-at-Aspen: Exciting New Shangri-la of Skiing," *Denver Post,* November 12, 1967, 17–20; Paul Anderson, "Laying a Foundation for Snowmass," *Aspen Times,* January 29, 1967; Anne M. Gilbert, "Re-Creation Through Recreation: Aspen Skiing from 1870–1970," (Aspen Historical Society, Aspen, CO, 1995), 90–91; Peggy Clifford, *To Aspen and Back Again: An American Journey* (New York: St. Martin's Press, 1979). Snowmass offers a useful barometer of the changes Janss's conceptions brought precisely because it was built from scratch; at Sun Valley, Janss transformed the community equally thoroughly, but it is harder to discern the precise impact at the Idaho resort because of its pre-existing superstructure.
36. Clifford, *To Aspen and Back,* 105–6.
37. "Snowmass-at-Aspen: Exciting New Shangri-la of Skiing," 17–20; Anderson, "Laying a Foundation for Snowmass"; Gilbert, "Re-Creation Through Recreation," 90–91.
38. Fradkin, "King of the Mountains"; Curtis Casewit, "Snowmass: Shangri-La in Ski County USA," *Colorful Colorado* (midwinter 1968): 64–70, 94; for Scottsdale, see Bradford Luckingham, *Phoenix: The History of a Southwestern Metropolis* (Tucson: University of Arizona Press, 1989), 264–66.
39. "Snowmass 67," Janss Development Company, Snowmass File, Aspen Historical Society, Aspen, CO; *Snowmass Villager* 1, no. 1 (October 23, 1967): 1.
40. *Snowmass Villager,* 1–3; Mary Eshbaugh Hayes, "The Norwegian Invasion," *Aspen Times,* December 6, 1984.
41. Malcolm J. Rohrbough, *Aspen: The History of a Silver-Mining Town, 1879–1893* (New York: Oxford University Press, 1986); James S. Allen, *The Romance of Commerce and Culture: Capitalism, Modernism, and the Chicago-Aspen Crusade for Cultural Reform* (Chicago: University of Chicago Press, 1983).
42. Dean MacCannell, *The Tourist: A New Theory of the Leisure Class* (New York: Schocken Books, 1976), 94, borrows from Erving Goffman, describing this phenomena as "front" and "back" cultures (94). MacCannell describes the role of back culture as providing a place for belonging to a self-identified authentic ideal, a reach for reality.
43. Tim Woodward, "Idaho's Most Famous Resort Area Maintains Western Flavor," *Idaho Daily Statesman,* October 3, 1976; see real estate advertisements in *Aspen Times,* February 1, 1963; February 8, 1963; April 12, 1963; July 19, 1963; January 5, 1967; March 2, 1967; and October 29, 1967, for examples of the increase in asking price of similar properties.
44. Woodward, "Idaho's Most Famous Resort Area Maintains Quaint Western Flavor."
45. Anderson, "Laying a Foundation for Snowmass"; Woodward, "Idaho's Most Famous Resort Area Maintains Quaint Western Flavor."
46. Woodward, "Idaho's Most Famous Resort Maintains Quaint Western Flavor."
47. Clifford, *To Aspen and Back,* 105–9, 133.
48. Ibid., xi; Bruce Berger, *Notes of a Half-Aspenite* (Aspen, CO: Ashley and Associates, 1987).

10. "POWDER APLENTY"

1. Peggy Clifford, *To Aspen and Back Again: An American Journey* (New York: St. Martin's Press, 1979); Peggy Clifford and John MacCauley Smith, "The Distressing Rebirth of Aspen," *Denver Post Empire Magazine,* August 16, 1970, 8; Hunter S. Thompson, "The Temptations of Jean-Claude Killy," in *The Great Shark Hunt* (New York: Fawcett Popular Library, 1979), 86–108.
2. Paul Perry, *Fear and Loathing: The Strange and Terrible Saga of Hunter S. Thompson* (New York: Thunder's Mouth Press, 1992), 130–33.
3. United Bank of Denver, "Economic Analysis of the Skiing Industry," November 1971, 6.
4. Clifford, *To Aspen and Back,* 122.
5. Jack Foster, "Steamboat—A Gallant Little City," *Rocky Mountain News,* February 21, 1947; "Uranium Deposit Large, Engineers Declare," *Steamboat Pilot,* June 3, 1954; Sureva Towler, *The History of Skiing at Steamboat Springs* (Steamboat Springs, CO: Sureva Towler, 1987), 92–95.
6. Towler, *The History of Skiing,* 109; Abbot Fay, *Ski Tracks in the Rockies: A Century of Colorado Skiing* (Denver: Cordillera Press, 1984), 52.
7. "Plans Under Way for Ski Lift, Runs on Storm Mountain," *Denver Post,* October 23, 1957; Towler, *The History of Skiing,* 109–11.
8. Towler, *The History of Skiing,* 112–16.
9. William Logan, "Steamboat Springs: Ski Town U.S.A., *Rocky Mountain News,* May 15, 1966; Towler, *The History of Skiing,* 116–18.
10. Towler, *The History of Skiing,* 109.
11. "Ski Complex Planned at Mt. Werner," *Steamboat Pilot,* August 10, 1967; "Steamboat Springs Spends $1 Million for Big Sports Setup," *Rocky Mountain News,* ca. 1964; Towler, *The History of Skiing,* 116–18; Fay, *Ski Tracks in the Rockies,* 52.
12. "Development Boom Strikes Steamboat Springs Area; Two New Lifts Installed," *Ski Time,* December 1968, 36; Peter Blake, "Steamboat Springs' Ship Coming In," *Rocky Mountain News,* January 1969; Towler, *The History of Skiing,* 118.
13. Fay, *Ski Tracks in the Rockies,* 64–67;
14. "Mt. Werner Ski Area Purchased by LTV," *High Country USA,* November 1969, 14; Towler, *The History of Skiing,* 119.
15. Towler, *The History of Skiing,* 119.
16. Ibid., 118–19.
17. John Rolfe Burroughs, "Ski Town, U.S.A.: Rapid Developments Bid Fair to Make Steamboat Springs, Colorado, the St. Moritz of the Rockies" (Steamboat Springs, CO: Steamboat Springs Winter Sports Club, 1962), 1–3.
18. Colorado Ski Country USA, "Ski Country Impact Study," Denver, 1973.
19. Blake, "Steamboat Springs' Ship Coming In."
20. Towler, *The History of Skiing,* 119.
21. Thompson R. Smith, "Destruction and Appropriation: Local Culture and the Corporation in Steamboat Springs," paper, 1982, courtesy of Thompson R. Smith.
22. Ibid., 4.
23. Ibid., 9–10; Towler, *The History of Skiing,* 119.
24. City of Steamboat Springs Community Committee, "City of Steamboat Springs Community Committee Report," May 1, 1984, Local History Section, Werner Memorial Library, Steamboat Springs, Colorado.
25. Peggy Clifford and John M. Smith, *Aspen/Dreams and Dilemmas: Love Letter to a*

Small Town (Chicago: Swallow Press, 1970), 162–64. Clifford, *To Aspen and Back,* 92–94.

26. Clifford, *To Aspen and Back,* 94–95.
27. Ibid., 95.
28. Clifford and Smith, *Aspen/Dreams and Dilemmas,* 164–68.
29. Clifford, *To Aspen and Back,* 97.
30. Sidney Hyman, *The Aspen Idea* (Norman: University of Oklahoma Press, 1975).
31. Annie Gilbert, "Re-creation Through Recreation: Aspen Skiing from 1870–1970" (Aspen, CO: Aspen Historical Society, 1995), 76–84.
32. Cecil Jones, "Corporate Cornice Above Aspen," *Rocky Mountain News,* February 8, 1970, 2; Charlie Meyers, "Aspen's Darcy Brown Sticks to His Guns," *Denver Post,* January 5, 1977; Alan Gersten, "Ski Firm's Fox-y Takeover Clouds Future for Aspen," *Rocky Mountain News,* January 1978; Malcolm J. Rohrbough, *Aspen: The History of a Silver-Mining Town, 1879–1893* (New York: Oxford University Press, 1986), 23–25, 106–7, 124–26, 169–70, 229–33; Gilbert, "Re-creation Through Recreation," 85–86.
33. Clifford, *To Aspen and Back,* 81–83.
34. Ibid., 83; Jeanette Darnauer, interview with D. R. C. Brown, April 10, 1979, Aspen Historical Society Tape Recording no. 10, Aspen Historical Society, Aspen, CO.
35. Brown interview, April 10, 1979; Clifford, *To Aspen and Back.*
36. Perry, *Fear and Loathing,* 124–29; Clifford, *To Aspen and Back,* 101.
37. Hunter S. Thompson, "The Battle for Aspen," *Rolling Stone* 67 (October 1, 1970), 30–37; Perry, *Fear and Loathing,* 123–24; Clifford, *To Aspen and Back Again,* 138.
38. Hunter S. Thompson, "Freak Power in the Rockies," in Thompson, *The Great Shark Hunt,* 199–202.
39. Clifford, *To Aspen and Back Again,* 138.
40. Interview with Terrell J. Minger, June 24, 1997; Jennifer J. Hammond, "Growth Management in Aspen, Colorado, 1960–1977," Aspen Historical Society, July 22, 1995, 24–25; Rick Reese, "Presentation to the Salt Lake Winter Olympics Feasibility Study Committee, Utah State Capitol, November 16, 1984, Salt Lake City, courtesy of Ed Marston and Rick Reese.
41. Charles R. Goeldner, *The Aspen Skier,* vol. 1, *Lift Survey* (Boulder: Business Research Division, University of Colorado, 1978), 5–7; Peggy Clifford, "The 'Aspenization' of the Rest of America," *Rocky Mountain News,* March 12, 1978; Blake Fleetwood, "Booming Aspen Worries About the 'Los Angelization' of the Rockies," *New York Times,* March 2, 1975, 20–22; Bob Whearley, "Aspen: Ski-Bums, Beats, Art, and Culture Characterize Town," *Denver Post,* January 20, 1963, 6B; Colorado Ski Country USA, "Lift Tickets Issued," ca. 1972, Steven Knowlton Collection, Denver Public Library; Carl Abbott, Stephen J. Leonard, and David McComb, *Colorado: A History of the Centennial State* (Niwot, CO: University Press of Colorado, 1982), 317; Charlie Meyers, *Colorado Ski Country* (Helena and Billings, MT: Falcon Press, 1987), Colorado Geographic Series no. 4, 43.
42. Goeldner, *Lift Survey,* 13; Clifford, *To Aspen and Back Again,* 230–32; Berger, *Notes of a Half-Aspenite.*
43. Gersten, "Ski Firm's Fox-y Takeover Clouds Future for Aspen"; Aspen Ski Company, "Looking at Aspen's Skiing Roots," Aspen Skiing, Vertical File, Aspen Historical Society.
44. Brown interview, April 10, 1979.
45. Donald Hough, *The Cocktail Hour in Jackson Hole* (rept.; Worland, WY: High Plains Publishing, 1956).

46. Hough, *The Cocktail Hour.*
47. Judy S. Clayton, "Snow King Was State's First Ski Area," *Jackson Hole Guide,* January 18, 1989, C5; Angus M. Thuermer Jr., "Father of Snow King: Neil Rafferty Built the First Ski Lift and Saw the King Mature," *Jackson Hole News,* January 25, 1989, 9; "Teton County Has Colorful Past," *Jackson Hole Guide,* February 24, 1966.
48. Edward A. Wyatt, "McCollister a Visionary with a Quick Temper," *Jackson Hole News,* July 24, 1991.
49. "New Million Dollar Ski Facility Gets Green Light," *Jackson Hole News,* December 26, 1963.
50. Ibid.; Wyatt, "McCollister a Visionary"; Drew Simmons, "Tram Turns 25 with Toasts, Trips," *Jackson Hole News,* August 7, 1991.
51. Jack Goodman, "New Snow Means Happiness for Jackson Hole," *New York Times,* February 9, 1969, AA23; Morten Lund, "Jackson Hole: The Ecstasy and the Agony," *Ski Magazine,* October 1967, 14–17.
52. "New Million Dollar Ski Facility Gets Green Light"; "Offering Circular: The Jackson Hole Corporation Inc., October 26, 1960," Teton County Historical Society; Wyatt, "McCollister a Visionary."
53. Wyatt, "McCollister a Visionary."
54. Joy Ufford, "Birth of J. H. Ski Resort Changed Valley Winter," *Jackson Hole Guide,* July 15, 1992, A9.
55. David Stump, "Ski Corp. Sold: Lawsuit Settled," *Jackson Hole Guide,* July 15, 1992; Michael Sellett, "New Owners Take Over Ski Corp.: It's Over! McCollister Sells Ski Area," *Jackson Hole News,* July 15, 1992.
56. J. Royal Horton, *Murder in Jackson Hole* (Moose, WY: Homestead Publishing, 1993), 28–30; interview with Angus Thuermer Jr., August 1994.
57. Angus M. Thuermer Jr., "New Owners Take Over Ski Area: Kemmerer, Resor Form New Team," *Jackson Hole News,* July 15, 1992; Allen Baker, "Ski Corp.: Duess Will get 49 Percent Despite Great Year," *Jackson Hole Guide,* July 19, 1989; David Stump, "Ski Corp. Sold: Lawsuit Settled," *Jackson Hole Guide,* July 15, 1992.
58. David Stump, "New Owner Has Strong Ties to Wyoming," *Jackson Hole Guide,* July 15, 1992.
59. Robert Righter, conversation with the author, August 1994. (Bob Righter and Sherry Smith were kind enough to host me during one of my stays in Jackson; they have an extraordinary view of the Grand Tetons, and I too would pay oodles of money for it!)

11. ENTERTAINMENT TOURISM

1. Jerome H. Skolnick, *House of Cards: The Legalization and Control of Casino Gambling* (Boston: Little, Brown, and Company, 1978), 135–44; Hal K. Rothman, "Colony, Capital, and *Casino:* Money and the Real Las Vegas," in *The Grit Beneath the Glitter: Tales from the Real Las Vegas,* ed. Mike Davis and Hal K. Rothman (Berkeley: University of California Press, 1998).
2. Rothman, "Colony, Capital, and *Casino*"; Eugene P. Moehring, *Resort City in the Sunbelt* (Reno: University of Nevada Press, 1989), 107–39, 203–60; John M. Findlay, *People of Chance: Gambling in American Society from Jamestown to Las Vegas* (New York: Oxford University Press, 1986), 135–45.
3. John M. Findlay, *Magic Lands: Western Cityscapes and American Culture After 1940* (Berkeley; University of California Press, 1991), 54–55; Karal Ann Marling, *As Seen on TV* (Cambridge: Harvard University Press, 1994), 86–127; Richard V. Francaviglia, *Main Street Revisited: Time, Space, and Image Building in Small-Town America* (Iowa

City: University of Iowa Press, 1996), 144–64; n.a., *Disneyland: Dreams, Traditions, and Transitions* (Anaheim: Walt Disney Company, n.d.), 1–22.

4. Monthly Report, Grand Canyon National Park, August 1945, September 1945, and October 1945, Series 7, Grand Canyon, RG 79, National Archives; Moehring, *Resort City;* Eric F. Goldman, *The Crucial Decade—and After : America, 1945–1960* (New York: Alfred A. Knopf, 1973), 4–5, 12–15; John A. Jakle, *The Tourist: Travel in Twentieth-Century North America* (Lincoln: University of Nebraska Press, 1985), 185–98; Bernard DeVoto, "The National Parks," *Fortune,* June 1947, 120–21; Bernard DeVoto, "Let's Close the National Parks," *Harper's,* October 1953, 49–52; Robert D. Baker, Robert S. Maxwell, Victor H. Treat, and Henry C. Dethloff, *Timeless Heritage: A History of the Forest Service in the Southwest* (Washington, DC: Department of Agriculture, 1988), 59–68, 131–33; Ronald A. Foresta, *America's National Parks and Their Keepers* (Washington, DC: Johns Hopkins University Press, 1984), 50–55.
5. Findlay, *People of Chance,* 111–16; Skolnick, *House of Cards,* 107–10; Moehring, *Resort City,* 41, 68; Richard Lilliard, *Desert Challenge: An Interpretation of Nevada* (New York: Alfred A. Knopf, 1942), 335–76; Russell R. Elliott with William D. Rowley, *History of Nevada,* 2d ed. (Lincoln: University of Nebraska Press, 1987), 284–85; Glenda Riley, *Divorce: An American Tradition* (New York: Oxford University Press, 1991), 135–44. For a community study of another "division point" on a railroad, see Paxton P. Price, "The Railroad, Rincon, and the River," *New Mexico Historical Review* 65, no. 4 (October 1990): 437–54.
6. Findlay, *People of Chance,* 115–17; Alan Hess, *Viva Las Vegas: After-Hours Architecture* (San Francisco: Chronicle Books, 1993), 14–26.
7. Findlay, *People of Chance,* 122–26; Moehring, *Resort City,* 42–43; Perry Kaufman, "The Best City of Them All: A History of Las Vegas, 1930–1960" (Ph.D. diss., University of California–Santa Barbara, 1974), 189–90.
8. Moehring, *Resort City,* 43–44; *Las Vegas Review-Journal,* April 4, 1941, 8; George Stamos, "The Great Resorts of Las Vegas and How They Began," *Las Vegas Sun Magazine,* April 1, 1979, 6–10; Hess, *Viva Las Vegas,* 26–32; Kaufman, "The Best City," 170–72.
9. Moehring, *Resort City,* 44–46; Findlay, *People of Chance,* 124–28; Hess, *Viva Las Vegas,* 32–33; Findlay, *Magic Lands,* 27–28, 65–70.
10. *Las Vegas Review Journal,* July 31, 1946; Robert Lacey, *Little Man: Meyer Lansky and the Gangster Life* (Boston: Little, Brown and Company, 1991), 151; Ed Reid and Ovid Demaris, *The Green Felt Jungle* (New York: Trident Press, 1963), 61–63. Although a little tarnished by age and its screedlike characteristics, *The Green Felt Jungle* remains an excellent source for sorting out the 1950s in Las Vegas.
11. Lacey, *Little Man,* 151–53; Hess, *Viva Las Vegas,* 42–43; Reid and Demaris, *The Green Felt Jungle,* 24–26.
12. Moehring, *Resort City,* 47–49; Findlay, *People of Chance,* 163–64; Hess, *Viva Las Vegas,* 38–46; Peter Wiley and Robert Gottlieb, *Empires in the Sun: The Rise of the New American West* (New York: G. P. Putnam's Sons, 1982), 191.
13. Moehring, *Resort City,* 6–12.
14. Ibid., 13–20.
15. Richard Lowitt, *The New Deal and the West* (Bloomington: Indiana University Press, 1984).
16. Elliott with Rowley, *History of Nevada,* 248, 275–85; Joseph Stevens, *Hoover Dam* (Norman: University of Oklahoma Press, 1988).
17. Elliott with Rowley, *History of Nevada,* 310; Richard W. Mingus, "Breakdown in the

Broker State: The CIO in Southern Nevada During World War II" (Master's thesis, University of Nevada, Las Vegas, 1995).

18. Moehring, *Resort City,* 31–40; Elliott with Rowley, *History of Nevada,* 313.
19. Reid and DeMaris, *The Green Felt Jungle,* 14–34; Ralph Pearl, *Las Vegas Is My Beat* (Seacaucus, NJ: Lyle Stuart, 1973), 23–33; Moehring, *Resort City,* 41–54; Findlay, *People of Chance;* Hal Rothman, "Selling the Meaning of Place: Tourism, Entrepreneurship and Community Transformation in the Twentieth-Century American West," *Pacific Historical Review* 65, no. 4 (November 1996): 525–59; Lacey, *Little Man,* 150–51.
20. Skolnick, *House of Cards,* 111–12; Burton B. Turkus and Sid Feder, *Murder Inc.* (New York: Farrar, Strauss, and Young, 1951).
21. Reid and Demaris, *The Green Felt Jungle,* 24–26; Hess, *Viva Las Vegas.*
22. Reid and Demaris, *The Green Felt Jungle,* 61–70; Moehring, *Resort City,* 74–77, 83–85; Wiley and Gottlieb, *Empires in the Sun.* Skolnick, *House of Cards,* details the federal and state response to the skimming that characterized these resorts (124–33).
23. Wiley and Gottlieb, *Empires in the Sun,* 197; Lacey, *Little Man,* 298; Skolnick, *House of Cards,* 127–31. Reid and Demaris, *The Green Felt Jungle,* provide a list of registered Las Vegas casino owners in 1963 (233–42). A glance shows significant representation by members of organized crime and their associates.
24. Wiley and Gottlieb, *Empires in the Sun,* 195; Pearl, *Las Vegas Is My Beat.*
25. Interview with Joyce Marshall, October 23, 1993; interview with Robert Guebard, November 22, 1993; interview with Cathleen Dooley Loucks, November 18, 1993; Wiley and Gottlieb, *Empires in the Sun,* 193–94; David Spanier, *Welcome to the Pleasuredome: Inside Las Vegas* (Reno: University of Nevada Press, 1992), 65–68.
26. Skolnick, *House of Cards,* 115–16, 127–31; Lacey, *Little Man,* 299–300; Moehring, *Resort City,* 132–35, 238.
27. Kenneth Hudson, *Air Travel: A Social History* (Totowa, NJ: Rowman and Littlefield, 1980); Horace Sutton, *Travelers, the American Tourist from Stagecoach to Space Shuttle* (New York: Morrow, 1980), 247–60. Jakle, *The Tourist,* 176–84; Reid and Demaris, *The Green Felt Jungle,* 59.
28. Moehring, *Resort City,* 238; Findlay, *People of Chance,* suggests that Las Vegas "amounted to little more than another subdivision of metropolitan Los Angeles" because before 1960, "Southern Californians amounted to between three-fifths and three-fourths of all visitors to Las Vegas." He also argues that Las Vegas "demonstrat[ed] its nationwide popularity" in the same time period as the "futuristic strip captured the imaginations of Americans" (134, 137, 138–39). By the 1970s Californians and the West made up a significantly smaller percentage of Las Vegas visitors. The lowest years for California visitation were 1979, when approximately 31 percent of visitors reported Golden State addresses, and 1988, when the total was 29 percent. See Las Vegas Convention and Visitors Bureau, *Las Vegas Visitor Profile Study* (Las Vegas: Las Vegas Convention and Visitors Bureau, 1975–1990); Nevada State Highway Department, *Nevada Out-of-State Visitor Survey* (Carson City, NV: Nevada State Highway Department, 1963).
29. Lacey, *Little Man,* 294–301; Reid and DeMaris, *Green Felt Jungle,* 31–35.
30. Wiley and Gottlieb, *Empires in the Sun,* 198.
31. Moehring, *Resort City,* 115–16, 244–45.
32. Steven Brill, *The Teamsters* (New York: Simon and Schuster, 1978), 22–24; Wiley and Gottlieb, *Empires in the Sun,* 197–200; Reid and Demaris, *The Green Felt Jungle,* 98–101.
33. Brill, *The Teamsters,* 208.

34. Reid and Demaris, *The Green Felt Jungle,* 62–63, 100–104; Moehring, *Resort City,* 242–43; Brill, *The Teamsters,* 208.
35. Moehring, *Resort City,* 238–41.
36. Susan Berman, *Easy Street* (New York: Dial Press, 1981).
37. Moehring, *Resort City,* 116–18; Brill, *The Teamsters,* 210.
38. Moehring, *Resort City,* 119.
39. Skolnick, *House of Cards,* 113–18, 122; Moehring, *Resort City,* 55; Ronald A. Farrell and Carole Case, *The Black Book and the Mob: The Untold Story of the Control of Nevada's Casinos* (Madison: University of Wisconsin Press, 1995).
40. Skolnick, *House of Cards,* 140–41; Moehring, *Resort City,* 55.
41. Moehring, *Resort City,* 118–19; Skolnick, *House of Cards,* 134–37; Wiley and Gottlieb, *Empires in the Sun,* 201–3; Donald L. Barlett and James B. Steele, *Empire: The Life, Legend, and Madness of Howard Hughes* (New York: W. W. Norton, 1979); Michael Drosnin, *Citizen Hughes* (New York: Holt, Rinehart, and Winston, 1985).
42. *Nevada Report* 1, no. 1 (July 15, 1969); 2; Skolnick, *House of Cards,* 134.
43. Lacey, *Little Man,* 299–301; Skolnick, *House of Cards,* 139–40.
44. Spanier, *Welcome to the Pleasuredome,* 35–38, 95–96, 135–66; Elliott with Rowley, *History of Nevada,* 333–36; Moehring, *Resort City,* 86–87, 243–44; Howard Stutz and David Finnigan, "New Resort to Open Door for Union," *Las Vegas Review Journal,* May 12, 1989, A1:5.
45. Vern Willis, "Kerkorian Has Played Major Role in LV Success," *Las Vegas Review-Journal,* January 23, 1983, J3–5; Skolnick, *House of Cards,* 142–45; Moehring, *Resort City,* 120–22; Hess, *Viva Las Vegas,* 97; Deke Castleman, *Las Vegas* (Oakland, CA: Compass American Guides, 1993), 119.

12. PURIFYING THE WAGES OF SIN

1. Regional Demographic for the State of Nevada, July 20, 1995, 1–4.
2. Ibid., 13.
3. Courtney Alexander, "Rise to Power: The Recent History of the Culinary Union in Las Vegas," in *The Grit Beneath the Glitter: Tales from the Real Las Vegas,* ed. Mike Davis and Hal Rothman (Berkeley: University of California Press, 1998).
4. Most who work in the hotel and casino industry attribute their high wages to unionization. Even non-unionized resorts pay well; owners and managers are often prepared to pay higher than union scale and to offer more benefits to keep unions out; see interview with Joyce Marshall, October 23, 1993; interview with Robert Guebard, November 22, 1993; interview with Cathleen Dooley Loucks, November 18, 1993; interview with Paul Schmitt, November 17, 1993; David Spanier, *Welcome to the Pleasuredome; Inside Las Vegas* (Reno: University of Nevada Press, 1992), 35–38, 95–96, 135–66; Russell R. Elliott, *History of Nevada* (Lincoln: University of Nebraska Press, 1973), 333–36; Eugene P. Moehring, *Resort City in the Sunbelt: Las Vegas, 1930–1970* (Reno: University of Nevada Press, 1989), 86–87, 243–44; Howard Stutz and David Finnigan, "New Resort to Open Door for Union," *Las Vegas Review Journal,* May 12, 1989, A1:5.
5. This was my personal experience in August 1992. It was the longest line I've ever waited in! See also Regional Demographics for the State of Nevada, July 20, 1995, 14.
6. This is observational data gleaned from asking students about their family histories during eight consecutive semesters of teaching introductory history in classes of over 100.
7. Regional Demographics for the State of Nevada, July 20, 1995, 11.
8. Phyllis Darling, letter to Hal Rothman, April 1994.

9. Alan Hess, *Viva Las Vegas: After Hours Architecture* (San Francisco: Chronicle Books, 1993), 88–94.
10. Nicholas Pileggi, *Casino* (London: Faber and Faber, 1996), 224–36, gives Glick's ex post facto account (120–33); Steven Brill, *The Teamsters* (New York: Simon and Schuster, 1978), 232–37; Ned Day, *The Mob on the Run* (television documentary, KLAS-8, Las Vegas, 1987).
11. Pileggi, *Casino,* 224–36; Day, *The Mob on the Run;* Hess, *Viva Las Vegas,* 91–93.
12. Jerome H. Skolnick, *House of Cards: Legalization and Control of Casino Gambling* (Boston: Little, Brown, 1978), 206–21, offers the most analytical account; see also Pileggi, *Casino,* 175–215; Brill, *The Teamsters,* 232–37; and Day, *The Mob on the Run.*
13. Day, *The Mob on the Run.*
14. Skolnick, *House of Cards,* 172–75; Ed Reid and Ovid Demaris, *The Green Felt Jungle* (New York: Pocket Books, 1964), 172–85; Hank Messick, *Lansky* (New York: Berkley Publishing, 1971).
15. Peter Wiley and Robert Gottlieb, *Empires in the Sun: The Rise of the New American West* (New York: Putnam, 1982), 204–6, give the best description of the inner workings of the efforts to use regulatory powers to divest mobsters of their position in Las Vegas; see also Skolnick, *House of Cards,* 135–45.
16. Robert Macy, "Kirk Kerkorian Still 'Very Bullish' on Vegas," *Las Vegas Review Journal,* April 24, 1986, D1–2; Wiley and Gottlieb, *Empires in the Sun,* 206–9.
17. Hess, *Viva Las Vegas,* 101–3.
18. John M. Findlay, *People of Chance: Gambling in American Society from Jamestown to Las Vegas* (New York: Oxford University Press, 1986), 110–35. Richard O. Davies, *The Age of Asphalt: The Automobile, the Freeway, and the Condition of Metropolitan America* (New York: J. B. Lippincott, 1975); Earl Pomeroy, *In Search of the Golden West* (Lincoln: University of Nebraska Press, 1957), 218–32.
19. Jack E. Sheehan, "Milken Gives Wynn Key to Atlantic City," *Las Vegas Sun,* March 13, 1989, 1A–2A; Howard Stutz, "Drexel Paved Path of Gaming in 1980s," *Las Vegas Review Journal,* February 12, 1989, 1B–2B; Fen Montaigne, "What Makes Steve Wynn a Winner?" *Las Vegas Review Journal,* November 13, 1983, 4L–5L, 14L–15L; Sergio Lalli, "Wynn Plans Big Hotel on the Strip," *Las Vegas Review Journal,* October 30, 1986, A1:1–4; Sergio Lalli, "Wynn Envisions New Magic on the Strip," *Las Vegas Review Journal,* March 1, 1987, B1:3; Sergio Lalli, "Wynn Unveils Plans for Strip Resort," *Las Vegas Review Journal,* May 28, 1987, B1:1; "Planning Board to Review Wynn Resort," *Las Vegas Review Journal,* June 16, 1987, B2:4; Ed Vogel, "Wynn Applauds Las Vegas as Worldwide Vacation Spot," *Las Vegas Review Journal,* November 20, 1987, B1:5; Howard Stutz, "Steve Wynn's New Mirage Resort No Optical Illusion," *Las Vegas Review Journal,* December 10, 1988, B1:2; Howard Stutz, "Mirage License Clears Hurdle," *Las Vegas Review Journal,* October 12, 1989, B1:6; Ed Vogel, "Gaming Commission Grants License to Wynn to Operate the Mirage," *Las Vegas Review Journal,* October 27, 1989, B5:1; Robert Macy, "Here's a Peek Inside the Mirage," *Las Vegas Review Journal,* October 29, 1989, A1:2; Howard Stutz, "The Mirage to Become Reality," *Las Vegas Review Journal,* November 20, 1989, B1:2; Howard Stutz, "The Mirage Opens Doors to Public, Special Guests Today," November 22, 1989, 3B; Howard Stutz, "Thousands Welcome the Mirage," *Las Vegas Review Journal,* November 23, 1989, A1:2; Spanier, *Welcome to the Pleasuredome,* 36–38.
20. Jeff Burbank, "Four White Tigers Resort's First 'Guests,'" *Las Vegas Sun,* November 23, 1989, 1A, 5A; Stutz, "Drexel Paved Path of Gaming in 1980s," 1B; Spanier, *Welcome to the Pleasuredome,* 36–38.

21. Spanier, *Welcome to the Pleasuredome*, 17–59; Dial Torgerson, *Kerkorian: An American Success Story* (New York; Dial Press, 1974); Susan Gould, "Kirk Kerkorian," *Signature* 4 (1969); 1–5; "Kerkorian Ventures Range from Air Charter Service to Movie Theme Park," *Las Vegas Review Journal*, October 1, 1989, 8B; Vern Willis, "Kerkorian Has Played a Major Role in LV Success," *Las Vegas Review Journal*, January 23, 1983, J3; "MGM Grand Inc. Earns $6.2 Million Profit in '88," *Las Vegas Review Journal*, March 22, 1989, C7; Howard Stutz, "Kerkorian Poised for Vegas Return," *Las Vegas Review Journal*, October 1, 1989, B1:2; Ed Vogel, "Panel OKs Kerkorian's Plan to Sell Stock to Finance Park," *Las Vegas Review Journal*, October 27, 1989, 5B; Howard Stutz, "MGM Cleared for Marina Takeover," *Las Vegas Review Journal*, December 7, 1989, B1:2; Howard Stutz, "Gamers Approve Kerkorian Deal," *Las Vegas Review Journal*, December 22, 1989, B1; Jay Greene, "Kerkorian: Mysterious and Rich," *Las Vegas Sun*, April 8, 1991, B4; Lynn Waddell, "Again, Kerkorian Operates on a Grand Scale," *Las Vegas Sun*, October 7, 1991, A1; Lynn Waddell, "MGM Gets Big Boost," *Las Vegas Sun*, May 16, 1991, A1; Lynn Waddell, "MGM Financing Nearly Complete," *Las Vegas Sun*, April 7, 1992, A1.
22. Lynn Waddell, "Shot in the Arm: MGM Viewed as Possible Recession-buster," *Las Vegas Sun*, October 8, 1991, A1; Dan Njegomir, "New Resort Proposed for Southern End of the Strip," Las Vegas *Review Journal*, September 23, 1988, B1:2; Howard Stutz, "Success Under the Big Top," Las Vegas *Review Journal*, November 11, 1989, 1B, 4B, 5B; Vern Willis, "Circus Circus, with Profitable History, Looks Good for Future," *Las Vegas Review Journal*, December 22, 1991; R. E. Tammariello, "Grand Slam Canyon Plans Unveiled," *Las Vegas Review Journal*, August 27, 1992, 1A, 3A; Lynn Waddell, "It's a Wonder: Circus Circus to Build Grand Slam Canyon," *Las Vegas Sun*, August 27, 1992, 1A, 7A; Cy Ryan, "LV Key to Nevada Economy," *Las Vegas Review Journal*, January 31, 1993, D1; Mike Weatherford, "The Adventure Begins: New Grand Slam Canyon Offers Thrills and Chills," *Las Vegas Review Journal*, August 22, 1993, 1J–8J; Jeff Rubio, "Las Vegas: A Sure Bet for the Entire Family," *Hemisphere* (1993); 119–21; Spanier, *Welcome to the Pleasuredome*, 83–85, 99–101; analysis of the major hotels and their themes courtesy of Gene Moehring.
23. Hunter S. Thompson, *Fear and Loathing in Las Vegas* (New York: Popular Library, 1971), 46; Drexel Burnham Lambert Research, "Circus Circus Enterprises," April 9, 1984, and "Souvenir Program and Guide, Circus Circus Casino, Las Vegas," ca. 1971, Circus Circus Collection, Special Collections, James Dickinson Library, University of Nevada, Las Vegas; interview with Joyce Marshall, October 23, 1993; "Hotelman Jay J. Sarno Dies," *Las Vegas Sun*, July 22, 1984, 4C; Jeff German, "Bennett King of the Hill," *Las Vegas Sun*, October 17, 1993, 3C. Circus Circus's occupancy rate is consistently over 99 percent.
24. Drexel Burnham Lambert Research, "Circus Circus Enterprises," April 9, 1984, and "Souvenir Program and Guide, Circus Circus Casino, Las Vegas"; interview with Joyce Marshall, October 23, 1993; "Hotelman Jay J. Sarno Dies," *Las Vegas Sun*, July 22, 1984, 4C; Jeff German, "Bennett King of the Hill," *Las Vegas Sun*, October 17, 1993, 3C.
25. Findlay, *People of Chance*, 142–43, 201–2, 205–8; David Rich Lewis, "Still Native: The Significance of Native Americans in the History of the Twentieth-Century West," *Western Historical Quarterly* 24, no. 2 (May 1993): 215; "Indian Gaming: Law and Legislation," *NARF Legal Review* 10 (Fall 1985): 1–5; Pauline Yoshihashi, "Indian Tribes Put Their Bets on Casinos," *Wall Street Journal*, August 5, 1991, B1.
26. Regional Demographic Data for Nevada, July 20, 1995, 12.

27. Alexander, "Rise to Power."
28. Kurt Andersen, "Las Vegas, U.S.A.," *Time*, January 10, 1994, 42–51.

13. THE MÉLANGE OF POSTMODERN TOURISM

1. David A. Kaplan and Daniel Glick, "The Corporate Moguls Play Musical Chairlifts," *Newsweek*, December 23, 1996, 37.
2. Martha Weinman Lear, "For Charity, the Buck Stops Here," *Denver Post*, March 11, 1985; Ted Conover, *Whiteout: Lost in Aspen* (New York: Random House, 1991), 108–9.
3. The person in question, a fortyish Hispano-Acadian native of Santa Fe, former University of New Mexico athlete, and a friend of the author, requested anonymity. He reiterated that he meant what he said.
4. John Denver, "Rocky Mountain High"; Conover, *Whiteout*, 6, also offers an outstanding explication of Denver's role in Aspen (78–84); William Philpott, "Visions of a Changing Vail: Fast-Growth Fallout in a Colorado Resort Town," (Master's thesis: University of Wisconsin, 1994).
5. John Rember, "My Life as a Tourist," *Idaho Ski Guide 95/96*, 6; Conover, *Whiteout*, 12, 25; Doug Oppenheimer and Jim Poore, *Sun Valley: A Biography* (Boise, ID: Beatty Books, 1976), 170–71; Dorice Taylor, *Sun Valley* (Sun Valley: Ex Libris Sun Valley, 1980), 97–105.
6. Andrés Résendez, "Caught Between Profit and Ritual" (Ph.D. diss. University of Chicago, 1997), has defined this problem with great thoroughness and care; Tim Sandlin, *The Pyms: Unauthorized Tales of Jackson Hole* (Jackson, WY: Jackson Hole Magazine, 1991); Deborah Frazier, "Folks in Colorado Resort Town Hold onto Old Ways Despite Boom," *Las Vegas Review Journal and Las Vegas Sun* (from Associated Press), January 19, 1997, 13B.
7. Conover, *Whiteout*, 5, 135, 260–62; Rember, "My Life as a Tourist," 7.
8. Interview with Donna Bottum, August 12, 1994; interview with Angus Thuermer Jr., August 4, 1994.
9. Interview with Angus Thuermer Jr., August 4, 1994; interview with Donna Bottum, August 12, 1994; John Rember, *Cheerleaders from Gomorrah: Tales from the Lycra Archipelago* (Lewiston, ID: Confluence Press, 1994).
10. Lisa Jones, "El Nuevo West: The Region's New Pioneers Buoy the Economy and Live on the Edge," *High Country News*, December 23, 1996, 1, 10–11.
11. Ibid., 1, 6.
12. Ibid., 8, 11.
13. Ibid., 9.
14. City of Steamboat Springs, "1989 Community Committee Report," prepared for Steamboat Springs City Council by the 1989 Community Committee, Bud Werner Memorial Library, Routt County History Section, Steamboat Springs, Colorado.
15. Raye Ringholz, *Paradise Paved: The Challenge to Growth in the New West* (Salt Lake City: University of Utah Press, 1996), 1–19; Joel Garreau, *Edge City: Life on the New Frontier* (New York: Doubleday, 1991).
16. Ivan Goldman, "Aspen: Haven for Refugees," *Denver Post*, August 18, 1974, 33, 46; Gersten, "Ski Firm's Fox-y Takeover Clouds Future for Aspen," *Rocky Mountain News*, January 18, 1978; Brad Smith, "Aspen's Rich Image Belies the Needs of the Town's Poor," *Rocky Mountain News*, March 25, 1985, 4A; "Natives Strangers in Their Own Town," *Denver Post*, February 21, 1988, 24; James Coates, "A$pen: The No Man's Land Between Rich and Poor Exemplifies Contrasts in the Chic Resort," *Denver Post*,

March 11, 1985; "Aspen Chamber of Commerce: Employment and Housing Information," n.d. (ca. 1985), in Circular File, Aspen, Western History Department, Denver Public Library; Conover, *Whiteout,* 87; Rember, "My Life as a Tourist," 6.

17. Kathleen K. Daily and Gaylord T. Guenin, *Aspen: The Quiet Years* (Aspen, CO: Red Ink, 1994), 35–38.
18. Conover, *Whiteout,* 39; Ray Ring, "The New West's Servant Economy," *High Country News,* April 17, 1995; "Pedro Lopez, Entrepreneur," *High Country News,* April 17, 1995, 10.
19. Conover, *Whiteout;* Ring, "The New West's Servant Economy."
20. Duane A. Smith, *Rocky Mountain Boom Town: A History of Durango* (Albuquerque: University of New Mexico Press, 1980), 174–79, and Arthur R. Gómez, *Quest for the Golden Circle: The Four Corners and the Metropolitan West, 1945–1970* (Albuquerque: University of New Mexico, 1989), 149–91. Andrew Gulliford, *Boomtown Blues: Colorado Oil Shale, 1885–1985* (Niwot, CO: University Press of Colorado, 1989), presents a strident example of the problems of communities that rely on temporary industries without even the limited diversity that a tourist economy offers. Gulliford told me that increasingly, the people who live near his summer home in Silt, Colorado, west of Glenwood Springs, commute to Aspen and the Roaring Fork Valley, almost seventy miles away, to work. Gulliford also observed that more and more of the workers are Hispanic and that a significant percentage are undocumented.
21. Gómez, *Quest for the Golden Circle,* 175–81; interview with Larry Hartsfield, December 17, 1989.
22. "Union Studying New Telluride Mining Contract," *Denver Post,* May 12, 1953; "Telluride Ski Development Planned," *Denver Post,* December 10, 1968, 49; Olga Curtis, "The Rebirth of Telluride," *Denver Post Empire Magazine,* November 14, 1971, 13–18; Bob Ewegen, "Telluride Fears Aspenizing," *Denver Post,* February 14, 1973, 41; Howard Bryan, "Telluride: Counterculture Takes a Seat on the Town Council," *Rocky Mountain News,* June 23, 1974, 3; Grace Lichtenstein, "Colorado Town Lures Youths with Sun, Scenery, Bagels," *New York Times,* April 16, 1975; "Gas Station Adds to Town's Dilemma," *Grand Junction Sentinel,* October 5, 1975, 15; Olga Curtis, "All Is Not Joy in Telluride," *Denver Post Empire Magazine,* August 22, 1976, 11; David Freed, "Telluride Faces Squabble over Resort Growth," *Rocky Mountain News,* February 18, 1981, 14; Diane Eicher, "Telluride: Despite Impending Growth, It's Still an Idealistic Town," *Denver Post,* January 30, 1983, 1–12, 14, 20; Gary Schmitz, "Telluride: A Call to Destiny," *Denver Post,* November 6, 1984, 1A, 6A, 7A; J. D. Reed and Robert C. Wurmstedt, "Gentrifying a Mountain Paradise," *Time,* February 11, 1985, 98; Mark Tatge, "High Tech Opens Town to New Long-Distance Breed of Professionals," *Denver Post,* August 17, 1986, 1F, 8F; J. Sebastian Sinisi, "Competing Visions Tug at Telluride," *Denver Post,* September 4, 1988, 1H, 2H; Joe Garner, "Telluride Grapples with Loss of Innocence," *Rocky Mountain News,* June 30, 1991, 28–30; Frazier, "Folks in Colorado Resort Town Hold onto Old Ways Despite Boom."
23. William Logan, "Durango: Tourism, Railroad Key to Future," *Rocky Mountain News,* June 10, 1966, 37; "$700,000 Lodge to Be Ready This Year at Durango Ski Site," *Denver Post,* July 16, 1969, 97; Colorado Ski Country USA, "Lift Tickets Issued," ca. 1972; Wayne Moorehead, "Newcomers Keep Pace with Region's History," *Durango-Cortez Herald,* November 9, 1975, 11; Jim Carrier, "One-Track Economy Has Its Bumps," *Denver Post,* July 3, 1988, 1G, 2G; Joe Garner, "'Puppies' Teething on Sports: Durango Lures Young, Restless," *Rocky Mountain News,* October 15, 1990, 10; Steve Cohen, "Snow Takes 1st Priority in Durango," *Denver Post,* February 12, 1989, 1T, 7T, 8T;

Kevin McCullen, "Resettlement of West Lures New Pioneers," *Rocky Mountain News,* March 21, 1993, 10; Goldman, "Aspen: Haven for Refugees," 46; author's conversation with Durango Colorado resident Larry K. Hartsfield, August 10, 1990; Smith, *Rocky Mountain Boom Town,* 176–77; Gómez, "Quest for the Golden Circle," 226–44.

24. Conover, *Whiteout,* 1–2.
25. Sandlin, *The Pyms.*
26. Rember, "My Life as a Tourist," 7.
27. Struthers Burt, *The Diary of a Dude Wrangler* (New York: Charles Scribners, 1924); Donald Hough, *The Cocktail Hour in Jackson Hole* (Worland, WY: High Plains Publishing, 1956); J. Royal Horton, *Murder in Jackson Hole* (Moose, WY: Homestead Publishing, 1993).
28. U.S. Forest Service, "Lake Catamount Resort Final Environmental Impact Statement, Routt National Forest, November 1990, vols. 1–2; Jean A. Garren, "Lake Catamount: An Independent Look at Atmosphere, Autos, Water and Growth. Some Questions Not Addressed in the D.E.I.S.," May 25, 1989, Bud Werner Memorial Library, Routt County History Section, Steamboat Springs, Colorado.
29. Scott Condon, "Looking Back at the Birth of Growth Control," *Aspen Times,* October 5–6, 1996, 1–6.
30. Bruce Selcraig, "Glitz and Growth Take a Major Hit in Santa Fe," *High Country News,* August 8, 1994; Bruce Selcraig, "Lack of Enchantment: Santa Fe's Boom Goes Flat," *High Country News,* February 5, 1996, 1, 14–16; Candelaro Versace, "A Tale of Two Mayors: Santa Fe's Embattled Debbie Jaramillo," *Crosswinds,* December 1995, 14–16.
31. Versace, "A Tale of Two Mayors," 14–16; Selcraig, "Lack of Enchantment," 1, 14–16.
32. Selcraig, "Glitz and Growth Take a Major Hit in Santa Fe," 10–11; Selcraig, "Lack of Enchantment," 16.
33. Quoted in *High Country News,* February 5, 1996, 15.

BIBLIOGRAPHIC ESSAY

In this book I attempt a synthesis, relying largely on primary sources. Historians have too long ignored tourism, especially in the United States and in the West. Only a handful of books have addressed the subject. By far the most outstanding and prescient is Earl Pomeroy's *In Search of the Golden West: The Tourist in Western America* (Lincoln: University of Nebraska Press, 1957), now more than forty years old but still the place from which all other studies of western tourism depart. John Jakle, *The Tourist in 20th Century America* (Lincoln: University of Nebraska Press, 1985), is the major exception to the trend of neglect since Pomeroy; although Jakle's main emphasis is on the processes by which visitors go from place to place, his work opens new doors. John F. Sears, *Sacred Places: American Tourist Attractions in the Nineteenth Century* (New York: Oxford University Press, 1989), and Michael Kammen, *The Mystic Chords of Memory: The Transformation of Tradition in American Culture* (New York: Alfred A. Knopf, 1991), also explore some facets of what I label cultural and heritage tourism. More recent works such as Dona Brown's *Inventing New England: Regional Tourism in the Nineteenth Century* (Washington, DC: Smithsonian Institution Press, 1996) and Leah Dilworth's *Imagining Indians in the Southwest: Persistent Visions of a Primitive Past* (Washington, DC: Smithsonian Institution Press, 1996) open the way for interpretations of tourism through cultural history. Marta Weigle and Barbara A. Babcock, eds., *The Great Southwest of the Fred Harvey Company and the Santa Fe Railway* (Phoenix: Heard Museum, 1996), also contribute to the discussion. Despite my efforts here, most of the great monographs about tourism in the American West remain to be written.

Younger scholars are engaged in a significant amount of historical work about tourism. The most important is Marguerite S. Shaffer's "See America First: Tourism and National Identity" (Ph.D. diss., Harvard University, 1994), which sets its own dimensions for the relationship between tourism and identity. Other studies show promise: Anne Gilbert Coleman, "The Unbearable Whiteness of Skiing" (Ph.D. diss., University of Colorado, 1996), and for the South, C. Brenden Martin, "Selling the Southern Highlands: Tourism and Community Development in the Mountain South" (Ph.D. diss., University of Tennessee, 1997), stand out, as does William Philpott, "Visions of a Changing Vail: Fast-Growth Fallout in a Colorado Resort Town" (master's thesis, University of Wisconsin, 1994). These younger scholars are pioneering a largely uncharted course. I hope to offer them a road map that, in the best scholarly tradition, they will soon discard for one of their own making.

The best work to date about tourism has come from social scientists, particularly geographers and sociologists. Dean MacCannell's two major works, *The Tourist: A New Theory of the Leisure Class* (New York: Schocken Books, 1976), and *Empty Meeting Grounds: The Tourist Papers* (New York: Routledge, 1993), have provided much context for the study of the field. MacCannell helps elucidate the subject but is bound by an academic sensibility that skews the emphasis to the topics that interest academics. In this his work, despite its obvious brilliance, reveals both class and educational biases that mitigate against the understanding of a larger tourist whole on its own terms. Geographers have provided much of the groundwork for this kind of study. Douglas Pearce is one of the best known; his voluminous research and that of many other geographers and miscellaneous social scientists are best compiled in a primer, Douglas Pearce, *Tourist Development,* 2d. ed. (New York: John Wiley and Sons, 1989). Here Pearce synthesizes the work of thousands of articles, providing a fine assessment of the state of social science research. Karl Kim's work on Hawaii, especially "Tourism on Our Terms: Tourism Planning in Hawaii," (report, Western Governors' Association, 1991), and "The Political Economy of Foreign Investment in Hawai'i," *Social Process in Hawaii* 35 (1994): 35–54, has added measurably to this study.

Most of the places in this book harbor historians of their own, some of whom focus on tourism. At the Grand Canyon, J. Donald Hughes, *In the House of Stone and Light: A Human History of the Grand Canyon* (Grand Canyon, AZ: Grand Canyon Natural History Association, 1978), offers a fine history of the park. In Santa Fe, Chris Wilson, *The Myth of Santa Fe: Creating a Modern Regional Tradition* (Albuquerque: University of New Mexico Press, 1997), does an outstanding job of showing how tourism became tradition. Although he and I mildly disagree on where the credit and blame lie, I can only wish his book had been published earlier; it would have saved me thousands of hours of research. Robert Righter's *Crucible for Conservation: The Creation of Grand Teton National Park* (Niwot, CO: Colorado Associated University Press, 1983), remains the standard for the Grand Teton region; David J. Saylor, *Jackson Hole, Wyoming: In the Shadow of the Tetons* (Norman: University of Oklahoma Press, 1970), offers the closest thing to a history of Jackson Hole that yet exists. Sureva Towler, *The History of Skiing at Steamboat Springs* (Steamboat Springs, CO: Sureva Towler, 1987), provides the first genuine look at local history there, and Doug Oppenheimer and Jim Poore, *Sun Valley: A Biography* (Boise, ID: Beatty Books, 1976), offer a look at that community. James Sloan Allen, *The Romance of Commerce and Culture: Capitalism, Modernism, and the Chicago-Aspen Crusade for Cultural Reform* (Chicago: University of Chicago Press, 1983), presents a powerful, influential, and comprehensive look at the phenomenon of Walter Paepcke and the Aspen he created. My friend and colleague Eugene P. Moehring's book *Resort City in the Sun Belt: Las Vegas, 1930–1970* (Reno: University of Nevada Press, 1989), offers an excellent look at the nuts and bolts of building a twentieth-century city. Robert Lacey, *Little Man: Meyer Lansky and the Gangster Life* (Boston: Little, Brown and Company, 1991), and Ed Reid and Ovid Demaris, *The Green Felt Jungle* (New York: Trident Press, 1963), dissect the mob era in Las Vegas. Alan Hess, *Viva Las Vegas: After-Hours Architecture* (San Francisco: Chronicle Books, 1993), provides the best look at the architecture of Las Vegas and through it, the growth of entertainment tourism.

Each of the activities included here has a history. Lawrence R. Borne's *Dude Ranching: A Complete History* (Albuquerque: University of New Mexico Press, 1983) is a long-overlooked but extremely significant work. Elizabeth Clair Flood, *Old-Time Dude Ranches out West: Authentic Ranches for Modern-day Dudes* (Salt Lake City: Gibbs-Smith, 1995), adds to Borne's story. Warren Belasco's *Americans on the Road: From Autocamp to Motel, 1910–1945* (Boston: MIT Press, 1979) is the most important explication of autocamping. There is no comprehensive history of the ski industry to date; the closest is E. John B. Allen's *From Skisport to Skiing: One Hundred Years of an American Sport* (Amherst: University of Massachusetts Press, 1993). Abbott Fay, *Ski Tracks in the Rockies: A Century of Colorado Skiing* (Denver: Cordillera Press, 1984), offers a general history of Colorado skiing. For gaming, the best book is Jerome H. Skolnick, *House of Cards: The Legalization and Control of Casino Gambling* (Boston: Little, Brown, and Company, 1978). John M. Findlay, *People of Chance: Gambling in American Society from Jamestown to Las Vegas* (New York: Oxford University Press, 1986), provides the cultural context. Another useful volume is Peter Wiley and Robert Gottlieb, *Empires in the Sun: The Rise of the New*

American West (New York: G. P. Putnam's Sons, 1982), which helps set the stage for understanding how western patterns of growth came to include service economies. Incredibly valuable also is Arthur R. Gómez's *Quest for the Golden Circle: The Four Corners and the Metropolitan West, 1945–1970* (Albuquerque: University of New Mexico, 1989), a vastly underappreciated and underrecognized work that has great implications for the study of the late twentieth-century West.

The real stories of these places have been told through the eyes of their residents, all of whom shape what they say to fit their position on the local ladder. Again, most places have their authors; typically, the more powerful and poignant the writing about a place, the greater the chance that resistance to change has proved futile. Memoirs constitute one category, but as all forms of autobiography, they are as important for where they stand as for what they say. For Jackson, Struthers Burt's *The Diary of a Dude Wrangler* (New York: Charles Scribners, 1924), is the most comprehensive explanation of the phenomenon of neonativity; Burt is the consummate neonative, always conscious of and even self-conscious about his position. His son, Nathaniel Burt, *Jackson Hole Journal* (Norman: University of Oklahoma Press, 1983), adds much but is so much a part of what has occurred that his explanations sound tailored to his audience in the way his father manufactured experience for visitors. Donald Hough, *The Cocktail Hour in Jackson Hole* (Worland, WY: High Plains Publishing, 1956), provides another take on Jackson. Women offer some of the most lucid and incisive explications of change. Sun Valley's Dorice Taylor presents the classic displaced neonative's tale in *Sun Valley* (Sun Valley, ID: Ex Libris Sun Valley, 1980). Raye Ringholz is both observer and participant, autobiographer and journalist in *Little Town Blues: Voices from a Changing West* (Salt Lake City: Peregrine Smith Books, 1992); Peggy Clifford, *To Aspen and Back Again: An American Journey* (New York: St. Martin's Press, 1979), defines Aspen and then analyzes its demise. Bruce Berger, *Notes of a Half-Aspenite,* (Aspen, CO: Ashley and Associates, 1987), offers another view. Las Vegas lends itself much more to neonative memoirs. John Rember, "On Going Back to Sawtooth Valley," in *Where the Morning Light's Still Blue: Personal Essays About Idaho,* ed. William Studebaker and Rick Ardinger (Moscow, ID: University of Idaho Press, 1994) gives a poignant look at the concept of home. Susan Berman, *Easy Street* (New York: Dial Press, 1981), offers an elegant and intimate look at Las Vegas; Hunter S. Thompson, *Fear and Loathing in Las Vegas* (New York: Popular Library, 1971), is far harder to categorize. Fiction writers such as John Rember and Tim Sandlin add measurably to the stories of places. John Rember, *Cheerleaders from Gomorrah: Tales from the Lycra Archipelago* (Lewiston, ID: Confluence Press, 1994), an only slightly veiled account of Sun Valley, offers one of the freshest literary voices to come from the West in years. Tim Sandlin, *The Pyms: Unauthorized Tales of Jackson Hole* (Jackson, WY: Jackson Hole Magazine, 1991), gives a satirical account of change, local identity, and the claims to place of individuals and groups.

The real sources for the study of tourism as recent history are the people and the places where tourism occurs. Conversations and libraries, coffeehouses and archives provided the raw material for this book as much as did books and articles. From Wallowa County, Oregon, to Santa Fe and from the coast to Kansas, everyone has a take on tourism. I've tried to reflect as many of those perspectives as I can.

INDEX